Sociology

Sociology
An Introductory Textbook and Reader

Daniel Nehring

Harlow, England • London • New York • Boston • San Francisco • Toronto • Sydney
Auckland • Singapore • Hong Kong • Tokyo • Seoul • Taipei • New Delhi
Cape Town • São Paulo • Mexico City • Madrid • Amsterdam • Munich • Paris • Milan

Pearson Education Limited
Edinburgh Gate
Harlow CM20 2JE
United Kingdom
Tel: +44 (0)1279 623623
Web: www.pearson.com/uk

First published 2013 (print and electronic)

ISBN: 978-1-4082-4452-4 (print)
       978-1-4082-4453-1 (PDF)
       978-0-273-78195-0 (eText)

British Library Cataloguing-in-Publication Data
A catalogue record for the print edition is available from the British Library

Library of Congress Cataloging-in-Publication Data
Nehring, Daniel.
  Sociology : an introductory textbook and reader / Daniel Nehring.
     pages cm
  Includes bibliographical references.
  ISBN 978-1-4082-4452-4 — ISBN 978-1-4082-4453-1 (PDF) — ISBN 978-0-273-78195-0 (eText)
  1. Sociology—Textbooks. 2. Sociology. I. Title.
  HM586.N44 2013
  301—dc23
                                                  2013005108

10 9 8 7 6 5 4 3 2 1
17 16 15 14 13

Print edition typeset in 9.5/12.5pt Giovanni by 75
Print edition printed in Great Britain by Henry Ling Ltd, at the Dorset Press, Dorchester, Dorset

NOTE THAT ANY PAGE CROSS REFERENCES REFER TO THE PRINT EDITION

Contents

List of readings

Chapter 5

Chapter 6

Acknowledgements

The idea for this book resulted from many discussions with Ken Plummer between 2009 and 2011. In the end, we did not end up writing it together. Nonetheless, many aspects of its structure and content are based on Ken's ideas. I am grateful for these ideas and for a thoroughly enjoyable period of collaborative work. Andrew Taylor provided crucial encouragement in the final stages of my work on the manuscript. Rina Arya read through the manuscript and offered many important suggestions. Robin West compiled the readings, and I would like to thank him for his quick and efficient help. Mary Lince and Jill Wallis assisted with the final revisions of the text. Finally, I would like to thank the anonymous reviewers who offered suggestions and constructive criticism at various stages of this project.

Publisher's acknowledgments

We are grateful to the following for permission to use copyright material:

Text

Extract on pages 4–7 from *The Rules of Sociological Method*, Macmillan (Durkheim, Emile and Lukes, Steven 1982) pp.50–55, Reproduced with the permission of Palgrave Macmillan; Extract on pages 8–14 from *The Sociological Imagination*, Oxford University Press, Inc. (Mills, C.W. 1959) pp.3–11, (c) Oxford University Press, Inc. By permission of Oxford University Press, USA; Extract on pages 19–22 from Simmel, G. 'The Problem of Sociology' in *Georg Simmel: On Individuality and Social Forms*, The University of Chicago Press (Levine, D.N. (ed) 1971) pp.23–27, Reprinted with permission of the University of Chicago Press; Extract on pages 29–32 from *Not for Profit: Why Democracy Needs the Humanities*, Princeton University Press (Nussbaum, Martha 2010) pp. 1–2, 9–10, 14–15 and 24–26, (c) 2010 by Princeton University Press. Reprinted by permission of Princeton University Press.; Extract on pages 40–7 from *Telling About Society*, The University of Chicago Press (Becker, S. Howard) pp.5–14; Extract on pages 140–8 from *Community and Society*, The Michigan State University Press (Tonnies, F. 1957) pp.35–37, 37–39 and 64–67; Extract on pages 150–6 from 'The Metropolis and Mental Life' in *On Individuality and Social Forms*, The University of Chicago Press (Levine, D. 1971) pp.324–333,

Reprinted with permission of the University of Chicago Press; Extract on pages 160–4 from *Southern Theory*, Polity (Connell, R. 2007) pp.4–9, World excluding Australasia and Asia reproduction rights granted by Polity Press. Republication rights in Australasia and Asia granted with permission of Allen & Unwin Book Publishers.; Extract on pages 68–75 from *The Essential Comte, Selected from Cours de Philosophie Positive*, Croom Helm (Edited by S. Andreski 1974) pp.19–20, 124–126, 138–142, Reproduced by permission of Taylor and Francis Books UK; Extract on pages 77–81 from *Principles of Sociology*, Palgrave (Edited by S. Andreski 1969) pp.1–2 and 7–12; Extract on pages 117–21 from *Weber, M. 'The Development of the Capitalist Frame of Mind' in The Protestant Ethic and the Spirit of Capitalism with Other Writings on the Rise of the West*, 4th E.d, Oxford University Press (Kalberg, S. 2009) pp.431–435, By permission of Oxford University Press, USA; Extract on pages 124–30 from *'The Self, The I and the Me' in The Production of Reality*, 4th Ed., Pine Forge Press (Jody O'Brien 2006) pp.250–254, Reproduced with permission of Sage Publications, Inc.; Extract on pages 94–114 from *Readings from Emile Durkheim*, Routledge (Edited by Thompson, K. 2004) pp.65–83, Reproduced by permission of Taylor and Francis Books UK; Extract on pages 172–7 from *Multiple Modernities*, Transaction Publishers (Eisenstadt, S. 2002) pp.1–8; Extract on pages 200–6 from *The Presentation of Self in Everyday Life*, Penguin (Goffman, Erving 1959) pp.28–36, Reprinted in the British Commonwealth, Australia and New Zealand with permission of Penguin Books Ltd; Extract on pages 200–6 from *The Presentation of Self in Everyday Life*, Bantam Doubleday Dell Group (Goffman, Erving 1959) pp.28–36, © 1959 by Erving Goffman. Republication in the rest of the World and digital rights granted by permission of Doubleday, a division of Random House, Inc. Any third party use of this material, outside of this publication, is prohibited. Interested parties must apply directly to Random House, Inc. for permission; Extract on pages 221–9 from Parts Unknown: Undercover Ethnography of the Organs-Trafficking Underworld, *Ethnography*, Vol 5, no.1, pp.30–31, 37–39 and 44–49 (Scheper-Hughes, Nancy 2004), Reprinted by permission of SAGE.; Extract on pages 231–8 from *The System of Modern Societies*, Prentice Hall (Parsons, T. 1971) pp.4–11, (c) 1971, Reprinted and Electronically reproduced by permission of Pearson Education, Inc., Upper Saddle River, New Jersey; Extract on pages 241–6 from *Challenging Codes: Collective Action in the Information Age*, Cambridge University Press (Melucci, Alberto 1996) pp.1–6, (c) Alberto Melucci 1996, published by Cambridge University Press. Reproduced with permission.; Extract on pages 179–90 from *Consumer Culture and Postmodernism*, Sage (Featherstone, M. 1990) pp.1–12, Reproduced by permission of SAGE Publications, London, Los Angeles, New Delhi and Singapore.; Extract on pages 209–18 from *The Commercialization of Intimate Life: Notes from Home and Work*, University of California Press (Hochschild, Arlie Russell 2003) pp.13–18 and 19–24, Reprinted with permission of the University of California Press; Extract on pages 248–53 from *Unhitched: Love, Marriage and Family Values from Hollywood to Western China*, New York University Press (Stacey, J. 2001) pp.49/50 and 60–64; Extract on pages 255–64 from *Jesus in Disneyland: Religion in Postmodern Times*, Polity Press (Lyon, David 2000) pp.1–10; Extract on pages 360–6 from *The Global City: New York, London, Tokyo*, Princeton University Press (Sassen, S. 1991) pp.3–9, (c) 1991 Princeton University Press. Reprinted by permission of Princeton University Press.; Extract on pages 280–93 from *Globalization and Culture*, Rowman and Littlefield (Nederveen Pieterse, J. 2009) pp.43–58; Extract on pages 306–14 from *The*

Network Society: Social Aspects of New Media, 2nd Ed., Sage (van Dijk, J 2006) pp.1–3, 19–20, 32–36 and 191–194, Reproduced by permission of SAGE Publications, London, Los Angeles, New Delhi and Singapore; Extract on pages 318–24 from *McDonaldization: The Reader*, Sage (George Ritzer 2002) pp.1–2 and 13–19; Extract on pages 326–37 from *Risk Society*, Polity Press (Beck, U. 1992) pp.19–27 and 87–90; Extract on pages 339–51 from *Culture and Materialism: Selected Essays*, Verso (2006) pp.170–186 (cut to 5 pages), Reproduced with permission of Verso.; Extract on pages 353–62 from *Personal Connections in the Digital Age*, Polity Press (Baym, N. 2010) pp.1–2 and 6–12; Extract on pages 372–79 from The New Capitalism, *Social Research: An International Quarterly*, Vol. 64, No.2, pp.161–168 and 172–175 (Sennett, R. 1997), Reproduced by permission of Social Research, www.socres.org; Extract on pages 382–88 from *The New Individualism*, Routledge (Elliott, A. and Lemert, C. 2006) pp.79–82 and 91–96, Reproduced by permission of Taylor and Francis Books UK; Extract on pages 299–309 from *Capitalism: A Very Short Introduction*, Oxford University Press (Fulcher, J. 2004) pp.1–19, (c) James Fulcher 2004. By permission of Oxford University Press.; Quote on pages 436–7 from http://siteresources.worldbank.org/INTPA/Resources/429966–1259774805724/Poverty_Inequality_Handbook_Ch01.pdf, Reproduced with permission of The World Bank.; Extract on pages 465–72 from *Climate Change and Society*, Polity Press (Urry, J. 2011) pp.5–7 and 114–121; Extract on pages 475–9 from *Mobile Lives*, Routledge (Elliott, A. and Urry, J. 2010) pp.87–91, Reproduced by permission of Taylor and Francis Books UK; Extract on pages 414–24 from *Gender Politics*, Pluto Press (Monro, S. 2005) pp.10–22; Extract on pages 437–47 from *Politics as Usual*, Polity Press (Pogge, T. 2010) pp.10–13, 20–24 and 57–62; Extract on pages 449–54 from *The Civil Sphere*, Oxford University Press (Alexander, J. 2006) pp.3–9, (c) 2006 by Oxford University Press, Inc. By permission of Oxford University Press, USA; Extract on pages 396–404 from *Modernity and the Holocaust*, Polity Press (Bauman, Z. 1989) pp.12–18 and 56–60; North American republication rights for *Modernity and the Holocaust* granted by Cornell University Press.

Photographs
(Key: b-bottom; c-centre; l-left; r-right; t-top)

Alamy Images: © The Art Gallery Collection 165cl, © Caro 474, © GL Archive 165br, © INTERFOTO 165c, 165cr, © Mary Evans Picture Library 165tl, 165bl, © Pictorial Press Ltd 165tr, © SOTK2011 165tc; **Corbis:** © Bettmann 239; **DK Images:** 207; **Getty Images:** Robert Nickelsberg 265, SAUL LOEB/AFP 241; **www.granger.com**: 165bc; **Daniel Nehring:** 254.

In some instances we have been unable to trace the owners of copyright material, and we would appreciate any information that would enable us to do so.

1 Sociology: A panorama

1.1 The world you live in

It is likely that you are reading this book as part of an undergraduate course in sociology or a related field. Studying for a degree can sometimes be a solitary experience, as you need to spend long periods of time reading and writing by yourself. But to what extent does your academic success actually depend only on yourself? On the one hand, dedication, an interest in your subjects, and intellectual abilities are certainly very important for you to do well. On the other hand, however, your achievements depend on a great many other people: lecturers who introduce you to different areas of study and offer advice on your writing, administrators who make sure that all your work is correctly processed and registered, librarians who obtain books and journals that are important for your studies, and friends and classmates with whom you can study and have a good time when you need to relax, just to name a few of the people you meet while at university. Your successes and failures at university, in this sense, do not only result from your own efforts; they are influenced by the actions of many others.

Some of these others you will meet in person every day, in lectures, seminars, and all the other activities you engage in. Significant events in your life, however, are also shaped by people you rarely encounter face-to-face. You are likely to have family members and friends who live far away from you, and you probably use things such as mobile phones, Facebook, MySpace, Skype, etc., to communicate with them as often as you can. While you are studying in London, they are in another part in the UK, or in Europe, or North America, or Brazil, or China, or Japan, and so forth. Nevertheless, they know a lot of what happens to you every day, and their views and ideas may be quite important to you.

Even more indirectly, you also depend on people and organisations you will perhaps never meet. Your ability to study, for instance, depends to a large degree on how much you need to pay in tuition fees every year. This is decided by government officials and policy makers of whose existence you may not even be aware. Nevertheless, their choices fundamentally determine your ability to pay for your studies. Even much simpler aspects of your life greatly depend on others. Being well clothed, for example, is, for most people, a very basic need, and dressing according to current fashion is quite important to many. You may know the brands of your clothes, and you may know the shops in which you like to buy them, but you are unlikely to know about the factories which actually produced them and the people who work in these factories. If you look at the labels of your trousers, shirts, or shoes, it is not improbable that you will find that they were made in countries that may be far away from you, like Indonesia or China or Bangladesh or Mexico. The low prices on which your ability to buy certain brands depends are, in turn, based on very low wage levels in these countries and, sometimes, highly exploitative working conditions, including excessive working hours, hazardous workplaces, and the use of child labour, just to name a few recurrent problems.[1] While you do not know the factory workers who made your clothes, your living conditions depend on theirs, and theirs on yours.

These examples show that the world today is a strikingly small place, in which our lives are connected to those of others both close and distant. They also show that our achievements are shaped by powerful social forces, which sometimes place us in highly unequal relationships with others. The study of these social forces is the subject matter of sociology. This book will introduce you to a variety of sociological perspectives that may fundamentally change your understanding of human social relationships.

1.2 The study of social facts

Two things are important when it comes to understanding what sociology is all about. On the one hand, sociology is characterised by a high level of diversity in the intellectual perspectives and views of the world that inform research. Sociology is practised by scholars in universities and other institutions in many places around the world. The understandings that these sociologists bring to their work may vary quite considerably, and controversies and disagreements about the best way to understand a social problem are quite common. This is to say that there is not one right way of doing sociology. As students of sociology, you will gradually familiarise yourselves with different theoretical perspectives and ways of doing research, and you will likely find that some of these perspectives seem much more meaningful to you than others.

On the other hand, most sociological perspectives do share some common ground. First of all, sociology generally concerns the study of social facts. The term 'social facts'

---

[1] If you would like to know more about these problems, a quick search on the internet will give you a lot to read. A good documentary film on the case of Indonesia is 'The Globalization Tapes' at http://www.freedocumentaries.org/int.php?filmID=95.

was introduced by Émile Durkheim, a French scholar who played a pivotal role in establishing sociology as an academic discipline in Western Europe in the late nineteenth and early twentieth century. In his book *The Rules of Sociological Method* (Durkheim 1895/1982), Durkheim presented the study of social facts as the proper subject matter of sociology. He argued that, in every society, individuals' lives are shaped by powerful social forces that are beyond their direct control or influence. He gives the following, now famous, example to illustrate this point:

> When I perform my duties as a brother, a husband or a citizen and carry out the commitments I have entered into, I fulfil obligations which are defined in law and custom and which are external to myself and my actions. Even when they conform to my own sentiments and when I feel their reality within me, that reality does not cease to be objective, for it is not I who have prescribed these duties; I have received them through education. (Durkheim 1895/1982: 50)

In other words, many of the things we do, or do not do, or cannot do in everyday life are not simply a matter of individual choice or preference. Rather, they are shaped by society's laws, customs, and generalised expectations towards individuals. These laws, customs, and generalised expectations are what Durkheim understands as 'social facts'.

An example may serve to clarify this point. In virtually all societies, there is a generalised expectation for individuals not to behave in an overly aggressive or violent manner. Public displays of aggression, such as shouting or arguing loudly in public, will likely affect our reputation with others, who may even ask us to act in a more acceptable manner. Physical violence, however, will provoke severe punishments. Practically all forms of violence elicit punishments of some sort, from brawling schoolchildren being sent home by their teacher, to violent adults being incarcerated for attacking others. Consequently, overly hard-tackling football players face expulsion from a match by the referee, and football hooligans may be detained by the police.

Moreover, it is important to note that most people seek to avoid confrontations and violence. Unlike hooligans, we generally know that violence is not accepted anywhere in our everyday lives, and we often feel uneasy, anxious, or worried at the mere thought of being involved in a violent confrontation. Such negative feelings are social in so far as they are a result of our education; throughout the early stages of our lives, parents, teachers and others will shame us and reprimand us for unruly or aggressive behaviour until their command not to be violent has become an important part of the way we feel about and judge our own behaviour. According to Émile Durkheim, non-violence, therefore, is a social fact: it is a standard of behaviour which is generally held in society, acts as an external force upon individuals' consciousness, persists above and beyond particular individuals' control, and compels individuals to act in particular ways.

Reading

Durkheim, Émile (1895/1982) *The Rules of Sociological Method*, London: The Macmillan Press, pp. 50–5

What is a Social Fact?

Before beginning the search for the method appropriate to the study of social facts it is important to know what are the facts termed 'social'.

The question is all the more necessary because the term is used without much precision. It is commonly used to designate almost all the phenomena that occur within society, however little social interest of some generality they present. Yet under this heading there is, so to speak, no human occurrence that cannot be called social. Every individual drinks, sleeps, eats, or employs his reason, and society has every interest in seeing that these functions are regularly exercised. If therefore these facts were social ones, sociology would possess no subject matter peculiarly its own, and its domain would be confused with that of biology and psychology.

However, in reality there is in every society a clearly determined group of phenomena separable, because of their distinct characteristics, from those that form the subject matter of other sciences of nature.

When I perform my duties as a brother, a husband or a citizen and carry out the commitments I have entered into, I fulfil obligations which are defined in law and custom and which are external to myself and my actions. Even when they conform to my own sentiments and when I feel their reality within me, that reality does not cease to be objective, for it is not I who have prescribed these duties; I have received them through education. Moreover, how often does it happen that we are ignorant of the details of the obligations that we must assume, and that, to know them, we must consult the legal code and its authorised interpreters! Similarly the believer has discovered from birth, ready fashioned, the beliefs and practices of his religious life; if they existed before he did, it follows that they exist outside him. The system of signs that I employ to express my thoughts, the monetary system I use to pay my debts, the credit instruments I utilise in my commercial relationships, the practices I follow in my profession, etc., all function independently of the use I make of them. Considering in turn each member of society, the foregoing remarks can be repeated for each single one of them. Thus there are ways of acting, thinking and feeling which possess the remarkable property of existing outside the consciousness of the individual.

Not only are these types of behaviour and thinking external to the individual, but they are endued with a compelling and coercive power by virtue of which, whether he wishes it or not, they impose themselves upon him. Undoubtedly when I conform to them of my own free will, this coercion is not felt or felt hardly at all, since it is unnecessary. None the less it is intrinsically a characteristic of these facts; the proof of this is that it asserts itself as soon as I try to resist. If I attempt to violate the rules of law they react against me so as to forestall my action, if there is still time. Alternatively, they annul it or make my action conform to the norm if it is already accomplished but capable of being reversed; or they cause me to pay the penalty for it if it is irreparable. If purely moral rules are at stake, the public conscience restricts any act which infringes them by the surveillance it exercises over the conduct of citizens and by the special punishments it has at its disposal. In other cases the constraint is less violent; nevertheless, it does not cease to exist. If I do not conform to ordinary conventions, if in my mode of dress I pay no heed to what is customary in my country and in my social class, the laughter I provoke, the social distance at which I am kept, produce, although in a more mitigated form, the same results as any real penalty. In other cases, although it may be indirect, constraint is no less effective. I am not forced to speak French with my compatriots, nor to use the legal currency, but it is impossible for me to do otherwise. If I tried to escape the necessity, my attempt would fail miserably. As an industrialist nothing prevents me from working with the processes and methods of the previous century, but if I do I will most certainly ruin myself. Even when in fact I can struggle free from these rules and successfully break them, it is never without being forced to fight against them. Even if in the end they are overcome, they make their constraining power sufficiently felt in the resistance that they afford. There is no innovator, even a fortunate one, whose ventures do not encounter opposition of this kind.

Here, then, is a category of facts which present very special characteristics: they consist of manners of acting, thinking and feeling external to the individual, which are invested with a coercive power by virtue of which they exercise control over him. Consequently, since they consist of representations and actions, they cannot be confused with organic phenomena, nor with psychical phenomena, which have no existence save in and through the individual consciousness. Thus they constitute a new species and to them must be exclusively assigned the term *social*. It is appropriate, since it is clear that, not having the individual as their substratum, they can have none other than society, either political society in its entirety or one of the partial groups that it includes – religious denominations, political and literary schools, occupational corporations, etc. Moreover, it is for such as these alone that the term is fitting, for the word 'social' has the sole meaning of designating those phenomena which fall into none of the categories of facts already constituted and labelled. They are consequently the proper field of sociology. It is true that this word 'constraint', in terms of which we define them, is in danger of infuriating those who zealously uphold out-and-out individualism. Since they maintain that the individual is completely autonomous, it seems to them that he is diminished every time he is made aware that he is not dependent on himself alone. Yet since it is indisputable today that most of our ideas and tendencies are not developed by ourselves, but come to us from outside, they can only penetrate us by imposing themselves upon us. This is all that our definition implies. Moreover, we know that all social constraints do not necessarily exclude the individual personality.

Yet since the examples just cited (legal and moral rules, religious dogmas, financial systems, etc.) consist wholly of beliefs and practices already well established, in view of what has been said it might be maintained that no social fact can exist except where there is a well defined social organisation. But there are other facts which do not present themselves in this already crystallised form but which also possess the same objectivity and ascendancy over the individual. These are what are called social 'currents'. Thus in a public gathering the great waves of enthusiasm, indignation and pity that are produced have their seat in no one individual consciousness. They come to each one of us from outside and can sweep us along in spite of ourselves. If perhaps I abandon myself to them I may not be conscious of the pressure that they are exerting upon me, but that pressure makes its presence felt immediately I attempt to struggle against them. If an individual tries to pit himself against one of these collective manifestations, the sentiments that he is rejecting will be turned against him. Now if this external coercive power asserts itself so acutely in cases of resistance, it must be because it exists in the other instances cited above without our being conscious of it. Hence we are the victims of an illusion which leads us to believe we have ourselves produced what has been imposed upon us externally. But if the willingness with which we let ourselves be carried along disguises the pressure we have undergone, it does not eradicate it. Thus air does not cease to have weight, although we no longer feel that weight. Even when we have individually and spontaneously shared in the common emotion, the impression we have experienced is utterly different from what we would have felt if we had been alone. Once the assembly has broken up and these social influences have ceased to act upon us, and we are once more on our own, the emotions we have felt seem an alien phenomenon, one in which we no longer recognise ourselves. It is then we perceive that we have undergone the emotions much more than generated them. These emotions may even perhaps fill us with horror, so much do they go against the grain. Thus individuals who are normally perfectly harmless may, when gathered together in a crowd, let themselves be drawn into acts of atrocity. And what we assert about these transitory outbreaks likewise applies to those more lasting movements of opinion which relate to religious, political, literary and artistic matters, etc., and which are constantly being produced around us, whether throughout society or in a more limited sphere.

Moreover, this definition of a social fact can be verified by examining an experience that is characteristic. It is sufficient to observe how children are brought up. If one views the facts as they are and indeed as they have always been, it is patently obvious that all education consists of a continual effort to impose upon the child ways of seeing, thinking and acting which he himself would not have arrived at spontaneously. From his earliest years we oblige him to eat, drink and sleep at regular hours, and to observe cleanliness, calm and obedience; later we force him to learn how to be mindful of others, to respect customs and conventions, and to work, etc. If this constraint in time ceases to be felt it is because it gradually gives rise to habits, to inner tendencies which render it superfluous; but they supplant the constraint only because they are derived from it. It is true that, in Spencer's view, a rational education should shun such means and allow the child complete freedom to do what he will. Yet as this educational theory has never been put into practice among any known people, it can only be the personal expression of a *desideratum* and not a fact which can be established in contradiction to the other facts given above. What renders these latter facts particularly illuminating is that education sets out precisely with the object of creating a social being. Thus there can be seen, as in an abbreviated form, how the social being has been fashioned historically. The pressure to which the child is subjected unremittingly is the same pressure of the social environment which seeks to shape him in its own image, and in which parents and teachers are only the representatives and intermediaries.

Thus it is not the fact that they are general which can serve to characterise sociological phenomena. Thoughts to be found in the consciousness of each individual and movements which are repeated by all individuals are not for this reason social facts. If some have been content with using this characteristic in order to define them it is because they have been confused, wrongly, with what might be termed their individual incarnations. What constitutes social facts are the beliefs, tendencies and practices of the group taken collectively. But the forms that these collective states may assume when they are 'refracted' through individuals are things of a different kind. What irrefutably demonstrates this duality of kind is that these two categories of facts frequently are manifested dissociated from each other. Indeed some of these ways of acting or thinking acquire, by dint of repetition, a sort of consistency which, so to speak, separates them out, isolating them from the particular events which reflect them. Thus they assume a shape, a tangible form peculiar to them and constitute a reality *sui generis* vastly distinct from the individual facts which manifest that reality. Collective custom does not exist only in a state of immanence in the successive actions which it determines, but, by a privilege without example in the biological kingdom, expresses itself once and for all in a formula repeated by word of mouth, transmitted by education and even enshrined in the written word. Such are the origins and nature of legal and moral rules, aphorisms and popular sayings, articles of faith in which religious or political sects epitomise their beliefs, and standards of taste drawn up by literary schools, etc. None of these modes of acting and thinking are to be found wholly in the application made of them by individuals, since they can even exist without being applied at the time.

Consider

1. What is a social fact? Define the concept in your own words.
2. Now draw up a list of as many examples as you can think of. Explain how each example matches Durkheim's definition of social facts.
3. 'The pressure to which the child is subjected unremittingly is the same pressure of the social environment which seeks to shape him in its own image, and in which parents and teachers are only the representatives and intermediaries.' Discuss.
4. Reread the last paragraph in the extract. What does Durkheim mean when he claims that certain modes of acting and thinking can exist without actually being applied at a given point in time? Can you think of any examples?
5. Why might it be important to study the workings of social facts? Summarise your own views, using sociological concepts and ideas from Durkheim and other relevant sources.

1.3 The sociological imagination

In their study of social facts, sociologists adopt a particular way of looking at the world. This perspective is often termed the 'sociological imagination', after a seminal eponymous book published by US sociologist C. Wright Mills in 1959. What is the sociological imagination? Answering this question, I will let Mills's work speak for itself. In the following, you will find the first of many readings from influential, groundbreaking and innovative sociological texts. One way to become a sociologist is to study the writings of other sociologists and become acquainted with their perspective on society and the language they use to describe this perspective. C. Wright Mills's work is foundational to contemporary sociology. Its key ideas, presented here, will provide you with a base that will make it easier for you to appreciate the more specialised concerns of sociological research discussed later on in this book.

Reading

Mills, C.W. (1959/1967), *The Sociological Imagination*, Harmondsworth: Penguin, pp. 9–17

The Promise

Nowadays men often feel that their private lives are a series of traps. They sense that within their everyday worlds, they cannot overcome their troubles, and in this feeling, they are often quite correct: what ordinary men are directly aware of and what they try to do are bounded by the private orbits in which they live; their visions and their powers are limited to the close-up scenes of job, family, neighbourhood; in other milieux, they move vicariously and remain spectators. And the more aware they become, however vaguely, of ambitions and of threats which transcend their immediate locales, the more trapped they seem to feel.

Underlying this sense of being trapped are seemingly impersonal changes in the very structure of continent-wide societies. The facts of contemporary history are also facts about the success and the failure of individual men and women. When a society is industrialized, a peasant becomes a worker; a feudal lord is liquidated or becomes a businessman. When classes rise or fall, a man is employed or unemployed; when the rate of investment goes up or down, a man takes new heart or goes broke. When wars happen, an insurance salesman becomes a rocket launcher; a store clerk, a radar man; a wife lives alone; a child grows up without a father. Neither the life of an individual nor the history of a society can be understood without understanding both.

Yet men do not usually define the troubles they endure in terms of historical change and institutional contradiction. The well-being they enjoy, they do not usually impute to the big ups and downs of the societies in which they live. Seldom aware of the intricate connexion between the patterns of their own lives and the course of world history, ordinary men do not usually know what this connexion means for the kinds of men they are becoming and for the kinds of history-making in which they might take part. They do not possess the quality of mind essential to grasp the interplay of man and society, of bio-graphy and history, of self and world. They cannot cope with their personal troubles in such ways as to control the structural transformations that usually lie behind them.

Surely it is no wonder. In what period have so many men been so totally exposed at so fast a pace to such earthquakes of change? That Americans have not known such catastrophic changes as have the men and women of other societies is due to historical facts that are now quickly becoming 'merely history'. The history that now effects every man is world history. Within this scene and this period, in the course of a single generation, one sixth of mankind is transformed from all that is feudal and backward into all that is modern, advanced, and fearful. Political colonies are freed; new and less visible forms of imperialism installed. Revolutions occur; men feel the intimate grip of new kinds of authority. Totalitarian societies rise, and are smashed to bits – or succeed fabulously. After two centuries of ascendancy, capitalism is shown up as only one way to make society into an industrial apparatus. After two centuries of hope, even formal democracy is restricted to a quite small portion of mankind. Everywhere in the underdeveloped world, ancient ways of life are broken up and vague expectations become urgent demands. Everywhere in the overdeveloped world, the means of authority and of violence become total in scope and bureaucratic in form.

Humanity itself now lies before us, the super-nation at either pole concentrating its most coordinated and massive efforts upon the preparation of the Third World War.

The very shaping of history now outpaces the ability of men to orient themselves in accordance with cherished values. And which values? Even when they do not panic, men often sense that older ways of feeling and thinking have collapsed and that newer beginnings are ambiguous to the point of moral stasis. Is it any wonder that ordinary men feel they cannot cope with the larger worlds with which they are so suddenly confronted? That they cannot understand the meaning of their epoch for their own lives? That – in defence of selfhood – they become morally insensible, trying to remain altogether private men? Is it any wonder that they come to be possessed by a sense of the trap?

It is not only information that they need – in this Age of Fact, information often dominates their attention and overwhelms their capacities to assimilate it. It is not only the skills of reason that they need – although their struggles to acquire these often exhaust their limited moral energy.

What they need, and what they feel they need, is a quality of mind that will help them to use information and to develop reason in order to achieve lucid summations of what is going on in the world and of what may be happening within themselves. It is this quality, I am going to contend, that journalists and scholars, artists and publics, scientists and editors are coming to expect of what may be called the sociological imagination.

1

The sociological imagination enables its possessor to understand the larger historical scene in terms of its meaning for the inner life and the external career of a variety of individuals. It enables him to take into account how individuals, in the welter of their daily experience, often become falsely conscious of their social positions. Within that welter the framework of modern society is sought, and within that framework the psychologies of a variety of men and women are formulated. By such means the personal uneasiness of individuals is focused upon explicit troubles and the indifference of publics is transformed into involvement with public issues.

The first fruit of this imagination – and the first lessons of the social science that embodies it – is the idea that the individual can understand his own experience and gauge his own fate only by locating himself within his period, that he can know his own chances in life only by becoming aware of those of all individuals in his circumstances. In many ways it is a terrible lesson; in many ways a magnificent one. We do not know the limits of man's capacities for supreme effort or willing degradation, for agony or glee, for pleasurable brutality or the sweetness of reason. But in our time we have come to know that the limits of 'human nature' are frighteningly broad. We have come to know that every individual lives, from one generation to the next, in some society; that he lives out a biography, and that he lives it out within some historical sequence. By the fact of his living he contributes, however minutely, to the shaping of this society and to the course of its history, even as he is made by society and by its historical push and shove.

The sociological imagination enables us to grasp history and biography and the relations between the two within society. That is its task and its promise. To recognize this task and this promise is the mark of the classic social analyst. It is characteristic of Herbert Spencer – turgid, polysyllabic, comprehensive; of E. A. Ross – graceful, muckraking, upright; of Auguste Comte and Emile Durkheim; of the intricate and subtle Karl Mannheim. It is the quality of all that is intellectually excellent in Karl Marx; it is the clue to Thorstein Veblen's brilliant and ironic insight, to Joseph Schumpeter's many-sided constructions of reality; it is the basis of the psychological sweep of W. E. H. Lecky no less than of the profundity and clarity of Max Weber. And it is the signal of what is best in contemporary studies of man and society.

No social study that does not come back to the problems of biography, of history, and of their intersections within a society, has completed its intellectual journey. Whatever the specific problems of the classic social analysts, however limited or however broad the features of social reality they have examined, those who have been imaginatively aware of the promise of their work have consistently asked three sorts of questions:

(1) What is the structure of this particular society as a whole? What are its essential components, and how are they related to one another? How does it differ from other varieties of social order? Within it, what is the meaning of any particular feature for its continuance and for its change?

(2) Where does this society stand in human history? What are the mechanics by which it is changing? What is its place within and its meaning for the development of humanity as a whole? How does any particular feature we are examining affect, and how is it affected by, the historical period in which it moves? And this period – what are its essential features? How does it differ from other periods? What are its characteristic ways of history-making?

(3) What varieties of men and women now prevail in this society and in this period? And what varieties are coming to prevail? In what ways are they selected and formed, liberated and repressed, made sensitive and blunted? What kinds of 'human nature' are revealed in the conduct and character we observe in this society in this period? And what is the meaning for 'human nature' of each and every feature of the society we are examining?

Whether the point of interest is a great power state or a minor literary mood, a family, a prison, a creed – these are the kinds of questions the best social analysts have asked. They are the intellectual pivots of classic studies of man in society – and they are the questions inevitably raised by any mind possessing the sociological imagination. For that imagination is the capacity to shift from one perspective to another – from the political to the psychological; from examination of a single family to comparative assessment of the national budgets of the world; from the theological school to the military establishment; from considerations of an oil industry to studies of contemporary poetry. It is the capacity to range from the most impersonal and remote transformations to the most intimate features of the human self – and to see the relations between the two. Back of its use there is always the urge to know the social and historical meaning of the individual in the society and in the period in which he has his quality and his being.

That, in brief, is why it is by means of the sociological imagination that men now hope to grasp what is going on in the world, and to understand what is happening in themselves as minute points of the intersections of biography and history within society. In large part, contemporary man's self-conscious view of himself as at least an outsider, if not a permanent stranger, rests upon an absorbed realization of social relativity and of the transformative power of history. The sociological imagination is the most fruitful form of this self-consciousness. By its use men whose mentalities have swept only a series of limited orbits often come to feel as if suddenly awakened in a house with which they had only supposed themselves to be familiar. Correctly or incorrectly, they often come to feel that they can now provide themselves with adequate summations, cohesive assessments, comprehensive orientations. Older decisions that once appeared sound, now seem to them products of a mind unaccountably dense. Their capacity for astonishment is made lively again. They acquire a new way of thinking, they experience a transvaluation of values: in a word, by their reflection and by their sensibility, they realize the cultural meaning of the social sciences.

2

Perhaps the most fruitful distinction with which the sociological imagination works is between 'the personal troubles of milieu' and 'the public issues of social structure'. This distinction is an essential tool of the sociological imagination and a feature of all classic work in social science.

Troubles occur within the character of the individual and within the range of his immediate relations with others; they have to do with his self and with those limited areas of social life of which he is directly and personally aware. Accordingly, the statement and the resolution of troubles properly lie within the individual as a biographical entity and within the scope of his immediate milieu – the social setting that is directly open to his personal experience and to some extent his wilful activity. A trouble is a private matter: values cherished by an individual are felt by him to be threatened.

Issues have to do with matters that transcend these local environments of the individual and the range of his inner life. They have to do with the organization of many such milieux into the institutions of a historical society as a whole, with the ways in which various milieux overlap and interpenetrate to form the larger structure of social and historical life. An issue is a public matter: some value cherished by publics is felt to be threatened. Often there is a debate about what the value really is and about what it is that really threatens it. This debate is often without focus if only because it is the very nature of an issue, unlike even widespread trouble, that it cannot very well be defined in terms of the immediate and everyday environments of ordinary men. An issue, in fact, often involves a crisis in institutional arrangements, and often too it involves what Marxists call 'contradictions' or 'antagonisms'.

In these terms, consider unemployment. When, in a city of 100,000, only one man is unemployed, that is his personal trouble, and for its relief we properly look to the character of the man, his skills, and his immediate opportunities. But when in a nation of 50 million employees, 15 million men are unemployed, that is an issue, and we may not hope to find its solution within the range of opportunities open to any one individual. The very structure of opportunities has collapsed. Both the correct statement of the problem and the range of possible solutions require us to consider the economic and political institutions of the society, and not merely the personal situation and character of a scatter of individuals.

Consider war. The personal problem of war, when it occurs, may be how to survive it or how to die in it with honour; how to make money out of it; how to climb into the higher safety of the military apparatus; or how to contribute to the war's termination. In short, according to one's values, to find a set of milieux and within it to survive the war or make one's death in it meaningful. But the structural issues of war have to do with its causes; with what types of men it throws up into command; with its effects upon economic and political, family and religious institutions, with the unorganized irresponsibility of a world of nation-states.

Consider marriage. Inside a marriage a man and a woman may experience personal troubles, but when the divorce rate during the first four years of marriage is 250 out of every 1,000 attempts, this is an indication of a structural issue having to do with the institutions of marriage and the family and other institutions that bear upon them.

Or consider the metropolis – the horrible, beautiful, ugly, magnificent sprawl of the great city. For many upper-class people, the personal solution to 'the problem of the city' is to have an apartment with private garage under it in the heart of the city, and forty miles out, a house by Henry Hill, garden by Garrett Eckbo, on a hundred acres of private land. In these two controlled environments – with a small staff at each end and a private helicopter connexion – most people could solve many of the problems of personal milieux caused by the facts of the city. But all this, however splendid, does not solve the public issues that the structural fact of the city poses. What should be done with this wonderful monstrosity? Break it all up into scattered units, combining residence and work? Refurbish it as it stands? Or, after evacuation, dynamite it and build new cities according to new plans in new places? What should those plans be? And who is to decide and to accomplish whatever choice is made? These are structural issues; to confront them and to solve them requires us to consider political and economic issues that affect innumerable milieux.

In so far as an economy is so arranged that slumps occur, the problem of unemployment becomes incapable of personal solution. In so far as war is inherent in the nation-state system and in the uneven industrialization of the world, the ordinary individual in his restricted milieu will be powerless – with or without psychiatric aid – to solve the troubles this system or lack of system imposes upon him. In so far as the family as an institution turns women into darling little slaves and men into their chief providers and unweaned dependants, the problem of a satisfactory marriage remains incapable of purely private solution. In so far as the overdeveloped megalopolis and the overdeveloped automobile are built-in features of the overdeveloped society, the issues of urban living will not be solved by personal ingenuity and private wealth.

What we experience in various and specific milieux, I have noted, is often caused by structural changes. Accordingly, to understand the changes of many personal milieux we are required to look beyond them. And the number and variety of such structural changes increase as the institutions within which we live become more embracing and more intricately connected with one another. To be aware of the idea of social structure and to use it with sensibility is to be capable of tracing such linkages among a great variety of milieux. To be able to do that is to possess the sociological imagination.

Consider

1. Who was C. Wright Mills? What can you find out about his life? Use the internet to find out as much as you can about his life and work. Here are three websites to get you started:

   C. Wright Mills's sociology
   http://www.faculty.rsu.edu/users/f/felwell/www/Theorists/Mills/

   C. Wright Mills: power, craftsmanship, and private troubles and public issues
   http://www.infed.org/thinkers/wright_mills.htm

   C. Wright Mills
   http://www.cwrightmills.org/

   Who wrote these websites? How reliable is the information presented on them? How can you tell?

2. This chapter gives you a basic outline of Mills's argument. Yet, as you may have noticed, it does not cover many other points Mills makes in the abstract you have just read. Consider the following tasks and questions:

   (a) Summarise the reading in your own words. What are the main points Mills is trying to make?

   (b) What is the sociological imagination? Give a definition in your own words.

   (c) 'No social study that does not come back to the problems of biography, of history and of their intersection within a society has completed its intellectual journey.' What does Mills mean by this? Mills explains this statement by raising three sets of important questions about society. Consider these when formulating your answer.

   (d) The next part of the reading, labelled Part 2 by Mills, considers the distinction between 'personal troubles of milieu' and 'public issues of social structures'. Explain this distinction in your own words. Can you come up with any examples of your own?

   (e) The sociological imagination enables us to better understand the events in our everyday lives. Do you agree with this statement? If so, why?

A perhaps surprising feature of *The Sociological Imagination* is that it very much seems to speak to contemporary concerns, even though more than five decades have passed since its publication. Terms such as 'indifference', 'uneasiness' and 'anxiety' would appear to render fitting descriptions of the life experience of young people in many parts of the world, and Mills's example of choice – unemployment – is most certainly a pressing concern to many in the contemporary world.

Let us use this example to further explore the sociological imagination. Mills argues that mass unemployment cannot merely be explained through individual shortcomings, it is the outcome of the interplay of large-scale social forces – social facts – beyond their direct control:

> When, in a city of 100,000, only one man is unemployed, that is his personal trouble, and for its relief we properly look to the character of the man, his skills, and his immediate opportunities. But when in a nation of 50 million employees, 15 million men are unemployed, that is an issue, and we may not hope to find its solution within the range of opportunities open to any one individual. The very structure of opportunities has collapsed. Both the correct statement of the problem and the range of possible solutions require us to consider the economic and political institutions of the society, and not merely the personal situation and character of a scatter of individuals. (Mills 1959/1967: 9)

This insight leads Mills to make an important distinction: on the one hand, there are individual troubles that result from the specific features of our character and personal lives. These troubles are of interest to psychologists and *in themselves* do not constitute the proper subject matter of sociology. On the other hand, there are 'the public issues of social structure' (Mills 1959/1967: 8). These concern the large-scale institutions and social forces out of which societies are built, such as the state, government, law, private corporations, labour markets, clothing fashions, national cuisines, and traffic rules, and in which individual lives are embedded. Individual biographies are played out within much larger historical processes and patterns, and it is the sociologist's task to make sense of the relationship between the two. 'The sociological imagination enables us to grasp history and biography and the relations between the two within society. That is its task and its promise' (Mills 1959/1967: 6).

In this sense, sociologists address three kinds of questions: First, how are the large-scale institutions and social forces of society organised at any particular time? How, for example, do labour markets, private corporations and governments interact to create employment opportunities for individuals? Second, how do the mechanisms by which these social forces operate change over time? Mass unemployment has become a pervasive feature of life in the Western world only in recent decades. How can this change be explained? Third, how do the social forces that are characteristic of a society at a particular time shape the world views and life events of the individuals it comprises? What, for instance, are the anxieties, worries and preoccupations which mass unemployment and labour instability engender in the women and men who face them every day?

Nearly 40 years after C. Wright Mills published *The Sociological Imagination*, US sociologist Richard Sennett (1998) pursued these questions (also see Chapter 5). Sennett was concerned with the origins and personal consequences of widespread labour instability in the USA. While American workers in the 1950s and 1960s might have been able to spend their whole career with the same employer, contemporary Americans' working lives are characterised by frequent layoffs and the need to be flexible and be ready to change work at any moment, often with the consequence of moving town and leaving behind families, friends and colleagues.

Sennett argues that this change has been brought about by a number of large-scale changes in US society over the past 40 years. Employment in industrial manufacturing has largely disappeared or moved abroad, and it has been replaced with service work that offers no long-term prospects. At the same time, companies have abandoned the ambition of retaining the same labour force over long periods, recruiting and laying off staff to suit their short-term needs and demanding utmost flexibility from their employees.

To illustrate these changes, Sennett vividly contrasts the image of the 1950s factory worker, who spent most of his life working at the same assembly line for the same company, with the contemporary service worker, who stays only for short periods with a particular employer, often has to have several jobs to make ends meet, and develops few or no ties with colleagues and company. This new world of work is, Sennett argues, increasingly unpredictable, with jobs terminating in dead-ends and large numbers of workers being laid off regardless of their actual performance of their work. Failure, in this sense, has become an ever-present threat:

> Failure is the great modern taboo. Popular literature is full of recipes for how to succeed, but largely silent about how to cope with failure. Coming to terms with failure, giving it a shape and a place in one's life history, may haunt us internally but seldom is discussed with others. [. . .] Failure is no longer the normal prospect facing only the very poor or disadvantaged; it has become more familiar as a regular event in the lives of the middle classes. The shrinking size of the elite makes achievement more elusive. The winner-take-all market is a competitive structure which disposes large numbers of educated people to fail. Downsizings and reengineerings impose on middle-class people sudden disasters which were in an earlier capitalism much more confined to the working classes. (Sennett 1998: 118)

From this diagnosis, Sennett goes on to link large-scale historical changes in the US economy and labour market to the everyday lives of common people. He thus builds the bridge between 'personal troubles of milieu' and 'public issues of social structure' that C. Wright Mills (1959/1967: 8) describes as a hallmark of the sociological imagination. Sennett reports that the demands of unstable and unpredictable employment place a heavy burden on workers' personal lives. He goes so far as to argue that a 'corrosion of character' is increasingly pervasive in the USA: from a young age on, Americans become used to a pattern of constant change in their lives, changing city, friends and jobs at regular intervals. They become accustomed to experiences of failure – being 'down-sized', being made redundant according to corporate needs regardless of their job performance – that are emotionally extremely hard to cope with. In the process, their ability to form a lasting attachment to others and create social ties built on trust has begun to wane. Social relationships are increasingly becoming unstable, and people are set adrift in lives over which they have less and less control:

> 'Who needs me?' is a question of character which suffers a radical challenge in modern capitalism. The system radiates indifference. It does so in terms of the outcomes of human striving, as in winner-take-all markets, where there is little connection between risk and reward. It radiates indifference in the organization of absence of trust, where there is no reason to be needed. And it does so through reengineering of institutions in which people are treated as disposable. Such practices obviously and brutally diminish the sense of mattering as a person, of being necessary to others. (Sennett 1998: 146)

In sum, Richard Sennett's research shows the sociological imagination at work. First, he shows how large-scale social forces – labour markets, corporations, public policies – interact with each other to provide workers with employment opportunities that are increasingly fragile and short-lived. Second, he explains how the characteristics of labour markets, corporations and public policies have changed over the past five decades and rendered the idea of stable, live-time employment obsolete. Third, and maybe most importantly, Sennett shows how these changes are moulding the everyday lives of women and men across the USA, requiring constant mobility and flexibility and making the task of maintaining deep, close, meaningful personal bonds harder and harder.

1.4 The study of society

So far, we have examined two approaches to thinking about sociology. First, sociology may be understood as the study of 'social facts'. As we have seen, social facts are forces above and beyond individuals' control that exert a powerful influence on their ways of thinking, feeling and acting in everyday life. Language, norms about aggressive behaviour in public places, or traffic laws that mandate that we drive on the correct side of the road, are just a few examples of the myriad social facts that shape the way we live.

Second, sociologists tend to look at the world from a special perspective – the 'sociological imagination'. The sociological imagination enables us to look at the world in ways that highlight how particular events in our lives are shaped by large-scale social forces or 'social facts'. For example, from a common-sense perspective, going to university to study for a degree is, first of all, an individual choice resulting from your personal motivations and interest. However, this individual choice is only meaningful in a social context in which there are actual opportunities for you to receive a university education, in which a university education is widely regarded as an important part of young people's personal and professional development, and in which obtaining a degree significantly improves your life chances in the long run. In other words, your personal choice to study for a degree is dependent on and shaped by the interplay of a variety of large-scale social forces – labour markets, educational institutions, cultural values emphasising the importance of formal education, etc. The sociological imagination allows us to recognise these social forces and study their effects on our lives.

However, these two observations on their own do not fully explain what sociology is all about. Specifically, they do not explain how social facts come to be and why we should assume that our lives are shaped by social forces beyond our control and not of our own making. For the idea of social facts to make sense, it is necessary to assume, in the first instance, that there is such a thing as 'society' and to explore what exactly we might understand by it. For this purpose, we turn to Georg Simmel. He was an early influential sociologist, and a significant concern of his work was to define the discipline of sociology and set it apart from other fields of intellectual enquiry. His writings set out basic sociological concepts with particular clarity and precision. In *The Problem of Sociology* (1908/1971) Simmel elaborates on his understanding of 'society'.

Reading

Simmel, G. (1908/1971), 'The Problem of Sociology', in *Georg Simmel: On Individuality and Social Forms*, edited by D. N. Levine, Chicago: The University of Chicago Press, pp. 23–7

The Problem of Sociology

1908

Society exists where a number of individuals enter into interaction. This interaction always arises on the basis of certain drives or for the sake of certain purposes. Erotic, religious, or merely associative impulses; and purposes of defense, attack, play, gain, aid, or instruction – these and countless others cause man to live with other men, to act for them, with them, against them, and thus to correlate his condition with theirs. In brief, he influences and is influenced by them. The significance of these interactions among men lies in the fact that it is because of them that the individuals, in whom these driving impulses and purposes are lodged, form a unity, that is, a society. For unity in the empirical sense of the word is nothing but the interaction of elements. An organic body is a unity because its organs maintain a more intimate exchange of their energies with each other than with any other organism; a state is a unity because its citizens show similar mutual effects. In fact, the whole world could not be called one if each of its parts did not somehow influence every other part, or, if at any one point the reciprocity of effects, however indirect it may be, were cut off.

This unity, or sociation, may be of very different degrees, according to the kind and the intimacy of the interaction which obtains. Sociation ranges all the way from the momentary getting together for a walk to the founding of a family, from relations maintained "until further notice" to membership in a state, from the temporary aggregation of hotel guests to the intimate bond of a medieval guild. I designate as the content – the materials, so to speak – of sociation everything that is present in individuals (the immediately concrete loci of all historical reality) – drive, interest, purpose, inclination, psychic state, movement – everything that is present in them in such a way as to engender or mediate effects upon others or to receive such effects. In themselves, these materials which fill life, these motivations which propel it, are not social. Strictly speaking, neither hunger nor love, work nor religiosity, technology nor the functions and results of intelligence, are social. They are factors in sociation only when they transform the mere aggregation of isolated individuals into specific forms of being with and for one another, forms that are subsumed under the general concept of interaction. Sociation is the form (realized in innumerably different ways) in which individuals grow together into a unity and within which their interests are realized. And it is on the basis of their interests – sensuous or ideal, momentary or lasting, conscious or unconscious, causal or teleological – that individuals form such unities.

In any given social phenomenon, content and societal form constitute one reality. A social form severed from all content can no more attain existence than a spatial form can exist without a material whose form it is. Any social phenomenon or process is composed of two elements which in reality are inseparable: on the one hand, an interest, a purpose, or a motive; on the other, a form or mode of interaction among individuals through which, or in the shape of which, that content attains social reality.

It is evident that that which constitutes society in every current sense of the term is identical with the kinds of interaction discussed. A collection of human beings does not become a society because each of them has an objectively determined or subjectively impelling life-content. It becomes a society only when the vitality of these contents attains the form of reciprocal influence; only when one individual has an effect, immediate or mediate, upon another, is mere spatial aggregation or temporal succession transformed into society. If, therefore, there is to be a science whose subject matter is society and nothing else, it must exclusively investigate these interactions, these kinds and forms of sociation. For everything else found within "society" and realized through it and within its framework is not itself society. It is merely a content that develops or is developed by this form of coexistence, and it produces the real phenomenon called "society" in the broader and more customary sense of the term only in conjunction with this form. To separate, by scientific abstraction, these two factors of form and content which are in reality inseparably united; to detach by analysis the forms of interaction or sociation from their contents (through which alone these forms become social forms); and to bring them together systematically under a consistent scientific viewpoint – this seems to me the basis for the only, as well as the entire, possibility of a special science of society as such. Only such a science can actually treat the facts that go under the name of sociohistorical reality upon the plane of the purely social.

Abstractions alone produce science out of the complexity or the unity of reality. Yet however urgently such abstractions may be demanded by the needs of cognition itself, they also require some sort of justification of their relation to the structure of the objective world. For only some functional relation to actuality can save one from sterile inquiries or from the haphazard formulation of scientific concepts. Certainly, naïve naturalism errs in assuming that the given itself contains the analytic or synthetic arrangements through which it becomes the content of a science. Nevertheless, the characteristics of the given are more or less susceptible to such arrangements. An analogy may help here. A portrait fundamentally transforms the natural human appearance, but one face is better suited than another to such a transformation into something radically alien. Remembering this helps us to appraise the greater or lesser appropriateness

of various scientific problems and methods. The right to subject sociohistorical phenomena to an analysis in terms of form and content (and to synthesize
the forms) rests upon two conditions which must be verified on a factual basis.
On the one hand, we must demonstrate that the same form of sociation can be
observed in quite dissimilar contents and in connection with quite dissimilar
purposes. On the other hand, we must show that the content is realized in using
quite dissimilar forms of sociation as its medium or vehicle. A parallel is found
in the fact that the same geometric forms may be observed in the most heterogeneous materials and that the same material occurs in the most heterogeneous
spatial forms. Similar relations obtain between logical forms and the material
contents of cognition.

Both of these conditions are undeniable facts. We do find that the same form of
interaction obtains among individuals in societal groups that are the most unlike
imaginable in purpose and significance. Superiority, subordination, competition,
division of labor, formation of parties, representation, inner solidarity coupled
with exclusiveness toward the outside, and innumerable similar features are
found in the state as well as in a religious community, in a band of conspirators
as in an economic association, in an art school as in a family. However diverse
the interests that give rise to these sociations, the forms in which the interests are
realized are identical. On the other hand, the identical interest may take on form
in very different sociations. Economic interest is realized both in competition
and in the planned organization of producers, in isolation from other groups
and in fusion with them. Although the religious contents of life remain identical,
at one time they demand an unregulated, at another time a centralized, form of
community. The interests upon which the relations between the sexes are based
are satisfied by an almost endless variety of family forms. The educational interest may lead to a liberal or to a despotic relation between teacher and pupil, to
individualistic interaction between them, or to a more collectivistic type of interaction between the teacher and the totality of his pupils. Hence, not only may the
form in which the most widely different contents are realized be identical, but a
content too may persist while its medium – the interactions of the individuals –
moves in a variety of forms. We see, then, that the analysis in terms of form
and content transforms the facts – which in their immediacy present form and
content as an indissoluble unity of social life – in such a way as to furnish the
legitimation of the sociological problem. This problem demands that the pure
forms of sociation be identified, ordered systematically, explained psychologically, and studied from the standpoint of their historical development. . . .

This conception of society implies a further proposition: A given number of
individuals may be a society to a greater or a smaller degree. With each formation of parties, with each joining for common tasks or in a common feeling or
way of thinking, with each articulation of the distribution of positions of submission and domination, with each common meal, with each self-adornment

for others – with every growth of new synthesizing phenomena such as these, the same group becomes "more society" than it was before. There is no such thing as society "as such"; that is, there is no society in the sense that it is the condition for the emergence of all these particular phenomena. For there is no such thing as interaction "as such" – there are only specific kinds of interaction. And it is with their emergence that society too emerges, for they are neither the cause nor the consequence of society but are, themselves, society. The fact that an extraordinary multitude and variety of interactions operate at any one moment has given a seemingly autonomous historical reality to the general concept of society. Perhaps it is this hypostatization of a mere abstraction that is the reason for the peculiar vagueness and uncertainty involved in the concept of society and in the customary treatises in general sociology. We are here reminded of the fact that not much headway was made in formulating a concept of "life" as long as it was conceived of as an immediately real and homogeneous phenomenon. The science of life did not establish itself on a firm basis until it investigated specific processes within organisms – processes whose sum or web life is; not until, in other words, it recognized that life consists of these particular processes.

Consider

1. Who was Georg Simmel? Use the internet to find out as much as you can about his life and work. Here is one website to help you with this task:

   Georg Simmel homepage http://www.socio.ch/sim/index_sim.htm

   Can you find any other websites on Georg Simmel? Who wrote these websites? How reliable is the information presented on them? How can you tell?
2. Again, this chapter introduces you to the most important arguments of the reading, but does not cover all of it. The following questions may help you to gain a fuller understanding. You may find this reading relatively difficult, and it may help you to look at some of the secondary sources recommended at the end of this chapter.
   (a) What are Simmel's main arguments throughout the reading? Draw up a list of his key points and explain each of them in your own words.
   (b) 'Society exists where a number of individuals enter into interaction.' Explain.
   (c) What does Simmel understand by 'sociation'? Define the concept, using examples of your own.
   (d) In developing his concept of society, Simmel distinguishes between the 'form' and the 'content' of social life. Can you explain this distinction in your own words? This is a particularly challenging question. It may help you to do some background reading on Simmel's work before answering it. In particular, you might start by looking at pp. 276–8 in George Ritzer's *Classical Sociological Theory* and building your answer on Ritzer's explanation.

(e) 'A given number of individuals may be a society to a greater or a smaller degree. With each formation of parties, with each joining for common tasks or in a common feeling or way of thinking, [. . .] with each common meal, with each self-adornment for others – with every growth of new synthesizing phenomena such as these, the same group becomes "more society" than it was before.' Explain this statement in reference to one of the following examples:
  (i) A football club
  (ii) A family
  (iii) A nation
  (iv) A political party
  (v) A religious group.

Let us consider the opening passages of Simmel's argument. Here, he presents the most basic aspects of his definition of society and develops a number of concepts that are still central to sociology today. Simmel begins by arguing that society 'exists where a number of individuals enter into interaction' (1908/1971: 23). First of all, the idea of social 'interaction' needs to be unravelled. Individuals come together and 'interact' or engage with each other to pursue their personal interests and objectives. As Simmel explains later on, such interests and objectives on their own are not social. However, in so far as their pursuit invariably requires people to come together and engage with each other, they form the base of social interaction and give such interaction a meaningful 'content' (Simmel 1908/1971: 24). Simmel states that their interests and objectives 'cause man [sic] to live with other men, to act for them, with them, against them, and thus to correlate his conditions with theirs' (1908/1971: 23). Importantly, Simmel here seems to presume that there is an intrinsic need for human beings to interact to achieve their interests. While he does not state this explicitly, Simmel here presents humans as inherently social beings, who unavoidably need to come together and do things with each other – and sometimes against each other – to survive and thrive. Based on their personal interests, drives and purposes, individuals unavoidably engage with each other, at the same time affecting the lives of others and being affected by them (Simmel 1908/1971: 24).

A simple example might help to clarify this point: I am hungry, and therefore I would like to eat. Moreover, I wish to eat a meal I enjoy. I decide to visit a Chinese restaurant and eat spicy stir fry frog, one of my favourite dishes. Considered on its own, my desire to have dinner is not social. It is related to my physical condition (hunger) and my very personal preferences (stir fry frog is not a common or popular dish in Great Britain). However, my dinner plans are social in so far as they require me to engage directly and indirectly with a variety of other people – the restaurant staff through whom I will place an order, the cook who will prepare the meal, the other guests in the restaurant, whose presence reminds me that I should display good table manners, and so forth. Moreover, my preferences as to food are the outcome of prior social interaction with others – for instance with my Chinese friends who introduced me to stir fry frog. I would not have been aware of, or taken an interest in this dish, had I not travelled to China and been invited to restaurants where my friends would order it for me. In this sense, my very own and personal preferences and choices are shaped by prior social interaction with others, and they require me to continue interacting with people in an ongoing manner. Likewise, my interaction with others has various consequences for their lives, affecting their way of thinking, and contributing to the success or failure of their actions.

Simmel builds his definition of society upon this insight into the foundational role of social interaction in human life. Through their ongoing interaction with each other, individuals come to form, in Simmel's words, a 'unity' (1908/1971: 23). Simmel uses the analogy of the organic body to characterise this unity: the bodies of a rose, a tiger and a boy are distinctive wholes or unities. At the same time, however, this unity is composed of and depends upon each of the single organs it comprises. These organs, in turn, depend upon each other for survival. In the same way, unities of human beings – states, tribes, cities, villages, football teams, dance clubs, companies, etc. – comprise different individuals with distinct interests, upon whose constructive interaction they depend. Student group presentations may serve as an example here. The success of a class presentation depends on all group members doing their share of preparatory work and demonstrating their knowledge during the presentation. If, out of a lack of time, interest, or mutual sympathy, the group members do not cooperate, the group does not function as a meaningful unity any more. The resulting class presentation may be weak, or it may depend on the efforts of a few isolated group members who decided to get it done on their own.

Simmel also terms this unity 'sociation' (1908/1971). Sociation may take many distinctive forms, from the fleeting engagement among a group of strangers who have come together to watch a concert or sports event to the durable, often lifelong belonging to a family or a nation. It is through such forms of sociation that society comes to be and that societies acquire their particular shape and character. For instance, European societies in the Middle Ages were generally shaped by religious forms of sociation. Churches played a pivotal role in community life, monasteries acted as central storehouses of knowledge, and the Catholic Church wielded inordinate political power, directly ruling some states and indirectly controlling others. Contemporary European societies are distinct from their medieval predecessors because, among other reasons, the political influence of the Catholic Church receded from the eighteenth century onwards, and religious freedom became a general right. Today, many different forms of religious and non-religious sociation co-exist happily – and sometimes unhappily – throughout the world. A vast variety of different kinds of religious practices and interaction can be observed in major metropolises, while, at the same time, the lives of many people are not motivated by any particular religion at all. Thus, the unities that constitute contemporary societies differ greatly from those that were prevalent centuries ago.

Simmel derives an important conclusion from his discussion of sociation:

> It is evident that that which constitutes society in every current sense of the term is identical with the kinds of interaction discussed. A collection of human beings does not become a society because each of them has an objective determined or subjectively impelling life content. (Simmel 1908/1971: 24)

In other words, a society only exists where people interact with each other in ways that sustain it and give it a specific form and character. Societies – large-scale unities of individuals – are built out of ongoing, meaningful social interaction. For instance, in an abstract sense, French society has existed continuously since the year 843 – for nearly 1,200 years. However, if you take a moment to consider what life in France would have typically been like in the year 1000 and in the year 2000, you will be confronted with very different kinds of society. The forms of sociation that characterise life in the modern, urbanised, industrialised, secular France of the 2000s have very little in common with those of rural, feudal, religious France under its medieval kings. The name 'France' covers a variety of very different societies. Each society acquires its character through the ongoing interaction of its members and the typical forms of sociation – cities, villages, farms, tribes, pubs, churches, families and so forth – to which this interaction gives rise. As people's beliefs and habits change, new technologies are discovered, and others are considered obsolete, so forms of sociation develop and societies are transformed.

1.5 What is sociology?

Based on these observations, we can now draw an initial sketch of sociology and its central concerns. To begin with, we can say that sociology is the study of society. On the one hand, this involves the examination of social facts, that is, large-scale social forces that mould the ways in which we live with each other. On the other hand, sociology is the study of social interaction, exploring the common forms in which individuals engage with each other in everyday life and which give their societies a distinctive character.

If you are observant, you may already have noted that sociologists take quite different approaches to the study of society. Some, such as Émile Durkheim, emphasise the role which social facts play in determining the nature of social life. Others, such as Georg Simmel, highlight the role which interaction between individuals in everyday life plays in forming society. In spite of these differences of emphasis, however, sociologists share a commitment to the sociological imagination. The sociological imagination offers us a view of the world that highlights how individual lives are shaped by and constitutive of the larger patterns and forces of society. The sociological imagination allows us to understand that human beings do not exist as isolated atoms, separate and

Sociology is the study of society.	Sociology is the study of social facts.	'A social fact is every way of acting, fixed or not, capable of exercising on the individual an external constraint; or again, every way of acting which is general throughout a given society, while at the same time existing in its own right independent of its individual manifestations' (Durkheim 1895/1982: 13).
	Sociology is the study of social interaction.	'Society exists where a number of individuals enter into interaction. This interaction always arises on the basis of certain drives or for the sake of certain purposes. [. . .] The significance of these interactions among men lies in the fact that it is because of them that the individuals, in whom these driving impulses are lodged, form a unity, that is, a society' (Simmel 1908/1971: 23).
Sociology is shaped by the sociological imagination.	Sociology understands individual lives through their larger social context.	'The sociological imagination enables us to grasp history and biography and the relations between the two within society' (Mills 1959/1967: 6).
		'Perhaps the most fruitful distinction with which the sociological imagination works is between "the personal troubles of milieu" and "the public issues of social structure". This distinction is an essential tool of the sociological imagination and a feature of all classic work in social science' (Mills 1959/1967: 8).

Figure 1.1   What is sociology? An initial approximation

independent from others and responsive purely to their own plans and motivations. Rather, our ways of thinking, feeling and acting are to a large extent the product of our encounters with others. At the same time, we also have an active influence on the ways in which others can lead their lives.

This work is meant to be an argument in favour of the sociological imagination. What follows will introduce you to the rich, diverse perspectives on the world which sociology offers. While working with this text, you will also have a chance to do sociology yourself and use sociological concepts and ideas to explore a variety of issues in your everyday lives. In this sense, we hope to offer you both a 'textbook' and a sociological toolkit.

In what follows, we expand on the basic characterisation of sociology developed above. In doing so, a number of common themes are introduced. Sociology is presented as an *activity* that allows us to better understand the world we live in and act upon this understanding. Sociology is not dead knowledge stored in arcane tomes in dusty libraries. There is no gap between the 'real world' and sociological knowledge. The importance of the many readings collected here – some of them decades or centuries old – lies in the fact that they contain keys to better making sense of society and the many small and large problems it poses. These readings are meaningful in so far as they may provide you with ideas that help you to think *creatively* about your social environment. We all grow up with common sense: beliefs about the way the world works that are largely taken for granted in the communities to which we belong. The sociological imagination allows us to *challenge common sense*, critically interrogate our taken-for-granted beliefs, and develop explanations of social problems that are original and surprising. Sociology in this sense is a *reflexive endeavour* that encourages us to question beliefs about the world we simply have assumed to be true and uncover alternative perspectives on the issues and problems that characterise our everyday lives.

We then introduce a further central aspect of sociology (Chapter 2). This expands upon the argument outlined above that sociological knowledge is fundamentally different from common sense, by describing sociology as the *systematic* study of the social world on the base of specific *tools and methods*. We will look at some of the methods of sociological enquiry, explain how these may form part of your studies, and give you opportunities to try out some of them yourselves.

You will then be introduced to the variety of substantive concerns and lines of enquiry that sociologists have developed in the pursuit of two fundamental questions: *What is society? How do large-scale social forces shape individuals' lives, and how do individuals shape the features of their social world?* We next examine the origins of sociology and introduce you to some of the most important arguments of the scholars who founded sociology (Chapter 3), and go on to outline some central concerns in contemporary sociology (Chapter 4). First, we look at certain social processes and institutional processes, such as capitalism or modernisation, that have shaped the contemporary world at large. Second, we examine central social dimensions of everyday life, looking in depth at issues such as the social nature of the self, the body and human emotions.

A further important theme (in Chapter 5) develops the notion that sociology is a *global project*. While sociology ostensibly emerged and developed in the universities of the Western imperial powers of the nineteenth and twentieth century, the discipline has in truth been shaped by concerns with worldwide social developments. In this context, the chapter introduces sociological concepts of *globalisation* and worldwide forms of social organisation. In the twenty-first century, sociology has become truly global, and sociologists all around the world use the sociological imagination to make sense of an increasingly wide variety of social phenomena and problems.

Our next concern (Chapter 6) is with the ways in which contemporary societies produce, sustain and regulate major forms of social difference and inequality. We look at social processes that are of major contemporary significance, such as mass media, consumption, religion and work, and ask how these processes are linked to major axes of inequality and difference – of class, race, sex and gender, and so forth – that define differences between human beings today.

We conclude (Chapter 7) by considering the question of how the sociological imagination may matter in public life and in your development as an individual, examining, first, the importance of sociological understandings of 'society' and social change, and then connecting the sociological imagination to broader arguments about human life in the contemporary world.

Our overall goal is to allow you to familiarise yourself with major concepts and processes of sociological enquiry and begin to appreciate the sociological imagination. This will require effort and engagement on your part. To make things easier, a range of guides, tools and exercises have been included that are meant to guide you and allow you to experiment with sociological ideas. However, the most important point to remember on your way through this text is that sociology is about creativity, an interest in looking at the world from fresh perspectives, and, simply, fun. This is not meant to be a stale compendium of knowledge to be memorised for reproduction in tests and essays. Rather, we encourage you to immerse yourself in the ideas introduced and draw on those that seem most interesting, valuable, or important to you to discover the world for yourselves.

The debate: Sociology's value

So far, we have skirted around an international hot-button issue that is likely to have a very direct impact on your studies. Universities, a distinctive form of centre of higher learning, are a creation of medieval Europe. Since the time the University of Bologna was founded in 1088, however, universities have little by little spread around the world, and they are now focal points for scholarship in a multiplicity of countries. At the same time, the meaning of scholarship and the roles it may play in society have changed very markedly over different periods. The outset of the twenty-first century is one such period of change. Recent years have witnessed significant transformations within capitalism as the globally dominant mode of organisation of social and economic life (see Chapter 5 for more on this). As a part of these transformations, the meaning of studying for a higher degree is being contested and remade in many places, the UK and the USA being very notable examples. The following reading introduces you to some aspects of the public debates that surround these issues. After the reading, you will find a set of questions that ask you to consider your own place in all this.

Reading

Nussbaum, Martha, 2010, *Not for Profit: Why Democracy Needs the Humanities*, Princeton: Princeton University Press, pp. 1–2, 9–10, 14–15, 24–6

I The Silent Crisis

We are in the midst of a crisis of massive proportions and grave global significance. No, I do not mean the global economic crisis that began in 2008. At least then everyone knew that a crisis was at hand, and many world leaders worked quickly and desperately to find solutions. Indeed, consequences for governments were grave if they did not find solutions, and many were replaced in consequence. No, I mean a crisis that goes largely unnoticed, like a cancer; a crisis that is likely to be, in the long run, far more damaging to the future of democratic self-government: a worldwide crisis in education.

Radical changes are occurring in what democratic societies teach the young, and these changes have not been well thought through. Thirsty for national profit, nations, and their systems of education, are heedlessly discarding skills that are needed to keep democracies alive. If this trend continues, nations all over the world will soon be producing generations of useful machines, rather than complete citizens who can think for themselves, criticize tradition, and understand the significance of another person's sufferings and achievements. The future of the world's democracies hangs in the balance.

What are these radical changes? The humanities and the arts are being cut away, in both primary/secondary and college/university education, in virtually every nation of the world. Seen by policy-makers as useless frills, at a time when nations must cut away all useless things in order to stay competitive in the global market, they are rapidly losing their place in curricula, and also in the minds and hearts of parents and children. Indeed, what we might call the humanistic aspects of science and social science – the imaginative, creative aspect, and the aspect of rigorous critical thought – are also losing ground as nations prefer to pursue short-term profit by the cultivation of the useful and highly applied skills suited to profit-making.

This crisis is facing us, but we have not yet faced it. We go on as if everything were business as usual, when in reality great changes of emphasis are evident all over. We haven't really deliberated about these changes, we have not really chosen them, and yet they increasingly limit our future. [. . .]

Education is not just for citizenship. It prepares people for employment and, importantly, for meaningful lives. Another entire book could be written about the role of the arts and humanities in advancing these goals. All modern democracies, however, are societies in which the meaning and ultimate goals of human life are topics of reasonable disagreement among citizens who hold many different religious and secular views, and these citizens will naturally differ about how far various types of humanistic education serve their own particular goals. What we can agree about is that young people all over the world, in any nation lucky enough to be democratic, need to grow up to be participants in a form of government in which the people inform themselves about crucial issues they will address as voters and, sometimes, as elected or appointed officials. Every modern democracy is also a society in which people differ greatly along many parameters, including religion, ethnicity, wealth and class, physical impairment, gender, and sexuality, and in which all voters are making choices that have a major impact on the lives of people who differ from themselves. One way of assessing any educational scheme is to ask how well it prepares young people for life in a form of social and political organization that has these features. Without support from suitably educated citizens, no democracy can remain stable.

I shall argue that cultivated capacities for critical thinking and reflection are crucial in keeping democracies alive and wide awake. The ability to think well about a wide range of cultures, groups, and nations in the context of a grasp of the global economy and of the history of many national and group interactions is crucial in order to enable democracies to deal responsibly with the problems we currently face as members of an interdependent world. And the ability to imagine the experience of another – a capacity almost all human beings possess in some form – needs to be greatly enhanced and refined if we are to have any hope of sustaining decent institutions across the many divisions that any modern society contains. [. . .]

To think about education for democratic citizenship, we have to think about what democratic nations are, and what they strive for. What does it mean, then, for a nation to advance? In one view it means to increase its gross national product per capita. This measure of national achievement has for decades been the standard one used by development economists around the world, as if it were a good proxy for a nation's overall quality of life.

The goal of a nation, says this model of development, should be economic growth. Never mind about distribution and social equality, never mind about the preconditions of stable democracy, never mind about the quality of race and gender relations, never mind about the improvement of other aspects of a human being's quality of life that are not well linked to economic growth. (Empirical studies have by now shown that political liberty, health, and education are all poorly correlated with growth.) One sign of what this model leaves out is the fact that South Africa under apartheid used to shoot to the top of development indices. There was a lot of wealth in the old South Africa, and the old model of development rewarded that achievement (or good fortune), ignoring the staggering distributional inequalities, the brutal apartheid regime, and the health and educational deficiencies that went with it.

This model of development has by now been rejected by many serious development thinkers, but it continues to dominate a lot of policy-making, especially policies influenced by the United States. The World Bank made some commendable progress, under James Wolfensohn, in recognizing a richer conception of development, but things then slipped badly, and the International Monetary Fund never made the sort of progress that the Bank did under Wolfensohn. Many nations, and states within nations, are pursuing this model of development. Today's India offers a revealing laboratory of such experiments, as some states (Gujarat, Andhra Pradesh) have pursued economic growth through foreign investment, doing little for health, education, and the condition of the rural poor, while other states (Kerala, Delhi, to some extent West Bengal) have pursued more egalitarian strategies, trying to ensure that health and education are available to all, that the infrastructure develops in a way that serves all, and that investment is tied to job creation for the poorest. [. . .]

How else might we think of the sort of nation and the sort of citizen we are trying to build? The primary alternative to the growth-based model in international development circles, and one with which I have been associated, is known as the Human Development paradigm. According to this model, what is important is the opportunities, or "capabilities," each person has in key areas ranging from life, health, and bodily integrity to political liberty, political participation, and education. This model of development recognizes that all individuals possess an inalienable human dignity that must be respected by laws and institutions. A decent nation, at a bare minimum, acknowledges that its citizens have entitlements in these and other areas and devises strategies to get people above a threshold level of opportunity in each.

The Human Development model is committed to democracy, since having a voice in the choice of the policies that govern one's life is a key ingredient of a life worthy of human dignity. The sort of democracy it favors will, however, be one with a strong role for fundamental rights that cannot be taken away from people by majority whim – it will thus favor strong protections for political liberty; the freedoms of speech, association, and religious exercise; and fundamental entitlements in yet other areas such as education and health. This model dovetails well with the aspirations pursued in India's constitution (and that of South Africa). The United States has never given constitutional protection, at least at the federal level, to entitlements in "social and economic" areas such as health and education; and yet Americans, too, have a strong sense that the ability of all citizens to attain these entitlements is an important mark of national success. So the Human Development model is not pie-in-the-sky idealism; it is closely related to the constitutional commitments, not always completely fulfilled, of many if not most of the world's democratic nations.

If a nation wants to promote this type of humane, people-sensitive democracy dedicated to promoting opportunities for "life, liberty and the pursuit of happiness" to each and every person, what abilities will it need to produce in its citizens? At least the following seem crucial:

- The ability to think well about political issues affecting the nation, to examine, reflect, argue, and debate, deferring to neither tradition nor authority
- The ability to recognize fellow citizens as people with equal rights, even though they may be different in race, religion, gender, and sexuality: to look at them with respect, as ends, not just as tools to be manipulated for one's own profit
- The ability to have concern for the lives of others, to grasp what policies of many types mean for the opportunities and experiences of one's fellow citizens, of many types, and for people outside one's own nation
- The ability to imagine well a variety of complex issues affecting the story of a human life as it unfolds: to think about childhood, adolescence, family relationships, illness, death, and much more in a way informed by an understanding of a wide range of human stories, not just by aggregate data
- The ability to judge political leaders critically, but with an informed and realistic sense of the possibilities available to them
- The ability to think about the good of the nation as a whole, not just that of one's own local group
- The ability to see one's own nation, in turn, as a part of a complicated world order in which issues of many kinds require intelligent transnational deliberation for their resolution

This is only a sketch, but it is at least a beginning in articulating what we need.

Discuss

1. How, if at all, are the transformations of higher education towards a 'for profit' model taking place in your own society? Do some background research.
2. 'Radical changes are occurring in what democratic societies teach the young, and these changes have not been well thought through. [. . .] If this trend continues, nations all over the world will soon be producing generations of useful machines, rather than complete citizens who can think for themselves, criticize tradition, and understand the significance of another person's suffering and achievements.' What does Nussbaum mean? Try to explain her ideas in your own words. Do you agree with her observations?
3. So what, in your view, is the value of studying sociology in the contemporary world? Attempt to link your question to Nussbaum's arguments.
4. What do you hope to achieve by studying for a degree? How will it shape your future?

1.6 Study resources

Guide to further reading

There are a number of good starting points to further explore the ideas presented in this chapter. To begin with, C. Wright Mills's *The Sociological Imagination* is a timeless classic and highly recommendable. There are various editions of the text available. Mills's *The Power Elite* (1956/1999) uses the idea of the sociological imagination to look at the entanglement of military, corporations, and political power in the USA. Even though it was originally published more than half a century ago, the book is still of contemporary relevance and makes for an interesting read. If you would like to read a contemporary assessment of Mills's sociology, you might look at the respective chapter in Graham Crow's *The Art of Sociological Argument* (2005).

We will explore the work of Émile Durkheim and Georg Simmel in greater detail in Chapter 5. However, to begin to familiarise yourself with their approaches to sociology, Rob Stones's *Key Sociological Thinkers* is a good starting point. George Ritzer's *Classical Sociological Theory* (2008) and Ian Craib's *Classical Social Theory* (1997) likewise offer good introductions to the work of both scholars.

The sociologist's toolkit

To become a sociologist and deal with the many tasks and challenges on the way, it will help you to build a set of resources on which you can rely. These are some initial suggestions, with more to come in the following chapters.

1. *Dealing with difficult language* Sociological knowledge is stored in books and articles that often use unfamiliar terms and concepts. Having a general dictionary to look up difficult words will help a lot. The *Oxford English Dictionary* is widely used, but there is a wide variety of other dictionaries. In addition, a sociological dictionary will allow you to quickly gain a basic understanding of sociological terms and concepts. *A Dictionary of Sociology* (Oxford University Press, 2009) is a good choice. Finally, there is a wide variety of study skills texts to help students deal with difficult readings. *The Study Skills Handbook* by Stella Cottrell is widely used, and you will be able to find many alternative texts.
2. *Building your own library* You will be able to find a wide variety of sociological books and journals in libraries. Nevertheless, it is very helpful to have a basic stock of books ready at all times to support your thinking. An introductory textbook such as this one, a textbook on sociological research methods, and a general overview of sociological theories will help you greatly in your studies. This book contains many

relevant suggestions, but you may wish to browse in bookshops to find the books you like best.

3. *Using the internet effectively* It is very important that you are clear about how to use and how not to use the internet. Websites are full of information that may seem relevant to your studies, but many of them do not contain trustworthy information. Intute (www.intute.ac.uk), even though it has not been updated for a while, still allows you to access a wide variety of high-quality materials and also contains a training suite that allows you to develop your internet skills. You can use this website as a starting point for your sociological discoveries online.

Works cited

Durkheim, Émile (1895/1982), *The Rules of Sociological Method*, London: The Macmillan Press.

Mills, C. Wright (1959/1967), *The Sociological Imagination*, London: Oxford University Press.

Sennett, R. (1998), *The Corrosion of Character: The Personal Consequences of Work in the New Capitalism*, New York: W. W. Norton.

Simmel, Georg (1908/1971), 'The Problem of Sociology', in *Georg Simmel: On Individuality and Social Forms*, edited by D. N. Levine, Chicago: The University of Chicago Press.

2 Doing sociology

2.1 Not a desk job: sociology as a form of practice

There are various perspectives from which to introduce sociology. First of all, we can examine the *world of ideas and theories* that constitute sociological knowledge of the world. What are the main ideas underlying the sociological imagination? What kinds of knowledge about different arenas of social life does the sociological imagination reveal? This is the dominant perspective we have adopted for this text. In addition, we highlight the ways in which particular strands of theory are grounded in the scholarship of certain influential scholars, whose work has inspired prominent approaches to the study of the social world. Chapter 1, for instance, introduced you to two such scholars, Émile Durkheim and C. Wright Mills. Durkheim's recognition of the existence of a distinct class of social facts, above and beyond the control of particular individuals, but nevertheless shaping their lives, has been foundational to most sociological enquiry to date. Written about sixty years later, Mills's outline of the contours of a distinctive sociological imagination has similarly shaped the world view of many generations of sociologists.

In addition, there is a further important perspective to take into account. If sociology consisted purely of 'ideas and theories', it would have very little connection to the multifaceted realities of everyday life around the world. Its proposals would quickly become stale and incapable of offering meaningful explanations of human life. As we will see in more detail in Chapter 3, sociology developed precisely as a response to the apparent incapability of derived theological and philosophical traditions to make sense of the vast changes that began to engulf the world from the late eighteenth century on. Sociology, hence, always needs to be understood as a *special form of practice*, of actively using the sociological imagination to engage with the social world. Sociology is in part about studying books and journal articles. This is necessary in order to develop an understanding of the sociological imagination and the various forms of sociological thought it has spawned. Crucially, however, sociology is also about going 'out there', observing, talking to people, learning about their lives and the communities in which these lives take place, and using the resulting understanding to offer fresh insights about the contemporary world, its origins, and its possible futures. Books and journal articles are only the very final outcome of this process of learning and understanding. *Sociology is a special form of practice, grounded in the sociological imagination, and geared towards the development of an understanding of the social world, its historical roots, and its developmental possibilities.*

At its most engaging, sociology consists of vivid ethnographies – first-hand narratives of the way of life of a particular group of people or community that result from months-long or even years-long involvement by the researcher. James Farrer (2002) visited nightclubs and discos in Shanghai over many months to witness contemporary young Chinese people's experiences of dating, sex and leisure. Roger Lancaster (1992) lived for years in Nicaragua to gain a first-hand understanding of the everyday lives of poor people in this Central American country. Meanwhile, American sociologist Nicole Constable (2003) spent substantial time in the virtual world of internet dating to make sense of the phenomenon of 'mail-order brides' and internet dating.

Equally, the findings of survey research, derived from abstract, computer-based statistical analysis and much dry office work, are grounded in meticulously planned and conducted interviews with dozens, hundreds, and sometimes even thousands of people. The British Household Panel Survey and the British Social Attitudes survey, for instance, paint a detailed picture of the domestic lives, attitudes and values of people in Great Britain. The work of sociologist Ronald Inglehart (e.g. Inglehart and Welzel 2005) even uses survey research to offer insights into social and political attitudes and values at a worldwide level!

In contrast, one reason that the research of early sociologists such as Auguste Comte or Herbert Spencer (see Chapter 3 for details) has fallen out of favour to some extent is that much of it resulted from armchair speculation. Instead of going out there to explore social life first-hand, or at least reading the work of their colleagues, both Comte and Spencer often limited themselves to developing grand theories with very little grounding in either direct observation or the scientific developments of their time.

In sociology degree courses, such as the one you are likely taking, there is often a division of labour between classes that introduce you to the discipline's fundamental body of ideas and classes that equip you with the tools for doing sociology. This book is intended for the former kind of class. Nonetheless, this chapter will also give you a general idea of the things sociologists do. This chapter should be read as a brief general introduction to sociological research, with recommendations of more detailed introductory texts to be found at the end.

We will begin with some matters you need to be aware of as students of sociology. 'Studying sociology' thus looks at very basic practical issues, from the role of reading, writing and, above all, critical and creative thinking in your degree programme, to the conventions of acknowledging the work of the scholars on which your writings are based. 'Doing sociological research' then sketches the ways in which professional sociologists go about planning and doing research and presenting their findings to a wide audience. During your studies, you will likely get to try out some of these skills and activities – particularly if your degree programme concludes with a dissertation. Here, we hope to give you a general sense of what you could do, and make you look at your world through the lens of a professional sociologist.

Reading
*grounding on ideas into
already existing ideas*

2.2 Studying sociology

Let's now consider the main activities in which you will become involved as part of your sociology degree. As a matter of course, you will find your own, very personal way of studying and your own, very personal preferences for certain aspects of sociology. However, I suggest that there are certain activities that will be central to your studies, regardless of how exactly you approach them. These are outlined in Figure 2.1.

Reading is crucial to sociology in two ways. First, to become a sociologist you must have a good understanding of the sociological imagination, sociological theories and the method sociologists use to study the world. This knowledge is stored in books and journal articles you will review as part of your studies. Second, while creativity and new ideas are central, sociologists ground these in already existing ideas about key social issues and problems. Scholarship, in sociology as much as in other fields, is a *cumulative process*, in which new ideas and discoveries are built upon old ones, which are extended, modified or debunked. This makes it easier for sociologists to avoid conceptual mistakes, and it allows them to use the sophisticated insights of previous scholars to construct their own arguments. Failure to read and to take into account the work of other scholars easily leads to ideas that may seem out of touch or irrelevant, as the mentioned cases of Herbert Spencer and Auguste Comte illustrate.

Sociological knowledge in books and articles, even in its most abstract form, ultimately stems from *empirical observation*, that is to say, from direct experience of the social world – from listening, watching, smelling, touching the things that go on

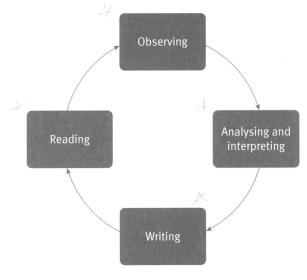

Figure 2.1   Sociology's foundational activities

around us. Sociologists use an array of methods of systematic enquiry to structure their observation of the world, and your studies will familiarise you with these. At first, it will be useful for you to relate the abstract sociological arguments you read to concrete experiences from your everyday life. Later on, you may be required to use sociological knowledge yourself to observe and engage with a certain place, community, or group of people as a base for a dissertation project. In any case, sociological knowledge stems from empirical observation, and it is only meaningful if you relate it back to the empirical world. Even for the most abstract argument you may read, there is a concrete example you can use to make it meaningful.

In turn, whether you read or observe first hand, your engagement with sociology should be guided by a certain frame of mind that involves *actively analysing and interpreting* what you read or see.

Anthropologist Harry Wolcott (1994: 12) explains that analysing 'addresses the identification of essential features and the systematic description of interrelationships among them – in short, how things work'. By gathering and analysing information, we can discover that unemployment is not an isolated, self-enclosed phenomenon; rather it is systematically related to a number of other social processes, such as the outsourcing of manufacturing abroad or the replacement of human with machine labour. Once we have identified such relationships, we are faced with questions of interpretation: ' "How does it all mean?" "What is to be made of all this?" ' (Wolcott 1994: 12). What are the social, economic and political implications of the decline of manufacturing in countries like the USA or Britain? Is this a development to be encouraged (e.g. because it leads to the creation of more highly-skilled, better-paid service jobs), or does it amount to a major social problem (e.g. due to the loss of jobs for the urban working classes and the exploitation of industrial labourers in the countries to which these jobs have been exported)? Based on the knowledge we have obtained from our analysis of the information we have gathered, we can proceed to formulate conclusions that are grounded in concrete evidence, rather than speculation or common sense. Thus, from this perspective, *sociology is geared towards the systematic analysis and interpretation of knowledge about the social world, with a view to the development of a better, clearer, more detailed understanding of significant social issues and problems.*

As a student of sociology, you are involved in this endeavour in particular through various forms of *writing*. You will mostly encounter writing in the form of essays, exams and dissertations. For each of these, you will be given a specific topic or question to consider. There are two basic approaches to writing about sociology during your degrees. One could be labelled the 'kitchen sink approach': you are given a topic, task or essay question to write about, and you proceed to write down everything you know about your subject matter, summarising from the different sources you have read. This will not take you very far, as it only requires you to repeat memorised knowledge, without making use of it to arrive at your own understanding of the problem or question you are considering.

Instead, in your writing, try to place a premium on using sociological ideas in creative ways. Demonstrate that you can draw on this knowledge to arrive at your own, original understanding of the world. Look at the topic you have been given to write about. Read relevant academic books and journal articles. Draw on what you have seen, read, heard elsewhere in your everyday lives for concrete examples. Then use what

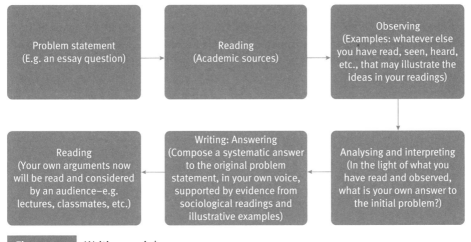

Figure 2.2   Writing sociology

you have learned to formulate your own answer, in your own voice, to the problem you are writing about. In this context, you can make selective use of the academic sources you have read and the examples you have developed to support your arguments. The key point, however, is that your writing must always consist of your own arguments, grounded in the sociological imagination. Writing, in a sense, is the end point of the sociological journey, as it allows you to systematise your ideas about whichever social phenomenon you are dealing with, give them a final shape, and put them forward to your readers for consideration. Figure 2.2 tries to summarise sociology's foundational activities from the point of view of writing.

Throughout this text, be you will find practical advice on each of the foundational activities in the various boxes. Moreover, you may turn to the 'guide to further reading' (at the chapter's end) for study skills books that contain much more detailed guidance on the issues sketched here. In the meantime, however, we will move on to consider how the four foundational activities inform the research of professional sociologists.

2.3 Doing sociological research: a quick and simple sketch

Telling about society

Let's begin by briefly re-examining what sociological stories about the world actually do. Obviously, sociologist are not the only ones to comment on the patterns and meanings of human life – poets, painters, playwrights, novelists, photographers and journalists, just to name a few, spend their lives dedicated to this task in one way or another. In fact, we all without any exception create our own very particular stories about the world as we move through our lives. In a recent book, sociologist Howard S. Becker (2007) considers these various ways of 'telling about society'. Below is a passage from the text.

Reading

Becker, Howard S. (2007), *Telling About Society*, Chicago: The University of Chicago Press, pp. 5–14

Who Tells?

We are all curious about the society we live in. We need to know, on the most routine basis and in the most ordinary way, how our society works. What rules govern the organizations we participate in? What routine patterns of behavior do others engage in? Knowing these things, we can organize our own behavior, learn what we want, how to get it, what it will cost, what opportunities of action various situations offer us.

Where do we learn this stuff? Most immediately, from our experience of daily living. We interact with all sorts of people and groups and organizations. We talk to people of all kinds in all kinds of situations. Of course, not *all* kinds: everyone's social experience of that face-to-face kind is limited by their social connections, their situation in society, their economic resources, their geographical location. You can get by with that limited knowledge, but in modern societies (probably in all societies) we need to know more than what we learn from personal experience. We need, or at least want, to know about other people and places, other situations, other times, other ways of life, other possibilities, other opportunities.

So we look for "representations of society," in which other people tell us about all those situations and places and times we don't know firsthand but would like to know about. With the additional information, we can make more complex plans and react in a more complex way to our own immediate life situations.

Simply put, a "representation of society" is something someone tells us about some aspect of social life. That definition covers a lot of territory. At one extreme lie the ordinary representations we make for one another, as lay folks, in the course of daily life. Take mapmaking. In many situations and for many purposes, this is a highly professionalized activity based on centuries of combined practical experience, mathematical reasoning, and scientific scholarship. But in many other situations, it's an ordinary activity we all do once in a while. I ask you to visit me sometime, but you don't know how to drive to where I live. I can give you verbal directions: "Coming from Berkeley, you take the first exit on the right off the Bay Bridge, turn left at the bottom of the ramp, go several blocks and turn left on to Sacramento, keep going until you hit Kearny, turn right and go up to Columbus . . . " I can suggest you consult a standard street map along with my directions, or I can just tell you that I live near the intersection of Lombard and Jones and let you use the map to find that spot. Or I can draw my own little map, personalized for you. I can show where you would start from – "your house" – and draw in the relevant streets, indicating where you should turn, how long each leg will be, what landmarks you will pass, and how you will know when you reach "my house." These days an Internet site will tell you all that, or you can let your GPS device do it for you.

Those are all representations of a portion of society, contained in a simple geographical relationship; a simpler and better way of saying it is that these are all ways of telling about society or some portion thereof. Some of the ways, the standard automobile map or the computer description, are made by highly trained professionals using a lot of specialized equipment and knowledge. The verbal description and the homemade map are made by people just like the people to whom they are given, people who have no more geographical knowledge or ability than any ordinarily competent adult. They all work, in different ways, to do the job of leading someone from one place to another.

My own professional colleagues – sociologists and other social scientists – like to talk as though they have a monopoly on creating such representations, as though the knowledge of society they produce is the only "real" knowledge about that subject. That's not true. And they like to make the equally silly claim that the ways they have of telling about society are the best ways to do that job or the only way it can be done properly, or that their ways of doing the job guard against all sorts of terrible mistakes we would otherwise make.

That kind of talk is just a standard professional power grab. Considering the ways that people who work in other fields – visual artists, novelists, playwrights, photographers, and filmmakers – as well as laypeople represent society will show analytic dimensions and possibilities that social science has often ignored that might otherwise be useful. I will concentrate on the representational work done by other kinds of workers, as well as that done by social scientists. Social scientists know how to do their job, and that's adequate for many purposes. But their ways aren't the only ways.

What are some of the other ways? We can categorize representational activities in many ways. We could talk about media – film vs. words vs. numbers, for instance. We might talk about the intent of the makers of the representations: science vs. art vs. reportage. Such a comprehensive review would serve many purposes well, but not my purpose of exploring generic problems of representation and the variety of solutions the world has so far produced. Looking at some major, highly organized ways of telling about society means attending to the distinctions among science, art, and reportage. Those are not so much distinct ways of doing something as they are ways of organizing what might be, from the point of view of materials and methods, pretty much the same activity. [. . .]

Telling about society usually involves an interpretive community, an organization of people who routinely make standardized representations of a particular kind ("makers") for others ("users") who routinely use them for standardized purpose. The makers and users have adapted what they do to what the others do, so that the organization of making and using is, at least for a while, a stable unity, a *world* (used in a technical sense I've developed elsewhere [Becker 1982] and will discuss more fully below).

Often enough, some people don't fit well into these organized worlds of makers and users. These experimenters and innovators don't do things as they are usually done, and therefore their works may not have many users. But their solutions to standard problems tell us a lot and open our eyes to possibilities more conventional practice doesn't see. Interpretive communities often borrow procedures and forms, using them to do something the originators in that other community never thought of or intended, producing mixtures of method and style to fit into changing conditions in the larger organizations they belong to.

This is all very abstract. Here's a more specific list of standard formats for telling about society, which have produced exemplary works of social representation worth inspecting carefully:

Fiction. Works of fiction, novels and stories, have often served as vehicles of social analysis. The sagas of families, classes, and professional groups by writers as dissimilar in aims and talent as Honoré de Balzac, Émile Zola, Thomas Mann, C. P. Snow, and Anthony Powell have always been understood to embody, and to depend on for their power and aesthetic virtues, complex descriptions of social life and its constituent processes. The works of Charles Dickens, taken singly and as a whole, have been understood (as he intended them to be) as a way of describing to a large public the organizations that produced the ills his society suffered from.

Drama. Similarly, the theater has often been a vehicle for the exploration of social life, most especially the description and analysis of social ills. George Bernard Shaw used the dramatic form to embody his understanding of how "social problems" came about and how deeply they penetrated the body politic. His *Mrs. Warren's Profession* explains the workings of the business of prostitution as it provided the livelihood of at least some of the British upper classes; and *Major Barbara* did the same for war and munitions making. Many playwrights have used drama for similar purposes (Henrik Ibsen, Arthur Miller, David Mamet).

To say that these works and authors deal in social analysis doesn't mean that that is "all" they do or that their works are "only" sociology in artistic disguise. Not at all. Their authors have purposes in mind beyond social analysis. But even the most formalist critic should realize that some part of the effect of many works of art depends on their "sociological" content and on the belief of readers and audiences that what these works tell them about society is, in some sense, "true."

Films. In the most obvious case, documentary film – Barbara Koppel's 1976 *Harlan County, U.S.A.* and Edgar Morin and Jean Rouch's 1961 *Chronique d'un été* are well known examples – has had as a primary object the description of society, often, but not necessarily overtly, in a reformist mode, aiming to show viewers what's wrong with current social arrangements. Fiction films also often mean to analyze and comment on the societies they present, many times those in which they are made. Examples range from Gillo Pontecorvo's pseudodocumentary *Battle of Algiers* (1966) to classic Hollywood fare like Elia Kazan's 1947 *Gentleman's Agreement.*

Photographs. Likewise, still photographers have, from the beginnings of the genre, often occupied themselves with social analysis. A well-defined genre of documentary photography has had a long and illustrious history. Some exemplary works of that genre include Brassaï's *The Secret Paris of the '30s* (1976), Walker Evans's *American Photographs* ([1938] 1975), and Robert Frank's *The Americans* ([1959] 1969).

So far I have talked about "artistic" modes of making representations of society. Other representations are more associated with "*science.*"

Maps. Maps, associated with the discipline of geography (more specifically, cartography), are an efficient way of displaying large amounts of information about social units considered in their spatial dimension.

Tables. The invention of the statistical table in the eighteenth century made it possible to summarize vast numbers of specific observations in a compact and comparable format. These compact descriptions help governments and others organize purposeful social action. A governmental census is the classical form of such use. Scientists use tables to display data others can use to evaluate their theories. Twentieth-century social scientists became increasingly dependent on the tabular display of quantitative data gathered specifically for that purpose.

Mathematical models. Some social scientists have described social life by reducing it to abstract entities displayed as mathematical models. These models, intentionally removed from social reality, can convey basic relations characteristic of social life. They have been used to analyze such varied social phenomena as kinship systems and the world of commercial popular music.

Ethnography. A classic form of social description has been the ethnography, a detailed verbal description of the way of life, considered in its entirety, of some social unit, archetypically but not necessarily a small tribal group. The method came to be applied, and is widely applied now, to organizations of all kinds: schools, factories, urban neighborhoods, hospitals, and social movements.

Somewhere between the extremes of art and science lie history and biography, usually devoted to detailed and accurate accounts of past events but often equally given to evaluating large generalizations about matters the other social sciences deal with. (Remember that all of today's sociological reports will be raw material for historians of the future, as masterworks of sociology like the Lynds' studies of "Middletown" have turned from social analysis into historical document.)

Finally, there are the sports, mavericks, and innovators I spoke of earlier. Some makers of representations of society mix methods and genres, experiment with forms and languages, and provide analyses of social phenomena in places we don't expect them and in forms we don't recognize as either art or science or that we see as some unusual and unfamiliar mixture of genres. So Hans Haacke, who can be called a conceptual artist, uses uncomplicated devices to lead users to unexpected conclusions. Georges Perec and Italo Calvino, members of the French literary group OULIPO (Motte 1998) devoted to esoteric literary experiments, made the novel, in one form or another, a vehicle for subtle sociological thinking. And in David Antin's "talk pieces," stories that may or may not be fictions convey complex social analyses and ideas. Like all such experiments, the work of these artists forces us to reconsider procedures we usually take for granted, and I'll discuss their work at length later in the book.

Facts

I must make an important distinction, even though it is fallacious and misleading and every word involved is slippery and indeterminate. I don't think those faults make much difference for my purpose here. It's the distinction between "fact" and "idea" (or "interpretation"). One part of any report on society (of any of the kinds I've just outlined) is a description of how things are: how some kinds of things are, in some place, at some time. This is how many people there are in the United States, as counted in the year 2000 by the U.S. Bureau of the Census. This is how many of them are women and how many are men. This is the age distribution of that population – so many below five, so many aged five to ten, all the way up. This is the racial composition of that population. This is the distribution of their incomes. This is that income distribution in racial and gender subgroups of the population.

Those are facts about the U.S. population (and, of course, similar facts are more or less available for all the other countries in the world). They are descriptions of what a person who went looking for such numbers would find, the evidence that results from the operations demographers and statisticians have undertaken in accordance with the procedures of their craft.

In the same way, anthropologists tell us, for instance, how *these* people living in *this* society reckon kinship: they recognize these categories of familial relationship and think this is how people related in those ways should behave toward one another; these are, in the classical phrase, their mutual rights and obligations. Anthropologists support their analyses with accounts of the facts about how those people talk and behave, contained in the field notes that report their on-the-spot observations and interviews, just as demographers support descriptions of the U.S. population with the data produced by the census. In either case, the professionals begin with evidence gathered in ways their craft peers recognize as sufficient to warrant the factual status of the results.

Now for the caveats. Thomas Kuhn long ago persuaded me that facts are never just facts but are rather, as he said, "theory-laden" (1970). Every statement of a fact presupposes a theory that explains what entities are out there to describe, what characteristics they can have, which of those characteristics can be observed and which can only be inferred from characteristics that are observable, and so on.

Theories often seem so obvious as to be self-evident. Does anyone need to argue that you can tell a human being when you see one and distinguish such a being from some other kind of animal? Does it need arguing that these human beings can be characterized as male or female? Or as black, white, Asian, or of another racial variety?

In fact, scientists and laypeople argue about things like that all the time, as the continually shifting racial categories in censuses all over the world make clear. Characteristics like gender and race don't appear in nature in an obvious way. Every society has ways of telling boys from girls and distinguishing members of racial categories its members think are important from one another. But these categories rest on theories about the essential characteristics of humans, and the nature of the categories and the methods of assigning people to them vary between societies. So we can never take facts for granted. There are no pure facts, only "facts" that take on meaning from an underlying theory.

Moreover, facts are facts only when they are accepted as such by the people to whom those facts are relevant. Am I indulging in a pernicious kind of relativism, or malicious wordplay? Maybe, but I don't think we have to discuss whether there is an ultimate reality science will eventually reveal in order to recognize that reasonable people, including reasonable scientists, often disagree on what constitutes a fact, and when a fact really is a fact. Those disagreements arise because scientists often disagree on what constitutes adequate evidence for the existence of a fact. Bruno Latour (1987, 23–29) has demonstrated, well enough to suit me and many others, that, as he so neatly puts it, the fate of a scientific finding lies in the hands of those who take it up afterward. If they accept it as fact, it will be treated as fact. Does that mean that any damn thing can be a fact? No, because one of the "actants," to use Latour's inelegant expression, that must agree with the interpretation is the object about which the statements of fact are made. I can say the moon is made of green cheese, but the moon will have to cooperate, exhibiting those characteristics that other people will recognize as green cheese-like, or else my fact will become an unacceptable nonfact. Worse yet, my fact may not even be disputed; it may just be ignored, so that you might say it doesn't exist at all, at least not in the discourse of scientists who study the moon. There may be an ultimate reality, but we are all fallible human beings and may be wrong, so all facts are disputable in the real world we live in. That fact is at least as obdurate and hard to talk away as any other scientific fact.

Finally, facts are not accepted in general or by the world at large, they are accepted or rejected by the particular audiences their proponents present them to. Does this mean science is situational and its findings therefore not universally true? I'm not taking a position on such ultimate questions of epistemology, just recognizing what's obvious: when we make a report about society, we make it to somebody, and who those somebodies are affects how we present what we know and how users react to what we present to them. Audiences differ – this is important – in what they know and know how to do, in what they believe and will accept, on faith or with evidence of some kind. Different kinds of reports routinely go to different kinds of audiences: statistical tables to people more or less trained to read them, mathematical models to people with highly specialized training in the relevant disciplines, photographs to a wide variety of lay and professional audiences, and so on.

Instead of facts supported by evidence that makes them acceptable as fact, then, we have facts based on a theory, accepted by some people because they have been gathered in a way acceptable to some community of makers and users.

Interpretations

It's not easy to separate interpretations from facts. Every fact, in its social context, implies and invites interpretations. People move easily and without much thought from one to the other. The same facts will support many interpretations. To say, to take a provocative example, that racial groups differ in IQ scores might well be a fact – that is, demonstrated by the use of tests commonly used by psychologists who make a business of such measurement. But to interpret such a finding as a demonstration that such differences are genetic – inherited and thus not easily changed – is not a fact, it's an interpretation of the meaning of the reported fact. An alternate interpretation says the fact demonstrates that the IQ test is culture specific and can't be used to compare different populations.

Neither do the findings about race, gender, and income we can find in the U.S. Census speak for themselves. Someone speaks for them, interpreting their

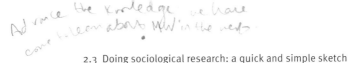

meaning. People argue more about interpretations than they do about facts. We can agree on the numbers describing the relations between gender, race, and income, but the same census data might be interpreted to show the existence of discrimination, the lessening of discrimination, the joint working of two disadvantaged conditions (being female, being black) on income, or many other possible stories.

A report about society, then, is an artifact consisting of statements of fact, based on evidence acceptable to some audience, and interpretations of those facts similarly acceptable to some audience.

Consider

1. What are the different representations of society that Becker identifies? How are they similar? What are the main differences you see between them? Where relevant, use your own examples to illustrate these questions.
2. How does Becker define 'facts' and 'interpretations' of the social world? What is their respective role in different representations of society?
3. Can any representation of social life be simply factual without involving any interpretations? Illustrate your answer with relevant examples.

One important question that results from Becker's arguments is what makes sociological accounts of the world distinctive and significant. What is the case for sociology, if we already have novelists, artists, journalists and so many others telling us about society? There are two answers to this question. One – considered in Chapter 1 – would point to the importance of the sociological imagination. The other, examined here, looks at the particular techniques that sociologists use to advance knowledge about the world.

We have already argued above that sociology distinguishes itself by grounding its explorations of social phenomena in *empirical observation*. However, journalists certainly ground their stories in careful investigative work, and even abstract works of art are grounded in some sort of engagement with events in the world. What makes sociological research distinctive is that it *builds upon the systematic use of specific methods of enquiry to generate knowledge about social phenomena* and that *it sets out its evidence and the interpretations built upon this evidence in an equally systematic manner*, so as to facilitate their appraisal by readers. In other words, sociologists have at their disposal an array of well-developed methods of enquiry that allow them to arrive at an understanding of society's issues and problems that is demonstrably trustworthy and believable.

For example, sociologist Elijah Anderson (1999) set out to understand the reasons for exceptionally high levels of violence in poor black inner-city neighbourhoods in the USA. Over a period of many months, he spent time with the residents of one particular inner-city area of Philadelphia. He concluded that, in the economically most deprived urban areas, where opportunities for work and formal education are extremely scarce, young people often negotiate their sense of self-worth and respect through a 'code of the street':

> At the extreme end of the street-oriented group are those who make up the criminal element. People in this class are profound casualties of the social and economic system, and they tend to embrace the street code wholeheartedly. [. . .] For them, people and situations are best approached both as objects of exploitation and as challenges possibly 'having to trick them,' and in most situations their goal is to avoid being 'caught up in the trick back.' [. . .] Consistently, they tend to approach all persons and situations as part of life's obstacles, as things to subdue or 'get over.' To get over, individuals develop an effective 'hustle' or 'game plan,' setting themselves up in a position to prevail by being 'slick' and outsmarting others. In line with this, one must always be wary of one's counterparts, to assume that they are involved with you only for what they can get out of the situation. (Anderson 1999: 36f.)

Anderson argues that, while many people in inner city areas follow another set of values and beliefs focused on 'decency', it is very hard to resist the code of the street. This is so because rewards for hard work and efforts to eschew violence are so unlikely – employers have fled the inner city, jobs are hard to come by and difficult to sustain, and making a living is a constant struggle against very bad odds.

To arrive at these conclusions, not only did Anderson spend a lot of time in poor central areas of Philadelphia, but he systematically gathered and recorded evidence for his ideas through specific techniques, such as sociological observation and interviews, and he used equally systematic and structured techniques to analyse this evidence before presenting it to his readers. It is these procedures that set Anderson's work apart from, say, journalistic reporting about urban poverty and violence, or TV shows like *The Wire*.

The systematic construction and display of evidence for statements about important social problems means that sociological research is particularly suited for the interrogation of *common sense* and the stereotypes and false beliefs that are often associated with it. At the time that these words are written (July 2011) a fierce political battle over government spending and public debts is being waged by politicians in the USA. Many of these politicians justify their calls for 'fiscal responsibility' and cuts to welfare benefits for the poor with common sense, and the argument that benefits make the poor and unemployed too lazy to work is frequently made. Studies such as Anderson's 'Code of the Street' have the power to credibly disqualify such myths, and it is here that sociology can make an important contribution to political life and public debates.

Approaches to sociological knowledge

In this context, it must be noted that sociologists often do not agree about the specific procedures to be used in research and the nature of evidence to be gathered. This may be seen as a particular strength of sociological enquiry, as it may lead to social phenomena being studied from a range of different and complementary perspectives. In any case, these differences of perspective may be quite fundamental. They are often rooted in widely varying *epistemological assumptions* about the kind of knowledge sociologists can and should produce. *Epistemology* is a long-established branch of Western philosophy that examines the ways in which humans gain knowledge about the world, and the nature of such knowledge. As we will see in the next chapter, sociology emerged simultaneously in various parts of the world and based on often quite different intellectual inspirations.

We can very broadly divide contemporary sociologists into two epistemological camps. To do so vastly oversimplifies matters, but it also amounts to a useful starting point for your discovery of sociological research (provided you keep in mind that there is much more to it than what is described here). On the one hand, there are *positivist* approaches to sociological research. Positivists see a close association between sociology and the natural sciences. Just as there are laws governing the natural world, as studied by, say, physics, chemistry or biology, there are assumed to be relatively stable patterns and regularities that organise people's behaviour. In order to study these regularities, positivist sociologists use methods meant to lead to objective scientific knowledge about social behaviour.

In contrast, *interpretivist* sociologists emphasise differences between the natural and the human world. In particular, unlike physical objects, such as rocks or chemical substances or the sun, human beings act in response to feelings, beliefs, attitudes, and so forth. If you hold a rock in your hand and then release it, it will fall to the floor no matter what. If you ask a good friend to lend you a substantial sum of money, your friend may be torn between the wish to honour your friendship and the risk that you may not repay the debt for some time – his response to your request is by no means certain, and it depends on a range of personal considerations. Therefore, interpretivist sociologists argue that we must look at the subjective meanings and motivations that inform people's behaviour in everyday life, rather than limiting ourselves to the study of externally observable patterns and regularities.

This is just the approach which Elijah Anderson took in his research. His findings about the causes of violence are all about the subjective understandings, motivations and attitudes which young people in deprived inner-city areas have towards themselves and others. His quoted discussion of the 'street-oriented group' provides a good illustration of this approach: Issues such as being 'slick' in one's dealings with others and developing a 'game plan' to avoid being manipulated are all about the forms of subjective life experience which economic destitution has brought about in some young people. In contrast, a scientifically minded positivist would have approached Anderson's subject matter from a very different perspective. Instead of focusing on the subjective life experiences of a relatively small group of people, such a researcher might have chosen to compare economic and crime statistics on many US cities, in order to understand under which conditions economic disadvantage might be associated with high levels of violence and criminal behaviour.

The previous paragraphs begin to suggest how many broadly divergent ways of doing sociology there are. This diversity inevitably leads to the question of how sociologists choose between various traditions of thinking about social life and doing research. Answers to this question in turn are diverse and controversial. John Scott (2011) argues that dissimilar perspectives on the social world may, in the best of cases, complement each other. He suggests that an appraisal of their logic and their ability to accurately describe observable social processes can guide researchers in their choices of perspective. However, others (e.g. Connell 2007; Hill Collins 1990) suggest that our judgements about what might constitute a logical and accurate description of social life are shaped and constrained by a variety of factors, from the cultural context in which our lives are situated to our gender or our political values. From this standpoint, it becomes quite difficult to state with any certainty why and in which ways a particular intellectual perspective 'works better' than another.

What these observations should leave you with at the beginning of your studies of sociology is a general awareness of the need, first, to be open but critical towards the ideas you will encounter and, second, to develop for yourself criteria by which you can assess the different takes on social life you encounter. John Scott (2011) correctly observes that theoretical and methodological choices, such as those you will face when you write research papers or dissertations, should not be a matter of whimsical choices from a sociological supermarket. You are therefore faced with the challenge of providing intellectually sound justifications for the positions you take. The development of your capacity to give such justifications is an important part of the courses you will take during your studies of sociology, and it is perhaps just as significant as simply acquiring knowledge about the discipline and its various fields.

Research process and practice

As the example of Elijah Anderson's research shows, the epistemological assumptions which sociologists hold may translate into quite different approaches to the practice of research. In fact, the whole process of sociological research may come to vary considerably. By *research process*, we understand the sequence of activities through which sociologists arrive at answers to the research questions and problems they pursue. Typically, the research process begins with the choice of a problem to study and concludes with the publication of a research report, often in the form of one or several journal articles or a book. The chains of activities researchers pursue in between may turn out to be somewhat different, however. Consider Figure 2.3 and Figure 2.4.

Any study invariably begins with the specification of a general research problem, that is to say of an issue or subject matter to be studied. So, for example, Elijah Anderson (1999) was puzzled by the phenomenon of urban violence in the USA. Around the same time, sociologist Arlie Russell Hochschild took note of extremely long working hours that were common in contemporary (1997) US society, with often serious consequences for family life.

Such a general research problem now needs to be narrowed down, so that its study becomes practically feasible. It would be quite impossible, both in terms of time and

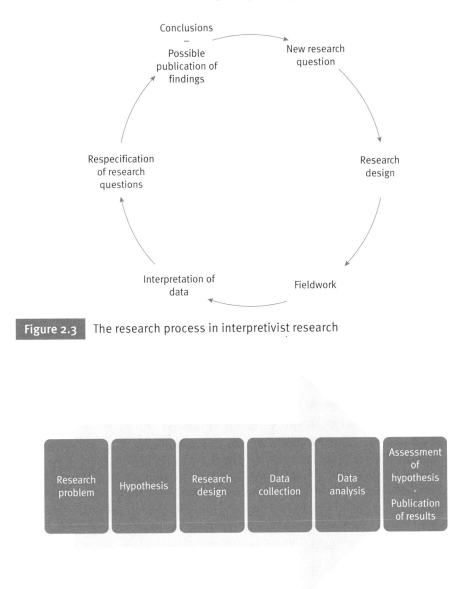

Figure 2.3   The research process in interpretivist research

Figure 2.4   The research process in positivist sociology

resources, to examine urban violence or the clash between work commitments and
family life (or any other topic) from every possible angle. It is here that the solutions
of interpretivists and positivists begin to differ. Interpretivists often prefer to work with
fairly loose and open-ended research questions that allow them to explore their subject matter in depth from different angles and deal with unanticipated issues when

they arise. So, for example, Nicole Constable (2003) writes that her interest in trans-national long-distance dating relationships was inspired by a chance encounter with an American man named Ben, who told her about his relationship with a Filipina he had met through a pen pal introduction service. This encounter led Constable to the following, very open question: 'Why would Ben (and tens of thousands of U.S. men), I wondered, decide to subscribe to a magazine or an Internet agency and write to women thousands of miles away in the hopes of finding a spouse?' (Constable 2003: 2). Constable explains that she presumed to know very little when she raised this question, gradually gaining an understanding of her subject matter and narrowing down the focus of her attention.

In contrast, positivist sociology begins with a much narrower focus. Instead of open-ended research questions, set hypotheses about the relationships of particular social phenomena (termed 'variables') are derived from a review of the extant academic lit-erature. Had Nicole Constable followed such an approach, her research might have departed from a hypothesis such as the following:

The more negative experiences American men have had with intimate partners of their own nationality, the more likely they are to participate in transnational long-distance dating relationships.

'Negative experiences' could be concretely measured through the number of break-ups, failed engagements, divorces, etc., which men have experienced. Had Constable chosen such an approach, her research would have lost much of its exploratory char-acter, instead limiting itself to rigorously testing the association between bad relation-ships in the past and participation in transnational dating.

Regardless of the approach chosen, the next step is always the formulation of a *research design*. A research design could be described as a kind of master plan accord-ing to which the project is to be executed. It attempts to specify in detail the technical aspects of the project and preview its various stages from beginning to end. As Figure 2.4 shows, positivists envision research as a tendentially linear process, in which a rigorous plan is formulated at the outset and then implemented to lead to a very specific set of conclusions. In contrast (Figure 2.3), interpretivist research is often imagined as a cycli-cal process, which emphasises exploration and leaves researchers free to move between different stages, re-visit and revise assumptions made at the outset, and flexibly gather evidence until a fully clear set of findings emerges.

In any case, such a plan allows the researcher to think through the various elements and stages of her work and develop a clear rationale for the choices she has made. Important elements of a research design typically include, among others, those out-lined in Figure 2.5 and Figure 2.6.

Now the main stage of the research process, often called *data collection* or *field-work*, begins. The researcher spends an often prolonged time in the field to pursue her research questions and put her research design into practice. Elijah Anderson reports that he conducted extensive fieldwork over many years in Philadelphia, both for *Code of the Street* and other books. This allowed him to gain the in-depth insights into urban

1. The choice of a *methodological framework* appropriate for the study. The term 'methodology' might be understood to refer to the overall principles of research, chosen according to the researcher's initial epistemological assumptions. *Quantitative* methodologies are often associated with positivist epistemologies. They involve sets of statistical techniques geared towards the objective measurement of social patterns and processes, to test specific hypotheses. *Qualitative* methodologies instead tend to focus on the in-depth exploration of subjective meanings and experiences of social life. In recent years, many sociologists have sought to transcend oppositions between qualitative and quantitative methodologies, integrating them into *mixed methodologies*.

2. The choice of a *population* and *setting* to be studied. Elijah Anderson (1999), for instance, studied violence in economically deprived inner-city areas in the USA (setting). His population consequently were the inhabitants of such areas, in particular poor African Americans.

3. The choice of a *sample* and *sampling strategy* from the study's population. Sampling deals with researchers' need to systematically select participants for their projects, as the meaning and relevance of their findings would otherwise be impossible to assess. For *Code of the Street*, Anderson chose one particular area of Philadelphia and its residents, arguing that the troubles faced by these people are in various ways typical or indicative of broader issues in urban America. Anderson's work is a good example of sampling in qualitative methodologies, in that it concentrates on a relatively small number of people in a particular place. In contrast, quantitative methodologies are often associated with efforts to study large samples, with a view to generalising to whole populations. Pre-election surveys are a prime instance of such efforts: hundreds and sometimes thousands of people are interviewed about their voting preferences, in order to predict the intentions of the electorate (often millions of people) as a whole.

4. The choice of *research methods* to be used to gain insights into the lives of one's participants. Research methods are formalised techniques which sociologist have developed to explore particular aspects of a social phenomenon. *In-depth interviews* (a conversation loosely structured by a set of pre-defined questions) allowed Elijah Anderson to understand his participants' experiences of violence in everyday life, while *participant observation* made it possible for him to engage with them for prolonged periods of time and witness first-hand some of the issues they had spoken about. In contrast to the qualitative research methods Anderson deployed, a prime example of quantitative methods would be the survey – an interview based on a series of standardised questions, in which answers are recorded in a similarly standardised, often numerical, format on a questionnaire.

5. The choice of techniques of *data analysis*. In-depth interviews are normally tape recorded and then transcribed into text files. The numerical information on survey questionnaires can be entered into spreadsheet software, such as SPSS or Excel. But what to do with all this information, how to make sense of it, and how to discover in it answers to one's research questions? For this, sociologists may rely on a range of formalised techniques of data analysis, including statistical methods and techniques for the analysis of textual and audiovisual materials. At least to some extent, it can be anticipated at the outset of the research process which data analysis strategies will be useful at the end.

6. The consideration of *practical and ethical aspects* of the planned project. This, for instance, involves questions about how to gain access to the chosen setting and population, how much time to spend there, and how to obtain the resources (e.g. transport, accommodation, time, money, a digital recorder to tape interviews, etc.) necessary for the project. It is also necessary for researchers to consider whether any elements of their work might be harmful to their participants, how to protect their anonymity in published materials, and so forth.

Figure 2.5 Research design – a basic framework

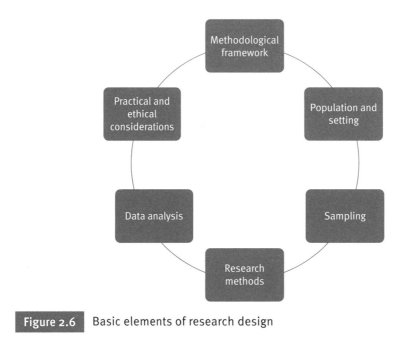

Figure 2.6   Basic elements of research design

everyday life that he sought. Likewise, large-scale quantitative studies can be very time-consuming. The British Household Panel Survey, for example, has been conducted annually since 1991 to gather information about a wide range of social and economic characteristics of British households. It is based on a sample of up to 9,000 households across the UK that allow representative insights into the domestic life of the population at large.

Fieldwork is best described as a 'messy affair', full of unanticipated twist and turns. While the development of a good research design ensures the methodological quality of a project, it is impossible to foresee what the actual encounters with dozens or even hundreds of participants may entail. Unanticipated problems may arise as much as unforeseen opportunities. Elijah Anderson's fieldwork for *Code of the Street* (1999) was shaped by his chance encounter with John Turner, a 21-year-old black man whose troubles – a lack of employment opportunities, problems with the law, a volatile personal life that had led him to have four children from three different women by the time he met Anderson – are illustrative of the struggles many young urban male African Americans face. Another such chance encounter led Harry Wolcott to publish a series of well-received journal articles on the life story of Brad, a schizophrenic young man whom Wolcott had met near his home. However, Wolcott's fortunes changed when he admitted to having had an intimate relationship with Brad, who on one occasion even attempted to murder the researcher (Wolcott 2002)! Even research conducted within an ideally linear positivist framework routinely has to cope with such changes and turnabouts. It is for this reason that not only good planning skills, but also creativity, a spirit of discovery, and the ability to improvise on the spot are important talents for fieldworkers to possess.

When fieldwork is complete, the researcher can systematise his records and turn them into a structured set of data ready for analysis. Qualitative researchers like Anderson or Wolcott will type up the fieldnotes they kept on their observations and the audio records of the interviews they conducted. Quantitative survey researchers will enter the numerical and textual data from their questionnaires into an electronic database, ready for statistical analysis. As discussed above, a range of techniques are then applied in the analysis of such data. Ideally, if the data are substantial and well organised enough, conclusions will emerge that allow the researcher to formulate an answer to his research question (as in Anderson's explanation of urban violence through the 'code of the street') or accept or reject her hypothesis (as in, hypothetically: 'findings suggest that the experience of numerous bad break-ups does indeed make American men more likely to participate in online long-distance dating'). In the end, these conclusions may form the base of a book, article, or dissertation – providing new insights into social life and raising question for future research.

2.4 How to become a sociologist

At the outset of the chapter, you had an overview of many of the challenges that you will face as students of sociology. The second part then looked at many of the things that professional sociologists do on a daily basis during their careers. So, what to make of all this information?

Maybe the best way to use this chapter is as a reference manual and launching pad for your future studies. The schematic overview of sociological research has hopefully alerted you to many of the 'big issues' of which you should be aware, and provided you with an initial, simple outline of key ideas. From here, you can move on to look at the complexities of sociological research, using, for instance, some of the sources suggested below.

Maybe the examples of real-life sociological research have also helped you to consider which aspects of the discipline interest you most. As we have stressed repeatedly, becoming a sociologist is, after all, about your creativity and your curiosity to find out more about the social world. On your way to becoming a sociologist, the readings in this text will maybe inspire you. At the end of your degree, you will likely be faced with a dissertation project that will require you to conduct your own small sociological research project. To manage this, you will need to be aware of the basic procedures that shape such research and be able to apply them yourself. This chapter has given you an idea of what will be required of you. More than anything, however, you will need a good research idea and the passion to study it in detail over a long period of time. Hopefully, this chapter has made you imagine some social issues and problems you would like to study for yourself.

The debate: Researching social life

This chapter has given you a very basic introduction to sociology as a form of practice and profession. There is still a lot more for you to find out, though. A good way to start is to look into the different tools and methods which sociologists use to study the world. Some of these have been around for a long time, while others have only been developed quite recently. Choose two tools (not all of them are 'methods' in the strictest sense) from the following – incomplete – list and find out more about them. There are lots of easily accessible readings, online videos, tutorials, etc., that you might look at. Give a brief definition of each of your chosen tools. Then compare them. What aspects of social life do they foreground? How do they differ from each other? Give examples of social phenomena they could help study.

1. Participant observation
2. In-depth interviews
3. Ethnography
4. Online ethnography
5. Auto-ethnography
6. Visual ethnography/sensory ethnography
7. Questionnaire surveys
8. Experiments
9. Oral history
10. Action research

Now consider how the knowledge gathered with these tools might be different from common-sense knowledge. How do sociological tools and research methods allow us to look at the world from the point of view of the sociological imagination?

2.5 Guide to further reading

There is a vast literature on sociological research methods. Moreover, the tools and methods that are of interest to sociologists overlap with other disciplines, such as anthropology, history, cultural studies, literature, economics, and so forth. Your first task might be to get a general overview of the field. Textbooks are useful for this, and Alan Bryman's widely used *Social Research Methods* (4th edn, 2012) is very comprehensive and up-to-date. Any other introductory textbook may be equally useful, but we suggest that you choose one that considers a wide variety of approaches to social research – qualitative, interpretive and quantitative positivist frameworks – and is not too heavily inclined towards one or another.

At some point, you will get a feeling for the methodological approaches that best match your views and interests. At this stage, you might take a look at current and innovative developments in your area of interest. For varieties of qualitative research, Norman Denzin and Yvonna Lincoln's *Handbook of Qualitative Research* (4th edn, 2011) is a good starting point. David de Vaus's *Surveys in Social Research* (6th edn, 2012) is a popular text on, as its title implies, quantitative survey research. Keith Punch's *Introduction to Social Research* (2005) compares quantitative and qualitative approaches, and John Cresswell's *Research Design* (3rd edn, 2008) is a practically focused introduction to the practice of qualitative, quantitative and mixed methods research. Again, with just a little bit of research, you will find lots of other books similar to the ones listed here. On the very latest developments in methods of social research, journals are, of course, the best source. There are specialist journals on a wide variety of approaches, such as *Qualitative Research*, *Ethnography*, or *Sociological Methodology*.

Finally, you will need to develop a sense of how to do sociological research yourself. Cresswell's *Research Design* is one useful source here. On qualitative research, there are a number of very useful texts by David Silverman, such as *Doing Qualitative Research* (2009) or *Interpreting Qualitative Data* (2011). These books are meant for postgraduate students, but they are written in a very lively and accessible manner, and you might find them very helpful. There are also numerous books on undergraduate research projects, such as Judith Bell's *Doing Your Research Project* (2010) or Martin Brett Davies's *Doing a Successful Research Project* (2007), among many others. These books provide guidance on the various steps of the research process, and they may help you a lot in taking a project from its early stages to its successful completion. However, they often only provide a general overview of the research process, and you will likely need to complement them with other, more specialised readings.

Works cited

Anderson, Elijah (1999), *Code of the Street: Decency, Violence, and the Moral Life of the Inner City*, London: W.W. Norton.

Becker, Howard S. (2007), *Telling About Society*, Chicago: The University of Chicago Press.

Bryman, Alan (2012), *Social Research Methods*, Oxford: Oxford University Press.

Connell, R. (2007), *Southern Theory: The Global Dynamics of Knowledge in Social Science*, Cambridge: Polity Press.

Constable, Nicole (2003), *Romance on a Global Stage: Pen Pals, Virtual Ethnography and 'Mail-Order' Marriages*, Berkeley: University of California Press.

Hill Collins, Patricia (1990), *Balck Feminist Thought: Knowledge, Consciousness and the Politics of Empowerment*, New York: HarperCollins.

Hochschild, Arlie Russell (1997), *The Time Bind: When Work Becomes Home and Home Becomes Work*, New York: Henry Holt and Company.

Inglehart, Ronald and Christian Welzel (2005), *Modernization, Cultural Change, and Democracy: The Human Development Sequence*, Cambridge: Cambridge University Press.

Scott, John (2011), *Conceptualising the Social World: Principles of Sociological Analysis*, Cambridge: Cambridge University Press.

Wolcott, H. (1994), *Transforming Qualitative Data: Description, Analysis, and Interpretation*, Thousand Oaks: Sage.

Wolcott, Harry F. (2002), *Sneaky Kid and Its Aftermath: Ethics and Intimacy in Fieldwork*, Lanham: Altamira Press.

3 Classical Western sociology

3.1 Making sense of classical sociology

This chapter will introduce you to some of the earliest sociologists and their ideas. First of all, let us consider the following question: When exactly did sociology begin? As we will see further on, this question is very problematic. For the moment, though, it allows us to point you to two key dates you may wish to keep in mind as general points of orientation.

The first of these dates is 14 July 1789. On this day, one of the most pivotal events of the French Revolution took place. A large mob, enraged by years of economic crisis, material deprivation and political repression, stormed the Bastille, an infamous prison in Paris symbolising the power of the French monarchy. In the aftermath of this insurrection, the monarchy fell, and France was temporarily reconstituted as a republic. Today, 14 July – Bastille Day – is celebrated in France as the beginning of the modern French nation. Indeed, this date marks a historical period characterised by large-scale social, economic, political and cultural upheaval with lasting transformative consequences across large parts of Europe. These transformations are today understood as central elements of the modernisation of European societies. Such processes of modernisation, and the nature of modern social life, have been a central preoccupation for sociologists since the beginnings of the discipline. Sociology developed as an intellectual perspective that made it possible to decipher the disorder, change and chaos that suddenly had seemed to envelop large parts of Europe.

Old frameworks of thought, such as theology and philosophy, struggled to arrive at comprehensive explanations for these massive changes. While remaining powerful, the social and political influence of Christianity in particular had gradually begun to wane. At the same time, new technologies of transportation and mass communication facilitated the quick spread of new ideas across large geographical spaces. There was thus both a need for new ways of explaining the world and a possibility for such new forms of thought to spread and become widely accepted. The eighteenth century and even more so the nineteenth century thus witnessed rapid developments in established areas of intellectual life, such as physics, and the emergence of original forms of thought, such as modern biology, anthropology and sociology.

The year 1839 might serve as a marker of sociology's beginnings. In this year, the French scholar Auguste Comte introduced the term 'sociology' to designate an original approach to the study of human life. In his multi-volume study, *Cours de Philosophie Positif*, published between 1830 and 1842, Comte sought to set out this new perspective. Developing his sociology, Comte meant to enable, amidst the upheaval and chaos of his time, the systematic analysis of patterns and regularities in the ways in which societies develop and change. For inspiration, Comte looked to the rapidly developing natural sciences, describing sociology as a kind of 'social physics', which would allow its students to uncover the 'laws' of social life, much as physicists sought to uncover the laws of nature.

Therefore, we might see early sociology as very much a product of a specific historical period and place: sociology was necessitated by the historical transformations Western Europe was undergoing during the time of Comte and other pioneering sociologists. At the same time, sociology was made possible by these transformations. They provided scholars with reasons to reconsider basic elements of human life, as well as with the opportunity to turn such inspiration into published works with a wide readership. The strictures of religiously defined morality and law had begun to recede towards the end of the eighteenth century, and many new ideas could now be voiced without being subdued by agents of church and state. Sociology also thrived because, little by little, it found a home in the burgeoning network of, first of all, Western European and, later on, North American universities. These universities concentrated learning and scholarship and provided a suitable institutional environment for the development of sophisticated bodies of knowledge. At the same time, the Industrial Revolution brought about massive social transformations that required new forms of scholarship to be adequately understood. The rise of industrial mass production, the formation of cities of largely unprecedented size around factories and mines, and the strikingly poor living conditions of the men, women and children who toiled in these factories and mines are just some examples of social phenomena that required urgent explanation. We might therefore say that sociology began in Western Europe in approximately 1839, in the context of a growing preoccupation with the nature of the rapid modernisation of society.

However, we wish to caution you against saying so without major qualifications. The view that sociology is, in terms of its origins, a distinctively Western intellectual project has a long history, and it is frequently found in textbooks on sociological theory and introductory sociology. In recent years, however, many scholars have begun to challenge and modify this narrative. This development is perhaps due to a broader 'global turn' in sociology, which has led to an increased awareness of social, cultural and intellectual interdependencies across world regions and entailed a re-examination of sociology's historical foundations.

The view that sociology developed in response to processes of modernisation unique to European societies is problematic. Scholars such as Gurminder Bhambra rightly point out that such narratives of sociology's history are distorted by Eurocentrism, that is, 'the belief, implicit or otherwise, in the world historical significance of events believed to have developed endogenously within the cultural-geographical sphere of Europe' (Bhambra 2008: 5). Early sociology is thus characterised by a paradox: on the one hand, many of its central assumptions about modernity and social change drew upon the supposed uniqueness and, in some ways, superiority of Europe. Most of those who consciously identified themselves with the label 'sociologist' early in the discipline's history were white European men living in the metropolitan centres of Western Europe. Even though many of them did write about non-European societies, they primarily did so to bring to the fore the distinctiveness of patterns and changes of social life in Europe. On the other hand, however, the social processes that brought about modernity and sociology as the study of modern life were not localised in Europe, and they were not uniquely European or Western. Foundational elements of modernity, such as the Renaissance, the Enlightenment or the Industrial Revolution, were all in some way connected to and enabled by much broader developments, such as the colonisation and economic exploitation of large parts of the world by Europeans, the slave trade, or strong extra-European influences on European intellectual life. This paradox in the history of sociology has attracted increasing attention in recent years, and sociology, both in terms of its past and its future, is more and more understood as a global rather than a European project.

The idea of sociology as a global project might guide your review of classical sociology in this chapter. If you browse through the following pages, you will find that most of the scholars whose work we explore were white men living and working in the urban centres of Europe and North America. We thus run the risk of reproducing the very Eurocentrism to which we have drawn your attention above. Nonetheless, there is a good reason for proceeding in this way. These scholars are often collectively described as the 'founders' or 'founding fathers' of sociology, and their works define the canon of classical sociology. By *canon* should be understood a set of texts whose ideas and concepts defined sociology in their own times and continue to influence sociological research in the present. As students of sociology, you must become familiar with these ideas and concepts, and it is only on this basis that you will be able to develop a critical appreciation of social life and sociology past and present.

In developing their own stories about society, contemporary sociologists frequently draw on, extend, criticise, and challenge the works of the discipline's founders, and there are broad continuities or 'traditions' in sociological research that reach from the nineteenth century into the present. Texts written 50 or 100 years ago do not directly address social phenomena you may find interesting, exciting, or worrisome today. The internet, Facebook, and global warming did not arrive until very recently. However, the canon of classical sociology may in fact offer you ideas with which you can make sense of these contemporary issues.

At the same time, we will also approach this canon from a critical perspective and highlight its limitations. In doing so, we would like to encourage you to actively engage with classical sociology: What tools does it offer us for making sense of social life? How can its ideas best be adapted to shed light on contemporary social issues and problems? How do those ideas need to be adjusted and re-evaluated in the light of contemporary perspectives on society? If you treat it as a thing of the past, classical sociology may seem staid and stale. However, if you interrogate it in relation to your concerns and interests in the present, you may find that the writings of sociology's founders have much to offer still, both as a resource and a site of inspiring disagreement.

To round off this general introduction to classical sociology, the following timeline provides you with a quick overview of the scholars discussed in this chapter and their major works.

Classical sociology: a very basic timeline

1798–1857	Auguste Comte	
	1798	Born in Montpellier, France
	1817	Becomes secretary of Claude Henri Saint-Simon
	1830–42	*Cours de Philosophie Positif*; translated into English by Harriet Martineau and published as *The Positive Philosophy of Auguste Comte* in 1853
	1844	*Discours sur l'Esprit Positif*; translated into English and published as *A General View of Positivism* in 1851
	1857	Died in Paris, France
1802–1876	Harriet Martineau	
	1802	Born in Norwich, England
	1832–34	Publication of *Illustrations of Political Economy*
	1836/1837	Publication of *Society in America* (2 volumes)
	1838	Publication of *How to Observe Morals and Manners*
	1876	Died in Ambleside, England
1818–1883	Karl Marx	
	1818	Born in Trier, Germany
	1843	Publication of *Zur Kritik der Hegelschen Rechtsphilosophie* (*A Contribution to the Critique of Hegel's Philosophy of Right*)
	1845	With Friedrich Engels, publication of *Die deutsche Ideologie* (*The German Ideology*)
	1848	With Friedrich Engels, publication of *Manifest der Kommunistischen Partei* (*Manifesto of the Communist Party*)
	1858	Publication of *Grundrisse der Kritik der politischen Ökonomie* (*Foundation of the Critique of Political Economy*)
	1859	Publication of *Zur Kritik der politischen Ökonomie* (*A Contribution to the Critique of Political Economy*)
	1867	Publication of the first volume of *Das Kapital* (*Capital*)
	1883	Died in London, England
	1885/1894	Posthumous publication by Friedrich Engels of the second and third volumes of *Das Kapital* (*Capital*)
1820–1903	Herbert Spencer	
	1820	Born in Derby, England
	1850	Publication of *Social Statics*

	1873	Publication of *The Study of Sociology*
	1864–91	*A System of Synthetic Philosophy.* Herbert Spencer's *System of Synthetic Philosophy* comprises ten volumes, published over a period of 17 years. These consider the nature and evolution of life from four linked perspectives: biology, psychology, sociology and ethics.
	1903	Died in Brighton, England
1855–1936	Ferdinand Tönnies	
	1855	Born in Oldenswort, Duchy of Schleswig (now Germany)
	1887	Publication of *Gemeinschaft und Gesellschaft* (*Community and Association*, published in English in 1889)
	1909	Publication of *Die Sitte* (*Custom*)
	1931	Publication of *Einführung in die Soziologie* (*An Introduction to Sociology*)
	1936	Died in Kiel, Germany.
1858–1917	Émile Durkheim	
	1858	Born in Epinal, France
	1893	Publication of *De la Division du Travail Social* (*The Division of Labour in Society*)
	1895	Publication of *Les Règles de la Méthode Sociologique* (*The Rules of Sociological Methods*)
	1897	Publication of *Le Suicide* (*Suicide*)
	1912	Publication of *Les Formes Elémentaires de la Vie Religieuse* (*The Elementary Forms of Religious Life*)
	1917	Died in Paris, France
1858–1917	Georg Simmel	
	1858	Born in Berlin, Kingdom of Prussia (now Germany)
	1900	Publication of *Philosophie des Geldes* (*The Philosophy of Money*)
	1903	Publication of *Die Großstadt und das Geistesleben* (*The Metropolis and Mental Life*)
	1908	Publication of *Soziologie (Sociology)*. This substantial study comprises many of Simmel's frequently cited essays, for instance on the stranger, secrecy, or 'metropolis and mental life'. It also sets out the general principles of Simmel's sociology of societal forms (see below).

	1917	Publication of *Grundfragen der Soziologie (Questions of Sociology)*
	1917	Died in Straßburg, Germany (now Strasbourg, France)
1860–1935	Jane Addams	
	1860	Born in Cedarville, Illinois, USA
	1902	Publication of *Democracy and Social Ethics*
	1907	Publication of *Newer Ideals of Peace*
	1910	Publication of *Twenty Years at Hull House*
	1922	Publication of *Peace and Bread in Times of War*
	1935	Died in Chicago, Illinois, USA
1863–1931	George Herbert Mead	
	1863	Born in South Hadley, Massachusetts, USA
	1931	Died in Chicago, Illinois, USA
	1932	Publication of *The Philosophy of the Present*
	1934	Publication of *Mind, Self and Society*
	1936	Publication of *Movements of Thought in the Nineteenth Century*
	1938	Publication of *The Philosophy of the Act*

In his lifetime, George Herbert Mead became a distinguished scholar, teaching at the University of Michigan and later at the University of Chicago, and publishing a very wide range of journal articles and other short papers. After his death, Mead's former students compiled some of his unpublished manuscripts and published them in the four books listed above. These books, and in particular *Mind, Self and Society*, are today frequently used as introductions to Mead's work. His other papers have been collected in numerous anthologies, and some of them are available online.

1864–1920	Max Weber	
	1864	Born in Erfurt, Kingdom of Prussia (now Germany)
	1896/1909	Publication of *The Agrarian Sociology of Ancient Civilization* (originally published in German as two individual papers)
	1904/1905/1917	Publication of *The Methodology of the Social Sciences* (comprises three individual essays originally published in German)
	1904/1905/1920	Publication of *The Protestant Ethic and the Spirit of Capitalism* (originally published as a two-part essay in 1904/1905 in German, then reissued in revised form in 1920)

| 1915–19 | Publication of *Die Wirtschaftsethik der Weltreligionen* (a comparative work in the sociology of religion that comprises essays on Confucianism, Taoism, Hinduism, Buddhism, and Judaism) |
| 1920 | Died in Munich, Germany |

1868–1963 W.E.B. Du Bois

1868	Born in Great Barrington, Massachusetts, USA
1899	Publication of *The Philadelphia Negro*
1903	Publication of *The Souls of Black Folk*
1915	Publication of *The Negro*
1924	Publication of *The Gift of Black Folk: The Negroes in the Making of America*
1940	Publication of *Dusk of Dawn: An Essay Toward an Autobiography of a Race Concept*
1963	Died in Accra, Ghana
1968	Posthumous publication of *The Autobiography of W.E.B. Du Bois*.

Consider

What do you make of this timeline? Taken at face value, it consists of a simple list of works written by various sociologists and their publication dates. You might thus be content with using this timeline for an overview of important early sociological studies and leave it at that. If you look more closely, though, you can learn quite a bit more. For instance, you can tell that many of the works that are now seen as 'classics' and part of a largely fixed canon actually had quite complicated publication histories. While George Herbert Mead published prolifically in his lifetime, the books that are now used to introduce students to his thinking were all put together and published after his death. The works of many of the scholars listed above were published originally in one language and then translated. For example, engagement with the work of Max Weber in the English-speaking world was initially hindered by a lack of translations and, in some cases, did not begin until years after his death. Sociology, in this sense, always has been not just books and written text, but a vibrant world of people communicating with each other, exchanging ideas, and sometimes also failing to pay sufficient attention to each other.

This is just one important issue to which the timeline points. In addition, there are others. Consider the following questions:

1. All the scholars included in this timeline came from a very small number of countries. Why is this?

2. Some of them were born in one country, but died in another. Why might this be? Compare the cases of Max Weber, Georg Simmel and Karl Marx. What do your findings tell you about the time in which these men developed their approaches to sociology?

3. Are there any commonalities between the issues these early sociologists considered in their works? You can gain some respective indications by just considering their titles, but you may find it necessary to do some further research to be able to answer this question.

4. The timeline's omissions likewise can be telling. For instance, it only includes ten names, but sociology surely was not founded by only a handful of people. Using relevant alternative resources, compile a file on other early sociologists who had a significant impact on the discipline in their respective countries. In doing so, try to cast your net as widely as possible and consider a variety of different countries.

5. The timeline is framed by several important developments, outlined on the preceding pages. Find out more about the following four: secularisation, the rise of the modern university, the Industrial Revolution, and colonialism. What does each of these terms refer to? How did these four developments shape social life in Europe in the nineteenth century? How did they influence the development of modern sociology?

3.2 Introducing classical sociologists

Let us now turn to a brief survey of the ideas of a small group of early sociologists. Their work has remained prominent over the years, and in many cases it still inspires the thinking of contemporary sociologists. Indeed, some of them, such as Max Weber, Karl Marx and Émile Durkheim, are frequently identified as 'founding fathers of sociology'. However, it must be clear from the outset that these men and women were not alone in developing sociology and that many other thinkers contributed greatly to this project. Therefore, you may view the following discussion as an introduction to some of the most seminal and lasting contributions of early sociologists and as a launch pad for further exploration.

Auguste Comte

Let us begin our discussion by returning to Auguste Comte. Comte was born in 1798, amidst the social and political upheaval of the French Revolution. For a number of years, he worked closely with Claude Henri de Saint-Simon. His experiences of the radical transformation of French society and his collaboration with Saint-Simon, a notable progressive scholar of his time, greatly inspired Comte. While remaining on the margins of academia for much of his life, Comte's writings demonstrate his abilities as a radically creative thinker preoccupied with the development of new ideas capable of making sense of a society in transition. His work did gain the attention of other noted scholars of his time, such as the English philosopher John Stuart Mill, and it inspired many political thinkers and revolutionaries throughout the nineteenth and early twentieth century. Comte's work is much less influential today, and there is no Comtean school of sociology. Nonetheless, his ideas continue to be significant as a central foundation for sociological thought.

As mentioned above, Comte proposed the term 'sociology' to define a new form of studying the world. In doing so, he sought a radical break from dominant forms of speculative theorising about society in philosophy and theology. In his *Cours de Philosophie Positive* (1830–42/1974), one of his major works, Comte favourably compares the natural sciences with the state of social thought in his time. Writing about the latter, he argues:

> Unfortunately this [i.e. the highly developed status of the natural sciences] does not apply to social phenomena, the theory of which has not yet issued from the theologico-metaphysical prison, to which thinkers appear to condemn it, as a fatal exception, for all time. The philosophic enterprise that I have initiated, without changing its nature or its goal, now becomes more difficult and more audacious, and assumes a new character: instead of estimating and improving, our present task is to create a whole order of scientific conceptions that no previous philosopher has so much as outlined, and which had never even been glimpsed before as a possibility. (Comte 1830–42/1974: 124)

Three important aspects of Comte's thinking are visible in this statement. First, there is his intent to distance himself from the failed enterprise of 'theologico-metaphysical' enquiry about the world. Second, he turned to the natural sciences as an inspiration in his search for alternatives. Finally, Comte viewed himself as an audacious innovator, poised to 'create a whole new order of scientific conceptions'.

Alongside his use of the label 'sociology', Comte also described this project as 'social physics'. Social physics, thus Comte, are, on the one hand, concerned with the study of 'social statics', that is, the analysis of the ways in which various parts of the social system of complex societies are linked and interact with each other. On the other hand, 'social dynamics' examine the laws by which societies change and different forms of social organisation succeed each other.

As a scholar living in the age of Enlightenment, Comte tended to view change in terms of a supposed natural progress towards more harmonious forms of social life, with achievements in scientific understanding playing a crucial role in such progress. For Comte, sociology formed part of a broader 'positive philosophy' encompassing various disciplines, including the mathematics, astronomy, physics and biology (Comte 1830–42/1974). Comte used the idea of a 'positive philosophy' or 'positivism' to present an alternative to the negative, destructive forms of thought that he saw as prevalent in his time.

At the same time, positivism for Comte also meant a particular mode of scientific enquiry. Comte argued that, in spite of the importance of theorising, knowledge of the world had to be established through its direct and methodical observation. He suggested that both the natural and the social world were governed by specific laws, which could be discerned through systematic scientific study. In his much-cited 'law of the three stages', Comte argued that the human mind progressed in three stages, from theological explanations of the world to metaphysical, that is, speculative philosophical, analyses, and, finally, to systematic scientific research in the positivist stage. Within this holistic model of science, the methods of enquiry to be used by sociologists in many ways were to parallel those employed by natural scientists.

While there is no Comtean school of sociology, the term positivism continues to be used by many sociologists worldwide to designate forms of enquiry that are modelled upon the natural sciences. One of Comte's legacies, in this sense, lies in his establishment of sociology *as a discipline built upon the systematic combination of empirical research and theorising*, rather than purely speculative enquiry. While many of his more specific proposals today seem far-fetched and obsolete, Auguste Comte established some general conceptual foundations for sociology on which it has continued to build and thrive.

Reading

Comte, Auguste (1830–42/1974), *The Essential Comte, Selected from Cours de Philosophie Positive*, edited by S. Andreski, London: Croom Helm, pp.19–20, 124–6, 138–42

Course in Positive Philosophy

I

Aim of the Course. General Considerations on the Nature and Importance of Positive Philosophy

The object of this first lecture is to set forth clearly the aim of this course, that is, to determine in exactly what spirit the various branches of natural philosophy will be considered.

No doubt the nature of this course will only be completely understood, and a definite opinion formed about it, when the various parts have been developed in their order. Such is the usual drawback of definitions, when the system of ideas is extensive and the definitions precede the ideas. There are two aspects to generalities: either they are the conspectus of a doctrine still to be established, or the summary of one already established. But even if it is only as a summary that they acquire all their force, as a conspectus they are still extremely important, for they characterise from the start the subject under consideration.

As we understand it, an absolutely indispensable preliminary to a study as vast and hitherto as indeterminate as that which we are about to undertake, is the strict delimitation of the field of research. In obedience to this logical necessity, I must now indicate the considerations that have led me to give this new course, and that will each be developed in the detail demanded by its very great importance.

In order to explain adequately the true nature and proper character of positive philosophy, it is necessary to survey as a whole the progress of the human spirit, for a concept is understood only through its history.

Studying the total development of the human intelligence in its various spheres of activity, from its first trial flights up to our own day, I believe I have discovered a fundamental law to which it is subjected from an invariable necessity, and which seems to me to be solidly established, either by rational proof drawn from a knowledge of our nature, or by the historical test, an attentive examination of the past. This law is that each of our principal conceptions, each branch of our knowledge, passes successively through three different theoretical states: the theological or fictitious, the metaphysical or abstract, and the scientific or positive. In other words, the human mind, by its nature, employs in all its investigations three methods of philosophising, of an essentially different and even opposed nature: first the theological, then the metaphysical, and finally the positive. Hence there are three mutually exclusive kinds of philosophy, or conception systems regarding the totality of phenomena: the first is the necessary starting-point of human intelligence; the third its fixed and final state; the second is only a means of transition.

In the theological state, the human mind, directing its search to the very nature of being, to the first and final causes of all the effects that it beholds, in a word, to absolute knowledge, sees phenomena as products of the direct and continuous action of more or less numerous supernatural agents, whose arbitrary intervention explains all the apparent anomalies of the universe.

In the metaphysical state, which at bottom is a mere modification of the theological, the supernatural agents are replaced by abstract forces, veritable entities (personified abstractions) inherent in the various types of being, and conceived as capable in themselves of engendering all observed phenomena, the explanation of which consists in assigning to each its corresponding entity.

Finally, in the positive state, the human mind, recognising the impossibility of attaining to absolute concepts, gives up the search for the origin and destiny of the universe, and the inner causes of phenomena, and confines itself to the discovery, through reason and observation combined, of the actual laws that govern the succession and similarity of phenomena. The explanation of the facts, now reduced to its real terms, consists in the establishment of a link between various particular phenomena and a few general facts, which diminish in number with the progress of science. [. . .]

VIII

Preliminary Considerations on the Necessity of Social Physics as suggested by the Analysis of the Present State of Society

In each of the five preceding parts of our study philosophic exploration has rested on a truly scientific state of the sciences, pre-existing and unanimously accepted, whose constitution, although only more or less complete up to the present, even with regard to the least complex and most closely studied phenomena, satisfies the conditions of positivity in all cases, including the most recent and most imperfect, and needs only an effort of rational appreciation, guided by incontestable rules, to designate the principal improvements yet to be made in order to detach real science from every indirect influence of ancient philosophy. Unfortunately this does not apply to social phenomena, the theory of which has not yet issued from the theologico-metaphysical prison, to which thinkers appear to condemn it, as a fatal exception, for all time. The philosophic enterprise that I have initiated, without changing its nature or its goal, now becomes more difficult and more audacious, and assumes a new character: instead of estimating and improving, our present task is to create a whole order of scientific conceptions that no previous philosopher has so much as outlined, and which had never even been glimpsed before as a possibility.

Such creation, even if happily accomplished, cannot at once lift this branch of natural philosophy, dealing with the most complex phenomena, to the rational level of the various fundamental sciences, even of those whose development is least advanced. All that we can attempt in our day is to bring its foundations so far forward that intelligent people will realise the possibilty of cultivating social science in the manner of the positive sciences; we can also see to it that its foundations are solidly established and its philosophic character defined. That will be sufficient for our most urgent intellectual needs, and even for the most imperious demands of social practice, especially today. Even when reduced to these dimensions, the enterprise is still too vast to be properly treated in lectures concerned with the positive philosophy as a whole. The new science can only figure here as an indispensable element, whose importance, it is true, merits its eventual predominance. I shall later expound all my ideas on this great subject in a special Treatise on political philosophy, with all the necessary explanations, and not without due comment on possible applications to the present transitional state of society. Here I must necessarily confine myself to the most general considerations, adhering as scrupulously as possible to the strictly scientific point of view, and not aiming at any other effect than the reduction to order of our intellectual anarchy, true source of our moral and political anarchy – with which latter subject I shall not here be directly concerned.

But the extreme novelty of the doctrine would render these scientific considerations almost unintelligible, and certainly inefficacious, if my exposition did not become, with regard to a science I am endeavouring to create, much more explicit and more specific than it needed to be in previous lectures, where I could suppose the reader to be sufficiently familiar with the basis of the subject. That is why, before opening up the subject methodically, I must devote this chapter to defining the significance of this philosophic departure, and the inanity of previous attempts at it.

The great and fundamental lacuna left in the system of positive philosophy by the deplorable state of prolonged infantilism in which social science still languishes, should suffice to demonstrate to any philosopher the necessity of an enterprise that will stamp the human mind, already prepared for it in so many ways, with the character of unity of method and homogeneity of doctrine, indispensable to its full speculative development and to the nobility and energy of its practical activity. But however weighty this enterprise, which in truth embraces all others, the point of view in politics today is too narrow and too superficial for even the best minds to be able to grasp its real meaning straight away and to derive from it sufficient motivation to endure the long and painful contention that its gradual accomplishment would involve. In its first stages no science can be cultivated or conceived apart from its corresponding art, as I showed in the seventh chapter, where we learned that the more complex the order of phenomena, the more intense and prolonged is this connection. If biological science, in spite of its advanced state, still appears too closely attached to the medical art, should we be surprised that statesmen are inclined to regard as a mere intellectual exercise any sociological speculation that is not immediately linked to practical effect? However blind such an attitude, it will be obstinately persisted in as the best safeguard against vague and chimerical utopias, although experience has abundantly proved its uselessness in this capacity, for it has not been able to prevent a daily flood of the most extravagant illusions. But I must allow for what is at bottom reasonable in this puerile prejudice and will devote this lecture to preliminary explanations of the link between the institution of what I call *social physics* and the deplorable ills of present society, as manifest to every thinking mind. From these elucidatory remarks every real statesman will understand, I hope, that the great labour I have set myself, although it does not pretend to any special immediate application, is undeniably of the greatest utility, without which indeed it would not merit the attention of those who are rightly absorbed by the obligation in which they find themselves of resolving the frightening revolutionary tension of modern society, an obligation every day more pressing, and apparently every day more difficult to discharge.

From the lofty standpoint that we have now attained, the social situation is seen in full light as characterised quite simply by the most widespread though temporary anarchy of the intellectual system, in an interregnum following on the increased decadence of the theologico-metaphysical philosophy, now in the last stages of decrepitude, coupled with the continuous but still incomplete development of positive philosophy, up till now too narrow, too specialised and too timid to take possession of the spiritual government of humanity. To this situation must be traced the origin of that vacillating and contradictory state of all the great social ideas which so disrupts moral and political life: but here we perceive also the system of operations, some philosophic, some political, which must gradually deliver society from its present fatal tendency to immediate dissolution, and lead it to a new organisation at once more progressive and more consistent than that which rested on theological philosophy. Such is the proposition which will emerge as proved, I hope, from the treatment that follows, and of which I will give here a preliminary sketch, whose purpose is to demonstrate in the political schools most opposed to one another an equal impotence, and the absolute necessity of bringing to these sterile and stormy struggles a new spirit capable, once its ascendancy has been gradually established, of guiding our society towards the final goal of that revolutionary movement that has been developing within it for three centuries. [. . .]

When one considers without prejudice the present state of social science in that frankly positive spirit which sound scientific study must everywhere develop today, one cannot help recognising, both in the method and the doctrine, a combination of the various features that have always distinguished the theologico-metaphysical infancy of the other branches of natural science. In a word the general situation of political science today is exactly analogous to that of astrology in relation to astronomy, of alchemy in relation to chemistry, and the cure-all in relation to medicine. Theological politics and metaphysical politics, despite their practical antagonism, can be lumped together without any serious inconvenience, and so simplify investigation, because at bottom the second is but a modification of the first from which it does not differ except in being less extreme, as we have already observed in connection with other natural phenomena, and as we shall see still more with social phenomena. Whether phenomena are referred to a direct and continuous supernatural intervention or explained by the mysterious virtue of corresponding entities, this merely secondary difference between ultimately identical concepts in no way prevents a common production of the same characteristic attributes, indeed less here than in any other philosophic subject. The characteristics consist, as to method, in the preponderance of imagination over observation, and as to doctrine, in the exclusive search for absolute ideas, whence results, as the aim of 'science' the exercise of an arbitrary and indefinite action upon phenomena, which are not regarded as subject to invariable natural laws. In a word the general spirit of human speculation in the theologico-metaphysical state is ideal in its procedures, absolute in its conceptions, and arbitrary in its applications. Now it cannot be doubted that these are still the dominant characteristics of social thought. If we reverse the triple aspect of the theologico-metaphysical spirit, its imagination taking precedence over observation, its absolute conceptions, and its arbitrary applications, we shall have the intellectual attitude necessary for the creation of positive sociology, and which must afterwards guide its entire development.

Positive philosophy is first of all characterised, in any subject by that necessary and permanent subordination of imagination to observation which constitutes the scientific spirit, as opposed to the theological or metaphysical spirit. Although such a philosophy offers to human imagination the widest and most fruitful of fields, as we have seen from our examination of the fundamental sciences, it restricts its activity to discovering or perfecting either the exact co-ordination of the facts as they stand, or the means of undertaking new investigations. It is this habitual tendency to subordinate scientific conceptions to the facts – it being the sole function of these conceptions to demonstrate the interconnection of the facts – that must be introduced into social studies, where vague and ill-defined observation still offers no sufficient foundation for truly scientific reasoning, and is continually being modified by imagination under the stimulus of very lively passions. By virtue of its greater complexity, and incidentally its more intimate connection with human passions, political speculation more than any other was bound to remain sunk in this deplorable situation where it still languishes, whilst simpler and less stimulating studies have one by one been extricated from it during the last three centuries. We must never forget that up to a more or less recent past every order of scientific conception has been in the same state of infancy from which, the more complex and specialised its nature, the later it was emancipated; indeed the most complex have been emancipated only in our time. The intellectual and moral phenomena of individual life for instance – except by a few advanced spirits – are still studied most of the time in almost as anti-scientific a manner as political phenomena. Thus only a superficial judgement can regard as peculiar to politics that disposition to vague and uncertain observation by which sophists and rhetoricians interpret known facts according to the whim of their imagination. The same vice has prevailed in every subject of human speculation; the only thing that is special in this case is that the vice is more ingrained, as a natural result of the greater complexity of the subject, according to my theory of the development of the human mind. These reflections lead one to consider the extension to social studies of that philosophic regeneration which all other scientific studies have experienced not only as possible but as certain and imminent, were it not for the much greater intellectual difficulty that they present and the hindrances arising from more direct contact with the principal passions. But this should only stimulate the true thinker to greater efforts.

If instead of mode of procedure, we consider the actual scientific conceptions in positive philosophy, we see that in contradistinction to theologico-metaphysical philosophy it has a constant tendency to make all those notions relative which had been considered absolute. This transition from the absolute to the relative constitutes one of the most important philosophic results of each one of the intellectual revolutions that have brought various orders of speculation out of the theological and metaphysical state to the scientific state. From the purely scientific point of view, and setting aside all idea of utility, it seems to me we may regard the contrast between the relative and the absolute as expressing the antipathy between modern and ancient philosophy. Every study of the inner nature of beings, of their primary and final causes, etc. must obviously be absolute, while every investigation of the laws of phenomena is eminently relative, since it presupposes that the progress of thought is dependent on the gradual improvement of observation, exact reality being never, in any subject, perfectly disclosed: so that the relative nature of scientific conceptions is inseparable from the true notion of natural laws, just as the chimerical attachment to absolute knowledge accompanies the use of theological fictions or metaphysical entities. Now there is no need to insist here on the obvious fact that this absolute spirit still characterises social speculation. Its various schools, both theological and metaphysical, are dominated by the idea of an unchanging political type, more or less vaguely defined, but always conceived in such a manner as to prevent any radical modification of the chief political conceptions according to the state of human civilisation. Although such a notion, which could not possibly be based on rational thinking, must at once engender great philosophic differences, especially today, yet less pronounced differences than they appear, yet each one of the opinions of which this type is the subject preserves the immobility of the type throughout all modifications of social history. The absolute spirit inherent in contemporary political science, with all its disadvantages, has at least constituted up till now the only means of controlling individual extravagances, and of preventing a flood of different opinions. The various philosophers who, impressed by the danger of this intellectual absolutism, have sometimes endeavoured to free themselves from it, but have not had the strength to rise to the conception of truly positive politics, have incurred the blame, still more grave, of presenting all political ideas as being by nature radically uncertain and even arbitrary, for they have destroyed the foundation of their present stability, without substituting a firmer basis. These ill-conceived attempts have even cast general discredit on any attempt to regenerate the spirit of politics. By losing its absoluteness it seems today, in the eyes of many respectable men in the various political parties, to have necessarily lost its stability, and consequently its morality. But these fears, although very natural, will easily be dissipated in the mind of anyone who appreciates the character of positive sociology, and considers the development of the previous branches of natural philosophy, where one certainly does not observe that in ceasing to be absolute, and becoming relative, scientific ideas have become in any way arbitrary. On the contrary it is clear that by this transformation these ideas have acquired a consistency and a stability very superior to their vague primitive immutability, each one of them being gradually involved in a system of relations of constantly increasing range and strength and tending more and more to prevent any serious aberration. Thus there is no risk at all of falling into a dangerous scepticism by destroying once and for all the absolute spirit that characterises so deplorably the prolonged infantilism of social science, provided this destruction is but the natural result of the passage of this science to the positive state. Operating this transition, positive philosophy will not fail to display its usual characteristic of never suppressing a means of intellectual co-ordination without immediately substituting another means, more wide-ranging and more efficacious. Is it not apparent that the transition from the absolute to the relative offers today in politics the only means of arriving at conceptions capable of eliciting unanimous and lasting assent?

Consider

1. Who was Auguste Comte? Following from the preceding outline, explore Comte's life in greater detail. Specifically, focus on the ways in which Comte's life experiences shaped his views as a scholar.
2. To what extent may it be assumed that a scholar's or artist's work is shaped by her or his life experiences? Answer this question in relation to Auguste Comte and two other scholars discussed in this chapter.
3. Based on the preceding extract from Comte's work, outline Comte's 'law of the three stages' in as much detail as possible.
4. 'Positive philosophy is first of all characterised, in any subject by that necessary and permanent subordination of imagination to observation which constitutes the scientific spirit, as opposed to the theological and metaphysical spirit.' Explain this statement in as much detail as possible. In particular, explain what Comte understands by 'the scientific spirit' and how this scientific spirit differs from theological and metaphysical enquiry.
5. How does Comte justify the need for his 'social physics'?

Herbert Spencer

While Auguste Comte made an important contribution to the foundation of Western sociology in the first half of the nineteenth century, Herbert Spencer rose to prominence in the century's second half. Born in Derby in 1820, Spencer spent his life mainly in England. Spencer was largely an autodidact, never acquiring a university degree or holding an academic position. Nevertheless, his works for a time gained him substantial international prominence and were read and commented upon widely in the later decades of the nineteenth century. Spencer met and engaged with many prominent scholars of his day and came to hold a distinguished position in British society. At the same time, however, he often failed to engage with the work of other scholars, and his own writings are largely derived from speculative theorising of the sort criticised by Comte and other scientifically minded thinkers. It is, at least in part, for this reason that Spencer's work has lost much of its direct influence upon contemporary sociology. Rather, it is significant in a broader sense, contributing to giving sociology a direction in its formative period and setting out some general themes that continue to be important to date.

Like Comte, Spencer drew much inspiration from the natural sciences, in particular biology, and he was equally concerned with uncovering a set of general laws governing the social world. Moreover, just as Comte's, Spencer's sociology was, to a great extent, driven by a strong interest in generating a better understanding of the large-scale social transformations of his time. However, while much of Comte's work deals with progress in human understanding of the world – consider the 'law of the three stages' – Spencer took a much greater interest in the historical development of the social system and its institutions themselves.

In doing so, Spencer drew heavily on ideas about evolution that were rising to increasing prominence in biology during his lifetime. Indeed, in his *Principles of Sociology* (Spencer 1874–96/1969), he uses the analogy of a biological organism to characterise sociology's concerns and objectives. Consider his paradigmatic statement on sociology in the text's opening:

> In Biology, the explanation of functions implies knowledge of the various physical and chemical actions going on throughout the organism. Yet these actions become comprehensible only as fast as the relations of structures and reciprocities of functions become known; nay, they cannot even be described without reference to the vital actions interpreted by them. Similarly in Sociology, it is impossible to explain the origin and development of those ideas and sentiments which are the leading agents in social evolution, without referring directly or by implication to the phases of that evolution. (Spencer 1874–96/1969: 1)

Just as a biological organism has to be understood in terms of the interdependence of its various organs – for example, liver, heart, lungs, and so forth, among human beings – the organism of society must be explained through the interaction of its various constituent elements – family, marriage, political organisation, religious bodies, etc. Likewise, the concept of evolution is, for Spencer, of essence in order to account for the ways in which both biological and societal organisms change and develop over time.

Spencer compared various types of societies, such as 'nomadic', 'semi-settled' and 'settled' societies, and used these comparisons to set out a number of general principles of social evolution (Spencer 1874–96/1969). Societies evolve over time, integrating greater numbers of individuals, areas of land, and so forth, and becoming gradually more stratified and complex. Through their ongoing interaction with each other, human beings establish social structures and institutions that become to a large extent independent of isolated individual acts. Spencer understood societies as adaptive bodies that tend towards a state of 'equilibrium'; in individuals goals correspond to the functional needs of society as a whole. A simple example for such equilibrium would be a labour market able to fill all the specialised positions of a highly complex economy – doctors, bakers, stock brokers, plumbers, etc. – with exactly the number of individuals available and in need of such labour.

Rather than in the details of his arguments, Spencer's contribution lies in his development of a broad set of concerns that continue to inspire sociologists. By conceptualising society as a living organism, he drew attention to the question of how increasingly complex and rapidly changing societies can maintain order and meet their members' basic needs. This question is certainly as topical in the early twenty-first century as it was in the late nineteenth century, providing Herbert Spencer's ideas with continued relevance.

Reading

Spencer, Herbert (1874–96/1969), *Principles of Sociology*, edited by S. Andreski, London: Macmillan, pp. 1–2, 7–12

The Scope of Sociology

§ 208. In Biology the explanation of functions implies knowledge of the various physical and chemical actions going on throughout the organism. Yet these actions become comprehensible only as fast as the relations of structures and reciprocities of functions become known; nay, they cannot even be described without reference to the vital actions interpreted by them. Similarly in Sociology, it is impossible to explain the origin and development of those ideas and sentiments which are leading agents in social evolution, without referring directly or by implication to the phases of that evolution.

§ 209. The phenomena of social evolution are determined partly by the external actions to which the social aggregate is exposed, and partly by the natures of its units; and these two sets of factors are themselves progressively changed as the society evolves.

§ 210. The development of the family stands first in order. The ways in which the fostering of offspring is influenced by promiscuity, by polyandry, by polygyny, and by monogamy, have to be traced; as have also the results of exogamous marriage and endogamous marriage. These, considered first as affecting the maintenance of the race in number and quality, have also to be considered as affecting the condition of adults. Moreover, beyond observing how the several forms of the sexual relations modify family-life, they have to be treated in connexion with public life; on which they act and which reacts on them. And then, after the sexual relations, there have to be similarly dealt with the parental and filial relations.

Sociology has next to describe and explain the rise and development of that political organization which in several ways regulates affairs – which combines the actions of individuals for purposes of tribal or national offence and defence; and which restrains them in certain of their dealings with one another, as also in certain of their dealings with themselves. It has to trace the relations of this co-ordinating and controlling apparatus, to the area occupied, to the amount and distribution of population, to the means of communication. It has to show the differences of form which this agency presents in the different social types, nomadic and settled, militant and industrial. It has to describe the changing relations between this regulative structure which is unproductive, and those structures which carry on production. It has also to set forth the connexions between, and reciprocal influences of, the institutions carrying on civil government, and the other governmental institutions simultaneously developing – the ecclesiastical and the ceremonial. And then it has to take account of those modifications which persistent political restraints are ever working in the characters of the social units, as well as the modifications worked by the reactions of these changed characters on the political organization. [. . .]

What Is a Society?

§ 212. This question has to be asked and answered at the outset. Until we have decided whether or not to regard a society as an entity; and until we have decided whether, if regarded as an entity, a society is to be classed as absolutely unlike all other entities or as like some others; our conception of the subject-matter before us remains vague.

It may be said that a society is but a collective name for a number of individuals. Carrying the controversy between nominalism and realism into another sphere, a nominalist might affirm that just as there exist only the members of a species, while the species considered apart from them has no existence; so the units of a society alone exist, while the existence of the society is but verbal. Instancing a lecturer's audience as an aggregate which by disappearing at the close of the lecture, proves itself to be not a thing but only a certain arrangement of persons, he might argue that the like holds of the citizens forming a nation.

But without disputing the other steps of his argument, the last step may be denied. The arrangement, temporary in the one case, is permanent in the other; and it is the permanence of the relations among component parts which constitutes the individuality of a whole as distinguished from the individualities of its parts. A mass broken into fragments ceases to be a thing; while, conversely, the stones, bricks, and wood, previously separate, become the thing called a house if connected in fixed ways.

Thus we consistently regard a society as an entity, because, though formed of discrete units, a certain concreteness in the aggregate of them is implied by the general persistence of the arrangements among them throughout the area occupied. And it is this trait which yields our idea of a society.

§ 213. But now, regarding a society as a thing, what kind of thing must we call it? It seems totally unlike every object with which our senses acquaint us. Any likeness it may possibly have to other objects, cannot be manifest to perception, but can be discerned only by reason. If the constant relations among its parts make it an entity; the question arises whether these constant relations among its parts are akin to the constant relations among the parts of other entities. Between a society and anything else, the only conceivable resemblance must be one due to *parallelism of principle in the arrangement of components*.

There are two great classes of aggregates with which the social aggregate may be compared – the inorganic and the organic. Are the attributes of a society in any way like those of a not-living body? or are they in any way like those of a living body? or are they entirely unlike those of both?

The first of these questions needs only to be asked to be answered in the negative. A whole of which the parts are alive, cannot, in its general characters, be like lifeless wholes. The second question, not to be thus promptly answered, is to be answered in the affirmative. The reasons for asserting that the permanent relations among the parts of a society, are analogous to the permanent relations among the parts of a living body, we have now to consider.

§ 214. When we say that growth is common to social aggregates and organic aggregates, we do not thus entirely exclude community with inorganic aggregates. Some of these, as crystals, grow in a visible manner; and all of them, on the hypothesis of evolution, have arisen by integration at some time or other. Nevertheless, compared with things we call inanimate, living bodies and societies so conspicuously exhibit augmentation of mass, that we may fairly regard this as characterizing them both. Many organisms grow throughout their lives; and the rest grow throughout considerable parts of their lives. Social growth usually continues either up to times when the societies divide, or up to times when they are overwhelmed.

Here, then, is the first trait by which societies ally themselves with the organic world and substantially distinguish themselves from the inorganic world.

§ 215. It is also a character of social bodies, as of living bodies, that while they increase in size they increase in structure. Like a low animal, the embryo of a high one has few distinguishable parts; but while it is acquiring greater mass, its parts multiply and differentiate. It is thus with a society. At first the unlikenesses among its groups of units are inconspicuous in number and degree; but as population augments, divisions and sub-divisions become more numerous and more decided. Further, in the social organism as in the individual organism, differentiations cease only with that completion of the type which marks maturity and precedes decay.

Though in inorganic aggregates also, as in the entire Solar System and in each of its members, structural differentiations accompany the integrations; yet these are so relatively slow, and so relatively simple, that they may be disregarded. The multiplication of contrasted parts in bodies politic and in living bodies, is so great that it substantially constitutes another common character which marks them off from inorganic bodies.

§ 216. This community will be more fully appreciated on observing that progressive differentiation of structures is accompanied by progressive differentiation of functions.

The divisions, primary, secondary, and tertiary, which arise in a developing animal, do not assume their major and minor unlikenesses to no purpose. Along with diversities in their shapes and compositions go diversities in the actions they perform: they grow into unlike organs having unlike duties. Assuming the entire function of absorbing nutriment at the same time that it takes on its structural characters, the alimentary system becomes gradually marked off into contrasted portions; each of which has a special function forming part of the general function. A limb, instrumental to locomotion or prehension, acquires divisions and sub-divisions which perform their leading and their subsidiary shares in this office. So is it with the parts into which a society divides. A dominant class arising does not simply become unlike the rest, but assumes control over the rest; and when this class separates into the more and the less dominant, these, again, begin to discharge distinct parts of the entire control. With the classes whose actions are controlled it is the same. The various groups into which they fall have various occupations: each of such groups also, within itself, acquiring minor contrasts of parts along with minor contrasts of duties.

And here we see more clearly how the two classes of things we are comparing, distinguish themselves from things of other classes; for such differences of structure as slowly arise in inorganic aggregates, are not accompanied by what we can fairly call differences of function.

§ 217. Why in a body politic and in a living body, these unlike actions of unlike parts are properly regarded by us as functions, while we cannot so regard the unlike actions of unlike parts in an inorganic body, we shall perceive on turning to the next and most distinctive common trait.

Evolution establishes in them both, not differences simply, but definitely-connected differences – differences such that each makes the others possible. The parts of an inorganic aggregate are so related that one may change greatly without appreciably affecting the rest. It is otherwise with the parts of an organic aggregate or of a social aggregate. In either of these, the changes in the parts are mutually determined, and the changed actions of the parts are mutually dependent. In both, too, this mutuality increases as the evolution advances. The lowest type of animal is all stomach, all respiratory surface, all limb. Development of a type having appendages by which to move about or lay hold of food, can take place only if these appendages, losing power to absorb nutriment directly from surrounding bodies, are supplied with nutriment by parts which retain the power of absorption. A respiratory surface to which the circulating fluids are brought to be aerated, can be formed only on condition that the concomitant loss of ability to supply itself with materials for repair and growth, is made good by the development of a structure bringing these materials. Similarly in a society. What we call with perfect propriety its organization, necessarily implies traits of the same kind. While rudimentary, a society is all warrior, all hunter, all hut-builder, all tool-maker: every part fulfils for itself all needs. Progress to a stage characterized by a permanent army, can go on only as there arise arrangements for supplying that army with food, clothes, and munitions of war by the rest. If here the population occupies itself solely with agriculture and there with mining – if these manufacture goods while those distribute them, it must be on condition that in exchange for a special kind of service rendered by each part to other parts, these other parts severally give due proportions of their services.

This division of labour, first dwelt on by political economists as a social phenomenon, and thereupon recognized by biologists as a phenomenon of living bodies, which they called the "physiological division of labour," is that which in the society, as in the animal, makes it a living whole. Scarcely can I emphasize enough the truth that in respect of this fundamental trait, a social organism and an individual organism are entirely alike. When we see that in a mammal, arresting the lungs quickly brings the heart to a stand; that if the stomach fails absolutely in its office all other parts by-and-by cease to act; that paralysis of its limbs entails on the body at large death from want of food, or inability to escape; that loss of even such small organs as the eyes, deprives the rest of a service essential to their preservation; we cannot but admit that mutual dependence of parts is an essential characteristic. And when, in a society, we see that the workers in iron stop if the miners do not supply materials; that makers of clothes cannot carry on their business in the absence of those who spin and weave textile fabrics; that the manufacturing community will cease to act unless the food-producing and food-distributing agencies are acting; that the controlling powers, governments, bureaux, judicial officers, police, must fail to keep order when the necessaries of life are not supplied to them by the parts kept in order; we are obliged to say that this mutual dependence of parts is similarly rigorous. Unlike as the two kinds of aggregates otherwise are, they are alike in respect of this fundamental character, and the characters implied by it.

Consider

1. Further explore Herbert Spencer's biography. Particularly consider the question of why Spencer might have taken a particular interest in biology as a base for his sociological writings.
2. What is a society? Discuss this question in relation to the preceding extract from Spencer's work.
3. In your own words, summarise Herbert Spencer's account of social evolution.
4. Spencer is often associated with theories of 'social Darwinism'. What is social Darwinism? Do you think that Spencer is rightly associated with those beliefs? Support your answer with references to Spencer's work.
5. What does Spencer understand by the 'progressive differentiation' of social structures? Support your argument with relevant examples of your own choice.

Karl Marx

Karl Marx was born to a prosperous middle-class family in the city of Trier in 1818. Trier at the time belonged to the Kingdom of Prussia, but would come to belong to the newly formed German state in 1871. This datum already points us to one of the key facts of Karl Marx's life, namely his exposure to the enormous social, political, and economic changes of his time. Marx witnessed the massive impoverishment and incipient social struggles of the Industrial Revolution, and he experienced – and indeed became involved in – the struggles between monarchist reactionaries and revolutionaries of various political inclinations that dominated much of the nineteenth century. Indeed, in part due to his involvement in radical politics, Marx was forced to leave Prussia after the failed revolution of 1848, spending the rest of his life in London, Great Britain, which at that time offered a measure of tolerance and political safety.

While Marx was strongly engaged in academic studies and obtained a doctorate, it would be inadequate to characterise him purely as an academic. Likewise, while Marx's work has been hugely influential in contemporary sociology, he would not have seen himself as a sociologist. Rather, Marx belonged to a generation of scholars who engaged with questions of their time across a variety of disciplines, including, in Marx's case, philosophy, history, economics and political science, to use contemporary labels. His work shares this holistic approach with the scholarship of Comte and Spencer, even though the latter two did identify themselves more clearly as sociologists. Moreover, an initial career in journalism led Marx to lifelong engagement as a political activist, based on a concern with international political oppression and economic exploitation after the Congress of Vienna (1815). He shared these concerns with Friedrich Engels, a noted social theorist and political activist, whom Marx had met in Paris in 1844. Marx and Engels shared a similar family background in Germany, as well as an intellectual and political orientation. These commonalities would entail decades of productive collaborative work, with Marx and Engels today being jointly recognised as the founders of modern Communism. They did not write out of a purely academic interest, and it is important to understand their works as a means to public engagement and political activism.

As such, the various studies and treatises which Marx and Engels composed individually or jointly continue to be of direct relevance in the contemporary world. Marx's thinking developed from his engagement with debates surrounding the work of German philosopher Georg Wilhelm Friedrich Hegel (1770–1831), which at the time had a dominant influence on German intellectual life. Hegel's work is part of a philosophical school known as 'German Idealism', and it relies to a large extent on metaphysical speculation to examine patterns and transformations of the world and human life.

Marx rejected Hegel's idealism, and his work indeed is known as a principal example of a *materialist conception of history*. By this is meant that Marx rejected the notion that the transformations which societies invariably undergo over time are primarily driven by changes in people's beliefs, political orientations, values, and so forth. Instead, Marx argued that social life in any particular historical period and societies' transformations over time are driven by their *material and economic organisation*, particularly in terms of the nature of property, whether private and individual or shared and collective, and the ensuing conflicts between large social groups or *social classes* with divergent economic interests. As Marx and Engels argued in their *Manifesto of the Communist Party* (1848/1983: 203), the 'history of all hitherto existing society is the history of class struggles'.

On the base of these fundamental assumption, Marx explored the nature of class struggle and economic exploitation in a wide variety of contexts, accounting for developments both in Europe and at the wider international level, for instance in the context of the colonial exploitation of India by the British Empire. Moreover, historical research led Marx to conclude that history was characterised by a gradual narrowing of class struggles in the modern capitalist era towards a conflict between the divergent interests of, on the one hand, the *industrial bourgeoisie*, the wealthy owners of the means of production, that is, machines, factories, tools, various forms of capital, etc., and, on the other hand, the *proletariat*, the working masses who, deprived of significant ownership, have to resort to selling their labour to survive. Marx argued that, due to economic contradictions inherent in capitalism and to a gradual growth in the proletariat's awareness of their own alienated, deprived condition and interests – their *class consciousness* – capitalism would eventually be destabilised. A proletarian revolution would ensue, paving the way for a new form of social life, characterised by economic, social and political equality.

Reading

Marx, Karl, and Friedrich Engels (1848/1983), *Manifesto of the Communist Party*, in *The Portable Karl Marx*, edited by E. Kamenka, New York: Penguin Books, pp. 203–17

Manifesto of the Communist Party

A spectre is haunting Europe – the spectre of communism. All the powers of old Europe have entered into a holy alliance to exorcise this spectre: Pope and Tsar, Metternich and Guizot, French Radicals and German police-spies.

Where is the party in opposition that has not been decried as communistic by its opponents in power? Where is the opposition that has not hurled back the branding reproach of communism, against the more advanced opposition parties, as well as against its reactionary adversaries?

Two things result from this fact:

I. Communism is already acknowledged by all European powers to be itself a power.

II. It is high time that Communists should openly, in the face of the whole world, publish their views, their aims, their tendencies, and meet this nursery tale of the spectre of communism with a manifesto of the party itself.

To this end, Communists of various nationalities have assembled in London and sketched the following manifesto, to be published in the English, French, German, Italian, Flemish and Danish languages.

I. Bourgeois and Proletarians

The history of all hitherto existing society is the history of class struggles.

Freeman and slave, patrician and plebeian, lord and serf, guild-master and journeyman, in a word, oppressor and oppressed, stood in constant opposition to one another, carried on an uninterrupted, now hidden, now open fight, a fight that each time ended, either in a revolutionary reconstitution of society at large, or in the common ruin of the contending classes.

In the earlier epochs of history, we find almost everywhere a complicated arrangement of society into various orders, a manifold gradation of social rank. In ancient Rome we have patricians, knights, plebeians, slaves; in the Middle Ages, feudal lords, vassals, guild-masters, journeymen, apprentices, serfs; in almost all of these classes, again, subordinate gradations.

The modern bourgeois society that has sprouted from the ruins of feudal society has not done away with class antagonisms. It has but established new classes, new conditions of oppression, new forms of struggle in place of the old ones.

Our epoch, the epoch of the bourgeoisie, possesses, however, this distinctive feature: It has simplified the class antagonisms. Society as a whole is more and more splitting up into two great hostile camps, into two great classes directly facing each other – bourgeoisie and proletariat.

From the serfs of the Middle Ages sprang the chartered burghers of the earliest towns. From these burgesses the first elements of the bourgeoisie were developed.

The discovery of America, the rounding of the Cape, opened up fresh ground for the rising bourgeoisie. The East-Indian and Chinese markets, the colonisation of America, trade with the colonies, the increase in the means of exchange and in commodities generally, gave to commerce, to navigation, to industry, an impulse never before known, and thereby, to the revolutionary element in the tottering feudal society, a rapid development.

The feudal system of industry, in which industrial production was monopolised by closed guilds, now no longer sufficed for the growing wants of the new markets. The manufacturing system took its place. The guild-masters were pushed aside by the manufacturing middle class; division of labour between the different corporate guilds vanished in the face of division of labour in each single workshop.

Meantime the markets kept ever growing, the demand ever rising. Even manufacture no longer sufficed. Thereupon, steam and machinery revolutionised industrial production. The place of manufacture was taken by the giant, modern industry, the place of the industrial middle class by industrial millionaires, the leaders of whole industrial armies, the modern bourgeois.

Modern industry has established the world market, for which the discovery of America paved the way. This market has given an immense development to commerce, to navigation, to communication by land. This development has, in its turn, reacted on the extension of industry; and in proportion as industry, commerce, navigation, railways extended, in the same proportion the bourgeoisie developed, increased its capital, and pushed into the background every class handed down from the Middle Ages.

We see, therefore, how the modern bourgeoisie is itself the product of a long course of development, of a series of revolutions in the modes of production and of exchange.

Each step in the development of the bourgeoisie was accompanied by a corresponding political advance of that class. An oppressed class under the sway of the feudal nobility, an armed and self-governing association in the medieval commune; here independent urban republic (as in Italy and Germany), there taxable "third estate" of the monarchy (as in France); afterwards, in the period of manufacture proper, serving either the semi-feudal or the absolute monarchy as a counterpoise against the nobility, and, in fact, cornerstone of the great monarchies in general – the bourgeoisie has at last, since the establishment of modern industry and of the world market, conquered for itself, in the modern representative state, exclusive political sway. The executive of the modern state is but a committee for managing the common affairs of the whole bourgeoisie.

The bourgeoisie, historically, has played a most revolutionary part.

The bourgeoisie, wherever it has got the upper hand, has put an end to all feudal, patriarchal, idyllic relations. It has pitilessly torn asunder the motley feudal ties that bound man to his "natural superiors," and has left no other nexus between man and man than naked self-interest, than callous "cash payment." It has drowned the most heavenly ecstasies of religious fervour, of chivalrous enthusiasm, of philistine sentimentalism, in the icy water of egotistical calculation. It has resolved personal worth into exchange value, and in place of the numberless indefeasible chartered freedoms, has set up that single, unconscionable freedom – Free Trade. In one word, for exploitation, veiled by religious and political illusions, it has substituted naked, shameless, direct, brutal exploitation.

The bourgeoisie has stripped of its halo every occupation hitherto honoured and looked up to with reverent awe. It has converted the physician, the lawyer, the priest, the poet, the man of science, into its paid wage labourers.

The bourgeoisie has torn away from the family its sentimental veil, and has reduced the family relation to a mere money relation.

The bourgeoisie has disclosed how it came to pass that the brutal display of vigour in the Middle Ages, which reactionaries so much admire, found its fitting complement in the most slothful indolence. It has been the first to show what man's activity can bring about. It has accomplished wonders far surpassing Egyptian pyramids, Roman aqueducts, and Gothic cathedrals; it has conducted expeditions that put in the shade all former exoduses of nations and crusades.

The bourgeoisie cannot exist without constantly revolutionising the instruments of production, and thereby the relations of production, and with them the whole relations of society. Conservation of the old modes of production in unaltered form was, on the contrary, the first condition of existence for all earlier industrial classes. Constant revolutionising of production, uninterrupted disturbance of all social conditions, everlasting uncertainty and agitation distinguish the bourgeois epoch from all earlier ones. All fixed, fast frozen relations, with their train of ancient and venerable prejudices and opinions, are swept away, all new-formed ones become antiquated before they can ossify. All that is solid melts into air, all that is holy is profaned, and man is at last compelled to face with sober senses his real conditions of life and his relations with his kind.

The need of a constantly expanding market for its products chases the bourgeoisie over the whole surface of the globe. It must nestle everywhere, settle everywhere, establish connections everywhere.

The bourgeoisie has through its exploitation of the world market given a cosmopolitan character to production and consumption in every country. To the great chagrin of reactionaries, it had drawn from under the feet of industry the national ground on which it stood. All old-established national industries have been destroyed or are daily being destroyed. They are dislodged by new industries, whose introduction becomes a life and death question for all civilised nations, by industries that no longer work up indigenous raw material, but raw material drawn from the remotest zones; industries whose products are consumed, not only at home, but in every quarter of the globe. In place of the old wants, satisfied by the production of the country, we find new wants, requiring for their satisfaction the products of distant lands and climes. In place of the old local and national seclusion and self-sufficiency, we have intercourse in every direction, universal inter-dependence of nations. And as in material, so also in intellectual production. The intellectual creations of individual nations become common property. National one-sidedness and narrow-mindedness become more and more impossible, and from the numerous national and local literatures there arises a world literature.

The bourgeoisie, by the rapid improvement of all instruments of production, by the immensely facilitated means of communication, draws all, even the most barbarian, nations into civilisation. The cheap prices of its commodities are the heavy artillery with which it batters down all Chinese walls, with which it forces the barbarians' intensely obstinate hatred of foreigners to capitulate. It compels all nations, on pain of extinction, to adopt the bourgeois mode of production; it compels them to introduce what it calls civilisation into their midst, i.e., to become bourgeois themselves. In one word, it creates a world after its own image.

The bourgeoisie has subjected the country to the rule of the towns. It has created enormous cities, has greatly increased the urban population as compared with the rural, and has thus rescued a considerable part of the population from the idiocy of rural life. Just as it has made the country dependent on the towns, so it has made barbarian and semi-barbarian countries dependent on the civilised ones, nations of peasants on nations of bourgeois, the East on the West.

The bourgeoisie keeps more and more doing away with the scattered state of the population, of the means of production, and of property. It has agglomerated population, centralised means of production, and has concentrated property in a few hands. The necessary consequence of this was political centralisation. Independent, or but loosely connected provinces, with separate interests, laws, governments, and systems of taxation, became lumped together into one nation, with one government, one code of laws, one national class interest, one frontier and one customs tariff.

The bourgeoisie, during its rule of scarce one hundred years, has created more massive and more colossal productive forces than have all preceding generations together. Subjection of nature's forces to man, machinery, application of chemistry to industry and agriculture, steam navigation, railways, electric telegraphs,

clearing of whole continents for cultivation, canalisation of rivers, whole populations conjured out of the ground – what earlier century had even a presentiment
that such productive forces slumbered in the lap of social labour?

We see then: the means of production and of exchange, on whose foundation
the bourgeoisie built itself up, were generated in feudal society. At a certain stage
in the development of these means of production and of exchange, the conditions under which feudal society produced and exchanged, the feudal organisation of agriculture and manufacturing industry, in one word, the feudal relations
of property became no longer compatible with the already developed productive
forces; they became so many fetters. They had to be burst asunder; they were
burst asunder.

Into their place stepped free competition, accompanied by a social and political constitution adapted to it, and by the economic and political sway of the
bourgeois class.

A similar movement is going on before our own eyes. Modern bourgeois society with its relations of production, of exchange and of property, a society that
has conjured up such gigantic means of production and of exchange, is like the
sorcerer who is no longer able to control the powers of the nether world whom
he has called up by his spells. For many a decade past the history of industry and
commerce is but the history of the revolt of modern productive forces against
modern conditions of production, against the property relations that are the conditions for the existence of the bourgeoisie and of its rule. It is enough to mention the commercial crises that by their periodical return put the existence of the
entire bourgeois society on its trial, each time more threateningly. In these crises
a great part not only of the existing products, but also of the previously created
productive forces, are periodically destroyed. In these crises there breaks out an
epidemic that, in all earlier epochs, would have seemed an absurdity – the epidemic of over-production. Society suddenly finds itself put back into a state of
momentary barbarism; it appears as if a famine, a universal war of devastation
had cut off the supply of every means of subsistence; industry and commerce
seem to be destroyed. And why? Because there is too much civilisation, too much
means of subsistence, too much industry, too much commerce. The productive
forces at the disposal of society no longer tend to further the development of the
conditions of bourgeois property; on the contrary, they have become too powerful for these conditions, by which they are fettered, and so soon as they overcome
these fetters, they bring disorder into the whole of bourgeois society, endanger
the existence of bourgeois property. The conditions of bourgeois society are too
narrow to comprise the wealth created by them. And how does the bourgeoisie
get over these crises? On the one hand, by enforced destruction of a mass of productive forces; on the other, by the conquest of new markets, and by the more
thorough exploitation of the old ones. That is to say, by paving the way for more
extensive and more destructive crises, and by diminishing the means whereby
crises are prevented.

The weapons with which the bourgeoisie felled feudalism to the ground are now turned against the bourgeoisie itself.

But not only has the bourgeoisie forged the weapons that bring death to itself; it has also called into existence the men who are to wield those weapons – the modern working class – the proletarians.

In proportion as the bourgeoisie, i.e., capital, is developed, in the same proportion is the proletariat, the modern working class, developed – a class of labourers, who live only so long as they find work, and who find work only so long as their labour increases capital. These labourers, who must sell themselves piecemeal, are a commodity, like every other article of commerce, and are consequently exposed to all the vicissitudes of competition, to all the fluctuations of the market.

Owing to the extensive use of machinery and to division of labour, the work of the proletarians has lost all individual character, and, consequently, all charm for the workman. He becomes an appendage of the machine, and it is only the most simple, most monotonous, and most easily acquired knack, that is required of him. Hence, the cost of production of a workman is restricted, almost entirely, to the means of subsistence that he requires for his maintenance, and for the propagation of his race. But the price of a commodity, and therefore also of labour, is equal to its cost of production. In proportion, therefore, as the repulsiveness of the work increases, the wage decreases. Nay more, in proportion as the use of machinery and division of labour increases, in the same proportion the burden of toil also increases, whether by prolongation of the working hours, by increase of the work exacted in a given time, or by increased speed of the machinery, etc.

Modern industry has converted the little workshop of the patriarchal master into the great factory of the industrial capitalist. Masses of labourers, crowded into the factory, are organised like soldiers. As privates of the industrial army they are placed under the command of a perfect hierarchy of officers and sergeants. Not only are they slaves of the bourgeois class, and of the bourgeois state; they are daily and hourly enslaved by the machine, by the overseer, and, above all, by the individual bourgeois manufacturer himself. The more openly this despotism proclaims gain to be its end and aim, the more petty, the more hateful and the more embittering it is.

The less the skill and exertion of strength implied in manual labour, in other words, the more modern industry becomes developed, the more is the labour of men superseded by that of women. Differences of age and sex have no longer any distinctive social validity for the working class. All are instruments of labour, more or less expensive to use, according to their age and sex.

No sooner is the exploitation of the labourer by the manufacturer, so far at an end, that he receives his wages in cash, than he is set upon by the other portions of the bourgeoisie, the landlord, the shopkeeper, the pawnbroker, etc.

The lower strata of the middle class – the small trades-people, shopkeepers, and retired tradesmen generally, the handicraftsmen and peasants – all these sink gradually into the proletariat, partly because their diminutive capital does not suffice for the scale on which modern industry is carried on, and is swamped in the competition with the large capitalists, partly because their specialised skill is rendered worthless by new methods of production. Thus the proletariat is recruited from all classes of the population.

The proletariat goes through various stages of development. With its birth begins its struggle with the bourgeoisie. At first the contest is carried on by individual labourers, then by the work people of a factory, then by the operatives of one trade, in one locality, against the individual bourgeois who directly exploits them. They direct their attacks not against the bourgeois conditions of production, but against the instruments of production themselves; they destroy imported wares that compete with their labour, they smash to pieces machinery, they set factories ablaze, they seek to restore by force the vanished status of the workman of the Middle Ages.

At this stage the labourers still form an incoherent mass scattered over the whole country, and broken up by their mutual competition. If anywhere they unite to form more compact bodies, this is not yet the consequence of their own active union, but of the union of the bourgeoisie, which class, in order to attain its own political ends, is compelled to set the whole proletariat in motion, and is moreover yet, for a time, able to do so. At this stage, therefore, the proletarians do not fight their enemies, but the enemies of their enemies, the remnants of absolute monarchy, the landowners, the non-industrial bourgeois, the petty bourgeoisie. Thus the whole historical movement is concentrated in the hands of the bourgeoisie; every victory so obtained is a victory for the bourgeoisie.

But with the development of industry the proletariat not only increases in number; it becomes concentrated in greater masses, its strength grows, and it feels that strength more. The various interests and conditions of life within the ranks of the proletariat are more and more equalised, in proportion as machinery obliterates all distinctions of labour, and nearly everywhere reduces wages to the same low level. The growing competition among the bourgeois, and the resulting commercial crises, make the wages of the workers ever more fluctuating. The unceasing improvement of machinery, ever more rapidly developing, makes their livelihood more and more precarious; the collisions between individual workmen and individual bourgeois take more and more the character of collisions between two classes. Thereupon the workers begin to form combinations (trade unions) against the bourgeois; they club together in order to keep up the rate of wages; they found permanent associations in order to make provision beforehand for these occasional revolts. Here and there the contest breaks out into riots.

Now and then the workers are victorious, but only for a time. The real fruit of their battle lies, not in the immediate result, but in the ever expanding union of the workers. This union is helped on by the improved means of communication that are created by modern industry, and that place the workers of different localities in contact with one another. It was just this contact that was needed to centralise the numerous local struggles, all of the same character, into one national struggle between classes. But every class struggle is a political struggle. And that union, to attain which the burghers of the Middle Ages, with their miserable highways, required centuries, the modern proletarians, thanks to railways, achieve in a few years.

This organisation of the proletarians into a class, and consequently into a political party, is continually being upset again by the competition between the workers themselves. But it ever rises up again, stronger, firmer, mightier. It compels legislative recognition of particular interests of the workers, by taking advantage of the divisions among the bourgeoisie itself. Thus the Ten-Hours Bill in England was carried.

Altogether, collisions between the classes of the old society further in many ways the course of development of the proletariat. The bourgeoisie finds itself involved in a constant battle. At first with the aristocracy; later on, with those portions of the bourgeoisie itself, whose interests have become antagonistic to the progress of industry; at all times with the bourgeoisie of foreign countries. In all these battles it sees itself compelled to appeal to the proletariat, to ask for its help, and thus, to drag it into the political arena. The bourgeoisie itself, therefore, supplies the proletariat with its own elements of political and general education, in other words, it furnishes the proletariat with weapons for fighting the bourgeoisie.

Further, as we have already seen, entire sections of the ruling classes are, by the advance of industry, precipitated into the proletariat, or are at least threatened in their conditions of existence. These also supply the proletariat with fresh elements of enlightenment and progress.

Finally, in times when the class struggle nears the decisive hour, the process of dissolution going on within the ruling class, in fact within the whole range of old society, assumes such a violent, glaring character, that a small section of the ruling class cuts itself adrift, and joins the revolutionary class, the class that holds the future in its hands. Just as, therefore, at an earlier period, a section of the nobility went over to the bourgeoisie, so now a portion of the bourgeoisie goes over to the proletariat, and in particular, a portion of the bourgeois ideologists, who have raised themselves to the level of comprehending theoretically the historical movement as a whole.

Of all the classes that stand face to face with the bourgeoisie to-day, the proletariat alone is a really revolutionary class. The other classes decay and finally disappear in the face of modern industry; the proletariat is its special and essential product.

The lower middle class, the small manufacturer, the shopkeeper, the artisan, the peasant, all these fight against the bourgeoisie, to save from extinction their existence as fractions of the middle class. They are therefore not revolutionary, but conservative. Nay, more, they are reactionary, for they try to roll back the wheel of history. If by chance they are revolutionary, they are so only in view of their impending transfer into the proletariat; they thus defend not their present, but their future interests; they desert their own standpoint to place themselves at that of the proletariat.

The "dangerous class," the social scum, that passively rotting mass thrown off by the lowest layers of old society, may, here and there, be swept into the movement by a proletarian revolution; its conditions of life, however, prepare it far more for the part of a bribed tool of reactionary intrigue.

In the conditions of the proletariat, those of old society at large are already virtually swamped. The proletarian is without property; his relation to his wife and children has no longer anything in common with the bourgeois family relations; modern industrial labour, modern subjection to capital, the same in England as in France, in America as in Germany, has stripped him of every trace of national character. Law, morality, religion, are to him so many bourgeois prejudices, behind which lurk in ambush just as many bourgeois interests.

All the preceding classes that got the upper hand, sought to fortify their already acquired status by subjecting society at large to their conditions of appropriation. The proletarians cannot become masters of the productive forces of society, except by abolishing their own previous mode of appropriation, and thereby also every other previous mode of appropriation. They have nothing of their own to secure and to fortify; their mission is to destroy all previous securities for, and insurances of, individual property.

All previous historical movements were movements of minorities, or in the interest of minorities. The proletarian movement is the self-conscious, independent movement of the immense majority, in the interest of the immense majority. The proletariat, the lowest stratum of our present society, cannot stir, cannot raise itself up, without the whole superincumbent strata of official society being blown to pieces.

Though not in substance, yet in form, the struggle of the proletariat with the bourgeoisie is at first a national struggle. The proletariat of each country must, of course, first of all settle matters with its own bourgeoisie.

In depicting the most general phases of the development of the proletariat, we traced the more or less veiled civil war, raging within existing society, up to the point where that war breaks out into open revolution, and where the violent overthrow of the bourgeoisie lays the foundation for the sway of the proletariat.

Hitherto, every form of society has been based, as we have already seen, on the antagonism of oppressing and oppressed classes. But in order to oppress a class, certain conditions must be assured to it under which it can, at least, continue its slavish existence. The serf, in the period of serfdom, raised himself to membership in the commune, just as the petty bourgeois, under the yoke of feudal absolutism, managed to develop into a bourgeois. The modern labourer, on the contrary, instead of rising with the progress of industry, sinks deeper and deeper below the conditions of existence of his own class. He becomes a pauper, and pauperism develops more rapidly than population and wealth. And here it becomes evident that the bourgeoisie is unfit any longer to be the ruling class in society, and to impose its conditions of existence upon society as an overriding law. It is unfit to rule because it is incompetent to assure an existence to its slave within his slavery, because it cannot help letting him sink into such a state, that it has to feed him, instead of being fed by him. Society can no longer live under this bourgeoisie, in other words, its existence is no longer compatible with society.

The essential condition for the existence and for the sway of the bourgeois class, is the formation and augmentation of capital; the condition for capital is wage labour. Wage labour rests exclusively on competition between the labourers. The advance of industry, whose involuntary promoter is the bourgeoisie, replaces the isolation of the labourers, due to competition, by their revolutionary combination, due to association. The development of modern industry, therefore, cuts from under its feet the very foundation on which the bourgeoisie produces and appropriates products. What the bourgeoisie therefore produces, above all, are its own grave-diggers. Its fall and the victory of the proletariat are equally inevitable.

Consider

1. How might the social, political, and economic conditions of the time have influenced Marx's arguments in the *Manifesto*?

   To answer this question, you may wish to examine the socio-economic consequences of the Industrial Revolution and the nature of the political system that followed the Congress of Vienna in 1815. A look at the revolutions of the year 1848 may allow you to understand the specific historical context in which the *Manifesto* was written.

2. How have Marx's and Engels's ideas influenced social and political life in the world? Give examples from different historical periods and geographical contexts.

3. Summarise Marx's and Engels's materialist conception of history in your own words, in reference to the preceding extract.

4. According to Marx and Engels, what are the main aspects of class struggle between the bourgeoisie and capitalism? Answering this question, give relevant examples of class struggle in the contemporary world.

5. 'The history of all hitherto existing society is the history of class struggles.' Critically discuss this statement.

6. The preceding extract only covers a limited part of Marx's and Engels's work. Two examples of concepts that have retained powerful influence over the years are *ideology* and *alienation*. Research the meaning of both terms in Marxist theory and formulate a short definition in your own words. Can you think of any contemporary examples to illustrate them?

7. Compare and contrast Karl Marx's materialist approach to history with Herbert Spencer's theory of societies' evolution. What are their main similarities and differences?

Émile Durkheim

Émile Durkheim contributed much to the establishment of sociology as an independent academic discipline, both by developing its distinctive perspective and conceptual
tools and by creating a space for it in academic institutions. Durkheim was born into
a family of rabbis in north-eastern France in 1858. He in many ways detached himself
from his family's religious heritage, instead taking an interest in new developments in
the sciences. Through studies in France and Germany, Durkheim came to teach at the
University of Bordeaux, where he offered the first ever social science course. Later in his
life, Durkheim would be named the first professor of sociology in France. Moreover,
with *L'Année Sociologique*, Durkheim founded one of the world's first sociology journals, which still exists today. Durkheim was a noted scholar in his lifetime, and his
works have earned him lasting central influence on the concerns, ideas and methods of
sociology across the twentieth and into the twenty-first century.

Durkheim's works cover a wide variety of subject matter, including, for example,
religion, education, processes of socio-economic differentiation in modern societies,
crime and the social origins of suicide. All these studies share a number of overarching
concerns. Durkheim had a strong interest in legitimising sociology as an independent
academic discipline. In his lifetime, sociology was not widely recognised at all, and in
some quarters the work of scholars such as Comte was considered to be quite scandal-
ous. Therefore, it was necessary to, first, demonstrate the possibility and importance of
a distinctively sociological perspective on social life and, second, to carve out a niche
for sociology in the academic institutions that tend to concentrate intellectual life. His
varied works are geared towards these objectives.

One of his early works, more on which you will read further on, is *Suicide* (Durkheim
(1897/2004)). Suicide might seem to be an odd subject matter for a sociologist, in so
far as taking one's life is certainly one of the most personal and solitary acts imaginable.
However, it is precisely due to this common-sense assumption that Durkheim picked this
topic. Demonstrating that suicide, against common sense, is a profoundly *social act* would
allow him to make a profound impression on his readers as to the novel and important
insights offered by sociology. In addressing this task, Durkheim therefore was not concerned with the explanation of particular individuals' personal motivations for taking their
lives. Instead, his overriding interest lay with explaining why, according to statistics on
suicide rates, people in particular times or social groups seemed to be more likely to commit suicide than others. This interest was grounded in Durkheim's (1895/1982) development of a distinctively sociological method of exploring social life, built around the idea of
'social facts' already discussed in Chapter 1. Using his new sociological method, Durkheim
proposed that such broad variations in suicide rates could be understood through the realisation that, beyond specific personal reasons for suicide, there were broader social causes
at work. Within different historical time periods or in different societies, different collective
outlooks on life and forms of social integration prevail. These, Durkheim concluded, had a
significant impact on individuals' likelihood to commit suicide. Thus, even one of the most
personal acts imaginable is ultimately shaped by the nature and features of wider society.

Durkheim's attention to topics such as suicide was grounded in a broader interest: Durkheim, just as the other early sociologists discussed in this chapter, worried about the nature of the rapid changes modern Western societies were undergoing in his time and sought to provide his contemporaries with a better understanding of these processes. Specifically, Durkheim was concerned about problems of *anomie* in modern societies, that is, a lack of norms and values that may guide individuals in their everyday lives and an overall breakdown of moral order. Durkheim developed this concern in another of his early works, *The Division of Labour in Society* (Durkheim 1984). Here, he charted the development of modern societies and changes in the forms of social solidarity which modernisation entails. Traditional, small-scale, rural societies, Durkheim concluded, are characterised by relatively simple forms of economic life, requiring little specialisation of the tasks to be performed by the members of a community and leading them to co-exist in close union with each other. In an isolated rural village of, say, the European Middle Ages, individuals would be likely to know all the members of their community, be dependent on mutual cooperation, and be exposed to their disapproval if they misbehaved. Durkheim labelled this form of co-existence *'mechanical solidarity'*. In contrast, in modern, urban societies, we are skilled only to perform a very narrow range of tasks – sociology lecturers, for example, know how to give a lecture or write a paper, but we may be at a loss when it comes to building a house or assembling a car – and we mostly do not know all those on whom we depend for our day-to-day survival. We are dependent on others through this diversification and narrowing of economic functions, but there may be little in the way of moral control and guidance, leading to a potential for anomie and moral disorientation. Durkheim labelled this mostly economic form of co-existence 'organic solidarity'. With his concern with social solidarity and the bonds that hold – or do not hold – society together, Durkheim inspired sociologists for generations to come. Indeed, as we shall see in later chapters, Durkheim's arguments in many ways coincide with those made by sociologists today, in the early twenty-first century!

Reading

Thompson, K., ed. (1985/2004), *Readings from Émile Durkheim*, London: Routledge, pp. 65–83

Suicide

Edited and translated from: *Le Suicide: étude de sociologie*, Paris, Alcan, 1897. Translation by Margaret Thompson.

Preface

Instead of taking pleasure in metaphysical meditation on social themes, the sociologist should take as the object of his research groups of clearly circumscribed facts, which are capable of ready definition and have recognizable limits, and he must adhere strictly to them. [. . .]

We have chosen suicide for this particular study from among many different subjects that we have had occasion to study during the course of our teaching because it seemed to be a particularly opportune example, and one which is unusually easily defined. Even so, some preliminary work has been necessary to outline it. On the other hand, in compensation, when one focuses in this way, one succeeds in finding real laws that demonstrate the possibilities of sociology much better than any dialectical argument. We shall be examining the laws that we hope to have established. We are quite likely to have made a few mistakes or to have made inductions beyond the observable facts. But at least each proposition is accompanied by proofs, which we have tried to make as plentiful as possible. Above all, we have tried hard to separate the arguments and the interpretations from the facts in each case. [. . .]

Sociological method as we practise it is entirely based on the fundamental principle that social facts must be studied as things; that is, as realities external to the individual. No precept has been more challenged, but none is more fundamental. For sociology to be possible it must first have an object, and one which is exclusive to sociology. It must take cognizance of a reality which does not belong to other sciences. But if there is – nothing real beyond individual consciousness then sociology must disappear for lack of any subject of its own. The only objects to which this observation might be applied are mental states of the individual, since nothing else exists. However, that is the field of psychology. In fact, from this point of view, everything of significance, for example concerning marriage, the family, or religion, consists of individual needs to which these institutions are simply a response – paternal love, filial love, sexual desire, what used to be called religious instinct, etc. The institutions themselves, with their diverse and complex historical forms, become negligible and of little significance. [. . .]

But it seems hardly possible to us, on the contrary, that there will not emerge from every page of this book, evidence that the individual is dominated by a moral reality which transcends him – collective reality. When one sees that each population has its own suicide rate and that this rate is more constant than the general mortality, and that, if it changes, it does so according to a coefficient of growth specific to that society; when it seems that variations according to different times of the day, month and year merely reflect the rhythm of social life; and when one observes that marriage, divorce, family, religious society, the army, etc., affect it according to definite laws, some of which can even be expressed in numerical form, one stops seeing these states and institutions as just inconsequential, ineffective ideological arrangements. Rather, they are felt to be real, living, active forces, which, because of the way in which they determine the individual, adequately demonstrate that they do not depend on him; even if the individual enters as an element in the emerging combination, to the extent that these forces become formed, they are imposed upon him. In these circumstances it becomes clear that sociology can and must be objective, since it confronts realities which are as definite and substantial as the realities that concern the psychologist or biologist.

Introduction

Since the word suicide keeps occurring in the course of this discussion, it might seem as if everyone knows its meaning, and that definition is superfluous. But, in reality, words in everyday language, like the concepts they express, are always ambiguous, and the scholar who uses them in their usual sense, without submitting them to further definition, risks serious confusion. [. . .]

The first task, therefore, must be to determine the order of facts that we intend to study under the label of suicide. Accordingly, we shall inquire whether, among the different kinds of death, there are some which have common characteristics that are objective enough to be recognized by any honest observer, specific enough not to be found elsewhere, but, at the same time, sufficiently similar to those generally called suicides so that we can keep the same expression without distorting the usual meaning. If such are found, we can group together under this label all the facts which show these distinctive characteristics, regardless of whether the class thus formed fails to include all cases labelled in this way or, inversely, includes some which are normally classified otherwise. What is important is not simply to express more precisely what the average person understands by the term suicide, but to establish a category of objects which can be usefully classified in this way and have an objective basis, corresponding to a definite order of things. [. . .]

So we come to the first formula: the term suicide is applied to any death which results directly or indirectly from a positive or negative act carried out by the victim himself.

But this definition is incomplete; it fails to distinguish between two very different sorts of deaths. The same classification and treatment cannot be given to the death of a person in a hallucinatory state who throws himself from a high window, believing it to be at street level, and to the death of a sane person who takes his life knowing what he is doing. In one sense there are a few deaths that are not the direct or indirect consequence of some steps taken by the person concerned. The causes of death are more often external than internal and they affect us only if we venture into their sphere of action.

Shall it be said that suicide exists only if the act resulting in death was carried out by the victim with this result in mind? That only he who wished to kill himself really kills himself and that suicide is intentional homicide of oneself? In the first place, this would be defining suicide by a characteristic which, whatever its interest and importance might be, would at least suffer from not being easily recognizable because it is not easy to observe. How do we know what the agent's motive was and whether, when he took his decision, it was in fact death that he desired or whether he had some other aim? Intention is too intimate a thing to be understood from outside other than by gross approximation. It even escapes self-observation. How often do we mistake the real reasons for our actions? We are constantly explaining actions deriving from petty feelings or blind routine as being due to noble passions or lofty considerations.

Besides, in general, an act cannot be defined by the ends that the actor is pursuing, for an identical pattern of behaviour can be adapted to many different ends without changing its nature. And indeed, if suicide existed only when the intention to kill oneself was present, then the term suicide could not be used for facts which, despite apparent differences, are basically identical to those generally called suicide and which cannot be called by any other name without rendering the term useless. The soldier who goes out in front to face certain death to save his regiment does not want to die, and yet he is not the author of his own death in the same way as the industrialist or merchant who kills himself to avoid the shame of bankruptcy? The same can be said of the martyr who dies for his faith, the mother who sacrifices herself for her child, etc. Whether the death is simply accepted as a regrettable but inevitable condition given the purpose, or whether it is expressly desired and sought for its own sake, in both cases the person renounces his existence, and the different ways of doing so can be only varieties of a single class. They possess too many fundamental similarities not to be combined in the same generic expression, though subsequent distinctions of types within this established genus are necessary. Certainly, in popular usage, suicide is first and foremost the act of despair of the man who does not wish to live. But, in fact, though one is still attached to life at the moment of leaving it, it is abandoned none the less; and there are clearly essential characteristics common to all acts in which a living person gives up what must be his most precious possession. On the other hand, the diversity of motives which might have prompted these decisions can give rise to only secondary differences. So when devotion goes as far as the definite sacrifice of life, it is, scientifically speaking, a suicide; we shall see later of what sort it is.

What is common to all possible forms of this supreme renunciation is that the determining act is carried out in full knowledge; the victim, at the moment of acting, knows what must be the result of his action, whatever the reason that led him to act in that way. All deaths which have this particular characteristic are clearly distinct from all others where the victim is either not the agent of his own death, or is its unconscious agent. They differ by an easily recognizable characteristic, for it is not an insoluble problem to discern whether or not the individual knew in advance the natural consequences of his action. Therefore, they form a definite, homogeneous group, distinguishable from any other, and consequently they must be designated by a special term. The term suicide is appropriate and there is no reason to create another, for the vast majority of deaths that are so designated are in fact part of this group. We can say conclusively, therefore, that: *suicide is applied to every case of death which results directly or indirectly from a positive or negative act, carried out by the victim himself, knowing that it will produce this result.* An attempt is an act defined in the same way, but falling short of actual death. [. . .]

But if the act is defined this way, is it of interest to the sociologist? Since suicide is an individual act which affects only the individual, and would seem to depend exclusively on individual factors it must therefore belong to the field of psychology. Surely one ordinarily explains the suicide's decision in terms of his temperament, character, and biographical events?

At this point it is not necessary to consider to what extent and under what conditions it is legitimate to study suicides in this way, but there is no doubt that they can be viewed in an entirely different light. If, instead of seeing suicides only as isolated, individual events that need to be examined separately, one considers all suicides committed in a particular society during a specific time period as a whole, it is evident that the total thus obtained is not simply a sum of independent units, a collective total, but constitutes in itself a new fact *sui generis*, which has its own unity and individuality, and therefore, its own pre-eminently social nature. In fact, for a particular society, provided that the observation is not carried out over too long a period, the statistics are almost invariable. [. . .] This is because the circumstances of life of whole populations remain essentially the same from year to year. Sometimes there are greater variations; but they are somewhat exceptional. They are always contemporaneous with some crisis which temporarily affects the social state. [. . .]

At every moment of its history each society has a certain tendency towards suicide. The relative intensity of this tendency is measured by taking the relationship between the total of voluntary deaths and the population of all ages and sexes. We shall call this numerical datum *the rate of mortality due to suicide, characteristic of the society under consideration*. It is generally calculated in proportion to a million or a hundred thousand inhabitants. [. . .]

The suicide rate therefore constitutes an order of facts which is unified and definite, as is shown by both its permanence and its variability. The permanence would be inexplicable if it was not related to a group of distinctive characteristics, united with each other, which assert themselves simultaneously despite the diversity of accompanying circumstances; and the variability testifies to the individual and concrete nature of these same characteristics, since they vary with the individual character of society itself. In short, these statistical data expresses the tendency to suicide with which each society is collectively afflicted. We will not say at this point what this tendency consists of, whether it is a *sui generis* state of the collective mind, with its own reality, or wheather it represents only the sum of individual states. Although the preceding considerations are difficult to reconcile with this latter hypothesis, we reserve this problem for treatment later in the course of this work. Whatever one's opinion on this matter, such a tendency certainly exists in one form or another. Every society is predisposed to produce a certain number of voluntary deaths. This predisposition can therefore be the object of a special study which belongs to sociology. This is the study we are about to undertake.

Our intention is not to compile an exhaustive inventory of all the conditions that give rise to individual suicides, but simply to examine those on which the definite fact that we have called the social suicide rate depends. These two questions are very distinct, even though they may be related. In fact, there are certainly many individual conditions which are not sufficiently general to affect the relationship between the total number of voluntary deaths and the population. They may perhaps cause this or that individual to kill himself, but not cause the society as a whole to have a greater or lesser tendency towards suicide. Since they are not related to a certain condition of social organization, they have no social consequences. They are, therefore, of interest to the psychologist, but not the sociologist. The sociologist studies causes which affect not the isolated individual but the group. Therefore, among the factors of suicide, the only ones which concern him are those which affect society as a whole. The suicide rate is the product of these factors. This is why we must confine our attention to them. [. . .]

How to Determine Social Causes and Social Types

The results of the preceding section are not entirely negative. We have in fact established that for each social group there exists a specific tendency towards suicide, which is explained neither by the organic psychological constitution of individual nor by the nature of the physical environment. Therefore, through a process of elimination, it must necessarily depend on social causes and be in itself a collective phenomenon; certain facts that we have examined, particularly geographical and seasonal variations in suicide, have led us directly to this conclusion. [. . .]

Unfortunately, classification of suicides of sane persons according to their morphological forms or characteristics is impracticable because there is a total lack of the necessary documentation. To be viable it would need good descriptions of many individual cases. One would need to know the suicide's psychological state at the moment of his decision, how he prepared to carry it out, how it was finally executed, whether he was agitated or depressed, calm or excited, anxious or irritated, etc. [. . .]

But we can achieve our end by another method, by reversing the order of study. In effect, there can be only as many different types of suicide as there are different causes. For each type to have its own nature, it must also have special conditions of existence. The same antecedent or group of antecedents cannot sometimes produce one result and sometimes another, otherwise the difference between the second and the first would itself be without cause, which would deny the principle of causality. Any specific difference observed in the causes, therefore, implies a similar difference between the effects. Consequently we can determine the social types of suicide by classifying the causes which produce them, rather than by classifying them directly according to their previously described characteristics. Without seeking to know why they are different from each other, we shall first study the social conditions which are responsible for them; then we shall group these conditions according to their similarities and differences into a certain number of separate classes, and we can be sure that a specific type of suicide will correspond to each of these classes. In a word, instead of being morphological, our classification will be aetiological from the start. [. . .] Thus we shall proceed from causes to effects and our aetiological classification will be complemented by a morphological classification, which will serve to verify the former, and vice versa.

In all respects, this reverse method is the only one suitable for the special problem that we have raised. We must not forget that it is the social suicide rate that we are studying. The only types of interest to us, therefore, are those which contribute to its formation and bring about its variations. It has not been established that all individual sorts of voluntary death have this property. There are some which, though general to a certain degree, are not linked or not sufficiently linked to the moral character of society to enter as a characteristic element into the special physiognomy of each people in relation to suicide. [. . .]

But how do we get at the causes?

In the legal statements which are made every time a suicide is committed, a note is made of the motive (family troubles, physical or other pain, guilt, drunkenness, etc.) which seems to have been the determining cause, and in the statistical records of almost every country there is a special table containing the results of these enquiries under the title: 'Presumed motives for suicides'. It would seem natural to take advantage of this work that has already been done and to begin our research by comparing these documents. They appear to show the immediate antecedents of different suicides; it would seem to be a good method for understanding the phenomenon that we are studying to return firstly to the most immediate causes, and then to proceed to other more distant causes in the series of phenomena, if it seems necessary.

But, as Wagner commented long ago, what are taken to be statistics about suicide motives are in reality statistics about the opinions concerning such motives as held by officials, often minor ones, responsible for providing such statistical information. Unfortunately, as we are aware, official statements are often very faulty even when they refer to obvious material facts that are comprehensible to any conscientious observer and require nothing in the way of evaluation. How much more suspect must they be considered to be when they attempt not simply to record a completed act but to interpret and explain it! It is always a difficult problem to specify the cause of a phenomenon. The scholar requires all sorts of observations and experiments to resolve just one of these questions. Human volition is the most complex of all phenomena. Consequently one must question the worth of these improvised judgements which, based on some hastily collected bits of information, claim to assign a specific origin to each individual case. As soon as some of the facts commonly believed to lead to despair are thought to have been discovered in the victim's past then further search is considered useless and, if the victim is supposed to have recently lost money, experienced family problems, or indulged a taste for alcohol, responsibility is assigned to his drunkenness, domestic unhappiness, or financial loss. Such suspect data cannot be taken as the basis of an explanation for suicide.

Furthermore, even if such data had more credibility, they would not be very useful, because the motives attributed to suicides, whether right or wrong, are not their true causes. The proof of this is that the proportion of cases attributed by the statistics to each of these presumed reasons remains almost identically the same, whereas the absolute numbers, on the contrary, show extreme variations. In France, from 1856 to 1878, suicides rose about 40%, and by more than 100% in Saxony during the period 1854–1880 (1,171 cases instead of 547). Yet in both these countries each category of motives retains the same relative importance from one period to the next.

If one considers that the figures reported here are, and can only be, gross approximations, and that, consequently, too much importance should not be attached to small differences, it can be seen that they remain effectively constant. But for the contributory share of each presumed reason to have remained proportionally the same while suicide is twice as prevalent, would require us to accept that each has doubled its effect. It cannot be fortuitous that they all became twice as fatal at the same time. We are forced to conclude that they all depend on a more general state, which they all more or less faithfully reflect. This is what makes them to varying degrees productive of suicide and, consequently, is its true determining cause. It is this state that we must study, without wasting time on any distant repercussions that it might have on the consciousness of individuals. [. . .]

The reasons ascribed for suicide, or the reasons which the suicide gives for his act, are often only apparent causes. Not only are the reasons merely individual repercussions of a general state, they also express this state very unfaithfully, since they remain the same whilst it does not. It might be said that they reveal the individual's weak points, through which the external current bringing pressure for self-destruction finds its easiest point of entry. But they are not part of this current itself, and therefore they cannot help us to understand it.

So we are not sorry that certain countries like England and Austria have stopped collecting these supposed causes of suicide. Statistical efforts should be given a different direction. Instead of trying to solve these insoluble problems of moral casuistry, they should be concerned with noting more carefully the social concomitants of suicide. In any case, we are making it a rule not to introduce into our research any data that are suspect or not very informative; in fact specialists in suicide have never succeeded in producing any interesting laws from such data. We shall therefore refer to them only occasionally when they seem to be particularly significant and to offer special guarantees. We shall proceed immediately to seek to determine the causes leading to suicide without concerning ourselves with the forms they may assume in individual cases. In order to achieve this we will leave to one side the individual, with his motives and ideas, and examine the different social environments (religious beliefs, family, political society, occupational groups, etc.) as a function of which variations in suicide occur. Only then shall we return to the individual to study how these general causes become individualized to produce the resulting homicidal effects. [. . .]

Egoistic Suicide

First we will consider the ways in which different religious denominations affect suicide.

A brief glance at a map of suicide in Europe makes it clear immediately that in the really Catholic countries such as Spain, Portugal and Italy, suicide has not developed very much, whilst in Protestant countries like Prussia, Saxony and Denmark, it is at its maximum. [. . .] Obviously these are not all on the same level intellectually and morally; but the similarities are sufficiently marked to enable us to attribute to denominational differences the evident contrast that they present with respect to suicide.

However, this first comparison is still too summary. Despite the existence of some similarities, the populations of these different countries do not have identical social environments. The civilizations of Spain and Portugal are much lower than that of Germany and this inferiority could conceivably be the reason for the lower level of suicide that we have noted. In order to avoid this source of error and to establish more definitely the influence of Catholicism and Protestantism on the tendency to suicide, the two religions need to be compared in the context of a single society.

Among the major German states, Bavaria has by far the fewest suicides. There have been scarcely 90 per million inhabitants each year since 1874, while Prussia has 133 (1871–75), the duchy of Baden 156, Wurtemberg 162, Saxony 300. And Bavaria also has the most Catholics: 713.2 to 1,000 inhabitants. On the other hand, comparison of the different Bavarian provinces shows suicides to vary in direct proportion to the number of Protestants and in inverse proportion to that of Catholics. [. . .]

Switzerland provides us with an interesting case from the same point of view. Because German and French populations co-exist there, it is possible to observe separately the influence of religious denominations on each race. In fact, its influence is the same on both. Catholic cantons are shown to have four or five times fewer suicides than Protestant cantons, whatever the nationality. [. . .]

Thus, everywhere without exception, Protestants evidence many more suicides than members of other denominations.

The propensity of Jews to commit suicide is always less than that of Protestants; in general terms, though to a lesser degree, it is also lower than that of Catholics. Occasionally, however, this latter relationship is reversed, particularly in the recent period. [. . .] It is still very rare for them to exceed the Catholic rate. Furthermore, it has to be remembered that Jews live more exclusively in cities and work in intellectual occupations more than members of other denominations. For this reason they have a greater inclination to commit suicide than adherents of other denominations, owing to reasons other than religion. Therefore, if the Jewish rate is so low, despite this aggravating circumstance, it must be assumed that this religion has the fewest suicides of all, other things being equal.

Having established these facts, how are they to be explained?

Bearing in mind that Jews tend to be in a small minority everywhere, and that in most of the societies where the previous observations were made Catholics were in a minority, it is tempting to find in these facts the cause that explains the relative rarity of voluntary deaths in these two denominations. Clearly, where minority denominations face the hostility of surrounding populations they are obliged to exercise strict control and very rigorous discipline over themselves in order to exist. [. . .]

But, firstly, suicide is insufficiently an object of public condemnation for the small amount of blame it incurs to have such an influence, even for those minorities which have to pay special attention to public opinion because of their situation [. . .] Anyway, this explanation would not account for the respective situations of Protestants and Catholics [. . .] whatever the proportional distribution of these two denominations in the population, wherever it has been possible to compare them with regard to suicide, Protestants are found to kill themselves much more frequently than Catholics. [. . .] Therefore, even if the great difference between the two religions was partly caused by the need for minorities to exercise prudence, the largest share is certainly due to other causes.

We shall discover these other causes in the character of the two religious systems. Nevertheless, they both prohibit suicide with equal strength; not only do they morally condemn it with great severity, but also they both teach that a new life begins beyond the grave where men are punished for their evil deeds, and suicide is regarded as one of these just as much by Protestantism as by Catholicism. Finally, in both religions these prohibitions are regarded as being of divine origin; they are not represented as the logical conclusion of correct reasoning, but their authority is found in God himself. Thus, if Protestantism is less conducive to the development of suicide, it is not due to a different attitude to that of Catholicism. Therefore, since both religions have the same teaching on this particular subject, the different effect that they have on suicide must derive from one of the more general differentiating characteristics.

The only fundamental difference between Catholicism and Protestantism is that the latter allows free inquiry to a much greater extent than the former. [. . .]

The first conclusion that we reach, therefore, is that the propensity for suicide of Protestantism must relate to the spirit of free inquiry that characterizes this religion. This relationship needs to be properly understood. Free inquiry itself is merely the effect of another cause. [. . .] the overthrow of traditional beliefs. [. . .]

So if Protestantism allows more freedom to individual thought than Catholicism, it is because it has fewer common beliefs and practices. Now, a religious society cannot exist without a collective creed and the more extensive the creed the more unified and strong is the society. [. . .] Thus we arrive at the conclusion that the superiority of Protestantism with respect to suicide results from it being a less strongly integrated church than the Catholic church.

This also explains the case of Judaism. In fact, the criticism to which Jews have for long been subjected to by Christianity has given rise to feelings of exceptional solidarity among them. [. . .] Furthermore, the ostracism to which they are subjected is only one of the causes leading to this result; the very character of Jewish beliefs must make a large contribution to it. Like all early religions, in reality Judaism fundamentally consists of a set of practices that minutely govern all details of life and leave little latitude to individual judgement. [. . .]

Two important conclusions emerge from this chapter.

First, we see why in general suicide increases with knowledge. But knowledge does not determine this increase. It is innocent in this respect and it would be totally unjust to accuse it; the example of the Jews demonstrates this point. But these two facts are simultaneous products of a single general condition which appears in different forms. Man seeks knowledge and he kills himself because the religious society of which he forms part has lost its cohesion; but he does not kill himself because of his knowledge. It is not the learning that he acquires which disorganizes religion; but because religion becomes disorganized, his need for learning is awakened. [. . .]

If religion protects man against the desire to kill himself, it is not because it preaches respect for his person based on arguments *sui generis*, but because it is a society. What constitutes this society is the existence of a certain number of beliefs and practices common to all the faithful which are traditional and therefore obligatory. The more numerous and strong these collective states are, the more strongly integrated is the religious community, and the greater its preservative value. The particular details of the dogmas and rites are secondary. The essential thing is that they are capable of supporting a sufficiently intense collective life. Because the Protestant church does not have the same degree of consistency as the others, it does not have the same moderating effect on suicide. [. . .]

But if religion preserves men from suicide simply because, and to the extent that, it constitutes a society, so too other societies probably have the same effect. Let us consider the family and political society from this perspective.

If one's attention is confined to absolute figures, then unmarried people seem to commit suicide less than the married. [. . .] Certainly, if one follows popular opinion and considers suicide to be an act of despair caused by the difficulties of existence, this opinion appears plausible. The unmarried person does in fact have an easier life than the married. Is it not true that marriage entails all sorts of burdens and responsibilities? In order to preserve the family in the present and for the future, does it not require more sacrifices and suffering than it takes to meet the needs of an unmarried person? However obvious this may seem, such *a priori* reasoning is completely false and only seems to be supported by the facts because they have been poorly analyzed [. . .] we must remember that a considerable number of the unmarried are less than 16 years old, while all the married are older. Up to the age of 16 the tendency towards suicide is very slight because of the age factor, without considering others. [. . .] The only way to avoid these difficulties is to calculate the rate of each group separately, at each age. With such procedures one might, for example, compare unmarried people aged from 25 to 30 years with married and widowed persons of the same age, and similarly for other periods; the effect of married status would thus be isolated from all the other factors and all its possible variations would be evident. [. . .]

Thus, when we say that the 'coefficient of preservation' of husbands aged 25 compared to unmarried men is 3, we mean that if the tendency to suicide of married persons of this age is represented by 1, that of unmarried people the same age must be represented by 3. Obviously, when the coefficient of preservation drops below unity, it really becomes a coefficient of aggravation.

The laws derived from these tables may be formulated thus:

(1) Too early marriages have an aggravating influence on suicide, especially for men. [. . .]
(2) From the age of 20 onwards married people of both sexes benefit from a coefficient of preservation in comparison with single people. [. . .]
(3) The coefficient of preservation of married people compared with single people varies according to sex. [. . .] We can say that the sex which is most favoured by marriage varies according to the society, and the extent of the difference between the rate of the two sexes itself varies depending on which sex is most favoured. [. . .]
(4) Widowhood reduces the coefficient of married people of both sexes, but usually it does not eliminate it completely. Widowed people kill themselves more often than married people, but in general less than single people.

   The coefficient of preservation of widowed people, like that of married people, in comparison with unmarried people, varies with sex. [. . .] We can state in the same terms, therefore, that the more favoured sex in the state of widowhood varies according to the society, and the differences between the two sexes itself varies depending on which sex is most favoured.

Having established the facts, let us look for the explanations.

The immunity enjoyed by married people can only be attributed to one of the following two causes:

It may be due to the influence of the domestic environment. It would then be the influence of the family which would neutralize any suicidal tendency or would prevent it from being realized.

Or it may be due to what might be called matrimonial selection. Marriage in fact operates a sort of automatic selection in the population as a whole. Not everyone who wants to marry does so; there is little chance of creating a successful family if one does not possess certain qualities of health, fortune and morality. [. . .]

It is in the constitution of the family group, therefore, that we must discover the principal cause of the phenomonon we are studying.

But, however interesting this result may be, it requires further definition; for the family environment is made up of different elements. For both husband and wife the family includes: (1) the wife or husband; (2) the children. Is the beneficial effect of the family on the suicidal tendency due to the former or the latter? To put it another way, the family consists of two different forms of association:

the conjugal group and the family group proper. These two social entities do not share the same origin or character, and as a result it is unlikely that they have the same effects. Whilst one derives from a contract and an elective affinity, the other springs from a natural phenomenon, consanguinity; the former unites two members of the same generation, the latter joins one generation to the next; the latter is as old as humanity, the former became organized at a relatively later date. [. . .]

One proof of the slight effect of marriage is the fact that the marriage rate has not changed very much since the first decades of the century, while suicide has tripled. [. . .]

But the slight effect of marriage is revealed particularly clearly in the case of women when it does not find its natural fulfilment in children. [. . .] In France, married but childless women commit suicide half again as often as unmarried women of the same age. We have already noted that generally the wife benefits less from family life than the husband. Now we can see the cause of this; taken by itself, conjugal life is harmful to the woman and aggravates her tendency to suicide.

If, nevertheless, most wives have appeared to enjoy a favourable coefficient of preservation, this is because childless households are the exception and consequently the presence of children remedies and reduces the bad effects of marriage in most cases. [. . .]

From [. . .] the preceding remarks it appears that marriage certainly has its own preservative effect against suicide. But it is very limited and of benefit to one sex only [. . .] (T)he fact remains that the family is the essential factor in the immunity of married people, that is, the family as the whole group of parents and children. Obviously, as husband and wife are members, they also share in producing this result, not as husband or wife, however, but as father or mother, as functionaries of the family association. If the disappearance of one increases the chances of the other committing suicide, it is not because the personal bonds that united them are broken, but because the family suffers a disaster, the shock of which is borne by the survivor. We shall reserve the special effect of marriage for a later study, but it can be said that domestic society, like religious society, acts as a powerful counter-agent against suicide.

This immunity even increases with the density of the family, that is with the increase in the number of its elements. [. . .] Our previous conclusion may thus be completed to read: just as the family is a strong safeguard against suicide, so the more strongly it is constituted the greater its protection.

If it had not been for the fact that statistics were so late in being developed, it would have been easy to show by the same method that this law applies to political societies. History teaches that suicide, which is generally rare in societies that are young in evolution and concentration, increases as societies disintegrate. [. . .] Major political upheavals are sometimes said to increase the number of suicides. But Morselli has proved conclusively that the facts contradict their view. All the revolutions which have occurred in France this century reduced the number of suicides at the time. [. . .] Great national wars have the same effect as political upheavals. [. . .]

These facts can be interpreted in only one way; namely, that major social upheavals and great popular wars rouse collective sentiments, stimulate a partisan spirit and patriotism, political and national faith, and by concentrating activity towards a single end, give rise, temporarily at least, to a stronger integration of society. The beneficial influence that we have demonstrated is not due to the crisis but to the struggles it gives rise to. Because they force men to close ranks and confront the common danger, the individual thinks less of himself and more of the common cause. [. . .]

We have, therefore, successively established the following three propositions:

Suicide varies inversely with the degree of integration of religious society.

Suicide varies inversely with the degree of integration of domestic society.

Suicide varies inversely with the degree of integration of political society.

[. . .]

So we come to this general conclusion: suicide varies inversely with the degree of integration of the social groups to which the individual belongs.

But society cannot disintegrate unless the individual simultaneously detaches himself from social life, unless his own ends become more important than common ends, that is to say, unless his personality begins to predominate over the collective personality. The weaker the groups to which he belongs become, the less he depends on them, and consequently relies only on himself and recognizes no other rules of conduct than those based on private interests. So if we agree to call this state 'egoism', where the individual ego asserts itself to excess in the face of the social ego, and at its expense, we can call the particular type of suicide that results from excessive individualism 'egoistic'.

Altruistic Suicide

In the natural order, no good is without limits. A biological quality can fulfil the ends which it is required to serve only on condition that it does not exceed certain limits. The same is true for social phenomena. If, as we have just seen, excessive individualism leads to suicide, insufficient individualism produces the same effects. When man is detached from society, he can easily kill himself, and this is also the case when he is too strongly integrated in society.

It has sometimes been said that suicide was unknown in lower societies. Expressed in these terms, the assertion is incorrect. It is true that egoistic suicide, as we have just described it, does not appear to be very common there. But there is another type which is found there in an endemic state. [. . .]

Suicide is therefore very common among primitive peoples. But it displays special characteristics. All the facts just considered fall into one of the following three categories:

(1) Suicides of men approaching old age or stricken with illness.

(2) Suicides of women on the death of the husband.

(3) Suicides of followers or servants on the death of their leaders.

In all these cases where a person kills himself it is not because he takes upon himself the right to do so, but, on the contrary, because *it is his duty*. If he fails in this obligation, he is punished by being dishonoured and, most often, by religious sanctions. [. . .]

For society to oblige certain members to kill themselves, it must be the case that the individual personality counts for very little. Since, as soon as such a personality begins to be formed, the right to life is the first right to be accorded to it. It is suspended only in very exceptional circumstances, such as war. But this weak individuation can itself have only one cause. For the individual to occupy so small a place in collective life he must be almost totally absorbed into the group and, consequently, be very strongly integrated. For the parts to have so little life of their own, the whole must form a compact and continuous mass. In fact we have shown elsewhere that this massive cohesion is characteristic of societies where the preceding practices are observed. [. . .]

We are therefore confronted with a type of suicide that differs from the preceding one by virtue of certain specific qualities. Whilst the latter is caused by excessive individuation, for the former it is insufficient individuation. [. . .] Having designated as 'egoism' the condition in which the ego pursues its own life and is obedient only to itself, the designation 'altruism' adequately expresses the opposite condition, where the ego is not its own property. It is blended with something other than itself, and the goal of conduct is external to itself, that is, in one of the groups in which it participates. Thus we call the suicide caused by intense altruism 'altruistic suicide'. But as it is also characteristically carried out as a duty, the designation should express this fact. So we will designate such a type 'obligatory altruistic suicide'.

It needs to be defined by the combination of these two adjectives, because not every altruistic suicide is necessarily obligatory. Some are not imposed by society so directly, having a more optional character. [. . .] The willingness of the Japanese to disembowel themselves for the slightest reason is well known. [. . .] A social prestige thus attaches to suicide, which is encouraged by this fact, and to decline this reward has effects similar to punishment. [. . .] But it even happens that the individual kills himself purely for the joy of sacrifice, despite the absence of a specific reason, because renunciation is itself considered praiseworthy. India provides the classic ground for this sort of suicide. The Hindu was predisposed to self-destruction under Brahminic influence. [. . .]

Thus we have constructed a second type of suicide, which itself consists of three forms: obligatory altruistic suicide, optional altruistic suicide, and acute altruistic suicide, the pure form of which is mystical suicide. [. . .]

Such suicides are unlikely to occur very widely in our own contemporary societies, where individual personality is increasingly freed from the collective personality. It cannot be denied that some people may have yielded to altruistic motives, such as soldiers who have preferred death to the humiliation of defeat [. . .] or those sad people who kill themselves to avoid disgracing their family.

When such people renounce life it is on account of something they love better than themselves. But these are isolated and exceptional cases, although there still exists a contemporary setting where altruistic suicide is chronic: specifically, the army.

In all European societies it is in fact generally the case that the suicidal propensity of soldiers is far higher than that of civilians of the same age. [. . .] Among all the components of modern society, it is the army that most resembles the structure of lower societies. It, too, constitutes a massive, compact group, which provides a rigid setting for the individual, and prevents any independent movement.

Anomic Suicide

But society is not simply something that attracts the sentiments and activities of individuals with unequalled force. It is also a power that controls them. There is a relationship between the way in which this regulating action is performed and the social suicide-rate.

The fact that economic crises have an aggravating effect on the suicide tendency is well-known. [. . .] But to what do these crises owe their influence? Is life more readily renounced as it becomes more difficult? This explanation is attractively simple; and it fits in with the popular idea of suicide. But it is contradicted by the facts. [. . .] Rather than an increase in poverty causing an increase in suicide, it is more the case that even fortunate crises, which have the effect of abruptly raising a country's prosperity, have an effect on suicide like economic disasters. [. . .] What proves even more conclusively that economic distress does not have the aggravating effect often attributed to it, is that it tends to give rise to exactly the opposite effect. [. . .] Poverty may even be considered a protection. In various French regions, those which have more people with independent means have higher numbers of suicides.

Thus, if industrial or financial crises increase suicides, it is not because they cause poverty, since crises of prosperity have the same result; rather, it is because they are crises, in other words, disturbances of the collective order. Every disturbance of equilibrium, even though it may involve greater comfort and a raising of the general pace of life, provides an impulse to voluntary death. [. . .]

No living person can be happy or even continue to exist if his needs are not sufficiently in proportion to his means. Otherwise, whether they require more than can be granted, or simply something different, those needs will be in constant conflict and bring only pain. Any action that cannot take place without pain tends not to be reproduced. Tendencies which are not satisfied atrophy, and since the tendency to live is simply the result of all the others, it cannot but weaken if other tendencies diminish. [. . .]

Human nature in itself cannot set variable limits to our needs. Consequently, in so far as it is left to the individual alone, these needs are unlimited. Without reference to any external regulating influence, our capacity for sensation is a bottomless abyss that nothing can satisfy.

But, then, if nothing external manages to restrict this capacity, it can only be a source of torment to itself. Unlimited desires are insatiable by definition, and insatiability is rightly considered a pathological symptom. [. . .]

Society alone can perform this moderating role, either directly and as a whole, or through the agency of one of its organs; for it is the only moral power superior to the individual, whose authority he accepts. [. . .] When society is disturbed, either by a painful crisis or by favourable, but abrupt, changes, it is temporarily incapable of exercising this action; and it is then that we get those sudden rises in the curve of suicides that were noted earlier.

In fact, in the case of economic disasters, a sort of declassification occurs whereby certain individuals are suddenly thrust into a lower position than they formerly occupied. They must then reduce their requirements, restrain their needs and learn to control themselves more. All the benefits of social influence are lost as far as they are concerned; their moral education has to begin again. Society cannot immediately adapt them to this new existence or teach them to exercise the additional restraint to which they are not accustomed. [. . .]

But the same applies if the crisis originates in a sudden increase in power and fortune. In this case, as the conditions of life are changed, the scale which regulated needs can no longer remain the same; for it varies according to social resources, since it largely determines the share of each class of producers. The scale is upset, but on the other hand, a new scale cannot be quickly improvised. It takes time for men and things to be reclassified by the public consciousness. As long as these liberated social forces have not regained their equilibrium, their respective values remain undetermined and therefore regulation is lacking for a while. One no longer knows what is fair, what are legitimate claims and hopes, and which are excessive. As a result, there is nothing to which one does not aspire. If this is a deep disturbance, it affects even the principles that regulate the distribution of different jobs between people. Since the relations between the various parts of society are necessarily changed, the ideas that express these relations must change. Any class that the crisis has particularly favoured is no longer resigned to its lot and, on the other hand, its good fortune awakens all sorts of jealousies above and below it. Appetites no longer accept limits on behaviour, since public opinion cannot restrain them. At the same time they are in a state of abnormal excitement simply because of the greater intensity of life in general. [. . .] This state of deregulation or 'anomie' is therefore further heightened by the fact that passions are less disciplined at the very moment when they need stronger discipline. [. . .]

If anomie never occurred except in intermittent spurts, as in the earlier cases, and in acute crises, it might well cause the social suicide rate to vary from time to time; but it would not be a regular constant factor. There is a sphere of life, however, where it is at present in a chronic state: the world of trade and industry.

For a century economic progress has mainly consisted of freeing industrial relations from regulations. Until recent times, it was the function of a whole system of moral forces to discipline them. First, there was religion, the influence of which was felt equally by workers and employers, poor and rich. It consoled the former and taught them to be content with their lot, stating that the social order was providential, that each class's share was fixed by God Himself, and by making them hope for compensation for present inequalities in a world to come. It restrained the latter by reminding them that earthly interests are not everything for man, that they must be subordinate to other, higher interests, and that in consequence they should not be pursued without regulation or to excess. Temporal power, for its part, moderated the scope of economic functions by its supremacy over them and the relatively subordinate position it gave them. At the heart of the business world itself, the occupational groups, by regulating salaries, prices and production, indirectly fixed the average level of income on which needs are partly based by the very force of circumstances. In describing this organization, we do not mean to propose it as a model. It is clear that, without profound changes, it would be inappropriate for present-day societies. All we are saying is that it existed, that it had useful effects, and that nothing has yet taken its place.

The reality is that religion has lost most of its power. And governmental power, rather than regulating economic life, has become its instrument and servant. Opposing schools of thought, such as orthodox economists and extreme socialists are in agreement about reducing it to a more or less passive role as intermediary between various social functions. The former want to make it simply the guardian of individual contracts; the latter expect it to attend to collective accounting, that is, to record consumer demands and transmit them to producers, to make an inventory of total income and redistribute it according to an established formula. But both refuse it power to subordinate other social organs to itself and to make them converge towards a single dominant aim. For both sides, nations are supposed to have as their only or principal objective the achievement of industrial prosperity; this is the implication of the dogma of economic materialism basic to both systems of thought, which are opposite only in appearance. As these theories merely express existing opinion, industry, instead of continuing to be regarded as a means to an end which transcends it, has become the supreme end for individuals and society. But then appetites thus awakened are freed from any limiting authority. By sanctifying these appetites, so to speak, this deification of material well-being has placed them above all human law. Restraining them seems like a kind of sacrilege. [. . .]

This is the reason for the excitement which predominates in this part of society, but which has spread to all the rest. A constant state of crisis and anomie exists there. From the top to the bottom of the scale, covetous desires are aroused without it being known where they might level out. [. . .]

Industrial and commercial functions are amongst the occupations which furnish the greatest number of suicides. They almost reach the level of the liberal professions, indeed they sometimes exceed it; they are certainly more affected than agriculture. The case of agriculture provides the best reminder of the constitution of the economic order as it used to be. The difference would be even more marked if, among industrial suicides, we distinguished beween employers and workers, for it is probably the former who are most affected by the condition to anomie. The high rate for those with independent means (720 per million) shows clearly that it is the better off who suffer most. This is because everything that enforces subordination reduces the effects of this condition. The lower classes have their horizon limited by those above them, and because of that their desires are more restrained. But those who have only empty space above them are almost inevitably lost in it, unless there is some force to hold them back.

Anomie, therefore, is a regular and specific factor in causing suicide in our modern societies. It is one of the sources feeding the annual totals. This is a new type that must be distinguished from the others. It differs from them in that it does not depend on the way in which individuals are attached to society, but on the way in which they are regulated by society. Egoistic suicide stems from the fact that men no longer see a reason for living; altruisitic suicide comes from the fact that this reason appears to them to lie outside life itself; the third kind of suicide, whose existence we have just established, comes from the fact that their activity is unregulated and they suffer as a consequence. Because of its origin, we shall call this last type 'anomic suicide'.

Certainly this type and egoistic suicide have ties of kinship. Both come from society's insufficient presence in individuals. But the sphere of its absence is not the same in both cases. In egoistic suicide society is deficient in truly collective activity, thus leaving it deprived of objects and meaning. In anomic suicide society has a weak presence in the really individual passions, leaving them without a restraining influence. The result is that, despite their ties, these two types remain independent of each other. We can offer to society everything social in us, but still be unable to limit our desires; without being an egoist one can live in a state of anomie, and vice versa. These two types of suicide do not draw their recruits from the same social environments; one has its main location in the intellectual occupations, the world of thought, the other is in the industrial or commercial world.

But economic anomie is not the only anomie that can lead to suicide.

[. . .] (T)hroughout Europe the number of suicides varies with that of divorces and separations. [. . .] One must seek the cause of this remarkable relationship, not in the predispositions of people's mental character, but in the intrinsic nature of divorce. At this point we may state as our first proposition: in all countries for which we have the necessary data, suicides of divorced people are extremely more numerous than those of other sections of the population. [. . .] What is the explanation? [. . .]

With regard to suicide, the more widely practised divorce is, the more marriage favours the wife and vice versa. [. . .]

Two consequences follow from this proposition.

The first is that only husbands contribute to the rise in the suicide rate in societies where divorce is frequent; by contrast, wives commit suicide less in those circumstances than elsewhere. If, therefore, divorce only develops in association with an improvement in women's moral situation, it cannot be accepted that divorce is linked to domestic society being in such a bad condition that it increases the tendency to suicide, for this increase would then occur for both husbands and wives. A weakening of the family spirit cannot have such opposite effects on the two sexes, on the one hand proving favourable to the mother but on the other hand having a serious effect on the father. Consequently, it is within the state of marriage and not of the family that the cause is to be found of the phenomenon we are studying. In fact, it is very likely that marriage acts in opposite ways on husband and wife. As parents they have the same objective, but as partners their interests are different and often opposed. It may well be the case that, in certain societies, particular aspects of the institution of marriage may benefit one and harm the other. Everything we have seen tends to prove that this is precisely the case with divorce.

Secondly, the same reason leads us to reject the hypothesis that this unfortunate state of marriage, to which divorce and suicide are closely related, derives from a greater frequency of matrimonial disputes; for such a cause should not result in increasing the wife's immunity any more than the weakening of family ties. If, where divorce is common, the suicide figures were really related to the number of conjugal quarrels, the wife should suffer as much as the husband. There is nothing in this situation which could give her special protection. Such a hypothesis is that much less tenable because divorce is more often asked for by the wife than by the husband (in 60% of French divorces and 83% of separations). So domestic disturbances are attributable to the man in the majority of cases. Hence, it would not be clear why, in countries where divorce is common, it is the man who commits suicide more frequently when it is he who causes more suffering to the wife, whilst the wife is less likely to commit suicide when her husband causes her to suffer more. Moreover, it has not been proved that the number of marriage quarrels increases in proportion to the number of divorces.

If we do not accept this hypothesis, there is only one other that is possible. The very institution of divorce, through its effect on marriage, must be the determining factor in suicide.

And what, in fact, is marriage? A regulation of relationships between the sexes, which extends not only to physical instincts that are active, but also to all kinds of feelings that civilization has gradually grafted on to the foundation of physical appetites. [. . .] By fixing the conjugal state for ever, it allows no way out and forbids all hopes, even legitimate ones. Even the man suffers from this immutability; but the disadvantages for him are largely compensated for by the advantages which he gains in other respects. Moreover, custom grants the man certain privileges which allow him to alleviate the rigour of the regime to some extent. On the other hand, for the woman there is neither compensation nor alleviation. For her, monogamy is a strict obligation. [. . .]

We thus come to the conclusion that is rather far removed from current ideas about marriage and its role. It is supposed to have been instituted for the benefit of the wife to protect her weakness against male capriciousness. Monogamy, particularly, is often presented as a sacrifice of man's polygamous instincts that he makes in order to raise and improve women's condition in marriage. In reality, whatever might have been the historical causes which made him impose this restriction, it is the man who benefits from it. The freedom that he has given up can thus only be a source of torment for him. The woman does not have the same reasons to give it up and, in this respect, one might say that, by submitting to the same rules, it is she who has made the sacrifice.[1]

The Social Element of Suicide

As a consequence of seeking the causes of the suicide tendency of each society in the nature of the societies themselves, and by leaving aside the individual, we have obtained completely different results. Whereas the relationships between suicide and biological or physical factors were uncertain and ambiguous, those between suicide and certain sorts of social environment were direct and constant. It is here that we finally encountered real laws, allowing us to attempt a methodical classification of types of suicide. [. . .]

From all these facts we can conclude that the social suicide rate can only be explained sociologically. It is the moral constitution of the society which always determines the quota of voluntary deaths. For each population there is a collective force with a particular strength which impels men to kill themselves.

Consider

1. How is suicide a social, rather than a purely individual, act? Answer this question in reference to the reading from Durkheim's work.

---

[1]From these considerations we can see that there is a type of suicide that is the opposite of anomic suicide, just as egoistic and altruistic suicide are opposites. This one results from excessive regulation; the type committed by people whose future is mercilessly blocked, whose passions are violently suppressed by an oppressive discipline. It is the suicide of very young husbands, of the childless married woman. To complete the picture, we must therefore establish a fourth type of suicide. But it is so unimportant today, and it is so very difficult to find examples other than the ones quoted, that it seems pointless to dwell on it. Yet it could be of historical interest. Are not slave suicides, which are thought to be common in certain circumstances (V. Corre, *Le Crime en pays créoles*, p. 48) and, in fact, all those suicides attributable to excesses of physical or moral despotism, examples of this type? To bring out the ineluctable, inflexible character of the rule which cannot be changed, and in contrast to the expression 'anomie' that we have been using, we might call this 'fatalistic suicide'.

2. What are the different types of suicide Durkheim identifies? What are their causes? Give examples of your own for each type of suicide.
3. What is anomie? Give examples of anomie in contemporary society.
4. Should suicide be considered a result of individual mental problems? Critically discuss Durkheim's work in relation to this question.
5. 'Perhaps the most fruitful distinction with which the sociological imagination works is between "the personal troubles of milieu" and "the public issues of social structure." This distinction is an essential tool of the sociological imagination and a feature of all classic work in social science' (Mills 1959/1967: 8).

   Discuss this statement in relation to Émile Durkheim's work on suicide.
6. Durkheim covered a wide range of other subject matters in his other writings. Draw up a list of his major works. What are their topics? Why are these topics of sociological importance? What were the main arguments Durkheim pursued in these publications? This question will require you to do substantial background research. Many of Durkheim's publications are now readily accessible online. Likewise, there are many books that offer summaries and overviews of Durkheim's work.

Modernity and rationalisation: Max Weber

Max Weber is one of those early sociologists whose work has retained vast influence even almost a century after his death. Weber made a significant contribution to establishing sociology in Germany and beyond. At the same time, he is renowned for his contributions to history and political economy, and his studies have retained a broad international audience across all these disciplines.

Max Weber was born in the city of Erfurt in 1864, just a few years before the foundation of a unified German state in 1871. German society in Weber's lifetime experienced a flourishing of science and industry and a growing sense of nationalism and Germany's role as a world power in competition with other world powers. However, the industrialisation and modernisation of the German nation had also brought about significant social and political tensions, as well as the formation of an impoverished urban working class. All these issues informed Weber's work in significant ways. Weber himself was born into a wealthy upper-middle-class family. His father was a prominent politician, and Weber's youth was characterised by frequent encounters with leading thinkers and intellectuals. After studying law at the universities of Heidelberg and Berlin, Weber eventually began an academic career. At the same time, he took a strong interest in politics and public policy debates, to which he contributed in various forms throughout his adult life. One might imagine Weber as a kind of 'public intellectual', doing important scholarly work, but at the same time occupying a prominent and visible space in public life and the media.

Weber's sociology is important in a number of ways. First, Weber contributed to the development of a distinctive theoretical and methodological perspective on social life. This perspective is grounded in the notion that the working of society at large can only be understood by examining the *subjective meanings* of individual people's actions in everyday life. Consider Weber's famous definition of sociology at the outset of *Economy and Society*:

> Sociology (in the sense in which this highly ambiguous word is used here) is a science which attempts to understand social action through a causal explanation of its course and effects. 'Action' is the human behaviour to which the acting individual (or individuals) attaches a subjective meaning. Action in this sense may be either external or internal behaviour, failure or refrain. Action is 'social' if the acting individual takes account of the behaviour of others and is thereby oriented in its course. (Weber (1956/1978): 4)

In order to understand social life, we must turn to its basic constituents: the individuals who engage in a myriad ways on a daily basis all around the planet. As sociologists, we are interested in those parts of individuals' behaviour that are distinctively *social*, that is to say actions which, in the meaning we attribute to them, in some way rely on the behaviour of others. From this perspective, even seemingly random mishaps may become meaningful social acts: I walk into the room, slip, fall, and in the process spill drink and food all over my clothes. The friends and colleagues who are present laugh at my mishap and its messy consequences. My face turns red, and I feel embarrassed. How will the others react, and what will they think of me now? Even such an apparently insignificant slip may be a highly significant social act, through the meaning I (self-image) and others (reputation) attribute to it, with possibly significant consequences for future social interaction (I now feel too awkward to attend dinner parties for quite some time).

Weber considered a wide range of theoretical, methodological and empirical issues, such as the role of values in sociological enquiry, problems of subjectivity and objectivity, the formation of modern bureaucracy, problems of social stratification, the sources of social authority and power, and the historical development and social impact of various world religions. As with Émile Durkheim, much of Weber's work was inspired by an overarching concern with the consequences of the rapid social transformation of his time and the nature of modern life. Specifically, Weber took an interest in the relationship between religious beliefs and processes of rationalisation. In this context, Weber developed a number of comparative studies on major world religions. Moreover, in one of his most-cited works, *The Protestant Ethic and the Spirit of Capitalism* (1905/2009), Weber focuses on the association between the rise of capitalism in the Western world, processes of rationalisation and the spread of certain forms of Protestant Christianity. Let us now turn to this study and examine Weber's arguments in detail.

Reading

Weber, M., The Development of the Capitalist Frame of Mind', in Kalberg, S. (2009), *The Protestant Ethic and the Spirit of Capitalism with Other Writings on the Rise of the West* (4th edn), New York: Oxford University Press, pp. 431–5

Weber's Summary Statements on "*The Protestant Ethic* Thesis"

A. The Development of the Capitalist Frame of Mind (1919–1920)

> From: Pp. 352–57, 367–69 in *General Economic History.* Translated by Frank H. Knight and revised by Stephen Kalberg (New York: Simon & Schuster, 1927).

It is a widespread error that the increase of population should be viewed as the decisive agent in the unfolding of Western capitalism. Karl Marx claimed, in opposition to this view, that every economic epoch has its own law of population. Although untenable in this general form, this position is justified in the present case.

The growth of population in the West proceeded most rapidly from the beginning of the eighteenth century to the end of the nineteenth. China experienced in the same period a population growth of at least equal degree – from 60 or 70 to 400 million (allowing for the inevitable exaggerations). This corresponds approximately to the increase in the West.

Nonetheless, the development of capitalism moved backward in China rather than forward, for the population increase took place in different strata than in the West, rendering China a swarming mass of peasants. The increase of a class, which corresponded to our proletariat, was involved only to the extent that a foreign market made possible the employment of coolies. ("Coolie" is originally an expression from India; it signifies neighbor or fellow member of a clan.) The growth of population in Europe did indeed favor the development of capitalism to the extent that the system, in a small population, would have been unable to secure the necessary labor force. In itself, however, it never called forth this development.

Nor can the *inflow of precious metals* be regarded, as Sombart implies, as the primary cause of the appearance of [modern] capitalism. It is certainly true that, in a given situation, an increase in the supply of precious metals may give rise to price revolutions, such as took place after 1530 in Europe. And if then other favorable conditions are present – a certain form of labor organization is crystallizing – the development of capitalism may be stimulated by the fact that large stocks of cash come into the hands of certain groups.

But the case of India proves that such an importation of precious metal will not alone bring about capitalism. In India, in the period of the Roman empire [44 B.C.E. to 476 A.C.], an enormous mass of precious metal – some 25 million *sestertii* annually – was collected in exchange for domestic goods. This inflow, however, gave rise to commercial capitalism to only a slight extent. The greater part of the precious metal disappeared into the hoards of the rajahs instead of being converted into cash and applied to the establishment of enterprises of a rational capitalist character. This indicates that the tendency that results from an inflow of precious metal depends entirely upon the formation of the labor organization.

The precious metal from America, after the discovery, flowed largely to Spain; but there a decline of capitalist development took place parallel with the importation. There followed, on the one hand, the suppression of the *comune-ros* [small towns] and the destruction of the commercial policies of the Spanish grandees and, on the other hand, the use of the money to meet military goals. Consequently, the stream of precious metal flowing through Spain scarcely touched it. Rather, it fertilized other countries that, since the fifteenth century, had been already undergoing a process of transformation in the organization of labor favorable to capitalism.

Hence, neither the growth of population nor the importation of precious metal called forth [modern] Western capitalism. The external conditions for the development of [modern] capitalism are, rather, first, geographical in character. In China and India the enormous costs of transportation, connected with their decisively inland commerce, necessarily formed serious obstructions for those classes in a position to make profits through trade and to use trading capital in the construction of a capitalist system. However, in the West the position of the Mediterranean as an inland sea, and the abundant interconnections through rivers, favored the development of international commerce.

Nonetheless, this factor must not be overestimated. The civilization of Antiquity was distinctively coastal. Here the opportunities for commerce were very favorable (thanks to the character of the Mediterranean Sea) in contrast to the Chinese waters with their typhoons – and yet no capitalism arose in Antiquity. Capitalist development, even in the modern period, was much more intense in [modern] Florence than in Genoa or Venice. Capitalism in the West was born in the industrial cities of the interior rather than in those cities which were centers of sea trade.

Military requirements were also favorable, though not as such. Instead, they were facilitating because of the special nature of the particular needs of the Western armies. Favorable also was the luxury demand, though again not in itself. In many cases it led to the development of irrational forms, such as small workshops in France and compulsory settlements of workers in connection with the courts of many German princes. In the last resort the groups which pro-duced capitalism were bound up with the rational permanent enterprise, rational accounting, rational technology, and rational law – but again not these alone. Necessary complementary forces were the rational spirit, the rationalization of the conduct of life in general, and a rational economic ethic.

At the beginning of all ethics and economic relations is *traditionalism*, the sanctity of tradition, and the exclusive reliance upon trade and industry as inherited from the fathers. This traditionalism survives far down into the present; only a human lifetime ago it proved futile to double the wages, in the hope of inducing increased exertions, of an agricultural laborer in Silesia who cultivated a certain tract of land on a contract basis. He would simply have reduced by half the work expended: with this half he would have been able to earn twice as much as before (sic). This general incapacity and indisposition to depart from the beaten path is the motive for the maintenance of tradition.

Primitive traditionalism may, however, undergo essential intensification as a consequence of two circumstances. First, material interests may be tied up with the maintenance of tradition. When, for example, in China the attempt was made to change certain roads or to introduce more rational means or routes of transportation, the perquisites of certain officials were threatened. And the same was the case in the Middle Ages in the West and in the modern era with the introduction of the railroad.

Such special interests of officials, landholders, and merchants assisted decisively in restricting a tendency toward rationalization. Stronger still is the effect of the stereotyping of trade on magical grounds. Here a deep repugnance exists to undertaking any change in the established conduct of life because supernatural evils are feared. Generally some injury to economic privilege is concealed in this opposition, but its effectiveness depends on a general belief in the potency of feared magical processes.

Traditional obstructions are not overcome by the economic impulse alone. The notion that our rational and capitalist era is characterized by a stronger economic interest than other periods is childish; the moving spirits of modern capitalism are not possessed of a stronger economic impulse than, for example, an oriental trader. The unchaining of the economic interests alone has produced only irrational results. Men such as Cortez and Pizarro, who were perhaps its strongest embodiment, were far from having an idea of a rational economic life. If the economic impulse in itself is universal, it is an interesting question as to the relations under which it becomes rationalized and rationally tempered in such fashion as to produce rational institutions of the character of the [modern] capitalist enterprise.

Originally, two opposite postures toward the pursuit of gain existed in combination [see 1927, pp. 312–13]. Internally, there was attachment to tradition and to the relations of piety among fellow members of the tribe, clan, and house-community, with the exclusion of the unrestricted quest for gain within the circle of those bound together by religious ties. Externally there was absolutely unrestricted play of the spirit of gain in economic relationships – every foreigner is seen as an enemy in respect to whom ethical restrictions do not apply. Here the ethics of internal and external relations are categorically different. The course of development involves the bringing in of calculation into the traditional brotherhood, thereby displacing the old religious relationships.

As soon as accountability is established within the family community, and economic relations are no longer strictly communistic, there is an end to the naive trust and its repression of the economic impulse. This side of the development is especially characteristic of the West. At the same time there is a tempering of the unrestricted quest for gain with the adoption of economic interests into the internal [family] economy. The result is a regulated economic life with the economic impulse functioning within bounds.

In detail, the course of development has varied. . . . The final result is the unusual fact that the germs of modern capitalism must be sought in a region where officially a theory was dominant which was distinct from that of the East and of classical Antiquity and in principle strongly hostile to capitalism. The *ethos* of the classical economic morality is summed up in the old judgment passed on the merchant, which was probably taken from primitive Arianism: *homo mercator vix aut numquam potest Deo placere* (he may conduct himself without sin but cannot be pleasing to God). This proposition was valid down to the fifteenth century, and the first attempt to modify it slowly matured in Florence under pressure of the shift in economic relations. . . .

* * *

The development of the concept of the calling quickly gave to the modern entrepreneur a fabulously clear conscience – and also to industrious workers. The employer gave to his employees – as the wages for their ascetic devotion to the calling and for cooperating in his ruthless exploitation of them through capitalism – the prospect of eternal salvation. This prospect, in an age when ecclesiastical discipline took control of the whole of life to an extent inconceivable to us now, represented a reality quite different from any it has today.

The Catholic and Lutheran churches also recognized and practiced ecclesiastical discipline. But in the Protestant ascetic communities admission to the Lord's Supper was conditioned on ethical fitness, which in turn was identified with business honor – while no one inquired into the content of one's faith. Such a powerful, unconsciously refined organization for the production of capitalist individuals has never existed in any other church or religion; in comparison with it what the Renaissance did for capitalism shrinks into insignificance. Its practitioners occupied themselves with technical problems and were experimenters of the first rank. Experimentation, which began in the realms of art and mining, was taken over into science [see 2005, pp. 324–25].

The worldview of the Renaissance, however, determined the politics of rulers in a large measure, even though it failed to transform the soul of mankind, as did the innovations of the Reformation. Almost all the great scientific discoveries of the sixteenth and seventeenth centuries grew on the soil of Catholicism. Copernicus was a Catholic, and Luther and Melanchthon repudiated his discoveries. Scientific progress and Protestantism must not at all be unquestioningly identified. The Catholic church has indeed occasionally obstructed scientific progress; however, the ascetic sects of Protestantism have also wished to know little about pure science – except when it concerned the real needs of daily life.

Conversely, Protestantism's unique achievement was to have placed science in the service of technology and the economy (see p. 447).

The religious root of modern humanity oriented to the economy is dead. Today the concept of the calling stands as a *caput mortuum* in the world. Ascetic religiosity has been displaced by a pessimistic, though by no means ascetic, view of the world, such as portrayed in [Bernard de] Mandeville's "fable of the bees" [1729]. Private vices are here understood as, under certain conditions, in service to the civic realm. With the complete disappearance of all the remains of the original enormous religious pathos of the sects, the optimism of the Enlightenment, which believed in the harmony of interests, appeared as the heir of Protestant asceticism in the field of economic ideas [see p. 158]. The princes and writers of the later eighteenth and early nineteenth centuries were guided by its hand.

Economic ethics arose against the background of the ascetic ideal, and now it has been stripped of its religious meaning. The working class, as long as the promise of eternal happiness could be held out to it, could accept its lot. When this consolation fell away, however, the appearance of society's strains and stresses became inevitable. They have grown uninterruptedly since then. This era had been reached by the conclusion of capitalism's early period At this point capitalism had reached the end of its early period and had embarked upon, in the nineteenth century, an age of iron.

Consider

1. Explore how Weber's ideas of rationalisation might apply to any of the following contemporary organisations:
   - Airports
   - Universities
   - Fast-food restaurants
   - Banks.
2. How did processes of rationalisation shape social life in Western Europe in Weber's times? Discuss this question in relation to any historical examples of your own choice. To discuss this question, you will need to investigate further and look at alternative sources.
3. In your own words, describe what Weber understood by the titular 'Protestant ethic' in the above reading.
4. How does the Protestant ethic, according to Weber, shape the spirit of economic activity in capitalism?
5. How well has Weber's argument stood the test of time? Consider this question in the light of the relatively recent rise of Japan and China to economic world power status.
6. Both Karl Marx and Max Weber took great interest in the social origins and consequences of the rise of modern capitalism. Examine the main similarities and differences between Marx's historical materialism and Weber's arguments on the spirit of capitalism.

7. Weber pursued the theme of rationalisation in a number of his other writings, on subject matters such as bureaucracy or power. Explore some of his respective works and summarise Weber's arguments. This question involves several tasks. First of all, you need to find out where Weber wrote about bureaucracy or power. A way to begin would be to look at some of the numerous books that summarise Weber's work. Morrison's *Marx, Durkheim, Weber* is one good starting point, but there are many others. Second, as part of your literature search, you need to source Weber's works, once you have their titles. Your local library is likely to have them, and many of them are also accessible online. Finally, once you have the books you need, you need to identify what to read and how. Look at the books' tables of content and indices to find passages that seem particularly noteworthy, interesting, or important. Then read selectively and keep notes on your findings. Remember: it is not necessary for you to produce a comprehensive overview of Weber's work. The purpose of this exercise is for you to gain a general understanding of the scope of Weber's work and some of his key ideas. How much can you find out in a short space of time?

The social self: George Herbert Mead

So far, we have only looked at the work of European scholars who have had a lasting impact on sociological thought. However, while early sociology was closely bound up with certain institutional changes in European societies, it quickly acquired broader international recognition. The development of American sociology is one example of sociology's global spread. The first sociology department in the USA was founded by Albion Small at the University of Chicago in 1892. In the USA, sociology was therefore formally recognised as a distinctive discipline earlier than in Europe. In France, the first sociology department was set up in 1895, while in Germany and Britain the discipline only began to be institutionalised in the early twentieth century.

The University of Chicago has remained a focal point for innovative developments in sociology. In the first half of the twentieth century, the *Chicago School of Sociology* quickly rose to prominence. From approximately the beginning of the 1920s onwards, sociologists such as Robert Park, Louis Wirth, Florian Znaniecki, Ernest Burgess and Edwin Sutherland published seminal studies that defined fields such as urban sociology and criminology. Later on, in the 1950s and 1960s, a second wave of Chicago sociologists coalesced around a common interest in symbolic interactionism and ethnographic research (see Chapter 4). Today, the University of Chicago still is at the forefront of developments in US sociology.

Among all these scholars, George Herbert Mead (1863–1931) occupies a particularly prominent place in contemporary sociology courses. While Mead did teach at the University of Chicago, he was affiliated with the philosophy department rather than the sociology department, and his work has had a lasting impact on a variety of fields, including philosophy and social psychology, as well as sociology. This illustrates the fact that, since its earliest days, sociological thought has intersected with developments in many other fields, often rendering disciplinary boundaries somewhat arbitrary.

One of Mead's most frequently cited works is *Mind, Self and Society* (1934/1967). Alongside three other volumes, this book was compiled after Mead's death by three of his former students, on the base of lecture notes and other unpublished materials. While Mead himself had written a number of influential papers in his lifetime, he had never summarised and systematised his thought in a book-length account. *Mind, Self and Society* in many ways fills this gap. In it, Mead describes his understanding of social life through the term *social behaviourism*. By using the term 'behaviourism', Mead seeks to draw attention to the fact that psychology, in his own words, 'cannot very well be made a study of the field of consciousness alone; it is necessarily a study of a more extensive field' (Mead 1934/1967: 4). This more extensive field is the influence of our environment on our psychic life and our behaviour. Mead's definition of the field of social psychology further clarifies this:

> Social psychology studies the activity or behavior of the individual as it lies within the social process; the behavior of an individual can be understood only in terms of the behavior of the whole social group of which he is a member, since his individual acts are involved in larger, social acts which go beyond himself and which implicate the other members of that group. (Mead 1934/1967: 6f.)

Here Mead points out that our ways of thinking, feeling and acting – our behaviour – lies within and is moulded by the features of the social spaces in which we lead our lives. Our individual acts, which in Mead's terminology also include inner, cognitive or emotional, processes, can only be explained through the interaction. In other words, Mead highlights the ways in which our selves, even though we might experience them as enclosed, bounded and distinctively our own, are inseparably entwined with the social worlds in which we conduct our everyday lives.

Mead's self is thus a *social self*, which emerges through our experiences of the world around us. Our self – our characteristic ways of thinking, feeling and acting that make us different from others – is not some sort of biological or inborn quality. Through our socialisation and our ongoing interactions with others in everyday life, our self is made, changes and develops. Social interaction and the *symbolic meanings* which are conveyed through interaction are thus central to who we are and who we may become.

A simple example may clarify these points: You take a class which you like. The teacher is nice, and you like the subject matter. You want to do well and so you work hard on your essay. When the teacher returns the essay, you notice that you got a high mark. Moreover, the teacher praises you in front of the class for your good work. Immediately, this experience makes you feel happy and pleased at the reward for your effort. More profoundly, however, it has an impact on your self, by making you see yourself as a good student capable of doing well at university. Through this insight, you feel more confident about your abilities, which in turn may allow you to do similarly well in future coursework.

Mead proposed that social interaction's entwinement with the self can be explained through our capacity to *reflexively take the role of others*: seeing ourselves reflected in the minds of others, understanding their intentions towards us, anticipating their reactions to our own behaviour, and appreciating their evaluations of our selves. Through such reflexivity – by continuously envisioning how others see us and respond to us – we develop an understanding of who we are and what our place in the world is. While being a good student is certainly a matter of your inner conviction, this conviction can only be sustained if it is confirmed by your teacher's assessment: the more high marks you score, the more certain you can be that academic achievement is a part of who you are, while a series of poor results may seriously dent your self-esteem.

Reading

Mead, George Herbert (1934/2006), 'The Self, the I, and the Me', in *The Production of Reality* edited by Jody O'Brien (4th edn), Thousand Oaks: Pine Forge Press, pp. 250–4

The Self, the I, and the Me

[. . .]

We can distinguish very definitely between the self and the body. The body can be there and can operate in a very intelligent fashion without there being a self involved in the experience. The self has the characteristic that it is an object to itself, and that characteristic distinguishes it from other objects and from the body. It is perfectly true that the eye can see the foot, but it does not see the body as a whole. We cannot see our backs; we can feel certain portions of them, if we are agile, but we cannot get an experience of our whole body. There are, of course, experiences which are somewhat vague and difficult of location, but the bodily experiences are for us organized about a self. The foot and hand belong to the self. We can see our feet, especially if we look at them from the wrong end of an opera glass, as strange things which we have difficulty in recognizing as our own. The parts of the body are quite distinguishable from the self. We can lose parts of the body without any serious invasion of the self. The mere ability to experience different parts of the body is not different from the experience of a table. The table presents a different feel from what the hand does when one hand feels another, but it is an experience of something with which we come definitely into contact. The body does not experience itself as a whole, in the sense in which the self in some way enters into the experience of the self.

It is the characteristic of the self as an object to itself that I want to bring out. This characteristic is represented in the word "self," which is a reflexive, and indicates that which can be both subject and object. This type of object is essentially different from other objects, and in the past it has been distinguished as conscious, a term which indicates an experience with, an experience of, one's self. It was assumed that consciousness in some way carried this capacity of being an object to itself. In giving a behavioristic statement of consciousness we have to look for some sort of experience in which the physical organism can become an object to itself.

When one is running to get away from someone who is chasing him, he is entirely occupied in this action, and his experience may be swallowed up in the objects about him, so that he has, at the time being, no consciousness of self at all. We must be, of course, very completely occupied to have that take place, but we can, I think, recognize that sort of a possible experience in which the self does not enter. We can, perhaps, get some light on that situation through those experiences in which in very intense action there appears in the experience of the individual, back of this intense action, memories, and anticipations. Tolstoi as an officer in the war gives an account of having pictures of his past experience in the midst of his most intense action. There are also the pictures that flash into a person's mind when he is drowning. In such instances there is a contrast between an experience that is absolutely wound up in outside activity in which the self as an object does not enter, and an activity of memory and imagination in which the self is the principal object. The self is then entirely distinguishable from an organism that is surrounded by things and acts with reference to things, including parts of its own body. These latter may be objects like other objects, but they are just objects out there in the field, and they do not involve a self that is an object to the organism. This is, I think, frequently overlooked. It is that fact which makes our anthropomorphic reconstructions of animal life so fallacious. How can an individual get outside himself (experientially) in such a way as to become an object to himself? This is the essential psychological problem of selfhood or of self-consciousness; and its solution is to be found by referring to the process of social conduct or activity in which the given person or individual is implicated. The apparatus of reason would not be complete unless it swept itself into its own analysis of the field of experience; or unless the individual brought himself into the same experiential field as that of the other individual selves in relation to whom he acts in any given social situation. Reason cannot become impersonal unless it takes an objective, non-affective attitude toward itself; otherwise we have just consciousness, not *self*-consciousness. And it is necessary to rational conduct that the individual should thus take an objective, impersonal attitude toward himself, that he should become an object to himself. For the individual organism is obviously an essential and important fact or constituent element of the empirical situation in which it acts; and without taking objective account of itself as such, it cannot act intelligently, or rationally.

The individual experiences himself as such, not directly, but only indirectly, from the particular standpoints of other individual members of the same social group, or from the generalized standpoint of the social group as a whole to which he belongs. For he enters his own experience as a self or individual, not directly or immediately, not by becoming a subject to himself, but only in so far as he first becomes an object to himself just as other individuals are objects to him or in his experience; and he becomes an object to himself only by taking the attitudes of other individuals toward himself within a social environment or context of experience and behavior in which both he and they are involved.

The importance of what we term "communication" lies in the fact that it provides a form of behavior in which the organism or the individual may become an object to himself. It is that sort of communication which we have been discussing – not communication in the sense of the cluck of the hen to the chickens, or the bark of a wolf to the pack, or the lowing of a cow, but communication in the sense of significant symbols, communication which is directed not only to others but also to the individual himself. So far as that type of communication is a part of behavior it at least introduces a self. Of course, one may hear without listening; one may see things that he does not realize; do things that he is not really aware of. But it is where one does respond to that which he addresses to another and where that response of his own becomes a part of his conduct, where he not only hears himself but responds to himself, talks and replies to himself as truly as the other person replies to him, that we have behavior in which the individuals become objects to themselves.

Such a self is not, I would say, primarily the physiological organism. The physiological organism is essential to it, but we are at least able to think of a self without it. Persons who believe in immortality, or believe in ghosts, or in the possibility of the self leaving the body, assume a self which is quite distinguishable from the body. How successfully they can hold these conceptions is an open question, but we do, as a fact, separate the self and the organism. It is fair to say that the beginning of the self as an object, so far as we can see, is to be found in the experiences of people that lead to the conception of a "double." Primitive people assume that there is a double, located presumably in the diaphragm, that leaves the body temporarily in sleep and completely in death. It can be enticed out of the body of one's enemy and perhaps killed. It is represented in infancy by the imaginary playmates which children set up, and through which they come to control their experiences in their play.

The self, as that which can be an object to itself, is essentially a social structure, and it arises in social experience. After a self has arisen, it in a certain sense provides for itself its social experiences, and so we can conceive of an absolutely solitary self. But it is impossible to conceive of a self arising outside of social experience. When it has arisen we can think of a person in solitary confinement for the rest of his life, but who still has himself as a companion, and is able to think and to converse with himself as he had communicated with others. That process to which I have just referred, of responding to one's self as another responds to it, taking part in one's own conversation with others, being aware of what one is saying and using that awareness of what one is saying to determine what one is going to say thereafter – that is a process with which we are all familiar. We are continually following up our own address to other persons by an understanding of what we are saying, and using that understanding in the direction of our continued speech. We are finding out what we are going to say, what we are going to do, by saying and doing, and in the process we are continually controlling the process itself. In the conversation of gestures what we say calls out a certain response in another and that in turn changes our own action, so that we shift from what we started to do because of the reply the other makes. The conversation of gestures is the beginning of communication. The individual comes to carry on a conversation of gestures with himself. He says something, and that calls out a certain reply in himself which makes him change what he was going to say. One starts to say something, we will presume an unpleasant something, but when he starts to say it he realizes it is cruel. The effect on himself of what he is saying checks him; there is here a conversation of gestures between the individual and himself. We mean by significant speech that the action is one that affects the individual himself, and that the effect upon the individual himself is part of the intelligent carrying-out of the conversation with others. Now we, so to speak, amputate that social phase and dispense with it for the time being, so that one is talking to one's self as one would talk to another person.

This process of abstraction cannot be carried on indefinitely. One inevitably seeks an audience, has to pour himself out to somebody. In reflective intelligence one thinks to act, and to act solely so that this action remains a part of a social process. Thinking becomes preparatory to social action. The very process of thinking is, of course, simply an inner conversation that goes on, but it is a conversation of gestures which in its completion implies the expression of that which one thinks to an audience. One separates the significance of what he is saying to others from the actual speech and gets it ready before saying it. He thinks it out, and perhaps writes it in the form of a book; but it is still a part of social intercourse in which one is addressing other persons and at the same time addressing one's self, and in which one controls the address to other persons by the response made to one's own gesture. That the person should be responding to himself is necessary to the self, and it is this sort of social conduct which provides behavior within which that self appears. I know of no other form of behavior than the linguistic in which the individual is an object to himself, and, so far as I can see, the individual is not a self in the reflexive sense unless he is an object to himself. It is this fact that gives a critical importance to communication, since this is a type of behavior in which the individual does so respond to himself.

We realize in everyday conduct and experience that an individual does not mean a great deal of what he is doing and saying. We frequently say that such an individual is not himself. We come away from an interview with a realization that we have left out important things, that there are parts of the self that did not get into what was said. What determines the amount of the self that gets into communication is the social experience itself. Of course, a good deal of the

self does not need to get expression. We carry on a whole series of different relationships to different people. We are one thing to one man and another thing to
another. There are parts of the self which exist only for the self in relationship to
itself. We divide ourselves up in all sorts of different selves with reference to our
acquaintances. We discuss politics with one and religion with another. There are
all sorts of different selves answering to all sorts of different social reactions. It is
the social process itself that is responsible for the appearance of the self; it is not
there as a self apart from this type of experience.

A multiple personality is in a certain sense normal, as I have just pointed
out. There is usually an organization of the whole self with reference to the
community to which we belong, and the situation in which we find ourselves.
What the society is, whether we are living with people of the present, people
of our own imaginations, people of the past, varies, of course, with different
individuals. Normally, within the sort of community as a whole to which we
belong, there is a unified self, but that may be broken up. To a person who is
somewhat unstable nervously and in whom there is a line of cleavage, certain
activities become impossible, and that set of activities may separate and evolve
another self. Two separate "me's" and "I's," two different selves, result, and that
is the condition under which there is a tendency to break up the personality.
There is an account of a professor of education who disappeared, was lost to the
community, and later turned up in a logging camp in the West. He freed himself
of his occupation and turned to the woods where he felt, if you like, more at
home. The pathological side of it was the forgetting, the leaving out of the rest of
the self. This result involved getting rid of certain bodily memories which would
identify the individual to himself. We often recognize the lines of cleavage that
run through us. We would be glad to forget certain things, get rid of things the
self is bound up with in past experiences. What we have here is a situation in
which there can be different selves, and it is dependent upon the set of social
reactions that is involved as to which self we are going to be. If we can forget
everything involved in one set of activities, obviously we relinquish that part of
the self. Take a person who is unstable, get him occupied by speech, and at the
same time get his eye on something you are writing so that he is carrying on two
separate lines of communication, and if you go about it in the right way you can
get those two currents going so that they do not run into each other. You can get
two entirely different sets of activities going on. You can bring about in that way
the dissociation of a person's self. It is a process of setting up two sorts of communication which separate the behavior of the individual. For one individual it
is this thing said and heard, and for the other individual there exists only that
which he sees written. You must, of course, keep one experience out of the field
of the other. Dissociations are apt to take place when an event leads to emotional
upheavals. That which is separated goes on in its own way.

The unity and structure of the complete self reflects the unity and structure
of the social process as a whole; and each of the elementary selves of which it

is composed reflects the unity and structure of one of the various aspects of that process in which the individual is implicated. In other words, the various elementary selves which constitute, or are organized into, a complete self are the various aspects of the structure of that complete self answering to the various aspects of the structure of the social process as a whole; the structure of the complete self is thus a reflection of the complete social process. The organization and unification of a social group is identical with the organization and unification of any one of the selves arising within the social process in which that group is engaged, or which it is carrying on.

The phenomenon of dissociation of personality is caused by a breaking up of the complete, unitary self into the component selves of which it is composed, and which respectively correspond to different aspects of the social process in which the person is involved, and within which his complete or unitary self has arisen; these aspects being the different social groups to which he belongs within that process. . . .

Rational society, of course, is not limited to any specific set of individuals. Any person who is rational can become a part of it. The attitude of the community toward our own response is imported into ourselves in terms of the meaning of what we are doing. This occurs in its widest extent in universal discourse, in the reply which the rational world makes to our remark. The meaning is as universal as the community; it is necessarily involved in the rational character of that community; it is the response that the world made up out of rational beings inevitably makes to our own statement. We both get the object and ourselves into experience in terms of such a process; the other appears in our own experience insofar as we do take such an organized and generalized attitude.

If one meets a person on the street whom he fails to recognize, one's reaction toward him is that toward any other who is a member of the same community. He is the other, the organized, generalized other, if you like. One takes his attitude over against one's self. If he turns in one direction one is to go in another direction. One has his response as an attitude within himself. It is having that attitude within himself that makes it possible for one to be a self. That involves something beyond the mere turning to the right, as we say, instinctively, without self-consciousness. To have self-consciousness one must have the attitude of the other in one's own organism as controlling the thing that he is going to do. What appears in the immediate experience of one's self in taking that attitude is what we term the "me." It is that self which is able to maintain itself in the community, that is recognized in the community insofar as it recognizes the others. Such is the phase of the self which I have referred to as that of the "me."

Over against the "me" is the "I." The individual not only has rights, but he has duties; he is not only a citizen, a member of the community, but he is one who reacts to this community and in his reaction to it, as we have seen in the conversation of gestures, changes it. The "I" is the response of the individual to the attitude of the community as this appears in his own experience. His response to that organized attitude in turn changes it. As we have pointed out, this is a change which is not present in his own experience until after it takes place. The "I" appears in our experience in memory. It is only after we have acted that we know what we have done; it is only after we have spoken that we know what we have said. The adjustment to that organized world which is present in our own nature is one that represents the "me" and is constantly there. But if the response to it is a response which is of the nature of the conversation of gestures, if it creates a situation which is in some sense novel, if one puts up his side of the case, asserts himself over against others and insists that they take a different attitude toward himself, then there is something important occurring that is not previously present in experience.

Consider

1. What does Mead mean when he states that we 'can distinguish very definitely between the self and the body'? Explain this argument in your own words.
2. How is the self reflexive? Can you give any examples of the self's reflexivity?
3. 'The self, as that which can be an object to itself, is essentially a social structure, and it arises in social experience.' Discuss.
4. Explains Mead's distinction between the 'I' and the 'me'. How is this distinction relevant to our understanding of the social nature of the self? This is a difficult question, and you may need to do some background reading on Mead's work to be able to answer it.
5. Both George Herbert Mead and Max Weber (see above) place a great emphasis on the role of subjective meanings in social interaction. Based on the readings in this book, as well as relevant background research, compare and contrast their respective approaches.
6. While Mead's work is taught particularly often in sociology courses, the work of other Chicago sociologists also had a lasting impact. Look into the work of at least one of the following scholars to find out more about it:
   (a) Ernest Burgess
   (b) Louis Wirth
   (c) Florian Znaniecki
   (d) Edwin Sutherland
   (e) Robert Park
   (f) Clifford Shaw.

W.E.B. Du Bois: Perspectives on race and social conflict

William Edward Burghardt Du Bois is the second American sociologist whose work we consider in this chapter. Du Bois's work is notable for its insights into patterns of racial inequality and conflict in US society. As such, it has been foundational for much sociological research on social inequalities and particularly on issues of race. Born in 1868 into a family of African and European ancestry, Du Bois lived in a time in which

US society, particularly in the South, was characterised by pervasive racism, Jim Crow laws, and segregation. Du Bois was nonetheless able to acquire a privileged education, which led in 1895 to a PhD from Harvard University, then and now an institution for academic and social elites. His studies also allowed him to visit the University of Berlin and develop ties with some of the leading German intellectuals of the time.

His later career combined groundbreaking scholarship with groundbreaking activism on behalf of African Americans. Between 1894 and 1910 and for a shorter period later in life, Du Bois held a number of academic appointments, the longest and most notable one at Atlanta University, a historically black university in the Deep South. In 1905, Du Bois participated in the foundation of the Niagara Movement. The Niagara Movement sought to decisively challenge segregation and the racist discrimination of African Americans, and it rejected proposals for accommodation with the current state of affairs. In 1910, Du Bois became the Director of Publications and Research for the newly formed National Association for the Advancement of Colored People (NAACP). In the NAACP's magazine *The Crisis*, Du Bois found a platform to publish his views on important social and political issues and advocate on behalf of African Americans. Towards the end of his life, Du Bois lost his faith in Americans' ability to constructively resolve the problems posed by entrenched racism. He retired to Ghana, adopted Ghanaian citizenship, and died in Accra in 1963.

Du Bois's life story deserves attention because it allows us to highlight certain important features of the sociological project at large. First, there is the inextricable entwinement of personal experience and academic research. There is an important tradition in sociology that advocates an objective and value-neutral stance towards one's topics of enquiry. While there are many ways to be a sociologist, Du Bois's life story perhaps does suggest that objectivity and value neutrality are neither easily achievable nor necessarily desirable. We discuss Du Bois in this book because he is commonly recognised as a sociologist whose achievements have had a lasting and significant impact. The significance of Du Bois's work in turn stems from his deep commitment to the explanation and improvement of the African American's social, economic and political situation. In other words, Du Bois became an important sociologist through his commitment to certain values and not through the adoption of a distant, tempered and forcibly neutral gaze on the lives of African Americans.

Du Bois's scholarship is highly complex, and it is notable for both theoretically significant insights and rigorous empirical research. To begin with, through his writings, he sought to foreground the centrality of the relationships between 'races' in American life. Consider the following statement from *The Conservation of Races*, a treatise published in 1897:

> The American Negro has always felt an intense personal interest in discussions as to the origins and destinies of races: primarily because back of most discussions of race with which he is familiar, have lurked certain assumptions as to his natural abilities, as to his political, intellectual and moral status, which he felt were wrong. He has, consequently, been led to deprecate and minimize race distinctions, to believe intensely that out of one blood God created all nations, and to speak of human brotherhood as though it were the possibility of an already dawning

to-morrow. Nevertheless, in our calmer moments we must acknowledge that human beings are divided into races; that in this country the two most extreme types of the world's races have met, and the resulting problem as to the future relations of these types is not only of intense and living interest to us, but forms an epoch in the history of mankind. (Du Bois 1897/2007: 6)

Here, Du Bois asserts the existence of human 'races'.[1] His claim that, in the USA, 'the two most extreme types of the world's races have met' then highlights the depth and the extent of racial conflict and strife. Later in the text, he concludes that 'the advance guard of the Negro people – the 8,000,000 people of Negro blood in the United States of America – must soon come to realize that if they are to take their just place in the van of Pan-Negroism, then their destiny is NOT absorption by the white Americans' (Du Bois 1897/2007). Du Bois thus rejects ideas of a cultural assimilation or blending of African Americans with whites, as advocated by some African American politicians of his time. His use of the term 'Pan-Negroism' refers to a political movement that is also often labelled *Pan-Africanism*. Pan-Africanism seeks to foreground the cultural achievements of people of African descent around the world and inspire unity. In part through Du Bois's influence, it gained in importance during the early twentieth century and then came to even greater prominence from the US civil rights movement of the 1960s and 1970s onwards.

Beyond these general arguments, Du Bois constructed a detailed analysis of the social conditions experienced by African Americans. Three notable works in this regard are *The Philadelphia Negro* (Du Bois 1899), *The Negro Church* (Du Bois 1903) and *The Souls of Black Folk* (Du Bois 1903/2009). In these and other publications, Du Bois covers a very wide range of topics, such as religion, crime, marriage, and the many facets of social inequality in American life. The following extract from *The Souls of Black Folk* is particularly noteworthy, offering deep insights into the ways in which ideas of race structure social interaction.

Reading

Du Bois, W.E.B (1903/1996), *The Souls of Black Folk*, New York: Penguin, pp. 3–12

1

Of our Spiritual Strivings

Between me and the other world there is ever an unasked question: unasked by some through feelings of delicacy; by others through the difficulty of rightly framing it. All, nevertheless, flutter round it. They approach me in a half-hesitant sort of way, eye me curiously or compassionately, and then, instead of saying directly, How does it feel to be a problem? they say, I know an excellent colored man in

---

[1] The idea that there are human 'races' reflects views current in Du Bois's time, but has now become quite problematic (see Chapter 5 for a discussion of this issue).

my town; or, I fought at Mechanicsville; or, Do not these Southern outrages make your blood boil? At these I smile, or am interested, or reduce the boiling to a simmer, as the occasion may require. To the real question, How does it feel to be a problem? I answer seldom a word.

And yet, being a problem is a strange experience, – peculiar even for one who has never been anything else, save perhaps in babyhood and in Europe. It is in the early days of rollicking boyhood that the revelation first bursts upon one, all in a day, as it were. I remember well when the shadow swept across me. I was a little thing, away up in the hills of New England, where the dark Housatonic winds between Hoosac and Taghkanic to the sea. In a wee wooden schoolhouse, something put it into the boys' and girls' heads to buy gorgeous visiting-cards – ten cents a package – and exchange. The exchange was merry, till one girl, a tall newcomer, refused my card, – refused it peremptorily, with a glance. Then it dawned upon me with a certain suddenness that I was different from the others; or like, mayhap, in heart and life and longing, but shut out from their world by a vast veil. I had thereafter no desire to tear down that veil, to creep through; I held all beyond it in common contempt, and lived above it in a region of blue sky and great wandering shadows. That sky was bluest when I could beat my mates at examination-time, or beat them at a foot-race, or even beat their stringy heads. Alas, with the years all this fine contempt began to fade; for the worlds I longed for, and all their dazzling opportunities, were theirs, not mine. But they should not keep these prizes, I said; some, all, I would wrest from them. Just how I would do it I could never decide: by reading law, by healing the sick, by telling the wonderful tales that swam in my head, – some way. With other black boys the strife was not so fiercely sunny: their youth shrunk into tasteless sycophancy, or into silent hatred of the pale world about them and mocking distrust of everything white; or wasted itself in a bitter cry, Why did God make me an outcast and a stranger in mine own house? The shades of the prison-house closed round about us all: walls strait and stubborn to the whitest, but relentlessly narrow, tall, and unscalable to sons of night who must plod darkly on in resignation, or beat unavailing palms against the stone, or steadily, half hopelessly, watch the streak of blue above.

After the Egyptian and Indian, the Greek and Roman, the Teuton and Mongolian, the Negro is a sort of seventh son, born with a veil, and gifted with second-sight in this American world, – a world which yields him no true self-consciousness, but only lets him see himself through the revelation of the other world. It is a peculiar sensation, this double-consciousness, this sense of always looking at one's self through the eyes of others, of measuring one's soul by the tape of a world that looks on in amused contempt and pity. One ever feels his two-ness, – an American, a Negro; two souls, two thoughts, two unreconciled strivings; two warring ideals in one dark body, whose dogged strength alone keeps it from being torn asunder.

The history of the American Negro is the history of this strife – this longing to attain self-conscious manhood, to merge his double self into a better and truer self. In this merging he wishes neither of the older selves to be lost. He would not Africanize America, for America has too much to teach the world and Africa. He would not bleach his Negro soul in a flood of white Americanism, for he knows that Negro blood has a message for the world. He simply wishes to make it possible for a man to be both a Negro and an American, without being cursed and spit upon by his fellows, without having the doors of Opportunity closed roughly in his face.

This, then, is the end of his striving: to be a co-worker in the kingdom of culture, to escape both death and isolation, to husband and use his best powers and his latent genius. These powers of body and mind have in the past been strangely wasted, dispersed, or forgotten. The shadow of a mighty Negro past flits through the tale of Ethiopia the Shadowy and of Egypt the Sphinx. Throughout history, the powers of single black men flash here and there like falling stars, and die sometimes before the world has rightly gauged their brightness. Here in America, in the few days since Emancipation, the black man's turning hither and thither in hesitant and doubtful striving has often made his very strength to lose effectiveness, to seem like absence of power, like weakness. And yet it is not weakness, – it is the contradiction of double aims. The double-aimed struggle of the black artisan – on the one hand to escape white contempt for a nation of mere hewers of wood and drawers of water, and on the other hand to plough and nail and dig for a poverty-stricken horde – could only result in making him a poor craftsman, for he had but half a heart in either cause. By the poverty and ignorance of his people, the Negro minister or doctor was tempted toward quackery and demagogy; and by the criticism of the other world, toward ideals that made him ashamed of his lowly tasks. The would-be black *savant* was confronted by the paradox that the knowledge his people needed was a twice-told tale to his white neighbors, while the knowledge which would teach the white world was Greek to his own flesh and blood. The innate love of harmony and beauty that set the ruder souls of his people a-dancing and a-singing raised but confusion and doubt in the soul of the black artist; for the beauty revealed to him was the soul-beauty of a race which his larger audience despised, and he could not articulate the message of another people. This waste of double aims, this seeking to satisfy two unreconciled ideals, has wrought sad havoc with the courage and faith and deeds of ten thousand thousand people, – has sent them often wooing false gods and invoking false means of salvation, and at times has even seemed about to make them ashamed of themselves.

Away back in the days of bondage they thought to see in one divine event the end of all doubt and disappointment; few men ever worshipped Freedom with half such unquestioning faith as did the American Negro for two centuries. To him, so far as he thought and dreamed, slavery was indeed the sum of all villainies, the cause of all sorrow, the root of all prejudice; Emancipation was the key to a promised land of sweeter beauty than ever stretched before the eyes of wearied Israelites. In song and exhortation swelled one refrain – Liberty; in his tears and curses the God he implored had Freedom in his right hand. At last it came, – suddenly, fearfully, like a dream. With one wild carnival of blood and passion came the message in his own plaintive cadences: –

"Shout, O children!
Shout, you're free!
For God has bought your liberty!"

Years have passed away since then, – ten, twenty, forty; forty years of national life, forty years of renewal and development, and yet the swarthy spectre sits in its accustomed seat at the Nation's feast. In vain do we cry to this our vastest social problem: –

"Take any shape but that, and my firm nerves
Shall never tremble!"

The Nation has not yet found peace from its sins; the freedman has not yet found in freedom his promised land. Whatever of good may have come in these years of change, the shadow of a deep disappointment rests upon the Negro people, – a disappointment all the more bitter because the unattained ideal was unbounded save by the simple ignorance of a lowly people.

The first decade was merely a prolongation of the vain search for freedom, the boon that seemed ever barely to elude their grasp, – like a tantalizing will-o'-the-wisp, maddening and misleading the headless host. The holocaust of war, the terrors of the Ku-Klux Klan, the lies of carpet-baggers, the disorganization of industry, and the contradictory advice of friends and foes, left the bewildered serf with no new watch-word beyond the old cry for freedom. As the time flew, however, he began to grasp a new idea. The ideal of liberty demanded for its attainment powerful means, and these the Fifteenth Amendment gave him. The ballot, which before he had looked upon as a visible sign of freedom, he now regarded as the chief means of gaining and perfecting the liberty with which war had partially endowed him. And why not? Had not votes made war and emancipated millions? Had not votes enfranchised the freedmen? Was anything impossible to a power that had done all this? A million black men started with renewed zeal to vote themselves into the kingdom. So the decade flew away, the revolution of 1876 came, and left the half-free serf weary, wondering, but still inspired. Slowly but steadily, in the following years, a new vision began gradually to replace the dream of political power, – a powerful movement, the rise of another ideal to guide the unguided, another pillar of fire by night after a clouded day. It was the ideal of "book-learning"; the curiosity, born of compulsory ignorance, to know and test the power of the cabalistic letters of the white man, the longing to know. Here at last seemed to have been discovered the mountain path to Canaan; longer than the highway of Emancipation and law, steep and rugged, but straight, leading to heights high enough to overlook life.

Up the new path the advance guard toiled, slowly, heavily, doggedly; only those who have watched and guided the faltering feet, the misty minds, the dull understandings, of the dark pupils of these schools know how faithfully, how pit-eously, this people strove to learn. It was weary work. The cold statistician wrote down the inches of progress here and there, noted also where here and there a foot had slipped or some one had fallen. To the tired climbers, the horizon was ever dark, the mists were often cold, the Canaan was always dim and far away. If, however, the vistas disclosed as yet no goal, no resting-place, little but flattery and criticism, the journey at least gave leisure for reflection and self-examination; it changed the child of Emancipation to the youth with dawning self-conscious-ness, self-realization, self-respect. In those sombre forests of his striving his own soul rose before him, and he saw himself, – darkly as through a veil; and yet he saw in himself some faint revelation of his power, of his mission. He began to have a dim feeling that, to attain his place in the world, he must be himself, and not another. For the first time he sought to analyze the burden he bore upon his back, that dead-weight of social degradation partially masked behind a half-named Negro problem. He felt his poverty; without a cent, without a home, with-out land, tools, or savings, he had entered into competition with rich, landed, skilled neighbors. To be a poor man is hard, but to be a poor race in a land of dollars is the very bottom of hardships. He felt the weight of his ignorance, – not simply of letters, but of life, of business, of the humanities; the accumulated sloth and shirking and awkwardness of decades and centuries shackled his hands and feet. Nor was his burden all poverty and ignorance. The red stain of bastardy, which two centuries of systematic legal defilement of Negro women had stamped upon his race, meant not only the loss of ancient African chastity, but also the hereditary weight of a mass of corruption from white adulterers, threatening almost the obliteration of the Negro home.

A people thus handicapped ought not to be asked to race with the world, but rather allowed to give all its time and thought to its own social problems. But alas! while sociologists gleefully count his bastards and his prostitutes, the very soul of the toiling, sweating black man is darkened by the shadow of a vast despair. Men call the shadow prejudice, and learnedly explain it as the natural defence of culture against barbarism, learning against ignorance, purity against crime, the "higher" against the "lower" races. To which the Negro cries Amen! and swears that to so much of this strange prejudice as is founded on just hom-age to civilization, culture, righteousness, and progress, he humbly bows and meekly does obeisance. But before that nameless prejudice that leaps beyond all this he stands helpless, dismayed, and well-nigh speechless; before that personal disrespect and mockery, the ridicule and systematic humiliation, the distortion of fact and wanton license of fancy, the cynical ignoring of the better and the boisterous welcoming of the worse, the all-pervading desire to inculcate disdain for everything black, from Toussaint to the devil, – before this there rises a sicken-ing despair that would disarm and discourage any nation save that black host to whom "discouragement" is an unwritten word.

But the facing of so vast a prejudice could not but bring the inevitable self-questioning, self-disparagement, and lowering of ideals which ever accompany repression and breed in an atmosphere of contempt and hate. Whisperings and portents came borne upon the four winds: Lo! we are diseased and dying, cried the dark hosts; we cannot write, our voting is vain; what need of education, since we must always cook and serve? And the Nation echoed and enforced this self-criticism, saying: Be content to be servants, and nothing more; what need of higher culture for half-men? Away with the black man's ballot, by force or fraud, – and behold the suicide of a race! Nevertheless, out of the evil came something of good, – the more careful adjustment of education to real life, the clearer perception of the Negroes' social responsibilities, and the sobering realization of the meaning of progress.

So dawned the time of *Sturm und Drang:* storm and stress today rocks our little boat on the mad waters of the world-sea; there is within and without the sound of conflict, the burning of body and rending of soul; inspiration strives with doubt, and faith with vain questionings. The bright ideals of the past, – physical freedom, political power, the training of brains and the training of hands, – all these in turn have waxed and waned, until even the last grows dim and overcast. Are they all wrong, – all false? No, not that, but each alone was over-simple and incomplete, – the dreams of a credulous race-childhood, or the fond imaginings of the other world which does not know and does not want to know our power. To be really true, all these ideals must be melted and welded into one. The training of the schools we need to-day more than ever, – the training of deft hands, quick eyes and ears, and above all the broader, deeper, higher culture of gifted minds and pure hearts. The power of the ballot we need in sheer self-defence, – else what shall save us from a second slavery? Freedom, too, the long-sought, we still seek, – the freedom of life and limb, the freedom to work and think, the freedom to love and aspire. Work, culture, liberty, – all these we need, not singly but together, not successively but together, each growing and aiding each, and all striving toward that vaster ideal that swims before the Negro people, the ideal of human brotherhood, gained through the unifying ideal of Race; the ideal of fostering and developing the traits and talents of the Negro, not in opposition to or contempt for other races, but rather in large conformity to the greater ideals of the American Republic, in order that some day on American soil two world-races may give each to each those characteristics both so sadly lack. We the darker ones come even now not altogether empty-handed: there are to-day no truer exponents of the pure human spirit of the Declaration of Independence than the American Negroes; there is no true American music but the wild sweet melodies of the Negro slave; the American fairy tales and folklore are Indian and African; and, all in all, we black men seem the sole oasis of simple faith and reverence in a dusty desert of dollars and smartness. Will America be poorer if she replace her brutal dyspeptic blundering with light-hearted but determined Negro humility? or her coarse and cruel wit with loving jovial good-humor? or her vulgar music with the soul of the Sorrow Songs?

Merely a concrete test of the underlying principles of the great republic is the Negro Problem, and the spiritual striving of the freedmen's sons is the travail of souls whose burden is almost beyond the measure of their strength, but who bear it in the name of an historic race, in the name of this the land of their fathers' fathers, and in the name of human opportunity.

And now what I have briefly sketched in large outline let me on coming pages tell again in many ways, with loving emphasis and deeper detail, that men may listen to the striving in the souls of black folk.

Consider

1. What does Du Bois mean when he writes that 'the Negro is [. . .] born with a veil' and possesses a 'double consciousness'? Explain this idea in your own words.
2. To what extent are the ideas of 'the veil' and 'double consciousness' relevant in contemporary social life? Illustrate your arguments with concrete examples.
3. Summarise Du Bois's argument in 'Of our spiritual strivings'. How does he describe the situation of African Americans? What goals would he like African Americans to achieve?
4. To what extent and in which ways has the situation of African Americans changed since Du Bois's time? Support your argument with relevant background research.
5. Many of Du Bois's key works are now freely available online, on websites such as Project Gutenberg. Examine the themes and major arguments covered in any one of the following works and write a report on your findings:
   (a) *The Souls of Black Folk*
   (b) *Darkwater*
   (c) *The Negro*
   (d) *The Conservation of Races*.

Social association in the modern world: Ferdinand Tönnies

We now turn to another German sociologist, Ferdinand Tönnies. As with many of the scholars introduced in this chapter, his lifetime spans the second half of the nineteenth century and the first decades of the twentieth century. Like Weber, Tönnies published widely around a variety of subject matters, including theoretical treatises on the work of scholars such as Thomas Hobbes, Friedrich Nietzsche and Karl Marx, legal and political research, and studies on the social problems brought about by the rapid industrialisation of Germany. On the whole, we may say that Tönnies, just like the other early sociologists in this chapter, was driven by an interest in and concern about the consequences of the rapid modernisation of society. This is evident, for instance, in his last major work, *Geist der Neuzeit* (published in 1935; the title might be rendered as *The Spirit of Modernity*), in which Tönnies develops a detailed historical exploration of the formation of modern societies.

Tönnies's most frequently cited and most widely known work, *Community and Civil Society* (Tönnies 1887/1957), is likewise geared towards these concerns. We might say that Tönnies here picks up on concerns about the nature of *social solidarity* in modern societies, much as Émile Durkheim did in France. The works of both Durkheim and Tönnies consider two questions: First, what are the factors that hold large, complex, diverse, and often quite unequal modern societies together and make their members cooperate with each other? Second, how did forms of social solidarity change over time, and how did distinctively modern solidarities come about? Beyond these very general questions, there are notable differences between Durkheim and Tönnies, though.

Tönnies addresses the problem of social solidarity by distinguishing between two basic ways of living together: *Gemeinschaft*, best translated into English as *community*, and *Gesellschaft*, for which simple translations would be *society* or *association*. Tönnies begins his argument in *Community and Civil Society* with a comparison of these two ways of life. Both, he argues, refer to the ways in which '[h]uman wills stand in manifold relations to one another' (Tönnies 1887/1957: 33), that is to say, to the various ways in which individuals engage with each other on the base of their varying and sometimes divergent interests and motives. Some of these forms of social engagement can be destructive and conflictual, while others may be grounded in cooperation and goodwill.

'Community' and 'society' both refer to cooperative forms of social engagement and designate, in essence, two different forms of holding society together. Tönnies (1887/1957: 33) describes community as a form of social engagement that is 'real' and 'organic', and he cites the relationships between mother and child, between husband and wife, and between brother and sister as prime instances of communal living. The term 'organic' – used with different meanings by scholars like Spencer and Durkheim – here points to a sort of natural and effortless way of living together in harmony, by virtue of being born into the same family and experiencing a strong sense of unity as a result. Describing community, Tönnies (1887/1957: 37) also writes of a 'perfect unity of human wills'.

'Society', in contrast, refers to a much more artificial and abstract sense of living together with others. An example of what Tönnies meant when writing about 'society' would be the complexities of life in a large modern metropolis. Modern cities often comprise a vast variety of social and economic activities – supermarkets, hospitals, business companies, universities, families, government offices, public services, restaurants, and so forth. The people living in a city mostly do not know each other, and simultaneously they depend on many of those unknown others for things they themselves cannot do: providing their food and other daily needs, collecting their waste, providing health care and public safety, etc.

Tönnies was interested in how it may be that individuals manage to actually meet each other's needs in such complex and anonymising social circumstances. He argued that, in 'society', individuals tend to act out of self-interest, being mostly unaware of the specific motives and interests of others. However, under ideal conditions, society is constructed in such a way that this mainly self-directed pursuit of one's interests also manages to fulfil the needs of others: I take an interest in reading about society and decide to study sociology. I finally become a lecturer in sociology, conducting research and teaching at a university. I do so primarily to follow my own inclinations. Nevertheless, I also help satisfy the needs of others, for instance by providing students with the education they will need to perform the most skilled jobs in contemporary society.

By outlining these types of association or social engagement, Tönnies sought to provide sociologists with conceptual tools that would allow them to look at the often much more conflictual patterns of everyday life in modern societies and determine the fault lines and breakdowns that prevent individuals from living together in ways that meet everybody's needs.

Reading

Tönnies, F. (1887/2001) *Community and Civil Society*, Cambridge: Cambridge University Press, pp. 17–21, 22–4, 52–4

The argument

The wills of human beings interact in many different ways. Every such relationship is reciprocal – on the one side active or assertive, on the other passive or acquiescent. These interactions are of such a kind that they tend either to support the mental and physical well-being of the other party or to destroy them – they are either positive or negative. My theory will concentrate on investigating only relationships that are based on positive mutual affirmation. Every relationship of this kind involves some kind of balance between unity and diversity. This consists of mutual encouragement and the sharing of burdens and achievements, which can be seen as expressions of people's energies and wills. The social group brought into existence by this positive relationship, envisaged as functioning both inwardly and outwardly as a unified living entity, is known by some collective term such as a *union, fraternity* or *association*.[1] The relationship itself, and the social bond that stems from it, may be conceived either as having real organic life, and that is the essence of *Community* [*Gemeinschaft*]; or else as a purely mechanical construction, existing in the mind, and that is what we think of as *Society* [*Gesellschaft*]. If we look at the ways in which these two terms are applied we shall see that they are conventionally used in German as synonyms. Up till now they have been confused in technical terminology, being employed interchangeably. So a few observations at the outset may establish their contrasting usages.

All kinds of social co-existence that are familiar, comfortable and exclusive are to be understood as belonging to *Gemeinschaft*. *Gesellschaft* means life in the public sphere, in the outside world. In *Gemeinschaft* we are united from the moment of our birth with our own folk for better or for worse. We go out into *Gesellschaft* as if into a foreign land. A young man is warned about mixing with bad society: but 'bad community' makes no sense in our language. Lawyers may use the term

---

[1] *eine Verbindung* – translatable as union, association, connection, combination, alliance, etc. Elsewhere in the book Tönnies uses the word specifically to mean the kind of holistic organic bonding that he attributes to *Gemeinschaft*, but here it is used in a more general way to cover groups in both *Gemeinschaft* and *Gesellschaft*.

'domestic society'[2] when they are thinking of such a relationship merely in its social and public aspects, but 'domestic *community*' with its infinite effects upon the human soul will be understood intuitively by anyone who has ever experienced it. In the same way an engaged couple recognise that in entering into marriage they are embarking upon a total community of life (*communio totius vitae*); but a 'society of life' would be a contradiction in terms.[3] You can 'keep someone company', but no one can offer another person 'community' in that casual way. You may be received into a religious community; but religious *societies*, like other bodies set up for whatever purpose, exist only for some extraneous goal, such as serving the state or to promote some theory. We have a community of language, custom, belief; but a society for purposes of business, travel, or scientific knowledge. Commercial partnerships are of particular importance; but even though a certain fellowship and community may exist among business partners, we would hardly speak of a 'commercial community'. And it would sound quite revolting to make the linguistic compound 'joint-stock community'. On the other hand community of ownership certainly exists, as in the case of fields, woods and pasture. No one would describe the common ownership of property between man and wife as a 'society of property'.[4]

Thus many differences between the two concepts become apparent. In the most universal sense we could speak of a Community that is *inclusive* of all mankind, such as the Church claims to be. But ordinary human 'Society' we understand simply as individuals living alongside but independently of one another. In recent times there has been talk, in academic discussion, of the 'Society' of a country as opposed to 'the state'; and we shall make use of this conception here, though its meaning only becomes fully apparent in terms of a more deep-seated contrast with the 'Community' of the common people. Community [*Gemeinschaft*] is old, Society [*Gesellschaft*] is new, both as an entity and as a term. This has been recognised by an author whose teaching of political theory is otherwise more notable for its broadness of range than for deep penetration.

---

[2] *die häusliche Gesellschaft* was the term used to define a three-generational household unit, made up of a married couple, elderly parents and children, under the Prussian Natural Law Code of 1794 (*Deutsches Rechtswörterbuch (Wörterbuch der älteren deutschen Rechtssprache)*, 7 vols. (Weimar: L. Böhlaus Nachfolger, 1914–83), vol. IV, p. 503).

[3] *Communio totius vitae*: not a term commonly used by Roman lawyers, but *communio* implied an indissoluble partnership. Tönnies may have had in mind early Roman marriage laws, before the erosion of restrictions on divorce under the later Roman republic and the empire. *Societas vitae*, on the other hand, *was* a term in Roman law (T. Mommsen, *The Digest of Justinian* (1870), English trans. Alan Watson, vols. I–IV (Philadelphia: University of Pennsylvania Press, 1985), vol. II, book xxv, p. 733).

[4] *eine Güter-Gesellschaft* = a contract-based property partnership which could be dissolved by agreement of the parties. Again, not a standard Roman law term, but it had been used in the Roman law-based code of Baden in 1808 (*Deutsches Rechtswörterbuch*, vol. IV, p. 1327).

"The entire concept of Society in the social and political sense", states Bluntschli (*Staatswörterbuch*, IV), "has its natural basis in the habits and the outlook of the *third estate*. It is not really an idea referring to the whole people, but merely to the concept of the third estate . . . it is the latter's notion of 'Society' that has become the source of collective prejudices and trends, while at the same time becoming the vehicle of their expression . . . Wherever urban culture flourishes, 'Society' also appears as its indispensable medium. Country people know little of it."[5] On the other hand, everyone who praises rural life has pointed to the fact that people there have a stronger and livelier sense of Community. Community means genuine, enduring life together, whereas Society is a transient and superficial thing. Thus *Gemeinschaft* must be understood as a living organism in its own right, while *Gesellschaft* is a mechanical aggregate and artefact.

2

Everything that is 'real' is organic,[6] in the sense that it must be seen in conjunction with the whole material world, which governs its nature and movements. Thus the power of magnetic attraction in all its many forms makes the universe, as our consciousness apprehends it, into a single whole.[7] The action of this whole expresses itself in the movements by means of which two bodies change their relative positions. But in order to be observed and considered scientifically, a whole must be carefully defined if it is to be of any significance; and each whole of this kind will be seen to consist of smaller wholes which have a particular direction and speed of movement in relation to each other. Attraction itself remains either unexplained (as a remote cause), or is thought of as a mechanical response to external contact, although happening for no known reason. Thus, as we know, masses of matter divide up into identical molecules which attract each other with greater or lesser magnetic force and which in their aggregate state form bodies. The molecules are split into different (chemical) atoms, whose difference remains to be explained by further analysis of various arrangements of the same atomic particles. Pure theoretical mechanics, however, assumes the existence of infinitesimal centres of force as the source of specific actions and reactions – an idea that

---

[5] J. G. Bluntschli and R. Bradter, *Deutsches Staatswörterbuch*, 12 vols. (Stuttgart and Leipzig: 1859), vol. IV, p. 247. By the 'third estate' Bluntschli and earlier users of the term meant, not the mass of the people, but those with a stake in civil society, i.e. the *bürgerlich* class.

[6] Almost certainly meant as an echo of Hegel's 'alles Wirkliche ist vernünftig' (F. Tönnies, 'Neue Philosophie der Geschichte: Hegel, Marx, Comte', *Archiv für Geschichte der Philosophie*, vol. 7 (1894), p. 487). In this second paragraph (and at many later points in the book) Tönnies abruptly switches from treating human relations as purely social arrangements to discussing them as though they were 'bodies' and 'forces' in the natural world. The reader should bear in mind his claim, not always crystal clear in the text, that his biological and mechanical models were not literal but analogical.

[7] cf. Clerk Maxwell, *Matter and Motion*, particularly pp. 1–35.

comes very close to something like 'metaphysical' atoms.[8] The total sum therefore cannot be altered by any disturbance in the constituent parts. For all practical purposes, however, the physical molecules are treated as being indistinguishable from the body of which they form a part. All true masses may be expressed in terms of specific gravity or measured by reference to quantities of other stable substances. But the moving units that compose the whole are merely hypothetical concepts required for purposes of scientific analysis. Strictly speaking, only the ultimate units, the metaphysical atoms, are the proper units of measurement – somethings which are nothings, or nothings which are somethings! – and here one must be mindful of the merely relative significance of all concepts of size.[9]

Nevertheless, although this may be an anomaly from the viewpoint of mechanics, bodies do in fact exist beyond these combinable and combining particles of inanimate matter. These bodies appear in every respect to be natural totalities, which function as a whole in relation to their parts: that is to say, they are organic bodies. We human beings, trying to understand what is going on around us, belong to bodies of this kind. Each of us has, apart from an indirect knowledge of all possible bodies, an immediate knowledge of his own body.[10] We are driven to the conclusion that some kind of 'conscious' life is bound up with *every* living body; and that through this conscious life the body has an objective existence in the same way that we know that we ourselves exist.

However, objective observation teaches us no less plainly that the whole is not merely the sum of its parts; on the contrary, the parts are dependent on and conditioned by the whole, so that the whole itself possesses intrinsic reality and substance. Human power can produce only inorganic things from organic raw materials, splitting them up and combining them again; and in much the same way both objects and concepts are hammered into a coherent shape by the process of scientific analysis. Phenomena can be brought to life by an original outlook and creative imagination, or by folk belief and inspired poetry; and this creativity, this use of the imagination, also occurs in science. But science has to treat living things as dead objects in order to grasp their interconnections. It translates all states and forces into motions, and represents all motions as amounts of work performed, i.e. as energy expended. It does this in order to understand everything as part of a uniform process and to measure things against one another as though they were interchangeable. This is valid in so far as the assumed uniformity really exists, and certainly the field of possibilities is in theory unlimited; the goal of theoretical understanding, and other related goals, is thus achieved.

---

[8]*Ibid.*, pp. 50–1.

[9]Lange, *History of Materialism*, vol. II, pp. 386–9; Clerk Maxwell, *Scientific Papers*, vol. II, pp. 451–84.

[10]cf. A. Schopenhauer, *The World as Will and Representation*, (1818), trans. E. F. J. Payne, 2 vols. (New York: Dover, 1969), vol. I, pp. 104–5.

But the inexorable processes of organic growth and decay cannot be understood by mechanical means. In this area concepts themselves are part of reality – living, changing and developing, like the inner core of an individual being. If science comes into play here it changes its nature, drops its analytical, rational stance for an intuitive and dialectical one – and turns into philosophy. Moreover the present study is not concerned with genuses and species; we are not considering people with regard to race, nation or tribe as *biological* units, but in the *sociological* sense. We are therefore looking at human relationships and connections either as living entities, or conversely as artificially constructed ones. One finds a counterpart and analogue to this dichotomy in the theory of the individual *will*; so the task of the second part of this study will be to present the problem in its *psychological* aspects.

The Theory of *Gemeinschaft*

I

In tune with the argument so far, the theory of *Gemeinschaft* is based on the idea that in the original or natural state there is a complete unity of human wills. This sense of unity is maintained even when people become separated. It takes various forms, depending on how far the relationship between *differently situated* individuals is predetermined and 'given'. The common root of these relationships is the all-embracing character of the sub-conscious, 'vegetative'[1] life that stems from birth: human wills, each one housed in a physical body, are related to one another by *descent* and kinship; they remain united, or become so out of necessity. This direct mutual affirmation is found in its most intense form in three types of relationships: namely, (1) that between a mother and her child; (2) that between a man and a woman as a couple, as this term is understood in its natural or biological sense; and (3) that between those who recognise each other as brothers and sisters, i.e. offspring at least of the same mother. While the seed of *Gemeinschaft*, or the bias of human minds towards it, is to be seen in any relationship of kinsfolk, these three are of special importance as containing the seeds which are strongest and most readily nurtured. Each of them is significant in it own special way.

A) The relationship between mother and child is most deeply rooted in pure instinct and *pleasure*;[2] and at the same time the shading over from a physical to a purely spiritual[3] relationship is here at its most apparent, particularly at the very beginning. The relationship implies a long duration, because the mother

---

[1] *vegetative* – the term applied by Tönnies to the sphere of organic life below the level of either sensation or thought, such as digestion or blood circulation.

[2] *der Gefallen* = pleasure, liking, preference. The term is linked in this paragraph with *die Gewöhnung* (custom, habit) and *das Gedächtnis* (memory) to form one of Tönnies's favourite rhetorical triads.

[3] *geistig* = spiritual, mental, intellectual, psychological.

is responsible for the nurture, protection and management of the child until it is capable of nourishing, protecting and managing itself. As this happens, the relationship loses its element of necessity, and separation becomes more likely. This tendency can, however, be counteracted by other factors, such as by growing *accustomed* to one another and sharing *memories* of the joy they have given each other, or else by the gratitude of the child for all the trouble the mother has taken on its behalf. These direct mutual connections are reinforced by others which link the pair with matters outside themselves – pleasure, habit, and memory unite them with things in their environment which from the beginning were agreeable, or which became so; for example, familiar, helpful, loving people, such as the father may be, if he lives together with his wife, or the brothers and sisters of the mother or the child, and so on.

B) The *sexual instinct* does not make permanent co-habitation necessary; to begin with it leads less to equal partnership than to one-sided subjugation of the woman, who, being by nature weaker, can be reduced to slavery and a mere object of possession. Thus the relationship between a *married couple*, regarded independently of family networks and related social forces, must be maintained chiefly by accommodation to each other, if the relationship is to be moulded into one of permanent mutual affirmation. Contributory factors already mentioned understandably play their part here, particularly the relation with children they have produced together, as well as the sharing of household and possessions.

C) Between *siblings* there is no such fundamental, instinctive liking and natural recognition of one another as there is between a mother and her child, or between partners of the opposite sex. The husband–wife relationship can, of course, coincide with the brother–sister one, and there is good reason to believe that this was frequently the case among many tribes at an earlier period of human history. We must remember that wherever and whenever descent was reckoned on the mother's side, the corresponding generations of cousins were described and regarded as brothers and sisters. This was so common that the restricted meaning of the term *Geschwister*,[4] as in many other cases, dates from a much later outlook. Through similar developments among the most important ethnic groups, marriage between brothers and sisters came to be eliminated; where exogamy was practised this meant no marriage with blood relatives, although more distant relatives might be permitted to marry. As a result, the love between siblings can be regarded as the most 'human' of relationships between human beings, even though it is based essentially on ties of blood.[5] It is evident in this case, that in contrast to the other types of relationship, instinct is at its weakest, and instead *memory*[6] seems to play the strongest part in creating, maintaining and consolidating emotional ties. When children of the same mother live together

---

[4] *die Geschwister* = siblings, brother(s) and sister(s).

[5] i.e human as opposed to merely 'natural'

[6] *das Gedächtnis* = memory or recollection, but often used by Tönnies to mean something rather broader, like a shared 'frame of reference'.

and remain together, they are almost bound to connect their individual recollections of happy impressions and experiences with the characters and activities of the others (if we discount all the causes of enmity that may work in the opposite direction). The more this group is threatened from outside, the more bonding together will be likely to occur, because circumstances impose the need to stick together, to fight and act collectively. The *habit* derived from this co-operation makes life together easier and more cherished. At the same time we can expect the highest degree of *similarity* of character and abilities among brothers – even though differences in intelligence and experience, in so far as these are purely human factors, may well be accentuated.

The theory of *Gesellschaft*

19

The theory of *Gesellschaft* takes as its starting point a group of people who, as in *Gemeinschaft*, live peacefully alongside one another, but in this case without being essentially united – indeed, on the contrary, they are here essentially detached. In *Gemeinschaft* they stay together in spite of everything that separates them; in *Gesellschaft* they remain separate in spite of everything that unites them. As a result, there are no activities taking place which are derived from an *a priori* and pre-determined unity and which therefore express the will and spirit of this unity through any individual who performs them. Nothing happens in *Gesellschaft* that is more important for the individual's wider group than it is for himself. On the contrary, everyone is out for himself alone and living in a state of tension against everyone else. The various spheres of power and activity are sharply demarcated, so that everyone resists contact with others and excludes them from his own spheres, regarding any such overtures as hostile. Such a *negative* attitude is the normal and basic way in which these power-conscious people relate to one another, and it is characteristic of *Gesellschaft* at any given moment in time. Nobody wants to do anything for anyone else, nobody wants to yield or give anything unless he gets something in return that he regards as at least an *equal* trade-off. Indeed it is essential that it should be more desirable to him than whatever he has already, for only by getting something that seems better can he be persuaded to give up something good. If everyone shares such desires, it is obvious that occasions may arise when object 'a' may be better for person 'B' than object 'b', and likewise object 'b' may be better for person 'A' than object 'a'; it is, however, *only* in the context of such relations that 'a' can be better than 'b' at the same time as 'b' is better than 'a'. This provokes the question: can we in any sense at all speak of the 'quality' or 'value' of things independently of such relationships?

The answer is this: as will be demonstrated, all goods are assumed to be separate from each other, and so are their owners. Whatever anyone has and enjoys, he has and enjoys to the *exclusion* of all others – in fact, there is no such thing as a 'common good'. Such a thing *can* only exist by means of a *fiction* on the part of the individuals concerned. It is only possible when they *invent* or manufacture a common personality with its own will, to whom the common *value system* has to relate. Such fictions are not of course invented without sufficient reason. But sufficient reason does indeed exist in the simple act of giving and receiving an object, because during this process contact takes place and *common ground* emerges which is sought by both parties. This lasts as long as the time taken for the "transaction", which can be almost no time at all or can be envisaged as extending for as long as you like. During this period the object which is being released from the sphere of 'A' has ceased to be completely under his will and control, but has not yet passed completely under the will and control of 'B'. It is still under the *partial* control of 'A' but *already* under the *partial* control of 'B'. It is dependent on both parties, in so far as their wills are acting in unison, as is the case while the will to give and receive continues. During this moment or period the object being exchanged represents common good or *social value*. The shared *will* to complete the transaction *can* be seen as constituting a sort of common or *unified* will, in that it *requires* each party to continue with the twofold act until it is completed. This 'will' *must* necessarily be regarded as a unity, since it is considered to be a 'person', or at least 'personality' is imputed to it; for to think of something as a 'being' or a 'thing' is the same as thinking of it as having a coherent unified identity.

Here, however, we must be careful to distinguish whether and to what extent such a fictitious entity exists *only* in theory, as a *philosophical* construct or hypothesis; or whether and when it also exists in the minds of the parties who conjured it up for a particular purpose (assuming that they are in fact capable of shared willing and acting). And the scene is different again if the two parties are conceived as mere *participants* in the creation of something objective in the scientific sense (meaning something that "everybody" necessarily *has* to think). It must of course be understood that every act of giving and receiving which happens in the way we have described *implicitly* involves a social will. Now such an action is inconceivable without its own intrinsic rationale or purpose i.e. the assumed exchange of gifts; which requires that the one action cannot precede the other – they have to take place at the same time. To put the thought in a different way, offer and acceptance on both sides must exactly *coincide*. So the *exchange* itself, as a unified single act, forms the *content* of the fictitious social will. In relation to this will the goods or values exchanged are exactly *equal*. This equality constitutes the judgement of value, which is *binding* for both parties, because they were united in making it. It may last only for the period or moment of the exchange, but within these limits it must look like a judgement which has been reached by "everybody", if it is going to be objective or universally valid. Therefore everyone is deemed to have one and the same will; the will to exchange becomes universal. Everyone takes part in and endorses the individual act, so that it becomes an entirely public act.

On the other hand, the general public may reject that individual act. They may say: a is not equal to b, it is greater or smaller than b, which means that things are not being exchanged according to their proper values. The true value is what everyone regards as its value, as recognised by Society in general; it is accepted as the rational and correct value, only when everyone has agreed on it as a matter of necessity rather than chance. The will of the people can be imagined as united and concentrated in the person of a skilled judge who weighs, measures and passes an *objective* judgement. All members of the public *have* to recognise this and behave accordingly, if they are themselves rational and capable of objective thought, and thus use the same criteria for weighing things up.

Consider

1. What does Tönnies understand by 'community'? Summarise his argument in your own words and provide relevant contemporary examples.
2. What does Tönnies understand by 'society'? Summarise his argument in your own words and provide relevant contemporary examples.
3. 'The theory of the Gesellschaft deals with the artificial construction of an aggregate of human beings which superficially resembles the Gemeinschaft in so far as the individuals live and dwell together peacefully. However, in the Gemeinschaft they remain essentially united in spite of all separating factors, whereas in the Gesellschaft they are essentially separated in spite of all uniting factors.'

   Explain Tönnies's statement in your own words. Provide relevant examples to illustrate his argument.
4. To what extent do people in the contemporary world live in 'community', and to what extent do they live in 'society'? Provide examples to illustrate your points.
5. Compare Tönnies's work on 'community' and 'society' with Durkheim's arguments about 'mechanical' and 'organic' solidarity in modern life. What are the main similarities and differences you can find? To answer this question, you may conduct some background research, in particular on the work of Émile Durkheim.

The social forms of modern life: Georg Simmel

While the other German scholars discussed in this chapter – Weber, Tönnies, Marx, Engels – attracted a wide following both within and beyond the academic world in their own lifetimes, Georg Simmel has only relatively recently come to be regarded as one of the foundational figures of sociology's childhood years. Born in 1858 in Berlin, Simmel published a wide variety of works, often in the form of short essays that spoke to concerns in both philosophy and sociology. He had close associations with leading intellectuals of his time, and his work gained him some public attention. At the same time, his publications received relatively little attention from the mainstream academics of his time, and Simmel's efforts were not recognised with a regular professorship until shortly before his death. In a time of rampant Antisemitism, Simmel was exposed to discrimination by leading academics due to his Jewish heritage. Moreover, the highly original and eclectic character of his writings may have contributed to his lack of immediate recognition. In many ways, we might think of Simmel as a man ahead of his time.

We have already explored Simmel's understanding of sociology, (see Chapter 1), so we do not need to address this topic here. What is more important now is a brief general overview of the various theoretical and substantive issues which Simmel sought to address in his writings. To understand Simmel, it is important to remember that he lived in a time in which sociology had not yet fully established itself as a discipline. While Simmel did in part view himself as a sociologist, he also sought to relate to the concerns of philosophy, and many of his writings are thus characterised by a very high level of abstraction and references to philosophical ideas and concepts.

Simmel's sociology can be described, first of all, as the *sociology of social forms*. Drawing on the ideas of Immanuel Kant, Simmel distinguished between the *content* and the *form* of social interaction. The *content* of social life lies in the social encounters and events that happen every day all around the world in an infinite variety. *Social forms*, in contrast, are abstract features, patterns and characteristics which the observant sociologist may identify among everyday social encounters. While no two human beings are alike and no two encounters between human beings are the same, the places which individuals occupy in such encounters and the characteristics of these encounters may show general commonalities. Many of Simmel's writings are concerned with outlining such commonalities. They deal with particular forms of social interaction, such as conflict, domination, or sociability, and the types of individuals involved in them – the stranger, the pauper, the adventurer, the nobleman, and so forth. In Simmel's account, for example, the stranger is a kind of person who in some ways always remains detached from a particular place or social group, even though he may temporarily form part of it and participate in its activities. Imagine that you invite your best friend to spend a weekend with your family. Your friend will be welcome to participate in all the things you do with your family members, and you may very much enjoy your time together. Yet your friend is not a family member, and her permanent presence in your home would be unwelcome. She is not family; she is a stranger.

Beyond his more micro-sociological interest in the forms of social life, Simmel took an equal interest in large-scale cultural and economic patterns of modern life. Through their everyday interaction, individuals produce the world they live in, Simmel argued. However, over time, particular cultural patterns may become stable and routinised and be taken for granted, taking on a life of their own beyond particular individuals' ability to change them. Simmel called these stable large-scale patterns of everyday life 'objective culture'. One instance of his interest in objective culture would be a major study on the role of money in modern life (Simmel 1900/2011). Another important study considered the nature of life in a modern city. In the following, we will examine Simmel's arguments in this study.

Reading

Simmel, G., 'The Metropolis and Mental Life', in Levine, D. (1903/1971), *On Individuality and Social Forms*, Chicago: The University of Chicago Press, pp. 324–33

The Metropolis and Mental Life

The deepest problems of modern life flow from the attempt of the individual to maintain the independence and individuality of his existence against the sovereign powers of society, against the weight of the historical heritage and the external culture and technique of life. This antagonism represents the most modern form of the conflict which primitive man must carry on with nature for his own bodily existence. The eighteenth century may have called for liberation from all the ties which grew up historically in politics, in religion, in morality and in economics in order to permit the original natural virtue of man, which is equal in everyone, to develop without inhibition; the nineteenth century may have sought to promote, in addition to man's freedom, his individuality (which is connected with the division of labor) and his achievements which make him unique and indispensable but which at the same time make him so much the more dependent on the complementary activity of others; Nietzsche may have seen the relentless struggle of the individual as the prerequisite for his full development, while Socialism found the same thing in the suppression of all competition – but in each of these the same fundamental motive was at work, namely the resistance of the individual to being levelled, swallowed up in the social-technological mechanism. When one inquires about the products of the specifically modern aspects of contemporary life with reference to their inner meaning – when, so to speak, one examines the body of culture with reference to the soul, as I am to do concerning the metropolis today – the answer will require the investigation of the relationship which such a social structure promotes between the individual aspects of life and those which transcend the existence of single individuals. It will require the investigation of the adaptations made by the personality in its adjustment to the forces that lie outside of it.

The psychological foundation, upon which the metropolitan individuality is erected, is the intensification of emotional life due to the swift and continuous shift of external and internal stimuli. Man is a creature whose existence is dependent on differences, i.e., his mind is stimulated by the difference between present impressions and those which have preceded. Lasting impressions, the slightness in their differences, the habituated regularity of their course and contrasts between them, consume, so to speak, less mental energy than the rapid telescoping of changing images, pronounced differences within what is grasped at a single glance, and the unexpectedness of violent stimuli. To the extent that the metropolis creates these psychological conditions – with every crossing of the street, with the tempo and multiplicity of economic, occupational and social life –

it creates in the sensory foundations of mental life, and in the degree of awareness necessitated by our organization as creatures dependent on differences, a deep contrast with the slower, more habitual, more smoothly flowing rhythm of the sensory-mental phase of small town and rural existence. Thereby the essentially intellectualistic character of the mental life of the metropolis becomes intelligible as over against that of the small town which rests more on feelings and emotional relationships. These latter are rooted in the unconscious levels of the mind and develop most readily in the steady equilibrium of unbroken customs. The locus of reason, on the other hand, is in the lucid, conscious upper strata of the mind and it is the most adaptable of our inner forces. In order to adjust itself to the shifts and contradictions in events, it does not require the disturbances and inner upheavals which are the only means whereby more conservative personalities are able to adapt themselves to the same rhythm of events. Thus the metropolitan type – which naturally takes on a thousand individual modifications – creates a protective organ for itself against the profound disruption with which the fluctuations and discontinuities of the external milieu threaten it. Instead of reacting emotionally, the metropolitan type reacts primarily in a rational manner, thus creating a mental predominance through the intensification of consciousness, which in turn is caused by it. Thus the reaction of the metropolitan person to those events is moved to a sphere of mental activity which is least sensitive and which is furthest removed from the depths of the personality.

This intellectualistic quality which is thus recognized as a protection of the inner life against the domination of the metropolis, becomes ramified into numerous specific phenomena. The metropolis has always been the seat of money economy because the many-sidedness and concentration of commercial activity have given the medium of exchange an importance which it could not have acquired in the commercial aspects of rural life. But money economy and the domination of the intellect stand in the closest relationship to one another. They have in common a purely matter-of-fact attitude in the treatment of persons and things in which a formal justice is often combined with an unrelenting hardness. The purely intellectualistic person is indifferent to all things personal because, out of them, relationships and reactions develop which are not to be completely understood by purely rational methods – just as the unique element in events never enters into the principle of money. Money is concerned only with what is common to all, i.e., with the exchange value which reduces all quality and individuality to a purely quantitative level. All emotional relationships between persons rest on their individuality, whereas intellectual relationships deal with persons as with numbers, that is, as with elements which, in themselves, are indifferent, but which are of interest only insofar as they offer something objectively perceivable. It is in this very manner that the inhabitant of the metropolis reckons with his merchant, his customer, and with his servant, and frequently with the persons with whom he is thrown into obligatory association. These relationships stand in distinct contrast with the nature of the smaller circle in which the inevitable knowledge of individual characteristics produces, with an equal inevitability, an emotional tone in conduct, a sphere which is beyond the mere objective weighting of tasks performed and payments made. What is essential here as regards the economic-psychological aspect of the problem is that in less advanced cultures production was for the customer who ordered the product so that the producer and the purchaser knew one another. The modern city, however, is supplied almost exclusively by production for the market, that is, for entirely unknown purchasers who never appear in the actual field of vision of the producers themselves. Thereby, the interests of each party acquire a relentless matter-of-factness, and its rationally calculated economic egoism need not fear any divergence from its set path because of the imponderability of personal relationships. This is all the more the case in the money economy which dominates the metropolis in which the last remnants of domestic production and direct barter of goods have been eradicated and in which the amount of production on direct personal order is reduced daily. Furthermore, this psychological intellectualistic attitude and the money economy are in such close integration that no one is able to say whether it was the former that effected the latter or *vice versa*. What is certain is only that the form of life in the metropolis is the soil which nourishes this interaction most fruitfully, a point which I shall attempt to demonstrate only with the statement of the most outstanding English constitutional historian to the effect that through the entire course of English history London has never acted as the heart of England but often as its intellect and always as its money bag.

In certain apparently insignificant characters or traits of the most external aspects of life are to be found a number of characteristic mental tendencies. The modern mind has become more and more a calculating one. The calculating exactness of practical life which has resulted from a money economy corresponds to the ideal of natural science, namely that of transforming the world into an arithmetical problem and of fixing every one of its parts in a mathematical formula. It has been money economy which has thus filled the daily life of so many people with weighing, calculating, enumerating and the reduction of qualitative values to quantitative terms. Because of the character of calculability which money has there has come into the relationships of the elements of life a precision and a degree of certainty in the definition of the equalities and inequalities and an unambiguousness in agreements and arrangements, just as externally this precision has been brought about through the general diffusion of pocket watches. It is, however, the conditions of the metropolis which are cause as well as effect for this essential characteristic. The relationships and concerns of the typical metropolitan resident are so manifold and complex that, especially as a result of the agglomeration of so many persons with such differentiated interests, their relationships and activities intertwine with one another into a many-membered organism. In view of this fact, the lack of the most exact punctuality in promises and performances would cause the whole to break down into an inextricable chaos. If all the watches in Berlin suddenly went wrong in different ways even only as much as an hour, its entire economic and commercial life would be derailed for some time. Even though this may seem more superficial in its significance, it transpires that the magnitude of distances results in making all waiting and the breaking of appointments an ill-afforded waste of time. For this reason the technique of metropolitan life in general is not conceivable without all of its activities and reciprocal relationships being organized and coordinated in the most punctual way into a firmly fixed framework of time which transcends all subjective elements. But here too there emerge those conclusions which are in general the whole task of this discussion, namely, that every event, however restricted to this superficial level it may appear, comes immediately into contact with the depths of the soul, and that the most banal externalities are, in the last analysis, bound up with the final decisions concerning the meaning and the style of life. Punctuality, calculability, and exactness, which are required by the complications and extensiveness of metropolitan life are not only most intimately connected with its capitalistic and intellectualistic character but also color the content of life and are conducive to the exclusion of those irrational, instinctive, sovereign human traits and impulses which originally seek to determine the form of life from within instead of receiving it from the outside in a general, schematically precise form. Even though those lives which are autonomous and characterised by these vital impulses are not entirely impossible in the city, they are, none the less, opposed to it *in abstracto*. It is in the light of this that we can explain the passionate hatred of personalities like Ruskin and Nietzsche for the metropolis – personalities who found the value of life only in unschematized individual expressions which cannot be reduced to exact equivalents and in whom, on that account, there flowed from the same source as did that hatred, the hatred of the money economy and of the intellectualism of existence.

The same factors which, in the exactness and the minute precision of the form of life, have coalesced into a structure of the highest impersonality, have, on the other hand, an influence in a highly personal direction. There is perhaps no psychic phenomenon which is so unconditionally reserved to the city as the blasé outlook. It is at first the consequence of those rapidly shifting stimulations of the nerves which are thrown together in all their contrasts and from which it seems to us the intensification of metropolitan intellectuality seems to be derived. On that account it is not likely that stupid persons who have been hitherto intellectually dead will be blasé. Just as an immoderately sensuous life makes one blasé because it stimulates the nerves to their utmost reactivity until they finally can no longer produce any reaction at all, so, less harmful stimuli, through the rapidity and the contradictoriness of their shifts, force the nerves to make such violent responses, tear them about so brutally that they exhaust their last reserves of strength and, remaining in the same milieu, do not have time for new reserves to form. This incapacity to react to new stimulations with the required amount of energy constitutes in fact that blasé attitude which every child of a large city evinces when compared with the products of the more peaceful and more stable milieu.

Combined with this physiological source of the blasé metropolitan attitude there is another which derives from a money economy. The essence of the blasé attitude is an indifference toward the distinctions between things. Not in the sense that they are not perceived, as is the case of mental dullness, but rather that the meaning and the value of the distinctions between things, and therewith of the things themselves, are experienced as meaningless. They appear to the blasé person in a homogeneous, flat and gray color with no one of them worthy of being preferred to another. This psychic mood is the correct subjective reflection of a complete money economy to the extent that money takes the place of all the manifoldness of things and expresses all qualitative distinctions between them in the distinction of "how much." To the extent that money, with its colorlessness and its indifferent quality, can become a common denominator of all values it becomes the frightful leveler – it hollows out the core of things, their peculiarities, their specific values and their uniqueness and incomparability in a way which is beyond repair. They all float with the same specific gravity in the constantly moving stream of money. They all rest on the same level and are distinguished only by their amounts. In individual cases this coloring, or rather this de-coloring of things, through their equation with money, may be imperceptibly small. In the relationship, however, which the wealthy person has to objects which can be bought for money, perhaps indeed in the total character which, for this reason, public opinion now recognizes in these objects, it takes on very considerable proportions. This is why the metropolis is the seat of commerce and it is in it that the purchasability of things appears in quite a different aspect than in simpler economies. It is also the peculiar seat of the blasé attitude. In it is brought to a peak, in a certain way, that achievement in the concentration of purchasable things which stimulates the individual to the highest degree of nervous energy. Through the mere quantitative intensification of the same conditions this achievement is transformed into its opposite, into this peculiar adaptive phenomenon – the blasé attitude – in which the nerves reveal their final possibility of adjusting themselves to the content and the form of metropolitan life by renouncing the response to them. We see that the self-preservation of certain types of personalities is obtained at the cost of devaluing the entire objective world, ending inevitably in dragging the personality downward into a feeling of its own valuelessness.

Whereas the subject of this form of existence must come to terms with it for himself, his self-preservation in the face of the great city requires of him a no less negative type of social conduct. The mental attitude of the people of the metropolis to one another may be designated formally as one of reserve. If the unceasing external contact of numbers of persons in the city should be met by the same number of inner reactions as in the small town, in which one knows almost every person he meets and to each of whom he has a positive relationship, one would be completely atomized internally and would fall into an unthinkable mental condition. Partly this psychological circumstance and partly the privilege of suspicion which we have in the face of the elements of metropolitan life (which are constantly touching one another in fleeting contact) necessitates in us that reserve, in consequence of which we do not know by sight neighbors of years standing and which permits us to appear to small-town folk so often as cold and uncongenial. Indeed, if I am not mistaken, the inner side of this external reserve is not only indifference but more frequently than we believe, it is a slight aversion, a mutual strangeness and repulsion which, in a close contact which has arisen any way whatever, can break out into hatred and conflict. The entire inner organization of such a type of extended commercial life rests on an extremely varied structure of sympathies, indifferences and aversions of the briefest as well as of the most enduring sort. This sphere of indifference is, for this reason, not as great as it seems superficially. Our minds respond, with some definite feeling, to almost every impression emanating from another person. The unconsciousness, the transitoriness and the shift of these feelings seem to raise them only into indifference. Actually this latter would be as unnatural to us as immersion into a chaos of unwished-for suggestions would be unbearable. From these two typical dangers of metropolitan life we are saved by antipathy which is the latent adumbration of actual antagonism since it brings about the sort of distanciation and deflection without which this type of life could not be carried on at all. Its extent and its mixture, the rhythm of its emergence and disappearance, the forms in which it is adequate – these constitute, with the simplified motives (in the narrower sense) an inseparable totality of the form of metropolitan life. What appears here directly as dissociation is in reality only one of the elementary forms of socialization.

   This reserve with its overtone of concealed aversion appears once more, however, as the form or the wrappings of a much more general psychic trait of the metropolis. It assures the individual of a type and degree of personal freedom to which there is no analogy in other circumstances. It has its roots in one of the great developmental tendencies of social life as a whole; in one of the few for which an approximately exhaustive formula can be discovered. The most elementary stage of social organization which is to be found historically, as well as in the present, is this: a relatively small circle almost entirely closed against neighboring foreign or otherwise antagonistic groups but which has however within itself such a narrow cohesion that the individual member has only a very slight area for the development of his own qualities and for free activity for which he himself is responsible. Political and familial groups began in this way as do political and religious communities; the self-preservation of very young associations requires a rigorous setting of boundaries and a centripetal unity and for that reason it cannot give room to freedom and the peculiarities of inner and external development of the individual. From this stage social evolution proceeds simultaneously in two divergent but none the less corresponding directions. In the measure that the group grows numerically, spatially, and in the meaningful content of life, its immediate inner unity and the definiteness of its original demarcation against others are weakened and rendered mild by reciprocal interactions and interconnections. And at the same time the individual gains a freedom of movement far beyond the first jealous delimitation, and gains also a peculiarity and individuality to which the division of labor in groups, which have become larger, gives both occasion and necessity. However much the particular conditions and forces of the individual situation might modify the general scheme, the state and Christianity, guilds and political parties and innumerable other groups have developed in accord with this formula. This tendency seems, to me, however to be quite clearly recognizable also in the development of individuality within the framework of city life. Small town life in antiquity as well as in the Middle Ages imposed such limits upon the movements of the individual in his relationships with the outside world and on his inner independence and differentiation that the modern person could not even breathe under such conditions. Even today the city dweller who is placed in a small town feels a type of narrowness which is very similar. The smaller the circle which forms our environment and the more limited the relationships which have the possibility of transcending the boundaries, the more anxiously the narrow community watches over the deeds, the conduct of life and the attitudes of the individual and the more will a quantitative and qualitative individuality tend to pass beyond the boundaries of such a community.

Consider

1. 'The deepest problems of modern life flow from the attempt of the individual to maintain the independence and individuality of his existence against the sovereign powers of society, against the weight of the historical heritage and the external culture and technique of life.' Explain the meaning of Simmel's statement in your own words. Provide relevant contemporary examples to support your arguments.

2. What are, according to Simmel, the typical consequences of urban life for individuals' mental condition and attitude towards others? How do these differ from rural life? Why?

3. What is, according to Simmel, the role which the money economy plays in the nature of modern urban life? Provide contemporary examples to illustrate your arguments.

4. 'There is perhaps no psychic phenomenon which is so unconditionally reserved to the city as the blasé outlook.' Discuss.

5. Simmel wrote about urban life in early twentieth-century Germany. To what extent do his arguments apply to contemporary urban life and to cities in other regions of the world? Discuss this question based on relevant examples.

6. Another interesting aspect of Simmel's work is his enquiry into money. Where did Simmel write about money? Conduct a literature search and obtain some of the relevant sources. What are Simmel's main arguments about the role of money in social life? Try to gain a quick overview of Simmel's ideas and summarise them in your own words.

3.3 The story of sociology

Classical sociology: Why?

We are now in a good position to summarise the findings of this chapter and offer some conclusions about the contemporary significance of classic sociology. We may generally say that the earliest sociologists defined a set of lasting concerns for sociology, which have continued to influence the interests and outlook of their successors. In addition, they established the importance of a distinctively sociological perspective on the world. It is here that the importance of classical sociology lies. It might be possible to study only contemporary sociology's analyses of social life in the present. However, this would prevent you from gaining a thorough understanding of, on the one hand, the origins and connections of the various perspectives and conceptual frameworks contemporary sociology has to offer, as these tend to be deeply rooted in earlier or 'classical' intellectual debates. For example, current discussions about the nature of today's global consumer culture – fast food, credit cards, pop music, movies, etc. – often consist of arguments built upon the works of classical sociologists like Karl Marx, Max Weber or Georg Simmel. If you have not read Marx, Weber or Simmel, you will not be able to fully understand these current discussions, interesting as they may seem. On the other hand, social life in the present has itself been shaped by powerful influences from the past. It is impossible, for example, to quite understand today's expressions of consumerism without an exploration of the origins of capitalism and associated modes of industrial mass production of cheap consumer goods. You might think of it like this: studying sociology without paying attention to history and the classics is like living in a house without a fundament. For a while, you might have a home, but, ultimately, the house will sink into the ground, and you will be lost.

Sociology's central concerns: the explanation of social patterns and social change

So what, then, is sociology all about? To begin with, this chapter suggests that sociology is concerned with the explanation of social patterns and social change. Let's unpick this statement step by step. First of all, sociology offers the insight that social life is somehow patterned or structured. Human life does not consist simply of encounters between individuals, unconstrained by outside concerns. Sociology suggests that there is an array of social forces, above and beyond individuals' direct control, that systematically structure their everyday lives, providing them with a language to speak, culturally specific ways to think and feel, modes of economic activity that allow for their material subsistence, and so forth. We first encountered this idea in the form of Durkheim's concept of social facts, in Chapter 1. In this chapter, we have examined a range of alternative ways of thinking about social structures and patterns. For example, Max Weber's

The Protestant Ethic and the Spirit of Capitalism points us to the role which *culture*, that is to say the meanings and values we attach to certain ways of thinking, feeling, and acting, may play in sustaining certain patterns of life, in Weber's case capitalism. In contrast, Karl Marx was also concerned with explaining capitalism, but took a much greater interest in *economic divisions*, specifically the unequal ownership of the means of production, such as capital, tools, machinery, land, etc. Both Marxist and Weberian sociology have over the years managed to offer differing and complementary narratives of the nature of capitalism and its impact on everyday life.

Second, sociology recognises that the nature of social life is not fixed and unchangeable and offers *explanations of social change*. All the early sociologists whose work we have examined were concerned about the large-scale, unprecedented social changes occurring in their lifetime. Dissatisfied with the explanations offered by religion and philosophy, they sought to construct new ways of making sense of change, sometimes as a primarily intellectual exercise, and sometimes as a base for political activism, as in the case of Karl Marx.

Sociology's central concerns: the story of modernity

The topic of social change merits further attention. It would be insufficiently precise to say that the early sociologists simply assembled various perspectives on the nature of social change. To be specific, we might say that they were interested in the *origins and dynamics of modernity*. The concept of modernity is foundational to sociology (and will be dealt with in detail in later chapters). A preliminary definition is in order here, though. It is useful to approach the sociological meaning of modernity through the colloquial meaning of the term. In our everyday imagination, 'modernity' is above all associated with things that are 'modern': airports, smart phones, laptop computers, science fiction films, electric lighting and skyscrapers are all easily labelled 'modern'. In contrast, horse-drawn coaches, ancient temples, candlelight, handwritten books, and the Epic of Gilgamesh are not things we are likely to consider modern: they are old, or at least they are old-fashioned and traditional. Among Christians, religious marriage in church is a traditional way of legitimising a long-term intimate relationship. However, Christian religious marriage has come to matter less and less in modern societies: civil marriage by a government official constitutes a widely chosen alternative, more and more people choose not to marry at all, and the number of practising Christians has declined greatly in many parts of the world.

Modernity, in this sense, marks objects and ways of life that are somehow current, up-to-date, or also fashionable – things that do not belong to *tradition*. The story of modernity was introduced by sociologists and other intellectuals and artists to explain the massive transformation of Western European societies in the eighteenth and nineteenth centuries and in the run-up to this historical period. 'Modernity' is an answer to the question of how to describe the emergent societies that differed vastly from the agricultural, feudal, religiously dominated way of life that had prevailed in Europe for centuries. 'Modernity' was originally meant to describe the historical break with traditional ways of life that occurred in Western Europe in the lifetime of the early sociologists and is said to have gradually spread around the world since then.

The works of classical sociology discussed in this chapter can all be read as stories of modernity. They are all concerned with explaining institutions and social-structural arrangements fundamental to the rise of modernity in the Western world, as well as with accounting for the consequences of modernity for the nature of social life. Marx and Weber, for instance, examine from different perspectives the rise of capitalism in the West and the social inequalities and hierarchies of power and authority capitalism entails. Durkheim's sociology foregrounds the potential for anomie which modern societies entail through the loss of traditional forms of social solidarity. Simmel trains his eye on the social-psychological consequences – the much-cited blasé outlook – which life in a modern city entails. Du Bois in turn concerns himself with the underpinnings of modernity in the African slave trade and the brutal exploitation of slaves and their descendants in the USA. Sociology therefore began as the story of the rise of modernity in the West.

Sociology's Eurocentrism

Or so the story goes. As has already been suggested, there are important problems with established narratives of sociology's origins. This is a point that bears further consideration. Pervasive Eurocentric narratives of sociology's history are precise in a very narrow sense, in so far as many early sociologists indeed set themselves the task of explaining the emergence of a unique – modern, capitalistic, and so forth – way of life in the West. For instance, while Max Weber's works examined a wide variety of societies and world religions, his global concerns ultimately were meant to serve as a platform for a comprehensive explanation of the rise of capitalism in the West (and nowhere else). In part, this approach allowed for a justification of the establishment of sociology as an independent academic discipline different from anthropology, whose self-declared task was the study of the conquered subjects in the colonial empires many Western nations were building around the world.

However, manifold problems do arise from an association of sociology with modernity of the form pursued above. First, as was argued earlier, it would be inaccurate to attribute the rise of modernity to unique and self-enclosed developments in Western Europe and, later, North America. The story that modernity began in certain Western countries, due to unique local developmental conditions, and emanated from there to the rest of the world, is fundamentally misleading. Second, the scholars discussed above were indeed among the first to establish a discipline by the name of sociology at Western universities. However, the forms of thought and intellectual enquiry we would today label as 'sociological' are not, and never have been, unique to the West. These problems are obscured in established accounts of sociology's history, as found in many older introductory textbooks you may read. Recently, however, sociologists around the world have begun to unravel and rework the story of their discipline. The work of Raewyn Connell has been crucial to these efforts. To conclude this chapter, we will examine an extract from her recent book *Southern Theory* (2007).

Reading

Connell, R. (2007), *Southern Theory*, Cambridge: Polity, pp. 4–9

Origin stories

Open any introductory sociology textbook and you will probably find, in the first few pages, a discussion of founding fathers focused on Marx, Durkheim and Weber. The first chapter may also cite Comte, Spencer, Tönnies and Simmel, and perhaps a few others. In the view normally presented to students, these men created sociology in response to dramatic changes in European society: the Industrial Revolution, class conflict, secularisation, alienation and the modern state. This curriculum is backed by histories such as Alan Swingewood's (2000) *Short History of Sociological Thought*. This well-regarded British text presents a two-part narrative of 'Foundations: Classical Sociology' (centring on Durkheim, Weber and Marx), and 'Modern Sociology', tied together by the belief that 'Marx, Weber and Durkheim have remained at the core of modern sociology' (2000: x). Sociologists take this account of their origins seriously. Twenty years ago, a star-studded review of *Social Theory Today* began with a ringing declaration of 'the centrality of the classics' (Alexander 1987). In the new century, commentary on classical texts remains a significant genre of theoretical writing (Baehr 2002).

The idea of classical theory embodies a canon, in the sense of literary theory: a privileged set of texts, whose interpretation and reinterpretation defines a field (Seidman 1994). This particular canon embeds an internalist doctrine of sociology's history as a social science. The story consists of a foundational moment arising from the internal transformation of European society; classic discipline-defining texts written by a small group of brilliant authors; and a direct line of descent from them to us.

But sociologists in the classical period itself did not have this origin story. When Franklin Giddings (1896), the first professor of sociology at Columbia University, published *The Principles of Sociology*, he named as the founding father – Adam Smith. Victor Branford (1904), expounding 'the founders of sociology' to a meeting in London, named as the central figure – Condorcet.

Turn-of-the-century sociology had no list of classic texts in the modern sense. Writers expounding the new science would commonly refer to Comte as the inventor of the term, to Darwin as the key figure in the theory of evolution, and then to any of a wide range of figures in the landscape of evolutionary speculation. Witness the account of the discipline in the second edition of *Dynamic Sociology* (1897) by Lester Ward, later the founding president of the American Sociological Society. At the time of the first edition in 1883, Ward observed, the term 'sociology' had not been in popular use. However, in the intervening decade a series of brilliant scientific contributions had established sociology as a popular concept. There were now research journals, university courses, societies; and sociology 'bids fair to become the leading science of the twentieth century, as biology has been that of the nineteenth'. Ward listed 37 notable contributors to the new science. The list included Durkheim and Tönnies, but not Marx or Weber.

The list of notables became a common feature in the textbooks of sociology that multiplied in the United States from the 1890s, Giddings' *Principles* being one of the first. (Ward had included Giddings in his list, and Giddings politely included Ward in his.) The famous 'Green Bible' of the Chicago School, Park and Burgess's (1924) *Introduction to the Science of Sociology*, listed 23 'representative works in systematic sociology'. Simmel and Durkheim were among them, but not Marx, Weber or Pareto. Only one work by Weber was mentioned in this thousand-page volume, and then only in the notes.

As late as the 1920s, then, there was no sense that certain texts were discipline-defining classics demanding special study. Rather, there was a sense of a broad, almost impersonal advance of scientific knowledge, the notables being simply leading members of the pioneering crew. Sociologists accepted the view, articulated early in the history of the discipline by Charles Letourneau (1881: vi), who was to hold the first chair of sociology in the world, that: 'The commencement of any science, however simple, is always a collective work. It requires the constant labour of many patient workmen . . . '

We therefore have strong reasons to doubt the conventional picture of the creation of sociology. This is not just to question the influence of certain individuals. We must examine the history of sociology as a collective product – the shared concerns, assumptions and practices making up the discipline at various times, and the shape given that history by the changing social forces that constructed the new science.

Global difference and empire

Sociology as a teaching discipline and a public discourse was constructed during the final two decades of the nineteenth century and the first decade of the twentieth in the great cities and university towns of France, the United States, Britain, Germany and, a little later, Russia. The internalist foundation story interprets these places as the site of a process of modernisation, or capitalist industrialisation, with sociology seen as an attempt to interpret what was emerging here. 'It was above all a science of the new industrial society' (Bottomore 1987: 7).

The main difficulty with this view is that it does not square with the most relevant evidence – what sociologists at the time were writing. Most general textbooks of sociology, up to World War I, did not have a great deal to say about the modernisation of the society in which the authors lived. Giddings' *Readings in Descriptive and Historical Sociology* (1906), typical in this respect, ranged from polyandry in Ceylon via matrilineal survivals among the Tartars to the mining camps of California. It was so little focused on modernity that it took as its reading on 'sovereignty' a medieval rendering of the legend of King Arthur.

What is in college textbooks need not correspond to the research focus of sociology, but on this too we have abundant evidence. Between 1898 and 1913,

Émile Durkheim and his hard-working collaborators produced twelve issues of *L'année sociologique*, an extraordinarily detailed international survey of each year's publications in, or relevant to, sociology. In these twelve issues, nearly 2400 reviews were published. (I have counted only the reviews in large type, whatever their length, not the brief notices in small type in the early issues, nor the listings of titles without reviews.) The reviews concerning Western/Northern Europe and modern North America increase with time: they average 24 per cent of all reviews in the first six issues, 28 per cent in the next five issues, and 32 per cent in the bumper issue of the year before the war.

Modern industrial society was certainly included: the journal published reviews about the American worker, the European middle class, technology in German industries, books by the Webbs and by Sombart, Booth on London poverty, even a work by Ramsay MacDonald, later Labour prime minister of Britain. But works focused on the recent or contemporary societies of Europe and North America made up only a fraction of the content of *L'année sociologique*: about 28 per cent of all reviews. Even fewer were focused on 'the new industrial society', since the reviews on Europe included treatises on peasant folk-tales, witchcraft in Scotland, crime in Asturias and the measurements of skulls.

Twice as many of the reviews concerned ancient and medieval societies, colonial or remote societies, or global surveys of human history. Studies of holy war in ancient Israel, Malay magic, Buddhist India, technical points of Roman law, medieval vengeance, Aboriginal kinship in central Australia and the legal systems of primitive societies were more characteristic of sociology as seen in *L'année sociologique* than studies of new technology or bureaucracy.

The enormous spectrum of human history that the sociologists took as their domain was organised by a central idea: difference between the civilisation of the metropole and other cultures whose main feature was their primitiveness. I will call this the idea of global difference. Presented in many different forms, this contrast pervades the sociology of the late nineteenth and early twentieth centuries.

The idea of global difference was often conveyed by a discussion of 'origins'. In this genre of writing, sociologists would posit an original state of society, then speculate on the process of evolution that must have led from then to now. The bulk of the three volumes of Herbert Spencer's *Principles of Sociology*, first issued in the 1870s, told such a story for every type of institution that Spencer could think of: domestic institutions, political institutions, ecclesiastical institutions, and so on. Spencer acted as if the proof of social evolution were not complete without an evolutionary narrative, from origins to the contemporary form, for each and every case.

The formula of development from a primitive origin to an advanced form was widespread in Victorian thought (Burrow 1966). Sociologists simply applied a logic that their audience would find familiar. The same architecture is found in works as well known as Durkheim's *Division of Labour in Society* (1893) and as obscure as Fairbanks' *Introduction to Sociology* (1896).

In none of these works was the idea of an origin taken as a concrete historical question. It could have been, because historians' knowledge of early societies was growing dramatically in these decades. Troy, Mycenae and Knossos were excavated by Schliemann and Evans. Flinders Petrie systematised the archaeology of Egypt, and the first evidence of Sumerian culture was uncovered at Lagash and Nippur (Stiebing 1993). But sociologists were not interested in where and when a particular originating event occurred, nor were they concerned about when the major changes actually happened. Time functioned in sociological thought mainly as a sign of global difference.

Durkheim did not have to find a precise time in the past for 'segmentary societies'; they existed in his own day. Durkheim used the example of the Kabyle of Algeria as well as the ancient Hebrews, and made no conceptual distinction between the two. He knew about the Hebrews because the ancient texts were in his library. How did he know about Kabylia? Because the French had conquered Algeria earlier in the century, and at the time Durkheim wrote, French colonists were evicting the local population from the best land (Bennoune 1988). Given the recent history of conquest, peasant rebellion and debate over colonisation, no French intellectual could fail to know something about the Kabyle. Indeed, the social life of France's North African subjects was being documented in great detail by a series of private and official enquiries (Burke 1980).

Algeria was not an isolated case. In the dozen years before *Division of Labour* was published, the armies of the French republic had moved out from Algeria to conquer Tunisia; had fought a war in Indo-China, conquered Annam and Tonkin (modern Vietnam) and seized control of Laos and Cambodia; and had established a protectorate over Madagascar. Under the Berlin Treaty of 1885, French trading posts in Central and Western Africa became the basis of a whole new empire. While Durkheim was writing and publishing the *Division of Labor* and the *Rules of Sociological Method* (1895), French colonial armies were engaged in a spectacular series of campaigns against the Muslim regimes of inland North and West Africa which produced vast conquests from the Atlantic almost to the Nile.

All this was part of a larger process. The British empire, also a maritime empire with a pre-industrial history, similarly gained a new dynamism and grew to a vast size in the nineteenth century (Cain and Hopkins 1993). The thirteen-colony United States became one of the most dynamic imperial powers of the nineteenth century, with about 80 years of overland conquest and settlement (the 'westward expansion'), followed by a shorter period of overseas conquest. The Tsarist overland conquests, begun in earlier centuries, were extended to North-east and Central Asia. In the later part of the nineteenth century, they were consolidated by Russian settlement. Prussia's expansion as an imperial power began with conquest within Europe – in the process, setting up a relationship between dominant and conquered races in the East which became the subject of young Max Weber's (1894) first sociological research. German overseas colonies in Africa and the Pacific followed the formation of the Reich in 1871. By the time the system of rival empires reached its crisis in the Great War of 1914–18, the expansion of Western power to a global scale had reached its climax.

In this light, the making of sociology takes on a new significance. The places where the discipline was created were the urban and cultural centres of the major imperial powers at the high tide of modern imperialism. They were the 'metropole', in the useful French term, to the larger colonial world. The intellectuals who created sociology were very much aware of this.

Since Kiernan's (1969) remarkable survey *The Lords of Human Kind*, historians have begun to grasp the immense impact that the global expansion of North Atlantic power had on popular culture (MacDonald 1994) and intellectual life (Said 1993) in the metropole, as well as in the colonies. It would be astonishing if the new science of society had escaped the impact of the greatest social change in the world at the time. In fact, the relationship was intimate. Sociology was formed within the culture of imperialism, and embodied an intellectual response to the colonised world. This fact is crucial in understanding the content and method of sociology, as well as the discipline's wider cultural significance.

Consider

1. How does Connell define 'Southern Theory' in the preceding reading? Explain her arguments in her own words.
2. What does Connell understand by the 'idea of global difference'? How did this idea inform the work of the early sociologists? Do you agree with this idea? Why (not)?
3. Sociology is the story of modernity. Critically assess this statement in reference to Connell's arguments in the preceding reading.
4. How, if at all, does the preceding reading suggest possibilities for sociology as a truly global intellectual project? What might the nature of such a project be?

The debate: The gender of classical sociology

This chapter has discussed the work of nine sociologists (see Photo 3.1). All of them had a lasting impact upon the discipline in its early stages. With, perhaps, the exception of Auguste Comte and Herbert Spencer, all of them influence the thinking of contemporary sociologists in significant ways. All of them were men.

One reason for this lies in the marginalisation of women in the public life of the nations in which sociology first emerged. Female scholars, writers and activists did play a significant role in public life in the eighteenth, nineteenth, and early twentieth centuries. However, they did so in spite of substantial resistance, their contributions often being viewed as undesirable, unnecessary and unwanted. Western societies around the time of sociology's creation were by and large characterised by men's *patriarchal domination* over women (an issue we further explore in Chapter 6). For instance, the emergence of sociology coincides with a movement

Photo 3.1   Some early sociologists. From top left to bottom right: Auguste
Comte, Herbert Spencer, Karl Marx, Émile Durkheim, Max Weber,
Georg Simmel, Ferdinand Tönnies, George Herbert Mead, W. E. B.
Du Bois.

Sources: from top left to bottom right © Mary Evans Picture Library/Alamy; © SOTK2011/Alamy; © Pictorial Press Ltd/
Alamy; © The Art Gallery Collection/Alamy; © INTERFOTO/Alamy; © INTERFOTO/Alamy; © Mary Evans Picture Library/
Alamy; The Granger Collection, New York; © GL Archive/Alamy

that is today labelled as 'first-wave feminism'. First-wave feminism was concerned
with women's struggle for basic rights to participation in public life in countries
such as the UK and the USA, most notably through the right to vote. Women's
activism for basic equality in civic life, from political lobbying to pickets, demon-
strations and hunger strikes, met with much resistance, and activists often faced
reprisals and legal sanctions for their protest.

It is not surprising, then, that female scholars' access to academic positions and
events was relatively limited. As sociology emerged at and through universities, they
were severely disadvantaged, and it was difficult for their ideas to gain wide currency
and make an immediate impact upon the new discipline. For example, Max Weber
held several prestigious professorships and his views were immediately influential

among the academics of his time. He even made a number of noted interventions in the politics of imperial Germany. Weber's wife, Marianne Weber, was highly erudite and active as a scholar. However, while a number of her works were published in her lifetime, they did not attract the same attention as her husband's writings.

Moreover, universities, including sociology departments, remained largely closed to female scholars until roundabout the 1970s. This facilitated the formation of a canon of widely recognised scholarship around groups of male sociologists, while the interventions of early female sociologists still remained underappreciated. Georg Simmel, for instance, struggled to gain recognition for his work during his lifetime. Some of his works were well received, but he only gained a tenured position at a university very late in his life. In the years after his death, interest in Simmel grew steadily, and he is now recognised as one of early sociology's founders or key figures. Such recognition has not been given to early female sociologists to the same extent. Recent textbooks and writings on early sociologists have begun to identify a number of female scholars deserving of greater attention. However, they are not often and not to the same degree written about or discussed in sociology courses.

There is thus a wealth of underappreciated sociological knowledge for you to discover. This project will ask you to pick a small number of early female sociologists and look into their work and the social context in which they produced it. Let's begin with a list of names:

1. Mary Wollstonecraft
2. Marianne Weber
3. Harriet Martineau
4. Jane Addams
5. Any other early female sociologist.

Now choose two names on this list and explore the following questions.

1. What are the main areas of enquiry of your chosen thinkers? What are their main works? What are the most notable concepts or ideas they developed?
2. How might their work have been shaped by the social conditions of their lifetime?
3. Which contemporary sociologists have developed their ideas further? How?

To begin with, there are a few texts that summarise the work of early female sociologists. You might take a look at these:

Madoo Lengermann, Patricia and Niebrugge, Gillian (2008), 'Early Women Sociologists and Classical Sociological Theory: 1830–1930', in Ritzer, George, *Classical Sociological Theory*, New York, McGraw-Hill, pp. 299–330.

Madoo Lengermann, Patricia and Niebrugge, Gillian (2007) *The Women Founders: Sociology and Social Theory 1830–1930*, Long Grove, Waveland Press.

Both texts focus on Anglophone and US sociology, and it will be important for you to explore other settings, too. (Can you think of any ways to do so?)

Nevertheless, these are worthwhile sources to start with. Both books contain bibliographies in which you can look for further readings. Likewise, internet searches on websites such as google.com (general search engine), scholar.google.com (like Google, but for academic sources only), or INTUTE will allow you to quickly find a lot of information. The website of your university library may be another useful starting point, and if there is a subject librarian for sociology or the social sciences, it might be good to talk to her or him.

Works cited

Bhambra, Gurminder (2008), *Rethinking Modernity: Postcolonialism and the Sociological Imagination*, London: Palgrave Macmillan.

Comte, Auguste (1830–42/1974), *The Essential Comte, Selected from Cours de Philosophie Positive*, edited by S. Andreski, London: Croom Helm.

Connell, Raewyn (2007), *Southern Theory: The global dynamics of knowledge in social science*, Cambridge: Polity Press.

Du Bois, W.E.B. (1897/2007), *The Conservation of Races and the Negro*, Hazelton: Pennsylvania State University.

Du Bois, W.E.B. (1899), *The Philadelphia Negro: A Social Study*, Boston: Ginn & Co.

Du Bois, W.E.B. (1903), *The Negro Church*, Atlanta: The Atlanta University Press.

Du Bois, W.E.B. (1903/2009), *The Souls of Black Folk*, EconArch Institute.

Durkheim, Émile (1895/1982), *The Rules of Sociological Method*, London: Macmillan

Durkheim, Émile (1897/2004), *Suicide: A Study in Sociology*, London: Routledge and Kegan Paul.

Durkheim, Émile (1984), *The Division of Labour in Society*, Basingstoke: Macmillan.

Marx, Karl, and Friedrich Engels (1848/1983), *Manifesto of the Communist Party*, in *The Portable Karl Marx*, edited by E. Kamenka, New York: Penguin Books.

Mead, George Herbert (1934/1967), *Mind, Self and Society from the Standpoint of a Social Behaviorist*, Chicago: The University of Chicago Press.

Mills, C. Wright (1959/1967), *The Sociological Imagination*, London: Oxford University Press.

Simmel, Georg (1900/2011), *The Philosophy of Money*, London: Routledge.

Spencer, Herbert (1874–1896/1969), *Principles of Sociology*, edited by S. Andreski, London: Macmillan.

Tönnies, Ferdinand (1887/1957), *Community and Civil Society*, East Lansing: Michigan University Press.

Tönnies, Ferdinand (1935/1998), 'Das Geist der Neuzeit', in Clausen, Lars (ed.), *Ferdinand Tönnies Gesamtausgabe*, Vol. 22, Berlin: Walter de Gruyter, pp. 1–226.

Weber, Max (1905/2009), *The Protestant Ethic and the Spirit of Capitalism, with Other Writings on the Rise of the West*, New York: Oxford University Press.

Weber, Max (1956/1978), *Economy and Society: An Outline of Interpretive Sociology*, edited by Guenther Rot and Claus Wititch, Berkeley: University of California Press.

4 Individual and social process

4.1 Continuing sociology's story

In this chapter, we move into the terrain of contemporary sociology. The previous chapters introduced you to sociology's origins. In particular, they explored how the discipline emerged from concerns with the nature of modernity and related social processes, such as capitalism, modern urban life, or anomie and the problem of social cohesion in highly differentiated societies. Here, we build on this introduction and explain how sociology's narrative of modernity has involved since the time of the 'classics'. Moreover, we look at a range of social processes in the modern world that have become distinctive focal points of sociological enquiry.

We approach these issues from two perspectives: macrosociology and microsociology. *Macrosociology* is concerned with the analysis of social processes on a large scale, typically looking at societies and social groups as a whole in order to identify significant social patterns and trends. In other words, macrosociology tends to concentrate on the workings of *social structures*: durable patterns of social life that shape and constrain what individuals can and cannot achieve in their everyday lives. Instances of such social structures would be social class, which to a large extent determines individuals' socio-economic position, and language, which shapes the ways in which we can communicate with others.

A prime example of sociological research with such a focus would be the work of Émile Durkheim. Looking at suicide as a social problem, Durkheim was not concerned very much with the subjective experiences of particular distressed people who had attempted to take their lives. Instead, Durkheim sought to explain suicide as a social-structural problem: based on suicide statistics, he considered the distribution and variations of suicide rates in society at large. He then sought to link these variations to large-scale structural issues, arguing, for example, that suicide rates are lower in Catholic than in Protestant countries due to the greater social controls offered by Catholicism.

Microsociology, in contrast, focuses on small-scale social interaction and the ways in which social encounters in everyday life are shaped by the motivations, interests, beliefs and values which individuals bring to them. As such, microsociology highlights individuals' *agency*, that is to say our capacity to creatively mould and shape our lives and those of others through the various ways in which we engage with them in daily life. At the same time, microsociological research also can paint powerful portraits of the ways in which large social structures and forces may affect the lives of individuals and communities.

Among the studies we already encountered in previous chapters, the ethnographic research of Elijah Anderson (1999) is a seminal illustration of both aspects of microsociology. On the one hand, Anderson convincingly demonstrates how the abandonment of inner-city Philadelphia and the comprehensive lack of employment and education opportunities leave the area's residents in a situation with very few, if any, life choices. Anderson's arguments here are indicative of large-scale structural developments in many American cities over the past decades. On the other hand, his explanation of the high levels of violence in the neighbourhood he studied emphasises individual agency and the choices which young people and their families make about street culture as a means to economic survival and self-respect. While Anderson portrays his participants as victims of economic and political processes beyond their control, he nevertheless stresses the importance of the personal choices they make as to their involvement in the violence of the 'code of the street'.

This chapter introduces you to an array of important conceptual tools and perspectives which sociologists have developed for the study of social structures, agency, and the interplay between the two. At the level of macrosociology, we focus on two central issues of sociological enquiry, namely the nature of modern society and problems of social cohesion. Our exploration of microsociology touches upon a range of issues that shape individual experiences of everyday life, from emotions to the social nature of the self. Working your way through this chapter, you will acquire a basic understanding of some major lines of sociological enquiry. In this sense, the stage is also set for our analysis of contemporary forms of social change, social inequalities and globalisation in Chapters 5 and 6. Our discussion remains unavoidably short, given the breadth of the material to be covered. However, you might use it as a compendium that offers you a general overview of the breadth of contemporary sociological thinking, following up on particular points of interest through the guide to further reading at the chapter's end.

4.2 What is modernity?

To begin with, it is important to revisit and clarify the meaning of 'modernity', perhaps one of sociology's most central and lasting concerns. In earlier chapters, we saw that sociology emerged in the context of monumental social, cultural, economic and political transformations starting in the eighteenth century and has sought to make sense of these changes. Since then, modernity has remained a central object of sociological interest. But what exactly is modernity, and how does it shape life in the contemporary world?

The complexity of this question becomes immediately clear if you consider the broad range of things, ideas, practices and ways of life that seem 'modern' in your imagination. Smartphones are quintessentially modern, representing latest developments in communication technology. Facebook and other online social networks are definitely modern, having totally reshaped in just a few years the ways in which particularly young people communicate and interact with each other. Skyscrapers are modern, as they stand for recent achievements in architecture as well as the urbane way of life that is commonly associated with ideas of being modern. And so forth – an infinite list of examples immediately comes to mind.

There is no one generally accepted sociological definition – respective debates that began more than 200 years ago are still very much in progress. There are, however, some basic assumptions on which there is a consensus, and we can use these to make sense of the concept here. Katie Willis neatly summarises these as follows:

> 'modernity' has been used as a term to describe particular forms of economy and society based on the experiences of Western Europe. In economic terms, 'modernity' encompasses industrialization, urbanization and the increased use of technology within all sectors of the economy. This application of technology and scientific principles is also reflected within social and cultural spheres. What has been termed the 'Enlightenment' period in Western Europe in the late seventeenth and eighteenth centuries, involved the growing importance of rational and scientific approaches to understanding the world and progress. This was contrasted with previous understandings that were often rooted in religious explanations. [. . .] People defining development as 'modernity', look at development largely in economic terms. (Willis 2005: 2f.)

In this sense, we may say that modernity refers to:

1. A set of distinctive forms of social, economic, cultural and political organisations and institutions. (Examples: capitalism in its various forms; the practice of science and attendant institutions, such as universities; standardised 'Fordist' industrial mass production; forms of social inequality and exploitation based on class, race, and colonialism.)
2. Underlying systems of norms, values, and beliefs. (Examples: rational-scientific thought; laws held to be universal and applicable to all human beings, such as human rights.)
3. Modes of everyday life that have emerged from and are sustained by these forms of social organisation and norms, values, and beliefs. (Example: consumerism, based on the mass production of cheap, standardised goods.)

However, all this should not be taken to suggest that modernity refers to an essentially European or Western form of life. Early sociologists were primarily concerned with Western experiences of modernity. Yet, as we have seen in Chapter 3, the beginning of modernity in Europe and changes such as industrialisation or the Enlightenment were firmly bound up with developments elsewhere (Bhambra 2008). To give just one example, the growing wealth of many European countries since the sixteenth century that eventually facilitated industrialisation was grounded in the systematic colonial exploitation of the Americas (Lee 2011). In addition, through centuries of global trade and the advent of means of fast travel and communication, the things and ideas we identify as modern have become a truly global phenomenon. The iPhones that are ubiquitous on London's streets are manufactured in Shenzhen in southern China. Skyscrapers dominate the faces of cities like Hong Kong and Mexico City as much as those of Frankfurt and New York. While Facebook has hundreds of millions of users around the world, the Chinese social networking software QQ has almost as many.

The recognition of the diverse, global nature of modernity has led many scholars in recent years to write of 'multiple modernities'. While skyscrapers, iPhones and Facebook characterise the lives of many in global cities around the world, these lives have nonetheless not become uniform and indistinct. The things and ideas that we identify as 'modern' can be taken in many different ways and combined with the manifold traditional ways of life that have shaped human history around the world. Online social networking may be just as popular in the USA as it is in China, but the ways in which young people talk to each other online are nevertheless still shaped by local customs and conventions. Singapore is a typically modern, highly urbanised and technologically developed country, and its political and legal institutions are simultaneously rooted in its English colonial past and local forms of politics. McDonald's serves fast food on every continent, but its menu in India differs notably from that in Japan, according to local tastes and customs. This idea of multiple modernities is explored in detail by Israeli sociologist Shmuel Eisenstadt.

Reading

Eisenstadt, S. (2002), 'Multiple Modernities', in Eisenstadt, S. (ed.) *Multiple Modernities*, New Brunswick: Transaction Publishers, pp. 1–8

Multiple Modernities

I

The notion of "multiple modernities" denotes a certain view of the contemporary world – indeed of the history and characteristics of the modern era – that goes against the views long prevalent in scholarly and general discourse. It goes against the view of the "classical" theories of modernization and of the convergence of industrial societies prevalent in the 1950s, and indeed against the classical socio-logical analyses of Marx, Durkheim, and (to a large extent) even of Weber, at least in one reading of his work. They all assumed, even if only implicitly, that the cultural program of modernity as it developed in modern Europe and the basic institutional constellations that emerged there would ultimately take over in all modernizing and modern societies; with the expansion of modernity, they would prevail throughout the world.

The reality that emerged after the so-called beginnings of modernity, and especially after World War II, failed to bear out these assumptions. The actual developments in modernizing societies have refuted the homogenizing and hegemonic assumptions of this Western program of modernity. While a general trend toward structural differentiation developed across a wide range of institutions in most of these societies – in family life, economic and political structures, urbanization, modern education, mass communication, and individualistic orientations – the ways in which these arenas were defined and organized varied greatly, in different periods of their development, giving rise to multiple institutional and ideological patterns. Significantly, these patterns did not constitute simple continuations in the modern era of the traditions of their respective societies. Such patterns were distinctively modern, though greatly influenced by specific cultural premises, traditions, and historical experiences. All developed distinctly modern dynamics and modes of interpretation, for which the original Western project constituted the crucial (and usually ambivalent) reference point. Many of the movements that development in non-Western societies articulated strong anti-Western or even antimodern themes, yet all were distinctively modern. This was true not only of the various nationalist and traditionalist movements that emerged in these societies from about the middle of the nineteenth century until after World War II, but also, as we shall note, of the more contemporary fundamentalist ones.

The idea of multiple modernities presumes that the best way to understand the contemporary world – indeed to explain the history of modernity – is to see it as a story of continual constitution and reconstitution of a multiplicity of cultural programs. These ongoing reconstructions of multiple institutional and ideological patterns are carried forward by specific social actors in close connection with social, political, and intellectual activists, and also by social movements pursuing different programs of modernity, holding very different views on what makes societies modern. Through the engagement of these actors with broader sectors of their respective societies, unique expressions of modernity are realized. These activities have not been confined to any single society or state, though certain societies and states proved to be the major arenas where social activists were able to implement their programs and pursue their goals. Though distinct understandings of multiple modernity developed within different nation-states, and within different ethnic and cultural groupings, among communist, fascist, and fundamentalist movements, each, however different from the others, was in many respects international.

One of the most important implications of the term "multiple modernities" is that modernity and Westernization are not identical; Western patterns of modernity are not the only "authentic" modernities, though they enjoy historical precedence and continue to be a basic reference point for others.

In acknowledging a multiplicity of continually evolving modernities, one confronts the problem of just what constitutes the common core of modernity. This problem is exacerbated and indeed transformed with the contemporary deconstruction or decomposition of many of the components of "classical" models of the nation and of revolutionary states, particularly as a consequence of globalization. Contemporary discourse has raised the possibility that the modern project, at least in terms of the classical formulation that held sway for the last two centuries, is exhausted. One contemporary view claims that such exhaustion is manifest in the "end of history." The other view best represented is Huntington's notion of a "clash of civilizations," in which Western civilization – the seeming epitome of modernity – is confronted by a world in which traditional, fundamentalist, antimodern, and anti-Western civilizations – some (most notably, the Islamic and so-called Confucian groupings) viewing the West with animus or disdain – are predominant.

II

The cultural and political program of modernity, as it developed first in Western and Central Europe, entailed, as Björn Wittrock notes, distinct ideological as well as institutional premises. The cultural program of modernity entailed some very distinct shifts in the conception of human agency, and of its place in the flow of time. It carried a conception of the future characterized by a number of possibilities realizable through autonomous human agency. The premises on which the social, ontological, and political order were based, and the legitimation of that order, were no longer taken for granted. An intensive reflexivity developed around the basic ontological premises of structures of social and political authority – a reflexivity shared even by modernity's most radical critics, who in principle denied its validity. It was most successfully formulated by Weber. To follow James D. Faubian's exposition of Weber's conception of modernity:

> Weber finds the existential threshold of modernity in a certain deconstruction: of what he speaks of as the "ethical postulate that the world is a God-ordained, and hence somehow meaningfully and ethically oriented cosmos. . . . "

> . . . What Weber asserts – what in any event might be extrapolated from his assertions – is that the threshold of modernity may be marked precisely at the moment when the unquestioned legitimacy of a divinely preordained social order began its decline. Modernity emerges – or, more accurately, a range of possible modernities emerge – only when what had been seen as an unchanging cosmos ceases to be taken for granted. Countermoderns reject that reproach, believing that what is unchanging is not the social order, but the tasks that the construction and functioning of any social order must address. . . .

> . . . One can extract two theses: Whatever else they may be, modernities in all their variety are responses to the same existential problematic. The second:

whatever else they may be, modernities in all their variety are precisely those responses that leave the problematic in question intact, that formulate visions of life and practice neither beyond nor in denial of it but rather within it, even in deference to it. . . .

The degree of reflexivity characteristic of modernity went beyond what was crystallized in the axial civilizations. The reflexivity that developed in the modern program not only focused on the possibility of different interpretations of core transcendental visions and basic ontological conceptions prevalent in a particular society or civilization; it came to question the very givenness of such visions and the institutional patterns related to them. It gave rise to an awareness of the possibility of multiple visions that could, in fact, be contested.

Such awareness was closely connected with two central components of the modern project emphasized in early studies of modernization by both Daniel Lerner and Alex Inkeles. The first recognized among those either modern or becoming "modernized" the awareness of a great variety of roles existing beyond narrow, fixed, local, and familial ones. The second recognized the possibility of belonging to wider translocal, possibly changing, communities.

Central to this cultural program was an emphasis on the autonomy of man: his or her (in its initial formulation, certainly "his") emancipation from the fetters of traditional political and cultural authority. In the continuous expansion of the realm of personal and institutional freedom and activity, such autonomy implied, first, reflexivity and exploration; second, active construction and mastery of nature, including human nature. This project of modernity entailed a very strong emphasis on the autonomous participation of members of society in the constitution of the social and political order, on the autonomous access of all members of the society to these orders and to their centers.

From the conjunctions of these different conceptions arose a belief in the possibility that society could be actively formed by conscious human activity. Two complementary but potentially contradictory tendencies developed within this program about the best ways in which social construction could take place. The first, crystallized above all in the Great Revolutions, gave rise, perhaps for the first time in history, to the belief in the possibility of bridging the gap between the transcendental and mundane orders – of realizing through conscious human agency, exercised in social life, major utopian and eschatological visions. The second emphasized a growing recognition of the legitimacy of multiple individual and group goals and interests, as a consequence allowed for multiple interpretations of the common good.

III

The modern program entailed also a radical transformation of the conceptions and premises of the political order, the constitution of the political arena, and the characteristics of the political process. Central to the modern idea was the breakdown of all traditional legitimations of the political order, and with it the opening up of different possibilities in the construction of a new order. These possibilities combined themes of rebellion, protest, and intellectual antinomianism, allowing for new center-formation and institution-building, giving rise to movements of protest as a continual component of the political process.

These ideas, closely aligned with what were emerging as the defining characteristics of the modern political arena, emphasized the openness of this arena and of political processes, generally, together with a strong acceptance of active participation by the periphery of "society" in questions of political import. Strong tendencies toward the permeation of social peripheries by the centers, and the impingement of the peripheries on the centers, led, inevitably, to a blurring of the distinctions between center and periphery. This laid the foundation for a new and powerful combination of the "charismatization" of the center or centers with themes and symbols of protest; these, in turn, became the elemental components of modern transcendental visions. Themes and symbols of protest – equality and freedom, justice and autonomy, solidarity and identity – became central components of the modern project of the emancipation of man. It was indeed the incorporation of the periphery's themes of protest into the center that heralded the radical transformation of various sectarian utopian visions into central elements of the political and cultural program.

From the ideology and premises of the political program of modernity and the core characteristics of modern political institutions, there emerged three central aspects of the modern political process: the restructuring of center-periphery relations as the principal focus of political dynamics in modern societies; a strong tendency toward politicizing the demands of various sectors of society, and the conflicts between them; and a continuing struggle over the definition of the realm of the political. Indeed, it is only with the coming of modernity that drawing the boundaries of the political becomes one of the major foci of open political contestation and struggle.

IV

Modernity entailed also a distinctive mode of constructing the boundaries of collectivities and collective identities. New concrete definitions of the basic components of collective identities developed – civil, primordial and universalistic, transcendental or "sacred." Strong tendencies developed toward framing these definitions in absolutist terms, emphasizing their civil components. At the same time, connections were drawn between the construction of political boundaries and those of cultural collectivities. This made inevitable an intensified emphasis on the territorial boundaries of such collectivities, creating continual tension between their territorial and/or particular components and those that were broader, more universalistic. In at least partial contrast to the axial civilizations, collective identities were no longer taken as given, preordained by some transcendental vision and authority, or sanctioned by perennial custom. They constituted foci of contestation and struggle, often couched in highly ideological terms.

V

As the civilization of modernity developed first in the West, it was from its beginnings beset by internal antinomies and contradictions, giving rise to continual critical discourse and political contestations. The basic antinomies of modernity constituted a radical transformation of those characteristics of the axial civilizations. Centered on questions unknown to that earlier time, they showed an awareness of a great range of transcendental visions and interpretations. In the modern program these were transformed into ideological conflicts between contending evaluations of the major dimensions of human experience (especially reason and emotions and their respective place in human life and society). There were new assertions about the necessity of actively constructing society; control and autonomy, discipline and freedom became burning issues.

Perhaps the most critical rift, in both ideological and political terms, was that which separated universal and pluralistic visions – between a view that accepted the existence of different values and rationalities and a view that conflated different values and, above all, rationalities in a totalistic way. This tension developed primarily with respect to the very concept of reason and its place in the constitution of human society. It was manifest, as Stephen Toulmin has shown in a somewhat exaggerated way, in the difference between the more pluralistic conceptions of Montaigne or Erasmus as against the totalizing vision promulgated by Descartes. The most significant movement to universalize different rationalities – often identified as the major message of the Enlightenment – was that of the sovereignty of reason, which subsumed value-rationality (*Wertrationalität*), or substantive rationality, under instrumental rationality (*Zweckrationalität*), transforming it into a totalizing moralistic utopian vision.

Cutting across these tensions, there developed within the program of modernity continual contradictions between the basic premises of its cultural and political dimensions and major institutional developments. Of particular importance – so strongly emphasized by Weber – was the creative dimension inherent in visions leading to the crystallization of modernity, and the flattening of these visions, the "disenchantment" of the world, inherent in growing routinization and bureaucratization. This was a conflict between an overreaching vision by which the modern world became meaningful and the fragmentation of such meaning by dint of an unyielding momentum toward autonomous development in all institutional arenas – economic, political, and cultural. This reflects the inherently modern tension between an emphasis on human autonomy and the restrictive controls inherent in the institutional realization of modern life: in Peter Wagner's formulation, between freedom and control.

Consider

1. What does Eisenstadt understand by 'multiple modernities'? Summarise his arguments in your own words.
2. How might the notion of multiple modernities be applied to the contemporary world? Draw up a list of examples of 'local' and simultaneously 'modern'

forms of life in different societies around the world. You might consider areas such as fashion, popular culture (movies, music, etc.), politics, and so on.

3. How could the idea of multiple modernities be used to analyse the global spread of fast food? To answer this question, it would be useful to explore the websites of fast food chains in different countries (e.g. McDonald's in the USA, Mexico, China, India, etc.) and compare menus, presentation, etc. Also consider how global fast food might be associated with the spread of particular, fast-paced, urban forms of professional life.

4.3 From modernity to postmodernity

There is still more to be said about modernity and the nature of contemporary social life. Experiences of modernity vary considerably around the world, but, importantly, they have also changed over time. Steam engines defined modernity in the nineteenth century by enabling industrial mass production. Black-and-white television sets arrived in the 1950s and fundamentally changed modern forms of mass communication and media consumption. Yet none of these comes to mind as particularly modern today. In addition to our three-part definition above, we may therefore say that *modernity refers to forms of social life that are characterised by relentless, continuous change and innovation.* Consider the common experience of buying and using a computer. Your expensive laptop may be state-of-the-art today, but you know that it will be quickly superseded by faster processors, bigger hard drives, more powerful memory chips, and so forth – in a couple of years, it will be obsolete, and you may have to replace it.

This dynamic of incessant change has led some scholars to conclude that we have, in fact, left behind modernity and entered the era of *postmodernity.* Debates about postmodernity originated in Western Europe and North America, but they have resonated in other parts of the world as well (see, for instance, Beverley, Oviedo, *et al.* 1995). From a sociological point of view, some important features of the postmodern condition are the following:

1. The de-standardisation of forms of socio-economic organisation in industrialised nations; a transition to service economies in the countries that concentrated industrial power in the nineteenth and early twentieth century (post-industrialism); the global spread of industrial production to countries like China, Indonesia, Brazil, or Mexico; and the emergence of new, complex forms of social inequalities not simply based on class, race and colonialism (see Chapters 6 and 7).

2. In cultural terms, a trend towards the abandonment of Western Enlightenment 'grand narratives' of progress and scientific rationality; and a growing awareness of globalisation and the connectedness of societies around the world (attendant cultural trends are often collectively labelled 'postmodernism').

3. In terms of modes of everyday life, a growing importance of individualised, choice-focused lifestyles and forms of consumption and communication, particularly among middle classes and wealthy elites; the de-standardisation of ways of living together, exemplified by the rise of new family forms through rising rates of divorce and re-marriage, the legitimisation of gay and lesbian marriages, etc.; and the complex mixing of lifestyles and cultures of different origins and places, exemplified by the enormous popularity of Latin American dancing in Western Europe in recent years or the spread of global foods that are neither here nor there (e.g. Tex Mex interpretations of Mexican cuisine or Chinese restaurants whose food you will never find in China).

Mobile phones again serve as a prime example of many of these points. Bulky and prohibitively expensive as recently as twenty years ago, mobile phones gained currency in the 1990s and truly exploded onto the global scene in the 2000s, with the arrival of technology that turned them into music players, photo cameras, portable cinemas, and internet terminals as well. Mobile phones represent the decline of industrial production in the manufacturing powerhouses of the West, often being produced by newer industrial powers around the world. Culturally, they stand for a new sense of global connectedness, allowing cheap and easy communication even between remote and distant places. Moreover, they are a prime example of early twenty-first-century consumerism, focused on individual preferences and choices rather than standardised, mass-produced goods. This is evident in the popularity of customisable Smartphones, which allow their users to suit their tastes from thousands of applications, from portable Facebook to video games to electronic versions of Shakespeare's collected works. iPhones are not simple telephones – for those few who can afford them, they may be profound expression of personal tastes and identity.

Reading

Featherstone, M. (1990), *Consumer Culture and Postmodernism*, London: Sage, pp. 1–12

Modern and Postmodern: Definitions and Interpretations

Any reference to the term 'postmodernism' immediately exposes one to the risk of being accused of jumping on a bandwagon, of perpetuating a rather shallow and meaningless intellectual fad. One of the problems is that the term is at once fashionable yet irritatingly elusive to define. As the 'Modern-day Dictionary of Received Ideas' confirms, 'This word has no meaning. Use it as often as possible' (*Independent*, 24 December 1987). Over a decade earlier, in August 1975, another newspaper announced that 'postmodernism is dead', and that 'post-post-modernism is now the thing' (Palmer, 1977: 364). If postmodernism is an ephemeral fashion then some critics are clear as to who are responsible for its prominence: 'today's paid theorists surveying the field from their booklined studies in polytechnics and universities are obliged to invent movements because their careers – no less than those of miners and fishermen – depend on it. The more movements they can give names to, the more successful they will be' (Pawley, 1986). For other critics these strategies are not just internal moves within the intellectual and academic fields; they are clear indicators and barometers of the 'malaise at the heart of contemporary culture'. Hence 'It is not difficult to comprehend this cultural and aesthetic trend now known as Postmodernism – in art and architecture, music and film, drama and fiction – as a reflection of . . . the present wave of political reaction sweeping the Western world' (Gott, 1986). But it is all too easy to see postmodernism as a reactionary, mechanical reflection of social changes and to blame the academics and intellectuals for coining the term as part of their distinction games. Even though certain newspaper critics and para-intellectuals use the term in a cynical or dismissive manner, they confirm that postmodernism has sufficient appeal to interest a larger middle-class audience. Few other recent academic terms can claim to have enjoyed such popularity. Yet it is not merely an academic term, for it has gained impetus from artistic 'movements' and is also attracting wider public interest through its capacity to speak to some of the cultural changes we are currently going through.

Before we can look at the means of transmission and dissemination of the concept, we need a clearer notion of the range of phenomena which are generally included under the umbrella concept postmodernism. We therefore need to take account of the great interest and even excitement that it has generated, both inside and outside the academy, and to ask questions about the range of cultural objects, experiences and practices which theorists are adducing and labelling postmodern, before we can decide on its political pedigree or dismiss it as merely a short swing of the pendulum.

In the first place the broad range of artistic, intellectual and academic fields in which the term 'postmodernism' has been used, is striking. We have music (Cage, Stockhausen, Briers, Holloway, Tredici, Laurie Anderson); art (Rauschenberg, Baselitz, Mach, Schnabel, Kiefer; some would also include Warhol and sixties pop art, and others Bacon); fiction (Vonnegut's *Slaughterhouse Five*, and the novels of Barth, Barthelme, Pynchon, Burroughs, Ballard, Doctorow); film (*Body Heat*, *The Wedding, Blue Velvet, Wetherby*); drama (The theatre of Artaud); photography (Sherman, Levine, Prince); architecture (Jencks, Venturi, Bolin); literary theory and criticism (Spanos, Hassan, Sontag, Fielder); philosophy (Lyotard, Derrida, Baudrillard, Vattimo, Rorty); anthropology (Clifford, Tyler, Marcus); sociology (Denzin); geography (Soja). The very names of those included and excluded in the list will doubtless strike some as controversial. To take the example of fiction, as Linda Hutcheon (1984: 2) argues, some would wish to include the novels of Garcia Marquez and even Cervantes under the heading of postmodernism and others would want to refer to them as neo-baroque and baroque.

Scott Lash would want to regard Dada as postmodernism *avant la lettre* (Lash, 1988). There are those who work and write unaware of the term's existence and others who seek to thematize and actively promote it. Yet it can be argued that one of the functions of the interest in postmodernism on the part of critics, para-intellectuals, cultural intermediaries and academics has been to diffuse the term to wider audiences in different national and international contexts (this is one of the senses in which one can talk about the globalization of culture); and to increase the speed of interchange and circulation of the term between the various fields in the academy and the arts, which now want to, and have to, pay more attention to developments among their neighbours. In this sense it is possible that some greater agreement on the meaning of the term might eventually emerge as commentators in each particular field find it necessary to recapitulate and explain the multiplex history and usages of the term in order to educate new, academic audiences.

To work towards some preliminary sense of the meaning of postmodernism it is useful to identify the family of terms derived from 'the postmodern' and these can best be understood by contrasting them to those which derive from 'the modern'.

modern	postmodern
modernity	postmodernity
modernité	*postmodernité*
modernization	postmodernization
modernism	postmodernism

If 'the modern' and 'the postmodern' are the generic terms it is immediately apparent that the prefix 'post' signifies that which comes after, a break or rupture with the modern which is defined in counterdistinction to it. Yet the term 'postmodernism' is more strongly based on a negation of the modern, a perceived abandonment, break with or shift away from the definitive features of the modern, with the emphasis firmly on the sense of the relational move away. This would make the postmodern a relatively ill-defined term as we are only on the threshold of the alleged shift, and not in a position to regard the postmodern as a fully fledged positivity which can be defined comprehensively in its own right. Bearing this in mind we can take a closer look at the pairings.

Modernity–postmodernity

This suggests the epochal meaning of the terms. Modernity is generally held to have come into being with the Renaissance and was defined in relation to Antiquity, as in the debate between the Ancients and the Moderns. From the point of view of late nineteenth- and early twentieth-century German sociological theory, from which we derive much of our current sense of the term, modernity is contrasted to the traditional order and implies the progressive economic and administrative rationalization and differentiation of the social world (Weber, Tönnies, Simmel): processes which brought into being the modern capitalist-industrial state and which were often viewed from a distinctly anti-modern perspective.

Consequently, to speak of postmodernity is to suggest an epochal shift or break from modernity involving the emergence of a new social totality with its own distinct organizing principles. It is this order of change that has been detected in the writing of Baudrillard, Lyotard, and to some extent, Jameson (Kellner, 1988). Both Baudrillard and Lyotard assume a movement towards a post-industrial age. Baudrillard (1983a) stresses that new forms of technology and information become central to the shift from a productive to a reproductive social order in which simulations and models increasingly constitute the world so that the distinction between the real and appearance becomes erased. Lyotard (1984) talks about the postmodern society, or postmodern age, which is premised on the move to a post-industrial order. His specific interest is in the effects of the 'computerization of society' on knowledge and he argues that the loss of meaning in postmodernity should not be mourned, as it points to a replacement of narrative knowledge by a plurality of language games, and universalism by localism. Yet Lyotard, like many users of the family of terms, sometimes changes register from one term to the next and switches usages, preferring more recently to emphasize that the postmodern is to be regarded as part of the modern. For example, in 'Rules and Paradoxes and Svelte Appendix' he writes ' "postmodern" is probably a very bad term because it conveys the idea of a historical "periodization". "Periodizing", however, is still a "classic" or "modern" ideal. "Postmodern" simply indicates a mood, or better a state of mind' (Lyotard, 1986–7: 209). The other interesting point to note about Lyotard's use of postmodernity in *The Postmodern Condition*, is that where he talks about the changes in knowledge accompanying the move to the post-industrial society he still conceives this as occurring within capitalism, adding weight to the argument of critics that the move to the postmodern society is under-theorized in Lyotard's work (see Kellner, 1988). Although the move is assumed at some points, it is easier to avoid the accusations of providing a grand narrative account of the move to postmodernity and the eclipse of grand narratives, by insisting on a more diffuse notion of 'mood' or 'state of mind'. Fredric Jameson (1984a) has a more definite periodizing concept of the postmodern, yet he is reluctant to conceive of it as an epochal shift, rather postmodernism is the cultural dominant, or cultural logic, of the third great stage of capitalism, late capitalism, which originates in the post World War Two era.

Lyotard's invocation of a postmodern mood or state of mind points us towards a second meaning of modernity–postmodernity. The French use of *modernité* points to the experience of modernity in which modernity is viewed as a quality of modern life inducing a sense of the discontinuity of time, the break with tradition, the feeling of novelty and sensitivity to the ephemeral, fleeting and contingent nature of the present (see Frisby, 1985a). This is the sense of being modern associated with Baudelaire which, as Foucault (1986: 40) argues, entails an ironical heroicization of the present: the modern man is the man who constantly tries to invent himself. It is this attempt to make sense of the experience of life in the new urban spaces and nascent consumer culture, which developed in the second half of the nineteenth century, which provided the impetus for the theories of modern everyday life in the work of Simmel, Kracauer and Benjamin discussed by David Frisby (1985b) in his *Fragments of Modernity*. The experience of modernity also forms the subject matter of Marshall Berman's (1982) book *All That is Solid Melts into Air* in which he looks at the visions and idioms accompanying the modernization process which he pulls together under the term 'modernism'. Berman discusses the modern sensibility that is manifest in a wide range of literary and intellectual figures from Rousseau and Goethe in the eighteenth century to Marx, Baudelaire, Pushkin and Dostoevsky in the nineteenth.

Apart from the confusing use of modernism to take in the whole of the experience and the culture that accompanied the modernization process, Berman and many of those who are currently trying to delineate the equivalent experience of postmodernity focus upon a particularly restrictive notion of experience: that which appears in literary sources and is so designated by intellectuals. But we have to raise the sociological objection against the literary intellectual's licence in interpreting the everyday, or in providing evidence about the everyday lives of ordinary people. Of course, some intellectuals may have articulated well the experience of the shocks and jolts of modernity. Yet we need to make the jump from modernity or postmodernity as a (relatively restricted) subjective experience to outlining the actual practices, and activities which take place in the everyday lives of various groups. Certainly the descriptions of subjective experience may make sense within intellectual practices, and within aspects of the practices of particular audiences educated to interpret these sensibilities, but the assumption that one can make wider claims needs careful substantiation.

To take an example of the alleged experience of postmodernity (or *postmodernité*), we can refer to Jameson's (1984a) account of the Bonaventura Hotel in Los Angeles. Jameson gives a fascinating interpretation of the experience of the new hyperspace of postmodern architecture, which, he argues, forces us to expand our sensorium and body. Yet we get little idea how individuals from different backgrounds actually experience the hotel, or better still, how they incorporate the experience into their day-to-day practices. Perhaps for them to interpret the experience as postmodern they need guidelines to make sense of things they may not fully notice, or view through inappropriate codes. Hence, if we want to understand the social generation and interpretation of the experience of postmodernity we need to have a place for the role of cultural entrepreneurs and intermediaries who have an interest in creating postmodern pedagogies to educate publics. The same can be said for two other features of postmodern culture identified by Jameson: the transformation of reality into images and the fragmentation of time into a series of perpetual presents. Here we can take an example which encompasses both features: the media, which tends to be central to many discussions of the postmodern sensibility (one thinks for example of Baudrillard's simulational world, where 'TV is the world'). Yet for all the alleged pluralism and sensitivity to the Other talked about by some theorists one finds little discussion of the actual experience and practice of watching television by different groups in different settings. On the contrary, theorists of the postmodern often talk of an ideal-type channel-hopping MTV (music television) viewer who flips through different images at such speed that she/he is unable to chain the signifiers together into a meaningful narrative, he/she merely enjoys the multiphrenic intensities and sensations of the surface of the images. Evidence of the extent of such practices, and how they are integrated into, or influence, the day-to-day encounters between embodied persons is markedly lacking. Thus while learned references to the characteristic experiences of postmodernity are important we need to work from more systematic data and should not rely on the readings of intellectuals. In effect we should focus upon the actual cultural practices and changing power balances of those groups engaged in the production, classification, circulation and consumption of postmodern cultural goods, something which will be central to our discussion of postmodernism below.

Modernization–postmodernization

On the face of it, both terms seem to sit unhappily amidst discussion of modernity–postmodernity, modernism–postmodernism. Modernization has been regularly used in the sociology of development to point to the effects of economic development on traditional social structures and values. Modernization theory is also used to refer to the stages of social development which are based upon industrialization, the growth of science and technology, the modern nation state, the capitalist world market, urbanization and other infrastructural elements. (In this usage it has strong affinities with the first sense of modernity we discussed above.) It is generally assumed, via a loose base–superstructure model, that certain cultural changes (secularization and the emergence of a modern identity which centres around self-development) will result from the modernization process. If we turn to postmodernization it is clear that a concomitant detailed outline of specific social processes and institutional changes has yet to be theorized. All we have is the possibility of deriving the term from those usages of postmodernity which refer to a new social order and epochal shift mentioned above. For example, Baudrillard's (1983a) depiction of a postmodern simulational world is based upon the assumption that the development of commodity production coupled with information technology have led to the 'triumph of signifying culture' which then reverses the direction of determinism, so that social relations become saturated with shifting cultural signs to the extent that we can no longer speak of class or normativity and are faced by 'the end of the social'. Baudrillard, however, does not use the term 'postmodernization'.

Yet the term does have the merit of suggesting a process with degrees of implementation, rather than a fully fledged new social order or totality. One significant context for the utilization of the term 'postmodernization' is the field of urban studies and here we can point to the writings of Philip Cooke (1988) and Sharon Zukin (1988a). For Cooke, postmodernization is an ideology and set of practices with spatial effects which have been notable in the British economy since 1976. Zukin also wants to use postmodernization to focus on the restructuring of socio-spatial relations by new patterns of investment and production in industry, services, labour markets and telecommunications. Yet, while Zukin sees postmodernization as a dynamic process comparable to modernization, both she and Cooke are reluctant to regard it as pointing to a new stage of society, for both see it as taking place within capitalism. This has the merit of focusing on processes of production as well as consumption and the spatial dimension of particular cultural practices (the redevelopment of downtowns and waterfronts, development of urban artistic and cultural centres, and the growth of the service class and gentrification) which accompany them.

Modernism–postmodernism

As with the pairing modernity–postmodernity, we are again faced with a range of meanings. Common to them all is the centrality of culture. In the most restricted sense, modernism points to the styles we associate with the artistic movements which originated around the turn of the century and which have dominated the various arts until recently. Figures frequently cited are: Joyce, Yeats, Gide, Proust, Rilke, Kafka, Mann, Musil, Lawrence and Faulkner in literature; Rilke, Pound, Eliot, Lorca, Valery in poetry; Strindberg and Pirandello in drama; Matisse, Picasso, Braque, Cézanne and the Futurist, Expressionist, Dada and Surrealist movements in painting; Stravinsky, Schoenberg and Berg in music (see Bradbury and McFarlane, 1976). There is a good deal of debate about how far back into the nineteenth century modernism should be taken (some would want to go back to the bohemian avant-garde of the 1830s). The basic features of modernism can be summarized as: an aesthetic self-consciousness and reflexiveness; a rejection of narrative structure in favour of simultaneity and montage; an exploration of the paradoxical, ambiguous and uncertain open-ended nature of reality; and a rejection of the notion of an integrated personality in favour of an emphasis upon the de-structured, de-humanized subject (see Lunn, 1985: 34ff). One of the problems with trying to understand postmodernism in the arts is that many of these features are appropriated into various definitions of postmodernism. The problem with the term, as with the other related terms we have discussed, revolves around the question of when does a term defined oppositionally to, and feeding off, an established term start to signify something substantially different?

According to Kohler (1977) and Hassan (1985) the term 'postmodernism' was first used by Federico de Onis in the 1930s to indicate a minor reaction to modernism. The term became popular in the 1960s in New York when it was used by young artists, writers and critics such as Rauschenberg, Cage, Burroughs, Barthelme, Fielder, Hassan and Sontag to refer to a movement beyond the 'exhausted' high modernism which was rejected because of its institutionalization in the museum and the academy. It gained wider usage in architecture, the visual and performing arts, and music in the 1970s and 1980s and then was rapidly transmitted back and forth between Europe and the United States as the search for theoretical explanations and justifications of artistic postmodernism shifted to include wider discussions of postmodernity and drew in, and generated an interest in, theorists such as Bell, Kristeva, Lyotard, Vattimo, Derrida, Foucault, Habermas, Baudrillard and Jameson (see Huyssen, 1984). Amongst the central features associated with postmodernism in the arts are: the effacement of the boundary between art and everyday life; the collapse of the hierarchical distinction between high and mass/popular culture; a stylistic promiscuity favouring eclecticism and the mixing of codes; parody, pastiche, irony, playfulness and the celebration of the surface 'depthlessness' of culture; the decline of the originality/ genius of the artistic producer; and the assumption that art can only be repetition.

There is also a wider usage of the terms 'modernism' and 'postmodernism' which refers to broader cultural complexes: that is, modernism as the culture of modernity, and postmodernism as the emergent culture of postmodernity. Daniel Bell (1976) takes up this position in which he sees the fundamental cultural assumption of modernity, the ideal of the autonomous self-determining individual, as giving rise to the bourgeois entrepreneur in the economic realm and the artistic search for the untrammelled self (which finds its expression in modernism) in the cultural realm. For Bell modernism is a corrosive force, unleashing an adversarial culture which in conjunction with the hedonistic culture of mass consumption subverts traditional bourgeois values and the Puritan ethic. Bell's analysis is based on the notion of the disjunction of the three realms, the polity, culture and economy, so there is no sense in looking for a base–superstructural model in his work in which a shift in the economy or socio-economic order such as to the post-industrial society would give rise to a new culture of postmodernism. Rather, postmodernism is perceived as a heightening of the antinomian tendencies of modernism with desire, the instinctual, and pleasure unleashed to carry the logic of modernism to its furthest reaches exacerbating the structural tensions of society and disjunction of the realms (Bell, 1980). Jameson (1984a) too uses postmodernism to refer to culture in the broader sense and talks about postmodernism as a cultural logic, or cultural dominant, which leads to the transformation of the cultural sphere in contemporary society. While Jameson shows some reluctance in adopting the view of periodization which assumes a sudden shift and transformation of all aspects of culture, he follows Mandel (1975) and links the stages of modernism to monopoly capitalism and postmodernism to post-World War Two late capitalism. This suggests that he uses a form of the base–superstructural model. Yet he also goes part of the way along the same route as Baudrillard, without referring to him, to argue that postmodernism is based upon the central role of reproduction in the 'de-centred global network' of present-day multinational capitalism which leads to a 'prodigious expansion of culture throughout the social realm, to the point at which everything in our social life . . . can be said to have become "cultural"' (Jameson, 1984a: 85–7).

There is one further point that needs to be taken up from the work of Bell and Jameson before going on to look at the use of postmodernism as a cipher for fundamental cultural changes as well as the possible expansion of the significance of culture in contemporary Western societies. John O'Neill (1988) has argued that both Bell and Jameson adopt a nostalgic reaction to postmodernism, and are united against postmodernism in their 'will to order', their desire to renew the threatened social bond via religion (Bell) or the Marxist utopia (Jameson). Both have the merit or flaw, depending on where you stand, of wanting to totalize: to depict postmodernism in its degrees of connectedness and disjunction to the contemporary social order. They also want to judge postmodernism as negative; they have a distaste for it, a response which has not passed unnoticed on the part of those critics who welcome the playfulness and pluralistic, 'democratic' spirit of postmodernism, and would see Jameson (and by association, Bell) as nostalgically bemoaning the loss of authority of the intellectual aristocracy over the population (see Hutcheon, 1986–7; During, 1987).

For those who welcome postmodernism as a mode of critical analysis which opens up ironies, inter-textuality and paradoxes, attempts to devise a theory of postmodern society or postmodernity, or delineate the role of postmodernism within the social order, are essentially flawed efforts to totalize or systematize. In effect they are authoritarian grand narratives which are ripe for playful deconstruction. Critics are, for example, quick to point out this apparent inconsistency in Lyotard's *Postmodern Condition*. Kellner (1988), for example, argues that Lyotard's notion of postmodernity itself entails a master narrative, that we can't have a theory of the postmodern without one. It should be added that Lyotard (1988) has recently emphasized the need to move away from what he sees as the misunderstanding of his book as an example of totalizing reason. For those who take seriously the implications of postmodernism as a mode of critical theorizing or cultural analysis, the attempt to produce a sociological understanding must necessarily fail as it cannot avoid totalizations, systematizations and legitimation via the flawed grand narratives of modernity: science, humanism, Marxism, feminism etc. Sociological synthesis must be abandoned for playful deconstruction and the privileging of the aesthetic mode. A postmodern sociology so conceived would abandon its generalizing social science ambitions and instead parasitically play off the ironies, incoherences, inconsistencies and inter-textuality of sociological writings. There are, of course, lessons to be learned from a postmodern sociology: it focuses attention on the ways in which theories are built up, their hidden assumptions, and questions the theorist's authority to speak for 'the Other', who as many researchers are finding out, is now often actively disputing both the account and the authority of the academic theorist. Yet if we are to attempt to make sense of the emergence of postmodernism and the changes taking place in the culture of contemporary Western societies we need to move beyond the false oppositions of foundationalism and relativism, of single episte-mology and plural ontology, and investigate specific social and cultural processes and the dynamics of the production of particular funds of knowledge. In effect we must relinquish the attractions of a postmodern sociology and work towards a sociological account of postmodernism (see Chapter 3).

To follow such an approach would entail focusing on the interrelationship between three aspects or meanings of the culture of postmodernism. In the first place we can consider postmodernism in the arts and in the academic and intel-lectual fields. Here we could usefully employ the field approach of Bourdieu (1971, 1979) and focus upon the economy of symbolic goods: the conditions of supply and demand for such goods, the processes of competition and monop-olization, and the struggles between established and outsiders. We could, for example, direct attention to the act of *naming* as an important strategy of groups engaged in struggles with other groups; the use of new terms by outsider groups who have an interest in destabilizing existing symbolic hierarchies to produce a reclassification of the field more in line with their own interests; the conditions which are breaking down the barriers between sub-fields of the arts and academic subjects; the conditions which dictate changes in the demand for particular types of cultural goods by various state agencies, consumers, audiences and publics.

To adequately deal with the last areas, indeed to adequately conceptualize all the above areas, would take us outside the specific analysis of particular artistic and intellectual fields and their interrelationship. Here we would need to con-sider postmodernism in terms of a second 'level' of culture, what is often called the cultural sphere, and consider the means of transmission, and circulation to audiences and publics and the feedback effect of the audience response in gener-ating further interest amongst intellectuals. To focus on this second area we need to look at artists, intellectuals and academics as specialists in symbolic produc-tion and consider their relationship to other symbolic specialists in the media, and those engaged in consumer culture, popular culture and fashion occupations. Here we need to focus on the emergence of what Bourdieu (1984) calls the 'new cultural intermediaries', who rapidly circulate information between formerly sealed-off areas of culture, and the emergence of new communication chan-nels under conditions of intensified competition (Crane, 1987). We also need to consider the competition, changing balances of power and interdependences between specialists in symbolic production and economic specialists (cf. Elias, 1987b) within conditions of a growth in the former group's power potential as producers and consumers accompanying the growth of mass and higher educa-tion in Western nations in the postwar era. We need to examine some of the processes of de-monopolization and de-hierarchization of previously established and legitimate cultural enclaves which has brought about a phase of cultural declassification in the Western world (DiMaggio, 1987). Finally, in addition to considering these changes on an intrasocietal level we need also to consider the processes of intensified competition on an intersocietal level which is shifting the balance of power away from Western intellectuals and artists and their right to speak for humanity, as well as the emergence of genuine global cultural questions through what Roland Robertson (1990) has called 'globalization'. These processes point to changes within the broader cultural sphere which are worthy of investigation in their own right; processes which, it can be argued, the concept of postmodernism has served to sensitize us to.

The concept of postmodernism is not, however, merely an empty sign which can be manipulated by artists, intellectuals and academics as part of the power struggles and interdependencies within their particular fields. Part of its appeal is that it speaks to the above changes and also purports to illuminate changes in the day-to-day experiences and cultural practices of broader groups in society. It is here that the evidence is weakest and the possibility of simply relabelling experiences as postmodern which were formerly granted little significance, is most obvious. It is here that we face the problem of an adequate definition of postmodernism and find a good deal of loose conceptual confusion with notions of 'the loss of a sense of historical past', 'schizoid culture', 'excremental culture', 'the replacement of reality by images', 'simulations', 'unchained signifiers' etc., multiplying. Scott Lash (1988) has endeavoured to move to a tighter definition of postmodernism as involving de-differentiation and the figural, which are held to be central to postmodern regimes of signification; yet here too we possess little systematic evidence about day-to-day practices, and we need information in terms of the stock sociological questions 'who? when? where? how many?' if we are to impress colleagues that postmodernism is more than a fad. Yet there is also a sense in which postmodernism proceeds under its own steam, with the changes in the cultural sphere we have hinted at above, leading to the formation of new audiences and publics interested in postmodernism. Such audiences and publics may eventually adopt postmodern practices and become attuned to postmodern experiences under the guidance of pedagogues produced by cultural intermediaries and para-intellectuals. Such 'feed-back' could lead to postmodernism becoming translated into reality.

To summarize, there is, as yet, no agreed meaning to the term 'postmodern' – its derivatives, the family of terms which include postmodernity, *postmodernité*, postmodernization and postmodernism are often used in confusing and interchangeable ways. I have attempted to outline and discuss some of these meanings. Postmodernism is of interest to a wide range of artistic practices and social science and humanities disciplines because it directs our attention to changes taking place in contemporary culture. These can be understood in terms of (1) the artistic, intellectual and academic fields (changes in modes of theorization, presentation and dissemination of work which cannot be detached from changes in specific competitive struggles occurring in particular fields); (2) changes in the broader cultural sphere involving the modes of production, consumption and circulation of symbolic goods which can be related to broader shifts in the balance of power and interdependencies between groups and class fractions on both inter- and intra-societal levels; (3) changes in the everyday practices and experiences of different groups, who as a result of some of the processes referred to above, may be using regimes of signification in different ways and developing new means of orientation and identity structures. It is apparent that in recent years we have witnessed a dramatic upsurge of interest in the issue of culture. Culture, once on the periphery of social science disciplines, particularly in sociology, has now been thrust increasingly towards the centre of the field and some of the barriers between the social sciences and humanities are in the process of being dismantled (Featherstone, 1988). We can understand this in terms of two processes which must be inter-related: firstly, the way in which culture has shifted in the arsenal of social science concepts from something which is essentially explicable in terms of other factors to broader metacultural questions concerning the cultural underpinnng, or 'deep' cultural coding, of the social (see Robertson, 1988); secondly, the way in which the culture of contemporary Western societies seems to be undergoing a series of major transformations which must be investigated in terms of intrasocietal, inter-societal and global processes. It should be apparent that this is one reason for the rise of interest in postmodernism, and a further reason why as cultural theorists and researchers we should be interested in it.

Consider
1. How does Mike Featherstone describe the difference between modernity and postmodernity? Explain his arguments in your own words.
2. How does Featherstone define postmodernism? Summarise his arguments in your own words.
3. How does Featherstone describe the difference between modernisation and postmodernisation? Explain his arguments in your own words.
4. (Post)modernism, (post)modernity, (post)modernisation – can you explain the difference between the three terms? If necessary, use additional sources to answer this question.
5. Draw up a list of examples that illustrate forms of postmodern social life in the contemporary world. How do these example's illustrate Featherstone's arguments?

4.4 Culture

The term 'culture' encompasses a notably wide variety of meanings and uses, both in academia and in everyday language. Moreover, culture is a subject matter of inter-disciplinary enquiry, and sociological approaches are inseparably intertwined with ideas and proposals from fields such as cultural studies, anthropology, philosophy, literature, theatre and film. Here, we will attempt to disentangle some of the meanings of culture and point you to strands of research that have developed around the concept.

To begin with a definition, we might describe culture as *the beliefs, values, norms, practices, and material objects on which individuals draw to guide their actions in everyday life.* Implicit in this definition are various particular dimensions of culture that merit further consideration.

First of all, our definition suggests that culture consists of beliefs, values, and norms. *Beliefs are factual assumptions about the world we take for granted and to which we orient our conduct.* Having grown up in a world permeated by science, most of us take the spherical nature of the planet for granted, and few of us are afraid of travelling by plane for fear of falling off the edge of the world. *Next, values are judgements of the moral quality of things and behaviours.* While travelling by plane is factually relatively safe – there are few accidents compared to other means of transport, and no risk of falling off the edge of the world – frequent air travel is increasingly being challenged as morally dubious, given the pollution it causes and the drain it places on natural resources such as fossil fuels. *Norms, finally, are formal and informal rules of conduct we are firmly expected to follow and to which sanctions are attached.* Most societies have norms that closely circumscribe the use of physical violence. Running up to another player and pushing him to the ground will result in a red card and instant dismissal from a football match. Outside football, it may constitute a breach of the law and entail significant sanctions by police and the courts.

From this perspective, culture is inherent in our minds: we learn norms, values, and beliefs, and they thus structure our perceptions and feelings about the world and guide our actions. Culture thus refers to the *symbolic nature* of human life. Philosopher Ernst Cassirer argues that all human life experience and conduct is based on symbols, that is, *shared, commonly recognised meanings of things that are transmitted in society, particularly through language*:

> Man cannot escape from his own achievement. He cannot but adopt the conditions of his own life. No longer in a merely physical universe, man lives in a symbolic universe. Language, myth, art, and religion are parts of this universe. They are the varied threads which weave the symbolic net, the tangled web of human experience. All human progress in thought and experience refines upon and strengthens this net. No longer can man confront reality immediately; he cannot see it, as it were, face to face. [. . .] He has so enveloped himself in linguistic forms, in artistic images, in mythical symbols or religious rites that he cannot see or know anything except by the interposition of this artificial medium. (Cassirer 1944/1954: 43)

The study of culture, in this sense can be understood as the exploration of the symbolic universe of beliefs, values, norms, myths, and so forth on whose base we engage with reality, of the ways in which cultural symbols are shared and transmitted through language and other means of communication, and of the processes through which symbolic meanings change over time. Thus, sociologists have in recent years taken an increasing interest in the ways in which the foundational cognitive processes through which we perceive reality are structured by culture and thus variable in historical and geographical terms (Cerulo 2002). For example, American sociologist Eviatar Zerubavel (2007) writes about the cognitive organisation of denial and notes how individuals are trained not to spot 'the elephant in the room' in certain situations. He cites rules of etiquette as an example: the person who is talking to us from across the table at a formal dinner might just have dropped a big chunk of food in his lap, but it is in our best interest not to see and not respond, so as to avoid an awkward situation.

From this derives, second, an understanding of culture as *practice*. This concerns the *strategies or logics of action by which we conduct our everyday lives and manage the different social situations in which we engage.* Ann Swidler (2001) argues that, throughout our lives, we learn a broad repertoire of skills, habits and mental orientations on which we can draw to guide our conduct in particular situations. Thus, we possess skills to guide us in a formal dinner, by, for instance, making us overlook other people's mishaps. Equally, we possess the necessary mental orientations to use at an informal eat-out with friends at McDonald's – where pointing out the aforementioned mishaps and laughing about them might just be an important part of the fun! In this sense, culture is not something we passively acquire or internalise. Rather, culture is something we actively use to engage with the world of people and things that surround us, by, for instance, differentiating between two different types of social gatherings and behaving in a manner that allows us to enjoy both to the fullest.

Third, there is the world of *material culture*, that is to say *the physical objects that humans mould according to their distinctive beliefs, values and norms for their uses in everyday life, thus investing them with specific symbolic meanings.* From dinner utensils to books to airplanes, we are surrounded by such objects, and learning their meanings and uses is an important part of being seen by others as a competent member of society. Consider the difference between the cutlery used in Western societies and the chopsticks used in East and Southeast Asia. Both have a long history, and their mastery may be an important part of eating in a socially acceptable manner in the places where they are prevalent. Both also may carry a range of other cultural meanings. Plastic cutlery immediately evokes images of fast food, whereas golden forks and knives conjure images of luxury and elevated social status. Thus, much sociological research concerns itself with the analysis of material culture, the trajectories of production and consumption of cultural objects, the ways in which they are represented and acquire particular cultural meanings, and the regulation of their production and consumption in public and private life.

In this sense, no cultural aspect of human life is simply natural. Culture, in terms of the symbolic universe we live in, our practice of everyday life, and the objects we use in this practice, is created, re-created, or changed in and by society. Thus, it varies between places, between historical periods, and even between subcultures co-existing within societies. Exploring the diverse cultural forms of human life and their variations is the task of cultural sociology.

Reading

Zerubavel, Eviatar (2002), 'The Elephant in the Room', in *Culture in Mind*, edited by Karen A. Cerulo, New York: Routledge, pp. 21–7

The Elephant in the Room

Notes on the Social Organization of Denial
Eviatar Zerubavel

This chapter looks at a somewhat unusual aspect of cognition, namely that which does not enter our awareness. I am referring here to that which, at least potentially, could have entered awareness yet nevertheless does not. Furthermore, I am referring to that which is deliberately left out of our consciousness. In other words, I am talking about the active process of blocking certain information from entering our minds. In that respect, I follow Sigmund Freud's critical distinction between that which we simply forget and that which we actively repress from our awareness, thereby regarding ignoring as an active process of deliberately not noticing.

Let me add here that I do not intend to discuss the physiological level of perception. I will not address, for example, the natural constraints affecting what enters our visual field. That is something on which psychologists and biologists are much more qualified to comment. By the same token, I do not intend to address the physiology of other senses, such as hearing, taste, or smell, the disruption of which certainly blocks the flow of information into our minds. I also will ignore the individual dimension of perception and attention. I shall therefore refrain from addressing strictly psychological phenomena such as self-numbing or dissociation, which have to do with the way individuals manage to block certain information from entering their consciousness. Though absolutely fascinating, they are quite irrelevant to my distinctly sociological concern with cognition.

As I have demonstrated elsewhere, cognitive sociology addresses cognitive matters at a level that both cognitive individualism and universalism leave untouched between them. I am therefore particularly interested in the *social* organization of attention, a topic I first addressed in a 1993 article I wrote on horizons, further developed in a chapter of *Social Mindscapes* titled "The Social Gates of Consciousness," and am now expanding into a book. At the heart of this book lies a phenomenon I call "the elephant in the room." I regard it as the sociological equivalent of what psychologists call "denial."

What makes the metaphor of "the elephant in the room" so evocative is the choice of such a large animal. Unlike a grasshopper on a twig, which we are unable to notice because it is so well camouflaged that its outlines practically blend with the surrounding background, the elephant has a commanding visual presence that is objectively unavoidable. Thus if we manage not to notice it, it can only be as a result of a deliberate act of ignoring, since naturally it would be practically impossible not to notice it! Not noticing an elephant, in other words, involves blindness to the obvious.

Notice the visual aspect of ignoring in this case. What is so striking about the elephant is not its smell (as it would have been had I used the metaphor of a skunk), but its visual presence. Not noticing the elephant in the room is thus the equivalent of being blind (which might explain the particular choice of punishment that Oedipus inflicted upon himself). Note, in this regard, the abundance of unmistakably visual metaphors related to denial: having a "tunnel vision," wearing "blinders," turning a "blind eye" to the obvious, or "looking the other way." Consider also statements such as "this time I'll overlook what you just did," or the way we seem so much more easily to ignore that which is not in the "spotlight," not to mention the "blind spots" we all seem to have in certain areas!

Yet as we come to focus on the proverbial monkey who "sees no evil," let us not forget his colleagues who hear and speak no evil. The conditions of being deaf or mute certainly complement the picture we begin to get when addressing the phenomenon of mental "blindness." And I definitely see the sociology of ignoring as complementing the sociology of silence as well as the sociology of secrecy, first introduced by Georg Simmel ninety years ago. Secrets, as we very well know, certainly help solidify structures of denial and ignorance.

As someone who grew up in a household where every single room housed several such elephants, I think that I have developed a particular sociological sensitivity to instances where the obviously present nonetheless remains publicly unacknowledged or even actively denied. Yet I also believe that I am pointing here to a critical generic social phenomenon which sociologists in general cannot afford to ignore. Can you imagine, for example, formal, official, social life without the mental process of relegating the "informal" and "unofficial" to the domain identified by Erving Goffman as the "out of frame"? By the same token, can you envision everyday social interaction without the element of tact, which presupposes a display of what he called "civil inattention," – that is, assigning certain aspects of the situation an "unfocused" status so as to allow the interaction to flow more "smoothly"?

Blocking certain information from entering our awareness (not to mention from allowing it to circulate among different individuals' awarenesses) is often done quite blatantly. Christopher Columbus, for example, actually threatened to cut out the tongue of any participant in his second voyage to the Caribbean who would not testify back home that Cuba was indeed part of the mainland! Similarly, God banished Adam and Eve from the Garden of Eden for tasting from the Tree of Knowledge. Consider also, in this regard, judges' explicit instructions to court stenographers actually to strike certain statements from the official record, or the invention of the eraser, identified by my 14-year-old son last year as "the most deadly weapon of denial."

Yet blocking certain information from entering our awareness is also done in a more subtle manner. Consider the way in which Captain Jeffrey Purdie (the watch commander of the Secret Service uniformed division), referring to an incident when President Clinton's mistress angrily stormed out of the White House, instructed one of his subordinates: "As far as you're concerned, this never happened" (*New York Times*, September 12, 1998, p. B7). And note the striking contrast between this explicit denial of what he had experienced only a few hours earlier and what actually precipitated that statement, namely the way in which the president himself had told him earlier, "I hope you use your discretion" (*New York Times*, September 12, 1998, p. B7), which is only an implicit invitation to forget. I am sure that at least some readers have been in situations where they were practically told by a superior, referring to what they were actually in the middle of doing, "This conversation never happened."

From a sociological perspective, of course, it is even more striking when even such "subtle" statements need not be uttered at all because it is implicitly quite clear to all participants that they are not "supposed" to know what they clearly do know! This is the basis of the fascinating social phenomenon commonly known as a "conspiracy of silence." The difference between explicit "hushes" and such subtle conspiracies of silence is analogous to the difference between a direct order actually to remove a particular passage from the next edition of an official history textbook and the implicit manner in which traditional historiography, until quite recently, has ignored the role of women in human history. It is the difference between deliberate, active repression and more passive negotiation of "blind spots."

As demonstrated by Freud in his writings on denial, as well as by Simmel in his discussion of the blasé attitude often displayed by dwellers in large cities, blocking certain information from entering our awareness seems to serve some obvious psychological functions. Yet the common saying that "ignorance is bliss" has a rather significant social dimension as well. After all, in an effort to avoid internal turbulence, many social systems are quite willing to ignore any "inconvenient" information that might possibly generate such turbulence. That is why women who are well aware of the horrendous fact that their own daughters are being sexually molested by their husbands or boyfriends, for example, nonetheless often choose to overlook such disquieting information and, in a manner somewhat evocative of the proverbial ostrich, try to pretend that such abuse is not really taking place, thereby inevitably "enabling" its persistence. The very same phenomenon is also evident, of course, when, in the name of the survival of the organization as a whole, fellow workers often choose to ignore obvious injustices inflicted upon one of their members, particularly when he or she is structurally located at the bottom of the organizational totem pole.

Needless to say, such "conspiracies of silence" obviously have some very significant moral undertones, particularly when the act of ignoring inevitably allows – or even encourages – the perpetuation of some clear abuse of power. Hence the distinctive moral role of those stubborn disturbers of silence we call "whistle-blowers," whether at the level of the family (such as neighbors in the case of child abuse), the organization (such as workers who take the courageous step of filing a grievance against an abusive boss), or even the nation as a whole (such as Emile Zola or Anita Hill).

In order to appreciate fully the social aspect of the way in which our attention is organized, we need to focus on the normative dimension of such organization. As I have argued elsewhere, there are some unmistakably social *rules* of focusing our attention. A classic example is what Goffman called "rules of irrelevance," one of the most obvious manifestations of which is the way in which we "down-play" various aspects of situations in order to conduct what we consider "fair" competition. As Kristen Purcell has demonstrated in her work on the sociomental organization of such competition, entire aspects of competitive situations are often treated as socially irrelevant and, as such, officially bracketed and thereby systematically ignored. Statutes of limitations, of course, have the same effect by curbing our historical attention, so that certain "prehistorical" elements are bracketed out of our official awareness. Note also the social rules of establishing agendas of meetings, which include formal articulations of what is "on the table" and what is not, as manifested in the distinction between that which does or does not enter the official minutes of meetings.

Consider also various rules of etiquette, many of which involve tact-related ethical obligations to "look the other way" and ignore things we otherwise most likely would have noticed about other around us. As if to underscore the way in which ignoring complements secrecy, normative prohibitions against not being "discreet" are often complemented by similar prohibitions against being too "nosy." Hence the rules of "civil inattention," whereby we learn to be like those monkeys who see and hear no "evil." And when we do see or hear it, we are expected to pretend we didn't, so as to save the face of others with whom we interact, as evident within families of stutterers, alcoholics, or the terminally ill. This, mind you, involves not just individual "niceness" but actual social, normative pressure to be "tactful."

As Hans Christian Andersen reminds us in his delightful sociological parable "The Emperor's New Clothes," the only one who did see the emperor's naked body was the young boy who had still not learned how not to notice embarrassing things about others! In other words, not noticing involves learning, as it is obviously part of a process I call "optical socialization," as when we teach children how not to look too attentively at people who have physical deformities. By the same token, one needs to learn what to ignore officially when taking the minutes at a faculty meeting.

Such optical socialization is often done explicitly. In sharp contrast to professions that train their members to try to notice "everything" to the point of being deliberately "nosy" (police detectives, journalists, psychotherapists, insurance claim investigators), there are others that try systematically to regulate what enters their members' awareness. Note, for instance, the way lawyers are specifically trained to focus just on that which is legally "relevant" to their case, or the way scientists are taught to control in their research designs the variables they plan to examine in their experiments. In the same way that Betty Edwards has been training artists how not to focus on objects so as to be able to notice the spaces between them, Wayne Brekhus is now trying to train sociologists how not to focus on politically sensitive topics so as to be able to research the socially mundane. As Ludwig Fleck noted with regard to microbiologists looking through a microscope, one needs to learn how to focus in order to notice anything. Yet as Ruth Simpson is showing in her current study of the transition from miasmatic to bacteriological theories of disease, medical practitioners also had to learn how to ignore the communal dimension of epidemics in order to be able to "see" how diseases spread through germs. In order to notice things, one needs to also learn first what not to notice! As the judge instructs the jury in Billy Wilder's *Witness for the Prosecution*: "You must shun out from your minds everything except what will take place in this court." In other words, only by becoming partly blind can we come to see anything in a "focused" manner.

Yet part of such "optical socialization" is also done implicitly. By merely noticing on what the camera focuses, young television watchers also learn what society normally ignores! The media, of course, are not the only agents of such tacit process of delineating our horizons. By hearing our parents sum up in two minutes how we spent an entire day together, we also learn from a very young age that which merits social attention and that which can actually be ignored.

As I have shown elsewhere, this also applies to our concern. The striking manner in which our social environment leads different individuals to place the limits of their concern at the same place, which is often quite different from where members of other social environments place them (contrast, for example, meat-eaters' and vegans' respective spheres of moral concern) suggests a certain social "calibration" of concern. And the differences are not just between cultures or subcultures but also between different historical periods within each of those. My blindness as a child in the fifties toward the very existence of Arab-Israelis living only a few miles away from me is certainly not as widely shared by children growing up in my hometown Tel Aviv today.

And what is true of concern also applies to curiosity. Consider, for example, the social organization of reading. The social curbing of our curiosity is quite evident in any reading list for doctoral comprehensive exams, as well as in the inevitably parochial academic pattern of citing only sources lying within the essentially conventional confines of supposedly discrete bodies of "literature."

Such references to curiosity and concern clearly underscore the implicit tension between the sociological and psychological perspectives on the mental processes of attending and ignoring. Yet I believe that we should acknowledge the inherent differences between those two perspectives and not treat those processes as lying exclusively within the psychologist's domain, as they traditionally have been until now. The fact that someone represses the memory of a particular traumatic experience because it is too painful to remember certainly belongs within the domain of the psychology of denial. Yet when a superior tells a subordinate "this conversation didn't happen," it clearly calls for a *sociology* of denial. Similarly, when Kathryn Harrison describes in her book *The Kiss* the way she tried to numb her awareness of the sexual relations she was having with her father by making various attempts at a "selective self-anesthesia" that "leaves me awake to certain things and dead to others," she is referring to mechanisms of denial that are clearly *intra*psychic. Yet when she describes how her boyfriend, himself threatened by such forbidden relations, colludes with her in such process of joint forgetting, we are dealing not just with denial but also with "codenial," which is an *inter* psychic process, thereby acknowledging the social dimension of ignoring.

Only when both psychologists and sociologists turn their attention to the mental processes of attending and ignoring can we have a truly comprehensive understanding of those processes. That, of course, is one of the principal intellectual missions of cognitive sociology.

Consider
1. According to Eviatar Zerubavel, how are mental acts of denial shaped by culture? Summarise his arguments in as much detail as possible.
2. Provide example for the following concepts:
   * conspiracies of silence
   * rules of irrelevance
   * optical socialisation.
3. Based on the reading, attempt to formulate a sociological definition of denial in your own words.
4. Zerubavel mainly looks at the mental acts that facilitate denial in everyday life. How may we use the objects of material culture to engage in denial? Illustrate your arguments with relevant examples.
5. 'Man cannot escape from his own achievement. He cannot but adopt the conditions of his own life. No longer in a merely physical universe, man lives in a symbolic universe. [. . .] He has so enveloped himself in linguistic forms, in artistic images, in mythical symbols or religious rites that he cannot see or know anything except by the interposition of this artificial medium' (Cassirer 1944/1954: 43). Discuss.

4.5 Self and social interaction

We now return to a fundamental problem of sociology. In Chapter 1, we argued that the subject matter of sociology is the study of society, and we described society as something that is different from a mere agglomeration of individuals. Societies have distinctive characteristics that set them apart from others – language, typical beliefs, values and habits, architecture, food, etc. – and they shape the lives of the individuals they comprise in peculiar and powerful ways. Thus, we can confidently assume that there is such a thing as society. However, this statement leaves other fundamental questions unanswered. While human societies possess the power to shape and constrain individuals' lives, this does not mean that these societies are like beehives, comprising vast numbers of drones that follow set tasks and routines without being different from each other at all. Quite the contrary: individuality, that is to say the fact that people are different and distinct from each other in character, personality and temperament, is a generally accepted feature of living with each other in society. In fact, in many societies individuality is highly valued. For example, in contemporary Western societies, a prime motivation for individuals to start living together and begin a family is romantic love – the feeling of having found someone unique and special to share one's life with. Individuality is a key element of social life and constitutes the grounds on which people relate to each other, from heartfelt love to acrimonious conflict. Sociology thus needs to answer questions about the ways in which society shapes, enables, and constrains our individuality.

There is no agreement on the degree to which differences between individuals result from biological and inborn causes instead of the influence of social forces. Nonetheless, we may confidently assume that the latter is considerable. Sociologists describe it as *socialisation*, that is to say the social experiences through which individuals come to learn about their cultures' norms, values, beliefs and generalised rules for social interaction, and through which they acquire a general understanding of the world and their place in it. Socialisation is a complex and lifelong process. It begins with our learning of fundamental aspects of life in childhood. Do you remember how you began to learn language as an infant or were taught how to use the toilet? But socialisation also encompasses the remainder of our lives: for example, consider how, little by little, you 'learn the rules' when you arrive at a new place, like university or a new workplace, and how your way of being gradually changes in these new places. Socialisation thus involves learning from many different people, from your parents and schoolteachers to your boss at work and your classmates at university.

Through socialisation, you become a part of the society in which you live. However, at the same time, you acquire knowledge and skills that allow you to make choices that are your very own – whether to go to university or not, whether to read for an essay or go out to a party, whether to marry or live alone, and so on. Through all these choices, you little by little acquire a unique *biography*, a history of life events and the thoughts and feelings that are attached to them.

Such insights into the enmeshing of individual biography and social forces led sociologists early on to point to the *social nature of the self*. George Herbert Mead's account of the self, as discussed in Chapter 3, is one instance of such arguments. Through his social psychology, Mead drew attention to the ways in which the self is not a stable, self-enclosed property of individuals, but rather constantly moulded and remoulded through everyday interaction with others. In a similar vein, Mead's contemporary, Charles Horton Cooley, wrote of the *looking-glass self*, to highlight the crucial role which our perceptions of others' impressions of ourselves play in our self-perceptions:

> As we see our face, figure, and dress in the glass, and are interested in them because they are ours, and pleased or otherwise with them according as they do or do not answer to what we should like them to be; so in imagination we perceive in another's mind some thought of our appearance, manners, aims, deeds, character, friends, and so on, and are variously affected by it. (Cooley 1902/1998: 164)

Self and self-experience are thus closely bound up with *social interaction*, that is to say the features and dynamics of our encounters with others in everyday life. A detailed and vivid account of the embedding of the self in such everyday encounters can be found in the work of the Canadian sociologist Erving Goffman (1922–1982). Heavily influenced by Mead and Chicago School sociologists, Goffman developed a *dramaturgical model* of social interaction. Starting with *The Presentation of Self in Everyday Life* (1959), Goffman drew on the world of the theatre to envision social interaction in terms of the, more or less able and convincing, *performance* of certain *roles* by the individuals involved in a given situation. Crucially, the participants in such social encounters are concerned with *impression management*, that is, the control of the perceptions which others have of self and the situation at hand. In public situations, *'front stage'* in Goffman's terminology, impression management must be tight and controlled, whereas *'back stage'* performances may be considerably more relaxed.

A brief example may clarify these points. You and your live-in partner have invited friends for dinner. Just before they arrive, you have a terrible fight. Nonetheless, you tidy up your, normally quite messy, flat, turning it from the back-stage site of your disorderly self-expression into publicly acceptable front stage. Your partner has not yet forgiven you for your snide remarks during your fight. Nonetheless, as you do not know your friends that well, you put on big smiles all night long and pretend that nothing bad has happened. You perform the roles of a happy couple and manage your friends' impressions so that they will think of you as nice people and good hosts. In the end, the evening goes well, and you both go to bed happily, thinking that you are in fact good hosts and nice people.

Reading

Goffman, Erving (1959), *The Presentation of Self in Everyday Life*, London: Penguin, pp. 28–36

Performances

Belief in the Part One Is Playing

When an individual plays a part he implicitly requests his observers to take seriously the impression that is fostered before them. They are asked to believe that the character they see actually possesses the attributes he appears to possess, that the task he performs will have the consequences that are implicitly claimed for it, and that, in general, matters are what they appear to be. In line with this, there is the popular view that the individual offers his performance and puts on his show 'for the benefit of other people'. It will be convenient to begin a consideration of performances by turning the question around and looking at the individual's own belief in the impression of reality that he attempts to engender in those among whom he finds himself.

At one extreme, one finds that the performer can be fully taken in by his own act; he can be sincerely convinced that the impression of reality which he stages is the real reality. When his audience is also convinced in this way about the show he puts on – and this seems to be the typical case – then for the moment at least, only the sociologist or the socially disgruntled will have any doubts about the 'realness' of what is presented.

At the other extreme, we find that the performer may not be taken in at all by his own routine. This possibility is understandable, since no one is in quite as good an observational position to see through the act as the person who puts it on. Coupled with this, the performer may be moved to guide the conviction of his audience only as a means to other ends, having no ultimate concern in the conception that they have of him or of the situation. When the individual has no belief in his own act and no ultimate concern with the beliefs of his audience, we may call him cynical, reserving the term 'sincere' for individuals who believe in the impression fostered by their own performance. It should be understood that the cynic, with all his professional disinvolvement, may obtain unprofessional pleasures from his masquerade, experiencing a kind of gleeful spiritual aggression from the fact that he can toy at will with something his audience must take seriously.

It is not assumed, of course, that all cynical performers are interested in deluding their audiences for purposes of what is called 'self-interest' or private gain. A cynical individual may delude his audience for what he considers to be their own good, or for the good of the community, etc. For illustrations of this we need not appeal to sadly enlightened showmen such as Marcus Aurelius or Hsun Tzû. We know that in service occupations practitioners who may otherwise be sincere are sometimes forced to delude their customers because their customers show such a heartfelt demand for it. Doctors who are led into giving placebos, filling station attendants who resignedly check and recheck tyre pressures for anxious women motorists, shoe clerks who sell a shoe that fits but tell the customer it is the size she wants to hear – these are cynical performers whose audiences will not allow them to be sincere. Similarly, it seems that sympathetic patients in mental wards will sometimes feign bizarre symptoms so that student nurses will not be subjected to a disappointingly sane performance. So also, when inferiors extend their most lavish reception for visiting superiors, the selfish desire to win favour may not be the chief motive; the inferior may be tactfully attempting to put the superior at ease by simulating the kind of world the superior is thought to take for granted.

I have suggested two extremes: an individual may be taken in by his own act or be cynical about it. These extremes are something a little more than just the ends of a continuum. Each provides the individual with a position which has its own particular securities and defences, so there will be a tendency for those who have travelled close to one of these poles to complete the voyage. Starting with lack of inward belief in one's role, the individual may follow the natural movement described by Park:

> It is probably no mere historical accident that the word person, in its first meaning, is a mask. It is rather a recognition of the fact that everyone is always and everywhere, more or less consciously, playing a role. . . . It is in these roles that we know each other; it is in these roles that we know ourselves.
>
> In a sense, and in so far as this mask represents the conception we have formed of ourselves – the role we are striving to live up to – this mask is our truer self, the self we would like to be. In the end, our conception of our role becomes second nature and an integral part of our personality. We come into the world as individuals, achieve character, and become persons.

This may be illustrated from the community life of Shetland. For the last four or five years the island's tourist hotel has been owned and operated by a married couple of crofter origins. From the beginning, the owners were forced to set aside their own conceptions as to how life ought to be led, displaying in the hotel a full round of middle-class services and amenities. Lately, however, it appears that the managers have become less cynical about the performance that they stage; they themselves are becoming middle class and more and more enamoured of the selves their clients impute to them.

Another illustration may be found in the raw recruit who initially follows army etiquette in order to avoid physical punishment and eventually comes to follow the rules so that his organization will not be shamed and his officers and fellow soldiers will respect him.

As suggested, the cycle of disbelief-to-belief can be followed in the other direction, starting with conviction or insecure aspiration and ending in cynicism. Professions which the public holds in religious awe often allow their recruits to follow it in this direction not because of a slow realization that they are deluding their audience – for by ordinary social standards the claims they make may be quite valid – but because they can use this cynicism as a means of insulating their inner selves from contact with the audience. And we may even expect to find typical careers of faith, with the individual starting out with one kind of involvement in the performance he is required to give, then moving back and forth several times between sincerity and cynicism before completing all the phases and turning-points of self-belief for a person of his station. Thus, students of medical schools suggest that idealistically oriented beginners in medical school typically lay aside their holy aspirations for a period of time. During the first two years the students find that their interest in medicine must be dropped that they may give all their time to the task of learning how to get through examinations. During the next two years they are too busy learning about diseases to show much concern for the persons who are diseased. It is only after their medical schooling has ended that their original ideals about medical service may be reasserted.

While we can expect to find natural movement back and forth between cynicism and sincerity, still we must not rule out the kind of transitional point that can be sustained on the strength of a little self-illusion. We find that the individual may attempt to induce the audience to judge him and the situation in a particular way, and he may seek this judgement as an ultimate end in itself, and yet he may not completely believe that he deserves the valuation of self which he asks for or that the impression of reality which he fosters is valid. Another mixture of cynicism and belief is suggested in Kroeber's discussion of shamanism:

> Next, there is the old question of deception. Probably most shamans or medicine men, the world over, help along with sleight-of-hand in curing and especially in exhibitions of power. This sleight-of-hand is sometimes deliberate; in many cases awareness is perhaps not deeper than the foreconscious. The attitude, whether there has been repression or not, seems to be as towards a pious fraud. Field ethnographers seem quite generally convinced that even shamans who know that they are frauds nevertheless also believe in their powers, and especially in those of other shamans: they consult them when they themselves or their children are ill.

Front

I have been using the term 'performance' to refer to all the activity of an individual which occurs during a period marked by his continuous presence before a particular set of observers and which has some influence on the observers. It will be convenient to label as 'front' that part of the individual's performance which regularly functions in a general and fixed fashion to define the situation for those who observe the performance. Front, then, is the expressive equipment of a standard kind intentionally or unwittingly employed by the individual during his performance. For preliminary purposes, it will be convenient to distinguish and label what seem to be the standard parts of front.

First, there is the 'setting', involving furniture, décor, physical layout, and other background items which supply the scenery and stage props for the spate of human action played out before, within, or upon it. A setting tends to stay put, geographically speaking, so that those who would use a particular setting as part of their performance cannot begin their act until they have brought themselves to the appropriate place and must terminate their performance when they leave it. It is only in exceptional circumstances that the setting follows along with the performers; we see this in the funeral cortège, the civic parade, and the dream-like processions that kings and queens are made of. In the main, these exceptions seem to offer some kind of extra protection for performers who are, or who have momentarily become, highly sacred. These worthies are to be distinguished, of course, from quite profane performers of the pedlar class who move their place of work between performances, often being forced to do so. In the matter of having one fixed place for one's setting, a ruler may be too sacred, a pedlar too profane.

In thinking about the scenic aspects of front, we tend to think of the living-room in a particular house and the small number of performers who can thoroughly identify themselves with it. We have given insufficient attention to assemblages of sign-equipment which large numbers of performers can call their own for short periods of time. It is characteristic of Western European countries, and no doubt a source of stability for them, that a large number of luxurious settings are available for hire to anyone of the right kind who can afford them. One illustration of this may be cited from a study of the higher civil servant in Britain:

> The question how far the men who rise to the top in the Civil Service take on the 'tone' or 'colour' of a class other than that to which they belong by birth is delicate and difficult. The only definite information bearing on the question is the figures relating to the membership of the great London clubs. More than three-quarters of our high administrative officials belong to one or more clubs of high status and considerable luxury, where the entrance fee might be twenty guineas or more, and the annual subscription from twelve to twenty guineas. These institutions are of the upper class (not even of the upper-middle) in their premises, their equipment, the style of living practised there, their whole atmosphere. Though many of the members would not be described as wealthy, only a wealthy man would unaided provide for himself and his family space, food and drink, service, and other amenities of life to the same standard as he will find at the Union, the Travellers', or the Reform.

Another example can be found in the recent development of the medical profession where we find that it is increasingly important for a doctor to have access to the elaborate scientific stage provided by large hospitals, so that fewer and fewer doctors are able to feel that their setting is a place that they can lock up at night.

If we take the term 'setting' to refer to the scenic parts of expressive equipment, one may take the term 'personal front' to refer to the other items of expressive equipment, the items that we most intimately identify with the performer himself and that we naturally expect will follow the performer wherever he goes. As part of personal front we may include: insignia of office or rank; clothing; sex, age, and racial characteristics; size and looks; posture; speech patterns; facial expressions; bodily gestures; and the like. Some of these vehicles for conveying signs, such as racial characteristics, are relatively fixed and over a span of time do not vary for the individual from one situation to another. On the other hand, some of these sign vehicles are relatively mobile or transitory, such as facial expression, and can vary during a performance from one moment to the next.

It is sometimes convenient to divide the stimuli which make up personal front into 'appearance' and 'manner', according to the function performed by the information that these stimuli convey. 'Appearance' may be taken to refer to those stimuli which function at the time to tell us of the performer's social statuses. These stimuli also tell us of the individual's temporary ritual state: that is, whether he is engaging in formal social activity, work, or informal recreation; whether or not he is celebrating a new phase in the season cycle or in his life-cycle. 'Manner' may be taken to refer to those stimuli which function at the time to warn us of the interaction role the performer will expect to play in the oncoming situation. Thus a haughty, aggressive manner may give the impression that the performer expects to be the one who will initiate the verbal interaction and direct its course. A meek, apologetic manner may give the impression that the performer expects to follow the lead of others, or at least that he can be led to do so.

We often expect, of course, a confirming consistency between appearance and manner; we expect that the differences in social statuses among the interactants will be expressed in some way by congruent differences in the indications that are made of an expected interaction role. This type of coherence of front may be illustrated by the following description of the procession of a mandarin through a Chinese city:

> Coming closely behind . . . the luxurious chair of the mandarin, carried by eight bearers, fills the vacant space in the street. He is mayor of the town, and for all practical purposes the supreme power in it. He is an ideal-looking official, for he is large and massive in appearance, whilst he has that stern and forbidding aspect, as though he were on his way to the execution ground to have some criminal decapitated. This is the kind of air that the mandarins put on when they appear in public. In the course of many years' experience, I have never once seen any of them, from the highest to the lowest, with a smile on his face or a look of sympathy for the people whilst he was being carried officially through the streets.

But, of course, appearance and manner may tend to contradict each other, as when a performer who appears to be of higher estate than his audience acts in a manner that is unexpectedly equalitarian, or intimate, or apologetic, or when a performer dressed in the garments of a high position presents himself to an individual of even higher status.

In addition to the expected consistency between appearance and manner, we expect, of course, some coherence among setting, appearance, and manner. Such coherence represents an ideal type that provides us with a means of stimulating our attention to and interest in exceptions. In this the student is assisted by the journalist, for exceptions to expected consistency among setting, appearance and manner provide the piquancy and glamour of many careers and the sale-able appeal of many magazine articles. For example, a *New Yorker* profile on Roger Stevens (the real-estate agent who engineered the sale of the Empire State Building) comments on the startling fact that Stevens has a small house, a meagre office, and no letterhead stationery.

In order to explore more fully the relations among the several parts of social front, it will be convenient to consider here a significant characteristic of the information conveyed by front, namely, its abstractness and generality.

However specialized and unique a routine is, its social front, with certain excep-tions, will tend to claim facts that can be equally claimed and asserted of other, somewhat different, routines. For example, many service occupations offer their clients a performance that is illuminated with dramatic expressions of cleanliness, modernity, competence, and integrity. While in fact these abstract standards have a different significance in different occupational performances, the observer is encouraged to stress the abstract similarities. For the observer this is a wonderful, though sometimes disastrous, convenience. Instead of having to maintain a dif-ferent pattern of expectation and responsive treatment for each slightly different performer and performance, he can place the situation in a broad category around which it is easy for him to mobilize his past experience and stereotypical thinking. Observers then need only be familiar with a small and hence manageable vocabu-lary of fronts, and know how to respond to them, in order to orient themselves in a wide variety of situations. Thus in London the current tendency for chimney sweeps and perfume clerks to wear white lab coats tends to provide the client with an understanding that the delicate tasks performed by these persons will be per-formed in what has become a standardized, clinical, confidential manner.

Consider
1. To begin with, summarise Goffman's arguments in your own words. Give as many everyday examples as you can.
2. What does Goffman understand by a 'performance'? What are the various features of social situations that shape a performance?
3. What elements are necessary for the performance of a 'good student'? Formulate your answer using Goffman's terminology.

4.6 The social life of emotions

Emotions are a persistent part of everyday life. Feelings are with you in everything you do every day. Many of the things you do are routine, and they do not produce strong feelings in you. Nonetheless, even commonplace situations like getting up, get-ting washed, and getting dressed or attending the same, not very interesting, lecture week after week do carry feelings with them – boredom, the pleasure of being clean and putting on clothes that make you feel good about yourself, and so forth. Then, of course, there are the more exceptional situations: the end-of-year exam, the visit to the dentist's, a romantic encounter, the excitement of being at the airport, about to leave for a faraway place. Even images and memories can provoke strong feelings. Photo 4.1 illustrates this point quite well. Unless you happen to be reading this book in Australia or have an interest in biology, the Sydney funnel-web spider is of small significance to you. Yet spiders – and even pictures of spiders – provoke instant revulsion and fright in many of us (including myself). Even abstract symbols and ideas may lead to strong expressions of feeling – think of the range of emotions, from pride to hate, that are often associated with the flags of various countries. It, therefore, surely is correct to describe emotions as an ever-present texture of social life.

Still, some sociologists are troubled by the idea of a sociology of emotions. As we saw in the preceding chapters, early sociology legitimised itself as the science-like study of societies. While the idea of sociology as a science is nowadays hotly disputed, it continues to inform the work of many scholars. Within ideals of objective, rational, value-free research, there is no space for emotions – the feelings of the researcher, the feelings that shape his interaction with his participants, the feelings of the participants themselves.

Photo 4.1   Sydney funnel-web spider. Resident around Sydney in Australia, Funnel-web spiders are often found in shrubby and overgrown spaces. They may also enter swimming pools. These spiders are among the most dangerous in the world. They are quite fast, and during attacks they bite repeatedly and cling firmly to their victim. Sydney funnel-web spiders are highly poisonous, and their bites on occasion have been lethal to humans.

Source: DK Images

Moreover, emotions have often been portrayed as purely personal matters – issues of individual mental life that should concern psychologists but not sociologists.

Nonetheless, in recent years there has been significant interest in emotion's roles in social life. The development of new genres of sociological writing has given sociologists an enhanced range of tools to this end. One example of this trend is the emergence of *auto-ethnography*, which explores social phenomena and processes through the writer's personal experiences. For instance, in her much praised study 'Chronicling an Academic Depression', Barbara Jago (2002) explores her experiences of major depression and, in so doing, sheds light on issues such as the social dynamics of academic life, the social nature of self-experience, and medical discourses of mental illness. Her argument is difficult to capture in a short extract, but the following account of an encounter in a university parking lot does highlight her intimately personal style and her attention to emotions:

> Crossing the parking lot toward the back door, I walk past a former student, early twenty-something with long blond hair. A smart young woman if memory serves. She doesn't acknowledge me. Perhaps she is still angry that I bailed out halfway through the semester last year, diagnosed with major depression, abandoning three classes, unable to do the teaching I loved, taking medical leave and then long-term disability. Perhaps my professor self has been rendered invisible, obliterated by a depression haze. Perhaps she just doesn't know what to say. My eyes seek the refuge of the ground. (Jago 2002: 730)

Moreover, since the 1970s, the *sociology of emotions* has theorised the role of emotions in social life and examined the social dynamics of emotions in societies around the world. A widely cited pioneer in this field is the American sociologist Arlie Russell Hochschild. In particular, *The Managed Heart* (1983), a study on the work of flight attendants, is often mentioned as a key study on the social nature of emotions. While many of Hochschild's observations seem somewhat quaint in the world of high-security post-9/11 air travel, she does capture fundamental aspects of service work:

> The young trainee sitting next to me wrote on her notepad, 'Important to smile. Don't forget to smile.' The admonition came from the speaker in the front of the room, a crew-cut pilot in his early fifties, speaking in a Southern drawl: 'Now girls, I want you to go out there and really *smile*. Your smile is your biggest *asset*. I want you to go out there and use it. Smile. *Really* smile. Really *lay it on*.' (Hochschild 1983: 4; emphasis in original)

Relentless niceness is certainly a central aspect of what service workers are expected to 'do', from embattled call centre agents dealing with customer complaints to weary fast-food workers serving hamburgers or kebabs after midnight. Hochschild unpacks the ways in which flight attendants' emotions are *socially constructed* in and through the demands of working life in airports and aeroplanes. She concludes that flight attendants are required to strategically manage their emotions, identifying and performing the *feeling rules* that are attached to certain situations: 'Your smile is your biggest asset.' In doing so, the flight attendants engaged in what Hochschild terms *emotional labour*, which 'requires one to induce or suppress feeling in order to sustain the outward countenance that produces the proper state of mind in others – in this case, the sense of being cared for in a convivial and safe place' (Hochschild 1983: 7). However, performing emotional labour may have a steep cost, as Hochschild found that workers may become alienated from their own selves by treating themselves as instruments according to the requirements of their workplace.

The following extract comes from one of Hochschild's (2003) later studies on the commercialisation of intimate life and personal relationships in the contemporary world. Here, Hochschild describes the emotional textures in women's advice books in the USA.

Reading

Hochschild, Arlie Russell (2003), *The Commercialization of Intimate Life: Notes from Home and Work*, Berkeley: University of California Press, pp. 13–18, 19–24

1 The Commercial Spirit of Intimate Life and the Abduction of Feminism

Signs from Women's Advice Books

Best-selling advice books for women published in the United States in the later part of the past century offer a glimpse into an important future trend in American popular culture. This trend is a curious, latter-day parallel to the very different cultural shift Max Weber describes in *The Protestant Ethic and the Spirit of Capitalism*. Just as Protestantism, according to Max Weber, "escaped from the cage" of the church to be transposed into an inspirational "spirit of capitalism" that drove men to make money and build capitalism, so feminism may be "escaping from the cage" of a social movement to buttress a commercial spirit of intimate life that was originally separate from and indeed alien to it. Just as market conditions ripened the soil for capitalism, so a weakened family prepares the soil for a commercialized spirit of domestic life. Magnified moments in advice books tell this story.

The current cultural shift differs in the object of its ideas (love and not work), in the social sphere it most affects (the family and not the economy), and in the population most immediately influenced (women, not men). The cultural shift reflected in advice books concerns a more marginal ideology – feminism – and the commercial transmutation of it is a shift that is smaller, I hope, in scale. Like the earlier trend, this one represents the outcome of an ongoing cultural struggle, gives rise to countertrends, and is uneven in its effect. But the parallel is there.

To explore evidence of this shift, this parallel, let's turn to best-selling advice books for women published between 1970 and 1990 as a likely bellwether of trends in the popular ideas governing women's approach to intimate life. For, like other commercial and professional conveyors of guidance, advice books are becoming more important while traditional spheres of authority, families and to a degree churches, are becoming less so. Thus, while the counsel of parents, grandparents, aunts and uncles, ministers, priests, and rabbis holds relatively less weight than it did a century ago, that of professional therapists, television talk show hosts, radio commentators, video producers, and magazine and advice book authors assumes relatively more weight. While people turn increasingly to anonymous authorities, the emotional problems they wish to resolve are probably more perplexing than ever.

Like other commercially based advice-givers, the authors of advice books act as emotional investment counselors. They do readings of broad social conditions and recommend to readers of various types how, how much, and in whom to "invest" emotional attention. They recommend emotional practices – such as asking the reader to think of "praise" as "manipulation" – to cast doubt on the sincerity of one's own praise and to detach oneself from another person, as the advice book writer Robin Norwood recommends in this essay's epigraph. Writers also motivate their readers by hitching investment strategies to inspirational ideas and images buried in "magnified moments" inside the parable-like stories that make up much of these books.

Neither author nor reader, I imagine, is much aware that they are offering or receiving "emotional investment counseling." Rather, authors see themselves as giving, and readers see themselves as receiving, helpful advice. Sometimes it is. My basic point is that helping and being helped are matters of such overwhelming importance that any cultural shift that "thins out" the process through which we give care to one another or empties the content of help should make us stop and think about where we're going.

A Cultural Cooling: Trends and Countertrends

With these starting points, I propose that many best-selling advice books published in recent years have become cooler in their approach to intimate life. They reflect a cultural cooling. This does not mean that individuals need one another less, only that they are invited to *manage their needs more*. The trend also reflects a paradox. Earlier advice books were far more patriarchal, less based on open and equal communication, but, oddly, they often reflect more warmth. More recent advice books call for more open and more equal communication but propose cooler emotional strategies with which to engage those equal bonds. From the vantage point of the early feminist movement, modern advice books reaffirm one ideal (equality) but undermine another (emotionally rich social bonds).

Two trends in the literature bear on this "cooling." One supports the observation of cooling but doesn't link it to advice books. The other analyzes advice books but doesn't focus on cooling. Christopher Lasch, Ann Swidler, Francesca Cancian, and Mary Evans, among others, argue that "commitment" is a diminishing part in people's idea of love. Data from American national opinion polls document a decline over recent decades in commitment to long-term love. In their study of daytime soap opera heroes and heroines, Lee Harrington and Denise Bielby don't observe a shift away from the idea of lasting love, but they note a shift away from social practices that affirm it.

Analyses of the advice literature, on the other hand, say little about this cooling. Commentators have instead critiqued the authoritarianism, privatism, and ideology of victimhood implicit in many advice books. In *I'm Dysfunctional, You're Dysfunctional*, Wendy Kaminer critiques advice books in the Recovery Movement (based on the twelve-step program of Alcoholics Anonymous) for appealing to individual choice while giving orders and taking it away. In *Self-Help Culture: Reading Women's Readings* Wendy Simonds rightly argues a second point, namely that self-oriented quick-fix books deflect attention from problems in the public sphere that cause people to need private help in the first place. In "Beware the Incest-Survivor Machine" Carol Tavris critiques the cult of victimhood many survivor books seem to promote.

While there is much truth in all three critiques, I believe something else is also going on – a shift in the cultural premises about human attachment. Although there is much talk about the relative merit of this or that kind of family, current advice books take us down a weird cultural tunnel, which reveals the soil and root system that characterizes them all.

To get a good look at this soil, we can draw an imaginary line through the emotional core of each advice book by focusing on the best and worst "magnified moments" in it, the top and bottom of the personal experience the book portrays. This method works best with the therapeutic, interview, and autobiographical books.

Most books seem to have four parts. In one, the author establishes a tone of voice, a relationship to the reader, and connects the reader to a source of authority – the Bible, psychoanalysis, corporate expertise, Hollywood, or the school of hard knocks. In a second part the author didactically describes moral or social reality. "This is how men are," or "that's what the job market's like," they say, or "this is the rule" and how it bends under a variety of circumstances. In a third part the book describes concrete practices; for example, "with your boyfriend, listen, with your girlfriend, talk," or "Wear blue to a 'power breakfast meeting' at work." In a fourth and I believe most revealing part of the advice book, the author tells stories about personal experience. These stories are based on the lives of patients in an author's psychotherapeutic practice, interviewees, or the author's own life. Such stories tend to be either exemplary or cautionary. Exemplary stories tell the reader what to do and cautionary stories tell her what not to do.

Stories of both sorts contain magnified moments, episodes of heightened importance, either epiphanies, moments of intense glee or unusual insight, or moments in which things go intensely but meaningfully wrong. In either case, the moment stands out as metaphorically rich, unusually elaborate, and often echoes throughout the book.

One thing a magnified moment magnifies is the *feeling* a person holds up as ideal. It shows what a person, up until the experience began, *wanted* to feel. Thus there is an ideal expressed in the moment and there is culture within the ideal. Magnified moments reflect a feeling ideal both when a person joyously lives up to it or, in some spectacular way, does not. More than the descriptions of the author's authority or beliefs, more than the long didactic passages in advice books about what is or isn't true or right, magnified moments show the experience we wish. We can ask many questions about this experience. We may ask, for example: What is it precisely about a feeling that makes it seem wonderful or terrible? Against what ideal is it being compared? Who is on the scene during the moment? What relations are revealed, in reality or imagination? By interrogating the moment, so to speak, we ferret out the cultural premises that underlie it. About the advice to which these magnified moments lend support, we can ask many questions. About the experience, and the ideal against which it is measured, we may ask further questions. Does the advice support a general paradigm of trust or caution? Does it center on expressing one's emotional needs or marshaling strategic control over them? Is the book warm, in the sense of legitimizing a high degree of care and social support and offering scope for human needs? Or is it cool, in the sense of presuming the individual should get by with relatively little support and of presuming she or he has fewer needs?

Doorway Drama

We can draw one set of magnified moments from Marabel Morgan's *The Total Woman* (1973), an arch-reactionary traditional book (covertly addressed to modern readers) that is curiously warm. We can draw a very different set from Colette Dowling's *The Cinderella Complex* (1981), a modern advice book that is curiously cool.

From *The Total Woman:*

> If your husband comes home at 6:00, bathe at 5.00. In preparing for your six o'clock date, lie back and let go of the tensions of the day. Think about that special man who's on his way home to you. . . . Rather than make your husband play hide-and-seek when he comes home tired, greet him at the door when he arrives. Make homecoming a happy time. Waltzing to the door in a cloud of powder and cologne is a great confidence builder. Not only can you respond to his advances, you will want to. . . . For an experiment, I put on pink baby-doll pajamas and white boots after my bubble bath. I must admit that I looked foolish and felt even more so. When I opened the door that night to greet Charlie, I was unprepared for his reaction. My quiet, reserved, non-excitable husband took one look, dropped his briefcase on the doorstep, and chased me around the dining room table. We were in stitches by the time he caught me, and breathless with that old feeling of romance. . . . Our little girls stood flat against the wall watching our escapade, giggling with delight.

We all had a marvelous evening together, and Charlie forgot to mention the problems of the day.

What did Marabel Morgan feel? First, she felt delight and surprise at Charlie's response. Charlie was surprised, of course, but then so was Marabel – at the very fact that her act succeeded. In some ways, Morgan's peak moment is the same as other peak moments in advice books to women. She feels central, appreciated, in the middle of an experience she wants to have. But in other ways her moment is very different. For one thing, it's "fun," and fun in a certain kind of way. It is sexually exciting within the context of the family. It is marital and family fun. She is breathless in her husband's arms – not in a lover's arms. And her two girls are nearby, "flat against the wall" and "giggling." Sexual excitement is marital and marital fun includes the kids.

In addition to Morgan's husband and daughters, present in fantasy are a community of women who are also working on their marriages. After they have tried out a certain move at home, Morgan tells us, one "Total Woman" class member often calls another the next morning to see how it went. Spanning across families, a mirror opposite to the women's movement, a community of Christian wives are "watching the show" in each other's homes.

Marabel Morgan's big moment doesn't occur naturally, as when one is suddenly overcome by a magnificent rainbow or sunset. It is not spontaneous. Her moment is a well-planned, choreographed act. Sometimes instead of dressing in pink pajamas, she dresses as a pixie or a pirate, or comes to the door totally nude wrapped in cellophane. Her magnified moment is not an occasion for self-realization or revealing communication, not the "high" of sudden self-honesty or intimate communication. The act and the delighted response form a stylized, premodern form of communication in themselves. Marabel puts on her baby-doll suit. Charlie sees she means to please him. He is pleased. She receives his pleasure. They have communicated. *That* is the high point. At the same time, Morgan's act paradoxically doubles as a shield against intimate communication. With doorway surprises, she advises her readers to "keep him off guard." Whether she is pleasing Charlie or getting her way with him by working female wiles, whether she draws inspiration from the Bible or Hollywood, Marabel Morgan is approaching her husband in an old-fashioned way.
[. . .]

The No-Needs Modern

At the other end of the spectrum we find a moment from Colette Dowling's *The Cinderella Complex*:

> Powerful emotional experiences await those who are really living out their own scripts. A Chicago woman in her early forties who still lives with and loves her husband is also intensely involved with a man she works with.

He too is married, so their time together is limited. They look forward to the business trips they manage to take together several times a year. On one of these, the woman decided after a few days that she wanted to go skiing. The man was not a skier and in any event had further work to do in Boston. "I decided that I should ski by myself," she told me [Dowling]. "I got on a bus in the middle of the afternoon and as we wound up into the Vermont mountains, it began to snow. I remember sitting by myself on this greyhound bus, looking out the window and watching the lights come on in the little towns we passed through. I felt so good, so secure in the knowledge that I could be myself, do what I want – *and also be loved* – I started to cry."

Marabel Morgan is greeting Charlie in pink baby-doll pajamas at dinnertime while her children watch. The "Chicago woman" leaves her husband for her lover, then leaves her lover to ride a Greyhound bus up a mountain alone. One is in the thick of family life, the other pretty far outside it. One is acting; the other enjoying, perhaps, the release from acting. Morgan values fun; Dowling, aliveness and self-understanding. Morgan is onstage, Dowling's Chicago woman is offstage. In their magnified moments, Morgan's husband is the audience while the Chicago woman's husband functions more as a stage.

The drama in the Chicago woman's magnified moment doesn't take place between herself and her husband, but between her desire to be attached and her desire to be independent. For Dowling's woman, the drama does not take place through the enactment of a social role but in an emotional space outside her regular life, beyond the labors of love. For even when she is offstage, away from her marriage, she's not working on her "intense affair." The focus moves to her feeling in the bus, the mountains, the snow, the anonymous context within which she feels attached but independent. She comes alive focusing inward – figuring out a troubled boundary between herself and anyone else. Her feelings are in response to thinking about relationships, not in response to enacting them. If Morgan is inspired by her own success at breathing life into monogamous marriage, the Chicago woman is inspired, perhaps, by daring to challenge it.

Who is on the scene in the Chicago woman's epiphany? She's honest. But who is she honest with? Her husband? Her lover? Her children? A close friend? A community of women? It is really none of these. Elsewhere we discover a somewhat people-less career and the idea of exertion, excelling. Her exertion is private and internal, against her very dependency on others.

For Dowling we're our best when we are by ourselves facing the elements alone, as in the myth of the cowboy, the Jack London trapper in a forest, Hemingway's man and the sea. Others of Dowling's positive moments are stories about women being sprung free into professional success, erotic freedom, and autonomy. In her final chapter she describes a scene from the life of Simone de Beauvoir, who broke her dependence on her life's partner, the philosopher Jean-Paul Sartre, through a series of fierce missions "climbing every peak, clambering down every gully . . . exploring every valley . . . around Marseilles, through challenging solitary ten hour hikes, 25 miles each day. . . . Simone de Beauvoir's hikes became both the method and the metaphor of her rebirth as an individual," Dowling says. She quotes de Beauvoir: "Alone I walked the mists that hung over the summit of Sainte Victoire, and trod along the ridge of the Pilon de Roi, bracing myself against a violent wind which sent my beret spinning down into the valley below. . . . When I was clambering over rocks and mountains or sliding down screes, I would work out shortcuts, so that each expedition was a work of art in itself." Once she charged up a steep gorge, unable to go back the way she came, but, upon reaching a fault in the rock, was unable to jump across. Backtracking down the treacherous rocks, triumphantly she concludes, *I knew that I could now rely on myself."*

In her most dreadful moment, Dowling feels the opposite of this. She begins the book with this passage:

> I am lying alone on the third floor of our house with a bad bout of the flu, trying to keep my illness from the others. The room feels large and cold and as the hours pass, strangely inhospitable. I begin to remember myself as a little girl, small, vulnerable, helpless. By the time night falls I am utterly miserable, not so sick with flu as with anxiety. "What am I doing here, so solitary, so unattached, so . . . floating?" I ask myself. How strange to be so disturbed, cut off from family, from my busy, demanding life . . . disconnected. More than air and energy and life itself what I want is to be safe, warm, taken care of.

This desire to be "safe, warm, taken care of" forms the basis of the dreaded "Cinderella Complex," which, Dowling goes on to generalize, is the "chief force holding women down today." Elsewhere in the book, Dowling points to the waste of brains when women don't have careers. She cites the Stanford Gifted Child Study of 600 California children with IQs above 135. She notes that most male geniuses have had high-level professional careers while most women geniuses have not. This isn't good for society, she says, or fair to women; in this, Dowling's advice book is clearly feminist and modern.

The Total Woman and *The Cinderella Complex* are guided by different inspirations. Morgan tries to have fun, she likes to act and feel exuberantly playful in the confines of a unitary patriarchal world. The dangerous feelings for her are anger, assertiveness, strivings outside the home, feelings that do not fit that patriarchal world. Dowling, on the other hand, strives to be honest with herself, to control and tame her needs in a sparsely populated and socially dispersed world. For her, the dangerous feeling is the desire to be "safe, warm, and taken care of." Indeed, her fear of being dependent on another person evokes the image of the American cowboy, alone, detached, roaming free with his horse. The American cowboy has long been a model for men struggling against the constraints of corporate capitalism. Now Dowling embraces this ideal for women. On the ashes of Cinderella, then, rises a postmodern cowgirl.

The two authors differ in their ideas about what is exciting: attaching yourself to a man or detaching yourself from him. They differ in their policies toward emotion management: one advises women to suppress any assertion of will in the service of binding them to men; the other advises women to suppress any feeling that would bind them to men too closely. They differ in the place they accord autonomy in the ideal feminine self and ultimately in their views about danger and safety in the world for women.

Although the advice books I've studied don't line up in the same rows on all dimensions, if we sort them according to their views on the role of women, roughly a third lean toward the "traditional" model. Examples are the humorous Erma Bombeck's *Motherhood: The Second Oldest Profession* (1983), her *The Grass Is Always Greener over the Septic Tank* (1976), and James Dobson's *Parenting Isn't for Cowards* (1987). Roughly two-thirds lean toward the modern model, of which *The Cinderella Complex* is an especially individualistic example. We find a lighter, more saucy version of it in Helen Gurley Brown's *Having It All* (1982). Equally searching but less focused on autonomy are Susan Forward and Joan Torres's *Men Who Hate Women and the Women Who Love Them* (1987), Robin Norwood's *Women Who Love Too Much* (1985), Connell Cowan and Melvyn Kinder's *Smart Women, Foolish Choices* (1985), and Barbara De Angelis's *Secrets about Men Every Woman Should Know* (1990).

Most of these "modern" books whisper to the reader, "Let the emotional investor beware." If Morgan counsels women to accumulate domestic capital and invest at home, Dowling cautions women to invest in the self as a solo enterprise. Most advice books of the 1970s and 1980s are spin-offs or mixtures of these two investment strategies. Gaining the edge during this period, then, is the postmodern cowgirl who devotes herself to the ascetic practices of emotional control and expects to give and receive surprisingly little love from other human beings.

A handful of books are warm moderns, emphasizing equality *and* social attachment, sharing *and* commitment. Examples are the Boston Women's Health Book Collective's *Ourselves and Our Children* (1978) and Harriet Lerner's *The Dance of Anger* (1985). It is my impression – though I've not taken a systematic look at women's advice books since 1990 – that the supply of warm modern books has expanded, although not that much.

The Cool Modern and the Commercial Spirit of Intimate Life

Cool modern advice books reveal a newly unfolding paradox that is reminiscent of an earlier paradox. In *The Protestant Ethic and the Spirit of Capitalism*, Weber describes a set of beliefs held by a variety of Protestant sects – a belief in ascetic self-control, frugality, hard work, and devotion to a calling. He traces the way in which these *religious* ideas were adapted to a *material* purpose. The idea of devotion to a calling came to mean devotion to making money. The idea of self-control came to mean careful saving, spending, and capital reinvestment.

The Protestant Ethic "escaped the cage" to become part of a new hybrid "spirit of capitalism."

Comparing the origin of these motivational ideas and their ultimate destination, Weber made this significant comment:

> Today the spirit of religious asceticism – whether finally, who knows? – has escaped from the cage. But victorious capitalism, since it rests on mechanical foundations, needs its support no longer. The rosy blush of its laughing heir, the Enlightenment, seems also to be irretrievably fading and the idea of duty in one's calling prowls about in our lives like the ghost of dead religious beliefs.

The original religious ideas jumped the churchyard fence to land in the marketplace. Luther and Calvin would have been aghast at the leap their ideas took. As Weber notes, wryly:

> . . . it is not to be understood that we expect to find any of the founders or representatives of these religious movements considering the promotion of what we have called the spirit of capitalism as in any sense the end of his life work. We cannot well maintain that the pursuit of worldly goods, conceived as an end in itself, was to any of them of positive ethical value.

Work devoted to a calling as the religious fathers originally intended it was a task set by God, and it led to salvation. In Benjamin Franklin's capitalist hands (his 1736 advice book was called *Necessary Hints to Those Who Would Be Rich*), a calling led elsewhere.

Now, has another set of beliefs jumped another fence? Is a more marginal belief system, feminism, escaping from the cage of a social movement to buttress a commercial spirit of intimate life? The feminism represented, for example, by Charlotte Gilman or Lucretia Mott, or by the mid-1970s second-wave feminists whose thinking is reflected in the best-selling advice book *Our Bodies, Ourselves,* has "escaped the cage" into a commercial arena. Like Calvin, the feminist founders might have worried at the cultural trends weaving themselves around their core ideals. "Equality, yes," they might say were they alive today, "but why allow the worst of capitalist culture to establish the *cultural basis* of it?" "Autonomy, yes," they might say, "but the standalone cowgirl – why?"

The analogy, then, is this: Feminism is to the commercial spirit of intimate life as Protestantism is to the spirit of capitalism. The first legitimates the second. The second borrows from but also transforms the first. Just as certain prior conditions prepared the soil for the spirit of capitalism to take off – the decline of feudalism, the growth of cities, the rising middle class – so, too, certain prior conditions ripen the soil for the takeoff of the commercial spirit of intimate life. The preconditions now are a weakening of the family, the decline of the church, and loss of local community – traditional shields against the harsher effects of capitalism.

Given this backdrop, a commercial culture has moved in, silently borrowing from feminism an ideology that made way for women in public life. From feminism these books draw a belief in the equal worth of men and women. Modern books begin with the idea that women think too little of themselves. Their human needs are not met. The authors of these books genuinely seek, I believe, to uplift women, to raise women's worth in their own eyes and the eyes of others. This idea is what makes cool modern books *modern*. This idea of equality makes them a powerful challenge to Marabel Morgan; it's what makes her advice seem old-fashioned, invalid, silly.

What advice books blend with feminism, however, is a commercial spirit of intimate life. And here I move well beyond analogy. For, it seems also true that part of the *content* of the spirit of capitalism is being *displaced* onto intimate life; this is, in fact, partly what the commercial spirit of intimate life *is*. The ascetic self-discipline that the early capitalist applied to his bank account the twenty-first-century woman applies to her appetite, her body, her love. The devotion to a "calling," which the early capitalist applied to earning money, the latter-day woman applies to "having it all." The activism, the belief in working hard and aiming high, the desire to go for it, to be saved, to win, to succeed, which the early capitalists used to build capitalism in a rough-and-tumble marketplace, many advice books urge women to transfer to love in a rapidly changing courtship scene.

The commercial spirit of intimate life is made up of images that prepare the way for a paradigm of distrust. These are images of "me" and "you" and "us" that are psychologically defended and shallow. It is also made up of a way of relating to others associated with the paradigm, a spirit of instrumental detachment that fits the emptied slots where a deeper "me," "you," and "us" might be.

Cool modern books prepare the self for a commercial spirit of intimate life by offering as ideal a self well defended against getting hurt. In Dowling's worst magnified moment, she leaps away in fright from her own desire to be "safe, warm, comforted." She ardently seeks to develop the capacity to endure emotional isolation. Parallel to the image of the low-needs self is the image of the self that ministers to itself. Who helps the self? The answer is the self. In appendix 4 of *Women Who Love Too Much*, Robin Norwood offers private affirmations: "Twice daily, for three minutes each time, maintain eye contact with yourself in a mirror as you *say out loud*, '(your name), I love you and accept you exactly the way you are.'" The heroic acts a self can perform, in this view, are to detach, to leave, and to depend on and need others less. The emotion work that matters is control of the feelings of fear, vulnerability, and the desire to be comforted. The ideal self doesn't need much, and what it does need it can get for itself.

Consider

1. Summarise Hochschild's argument in your own words.
2. What are the main contrasts Hochschild draws between 'warm' and 'cool' emotional styles of intimate life?
3. Do you agree with Hochschild's diagnosis of the rise of a 'cool modern' approach to couple relationships and love? Why? Support your answer with relevant examples from everyday life.
4. Why, if at all, should emotions form an important part of sociological enquiry? You may need to do some background research to be able to answer this question.

4.7 Making the social body

In 1968, US anthropologist Donn V. Hart published a study on sexual experiences and practices in the Philippines, a subject matter that, he admitted, was poorly understood among Western anthropologists of his time. Through extensive fieldwork in the Visayan Islands, Hart identified two noteworthy categorisations of sexual practice, báyot and lakín-on. He defined them as follows:

> English translations of *báyot* and *lakín-on* (from *laláki*, "male") indicate that the two terms are synonyms for homosexuality, transvestism, hermaphroditism, lesbianism, and general deviance from sexual norms (Hermosisima and Lopez 1966). These two vernacular words have the identical calibrated meaning of the popular use of berdache in anthropological literature (Angelino and Shedd 1955: 121). In Siaton and Dumaguete, báyot and lakín-on may refer respectively to men or women who only slightly exhibit physical stigmata or behavioral characteristics thought typical of the opposite sex, to transvestites, or to overt, aggressive homosexuals who do not cross-dress. The Cebuan vocabulary, however, distinguishes between degrees of 'bayotness.' A slightly effeminate man is *dalopapa* or *binabáye* (Tag. binabaeng). When these terms are used in reference to a chicken, they describe a rooster with henlike plumage (Hermosisima and Lopez 1966: 69). *Babae-babae* (from babáye, 'female') or *báyot-bayot* are more effeminate males, who do not cross-dress and who usually are not considered active sexual inverts. (Hart 1968)

We might understand these characterisations as exercises in cultural translation. Hart wrote about a subject matter of which his readers would likely have had no knowledge or understanding. He was thus faced with the task of re-rendering báyot and lakín-on in terms that would have made sense for Americans in the late 1960s. In turn, nearly half a century later, words such as 'lesbianism' are beginning to sound slightly odd; sexual cultures in the USA themselves have changed, and anthropologists today would likely use somewhat different language.

This illustrates a basic point: bodies feel natural; they seem to be biological givens. You are born into your body, you inhabit it, and you likely feel quite attached to it. It shares lots of features with others' bodies, and yet it is uniquely your own, as a glance into a mirror will confirm. Yet bodies are anything but simple affairs, and the way you experience your body and those of others around you is fashioned through a variety of complex social processes. It is from this recognition that sociological accounts of the body depart.

According to Chris Shilling (2005), four recent social trends have motivated such sociological interest. First, technological changes now allow significant modifications of bodies and raise questions – and, sometimes, concern – about the boundaries between nature and technology. Bodies broken in accidents can now be fixed, restored, or even recomposed – think about recent reports of successful face transplants. Through surgical intervention, bodies can now be transformed from 'male' into 'female' and vice versa. Artificial organs can replace or complement those with which we were born. And so forth. Bodies, according to Shilling (2003; 2005) have become *body projects*: they have been opened to potentially continuous transformation according to the norms, values and desires of society and individuals.

Second, bodies are social objects through their *commercialisation*. In mundane ways, such commercialisation occurs through the advertisement and sale of a wide range of cosmetic products. From shampoo to skin-lightening cream, people buy cosmetics to render their bodies desirable, with the advertising industry playing a major part in what amounts to desirability. In much less mundane ways, an often criminal 'organ economy' (Lundin 2012) now facilitates the purchase and sale of body parts to extend and enhance the lives of some, often at the expense of others.

Third, modern bodies are subject to often highly detailed *regimes of social control* or *governmentality*. 'Instrumental here was Foucault's (1970, 1979a, 1979b) analysis of how modernity's creation of "man" was accompanied by a shift in the target of governmental discourses (the fleshy body gave way to the mindful body as a focus of concern); in the object of discourse (preoccupation with matters of death was replaced by interest in structuring life); and in the scope of discourse (the control of anonymous individuals gave way to the management of differentiated populations)' (Shilling 2005). A useful example here are the increasingly tight regimes of scanning, surveying and sorting bodies that have been introduced at airports around the world through the US 'war on terror'.

Fourth, *social movements* have in recent decades played a major part in debates about how human bodies may or may not be used. This concerns, for instance, feminists' challenges of arguments about women's supposedly biologically grounded inferiority to men. Public debates and struggles about abortion are another notable example of contemporary importance.

Implicit in the preceding points is an understanding of the historical and socio-cultural mutability of the ways in which we understand, experience and act on our bodies. The German-English sociologist Norbert Elias (1897–1990) documented this mutability in enormous detail in *The Civilizing Process* (1939/2000). *The Civilizing Process* argues that historical changes in European societies from the Middle Ages onwards entailed an ever tighter and more detailed control over bodily expression in everyday life. Table manners, dress codes, and rules for one's behaviour in the presence of others gradually imposed self-control and discipline on individuals and taught them how to hide many of their bodily functions and expressions from view.

Reading

Scheper-Hughes, Nancy (2004), 'Parts unknown: Undercover ethnography of the organs-trafficking underworld', *Ethnography*, 5(1), pp. 30–1, 37–9, 44–9

In a poignant scene from producer Stephen Frears' neo-Gothic film 'Dirty Pretty Things', which treats the traffic in human frailty and vulnerability in the shadowy underworld of immigrant London, Okwe, a politically framed, haunted and hunted Nigerian doctor-refugee who is hiding out as a hotel receptionist, delivers a freshly purloined human kidney in a Styrofoam cooler to a sleazy body-parts broker in the underground parking lot of the sham elegant hotel staffed almost entirely by new immigrants, many of them (like Okwe) desperate illegals and refugees on the lam.

'How come I've never seen you before?' the English broker (one of the very few Anglo-speaking white people to appear in the film) asks Okwe before gingerly accepting the strangely animate and 'priceless' parcel handed over to him. Barely concealing his rage, Okwe replies between clenched teeth in his finely accented Nigerian English: 'Because we are the people you never see. We are the invisible people, the ones who clean your homes, who drive your taxis, who suck your cocks'. And, now it goes without saying, who provide you with their 'spare' body parts.

Little did Steven Knight, the London-based scriptwriter of 'Dirty Pretty Things', realize how close to the mark his imaginative portrayal of the global transplant underworld had struck. 'Why set this drama in a hotel?' I asked a Miramax film representative, noting that a three-star 'hospit-el' (as such medical and 'transplant tourist-trap' clinics are called in the Philippines) would have worked just as well and not let the world's transplant outlaws off the hook so easily. But the film is not a documentary but a social thriller which blends aspects of the global urban legends about child kidnapping for organs and prostitutes drugging unsuspecting barflies who wake up in a hotel bathtub minus a kidney (see Scheper-Hughes, 1996, 2001b, 2002; White, 1997) with the very real social dramas of human trafficking for transplantable organs and tissues (see Andrews and Nelkin, 2001; Rothman et al., 1997; Scheper-Hughes, 2000, 2001a, 2001c, 2002, 2003a, 2003b; Sharp, 2000). The back-door/backstage scenes of organs and tissues procurement combine aspects of the real, the unreal and the uncanny.

To a great many social scientists and folklorists like the tireless Véronique Campion-Vincent (1997) and the prolific Alan Dundes (1991), the organs theft story is little more than a contemporary variant of ancient body-stealing motifs that include the liver-eating Pishtaco monsters of the Andes (Oliver-Smith, 1969) and blood libel slanders that once accused European Jews of eating Christian babies or drinking their blood (Dundes, 1991). If the organ- and baby-stealing rumors provide an endless supply of good copy for journalists in global outposts (see, for example, 'Russian Woman Tries to Sell Grandson for His Organs') and Gothic subtexts to novels and films, the organ-stealing motif is also a great source of entertainment among the more sophisticated.

During a reception at the University of California following a lecture by the celebrated South African writer J.M. Coetzee (whom I had got to know at the University of Cape Town), the prickly author asked me what in the world I was now up to. I mumbled, 'fieldwork on the global traffic in human organs', as I quickly turned my head to avoid a topic that was hardly apropos to the festive occasion. But an acquaintance from the English department, who had joined the circle around Coetzee, broke in (thinking, no doubt, of films like 'Coma', 'Jesus of Montreal', and 'Central Station') to say: *Fabulous topic*! I suppose you have been going to a lot of movies lately'. 'Actually', I replied, 'I have been going to quite a few morgues'.

So, take the ethnographer. She has chosen to investigate a hidden and taboo subject, as forbidden a topic as witchcraft, incest or pedophilia. Using the traditional method of 'snowballing' – one patient, one surgeon, one hospital, one mortuary, one eye bank leading to the next – she begins to uncover a string of clues that will eventually take her from Brazil to Argentina and Cuba, and from South Africa to Israel, the West Bank and Turkey, and from Moldova in Eastern Europe to the Philippines in Southeast Asia. Finally, the clues lead her back to transplant units in Baltimore, Philadelphia and New York City. What she discovers is an extensive and illicit traffic in human organs and tissues procured from the bodies of vulnerable populations – some very dead, some in that 'dead/not quite dead' status known as brain death and a great many of them still very much alive.

Following new paths in the global economy, she discovers not one but *several* organs-trade circuits and triangles circulating body parts and living bodies – buyers, sellers, brokers and surgeons – often traveling in reverse directions. She finds that strange rumors and metaphors do at times harden into 'real' ethnographic facts. She learns how effectively organ-theft jokes, science fiction novels and urban legends conceal and distract attention from the 'really real' covert traffic in humans and their body parts. But once her writings begin to give credence to the material grounds underlying some of the rumors, she finds herself isolated, her research disvalued as too 'positioned', too engaged and therefore lacking in methodological rigor or theoretical discernment. Worse, she is labeled as naïve for she has begun to buy into the assumptive world of her informants, many of them poor, Third World, medically and technologically unsophisticated. [. . .]

Breaking and entering into the secret world of transplant

As a blend of experimental, multi-sited, ethnographic research and of medical human rights documentation, this project attempts to pierce the secrecy surrounding organ transplantation and to 'make public' and transparent all practices regarding the harvesting, selling and distribution of human organs and tissues. These practices are protected not only by the invisibility and social exclusion of organ donors but also by the great social trust invested in transplant medicine as an unquestioned social and moral good.

From the outset I was stymied by unwritten codes of professional loyalty and secrecy and by the impunity enjoyed by a professional medical elite. Transplant surgeons vie only with the Vatican and its cardinals with respect to their assumption of privilege, irrefutability and of a kind of 'divine election' that seems to place them above (or outside) the mundane laws that govern ordinary mortals. Like other humans, transplant surgeons are sometimes rogues and outlaws and their behavior causes anger, exasperation and consternation among their colleagues. Yet, like child-molesting priests among Catholic clergy, these outlaw surgeons are protected by the corporate transplant professionals hierarchy.

When I began I did not know that I would face a wall of silence, preventing access to the field by outsiders to the profession. To say the least, transplantation is an opaque rather than a transparent practice. The national and international organizations governing and regulating transplant – UNOS (US), Eurotransplant (Europe), Rio Transplant (Brazil), INCUCAI (Argentina) – collect data and publish or otherwise provide ample statistical tables but no direct access to the confidential medical data or to their files to check or verify the aggregate data. I was amused when, during a visit to Eurotransplant, I was walked through the offices, laboratories and corridors and given an excellent general orientation that ended in front of a large enclosed room with full-length glass windows on all sides, the space where the real work of matching 'anonymous' donor organs to 'anonymous' recipients took place. I could not enter, much less observe, any aspects of the decision-making process that had to be taken on faith as being totally objective. 'See, all windows here – we are totally transparent!' I was told by the administrator in a Kafkaesque manner.

Getting access to available statistics on the circulation of organs and tissues was a Herculean task in some places and easy enough in others. Cuba had a paper shortage and only with great difficulty could I get two pieces of paper from a medical director at MINISAP (the Cuban Ministry of Public Health) with the numbers of transplants performed over the past five years. South Africa did not produce national statistics on transplant and organs sharing (each hospital kept their own data); São Paulo's Transplant Central (the regional board that monitored organs procurement and distribution) gave me access to aggregate data on waiting lists, but these lists turned out to include large numbers of dead patients as well as patients who had already been transplanted. Argentina's national system, INCUCAI, produced more statistics than I knew what to do with, but some of which did not 'jibe' with the data that came from the smaller regional centers of organs procurement and distribution.

In one instance I was angrily confronted by the director of kidney transplants in a large public hospital in Johannesburg about a public statement I had made to the effect that South Africa did not really have official and public waiting lists: 'How dare you say that!' Dr B. fumed. 'Of course we have waiting lists'. To prove it he took a small agenda book out of his jacket and showed me his own personal penciled-in list of transplant candidates. While this private waiting list was not exactly what I had in mind, the best and most reliable data did come from individual surgeons, hospitals, clinics, private doctors' offices and tissue banks where some individuals took the time to review their own clinical data with me.

The social world of transplant surgery is small and personal. At the upper echelons transplant medicine could even be described as a face-to-face society. Like other professionals, transplant surgeons meet frequently at international meetings where they share jokes, anecdotes and personal concerns as well as strategic information. Not infrequently, a transplant surgeon would be 'prepped' in advance of my visit by a colleague in another country who would suggest how to 'manage' the 'Organs Watch Lady'. I soon lost the kind of anonymity that makes traditional fieldwork possible, although, to be sure, this project was decidedly *un*traditional.

Despite this, I did gain considerable entrée into some corners of the secretive world of transplant medicine. I am grateful to the many transplant professionals around the world who took me in from the cold, as it were, and allowed me not only to observe them at work, but who patiently answered an endless number of impertinent questions (many of which they obviously ducked and deflected), and who in some cases gave me access to their personal data and files, an extraordinary trust that I will honor here by caution and discretion, but which provides the background to my discussion.

Perhaps one source of entrée derived from the markedly different status of anthropologists and surgeons. While surgeons occupy the highest and most prestigious ranks in modern medicine, anthropologists occupy the lower ranks in the social sciences, especially at a time when quantitative approaches and rational choice-based models of human behavior predominate. (Anthropologists concern themselves with the ineffable and the irrational aspects of human life that are not so easily quantified.) The benefit of our exclusion from the world of 'real' power and influence is that anthropologists are generally perceived as benign, even amusing characters. We enter our research sites open-handedly and often without complicated research protocols or standardized interview questions. We visit, observe as unobtrusively as possible and try to make ourselves at home in the world, wherever that may be.

And so, I sometimes brought the tea cakes for the mid-morning tea break at the kidney transplant unit of Groote-Schuur Hospital in Cape Town, while in nearby Chris Hani shantytown, I often accompanied anxious patients to and from local hospitals via crowded combi-taxis. In the Salt River Mortuary in Cape

Town I was drafted by mortuary police to accompany the bereaved relatives and friends into the viewing room to identify the dead, following a horrendous political massacre (Scheper-Hughes, 1994). On one occasion, when a young woman used my shoulder to cry on after having had to identify a dear friend who had been murdered in the above mentioned Heidleberg Pub massacre which took place during the last days of the apartheid state in South Africa, she suddenly looked up at me and asked: 'Who are you, anyway? What are you doing here?' – a question I often had to ask myself during the course of this project.

But anthropologists make ourselves 'useful' in other ways. Most of us can 'read' bodies and translate emotions across class, gender, language and culture. We know when a quiet patient is not so much calm and resigned as worried to death and we can translate those anxieties in terms of cultural views of the body, sickness, death and dying. As hunters and gatherers of human values, we are acutely conscious of, and sensitive to, ethical and moral quandaries that we interpret from a relativist rather than a universalistic perspective. Indeed, every operating room, like every Navajo family, ought to have its own anthropologist cloaked in native attire – surgical scrubs in this instance rather than fancy Navajo shawls.

[...]

Behind the scenes of the organ trade

Equally problematic were the covert methods I sometimes had to use to access information on covert and illegal (as well as often highly stigmatized) activities. In some sites I posed as a patient (or the relative of a patient) looking to purchase or otherwise broker a kidney. I sometimes visited transplant units and hospital wards unannounced, posing (if anyone bothered to ask) as a confused friend or family member looking for another part of the hospital. At times I introduced myself, honestly enough, to transplant staff and nurses as 'Dr Scheper-Hughes conducting an international study of transplant', while leaving it vague just what kind of 'doctor' I was.

In travelling incognito, as I did when investigating allegations of illegal organs and tissues harvesting at Montes de Oca, the Argentine asylum for the profoundly mentally retarded, I had only Laud Humphreys (1975) and his award-winning but ethically questionable observational study of impersonal sex in public bathrooms as a shaky reference point. Erving Goffman had once posed as a mental patient for his study of St Elizabeth's Psychiatric Hospital in Washington, DC, but such deceptions are no longer permissible for researchers operating under the strict guidelines of human subjects protection committees.

But there are times when one must ask just whom the codes are protecting. As I could see no way of having my research pass through the University of California's Human Subjects Protection Committee, I applied for an exceptional dispensation from the university's human subjects committee, requesting that, for the purpose of this study, I be viewed as a human rights investigative reporter with the same rights as my colleagues in the Berkeley School of Journalism.

Permission was eventually granted. How else, except in disguise, could I learn of the hidden suffering of an invisible, silenced and institutionalized population like the patients of Montes de Oca mental asylum (see Chaudhary, 1992)? What alternative methods of investigation exist in tortured circumstances like these? These new engagements required not only a certain militancy but also a constant self-reflexive and self-critical rethinking of professional ethics, the production of truth and the protection of one's research subjects.

I ran up against other problems, some of them more mundane but equally important. Research on covert behavior results, quite naturally, in a skewing of data. My writings on the organs traffic, to date, have emphasized illicit activities in the Middle East and in Southeast Asia where for complex reasons they are conducted more openly. I have written far less on the commerce in human organs in the US, parts of Latin America and in Europe where public denial, moral condemnation and official prohibition force the activities underground and make the work of documenting the activities far more daunting. In contrast, Iran sponsors an official government program, the only one of its kind that regulates the sale of kidneys from poor to rich. It is guardedly praised by some (see Al-Khader, 2002; Ghods, 2002) but criticized by others (see Zargooshi, 2001). Similar programs are being considered in the Philippines and Israel. In the US, more than half of all kidney transplants are using living donors, some 20 percent of whom are unrelated, 'altruistic' donors, a claim (or pretense) that many transplant centers in the US are reluctant to question (see Delmonico and Scheper-Hughes, 2002).

Meanwhile, multi-sited research (even when based on many return and follow-up trips) still runs the risk of being too thinly spread, and demanding a sacrifice of the normally leisurely pace of traditional ethnographic work. I have had to travel, observe, respond, reflect and write more quickly than I am accustomed to. One of the many ironies associated with this project was its funding via George Soros' fortune accumulated through his own global 'trafficking' in money-markets that had destabilized so many of the economies where the traffic in humans and in organs is now common, especially Eastern Europe and Southeast Asia. Another irony is that the knowledge garnered from this difficult research is being transformed – from flesh into words as it were – into a book that is every bit as much a commodity as the pink, healthy kidneys snatched from the poor. In a word, as my Brazilian favela friends often reminded me, 'Nancí, here no one is innocent'. Least of all the anthropologist herself.

Avraham R., a retired lawyer of 70, stepped gingerly out of his sedan at the curb of the Beit Belgia Faculty Club at the University of Jerusalem in July 2000. The dapper gent, a grandfather of five, had been playing a game of 'chicken' with me over the past two weeks, ducking my persistent phone calls. But whenever I'd catch him in the flesh, rather than getting his recorded message, Avraham was a wonderful conversationalist, speaking uninhibitedly, full of zest and at length. Israeli style, most of these conversations were exchanged on cell phones while each of us was driving somewhere else in an increasingly booby-trapped terrain. In Israel today cell phones are a lifeline to an anxious people constantly checking in with each other throughout the day. Indeed, during return fieldwork in Israel in March 2001, when I accompanied the controversial former *New York Times Magazine* writer, Mike Finkel, to the Middle East for 'his' (i.e. my) story on transplant tourism (Finkel, 2001), we were twice within earshot of exploding bombs. Finkel and I wondered, given the political situation, who in the world would care about a news report dealing with Mr Tati's 'poisoned kidney' that he purchased from a peasant in Turkey and that all but cost him his life, or with Mr Sibony's furlough from a jail in Tel Aviv gotten in exchange for a kidney for his lawyer.

Each time I asked the genial Avraham for a face-to-face interview he demurred: 'It's not to protect me', he said, 'but my family'. Then, one afternoon, worn down perhaps by my repeated requests, Avraham surprised me, not only agreeing to meet me but insisting that he come over to my comfortable quarters where he settled in over a few bottles of mineral water to explain why and how he had come to the decision to risk traveling to an undisclosed location in Eastern Europe to purchase a kidney from an anonymous displaced rural worker and to face transplant in a spartan operating room ('I have more medicines in my own medicine chest than they had in that hospital', he said) rather than remain on dialysis at Hadassah Hospital as his nephrologist had suggested.

Avraham was still active and proud of his distinguished military record that had left him with more than a few scars. His noticeable limp, he said, had nothing to do with the effects of his diabetes or his kidney disease diagnosed several years earlier. As a veteran of active military service Avraham was still eligible for a transplant, but at his age, his doctors warned, such a long operation was risky. Dialysis, they said, was really his best option. But Avraham protested that he was not yet ready for the 'medical trashheap', which is the way he and many other Israeli kidney patients now view hemodialysis. Also, like a growing number of Israeli kidney patients, he rejected the idea of a cadaver organ (the 'dead man's organ') as 'disgusting' and unacceptable:

> Why should I have to wait years for a kidney from somebody who was in a traffic accident, pinned under a car for many hours, then in miserable condition in the I.C.U. [intensive care unit] for days and only then, after all that trauma, have that same organ put inside me? That organ isn't going to be any good! Or worse, I could get the organ of an old person, or an alcoholic, or someone who died of a stroke. That kidney has already done its work! No, obviously, it's much better to get a kidney from a healthy person who can also benefit from the money I can afford to pay. Believe me, where I went the people were so poor they didn't even have bread to eat. Do you have any idea of what one, let alone 5000 dollars, means to a peasant? The money I paid him was 'a gift of life' equal to what I received.

Then, in December 2001, following one of several paths indicated by the Israeli kidney buyers I had met in Jerusalem and Tel Aviv, I found myself in a dank, freezing dug-out wine cave in Mingir, central Moldova, where a boyish young man with a rakish stud in his lower lip and a tattoo on his arm, drew each of us a glass of smoky red wine from a homemade barrel while debating just how much of his story he should tell. I knew only that, at the age of 19, Vladimir was one of 17 young men lured away from the village by a local kidney hunter, a former prostitute who began styling herself as an overseas employment broker during the difficult years in the late 1990s when 40 percent of the rural Moldovan labor force was working overseas. Nina arranged Vladimir's traveling papers and his bus fare to Istanbul, a 17-hour, bumpy, overnight ride from the capital city of Chisenau.

Vlad was told there was a job waiting for him at a dry cleaner's store. He was put up in a room with two other Moldovan villagers in a rundown hotel facing a notorious Russian 'suitcase market' in Askaray, Istanbul, a place where dozens of newly arrived guest workers from the former Soviet countries peddled smuggled goods and their labor for a variety of service jobs. After a week of anxious waiting Nina arrived to tell a young girl that her 'waitress' job was in a bar where lap dancing was expected. And Vlad was told that he was wanted for a lot more than pressing pants and shirts. He could start by selling some blood and after a 'match' was made, he would sell his 'best' and 'strongest' kidney for $2700 minus his rent and food. The patient was an Israeli waiting downtown in Istanbul's most famous five-star hotel. 'I had no choice', Vlad told me the next day. 'I was scared and this was my only chance to get home again'.

Just before ducking into the wine cellar to hide from the view of his elderly father who had warned his son against talking to outsiders, Vlad had stood his ground firmly at the rickety gate to his small home, refusing to let us in. Nervously chewing sunflower seeds and spitting them out rapidfire in our direction, Vladimir boldly demanded a 'fair price' – '200, OK, 100 dollars' – for an interview. When I slipped him a crisp $20.00 bill Vlad nodded his head and indicated that we should follow him down into the outdoor wine cellar. It was so cold that our cameras froze and all I could think about was my feet turning into bloodless blocks of ice while trying to shake out the fresh snow that had gotten inside my leather boots. We begged for another interview to take place somewhere, *anywhere*, that was indoors and warm. Vlad shook his head. That was impossible. He could not think of any place in the village where we would not be seen and he and his elderly father – the remains of what was once a strong rural family – subjected to ridicule, and opening a wound that was still fresh.

'People in this village despise us for what we have done', Vlad said, referring to the other young men of the village who had been either tricked into or had willingly sold a kidney abroad in the past three years. Mingir now has the distinction of being disparaged throughout the region as 'the little village of half-men'. 'They say we are no better than whores', he said bitterly. Since his return home, Vlad has barely spoken to his elderly father, a recent widower in his 70s. I asked if I might not talk to his father in an attempt to convince him that his son – rather than an incorrigible juvenile delinquent – was the victim of an increasingly widespread international medical human rights abuse. Vlad was doubtful but arranged a return visit the following day. Then, recovering his cool and his youthful braggadocio, Vlad warned us, with a cocky twist of his head, that it would cost us 'big time' if we wanted to photograph his scar. I assured Vlad that I didn't, having accumulated more than enough photos of those deforming saber-length scars running the length of the torsos of young, healthy peasants and urban laborers in various parts of the world.

According to Moldovan police and local human rights activists, more than 300 Moldovans have sold their kidneys abroad since 1998. At least 17 sellers are from Minjir, a rustic and hardscrabble village of 5000, while others come from surrounding villages and from the capital city of Chisenau. In an interview with Vasile Tarlev, Moldova's prime minister, he acknowledged that the trade is linked to organized crime, but that it was difficult to 'fight an enemy that doesn't show its face'. The country's intelligence service said that almost every day a Moldovan sells a kidney, despite the social stigma the trade engenders, especially in small villages. Because they have sold a priceless body part that can never be replaced, kidney sellers are held in even lower esteem than the young village women who have entered the active sex trade in order to survive the collapse of the local economy.

Consider
1. According to Nancy Scheper-Hughes, what are the rules and patterns of the human organ trade?
2. What is the current scope and extent of the human organ trade? What does it reveal about the commodification of human bodies? To answer these questions, you will need to do substantial background research.
3. Provide contemporary examples of the ways in which bodies have been opened to technological intervention and modification.
4. How are bodies in contemporary society subject to regimes of social control? How are these regimes being contested by social movements?
5. What are the main dimensions of the 'civilising process' described by Norbert Elias? To anwer this question, you will need to do substantial further research.
6. What do differences in Western European and Chinese table manners and eating habits reveal about the social regulation of the human body? To anwer this question, you will need to do substantial further research.

4.8 What holds society together? Social systems

We now return to another fundamental question of sociology: 'What holds society together?' As we have seen, this concern already troubled early sociologists, provoking, for instance, Émile Durkheim's research on social solidarity and anomie in complex modern societies. Scholars in Durkheim's times tended to imagine the world in terms of nation states – communities characterised by a common territory, government, and, often, cultural identity (more about this later on). Nation states continue to be significant forms of social and political organisation today, and the question may arise of what keeps the larger ones from breaking into separate parts. Indonesia has more than 200 million inhabitants spread across thousands of islands and belonging to many different ethnic groups. The states of the USA are spread across a huge continental land-mass, and its more than 300 million residents are characterised by great cultural, social and ethnic differences. Even in much smaller Italy, big cultural and socio-economic differences between northern and southern regions are obvious. Moreover, as argued above, social ties today often extend beyond the boundaries of nation states, and there are trends towards a truly global society. So, what holds such immensely complex, large-scale, and diverse social formations together?

To answer this question, we first look at the concept of the *social system* and consider arguments put forward by American sociologist Talcott Parsons (1902–1979). Parsons's work had a dominant influence on international sociology for much of the twentieth century. While this influence has lessened today, particularly in the English-speaking world, his ideas are still foundational to a sociological understanding of problems of social solidarity and cohesion. Parsons's work is an example of sociological *grand theorising*, that is to say, of efforts to formulate comprehensive theories of social life that explain the workings of societies at large.

Parsons's approach to problems of social solidarity is most evident in his famous 'AGIL scheme' (adaptation – goal attainment – integration – latency), described in detail in the reading below. He considered society as an integrated system, whose different elements must fulfil certain functions for it to remain stable and largely harmonious. Following Parsons's approach, you might imagine society as a kind of living organism or machine, which depends on the workings of each of its different organs or components to stay alive and function.

Specifically, Parsons argued that a social system must fulfil four basic functions. First, it must *adapt* to its environment. It might be argued that China has met the goal of adapting to a competitive global economy particularly well, by turning itself into the leading exporter of manufactured goods. Second, a social system must be able to set and meet *goals* for its future development. Again, China is a good example, having pursued a systematic state-led strategy of economic development since 1978 that has vastly improved the country's fortunes.

Third, a social system must achieve *integration* and maintain a degree of balance in the norms, values and beliefs that are prevalent. Political and cultural struggles between Christian fundamentalists and the secular mainstream of US society about issues such as abortion, gay and lesbian marriage, and the teaching of science in public schools are a good example here, as they are indicative of a certain lack of integration of different sectors of American society. Finally, and most abstractly, Parsons argued that social systems need to fulfil the function of *latency* or *pattern maintenance*, by maintaining the values, beliefs, norms and practices that help society achieve integration. The education system is a prime example of pattern maintenance, in so far as teachers and textbooks work to transmit certain understandings of the world to the youngest generations in society. At present, US society is experiencing profound struggles at the level of pattern maintenance, with, for instance, Christian fundamentalists attempting to re-adjust the teaching of subjects like history or biology to their world views, thus attempting to change the character of public education at large.

This brief summary barely scratches the surface of Parsons's vast theoretical system. Today, its influence having declined notably, it is perhaps most important for you to sensitise yourself to the general problem areas of social cohesion to which Parsons's ideas point. Each of the four elements of the AGIL scheme provides a distinct perspective on the question of what holds society together, and it is here that its contemporary importance lies. Later on we will deal with more recent and contemporary perspectives on social cohesion, conflict and inequalities. Each of these perspectives raises a distinct set of problems and questions, as you will see. Ultimately, however, they can be referred back to the more general problems which Parsons sought to identify. This is one very important reason why continued engagement with his work is certainly worthwhile.

Reading

Parsons, T. (1971), *The System of Modern Societies*, Englewood Cliffs: Prentice-Hall, pp. 4–11

Theoretical Orientations

Two

Action Systems and Social Systems

We consider social systems to be constituents of the more general system of action, the other primary constituents being cultural systems, personality systems, and behaviorial organisms; all four are abstractly defined relative to the concrete behavior of social interaction. We treat the three subsystems of actions other than the social system as constituents of its environment. This usage is somewhat unfamiliar, especially for the case of the personalities of individuals. It is justified fully elsewhere, but to understand what follows it is essential to keep in mind that neither social nor personality systems are here conceived as concrete entities.

The distinctions among the four subsystems of action are functional. We draw them in terms of the four primary functions which we impute to all systems of action, namely pattern-maintenance, integration, goal-attainment, and adaptation.

An action system's primary integrative problem is the coordination of its constituent units, in the first instance human individuals, though for certain purposes collectivities may be treated as actors. Hence, we attribute primacy of integrative function to the social system.

We attribute primacy of pattern-maintenance – and of creative pattern change – to the cultural system. Whereas social systems are organized with primary reference to the articulation of social relationships, cultural systems are organized around the characteristics of complexes of symbolic meaning – the codes in terms of which they are structured, the particular clusters of symbols they employ, and the conditions of their utilization, maintenance, and change as parts of action systems.

We attribute primacy of goal-attainment to the personality of the individual. The personality system is the primary *agency* of action processes, hence of the implementation of cultural principles and requirements. On the level of reward in the motivational sense, the optimization of gratification or satifaction to personalities is the primary goal of action.

The behavioral organism is conceived as the adaptive subsystem, the locus of the primary human facilities which underlie the other systems. It embodies a set of conditions to which action must adapt and comprises the primary mechanism of interrelation with the physical environment, especially through the input and processing of information in the central nervous system and through motor activity in coping with exigencies of the physical environment. These relationships are presented systematically in Table 4.1.

There are two systems of reality which are environmental to action in general and not constituents of action in our analytical sense. The first is the *physical environment*, including not only phenomena as understandable in terms of physics and chemistry, but also the world of living organisms so far as they are not integrated into action systems. The second, which we conceive to be independent of the physical environment as well as of action systems as such, we will call *"ultimate reality,"* in a sense derived from traditions of philosophy. It concerns what Weber called "problem of meaning" for human action and is mediated into action primarily by the cultural system's structuring of meaningful orientations that include, but are not exhausted by, cognitive "answers."

In analyzing the interrelations among the four subsystems of action – and between these systems and the environments of action – it is essential to keep in mind the phenomenon of *interpenetration*. Perhaps the best-known case of interpenetration is the *internalization* of social objects and cultural norms into the personality of the individual. Learned content of experience, organized and stored in the memory apparatus of the organism, is another example, as is the *institutionalization* of normative components of cultural systems as constitutive structures of social systems. We hold that the boundary between any pair of action systems involves a "zone" of structured components or patterns which must be treated theoretically as *common* to *both* systems, not simply allocated to one system or the other. For example, it is untenable to say that norms of conduct derived from social experience, which both Freud (in the concept of the Superego) and Durkheim (in the concept of collective representations) treated as parts of the personality of the individual, must be *either* that *or* part of the social system.

Table 4.1 Action.

Subsystems	Primary Functions
Social	Integration
Cultural	Pattern Maintenance
Personality	Goal Attainment
Behavioral Organism	Adaptation

* The shaded area represents the social subsystem's environment.
This table presents the barest schematic outline of the primary subsystems and their functional references for the *General System of Action*, of which the social system is one of four primary subsystems, that concentrated about integrative function. A somewhat more elaborate schema is presented in Table 4.1, p. 26 of *Societies*; and a general rationale of this schema has been presented in Parsons, "Some Problems of General Theory in Sociology" in John C. McKinney and Edward Tyriakian (eds.), *Theoretical Sociology* (New York: Appleton-Century-Crofts, 1970).

It is by virtue of the zones of interpenetration that processes of interchange among systems can take place. This is especially true at the levels of symbolic meaning and generalized motivation. In order to "communicate" symbolically, individuals must have culturally organized common codes, such as those of language, which are also integrated into systems of their social interaction. In order to make information stored in the central nervous system utilizable for the personality, the behavioral organism must have mobilization and retrieval mechanisms which, through interpenetration, subserve motives organized at the personality level.

Thus, we conceived social systems to be "open," engaged in continual interchange of inputs and outputs with their environments. Moreover, we conceive them to be internally differentiated into various orders of subcomponents which are also continually involved in processes of interchange.

Social systems are those constituted by states and processes of social interaction among acting units. If the properties of interaction were derivable from properties of the acting units, social systems would be epiphenomenal, as much "individualistic" social theory has contended. Our position is sharply in disagreement: it derives particularly from Durkheim's statement that society – and other social systems – is a "reality *sui generis.*"

The structure of social systems may be analyzed in terms of four types of independently variable components: values, norms, collectivities, and roles. [Values take primacy in the pattern-maintenance functioning of social systems, for they are conceptions of desirable types of social systems that regulate the making of commitments by social units.] Norms, which function primarily to integrate social systems, are specific to particular social functions and types of social situations. They include not only value components specified to appropriate levels in the structure of a social system, but also specific modes of orientation for acting under the functional and situational conditions of particular collectivities and roles. Collectivities are the type of structural component that have goal-attainment primacy. Putting aside the many instances of highly fluid group systems, such as crowds, we speak of a collectivity only where two specific criteria are fulfilled. First, there must be definite statuses of membership so that a useful distinction between members and nonmembers can generally be drawn, a criterion fulfilled by cases that vary from nuclear families to political communities. Second, there must be some differentiation among members in relation to their statuses and functions within the collectivity, so that some categories of members are expected to do certain things which are not expected of other members. A role, the type of structural component that has primacy in the adaptive function, we conceive as defining a class of individuals who, through reciprocal expectations, are involved in a particular collectivity. Hence, roles comprise the primary zones of interpenetration between the social system and the personality of the individual. A role is never idiosyncratic to a particular individual, however. A father is specific to his children in his fatherhood, but he is a father in terms of the role-structure of his society. At the same time, he also participates in various other contexts of interaction, filling, for example, an occupational role.

The reality *sui generis* of social systems may involve the independent variability of each of these types of structural components relative to the others. A generalized value-pattern does not legitimize the same norms, collectivities, or roles under all conditions, for example. Similarly, many norms regulate the action of indefinite numbers of collectivities and roles, but only specific sectors of their action. Hence a collectivity generally functions under the control of a large number of particular norms. It always involves a plurality of roles, although almost any major category of role is performed in a plurality of particular collectivities. Nevertheless, social systems are comprised of *combinations* of these structural components. To be institutionalized in a stable fashion, collectivities and roles must be "governed" by specific values and norms, whereas values and norms are themselves institutionalized only insofar as they are "implemented" by particular collectivities and roles.

The Concept of Society

We define society as the type of social system characterized by the highest level of self-sufficiency relative to its environments, including other social systems. Total self-sufficiency, however, would be incompatible with the status of society as a subsystem of action. Any society depends for its continuation as a system on the inputs it receives through interchanges with its environing systems. Self-sufficiency in relation to environments, then, means stability of interchange relationships and capacity to control interchanges in the interest of societal functioning. Such control may vary from capacity to forestall or "cope with" disturbances to capacity to shape environmental relations favorably.

The physical environment has an adaptive significance for a society in that it is the direct source of the physical resources which the society can exploit through its technological and economic mechanisms of production. The allocation of access to physical resources, in order to be linked with the division of labor through the ecological aspect of society, requires a territorial distribution of residential locations and economic interests among the various subgroupings of the population. The physical environment has a second significance for societies in that, because of the importance of physical force as a preventive of undesired action, effective societal goal attainment requires control of actions within a territorial area. Hence, there are two contexts of societal self-sufficiency that concern, respectively, economic and political functioning in relation to the physical environment, through technology and through the organized use of force in the military and police functions.

A third context of societal self-sufficiency concerns the personalities of individual members in a special mode of interpenetration with the organisms involved. The organism links directly to the territorial complex through the importance of the physical location of actions. But its main link with the social system involves the personality; this primary zone of interpenetration concerns the status of *membership*. A society can be self-sufficient only in so far as it is generally able to "count on" its members' performances to "contribute" adequately to societal functioning. No more than in the other interchanges involved in self-sufficiency, need this integration between personality and society be absolute. Yet one could not speak of a society as self-sufficient if the overwhelming majority of its members were radically "alienated."

The integration of members into a society involves the zone of interpenetration between the social and personality systems. The relation is basically tripartite, however, because parts of the cultural system as well as parts of the social structure are internalized in personalities, and because parts of the cultural system are institutionalized in the society.

At the social level, the institutionalized patterns of *value* are "collective representations" that define the *desirable types* of social system. These representations are correlative with the conceptions of types of social systems by which individuals orient themselves in their capacities as members. It is the members' consensus on value orientation with respect to their own society, then, that defines the institutionalization of value patterns. Consensus in this respect is certainly a matter of degree. Hence self-sufficiency in this context concerns the degree to which the institutions of a society have been *legitimized* by the consensual value commitments of its members.

At the cultural level, social values comprise only part of a wider system of value, since all other classes of objects in the action system must be evaluated too. Values are related to such other components of a cultural system as empirical knowledge, expressive symbol systems, and the constitutive symbolic structures that compose the core of religious systems. Ultimately, values are mainly legitimized in religious terms. In the context of cultural legitimation, then, a society is self-sufficient to the extent that its institutions are legitimized by values that its members hold with relative consensus *and* that are in turn legitimized by their congruence with other components of the cultural system, especially its constitutive symbolism.

It is essential to remember that cultural systems do not correspond exactly with social systems, including societies. The more important cultural systems generally become institutionalized, in varying patterns, in a number of societies, though there are also subcultures within societies. For example, the cultural system centering on Western Christianity has, with certain qualifications and many variations, been common to the whole European system of modernized societies. Two modes of the relation of one society to other societies are discussed in the present book. First, all societies we speak of as "politically organized" are involved with various other societies in "international relations" of various types, friendly or hostile. We shall extend this conception and regard these relations as themselves constituting a social system which can be analyzed with the same general concepts as other types of social system. Second, a social system may be involved with the social structure and/or the members and/or the culture of two or more societies. Such social systems are numerous and of many different kinds. American immigrant families often retain effective kinship relations with people in the "old country," so that their kinship systems have both American and foreign "branches." Something similar can be said of many business firms, professional associations, and religious collectivities. Although the Roman Catholic Church, for example, is a social system, it clearly is not a society since its self-sufficiency is very low by our criteria. Its control of economic resources through the organization of production is minimal; it lacks autonomous political control of territorial areas; in many societies, its members constitute a minority. Thus we must take account of both social systems which are "supersocietal" in being comprised of a plurality of societies and social systems that are "cross-societal" in that their members belong to a plurality of different societies.

The Subsystems of Society

In accord with our four-function scheme for analyzing systems of action, we treat a society as analytically divisible into four *primary* subsystems (as shown in Table 4.2). Thus, the pattern-maintenance subsystem is particularly concerned with the relations of the society to the cultural system and, through it, *ultimate reality*; the goal-attainment subsystem or the polity, to the personalities of individual members; the adaptive subsystem, or the economy, to the behavioral organism and, through it, the physical world. These divisions are clearest and most important for societies advanced on the scale of modernity. However, the complexity of the relationships, both among subsystems of action and among subsystems of society, prevent these divisions from ever

Table 4.2 Society (more generally, social system).

Subsystems	Structural Components	Aspects of Developmental Process	Primary Function
Societal Community	Norms	Inclusion	Integration
Pattern Maintenance or Fiduciary	Values	Value Generalization	Pattern Maintenance
Polity	Collectivities	Differentiation	Goal Attainment
Economy	Roles	Adaptive Upgrading	Adaptation

This table attempts to spell out, a little more elaborately, a four-function paradigm for the *society*, or other type of social system, conceived as an integrative subsystem of a general system of action. The societal community, which is the primary subsystem of reference for the present analysis, is placed in the left hand column; the other three follow it. Corresponding to this set is a classification in the second column, by the same functional criteria, of four main structural components of social systems. In the third column follows a corresponding classification of aspects of process of developmental change in social systems which will be used extensively in the analysis that follows. Finally, the fourth column repeats the designation of four primary functional categories.

Except for the developmental paradigm, this schema was first fully presented in the author's "General Introduction, Part II: An Outline of the Social System" in *Theories of Society*. For general comparison with Tables 4.1 and 4.2, please consult *Societies*, Tables 1 and 2, pp. 28 and 29, and the accompanying explanatory note.

being very neat. For example, kinship structures must be located in all three of the above-mentioned subsystems. Through their relation to food, sex, biological descent, and residence, they are involved with the organism and the physical environment. As the individual's primary source of early learning of values, norms, and modes of communication, they are very much involved with the pattern-maintenance system. As the primary source of socialized services, they are involved with the polity.

Within this framework, the core of a society as a social system is the fourth component, its integrative subsystem. Because we treat the social system as integrative for action systems generally, we must pay special attention to the ways in which it achieves – or fails to achieve – various kinds and levels of internal integration. We will call the integrative subsystem of a society the *societal community*.

Perhaps the most general function of a societal community is to articulate a *system* of norms with a collective organization that has unity and cohesiveness. Following Weber, we call the normative aspect the system of legitimate order; the collective aspect is the societal community as a single, bounded collectivity. Societal order requires clear and definite integration in the sense, on the one hand, of normative coherence and, on the other hand, of societal "harmony" and "coordination." Moreover, normatively-defined obligations must on the whole be accepted while conversely, collectivities must have normative sanction in performing their functions and promoting their legitimate interests. Thus, normative order at the societal level contains a "solution" to the problem posed by Hobbes – of preventing human relations from degenerating into a "war of all against all."

It is important not to treat a structure of societal norms as a monolithic entity. Hence we distinguish four components analytically, even though they overlap greatly in specific content. Our distinctions concern the grounds of obligations and rights as well as the nature of sanctioning noncompliance and rewarding compliance or unusual levels of performance.

Consider
1. How does Talcott Parsons define the idea of the 'social system'? Explain his arguments in your own words.
2. Parsons' arguments are very abstract. Give examples for the different elements of the social system he discusses.
3. How, if at all, could Parsons' notion of the social system be used to conceptualise a 'global society'? Where relevant, give contemporary examples to illustrate your arguments.
4. This is perhaps one of the most abstract and challenging readings you have encountered so far in this book. Think about the strategies you could use to make the reading more approachable and easier to understand.
5. How might such an abstract text provide you with interesting and worthwhile insights into your own everyday lives? Think about examples that connect your own experiences to the issues discussed by Parsons.

4.9 Power and politics

Implicit in the preceding arguments are sociological concerns with the workings of power and politics. *Power* has been defined in a variety of ways. Max Weber's now classical proposal is a useful starting point for our argument here:

'Power' [. . .] is the probability that one actor within a social relationship will be in a position to carry out his own will despite resistance, regardless of the basis on which this probability rests. (Weber 1956/1978: 53)

Note that Weber describes power broadly as a property of social relationships between 'actors' – that is, individuals, but also larger groups and organisations, such as states, corporations, political movements, and so forth. According to the characteristics of the social relationships such actors enjoy with others, they will be able to impose their will to a greater or lesser extent. Classroom relationships between lecturers and students are systematically arranged in such a way that lecturers possess the ability to conduct classes according to their preferences. The use of physical violence in many societies is circumscribed by states' regulation of access to weapons and claims to a 'monopoly on violence' on the part of state agents such as police and military forces.

On the one hand, in this sense, power is a matter of *politics*: the institutional arrangements in society through which power is allocated to different actors and collective decisions are made. A wide variety of political systems can be found across the planet and throughout human history, from authoritarian and monarchic systems that concentrate power in the hands of select groups of individuals, to democratic systems that seek to distribute power widely among the members of a society or social group and facilitate collective decision-making.

On the other hand, power is a matter of the often *informal* relationships and hierarchies of gender, sexual orientation, race, class, generation, and so forth, that characterise our everyday lives. As much as it operates through highly formalised organisational structures like the police, the hospital, the university, etc., power works through the beliefs, norms and values which we bring into our everyday encounters with others.

Sociological explanations of power and politics are, again, manifold. Explaining the origins of ruling capitalist elites, Marxist scholars tend to emphasise control over the means of production, that is, infrastructure, factories, machines, etc., and over the

Photo 4.2 Demonstrators holding signs protest in front of an F.W. Woolworth store in Harlem to oppose lunch counter discrimination practiced in Woolworth stores in Greensboro, Charlotte, and Durham, North Carolina. The demonstrators, who belong to an organization known as "CORE" (Congress of Racial Equality), are urging Harlem residents not to patronize Woolworth stores until discrimination ends in stores in the three southern cities.

Source: © Bettman/CORBIS

dominant beliefs, or ideologies, that justify such control over society's material base. From a Marxist perspective, politics is thus often described as an arena of fundamental conflict and class struggle.

In contrast, pluralist theorists such as Robert Dahl (1961) describe power as dispersed among different actors and interest groups in society, who must enter into competition and negotiation with each other to achieve their agendas. Moreover, there are many properties of individuals and social relationships that may translate into power, such as social status, material wealth, or personal prestige. These properties tend to be dispersed, rather than concentrated, rendering politics an arena of ongoing negotiation and the balancing of competing interests.

Focusing less on formal politics and more on the microsocial dynamics that structure our everyday encounters with issues such as sexuality, crime or mental health, Michel Foucault describes power as diffuse, pervasive in all social relationships, and operating through a multiplicity of practices. For instance, writing about the development of modern understandings of sexuality, Foucault (1998) highlights the power of discourses – bodies of ideas and specific modes of using language that carry particular norms, values and beliefs about, in this case, sex. Structuring our experiences of everyday life, discourses are invested with considerable power. Yet, they do not emanate from a single source of authority, such as a government or a ruler. Rather, they accrue through a multiplicity of distinct, small-scale acts, such as academic studies about sex, the continued publication of news that bring the matter to the public's attention, and so forth.

Moreover, there is considerable debate among sociologists about the nature of the arenas in which politics and power relations are played out today. For a long time, sociological analysis has emphasised *nation states* as their basic units of analysis. Bounded by clearly identified frontiers, encompassing a population with unique, if varied, characteristics, and established as a single state, nation states in the twentieth century were often seen as being synonymous with 'society' (Connell 2007). However, as we will see later on, contemporary processes of globalisation have in many ways worn down these apparently clear boundaries. Thus, today actors such as transnational political organisations, business corporations, international financial institutions, or social movements have a defining impact on our lives in many ways, and their actions are often beyond the control of single nation states.

One instance of this is the rise of *new social movements*. Social movements could, at a very general level, be defined in terms of the organised pursuit of certain social and political goals, often outside of the formal structures of state, government and political parties. Theorists such as Alberto Melucci (1996) argue that the many new social movements that have emerged since the late 1960s differ notably from their predecessors. On the one hand, they often focus on socio-cultural issues that transcend the economic conflicts characteristic of earlier social movement activity and thus broaden the scope of issues publicly perceived as politically significant. The global environmental movement is a very significant illustration of this. Struggles between lesbian, gay, bisexual and transgender (LGBT) rights movements and conservative

Photo 4.3 'Occupy Everything': Rallying against a global financial elite perceived as irresponsible and unaccountable, the Occupy movement quickly spread from certain focal points, such as New York, across the globe. Here, protesters march through the streets of Chicago, Illinois, 19 May 2012, on the eve of the NATO summit.

Source: SAUL LOEB/AFP/Getty Images

counter-movements are another significant example, as is the recent 'Occupy' movement that has sought to challenge the global political and economic dominance of the financial industry. Arguments about *human rights*, that is, rights that are universally applicable to all human beings, frame the activities of many social movements and other political actors and further illustrate the mentioned trend towards the erosion of the politically clearly bounded nation state.

Reading

Melucci, Alberto (1996), *Challenging Codes: Collective Action in the Information Age*, Cambridge: Cambridge University Press, pp. 1–6

Prophet: the one who speaks before

Movements in complex societies are disenchanted prophets. The charmed universe of the *heroes* has definitively dissolved under the impact of an era taking cognizance of itself as a planetary system riven by molecular change, as a system which constantly generates tensions and then in turn adapts to them by striving to control them. Movements are a sign; they are not merely an outcome of the crisis, the last throes of a passing society. They signal a deep transformation in the logic and the processes that guide complex societies.

Like the prophets, the movements 'speak before': they announce what is taking shape even before its direction and content has become clear. The inertia of the old categories may prevent us from hearing the message and from deciding, consciously and responsibly, what action to take in light of it. Without the capacity of listening to these voices, new forms of power may thus coalesce, though multiple and diffuse and no longer reducible to any linear and easily recognizable geometry.

Contemporary movements are prophets of the present. What they possess is not the force of the apparatus but the power of the word. They announce the commencement of change; not, however, a change in the distant future but one that is already a presence. They force the power out into the open and give it a shape and a face. They speak a language that seems to be entirely their own, but they say something that transcends their particularity and speaks to us all.

This book was born over the last twenty years as an attempt to listen to the voices and read the signs of precisely that which collective action is proclaiming. But the mind that sets about to regard the societal actors today must in a similar manner proceed within a disenchanted framework. The intellectuals who claim to represent the good conscience or the true ideology of a movement have always participated in preparing the way for the advent of the Prince, only to end up as either his victims or his courtiers. The contemporary transformations of social actors paralleling the shift in the focus of conflicts and the changes in the forms of power have rendered the situation even more problematic. Both passionate and critical, involved and detached, the analysis of collective action is confronted with new challenges it itself must recognize, lest 'those who speak before' should go unheeded and the walls of stone or of silence muffle their message.

When looking at contemporary movements, we can assume one of two different attitudes – that of 'resolving' or that of 'listening.' Modern technology with its practice of intervention, wherein success is measured in terms of the efficacy of the given technique, claims victory for the 'resolutionary' approach and renders listening impossible. Under the influence of the general predisposition to immediate remedial action, social movements are taken into consideration solely on account of their capacity (or lack thereof) to modernize institutions or to produce political reform. But this is to forget, or to ignore, that the reduction of contemporary social movements to their political dimensions alone is tantamount to solving the 'symptom', to suppressing the message contained in their specifically communicative character ('symptom' literally means 'to fall together') and simply moving about the problem in the background.

Reflection on the analysis of social movements, however, is not warranted for the sake of scholarship only. At the same time, it may become a topical antidote in society: the work of analysis can contribute to the culture of the movements themselves, enhancing their resistance to the illusion that the word they bear is sacred and undermining the urge to totality that will swiftly turn them into churches or new powers that be. Heightened awareness of the possibilities and constraints of action can transform the word of the movements into language, culture, and social relationships, and may out of collective processes build a practice of freedom.

The continuum which ranges from protest and rebellion by a social group to the formation of a mass movement and a large-scale collective mobilization comprises a huge variety of intermediate forms of action, and any attempt to classify them seems at first sight all too formidable an undertaking. Indeed, one doubts whether such an operation might even reward the effort, since it remains questionable whether any continuity or homogeneity among the phenomena considered can actually be found. Here, more than in any other field of sociology, misunderstandings reign supreme. Terms such as 'collective violence', 'collective behaviour', 'protest', 'social movements', or 'revolution' often denote diverse phenomena and generate ambiguities, if not outright contradictions. It is not by chance that this confusion rotates around phenomena which closely involve the fundamental processes whereby a society maintains and changes its structure. Whether wittingly or not, the debate on the significance of collective action always embraces the issue of power relationships, and on closer examination derives its energy from defending or contesting a specific position or form of dominance. But the increasing prominence of the problem does not first and foremost stem from an ideological confrontation. It is social reality itself which presents us with a variety of collective phenomena, of conflictual actions, of episodes of social revolt which evade interpretation guided by traditional political categories, thus calling for new tools of analysis. Behind random protest or manifestations of cultural revolt in our complex planetary society – which by now also includes the developing societies of the 'South' – there of course always lie diverse problems and social structures. In this situation, the increasing diffusion of these phenomena and their diversification is, paradoxically, matched by the inadequacy of the analytical tools available to us.

In a certain sense, then, this book constitutes a venture into the uncertain terrain of a theory still to be constructed. In this search – which at the present stage can only proceed by trial and error – the capacity of a theory to rely exclusively on its own analytical foundations is necessarily limited. From this fact derives the importance of the growing body of research into cases of social movements and episodes of collective action, which in recent years has enriched theoretical analysis with a large quantity of empirical material relating to actual behaviour in society. From this point of view, the nonlinear progress of any analysis that attempts to come to grips with the theme of social movements and collective action is also understandable, obliged as it is to rely upon overspecific observations to fill gaps in the theory, just as it is, by the same token, forced to run the risk of general hypotheses where empirical material is scarce or nonexistent on the other hand.

In the last thirty years, analysis of social movements and collective action has developed into an autonomous sector of theory formation and research within the social sciences, and the amount and quality of the work in the area has grown and improved. Not incidentally, the autonomy of the conceptual field relating to the analysis of social movements has developed parallel to the increasing autonomy of noninstitutional forms of collective action in complex systems. The social space of movements has become a distinct area of the system and no longer coincides either with the traditional forms of organization of solidarity or with the conventional channels of political representation. The area of movements is now a 'sector' or a 'subsystem' of the social.

Recognizing this autonomy forces us to revise dichotomies like 'state' and 'civil society', 'public' and 'private', 'instrumental' and 'expressive'. The crisis of such polar distinctions signals a change in our conceptual universe. The notion of 'movement' itself, which originally stood for an entity acting against the political and governmental system, has now been rendered inadequate as a description of the reality of reticular and diffuse forms of collective action.

Contemporary 'movements' assume the form of solidarity networks entrusted with potent cultural meanings, and it is precisely these meanings that distinguish them so sharply from political actors and formal organizations next to them. We have passed beyond the global and metaphysical conception of collective actors. Movements are not entities that move with the unity of goals attributed to them by ideologues. Movements are systems of action, complex networks among the different levels and meanings of social action. Collective identity allowing them to become actors is not a datum or an essence; it is the outcome of exchanges, negotiations, decisions, and conflicts among actors. Processes of mobilization, organizational forms, models of leadership, ideologies, and forms of communication – these are all meaningful levels of analysis for the reconstruction from the within of the action system that constitutes the collective actor. But, in addition, relationships with the outside – with competitors, allies, and adversaries – and especially the response of the political system and the apparatuses of social control define a field of opportunities and constraints within which the collective action takes shape, perpetuates itself, or changes.

Contemporary forms of collective action are multiple and variable. They are located at several different levels of the social system simultaneously. We must therefore begin by distinguishing between the field of conflict on the one hand and the actors that bring such conflict to the fore on the other. In the past, studying conflicts implied analysing the social condition of a group and submitting what was known of that condition to deductive reasoning in order to wrest the causes of the collective action from it. Today, we must proceed by first singling out the field of conflict, and then explain how certain social groups take action within it.

Since no actor is inherently conflictual, the nature of action assumes a necessarily temporary character, and it may involve different actors and shift its locus among the various areas of the system. This multiplicity and variability of actors makes the plurality of the analytical meanings contained within the same physical phenomenon even more apparent. The totality of a given empirical collective action is usually attributed a quasi-substantial unity, when it is instead the contingent outcome of the interaction of a multiple field of forces and analytically distinct processes.

The inner differentiation of action is reinforced by the fact that in a planetary system social reality becomes synchronic: in the contemporaneity created by the media system, all the 'geological strata' of human history are simultaneously present. In the unity of the present, movements thus contain in one problems and conflicts that have different historical roots. Adding to this, movements attract the forms of discontent and marginalization that the social system generates, while the forming elites exploit conflict to seek opportunity to affirm themselves or to consolidate their positions.

An analytical perspective that draws on these insights helps us clarify one of the issues recurrently debated over the last decades. It concerns the 'newness' of contemporary conflicts: What is 'new' in the 'new social movements' is still an open question. Bearing the responsibility of the one who introduced the term 'new social movements' into sociological literature, I have watched with dismay as the category has been progressively reified. 'Newness', by definition, is a relative concept, which at the time of its formulation in the context of the movements research had the temporary function of indicating a number of comparative differences between the historical forms of class conflict and today's emergent forms of collective action. But if analysis and research fail to specify the distinctive features of the 'new movements', we are trapped in an arid debate between the supporters and critics of 'newness'.

On the one hand, there are those who claim that many aspects of the contemporary forms of action can be detected also in previous phenomena in history, and that the discovery of their purported newness is in the first place attributable to the bias shown by numerous sociologists blinded by emotional involvement with their subject matter. On the other hand, the defenders of the novel character of contemporary movements endeavour to show that these similarities are only formal, or apparent, and that the meaning of the phenomena is changed when they are set in different systemic contexts.

However, both the critics of the 'newness' of the 'new movements' and the proponents of the 'newness paradigm' commit the same epistemological mistake: they consider contemporary collective phenomena to constitute unitary empirical objects, seeking then on this basis to define the substance of their newness or to deny or dispute it. When addressing empirical 'movements', one side in the debate sets out to mark out differences with respect to the historical predecessors, the other stresses continuity and comparability.

The controversy strikes one as futile. In their empirical unity, contemporary phenomena are made up of a variety of components, and if these elements are not analytically separated, comparison between forms of action that belong to mutually distinct historical periods becomes an idle activity. It will be extremely difficult to decide, for instance, the extent of the 'new' in the modern 'women's movement', as a global empirical phenomenon, compared with the first feminist movements of the nineteenth century. Paradoxically, the result of the debate on 'new movements' has been the accelerating decline of the image of movements-as-entities. Through comparative work on different historical periods and different societies, we know now that contemporary movements, like all collective phenomena, bring together forms of action which involve various levels of the social structure. These encompass different points of view and belong to different historical periods. We must, therefore, seek to understand this multiplicity of synchronic and diachronic elements and explain how they are combined in the concrete unity of a collective actor.

Consider:
1. Based on the materials in this section, formulate a definition of power in your own words. Illustrate it with as many examples as you can think of.
2. 'Movements in complex societies are disenchanted prophets.' Discuss.
3. What are the features of contemporary social movements that Alberto Melucci highlights in the reading?
4. Based on any TWO contemporary social movements of your choice, illustrate the features of social movements discussed in the reading.

4.10 Families and personal life

Families have been of long-standing interest to sociologists. They have often been seen as institutions that facilitate the reproduction of society through childbearing, the socialisation of children into prevalent norms, values, and ways of life, the provision of material and emotional security, and the normative regulation of sexuality. Moreover, families have often been seen as being closely associated with *kinship*, that is to say durable social bonds established through common ancestry, marriage, adoption and so forth. This perspective tends to emphasise the universality of families and, moreover, specific types of family. The classical and highly influential work of American sociologist Talcott Parsons is illustrative in this regard. In his seminal work *The Social System* (1951/1991), Parsons does emphasise significant historical and geographical variations in kinship and family arrangements. However, he goes on to argue (p. 108) that 'a stable attachment of a man to a woman with inclusion of sexual relations taken for granted, almost automatically results in a family'. Implicit in this statement is the assumption of lasting intimate relationship between two heterosexual partners as the centrepiece of family.

More recent research has departed at least to some extent from this perspective. For example, in their study on the nature of personal communities in contemporary Britain, Ray Pahl and Liz Spencer argue in favour of abandoning the sharp divide between family ties and other personal bonds that has characterised much sociological research:

> In the research project which forms the basis for the rest of this article, we began by assuming that people have a set of relationships which are likely to vary in commitment and givenness. We recognized the need to allow for family members and friends to play similar as well as contrasting roles. Rather than seeing a sharp division between the family as 'given' and friends as 'chosen', we were aware from other research (Finch and Mason, 1993) that family members with whom relationships were close and salient could be as much 'chosen' as the life-long soul-mate friend who, in turn, may come to be seen as 'given'. (Pahl and Spencer 2006: 203)

Pahl and Spencer here blur the lines between family and friends, and they reject the idea that families are by definition characterised by social ties that are particularly close or intimate. Instead, they suggest that the ways in which individuals form personal communities with others are variable and open-ended. Equally, there have been significant recent proposals by British sociologists to focus on the study of *personal life*, rather than simply looking at family (Smart 2007).

Similarly, in a paper published 20 years ago, Peter Nardi argues that for gay people, friends often fill the roles of family members:

> This is particularly so when the social institutions exclude certain kinds of interpersonal relationships. For gay men and lesbians, social approval of intimate relationships is typically absent or limited by legal, religious, and cultural norms. For some, their families of origin (parents, siblings, and other close relatives) may not acknowledge or legitimize gay people's friendships and relationships. In the context of these social constraints and the need to sustain a sense of self, friendship takes on the roles typically provided by heterosexual families [. . .]. (Nardi 1992: 109)

The exclusion of which Nardi writes here is evident in the previously cited classical work of Talcott Parsons. Parsons (e.g. 1951/1991: 107ff.) focuses on heterosexual intimate relationships and marriages as central elements of family life and kinship, and he only writes of homosexuality as a taboo. However, at least in some societies, things have changed notably since Nardi wrote his paper two decades ago. Civil unions, marriages, and adoptions by gay and lesbian couples are now legally recognised in a number of countries around the world.

Analysing the social and legal recognition of same-sex relationships and families in Spain, José Ignacio Pichardo (2011) argues that a radical change in cultural meanings of kinship and family has taken place since the 1980s. For instance, while in 1973 only 3 per cent of society accepted homosexuality, this proportion had risen to 66.2 per cent by 2004 (Pichardo 2011: 548). This 'revolution in the social relations of gender and sexuality'

(Pichardo 2011: 545) has entailed a string of cultural and legal changes, culminating in the 2005 legalisation of same-sex marriages.

Thus, families need to be understood as encompassing a diverse range of historically and culturally specific personal ties between individuals. At the same time, as the arguments of Nardi and Pichardo suggest, families may also be important sites of social inequality in terms of gender and sexuality. The long-standing exclusion of LGBT people from the realm of socially legitimate and publicly recognised family life is one instance of such inequalities. Feminist critiques of families as sites of women's exploitation are equally significant. We will explore these issues further later on.

For the moment, we will rather focus on families as diverse and multifarious arrangements of personal bonds. This issue is addressed well in Judith Stacey's (2011) very recent book *Unhitched: Love, Marriage, and Family Values from Hollywood to Western China*. The following excerpt from the book focuses on the issue of gay parenthood.

Reading

Stacey, J. (2011), *Unhitched: Love, Marriage, and Family Values from Hollywood to Western China*, New York: New York University Press, pp. 49–50, 60–5

2

Gay Parenthood and the End of Paternity as We Knew It

Gay fathers were once as unthinkable as they were invisible. Now they are an undeniable part of the contemporary family landscape. During the same time that the marriage promotion campaign in the United States was busy convincing politicians and the public to regard rising rates of fatherlessness as a national emergency, growing numbers of gay men were embracing fatherhood. Over the past two decades, they have built a cornucopia of family forms and supportive communities where they are raising children outside of the conventional family. Examining the experiences of gay men who have openly pursued parenthood against the odds can help us to understand forces that underlie the decline of paternity as we knew it. Contrary to the fears of many in the marriage-promotion movement, however, gay parenting is not a new symptom of the demise of fatherhood, but of its creative, if controversial, reinvention. When I paid close attention to gay men's parenting desires, efforts, challenges, and achievements, I unearthed crucial features of contemporary paternity and parenthood more generally. I also came upon some inspirational models of family that challenge widely held beliefs about parenthood and child welfare. [. . .]

Parent Seeking Partner

Armando Hidalgo, a Mexican immigrant, was thirty-four years old when I interviewed him in 2001. At that point, he was in the final stages of adopting his four-year-old black foster son, Ramón. Armando had been a teenage sexual migrant to Los Angeles almost twenty years earlier. He had run away from home when he was only fifteen in order to conceal his unacceptable sexual desires from his large, commercially successful, urban Mexican family. The youthful Armando had paid a coyote to help him cross the border. He had survived a harrowing illegal immigration experience which culminated in a Hollywood-style footrace across the California desert to escape an INS patrol in hot pursuit. By working at a Taco Bell in a coastal town, Armando put himself through high school. Drawing upon keen intelligence, linguistic facility, and a prodigious work ethic and drive, he had built a stable career managing a designer furniture showroom and he had managed to secure U.S. citizenship as well.

Four years after Armando's sudden disappearance from Mexico, he had returned there to come out to his family, cope with their painful reactions to his homosexuality and exile, and begin to restore his ruptured kinship bonds. He had made annual visits to his family ever since, and on one of these he fell in love with Juan, a Mexican language teacher. Armando said that he told Juan about his desire to parent right at the outset, and his new lover had seemed enthusiastic: "So, I thought we were the perfect match." Armando brought his boyfriend back to Los Angeles, and they lived together for five years.

However, when Armando began to pursue his lifelong goal of parenthood, things fell apart. To initiate the adoption process, Armando had enrolled the couple in the county's mandatory foster-care class. However, Juan kept skipping class and neglecting the homework, and so he failed to qualify for foster-parent status. This behavior jeopardized Armando's eligibility to adopt children as well as Juan's. The county then presented Armando with a "Sophie's choice." They would not place a child in his home unless Juan moved out. Despite Armando's primal passion for parenthood, "at the time," he self-critically explained to me, "I made the choice of staying with him, a choice that I regret. I chose him over continuing with my adoption." This decision ultimately exacted a fatal toll on the relationship. In Armando's eyes, Juan was preventing him from fulfilling his life-long dream of having children. His resentment grew, but it took another couple of years before his passion for parenthood surpassed his diminishing passion for his partner. That is when Armando moved out and renewed the adoption application as a single parent.

Ramón was the first of three children that Armando told me he had "definitely decided" to adopt, whether or not he found another partner. His goal was to adopt two more children, preferably a daughter and another son, in that order. Removed at birth from crack-addicted parents, Ramón had lived in three foster homes in his first three years of life, before the county placed him with Armando through its fost-adopt program. Ramón had suffered from food allergies, anxiety, and hyperactivity when he arrived, and the social worker warned Armando to anticipate learning disabilities as well. Instead, after nine months under Armando's steady, patient, firm, and loving care, Ramón was learning rapidly and appeared to be thriving. And so was Armando. He felt so lucky to have Ramón, whom he no longer perceived as racially different from himself: "To me he's like my natural son. I love him a lot, and he loves me too much. Maybe I never felt so much unconditional love."

In fact, looking back, Armando attributed part of the pain of the years he spent struggling to accept his own homosexuality to his discomfort with gay male sexual culture and its emphasis on youth and beauty. "I think it made me fear that I was going to grow old alone," he reflected. "Now I don't have to worry that I'm gay and I'll be alone." For in addition to the intimacy that Armando savored with Ramón, his son proved to be a vehicle for building much closer bonds with most of his natal family. Several of Armando's eleven siblings had also migrated to Los Angeles. Among these were a married brother, his wife, and their children, who provided indispensable back-up support to the single working father. Ramón adored his cousins, and he and his father spent almost every weekend and holiday with them.

Ramón had acquired a devoted, long-distance *abuela* (grandmother) as well. Armando's mother had begun to travel regularly from Mexico to visit her dispersed brood, and, after years of disapproval and disappointment, she had grown to admire and appreciate her gay son above all her other children. Armando reported with sheepish pride that during a recent phone call his mother had stunned and thrilled him when she said, "You know what? I wish that all your brothers were like you. I mean that they liked guys." Astonished, Armando had asked her, "Why do you say that?" She replied, "I don't know. I just feel that you're really good to me, you're really kind. And you're such a good father." Then she apologized for how badly she had reacted when Armando told the family that he was gay, and she told him that now she was really proud of him. "'Now I don't have to accept it,'" Armando quoted her, "'because there's nothing to accept. You're natural, you're normal. You're my son, I don't have to accept you.' And she went on and on. It was so nice, it just came out of her. And now she talks about gay things, and she takes a cooking class from a gay guy and tells me how badly her gay cooking teacher was treated by his family when they found out and how unfair it is and all."

Although Armando had begun to create the family he always wanted, he still dreamt of sharing parenthood with a mate who would be more compatible than Juan: "I would really love to meet someone, to fall in love." Of course, the man of his dreams was someone family-oriented: "Now that's really important, family-oriented, because I am very close to my family. I always do family things, like my nephews' birthday parties, going to the movies with them, family dinners, etcetera. But these are things that many gay men don't like to do. If they go to a straight family party, they get bored." Consequently, Armando was pessimistic about finding a love match. Being a parent, moreover, severely constrained his romantic pursuits. He didn't want to subject Ramón, who had suffered so much loss and instability in his life, to the risk of becoming attached to yet another new parental figure who might leave him. In addition, he didn't want Ramón "to think that gay men only have casual relationships, that there's no commitment." "But," he observed, with disappointment, "I haven't seen a lot of commitment among gay men." Armando took enormous comfort, however, in knowing that even if he never found another boyfriend, he will "never really be alone": "And I guess that's one of the joys that a family brings." Disappointingly, I may never learn whether Armando found a co-parent and adopted a sister and brother for Ramón, because I was unable to locate him again in 2008.

Adopting Diversity

[. . .] Gestational surrogacy, perhaps the newest, the most high-tech, and certainly the most expensive path to gay parenthood, is available primarily to affluent couples, the overwhelming majority of whom are white men who want to have genetic progeny. Adoption, on the other hand, is one of the oldest forms of "alternative" parenthood. It involves bureaucratic and social rather than medical technologies, and the county fost-adopt program which Armando and six other men in my study employed is generally the least expensive, most accessible route to gay paternity. Like Armando, most single, gay prospective parents pursue this avenue and adopt "hard-to-place" children who, like Ramón, are often boys of color with "special needs."

The demographics of contrasting routes to gay parenthood starkly expose the race and class disparities in the market value of children. Affluent, mainly white couples [. . .] can purchase the means to reproduce white infants in their own image, or even an enhanced, eugenic one, by selecting egg donors who have traits they desire with whom to mate their own DNA. In contrast, for gay men who are single, less privileged, or both, public agencies offer a grab bag of displaced children who are generally older, darker, and less healthy. Somewhere in between these two routes to gay paternity lie forms of "gray market," open domestic or international adoptions, or privately negotiated sperm-donor agreements with women, especially lesbians, who want to co-parent with men. Independent adoption agencies and the Internet enable middle-class gay men, again typically white couples, to adopt newborns in a variety of hues.

Bernardo Fernandez, a middle-class, black Latino, took the gray-market route to parenthood, and with intimate consequences almost opposite to Armando's. Bernardo adopted the first of two mixed-race children while he was single, but then he had the great fortune of falling in love with a gay man who also had always wanted to parent. Less fortunately, however, Bernardo's beloved was an Australian visitor to the United States, and U.S. immigration law does not grant family status to same-sex partners. His partner therefore applied for a work visa so that he could stay in the United States, but his tourist visa had expired, and he had been forced to return home. The prospects of receiving a work visa were not looking good, and Bernardo feared that in order to live together as a family, he and the children were going to have to migrate to Australia, because it did admit same-sex partners. In the meantime, Bernardo was spending the months between his lover's regular visits parenting alone.

Price does not always determine the route to parenthood that gay men choose, or the race, age, health, or pedigree of the children they agree to adopt. During the period of my initial research, only one white, middle-class couple in my study had chosen to adopt healthy white infants. Some affluent white men enthusiastically adopted children of color, even when they knew that the children had been exposed to drugs prenatally. Drew Greenwald, a very successful architect who could easily have afforded assisted reproductive technology (ART), was the most dramatic example of this. He claimed, "It never would have occurred to me to do surrogacy. I think it's outrageous because there are all these children who need good homes. And people have surrogacy, they say, in part it's because they want to avoid the complications of adoption, but in candor they are really in love with their own genes. . . . I just think there is a bit of narcissism about it." An observant Jew and the son of Holocaust survivors, Drew found gestational surrogacy particularly offensive. "The idea of having a different genetic mother and birth mother is a little too Nazi-esque for me, a little too much genetic engineering for me. I feel somewhat uncomfortable with that. I mean, someone can be good enough to carry the baby, but their genes aren't good enough? That's outrageous."

Drew had opted for independent, open, transracial adoption instead. When I first interviewed him in 2002, he had just adopted his second of two multiracial babies born to two different women who both had acknowledged using drugs during their pregnancies. Drew, like Bernardo, had been single when he adopted his first child, and parenthood proved to be a route to successful partnership for him as well. Soon after adopting his first infant, Drew reunited with James, a former lover who had fallen "wildly in love" with Drew's new baby. James moved in while Drew was in the process of adopting a second child, and they have co-parented together ever since. Indeed, parenthood is the "glue" that cemented a relationship between the couple that Drew believed might otherwise have failed. Shared parenting provided them with a "joint project, a focus, and a source of commitment." Drew acknowledged that he was not a romantic. He had questions, in fact, "about the very term *intimacy*" and considered sex to be an important but minor part of life. He and James were very "efficient" in servicing their sexual needs, he quipped. They devoted perhaps "a few minutes" of their over-stuffed weekly schedule to this activity, "mainly on Shabbas, and then we're back to our family life."

I was indulging in my guilty pleasure of reading the Style section of the Sunday *New York Times* one morning in the fall of 2008, when I stumbled across a wedding photo and announcement that Drew and James, "the parents of five adopted children," had just married. Several weeks later, on a conference trip to Los Angeles, I visited the bustling, expanded family household. I learned that the white birth mother of their second child had since had two more unwanted pregnancies, one with the same African American man as before and one with a black Latino. She had successfully appealed to Drew and James to add both of these mixed-race siblings to their family. After the first of these two new brothers had joined their brood, Drew and James began to worry that because only one of their children was a girl, she would find it difficult to grow up in a family with two dads and only brothers. And so they turned to the Internet, where they found a mixed-race sister for their first daughter. Three of the five children suffered from learning or attention-deficit difficulties, but Drew took this in stride. He was well aware, he said, that he and James had signed on "for all sorts of trauma, challenge, heartache" in the years ahead. He was both determined and financially able to secure the best help available for his children. Nonetheless, Drew acknowledged, "I fully expect that the kids will break my heart at some point in various ways, but it's so worth it." It was sufficiently worth it, apparently, that the year after my 2008 visit, I received an email from Drew announcing that their child head count had climbed to six, because their "jackpot birth mom" had given birth yet again. "We're up to four boys and two girls," Drew elaborated. "It's a lot, as you can imagine, but wonderful."

Consider

1. To what extent, if at all, can we describe families as universal social institutions? Support your arguments through relevant background research.
2. What are the social, cultural and political shifts that have facilitated as well as inhibited the legalisation of same-sex marriages? Gather respective information on ONE of the following countries:

   South Africa
   Norway
   Spain
   The Netherlands.

3. Summarise Judith Stacey's case study on gay parenting. What are the main issues in gay parenting the reading portrays?
4. According to the reading, how do experiences of gay parenting intersect with broader issues of gender, ethnicity and migration?

4.11 Religion

Religion has been a central concern for sociologists for a very long time. Scholars such as Max Weber, Karl Marx and Émile Durkheim sought to understand the roles which religious beliefs and practices may play in the development of modern societies. In the early twenty-first century, religion continues to be of acute significance around the world.

One of the most salient features of religious life today is its irreducible diversity; a wide variety of religious faiths are prevalent around the world. The *global religions* have an often defining influence on everyday life across substantial geographical regions and among very large populations. In addition, there are thousands of other, less wide-spread religious faiths. There are often very pronounced differences between the beliefs, norms and practices these religions advocate. This, in turn, requires us to show caution in attempting to draw out some general features of religious life today.

In such general terms, we might define religion as a matter of *faith*, that is to say convictions about the nature of the world and human life that are not necessarily grounded in proof. Examples of this would be the belief in life after death in Islam and Christianity, or in a very wide variety of deities or supreme beings in Hinduism. Furthermore, religions often encompass *cosmogonies*, that is to say explanations of the creation of the world, *norms of moral conduct* in everyday life, and *rituals*, that is, highly formalised behavioural routines that carry a particular symbolic meaning. Pujas in Buddhism and Hinduism are examples of rituals, as are sacrificial offerings to the gods in ancient Roman religion. Religions may thus serve as important *institutions* in society, and many religions are supported by extensive organisational structures. For instance, the spread of the Catholic Christian faith through large parts of the world has been supported by the organisational power of the Catholic Church. Church functionaries often wield considerable political power, and until the nineteenth century, they governed many territories in Europe directly.

Photo 4.4   Hall of Prayer for Good Harvests, Temple of Heaven, Beijing. Part of a temple complex originally constructed in the early fifteenth century. Chinese emperors and their retinues would come here to pray for good harvests. Mistakes in the performance of the respective rituals would be regarded as bad omens and might reflect badly upon the emperor's power.

Source: Author's photograph

In terms of their role in society, some sociologists have emphasised religions' capabilities to serve as sources of *social cohesion*. Émile Durkheim (1912/1995) argued that religions organise social life around *conceptions of the sacred*, that is, social objects that are held to be awe-inspiring and worthy of devotion, as opposed to *profane*, mundane, or ordinary things. In so doing, they serve as conduits of social control, cohesion, and generally accepted meanings of life. In contrast, other thinkers have emphasised the role of religion as a conduit of power that legitimises inequality and oppression. Karl Marx, for example, argued that religion 'is the sigh of the oppressed creature, the heart of a heartless world, just as it is the spirit of spiritless conditions' (Marx 1844/1983: 115).

More recently, many sociologists have focused on the apparent waning of religion as a significant force in public life. In some societies – the United Kingdom, Denmark and Sweden being notable examples – a majority of people is either *atheistic* altogether and denies adherence to any faith or regards faith as entirely a matter with little bearing upon the conduct of public life. This has led some sociologists to note a significant trend towards *secularisation*, that is, a decline of the binding power of religious faith in public and everyday life and the simultaneous rise of non-religious institutions, norms and values, particularly in the form of scientific explanations of the world (cf. Martin 2005). Others argue that the problem of secularisation refers specifically to the relationships and relative power between Christian churches and non-religious institutions, particularly the nation state, in the Western world (cf. Turner 2011: 133ff.). Others emphasise the 'post-secular' characteristics of contemporary social life, in which new forms of belief and spirituality are on the rise and longer established forms of religion find a new purchase in public life (Davie 2010). In the following reading, David Lyon examines the role of religion in contemporary Western societies, noting a peculiar encounter between resurgent Christian faith and features of capitalist consumerism as a sign of the times.

Reading

Lyon, David (2000), *Jesus in Disneyland: Religion in Postmodern Times*, Cambridge: Polity Press, pp. 1–11

Meeting Jesus in Disneyland

It is Disneyland that is authentic here! The cinema and TV are America's reality! The freeways, the Safeways, the skylines, speed, deserts – these are America, not the galleries, the churches, the culture.

Jean Baudrillard

The scene is Anaheim, California, home of Disneyland. Not unusually, 10,000 people are streaming through the turnstiles. Only today they are heading for a Harvest Day Crusade. In place of the regular attractions and rides, Christian artists perform at several stages through the park, and an evangelist, Greg Laurie, preaches a gospel message. While some find the juxtaposition somewhat incongruous (has not the Disney Corporation expanded its family values to include gays and lesbians? is beer not sold here?) the organizers have no qualms about it: "We saw Disneyland as an opportunity to bring God's kingdom to the Magic Kingdom. We felt that, as they opened the door to us to share Christ, we wouldn't turn down the opportunity just because other things take place there. Jesus is the example for this."

Jesus in Disneyland. A bizarre sounding collaboration. Or is it? Just why does it appear so odd? At first blush, the objection could be that an ancient, premodern religion is found side-by-side, or, more accurately, *interacting* with, the epitome of postmodern culture – the artificial, simulated, virtual, fantasy world of Disney. It is not as if this religious group is merely using the park as a stadium for its event. To a considerable extent they adopt the styles, the fashions, even the attitudes of Disneyland. And they are not alone. Other groups – such as at the annual evangelical Spring Harvest weeks at Butlin's Holiday Camps or at Christian events at Legoland in the UK, and at numerous Christian theme parks, such as Logosland in Ontario – use similar venues and methods.

It seems like an anachronism. Two vastly different historical eras are telescoped incongruously into one, within the gates of a theme park. Not only do the two seem historically out of place; culturally, too, they clash. The simply-dressed, sandal-clad, travelling rabbi who quietly admitted to close associates that he was God's promised Messiah – Jesus – also has connections with the self-advertising, technologically complex, consumer culture of comfortable California? Anachronism or not, such things occur, especially in America.

But the problem is not just one of oddity. This collusion – or collision – of cultures also takes place in a context that was once supposed to have erased most traces of conventional religion from daily life. It is often said that when premodern religions met modernity, from the seventeenth century onwards, relations were less than cordial. The scientific-technological revolution, the burgeoning of industrial capitalism, and the rise of urbanism and democratic polities often had an abrasive and corrosive effect on organized religion. The mathematician LaPlace took the trouble to inform the French emperor that he "had no need of the hypothesis" of God. For many others, the process was implicit, whereby the "hypothesis" was for all practical purposes quietly dropped. Religious vestiges gradually succumbed to the evolutionary forces of modernity. Or so the story goes.

All this, and more, makes it hard to account for the Jesus in Disneyland event. Yet it occurred. And, apart from a few raised eyebrows, it was not treated by those involved as an anomaly or an isolated California quirk. Perhaps the difficulty is in the eye of the beholder? Those accustomed to the predominantly secular discourse of contemporary politics, mass media, or academe apparently have a harder time coping with Jesus in Disneyland than those who actually attended this event. This is not meant to imply that there is no anomaly, or that the view from below, which cheerfully harmonizes the surface contradictions, is in fact superior or correct. Nor do I mean to propose, however, that the secular discourse has it right either. Rather, I suggest that both perspectives should be problematized – held up for serious and careful examination – as a prelude to a better accounting for the event.

In what follows, I offer just such a problematizing account, as an introduction to the broad themes of this book. While the Jesus in Disneyland event is interesting in its own right, it also opens a fascinating window on contemporary religion and society. Conventional religion – in this case Christianity, but similar analysis can be made of other religions – is caught at a curious cultural juncture. Disneyland captures several crucial features of this, as the theme parks epitomize the tensions of modernity. Both modern and postmodern elements may be discerned at Disneyland, and today religious life is drawn by the pull of both gravitational fields.

Disneyland is a social and cultural symbol of our times. In particular, Disneyland is a trope for the democratization of culture, including religion. An event like the one noted here raises questions about the deregulation of religion. Disneyland also points up the ambiguities and ironies of modernity and postmodernity, as well as their sources, the proliferation of new communications media, and the growth of consumerism. Disneyland as a cultural symbol also hints strongly at questions of authority and identity, and of time and space, each of which is crucial for a contemporary understanding of religion, spirituality, and faith.

Disney's social impact

There can be little doubt that Disney's influence is universal. Wherever it is possible to see a television or a cinema screen, Disney characters will not be strangers. And in more and more world tourist destinations, a Disney theme park is within reach. Plans for the latest are currently under way in Hong Kong. Disney's impact extends far beyond films or parks made by the Disney corporation. By the end of the twentieth century Disney had become a byword for commercial culture, a symbol for animated cartoon lives, a model for tourist activities, and a mode of imagination. But it was also a way of communicating, a herald of technological futures, an architectural inspiration, and a guide to city planning. In Melbourne, Australia, a recent festival celebrated a Disneyfied Winnie-the-Pooh as a "United Nations ambassador for international friendship!" Under these conditions, it would be surprising if Disney did not have a religious relevance.

There are two main concepts used in exploring Disney's social influence, Disneyfication and Disneyization. Each has something significant to offer, but it is worth distinguishing between them. Disneyfication tends to be used critically. *Spy* magazine, for instance, defines Disneyfication as "the act of assuming, through the process of assimilation, the traits and characteristics more familiarly associated with a theme park . . . than with real life." The same magazine reported a telephone interview with Walt Disney World, in which it asked about the possibility of laying on a "Fantasia wedding," featuring a transparent box of mice, with pinned-on ear enlargements. The Disney receptionist balked at this, explaining that Mickey himself would attend. "Why simulate it with a real mouse when you can have the genuine article there?", she asked. The author of this piece also observed that "Genuine Disneyfication must be tawdry, contrived, useless, and dripping with class panic."

More sociologically Chris Rojek focuses on the moral and political culture represented by the Disney leisure industry, coming to the caustic conclusion that Disney parks "encourage the consumer to relate to America as a spectacle rather than as an object of citizenship." Disneyfication makes social conflict temporary and abnormal, emphasizes individual rather than collective action, and generally acts as a mouthpiece for the American Way. The Disney world view fails to make sense of the present or to provide a plausible vision of the future, sacrificing "knowledge for staged spectacles organized around soundbites of history and culture." Thus for Rojek Disneyfication subtly organizes our lives, even while letting us think that we are in a realm of release and escape.

Umberto Eco takes a similarly critical line, applying it to the ongoing uncertainty generated by Disney in order to perpetuate consumption. Deep questions of good and evil are rendered shallow through this process. The cynical shows through all too readily. Eco thinks of America as the prominent hyper-reality, whose ideology "wants to establish reassurance through imitation. But profit defeats ideology, because the consumers want to be thrilled not only by the guarantee of the good but also by the shudder of the bad." Thus there must be metaphysical evil, "both with the same level of credibility, both with the same level of fakery. Thus, on entering his cathedrals of iconic reassurance, the visitor will remain uncertain whether his final destination is heaven or hell, and so will consume new promises."

Such critical approaches to Disney have much to commend them. Disneyfication may be viewed as a process that diminishes human life through trivializing it, or making involvement within it appear less than fully serious. No wonder Neil Postman wrote of "amusing ourselves to death." Yet the Disneyfication thesis also has limits. The negative approach is not necessarily helpful in all contexts. With no pretence at neutrality, the term Disneyization has been proposed as an analytical alternative. Alan Bryman proposes that it should be defined as "the process by which *the principles* of the Disney theme parks are coming to dominate more and more sectors of American society as well as the rest of the world." He isolates four elements of Disneyization, which are outlined below. As I shall show, each principle also resonates in significant ways with some major themes of this book.

The first aspect is "theming," which can of course be found in many contexts not directly touched by Disney. Thus cafés and bars may be themed, along with hotels and shopping malls. Well-known examples include the Hard Rock Café and the Subway outlets. Theming lends coherence to a site, giving it a story line.

Theming creates connections and thereby gives a particular ambience to a complete environment. Today, that environment may be physical, at a permanent theme park site. But it may also be virtual. All computer users have become aware of particular kinds of "environments" that are themed in idiosyncratic ways, the "Mac" environment, or the "Netscape" one, and so on. Theming may be seen as postmodern surrogates for narratives (even "metanarratives") which, however fragmentary or temporary, tell tales within which lives may be located.

Bryman's second aspect is the "dedifferentiation of consumption." This technical term refers to ways that "forms of consumption associated with different institutional spheres become interlocked with each other and increasingly difficult to distinguish." It is a breaking down of conventional cultural differences between kinds of consumption and between consuming and other activities. In the World Showcase of the EPCOT Center, visitors to Disneyland think they are sampling cultures from around the world, whereas in reality they are entering a thinly disguised shopping area. Conversely, sites where one expects to shop seem to spawn attractions. You can find rides and leisure zones within shopping malls. Airports and train stations provide evidence of the same phenomenon. Authentic crafts and current CDs can be bought, haircuts and massages obtained, tickets bought and checked. Increasingly, then, in more and more daily life contexts, one may expect to consume across a broad range of items. Such dedifferentation accentuates the consumer culture, in which consumption becomes an order of life. The dedifferentiated environment privileges consumer outlooks and consumer skills.

Thirdly, Disneyization means merchandising. Images and logos are used to promote goods for sale, or are themselves for sale. The parks are both places where such merchandise is sold and the source of images and logos. Likewise the films are a source of images and logos that appear on merchandise, sometimes even before a film has been released. Many others, from sports teams to universities, have learned the Disneyesque techniques and advantages of merchandising. From our point of view, merchandising points up the power of an image, both in its own right and as something that can be bought. Merchandising also refers to itself and thus connects with a more general trend towards self-referentiality, which is a prime component of the post-modern. A recent example of this is the picture of the classic Coke bottle that appears on Coke cans, to reassure imbibers that it is the "real thing."

Fourthly, Disneyization involves emotional labour. Rather as McDonald's restaurants attempt to control the ways their employees view themselves and how they feel, so the Disney Corporation encourages scripted interactions using its staff. Theme park employees are well known for their smiling friendliness and helpfulness. Disney employees are supposed to give the impression that they are having fun too and not really working. This focus on the self, and how the self is expressed, is again a feature of the postmodern. As we shall see, the modes of self-expression in postmodern times relate to the religious realm in interesting ways.

Bryman explores the possibility that while McDonaldization exudes some very modern features associated with bureaucratic organization, Disneyization portends a shift into the postmodern. Disneyization spells consumerism and a concern with the sign value of goods, with style and identity projects. Disneyization breaks down differences, is depthless, and deals in cultivated nostalgia and in playfulness about reality. These are certainly themes that I think are deeply significant, both for the worlds of Disney and for the worlds of the postmodern. How far these features are affecting – and are affected by – contemporary religious spheres remains to be seen.

Modern and postmodern

The Jesus in Disneyland event may be used as an exemplar for understanding religion and society relationships at the turn of the twenty-first century. In several significant respects, religion is being both Disneyfied and Disneyized. This is what makes Disneyland such a good trope for contemporary culture, both modern and, increasingly, postmodern. Disneyland encapsulates in concentrated form some leading trends, especially the preoccupation with consuming – fashion, film, and music – and the experience of spectacles made possible by high technology. While Disney's simulations by electronic media raise doubts about reality, and thus connect neatly with the postmodern, there are many other features of Disneyland that still seem thoroughly modern. High technology, to take the most obvious example, is also explicitly linked, through the high-tech EPCOT Center, with classic modern notions of progress and linear time.

How, after all, does one enter the Magic Kingdom? What sustains this world? Well, all major credit cards are accepted and these, along with the whole massive theme park system, are entirely dependent on the highest of high technology. Night and day, electric power flows into Disneyland to support the operation of machinery and its finely tuned computer-controlled system. Moreover, McDonaldization, which epitomizes principles of modernity such as bureaucratic organization and scientific management, is also present in the theme parks. Whatever else postmodern means, at Disneyland or elsewhere, it emphatically does not mean that consumer capitalism has collapsed or that modern technology has been jettisoned. Just the reverse. The modern and the postmodern are equally characteristic of Disneyland.

It is crucial to dispose of the idea that modernity has somehow ground to a halt, to be replaced by postmodern conditions. Rather, the prefix "post" is attached to "modernity" in order to alert us to the fact that modernity itself is now in question. This does not mean that the sense of an ending – evinced in much postmodern literature – is insignificant, only that it can be over-extended. Sociologically speaking, although the rediscovery of deep cultural influences has helped to balance the analysis of social structure, the danger is to imagine that somehow social settings are irrelevant to the emergence of new cultural landscapes. Postmodernity is a kind of interim situation where some characteristics of modernity have been inflated to such an extent that modernity becomes scarcely recognizable as such, but exactly what the new situation is – or even whether any new situation can become "settled" – is unclear.

The inflated characteristics of modernity, which give rise to postmodern premonitions, relate above all to communication and information technologies (CITs) and to the tilt towards consumerism. Both are bound up with the restructuring of capitalism that has been under way since at least the last quarter of the twentieth century. Some such as Manuel Castells focus on the former, arguing that present trends are best summed up in the notion of an "information age." Others such as Zygmunt Bauman center their analyses on the social consequences of the shift towards consumer capitalism. But as the social and cultural converge, not least under the influence of these trends, it makes more sociological sense to hold the two together. The growth of CITs and new media augments the power of the image, while encouraging such developments as positional pluralism. But the dynamic of the whole system may be traced increasingly to the demand that consumption levels be constantly raised.

So phrases like the end of modernity, though arresting, can be very misleading. When Italian philosopher Gianni Vattimo used this phrase as a book title he was referring to the exhaustion of modern *ideas*, a modern *ethos* or a modern *world-view*. For him, modernity starts with Descartes, and is characterized above all by a belief in progress. But this is undercut, especially by Nietzsche, when progress is shown to have become just routine, severed from its old religious roots in Augustine. For Nietzsche, the realization that "God is dead" breaks the spell of "higher values" or purposes that drive history. Consequently, some form of nihilism is all that is left. Modernity's dynamic lies dead.

Much postmodern writing, especially in literary contexts, picks up these philosophical threads and weaves them into a story of the cultural collapse of modernity. But a sociological understanding of modernity would be rather more ambivalent about its incipient demise. If, for example, one takes the pulse of transnational capitalism or of technological development – each encapsulated in the Disney empire – the patient would appear to be in thoroughly healthy shape. True, the once cherished hopes that modernity would reduce global disparities of wealth or diminish the likelihood of war are seldom mentioned today. Yet, to change the metaphor, much of modernity's machinery hums on as efficiently as ever.

Religion and social change

The Jesus in Disneyland event demonstrates how religion may spill over its older (modern) institutional boundaries, taking new and changing shapes, with a corresponding diversity of meanings. But, as I shall argue later, some traditional religious resonance with Disneyland also exists – the strong sense of a story line (what Jean-François Lyotard called metanarratives) and of hierarchical organization being perhaps the most palpable. Understanding this involves exploring the reality of religious phenomena, the characteristics of the social-cultural context in which they are located, and the relationships between the two. The background to this is the debate about religion and modernity, classically understood within overarching theories of secularization. Such theories were once the standard means of coming to grips with the fortunes of religion in modern conditions.

Secularization theories provided a handy catch-all concept within which all kinds of phenomena could be interpreted, from the emptying of church pews to the decreasing references to God in political speeches (except maybe in the USA or Islamic nations). Despite the arguably powerful contribution of religion to the rise of modernity, it was widely assumed that Max Weber was right to see Christianity thus acting as its own gravedigger. So an event like Jesus in Disneyland could be seen in the light of such secularization theory as an instance of the inner secularization of the churches (given that the USA still has high rates of church attendance), in which the church becomes less and less distinguishable from the rest of the world, and entertainment rather than obedience its real dynamic.

Although the secularization thesis still calls for critical attention (the burden of the next chapter), it is slowly but surely being supplanted by less self-assured approaches. Jesus in Disneyland might equally be seen, for example, as evidence of the transformation or restructuring of religion, or at least of its deregulation. What if, given the tarnished status of several myths that make American life legitimate, the Crusade Christians at Disneyland were associating themselves with the somewhat more resilient myth of technology? This would bolster Christian credibility by showing that believers can embrace high technology, and simultaneously counter any residual notion that Christians are obliged to be ascetically cut off from the real world. This interpretation would be in a venerable and plausible tradition.

Once religious activity is free of the secularization straitjacket, however, we discover all sorts of other ways to consider it sociologically. British sociologist James Beckford, for instance, concludes that religion is best thought of as a cultural resource. In this way, religion can be seen to "convey symbols of newly-perceived social realities," whether to do with ethnicity, ecology, or the emancipation of women, and to be combined in flexible and unpredictable ways with all kinds of ideas and values. Jesus in Disneyland represents one such curious combination. Without its crippling conceptual tether to local community or to social institution, religion may be re-thought in fresh ways. Without the academic presumption that religion's social significance declines in the modern world, its actual social significance may be gauged appropriately.

The self-assured secularization story has little space for spiritual and supra-rational quests, whether formally religious or not. They tend to be seen as socially insignificant. Although Max Weber foresaw what he expected would be attempts to escape from the iron cage of bureaucratic rationality into a world of gods and spirits, it was the iron cage itself that preoccupied sociologists for the longest time. So the later twentieth century's sacralization of the Self – as a means of finding some continuity for multiple identities – comes as a surprise. This is seen above all in the multifarious New Age movements – and their commercial parasites – but also in the "self-absorbed solipsism" of the cybersurfer, creating a customized cosmos inside a virtual reality headset, or even, perhaps, constructing a personal website on the Internet. In this case, paradoxically, the cage offers the escape!

Of course, Disneyland is itself a classic mode of escape (and this is a common Disneyfication theme). There, one may find release from the humdrum world of everyday reality, as well as from the tensions and the conflicts, the violence and the degradation that characterize the real world. It is, on the one hand, a controlled release into a fantasy world of childhood, but on the other, a means of organizing its subjects, and of moral regulation. It offers an attractive alternative reality while simultaneously ignoring the outside world of discrimination, disease, and death, and persuading its customers that the world beyond the park gates is really gray, monotonous, or boring. But it also portrays as normal a world in which good and evil are seldom ambiguous, in which right triumphs, where patriarchy rules – think of the *Lion King* – and which encourages robot-like passivity as a response. As one critic said, sanitizing the stories renders them cute rather than acute, and with their cutting edge blunted they lose "the pulse of life under the skin of events." This ordering of the world through media discourse is a theme that straddles the modern–postmodern debate.

To what extent is an event like Jesus in Disneyland a capitulation to consumerism, and to what extent does it represent a carefully controlled compromise with contemporary cultural realities? As we explore the worlds of the new media and of consumer identities in relation to expressions of faith and of religious commitment, we shall find, as in this event, that there are no simple answers. The demise of regulated, institutional religion seems to open space for all manner of alternatives, as varied as they are unpredictable. All we can comment on here is the contexts that increasingly constrain and enable those alternatives to appear. The taken-for-granted religious monopolies of yesterday have now lost much of their former power, and in Christian contexts this may as often be applauded as bemoaned, in the sense that religious commitment may now be unshackled from its less worthy cultural accoutrements. The question confronted by believers operating in those contexts now is, with which aspects of today's culture can contracts be made, and which – infantilism? consumerism? fun? nostalgia? – must be eschewed?

These, then, are the kinds of phenomena and the kinds of questions that cry out for renewed attention as sociology emerges from its secular space-warp. Part of the reason that such issues are on the agenda again is that radical questions are raised about the future of modernity itself. If modernity challenges religion, then what happens when modernity itself is challenged? Although the debate about postmodernity often generates more heat than light, the very existence of the debate enables us to take a critical look at time-honoured assumptions about both modernity and religion. Jesus in Disneyland may make more sense within some alternative frames, fashioned from fresh resources. Perhaps Jesus in Disneyland signals the arrival of the postmodern Christian?

Consider

1. 'Religious suffering is at once the *expression* of real suffering and the *protest* against real suffering. Religion is the sigh of the oppressed creature, the heart of a heartless world, just as it is the spirit of spiritless conditions. It is the *opium* of the people' (Marx 1844/1983: 115; emphasis in original).

Discuss

2. In which ways is Disneyland a 'social and cultural symbol of our times'? Summarise David Lyon's arguments about the Disneyfication and Disneyisation of society.
3. How is the Jesus in Disneyland event indicative of broader trends in religious life in Western societies?
4. How does David Lyon link his arguments about religion to the broader sociological themes of modernity and postmodernity? Support your answer with specific references to the reading.
5. How, if at all, is religion a significant social force in the contemporary world? Support your answer with specific examples.

4.12 Deviance

My discussion so far has avoided a set of issues that are both important and readily visible in everyday life. As I have argued above, our ways of thinking, feeling and acting are guided in important ways by norms, that is to say formal and informal rules of conduct we are firmly expected to follow and to which sanctions are attached. However, for a variety of reasons, we often violate such norms of acceptable conduct. Just as human beings are individuals with distinct selves, their behaviour never fully conforms to general standards of conduct. Through processes of socialisation, we come to know about and understand society's norms, but we do not necessarily and automatically put them into practice. Sociology therefore attempts to understand *deviance*: those forms of conduct and ways of being that violate social norms and are recognised as such violations by self and others.

Street gangs are one example of social groups that are frequently associated with deviance. They also serve to illustrate the sociological complexities involved in the study of deviance. Consider the case of the Mara Salvatruchas.

The Mara Salvatruchas are one result of the social upheaval and political conflict that have afflicted much of Central America since the 1970s. They are a transnational

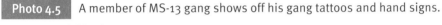

Photo 4.5   A member of MS-13 gang shows off his gang tattoos and hand signs.

Source: Robert Nickelsberg/Getty Images

street youth gang that emerged, more specifically, in the wake of civil war in El Salvador from 1980 to 1992 (Zilberg 2007). During the war, many Salvadorans fled to the USA. Jütersonke, Muggah and Rodgers describe the origins of the maras as follows:

> The *maras*, on the other hand, are linked to specific migratory patterns. There are reportedly just two *mara* groups, the Dieciocho (18) and the Salvatrucha (MS), operating in El Salvador, Guatemala and Honduras. The *maras* emerged directly from the 18th Street gang in Los Angeles, a group initially founded by Mexican immigrants in the 1960s. The 18th Street gang expanded during the late 1970s and early 1980s as a result of the influx of mainly Salvadoran and Guatemalan refugees who sought to incorporate into the gang as a form of social inclusion. By the latter half of the 1980s, a rival – possibly splinter – group founded by a second wave of Salvadoran refugees emerged, known as the Mara Salvatruchas ('*Salvatrucha*' being a combination of '*Salvadoreño*' and '*trucha*', meaning 'quick-thinking' or 'shrewd' in Salvadoran slang). The Dieciocho and the Salvatrucha rapidly became bitter rivals, frequently fighting each other on the streets of Los Angeles. As levels of intolerance began to grow and US immigration legislation acquired a more restrictive character, US-based gang members were repatriated to Central America. Between 1998 and 2005, the USA deported almost 46,000 convicts to Central America, in addition to 160,000 illegal immigrants caught without the requisite permit. Three countries – El Salvador, Guatemala and Honduras – received over 90% of the deportations from the USA (USAID, 2006: 18–19). (Jütersonke *et al.* 2009)

The maras have spread to many parts of the world. Police reports and media coverage tend to highlight the involvement of the maras in *crime*. Crime, in a sociological sense, refers to the violation of those norms that have been codified in *criminal law*. The contents of criminal law, in turn, are changeable, reflecting baseline assumptions in different societies and historical periods about intolerable forms of conduct that require prosecution by agents of the state. According to the US Federal Bureau of Investigation (http://www.fbi.gov/news/stories/2008/january/ms13_011408), the Mara Salvatruchas are involved in serious crimes, such as drug distribution, murder, rape and kidnapping.

However, it would be inaccurate to reduce the maras to their criminal activity. Research highlights that they developed in part as a response to the displacement their members experienced in Central America and in the new and often hostile territory of megacity Los Angeles in the USA. Their attraction may, in this sense, be related to the sense of security and belonging with which they provide their members. Photo 4.5 illustrates this point. The hand gesture and elaborate tattoos shown in the photograph are common displays of membership in the maras, and they create visible difference from outsiders. From this perspective, the Mara Salvatruchas might be described as a *subculture*. The term subculture, according to Hebdige (1979) refers to the expressive forms and rituals of groups that are in some sense subordinate in society. The formation of the maras, can, perhaps, be explained as a result of subordination and exclusion (Brotherton and Barrios 2009). In this sense, it might be said that the very hierarchies and forms of power that give society a definite, stable shape also bring about deviance by marginalising, excluding and branding as undesirable outsiders certain individuals and social groups:

> All social groups make rules and attempt, at some times and under some circumstances, to enforce them. Social rules define situations and the kinds of behavior appropriate to them, specifying some actions as 'right' and forbidding others as 'wrong.' When a rule is enforced, the person who is supposed to have broken it may be seen as a special kind of person, one who cannot be trusted to live the rules agreed on by the group. He is regarded as an *outsider*. (Becker 1963/1997: 1)

This is the opening paragraph of *Outsiders*, a now famous classic by US sociologist Howard S. Becker. In *Outsiders,* Becker considers the question of how societies, by creating norms and rules of appropriate conduct, label certain people as misfits and, in doing so, *produce* deviance. From this perspective, deviance comes to appear like a 'normal' and unavoidable part of social life.

Moreover, Becker's argument suggests it is also necessary to consider more extensively the development of formal *strategies of social control*. The emergence and spread of criminal law and criminal justice systems is just one example of such strategies. The French scholar Michel Foucault (1926–1984) traced the development of patterns of social control, power, and surveillance in Western society in great detail. Below, you will find an extract from his work.

Reading

Foucault, M. (1984), 'Panopticism', *The Foucault Reader*, edited by P. Rabinow, London: Penguin, pp. 206–13

Panopticism

(FROM *Discipline and Punish*)

. . . "Discipline" may be identified neither with an institution nor with an apparatus; it is a type of power, a modality for its exercise, comprising a whole set of instruments, techniques, procedures, levels of application, targets; it is a "physics" or an "anatomy" of power, a technology. And it may be taken over either by "specialized" institutions (the penitentiaries or "houses of correction" of the nineteenth century), or by institutions that use it as an essential instrument for a particular end (schools, hospitals), or by preexisting authorities that find in it a means of reinforcing or reorganizing their internal mechanisms of power (one day we should show how intrafamilial relations, essentially in the parents-children cell, have become "disciplined," absorbing since the classical age external schemata, first educational and military, then medical, psychiatric, psychological, which have made the family the privileged locus of emergence for the disciplinary question of the normal and the abnormal), or by apparatuses that have made discipline their principle of internal functioning (the disciplinarization of the administrative apparatus from the Napoleonic period), or finally by state apparatuses whose major, if not exclusive, function is to assure that discipline reigns over society as a whole (the police).

On the whole, therefore, one can speak of the formation of a disciplinary society in this movement that stretches from the enclosed disciplines, a sort of social "quarantine," to an indefinitely generalizable mechanism of "panopticism." Not because the disciplinary modality of power has replaced all the others; but because it has infiltrated the others, sometimes undermining them, but serving as an intermediary between them, linking them together, extending them, and, above all, making it possible to bring the effects of power to the most minute and distant elements. It assures an infinitesimal distribution of the power relations. . . .

The formation of the disciplinary society is connected with a number of broad historical processes – economic, juridico-political, and, lastly, scientific – of which it forms part.

1. Generally speaking, it might be said that the disciplines are techniques for assuring the ordering of human multiplicities. It is true that there is nothing exceptional or even characteristic in this: every system of power is presented with the same problem. But the peculiarity of the disciplines is that they try to define in relation to the multiplicities a tactics of power that fulfills three criteria: first, to obtain the

exercise of power at the lowest possible cost (economically, by the low expenditure it involves; politically, by its discretion, its low exteriorization, its relative invisibility, the little resistance it arouses); second, to bring the effects of this social power to their maximum intensity and to extend them as far as possible, without either failure or interval; third, to link this "economic" growth of power with the output of the apparatuses (educational, military, industrial, or medical) within which it is exercised; in short, to increase both the docility and the utility of all the elements of the system. This triple objective of the disciplines corresponds to a well-known historical conjuncture. One aspect of this conjuncture was the large demographic thrust of the eighteenth century; an increase in the floating population (one of the primary objects of discipline is to fix; it is an anti-nomadic technique); a change of quantitative scale in the groups to be supervised or manipulated (from the beginning of the seventeenth century to the eve of the French Revolution, the school population had been increasing rapidly, as had no doubt the hospital population; by the end of the eighteenth century, the peacetime army exceeded 200,000 men). The other aspect of the conjuncture was the growth in the apparatus of production, which was becoming more and more extended and complex; it was also becoming more costly and its profitability had to be increased. The development of the disciplinary methods corresponded to these two processes, or rather, no doubt, to the new need to adjust their correlation. Neither the residual forms of feudal power nor the structures of the administrative monarchy, nor the local mechanisms of supervision, nor the unstable, tangled mass they all formed together, could carry out this role: they were hindered from doing so by the irregular and inadequate extension of their network, by their often conflicting functioning, but above all by the "costly" nature of the power that was exercised in them. It was costly in several senses: because directly it cost a great deal to the treasury; because the system of corrupt offices and farmed-out taxes weighted indirectly, but very heavily, on the population; because the resistance it encountered forced it into a cycle of perpetual reinforcement; because it proceeded essentially by levying (levying on money or products by royal, seigniorial, ecclesiastical taxation; levying on men or time by *corvées* of press-ganging, by locking up or banishing vagabonds). The development of the disciplines marks the appearance of elementary techniques belonging to a quite different economy: mechanisms of power which, instead of proceeding by deduction, are integrated into the productive efficiency of the apparatuses from within, into the growth of this efficiency and into the use of what it produces. For the old principle of "levying-violence," which governed the economy of power, the disciplines substitute the principle of "mildness-production-profit." These are the techniques that make it possible to adjust the multiplicity of men and the multiplication of the apparatuses of production (and this means not only "production" in the strict sense, but also the production of knowledge and skills in the school, the production of health in the hospitals, the production of destructive force in the army).

In this task of adjustment, discipline had to solve a number of problems for which the old economy of power was not sufficiently equipped. It could reduce the inefficiency of mass phenomena: reduce what, in a multiplicity, makes it much less manageable than a unity; reduce what is opposed to the use of each of its elements and of their sum; reduce everything that may counter the advantages of number. That is why discipline fixes; it arrests or regulates movements; it clears up confusion; it dissipates compact groupings of individuals wandering about the country in unpredictable ways; it establishes calculated distributions. It must also master all the forces that are formed from the very constitution of an organized multiplicity; it must neutralize the effects of counterpower that spring from them and which form a resistance to the power that wishes to dominate it: agitations, revolts, spontaneous organizations, coalitions – anything that may establish horizontal conjunctions. Hence the fact that the disciplines use procedures of partitioning and verticality; that they introduce, between the different elements at the same level, as solid separations as possible; that they define compact hierarchical networks; in short, that they oppose to the intrinsic, adverse force of multiplicity the technique of the continuous, individualizing pyramid. They must also increase the particular utility of each element of the multiplicity, but by means that are the most rapid and the least costly, that is to say, by using the multiplicity itself as an instrument of this growth. Hence, it order to extract from bodies the maximum time and force, the use of those overall methods known as timetables, collective training, exercises, total and detailed surveillance. Furthermore, the disciplines must increase the effect of utility proper to the multiplicities, so that each is made more useful than the simple sum of its elements: it is in order to increase the utilizable effects of the multiple that the disciplines define tactics of distribution; reciprocal adjustment of bodies, gestures, and rhythms; differentiation of capacities; reciprocal coordination in relation to apparatuses or tasks. Lastly, the disciplines have to bring into play the power relations, not above but inside the very texture of the multiplicity, as discreetly as possible, as well articulated on the other functions of these multiplicities and also in the least expensive way possible: to this correspond anonymous instruments of power, coextensive with the multiplicity that they regiment, such as hierarchical surveillance, continuous registration, perpetual assessment and classification. In short, to substitute for a power that is manifested through the brilliance of those who exercise it, a power that insidiously objectifies those on whom it is applied; to form a body of knowledge about these individuals, rather than to deploy the ostentatious signs of sovereignty. In a word, the disciplines are the ensemble of minute technical inventions that made it possible to increase the useful size of multiplicities by decreasing the inconveniences of the power which, in order to make them useful, most control them. A multiplicity, whether in a workshop or a nation, an army or a school, reaches the threshold of a discipline when the relation of the one to the other becomes favorable.

If the economic take-off of the West began with the techniques that made possible the accumulation of capital, it might perhaps be said that the methods for administering the accumulation of men made possible a political take-off in relation to the traditional, ritual, costly, violent forms of power, which soon fell into disuse and were superseded by a subtle, calculated technology of subjection. In fact, the two processes – the accumulation of men and the accumulation of capital – cannot be separated; it would not have been possible to solve the problem of the accumulation of men without the growth of an apparatus of production capable of both sustaining them and using them; conversely, the techniques that made the cumulative multiplicity of men useful accelerated the accumulation of capital. At a less general level, the technological mutations of the apparatus of production, the division of labor, and the elaboration of the disciplinary techniques sustained an ensemble of very close relations. Each makes the other possible and necessary; each provides a model for the other. The disciplinary pyramid constituted the small cell of power within which the separation, coordination, and supervision of tasks were imposed and made efficient; and analytical partitioning of time, gestures, and bodily forces constituted an operational schema that could easily be transferred from the groups to be subjected to the mechanisms of production; the massive projection of military methods onto industrial organization was an example of this modeling of the division of labor following the model laid down by the schemata of power. But, on the other hand, the technical analysis of the process of production, its "mechanical" breaking-down, was projected onto the labor force, whose task it was to implement it: the constitution of those disciplinary machines in which the individual forces that they bring together are composed into a whole and therefore increased is the effect of this projection. Let us say that discipline is the unitary technique by which the body is reduced as a "political" force at the least cost and maximized as a useful force. The growth of a capitalist economy gave rise to the specific modality of disciplinary power, whose general formulas, techniques of submitting forces and bodies, in short, "political anatomy," could be operated in the most diverse political regimes, apparatuses, or institutions.

2. The panoptic modality of power – at the elementary, technical, merely physical level at which it is situated – is not under the immediate dependence or a direct extension of the great juridico-political structures of a society; it is nonetheless not absolutely independent. Historically, the process by which the bourgeoisie became, in the course of the eighteenth century, the politically dominant class was masked by the establishment of an explicit, coded, and formally egalitarian juridical framework, made possible by the organization of a parliamentary, representative regime. But the development and generalization of disciplinary mechanisms constituted the other, dark side of these processes. The general juridical form that guaranteed a system of rights that were egalitarian in principle was supported by these tiny, everyday, physical mechanisms, by all those systems of micropower that are essentially nonegalitarian and asymmetrical which we call the disciplines. And although, in a formal way, the representative regime makes

it possible, directly or indirectly, with or without relays, for the will of all to form the fundamental authority of sovereignty, the disciplines provide, at the base, a guarantee of the submission of forces and bodies. The real, corporal disciplines constituted the foundation of the formal, juridical liberties. The contract may have been regarded as the ideal foundation of law and political power; panopticism constituted the technique, universally widespread, of coercion. It continued to work in depth on the juridical structures of society, in order to make the effective mechanisms of power function in opposition to the formal framework that it had acquired. The "Enlightenment," which discovered the liberties, also invented the disciplines.

In appearance, the disciplines constitute nothing more than an infra-law. They seem to extend the general forms defined by law to the infinitesimal level of individual lives; or they appear as methods of training that enable individuals to become integrated into these general demands. They seem to constitute the same type of law on a different scale, thereby making it more meticulous and more indulgent. The disciplines should be regarded as a sort of counterlaw. They have the precise role of introducing insuperable asymmetries and excluding reciprocities. First, because discipline creates between individuals a "private" link, which is a relation of constraints entirely different from contractual obligation; the acceptance of a discipline may be underwritten by contract; the way in which it is imposed, the mechanisms it brings into play, the nonreversible subordination of one group of people by another, the "surplus" power that is always fixed on the same side, in inequality of position of the different "partners" in relation to the common regulation, all these distinguish the disciplinary link from the contractual link, and make it possible to distort the contractual link systematically from the moment it has as its content a mechanism of discipline. We know, for example, how many real procedures undermine the legal fiction of the work contract: workshop discipline is not the least important. Moreover, whereas the juridical systems define juridical subjects according to universal norms, the disciplines characterize, classify, specialize; they distribute along a scale, around a norm, hierarchize individuals in relation to one another and, if necessary, disqualify and invalidate. In any case, in the space and during the time in which they exercise their control and bring into play the asymmetries of their power, they effect a suspension of the law that is never total, but is never annulled either. Regular and institutional as it may be, the discipline, in its mechanism, is a "counterlaw." And, although the universal juridicism of modern society seems to fix limits on the exercise of power, its universally widespread panopticism enables it to operate, on the underside of the law, a machinery that is both immense and minute, which supports, reinforces, multiplies the asymmetry of power and undermines the limits that are traced around the law. The minute disciplines, the panopticisms of everyday, may well be below the level of emergence of the great apparatuses and the great political struggles. But, in the genealogy of modern society, they have been, with the class domination that traverses it, the political counterpart of the juridical norms according to which power was redistributed. Hence, no doubt, the importance that has been given for so long to the small techniques of discipline, to those apparently insignificant tricks that it has invented, and even to those "sciences" that give it a respectable face; hence the fear of abandoning them if one cannot find any substitute; hence the affirmation that they are at the very foundation of society, and an element in its equilibrium, whereas they are a series of mechanisms for unbalancing power relations definitively and everywhere; hence the persistence in regarding them as the humble but concrete form of every morality, whereas they are a set of physico-political techniques.

To return to the problem of legal punishments, the prison with all the corrective technology at its disposal is to be resituated at the point where the codified power to punish turns into a disciplinary power to observe; at the point where the universal punishments of the law are applied selectively to certain individuals and always the same ones; at the point where the redefinition of the juridical subject by the penalty becomes a useful training of the criminal; at the point where the law is inverted and passes outside itself, and where the counterlaw becomes the effective and institutionalized content of the juridical forms. What generalizes the power to punish, then, is not the universal consciousness of the law in each juridical subject; it is the regular extension, the infinitely minute web of panoptic techniques. . . .

Consider
1. Summarise Foucault's arguments in your own words.
2. What does Foucault understand by a 'disciplinary society'? Illustrate his arguments with examples of your own.
3. What does Foucault understand by the 'panoptic modality of power'? Can you think of any contemporary examples of this?
4. Do some research on the Mara Salvatruchas. Documentaries such as *Children of the War* or *MS13: World's Most Dangerous Gang* do offer some initial insights, in spite of their sensationalism. You will also easily be able to find a range of academic publications, official reports and other media documents. Consider how the materials you have found reflect issues of deviance, crime and social control, as discussed above.

4.13 Conclusion

This chapter has provided you with an array of basic sociological concepts on which you can draw to explore different facets of social life for yourself. The exercises we have suggested throughout the chapter might be a good starting point for this. Regardless, we believe that it is quite important that you treat the ideas put forward here as a 'sociological toolkit' that allows you to make sense of the world you live in, rather than purely academic matters. Even very abstract concepts such as postmodernism may speak in a significant way to your own experiences of everyday life. Another useful exercise is to return to the idea of the sociological imagination (discussed in Chapter 1). How do the concepts we have looked at in this chapter fulfil the promise of the sociological imagination? How do they relate individual biographies to large-scale historical developments? How do they connect personal troubles to big issues of public significance? Sociology only becomes truly meaningful if it speaks to such big issues of public significance. Thus, the more you try to look at these concepts outside the realm of university life, the easier it might become for you to develop a good understanding of what they mean.

From a more immediately academic perspective, this chapter has set out a range of substantive fields of sociological enquiry. While there are many more, the preceding pages may have given you an inkling of the vibrant diversity that is sociology today. From this point of view, you might consider which of these substantive fields are of particular interest to you. Thinking about this early on might help guide you in your reading, in future classes to take, and perhaps even in the choice of a dissertation topic!

The following chapters will now introduce you to further areas of sociological research. Both Chapter 5 and 6 will consider topics of special contemporary significance. While Chapter 5 introduces you to a range of issues around the broad themes of globalisation and social change, Chapter 6 highlights salient forms of social inequality and exploitation.

Research and debate: The social, the psychological and the sociological imagination

How is the psychological – our 'inner' mental life, our thoughts, our feelings – social? How are our personal experiences shaped by larger, social forces? These questions are foundational to the project of sociology, as this and the preceding chapters have shown. However, in many ways, they are not unique to sociology. Around the same time that sociology began to develop, other academic disciplines took shape that grappled with very similar questions. Anthropology, linguistics and psychology are particularly notable in this regard. In consequence, sociological research has always had an *interdisciplinary* character, with sociologists drawing on research in other fields, and scholars in other fields making substantial contributions to sociology. The work of George Herbert Mead (see Chapter 3) and the symbolic interactionists (see above) is one notable example of such interdisciplinarity. Symbolic interactionism is often cited as theory that lies at sociology's core. Nonetheless, it is deeply grounded in scholarship in social psychology and philosophy.

This project will ask you to look somewhat beyond sociology and somewhat beyond this book. Specifically, it asks you to compare three areas of enquiry:

1. Symbolic interactionism
2. Ethnomethodology and conversation analysis
3. Psychoanalysis.

Each of these three plays an important role in sociology, but is also grounded in other disciplines. How does each of these three areas of enquiry conceptualise the relationship between the social and the psychological? Summarise some of their core concepts and ideas. What are the most notable differences between them? In which ways do their arguments overlap? Finally, based on your findings, how would you yourself describe the relationship between the social and the psychological?

Works cited

Anderson, E. (1999), *Code of the street : decency, violence, and the moral life of the inner city*, London: W.W. Norton.

Becker, Howard S. (1963/1997), *Outsiders*, New York: Simon and Schuster.

Beverley, J., J. Oviedo. *et al.*, eds (1995), *The postmodernism debate in Latin America*, Durham: Duke University Press.

Bhambra, G. (2008), *Rethinking Modernity: Postcolonialism and the Sociological Imagination*, London: Palgrave Macmillan.

Brotherton, D. C. and L. Barrios (2009), 'Displacement and Stigma: The social-psychological crisis of the deportee', *Crime, Media, Culture* 5(1): 29–55.

Cassirer, E. (1944/1954), *An Essay on Man: An Introduction to a Philosophy of Human Culture*, New York: Doubleday Anchor Books.

Cerulo, K. A., ed. (2002), *Culture in Mind: Toward a Sociology of Culture and Cognition*, New York: Routledge.

Connell, R. (2007), *Southern Theory: The global dynamics of knowledge in social science*, Cambridge: Polity Press.

Cooley, Charles Horton (1902/1998), *On Self and Social Organisation*, edited by Hans-Joachim Schubert, Chicago: University of Chicago Press.

Dahl, R. A. (1961), *Who Governs?*, New Haven: Yale University Press.

Davie, G. (2010), *Resacralization. The New Blackwell Companion to the Sociology of Religion*, edited by B. S. Turner, Malden: Wiley-Blackwell.

Durkheim, É. (1912/1995), *The Elementary Forms of Religious Life*, New York: The Free Press.

Elias, N. (1939/2000), *The Civilizing Process: Sociogenetic and Psychogenetic Investigations*, Oxford, Blackwell.

Foucault, M. (1998), *The Will to Knowledge: The History of Sexuality Volume 1*, London: Penguin Books.

Goffman, E. (1959), *The Presentation of Self in Everyday Life*, Harmondsworth: Penguin Books.

Hart, D. V. (1968), 'Homosexuality and Transvestism in the Philippines : The Cebuan Filipino Bayot and Lakin-on', *Cross-Cultural Research* 3: 211–48.

Hebdige, D. (1979), *Subculture: The Meaning of Style*, London: Routledge.

Hochschild, A. R. (1983), *The Managed Heart: Commercialization of Human Feeling*, Berkeley: University of California Press.

Hochschild, A. R. (2003), *The Commercialization of Intimate Life: Notes from Home and Work*, Berkeley: University of California Press.

Jago, B. J. (2002), 'Chronicling an Academic Depression', *Journal of Contemporary Ethnography* 31(6): 72–957.

Jütersonke, O. *et al.* (2009), 'Gangs, Urban Violence, and Security Interventions in Central America', *Security Dialogue* 40(4–5): 373–97.

Lee, R. L. M. (2011), 'Modernity, Solidity and Agency: Liquidity Reconsidered', *Sociology* 45(4): 650–64.

Lundin, S. (2012), 'Organ economy: organ trafficking in Moldova and Israel', *Public Understanding of Science* 21(2): 226–241.

Martin, D. (2005), *On Secularization: Towards a Revised General Theory*, Aldershot: Ashgate.

Marx, K. (1844/1983), 'Contribution to the Critique of Hegel's Philosophy of Right: Introduction', in *The Portable Karl Marx*, edited by E. Kamenka, New York: Penguin Books (pp.115–24).

Melucci, A. (1996), *Challenging codes: Collective action in the information age*, Cambridge: Cambridge University Press.

Nardi, Peter (1992), 'That's What Friends are For: Friends as Family in the Gay and Lesbian Community', in *Modern Homosexualities: Fragments of Lesbian and Gay Experience*, edited by Ken Plummer, London: Routledge.

Pahl, Ray and Liz Spencer (2006), *Rethinking Friendship: Hidden Solidarities Today*, Princeton: Princeton University Press.

Parsons, Talcott (1951/1991), *The Social System*, London: Routledge.

Pichardo, J. I. (with Kerman Calvo) (2011), 'Sexualities Transformed? Inside Visions of Sexual, Social and Political Change in Spain', *Sexualities* 14(5): 503–622.

Shilling, C. (2003), *The Body and Social Theory*, London: Sage.

Shilling, C. (2005), *The Body in Culture, Technology and Society*, London: Sage.

Smart, C. (2007), *Personal Life: New Directions in Sociological Thinking*, Cambridge: Polity Press.

Swidler, A. (2001), *Talk of Love: How Culture Matters*, Chicago: University of Chicago Press.

Turner, B. S. (2011), *Religion and Modern Society: Citizenship, Secularisation and the State*, Cambridge: Cambridge University Press.

Weber, M. (1956/1978), *Economy and Society*, Berkeley: University of California Press.

Willis, K. (2005), *Theories and Practices of Development*, London: Routledge.

Zerubavel, E. (2007), *The Elephant in the Room: Silence and Denial in Everyday Life*, Oxford: Oxford University Press.

Zilberg, E. (2007), 'Gangster in guerilla face: A transnational mirror of production between the USA and El Salvador', *Anthropological Theory* 7(1): 37–57.

5 Globalisation and the modern world

5.1 Social change in the contemporary world

Having introduced you to a set of concepts foundational to contemporary sociological research (in Chapter 4), here, we connect these developments to the broader theme of *globalisation*. More than a media buzzword and a major object of interest for sociology, globalisation has become a driving force behind the changing face of human life in the early twenty-first century.

A good example of globalisation's importance are the world's global cities, already mentioned in the previous chapter. For instance, the distance between Hong Kong and London is nearly 10,000 kilometres, or 6,000 miles. Hong Kong has been a part of Chinese society for more than 2 millennia, while London has formed part of the European cultural universe for almost as long. In spite of their mutual remoteness, the two cities have become very close over the past two centuries. Through the imperialist expansion of Great Britain into China, and facilitated by technological breakthroughs in Europe, Hong Kong came to be a British colony in 1842. The foreign occupiers re-shaped Hong Kong to resemble their homeland: many places bear distinctively British names; Hong Kong's legal system builds upon English common law; and British goods, fashions and architecture came to be ubiquitous.

Today, having been independent from Britain and reintegrated into China as a 'special administrative region', Hong Kong retains close ties with Britain. The glass and steel architecture of the two cities' financial districts is indistinguishable, as are the office clothes worn by their denizens. Many globally operating corporations maintain headquarters in both Hong Kong and London, and fluid commercial and financial ties exist between the two cities. Many British professionals go to live and work in Hong Kong, just as London is an attractive destination for many from Hong Kong. Yet Hong Kong has retained its deep roots in southern Chinese culture and society. Both Chinese and English are official languages, and Cantonese is a predominant street language. Even a brief exploration of local ways of life, customs, values, cuisine, fashions, etc., makes it plain that Hong Kong forms part of the Chinese social world. Ultimately, however, it is a city of its own kind and character, to some extent a part of both worlds, yet quite fully in neither. This is one way in which globalisation has been remaking the world's metropolises.

This chapter seeks to unpack the social, economic, cultural and political processes that are collectively labelled 'globalisation'. In this context, it also introduces you to some major *institutions* in the contemporary world and considers how these institutions are being transformed by globalisation. Institutions are another major conceptual lens in sociological enquiry, referring to *durable social structures that tend to govern individuals' values, beliefs, interests and practices with regard to particular realms of social life*. In other words, institutions are social mechanisms that shape the ways in which we typically 'do' certain parts of our lives.

For instance, institutions called 'families', typically comprising a religiously married heterosexual couple, their children and perhaps other relatives, for a long time constituted the only socially acceptable way for people in most Western societies to experience intimate attachment, have sex, and raise children. This kind of family is by no means historically universal or prevalent throughout the world. Nonetheless, it has become culturally so deeply ingrained that its profound transformation by globalisation and other social forces is hard to tolerate for many. The ferocious opposition by traditionalists and religious fundamentalists in the USA to equal rights for sexual minorities and the legalisation of gay and lesbian marriages and adoptions is a testament to this.

The chapter begins with a detailed sociological exploration of the meanings of *globalisation*. On this base, we look at *capitalism* and *rationalisation* as social processes foundational to globalisation. You have already encountered these two themes in the work of Max Weber (in Chapter 3), and our discussion will allow us to point to important links between classical and contemporary sociology. We then consider another social process arguably central to globalisation: *risk*. Drawing on the work of German sociologist Ulrich Beck, we examine the theory that the risks brought about by modernisation and globalisation have acquired peculiar qualities, becoming potentially fundamental threats to human survival, while simultaneously remaining unpredictable and often invisible. Human uses of oil and nuclear energy and attendant recent catastrophes are key examples to consider here.

From here, we move on to look at a range of institutions and social processes and their transformation by globalisation: specifically, *consumer culture* and the fundamental role of *mass media* in contemporary social relationships, as well as the changing character of *religion, work*, and *family and personal life* under conditions of globalisation and ever more rapid social change.

On the following pages, you will experience the sociological imagination at perhaps its best. To begin with, you will find the issues discussed here to be more concrete and, perhaps, approachable than some of the topics discussed later. This is because all or most of these issues are likely to find a fairly direct expression in your own everyday lives. From man-made ecological disasters and the peculiar nature of risk in the contemporary world to the omnipresence of mass media and the changing nature of family life, you experience globalisation and are exposed to it on a daily basis. By making some sense of these influences, the present chapter shows you that sociology is more than just an academic exercise – it can truly make a difference and help you connect your own lives meaningfully to much larger social forces.

5.2 Globalisation

So, what exactly is globalisation? The example of Hong Kong immediately makes it evident that globalisation does not refer to a single social phenomenon or process. Rather, the term has been used by scholars to encompass a wide range of related developments, some of which have been playing out for a very long time. Moreover, researchers in various fields – sociology, cultural studies, history, politics, economics, business – have often arrived at notably different appraisals of these developments. Still, it is useful to begin our exploration of the idea with a single definition and then move on to more complex problems.

A good starting point here is the work of Australian sociologist Malcolm Waters, who defines globalisation as:

> A social process in which the constraints of geography on economic, political, social and cultural arrangements recede, in which people become increasingly aware that they are receding and in which people act accordingly. (Waters 1995: 5)

The notion of a waning of the constraints of geography refers to the new forms of translocal, transnational and often even transcontinental social life that Manuel Castells described as 'the network society'. Through advances in travel and communication technologies, *space* and physical distance are becoming less and less of an impediment to sustained social interaction. Already in the nineteenth century, it was possible for the British Empire to effectively control very remote territories, such as Hong Kong. Today, it is a routine affair for companies to spread their commercial affairs across the globe, for instance by having clothes produced cheaply in Indonesia before shipping them to the UK to be sold, all the while monitoring the process from headquarters in the USA. And many of our personal relationships don't exist in physical space at all any more, instead taking place in the virtual space of the internet, on social networking websites, in chat rooms, and so on. It is in this sense, that *time* has also become compressed. Twenty years ago, international telephone calls were unaffordably expensive for all but large corporations and the very wealthy, and a letter sent abroad would take weeks to arrive. Today, you can communicate instantaneously with anybody anywhere, as long as the other person has access to the internet or a mobile phone.

All these examples speak to a growing *global consciousness* throughout the world. Individuals, governments, non-governmental organisations, business companies, sports clubs, and so on, are increasingly aware of events, risks and opportunities around the world, and they act accordingly. News on the internet and TV tells us about global events almost instantly. All of us are aware of the vast differences in living conditions and opportunities in different places, and migration in search of a job, an education, or just basic safety is a key feature of life in the twenty-first century because of this. Football clubs, historically deeply rooted in their local communities, now scout for players internationally in order to be able to field the best team. Governments anticipate opportunities and risks on a global scale, and they accordingly participate in international organisations such as the United Nations, form alliances and trade partnerships, and sometimes go to war. The USA's action in Afghanistan and Iraq in the early 2000s is a prime example of this, as it highlights the US government's global awareness and its technological and logistical capacity to rapidly move military forces all around the world to plug perceived security risks and control strategic natural resources.

This global consciousness has found many expressions. Consequently, it is often useful to look in detail at particular *levels of globalisation*. For instance, *political globalisation* would examine the global extension of political processes, in the form of organisations such as the UN or the possibility for global political conflict and war. *Economic globalisation* refers to the growing importance of long-distance, transnational networks of production, consumption, trade and finance. *Cultural globalisation* concerns the ways in which values, beliefs, modes of life, and fashions spread around the world – think about the popularity of Western brands and fashion in China, or the great popularity of Japanese anime in the West, or the international success of Latin American music, or the global spread of fast food restaurants . . .

In the context of globalisation, such cultural forms and economic and political practices are often *localised* according to the traditions and requirements in particular societies. Earlier on, we mentioned how the global spread of McDonald's has involved the consideration of local culinary preferences – the company logo stays the same around the world, but the menu to choose from in, say, India, China and Mexico certainly isn't the same! An interesting example of economic globalisation and localisation is the development of Japan. In the late nineteenth century, the Japanese government and companies invested heavily into industrialisation and technological development, sometimes adapting successful Western practices to their own needs. This led to such success that, more than a half century later, Japan became renowned for the quality of its high-tech products. And this in turn meant that Western companies began to study the extraordinary success of Japan's corporations, adapting their models to work, for instance, in the USA. The global spread of business ideas had come full circle!

Beyond these general ideas, there is much controversy as to the exact nature and dynamics of globalisation. In order for you to gain a good understanding of sociological approaches to globalisation, a sense of these controversies is quite important. For this, we turn to a reading from the book *Globalization and Culture* (2009) by Jan Nederveen Pieterse.

Reading

Nederveen Pieterse, J. (2009), *Globalization and Culture*, Lanham: Rowman and Littlefield, pp. 42–58

Clash of Civilizations

In 1993 Samuel Huntington, as president of the Institute for Strategic Studies at Harvard University, published a controversial paper in which he argued that "a crucial, indeed a central, aspect of what global politics is likely to be in the coming years . . . will be the clash of civilizations. . . . With the end of the Cold War, international politics moves out of its Western phase, and its centerpiece becomes the interaction between the West and non-Western civilizations and among non-Western civilizations."

The imagery is that of civilizational spheres as tectonic plates at whose fault lines conflict, no longer subsumed under ideology, is increasingly likely. The argument centers on Islam: the "centuries-old military interaction between the West and Islam is unlikely to decline" (1993: 31–2). "Islam has bloody borders" (35). The fault lines include Islam's borders in Europe (as in former Yugoslavia), Africa (animist or Christian cultures to the south and west), and Asia (India, China). Huntington warns against a "Confucian-Islamic military connection" that has come into being in the form of arms flows between East Asia and the Middle East. Thus "the paramount axis of world politics will be the relations between 'the West and the Rest' " and "a central focus of conflict for the immediate future will be between the West and several Islamic-Confucian states" (48). He therefore recommends greater cooperation and unity in the West, between Europe and North America; the inclusion of Eastern Europe and Latin America in the West; cooperative relations with Russia and Japan; exploiting differences and conflicts among Confucian and Islamic states; and for the West to maintain its economic and military power to protect its interests.

The idea of dividing the world into civilizations has a long lineage. In Europe, it goes back to the medieval understanding of a tripartite world of descendants of the three sons of Noah (mentioned in Chapter 2 above). Arnold Toynbee's world history divided the world into civilizational spheres. It informs the approach of the "Teen Murti" school of Contemporary Studies in Delhi (Sardar and Van Loon 1997: 78). Kavolis (1988) divides the world into seven incommensurable civilizational systems based on religion: Christian, Chinese (Confucian-Taoist-Buddhist), Islamic, Hindu, Japanese (Shinto-Buddhist-Confucian), Latin American syncretism, and non-Islamic African. Galtung (1981) argues that each civilization has different ways of knowing the world. Dividing the world into civilizations is a cliché that echoes in every encyclopedia of world history; but it is also old fashioned and overtaken by new historiography and the emergence of "world history" (Prazniak 2000).

Huntington's position stands out for its blatant admixture of security interests and a crude rendition of civilizational difference. In view of its demagogic character it obviously belongs to the genre of "new enemy" discourse. In fact, it merges two existing enemy discourses, the "fundamentalist threat" of Islam and the "yellow peril," and its novelty lies in combining them.

Huntington recycles the Cold War: "The fault lines between civilizations are replacing the political and ideological boundaries of the Cold War as the flash points for crisis and bloodshed" (29). "The Velvet Curtain of culture has replaced the Iron Curtain of ideology as the most significant dividing line in Europe" (31). Hence there will be no "peace dividend." The Cold War is over but war is everlasting. This has been referred to as a new politics of containment and a new round of hegemonic rivalry, which is translated from an ideological into a civilizational idiom. Huntington's thesis has given rise to extensive debate and his argument has been widely rejected (e.g., Rashid 1997, Camilleri and Muzaffar 1998) while acknowledging that its contribution has been to present culture as a significant variable in international relations. Huntington has developed his thesis in a book (1996) and followed up with a wider treatment of culture (Harrison and Huntington 2000). I will not reiterate the debate here but bring up key points that show Huntington's view as one of three paradigms of cultural difference.

Huntington constructs the West as a "universal civilization," "directly at odds with the particularism of most Asian societies and their emphasis on what distinguishes one people from another" (41). The charge against "the Rest" is that they attempt modernization without westernization. This may be the actual danger: the specter of *different modernities* and thus the breakdown of western civilizational hegemony. By now, multiple modernities are an accepted theme (see Chapter 4 below).

The geopolitics is odd. Significant arms flows between the Middle East and East Asia do not involve Islamic countries but Israel and its arms sales to China, which have been of particular concern to the U.S. because they re-export high-tech equipment of U.S. origin. Another instance, which Huntington does cite, exchanges of military technology between Pakistan and China, also involves an American angle. Major concerns from an American security point of view, such as military relations between China and Iran (and more recently, arms exports from North Korea), are not mentioned.

What is overlooked in this geopolitical construction are the dialectics of the Cold War and the role the United States has been playing. It's not so much a matter of civilizational conflict as the unraveling of geopolitical security games most of which have been initiated by the U.S. in the first place (discussed in Johnson 2000), which the hegemon in its latter days can no longer control, so it calls on allied states to help channel them in a desirable direction. At the turn of the century, the British Empire in its latter days of waning economic and military power did the same, calling on the United States to "police" the Pacific, the Caribbean, and Latin America, on Japan to play a naval role in the China Sea, and to contain the Russian empire, and seeking allies in the European concert of powers. Then as now, the waning hegemon calls on "civilizational" affinities: the White Man's Burden and his civilizing mission, and now "democracy," freedom, and the virtues of the free market.

The sociologist Malcolm Waters formulates an interesting theorem according to which "material exchanges localize, political exchanges internationalize and symbolic exchanges globalize" (1995: 156). This is difficult to maintain because it ignores how microeconomic dynamics at the level of firms propel the macroeconomic process of globalization; but interesting in this context is the view that the cultural, symbolic sphere is the first to globalize; a perspective diametrically opposed to Huntington's thesis. This shows the oddity of Huntington's view: it is a *political* perspective on culture coined in conventional national security language. Culture is politicized, wrapped in civilizational packages that just happen to coincide with geopolitical entities. Obviously, there is much slippage along the way and all along one wonders: what is national security doctrine doing in a world of globalization and in the sphere of cultural representations? While Huntington focuses on fault lines between civilizations, his pessimism is matched by gloomy views on growing ethnic conflict (as in Moynihan 1993, Kaplan 1996).

Indeed the most remarkable element of the thesis is its surface claim of a clash of *civilizations*. Why is *culture* being presented as the new fault line of conflict? Huntington's framework is a fine specimen of what he blames Asian societies for: "Their emphasis on what distinguishes one people from another." At a general level, this involves a very particular way of reading culture. Compare Immanuel Wallerstein on "Culture as the ideological battleground of the modern world-system" (1991): note that culture and ideology are being merged in a single frame, and that culture is defined as "the set of characteristics which distinguish one group from another." Anthony King (1991: 13) uses a similar concept of culture as "collective articulations of human diversity."

If we would take this to its ultimate consequence then, for instance, bilingualism cannot be "cultural" because "it does not distinguish one group from another." Indeed any bicultural, intercultural, multicultural, or transcultural practices could not according to this definition be "cultural." Whichever mode of communication or intercourse different groups would develop to interact with one another would not be cultural for culture refers only to intergroup diversity. We have thus defined any form of intergroup or transnational culture out of existence for such per definition cannot exist. Intercultural diffusion through trade and migration, a lingua franca between cultures, returnees from abroad with bicultural experience, children of mixed parentage, travelers with multicultural experience, professionals interacting cross-culturally, the fields of cyberspace – all of these fall outside "culture."

Obviously, this notion of culture is one-sided to the point of absurdity. Diversity is one side of the picture but only one, and interaction, commonality or the possibility of commonality is another. In anthropology this is cultural relativism and Ruth Benedict's view of cultures as single wholes – a Gestalt or configuration that can only be understood from within and in its own terms. It implies a kind of "billiard ball" model of cultures as separate, impenetrable units (similar to the way states have been represented in the realist view of international relations). Over time, this generated ethnomethodology, ethnosociology, and a trend toward the indigenization of knowledge. This is an anomalous definition of culture. More common a definition in anthropology is that culture refers to behavior and beliefs that are learned and shared: learned so it is not "instinctual" and shared so it is not individual. Sharing refers to social sharing but there is no limitation as to the boundaries of this sociality. No territorial or historical boundaries are implied as part of the definition. This understanding of culture is open-ended. Learning is always ongoing as a function of changing circumstances and therefore culture is always *open*. To sharing there are no fixed boundaries other than those of common social experience, therefore there are no territorial limitations to culture. Accordingly culture refers as much to commonality as to diversity. In the next chapter, I refer to these fundamentally different notions of culture as territorial culture and translocal culture.

Cultural relativism represents an angle on culture that may be characterized as *culturalist differentialism* (Taguieff 1987, Al-Azmeh 1993). Its lineages are ancient. They are as old as the Greeks who deemed non-Greek speakers "barbarians." Next, this took the form of immutable cultural difference based on religion, separating the faithful from heathens, unbelievers and heretics. The romantics such as Johann Gottfried Herder revived this view of strong cultural boundaries, now in the form of language as the key to nationhood. Both nationalism and race thinking bear the stamp of cultural differentialism, one emphasizing territory and language, and the other biology as destiny. Nation and race have long been twin and at times indistinguishable discourses. During the era of nationalism, all nations claimed cultural distinction for their own nation and inferiority for others, usually in racial terms. "Jewishness," "Germanness," "Japaneseness," "Englishness," "Turkishness," "Greekness," and so forth, all imply an inward-looking take on culture and identity. They are creation myths of modern times. They all share the problem of boundaries: who belongs, and since when?

Cultural differentialism can serve as a defense of cultural diversity. It may be evoked by local groups resisting the steamroller of assorted "developers," by ecological networks, anthropologists, and artists, as well as travel agencies and advertisers promoting local authenticity. Culture and development, a growing preoccupation in development thinking, may turn "culture" into an asset (Schech and Haggis 2000; Nederveen Pieterse 2001c: chapter 5). It calls to mind the idea of the "human mosaic." An upside of this perspective may be local empowerment; the downside may be a politics of nostalgia, a conservationist posture that ultimately leads to the promotion of open-air museums. Either way the fallacy is the reification of the local, sidelining the interplay between the local and the global. The image of the mosaic is biased, as the anthropologist Ulf Hannerz (1992) points out, because a mosaic consists of fixed, discrete pieces whereas human experience, claims and postures notwithstanding, is fluid and open-ended. Accordingly critical anthropology opts for deterritorialized notions of culture such as flows and "traveling culture."

Hungtington's thesis is at odds with the common self-understandings of East and Southeast Asian societies, which run along the lines of East-West fusion, as in "Western technology, Asian values." The Confucian ethic may carry overtones of East Asian chauvinism but also represents an East-West nexus of a kind because the neo-Confucianism it refers to owes its status to its reinterpretation as an "Asian Protestant ethic." While Confucianism used to be the reason why East Asian countries were stagnating, by the late twentieth century it has become the reason why the "Tigers" have been progressing. In the process, Confucianism has been recoded as a cross-cultural translation of the Weberian thesis of the

Protestant ethic as the "spirit of modern capitalism." The Confucian ethic carries some weight in the "Sinic" circle of Singapore, Taiwan, China, and Korea; it carries less weight in Japan and no weight among the advocates of an "Asian way" such as Prime Minister Mahathir Mohamad of Malaysia and his "Look East" program (Mahathir and Ishihara 1995). Given the tensions between the ethnic Chinese and the "bumiputra" Malays in Malaysia, just as in Indonesia, here an Islamic-Confucian alliance is the least likely option.

While Huntington reproduces standard enemy images of "the Rest," he also rehearses a standard self-image of the West. "The West" is a notion conditioned by and emerging from two historical polarities: the North-South polarity of the colonizing and colonized world, and the East-West polarity of capitalism-communism and the Cold War. These were such overriding fields of tension that differences *within* the West/North, *among* imperialist countries and *within* capitalism faded into the background, subsiding in relation to the bigger issue, the seeming unity of imperialist or neocolonial countries and of the "free world" led by the U.S. In view of this expansionist history, we might as well turn the tables and say: the West has bloody borders. Thus, Huntington practices both Orientalism and Occidentalism. In reinvoking "the West," the differences between North America and Europe are papered over. In fact, historical revision may well show that there are much greater historical affinities, in particular similar feudal histories with their attendant consequences for the character of capitalisms, between Europe and Asia than between Europe and North America.

In his usual capacity as a comparative political scientist, Huntington (1991) observes a worldwide "third wave" of democratization. Apparently, at this level of discourse civilizational differences *are* receding. In this domain, Huntington follows the familiar thesis of convergence, that is, the usual modernization paradigm of growing worldwide standardization around the model of the "most advanced country," and his position matches Fukuyama's argument of the universal triumph of the idea of liberal democracy.

McDonaldization

The McDonaldization thesis is a version of the recent idea of the worldwide homogenization of societies through the impact of multinational corporations. McDonaldization, according to the sociologist George Ritzer, is "the process whereby the principles of the fast-food restaurant are coming to dominate more and more sectors of American society as well as the rest of the world" (1993: 19). The expression "the rest of the world" bears contemplating. The process through which this takes place is rationalization in Weber's sense, that is, through formal rationality laid down in rules and regulations. McDonald's formula is successful because it is efficient (rapid service), calculable (fast and inexpensive), predictable (no surprises), and controls labor and customers.

McDonaldization is a variation on a theme: on the classical theme of universalism and its modern forms of modernization and the global spread of capitalist relations. Diffusionism, if cultural diffusion is taken as emanating from a single center (e.g., Egypt), has been a general form of this line of thinking. From the 1950s, this has been held to take the form of Americanization. Since the 1960s, multinational corporations have been viewed as harbingers of American modernization. In Latin America in the 1970s, this effect was known as Coca-colonization. These are variations on the theme of cultural imperialism, in the form of consumerist universalism or global media influence. This line of thinking has been prominent in media studies according to which the influence of American media makes for global cultural synchronization (e.g., Schiller 1989, Hamelink 1983; a critical view is Morley 1994).

Modernization and Americanization are the latest versions of westernization. If colonialism delivered Europeanization, neocolonialism under U.S. hegemony delivers Americanization. Common to both is the modernization thesis, of which Marx and Weber have been the most influential proponents. Marx's thesis was the worldwide spread of capitalism. World-system theory is a current version of this perspective. With Weber, the emphasis is on rationalization, in the form of bureaucratization and other rational social technologies. Both perspectives fall within the general framework of evolutionism, a single-track universal process of evolution through which all societies, some faster than others, are progressing – a vision of universal progress such as befits an imperial world. A twentieth-century version of this line of thinking is Teilhard de Chardin's evolutionary convergence towards the noosphere.

Shannon Peters Talbott (1995) examines the McDonaldization thesis through an ethnography of McDonald's in Moscow and finds the argument inaccurate on every score. Instead of efficiency, queuing (up to several hours) and lingering are commonplace. Instead of being inexpensive, an average McDonald's meal costs more than a third of a Russian worker's average daily wage. Instead of predictability, difference and uniqueness attract Russian customers, while many standard menu items are not served in Moscow. Instead of uniform management control, McDonald's Moscow introduces variations in labor control ("extra fun motivations," fast service competitions, special hours for workers to bring their families to eat in the restaurant) and in customer control by allowing customers to linger, often for more than an hour on a cup of tea, to "soak up the atmosphere."

She concludes that McDonald's in Moscow does not represent cultural homogenization but should rather be understood along the lines of *global localization*. This matches the argument in business studies that corporations, also when they seek to represent "world products," only succeed if and to the extent that they adapt themselves to local cultures and markets. They should become insiders; this is the principle of "insiderization" for which the late Sony chairman Akio Morita coined the term *"glocalization,"* or "looking in both directions" (Ohmae 1992: 93). Firms may be multinational but "all business is local."

This can lead to counterintuitive consequences, as in the case of the international advertising firm McCann Erickson, whose Trinidad branch to justify a local presence promotes Trinidadian cultural specificity. "The irony is, of course, that . . .

it is advertising including transnational agencies which have become the major investors in preserving and promoting images of local specificity, retaining if not creating the idea that Trinidad is different, and inclucating this belief within the population at large" (Miller 1995: 9). The profitability of the transnational firm hinges on the profitability of the branch office whose interest lies in persuading the firm that only local advertising sells.

So far, this only considers the angle of the corporation. The other side of global localization is the attitude of customers. The McDonald's Moscow experience compares with adaptations of American fast food principles elsewhere, for instance in East Asia (Watson 1997). Here fast food restaurants though outwardly the same as the American models serve quite different tastes and needs. They are not down-market junk food but cater to middle class tastes. They are sought out for their "modern" aesthetics, are appreciated for food variation rather than uniformity, and generate "mixed" offspring, such as "Chinglish" or "Chamerican" restaurants in China. They offer a public space, a meeting place – in a sense culturally neutral because of its novelty – for new types of consumers, such as the consumer market of the young, of working women, and of middle class families. They function in similar ways in southern Europe and the Middle East. In wintry Tokyo, upstairs in Wendy's young students spend hours doing their homework, smoking and chatting with friends, because Japanese houses are small.

Thus, rather than cultural homogenization McDonald's and others in the family of western fast food restaurants (Burger King, KFC, Pizza Hut, Wendy's) usher in difference and variety, giving rise to and reflecting new, mixed social forms. Where they are imported, they serve different social, cultural, and economic functions than in their place of origin, and their formula is accordingly adapted to local conditions. In western metropoles, we now see oriental fast food restaurants and chains along with Latino, Middle Eastern, Turkish, and French eateries. Fast food may well have originated outside the West, in the street side food stalls of the Middle East, Asia, and Africa. American fast-food restaurants serve German food (hamburgers, frankfurters) with French (fries, dressing) and Italian elements (pizza) in American management style. American contributions besides ketchup are assembly-line standardization, in American Taylorist and managerial traditions, and marketing. Thus, it would make more sense to consider McDonaldization as a form of intercultural hybridization, partly in its origins and certainly in its present globally localizing variety of forms.

McDonaldization has sparked growing resistance and wide debate (Alfino et al. 1998, Smart 1999). In its home country, McDonald's is past its peak, its shares declining and franchises closing. Obesity as a national disease and changing diets, saturation of the fast food market, resistance, and litigation contribute to the decline. Beyond "rationalization" this takes us to the shifting shapes of contemporary capitalism. Is contemporary capitalism a homogenizing force? A stream of studies examines the cultures of late capitalism, a problematic often structured by world system thinking (Wallerstein 1990) or at least vocabulary (King 1991).

The commodification of labor, services, and information takes myriad forms, under headings each of which are another lament: McJobs, McInformation, McCitizens, McUniversity, McTourism, McCulture, McPrisons, McCourts (Gottdiener 2000, Ritzer 2002, Stojkovic et al. 1999). One study seeks "to intervene in discourses on transnational capitalism whose tendency is to totalize the world system" (Lowe and Lloyd 1997: 15), but in the process finds that "capitalism has proceeded not through global homogenization but through differentiation of labor markets, material resources, consumer markets, and production operations" (13). The economist Michael Storper finds a combined effect of homogenization and diversification across the world:

> The loss of "authentic" local culture in these places [smaller U.S. cities] is a constant lament. But on the other hand, for the residents of such places – or of Paris, Columbus, or Belo Horizonte, for that matter – there has been an undeniable increase in the variety of material, service, and cultural outputs. In short, the perceived loss of diversity would appear to be attributable to a certain rescaling of territories: from a world of more internally homogeneous localities, where diversity was found by traveling between places with significantly different material cultures to a world where one travels between more similar places but finds increasing variety within them. (Storper 2001: 114–15)

Most studies of capitalism and culture find diverse and hybrid outcomes. This suggests that capitalism itself hosts more diversity than is usually assumed – so the appropriate analytic would rather be capitalisms; and its cultural intersections are more diverse than is generally assumed. The rhizome of capitalism twins then with the rhizome of culture, which brings us to the theme of hybridization.

Hybridization: The Rhizome of Culture

Mixing has been perennial as a process but new as an imaginary. As a perspective, it differs fundamentally from the previous two paradigms. It does not build on an older theorem but opens new windows. It is fundamentally excluded from the other two paradigms. It springs from the taboo zone of race thinking because it refers to that which the doctrines of racial purity and cultural integrism could not bear to acknowledge the existence of: the half-caste, mixed-breed, métis. If it was acknowledged at all, it was cast in diabolical terms. Nineteenth-century race thinking abhorred mixing because, according to Comte de Gobineau and many others, in any mixture the "lower" element would predominate. The idea of mixing goes against all the doctrines of *purity* as strength and sanctity, ancient and classical, of which "race science" and racism have been modern, biologized versions.

Hybridization is an antidote to the cultural differentialism of racial and nationalist doctrines because it takes as its point of departure precisely those experiences that have been banished, marginalized, tabooed in cultural differentialism. It subverts nationalism because it privileges border-crossing. It subverts identity politics such as ethnic or other claims to purity and authenticity because it starts out from the fuzziness of boundaries. If modernity stands for an ethos of order and neat separation by tight boundaries, hybridization reflects a postmodern sensibility of cut'n'mix, transgression, subversion. It represents, in Foucault's terms, a "resurrection of subjugated knowledges" because it foregrounds those effects and experiences which modern cosmologies, whether rationalist or romantic, would not tolerate.

Hybridization goes under various aliases such as syncretism, creolization, métissage, mestizaje, crossover. Related notions are global ecumene, global localization, and local globalization. The next two chapters develop this perspective and discuss several objections to the hybridity thesis. Hybridization may conceal the asymmetry and unevenness in the process and the elements of mixing. Distinctions need to be made between different times, patterns, types, and styles of mixing; besides mixing carries different meanings in different cultural settings.

Hybridization occurs of course also among cultural elements and spheres *within* societies. In Japan, "Grandmothers in kimonos bow in gratitude to their automated banking machines. Young couples bring hand-held computer games along for romantic evenings out" (Greenfeld 1994: 230). Is the hybridization of cultural styles then typically an urban phenomenon, a consequence of urbanization and industrialization? If we look into the countryside virtually anywhere in the world, we find traces of cultural mixing: the crops planted, planting methods and agricultural techniques, implements and inputs used (seeds, fertilizer, irrigation methods, credit) are usually of translocal origin. Farmers and peasants throughout the world are wired, direct or indirect, to the fluctuations of global commodity prices that affect their economies and decision-making. The ecologies of agriculture may be local, but the cultural resources are translocal. Agriculture is a prime site of globalization (Richards 1996, Goodman and Watts 1997).

An interesting objection to the hybridization argument is that what are actually being mixed are cultural *languages* rather than *grammars*. The distinction runs between surface and deep-seated elements of culture. It is, then, the folkloric, superficial elements of culture – foods, costumes, fashions, consumption habits, arts and crafts, entertainments, healing methods – that travel, while deeper attitudes and values, the way elements hang together, the structural ensemble of culture, remain contextually bound. There are several implications to this argument. It would imply that contemporary "planetariza-tion" is a surface phenomenon only because "deep down" humanity remains divided in historically formed cultural clusters. Does this also imply that the new social technologies of telecommunication – from jet aircraft to electronic media – are surface phenomena only that don't affect deep-seated attitudes? If so, the implications would be profoundly conservative. A midway position is that the new technologies are profound in themselves while each historically framed culture develops its own takes on the new spaces of commonality.

Another issue is immigrant and settler societies where intermingling over time represents a historical momentum profound enough to engage cultural grammar and not just language. A prime example is North America. Probably part of the profound and peculiar appeal of American popular culture is precisely its mixed and "traveling" character, its "footloose" lightness, unhinged from the feudal past. In this culture, the grammars of multiple cultures mingle, and this intercultural density may be part of the subliminal attraction of American popular media, music, film, television: the encounter, and often enough the clash, but an intimate clash, of ethnicities, cultures, histories. The intermingling of cultural grammars then makes up the deeply human appeal of American narratives and its worldly character, repackaging elements that came from other shores, in a "Mississippi Massala."

Intercultural mingling itself is a deeply creative process not only in the present phase of accelerated globalization but stretching far back in time. Cees Hamelink notes: "The richest cultural traditions emerged at the actual meeting point of markedly different cultures, such as Sudan, Athens, the Indus Valley, and Mexico" (1983: 4). This sheds a different light on the language/grammar argument: presumably, some grammars have been mingling all along. Thus, a mixture of cultural grammars is part of the intrinsic meaning of the world religions (as against tribal, national religions). More fundamentally, the question is whether the distinction between cultural language and cultural grammar can be maintained at all, as a distinction between surface and depth. Certainly we know that in some spheres nothing has greater depth than the surface. This is the lesson taught by art and aesthetics. Superficial mingling then may have deep overtones. Even so we have been so trained and indoctrinated to think of culture in territorial packages of assorted "imagined communities" that to seriously address the windows opened and questions raised by hybridization in effect requires a decolonization of imagination.

A schematic précis of the three paradigms of cultural difference is in table 3.1.

Futures

The futures evoked by these three paradigms are dramatically different. McDonaldization evokes both a triumphalist Americanism and a gloomy picture of a global "iron cage" and global cultural disenchantment. The clash of civilizations likewise offers a horizon of a world of iron, a deeply pessimistic politics of cultural division as a curse that dooms humanity to lasting conflict and rivalry; the world as an archipelago of incommunicable differences, the human dialogue as a dialogue of war, and the global ecumene as an everlasting battlefield. The political scientist Benjamin Barber in *Jihad vs. McWorld* (1995) presents the clash between these two perspectives without giving a sense of the third option, mixing. Mixing or hybridization is open-ended in terms of experience as well as in a theoretical sense. Its newness means that its ramifications over time are not

Table 3.1 Three Ways of Seeing Cultural Difference.

Dimensions	Differentialism	Convergence	Mixing
Cosmologies	Purity	Emanation	Synthesis
Analytics	Territorial culture	Cultural centers and diffusion	Translocal culture
Lineages	Differences in language, religion, region. Caste.	Imperial and religious universalisms. Ancient "centrisms."	Cultural mixing of technologies, languages, religions
Modern times	Romantic differentialism. Race thinking, chauvinism. Cultural relativism.	Rationalist universalism. Evolutionism. Modernization. Coca-colonization.	Métissage, hybridization, creolization, syncretism
Present	"Clash of civilizations." Ethnic cleansing. Ethnodevelopment.	McDonaldization, Disneyfication, Barbiefication. Homogenization.	Postmodern views of culture, cultural flows, crossover, cut'n'mix
Futures	A mosaic of immutably different cultures and civilizations	Global cultural homogeneity	Open-ended ongoing mixing

predictable because it doesn't fit an existing matrix or established paradigm but itself signifies a paradigm shift.

Each paradigm represents a different politics of *multiculturalism*. Cultural differentialism translates into a policy of closure and apartheid. If outsiders are let in at all, they are preferably kept at arm's length in ghettos, reservations, or concentration zones. Cultural communities are best kept separate, as in colonial "plural society" in which communities are not supposed to mix except in the marketplace, or as in gated communities that keep themselves apart. Cultural convergence translates into a politics of assimilation with the dominant group as the cultural center of gravity. Cultural mixing refers to a politics of integration without the need to give up cultural identity while cohabitation is expected to yield new cross-cultural patterns of difference. This is a future of ongoing mixing, ever-generating new commonalities and new differences.

At a deeper level, each paradigm resonates with particular sensibilities and cosmologies. The paradigm of differentialism follows the principle of *purity*, as in ritual purity in the caste system, the *limpieza de sangre* in Spain after the Reconquest, and the preoccupation with purity of blood and lineage among aristocracies, a concern that was subsequently translated into thinking about "race" and class (Nederveen Pieterse 1989: Chapter 11). The paradigm of convergence follows the theory of *emanation*, according to which phenomena are the outward expressions of an ultimate numinous realm of being. In its sacred version, this reflects a theology and cosmogony of emanation outward from a spiritual center of power (as in Gnosticism). What follows upon the cycle of emanation, dissemination, and divergence is a cycle of "in-gathering," or a process of convergence. A temporal reflection of this cosmology is the ancient imperial system in which the empire is the circumference of the world and the emperor its center (as in the case of the Pharaoh, the emperor of China as the "middle of the middle kingdom," and imperial Rome) and divine kingship, in which the king embodies the land and the people. Western imperialism and its *mission civilisatrice* or White Man's Burden was a variation on this perspective. Since decolonization, the principle of radiation outward from an imperial center has retained its structure but changed its meaning, from positive to negative, as in dependency theory and the critique of cultural imperialism and Eurocentrism.

The third view is the synthesis that acts as the solvent between these polar perspectives. As such, it owes its existence to the previous two principles and is meaningful only in relation to them. It resolves the tension between purity and emanation, between the local and the global, in a dialectic according to which the local is in the global and the global is in the local. An example in which we see this synthetic motion in operation is Christmas: "The ability of this festival to become potentially the very epitome of globalization derives from the very same quality of easy syncretism which makes Christmas in each and every place the triumph of localism, the protector and legitimation for specific regional and particular customs and traditions" (Miller 1993: 25).

Each paradigm involves a different take on *globalization*. According to cultural differentialism, globalization is a surface phenomenon only: the real dynamic is regionalization, or the formation of regional blocs, which tend to correspond with civilizational clusters. Therefore, the future of globalization is interregional rivalry. According to the convergence principle, contemporary globalization is westernization or Americanization writ large, a fulfillment in installments of the classical imperial and the modernization theses. According to the mixing approach, the outcome of globalization processes is open-ended and current globalization is as much a process of easternization as of westernization, as well as of many interstitial influences.

In the end it turns out that the two clashing trends noted at the beginning, growing awareness of cultural difference and globalization, are not simply contradictory but interdependent. Growing awareness of cultural difference is a function of globalization. Increasing cross-cultural communication, mobility, migration, trade, investment, tourism, all generate awareness of cultural difference. The other side of the politics of difference is that the very striving for recognition implies a claim to equality, equal rights, same treatment: in other words, *a common universe of difference*. Accordingly, the clash between cultural diversity and globalization may well be considered a creative clash.

These views find adherents in each setting and their dispute echoes in every arena. Arguably, cultural self-understandings and empirical evidence confirm the third perspective more than the others do. Through most of Asia, ideas of East-West fusion are a dominant motif. In Africa, recombinations of local and foreign practices are a common notion. Latin America and the Caribbean are steeped in syncretism and creolization. But the imprint of other paradigms runs deep, disputes over identity and meaning are ubiquitous, and besides there is disagreement over the meaning and dynamics of hybridity. The next two chapters develop the theme of hybridity as a major departure in understanding cultural difference.

Consider
1. What is globalisation? Summarise the preceding definition in your own words.
2. What does Pieterse understand by the 'clash of civilizations'? Use examples of your own to support your arguments.
3. How does Pieterse define the McDonaldisation paradigm of globalisation? Again, give your own examples in support of your ideas.
4. Finally, what is hybridisation? What examples of hybridisation from your own everyday life can you think of?
5. Which of the three paradigms do you agree with? Why? Use sociological arguments and examples to construct your answer.
6. How does globalisation affect your own life? Consider this question from the point of view of cultural globalisation, economic globalisation and political globalisation.

5.3 Capitalism

Capitalism is a driving force of globalisation, and its international dominance is an important feature of life in the early twenty-first century. For these reasons, capitalism continues to be as central to sociological enquiry as it was in the times of Karl Marx and Max Weber. In brief, we might define capitalism as a form of organisation of economic life based on the primarily private ownership of the means of production (capital, machines, tools, production plants, etc.) and its deployment in the pursuit of financial profit. In addition, capitalism has important socio-cultural implications, shaping people's beliefs, values and interests in significant ways.

Consider the mobile phone you very likely own: you chose it from among dozens or hundreds of available models, based on considerations such as price, functionality and brand name. This telephone was manufactured by a private corporation, probably in a part of the world where labour costs are cheap, so as to keep costs down and maximise profits. From its point of assembly, it was transported by plane or ship for distribution and sale in your country, and probably many others. At some point, you decided that you needed a new mobile phone. Maybe you just wanted something cheap and functional, went out, and bought the cheapest model you could find. Maybe, however, you are brand conscious, and owning a technologically up-to-date gadget that is also 'cool' does matter to you. Such brand consciousness is not an accident – it's the result of living in a modern consumer culture (more on this later) and being constantly aware of the marketing campaigns which mobile phone companies use to paint their products in a favourable light. Your choice of product is ultimately your own, but the cultural environment in which you make it is moulded in significant ways by companies' efforts to maintain a healthy profit margin and survive in competition with other makers of similar products. This, in a nutshell, is one of the ways in which you encounter capitalism in your everyday life.

The rise of capitalism is often understood to have been associated with the Enlightenment and industrialisation in Europe. However, in different historical periods and in different places, capitalism has adopted many forms. In the Europe of the late nineteenth and early twentieth century, capitalism was driven by the rise of industrial manufacturing. Since then, however, Europe has transitioned into a post-industrial period, in which economic activity is increasingly built upon service work, such as financial services, banking, etc. Conversely, as we have argued before, new industrial powerhouses have emerged around the world, with China, India and Brazil being just a few examples.

Another major variation concerns the extent of state control over economic life. In the aftermath of a virtual collapse of the world economy in 1929, termed the 'Great Depression', governments around the world tended to adopt an active, interventionist role in economic life. They regulated the activities of private corporations by introducing more stringent laws on issues such as working hours and minimum wages and by controlling sectors of the economy central to public interests, such as health care, education and public transportation. Related approaches to economics are usually linked to the work of British economist John Maynard Keynes (1883–1946).

Since the late 1970s, a new international consensus, often associated with the term 'neoliberalism', has taken over in many countries. In many ways contrary to Keynesian economics, neoliberalism is based on the assumption that governments' control over economic affairs tends to be too slow and inefficient, given the extraordinary complexity of contemporary economic life. In order to ensure prosperity and economic growth, government regulation must recede, and private companies must be able to pursue their activities with as few constraints as feasible. In so far as it has been associated with fairly general international trends towards free trend and a deregulation of capitalist markets, some scholars argue that neoliberalism is virtual synonymous with globalisation in its present form. Indeed, the rise of neoliberal capitalism over the past 30 years has been astonishing, and even Communist China has long since endorsed many of its central assumptions.

However, the global turn to neoliberalism has entailed very significant problems. While it has led to an overall growth of wealth, it has equally led, for instance, to declining incomes for working class and middle class people in many countries and a huge growth in the unequal distribution of wealth. We will analyse these developments in much greater detail in the following chapter. For the moment, let us further examine the meaning and historical development of capitalism.

Reading

Fulcher, J. (2004), *Capitalism: A Very Short Introduction*, Oxford: Open University Press, pp. 1–18

What is capitalism?

Merchant capitalism

In April 1601 the English East India Company sent its first expedition to the East Indies. After some 18 months its four ships, *Ascension, Dragon, Hector*, and *Susan*, had returned from Sumatra and Java with a cargo mainly of pepper. The success of this venture led to a second expedition by the same ships, which left London in March 1604. On the return journey *Hector* and *Susan* set off first, but *Susan* was lost at sea and *Hector* was rescued by *Ascension* and *Dragon*, which found her drifting off South Africa with most of her crew dead. *Ascension, Dragon*, and *Hector* made it back to England in May 1606 with a cargo of pepper, cloves, and nutmegs. The shareholders in these two voyages made a profit of 95% on their investment.

Despite the similar success of the third expedition in 1607, the fourth one in 1608, consisting of the ships *Ascension* and *Union*, was a complete disaster. The *Ascension* reached the west coast of India but was there wrecked by its 'proud and headstrong master', who drove his ship aground after ignoring local warnings about shoaling waters. The *Union* called in at a Madagascan port, where the crew was ambushed and the captain killed, but nonetheless the ship made it to Sumatra and loaded a cargo. On her way back, the *Union* was wrecked off the coast of Brittany. The investors in this expedition lost all their capital.

Capitalism is essentially the investment of money in the expectation of making a profit, and huge profits could be made at some considerable risk by long-distance trading ventures of this kind. Profit was quite simply the result of scarcity and distance. It was made from the huge difference between the price paid for, say, pepper in the spice islands and the price it fetched in Europe, a difference that dwarfed the costs of the venture. What mattered was whether the cargo made it back to Europe, though market conditions were also very important, for the sudden return of a large fleet could depress prices. Markets could also become saturated if the high profitability of the trade led too many to enter it. A glut of pepper eventually forced the East India Company to diversify into other spices and other products, such as indigo.

A large amount of capital was needed for this trade. An *East Indianman*, as the ships engaged in this trade were called, had to be built, fitted out, armed with cannon against Dutch and Portuguese rivals, and repaired, if and when it returned. The Company's shipyards at Blackwall and Deptford, which were major employers of local labour, required financing. Capital was also needed to stock outgoing vessels with bullion and goods to pay for the spices, with munitions, and with food and drink for the large crews they carried. On the Company's third expedition, *Dragon* had a crew of 150, *Hector* 100, and *Consent* 30 – in all 280 mouths to feed, at least initially. One reason for the large crews was to make sure there were enough sailors to get the ships back after the hazards of the expedition had taken their toll.

The East India Company's capital was obtained largely but not entirely from the rich London merchants who controlled and administered it. Aristocrats and their hangers-on were another source, and one welcomed by the Company because of their influence at Court. The Company's privileges depended on royal favour. Foreign money was also involved, mainly from Dutch merchants excluded by the rival Dutch East Indies Company. They were also a useful source of intelligence about that company's activities.

The first 12 voyages were each financed separately, with capital committed to one voyage only and the profits of the voyage distributed among its shareholders, according to traditional merchant practices. This was, however, a risky way of financing long-distance trade, for it exposed capital to a long period of uncertainty in far-away and unknown places. Risk could be spread by sending out several ships on each expedition, so that not all the eggs were in one basket, but whole expeditions could, nonetheless, be lost, as in 1608. The company shifted to a method of finance that spread risks over a number of voyages and then became a fully fledged joint-stock company, with, after 1657, continuous investment unrelated to specific voyages. In 1688 trading in its stocks began on the London Stock Exchange.

Risk was also reduced through monopolistic practices. Like its counterparts abroad, the English East India Company was closely intertwined with the state, which granted it a monopoly for the import of oriental goods and gave it the right to export bullion to pay for them. In exchange the state, always short of money, gained revenue from customs duties on the large and valuable imports made by the company. There was certainly competition but it was international competition, in the Indies between the English, the Dutch, and the Portuguese, and as far as possible eliminated within each country. Outsiders were always trying to break into the trade, and one of the key privileges bestowed on the East India Company by the state was the right to take action against 'interlopers'.

Markets were manipulated by buying up stocks and holding back sales. In the 17th century Amsterdam merchants were particularly skilled in these practices and busily established monopolies not only in spices but in Swedish copper, whale products, Italian silks, sugar, perfume ingredients, and saltpetre (an ingredient of gunpowder). Large warehouses were crucial to this and Fernand Braudel comments that the warehouses of the Dutch merchants were bigger and more expensive than large ships. They could hold sufficient grain to feed the entire country for 10 to 12 years. This was not just a matter of holding goods back to force up prices, for large stocks also enabled the Dutch to destroy foreign competitors by suddenly flooding the whole European market with goods.

This was certainly capitalism, for long-distance trade required a heavy investment of capital in the expectation of large profits, but a free market capitalism it clearly was not. The secret of making high profits was to secure monopolies by one means or another, exclude competitors, and control markets in every way possible. Since profit was made from trading in scarce products rather than rationalizing production, the impact of merchant capitalism on society was limited. Most of the European population could get on with their daily work without being affected by the activities of these owners of capital.

Capitalist production

In the 1780s two Scots, James M'Connel and John Kennedy, travelled south to become apprentices in the Lancashire cotton industry. After gaining experience and making some money in the manufacture of cotton machinery, they set up their own firm in 1795 with an initial capital of £1,770. They soon made good profits from cotton spinning, achieving a return on capital of over 30% in 1799 and 1800. They accumulated capital rapidly and by 1800 their capital had risen to £22,000, by 1810 to £88,000. By 1820 the company had three mills and had established itself as the leading spinner of fine cotton in Manchester, the global metropolis of cotton spinning.

This soon became a very competitive industry, however, and profits could not be sustained at the high level of the early 1800s. This was, indeed, largely because high profits had resulted in expansion and attracted new entrants. There were already 344 cotton mills by 1819 but by 1839 there were 1,815. Technical advances enabled huge increases in productivity during the 1830s, and competition drove companies to invest heavily in the new machinery. The bigger mills built at this time contained 40,000 spindles, as compared with the 4,500 or so of their predecessors. The costs of this heavy investment in buildings and machinery, together with the downward pressure of increased productive capacity on yarn prices, depressed the industry's profitability to low levels in the 1830s.

Profit depended ultimately on the workers who turned raw cotton into yarn. M'Connel and Kennedy's labour force grew from 312 in 1802 to around 1,500 by the 1830s. Much of this was cheap child labour and at times nearly half those employed were under the age of 16. In 1819 there were 100 children under the age of 10, some as young as 7, who worked from 6.00 in the morning until 7.30 at night.

Apart from the occasional heavy cost of new factories and new machinery, wages were the company's main cost. Its annual wage bill was over £35,000 by 1811 and over £48,000 by the mid-1830s. Wage costs were minimized not just by holding wage rates down but also by replacing craft workers with less skilled and cheaper labour, as the invention of automatic machinery made this possible. The cyclical instability of the industry resulted in periodic slumps in demand, which forced employers to reduce wages and hours in order to survive.

As industrial capitalism developed, conflict over wages became increasingly organized. The spinners defended themselves against wage reductions through their unions, organizing at first locally but then regionally and nationally. In 1810, 1818, and 1830 there were increasingly organized strikes, but these were defeated by the employers, with the assistance of the state, which arrested strikers and imprisoned union leaders. The employers had created their own associations, so that they could 'black-list' union militants, answer strikes with 'lock-outs', and provide mutual financial support. Vigorous action by the spinners' unions does seem, nonetheless, to have been quite successful, for wages remained stable, in spite of declining profitability and employers' attempts to reduce them.

The exploitation of labour was not just a matter of keeping the wage bill down but also involved the disciplining of the worker. Industrial capitalism required regular and continuous work, if costs were to be minimized. Expensive machinery had to be kept constantly in use. Idleness and drunkenness, even wandering around and conversation, could not be allowed. The cotton mills did indeed have trouble recruiting labour because people simply did not like long, uninterrupted shifts and close supervision. Employers had to find ways of enforcing a discipline that was quite alien to the first generation of industrial workers. They commonly used the crude and negative sanctions of corporal punishment (for children), fines, or the threat of dismissal, but some developed more sophisticated and moralistic ways of controlling their workers.

Robert Owen introduced 'silent monitors' at his New Lanark mills. Each worker had a piece of wood, with its sides painted black for bad work, blue for indifferent, yellow for good, and white for excellent. The side turned to the front provided a constant reminder, visible to all, of the quality of the previous day's work. Each department had a 'book of character' recording the daily colour for each worker. Discipline was not only a factory matter, for Owen also controlled the community. He sent round street patrols to report drunkenness and fined the drunks next morning. He insisted on cleanliness and established detailed rules for the cleaning of streets and houses. There was even a curfew that required everyone to be indoors after 10.30 p.m. in the winter.

As E. P. Thompson has emphasized, disciplined work was regular, timed work. It meant turning up every day, starting on time, and taking breaks of a specified length at specified times. Employers had a long battle against the well-established tradition of taking off, as additional 'saint's days', 'St Monday', and even 'St Tuesday', to recover from weekend drinking. Time became a battleground, with some unscrupulous employers putting clocks forward in the morning and back at night. There are stories of watches being taken off workers, so that the employer's control of time could not be challenged. Significantly, timepiece ownership spread at the same time as the Industrial Revolution and at the end of the 18th century the government tried to tax the ownership of clocks and watches.

Industrial capitalism not only created work, it also created 'leisure' in the modern sense of the term. This might seem surprising, for the early cotton masters wanted to keep their machinery running as long as possible and forced their employees to work very long hours. However, by requiring continuous work during work hours and ruling out non-work activity, employers had separated out leisure from work. Some did this quite explicitly by creating distinct holiday periods, when factories were shut down, because it was better to do this than have work disrupted by the casual taking of days off. 'Leisure' as a distinct non-work time, whether in the form of the holiday, weekend, or evening, was a result of the disciplined and bounded work time created by capitalist production. Workers then wanted more leisure and leisure time was enlarged by union campaigns, which first started in the cotton industry, and eventually new laws were passed that limited the hours of work and gave workers holiday entitlements.

Leisure was also the creation of capitalism in another sense, through the commercialization of leisure. This no longer meant participation in traditional sports and pastimes. Workers began to pay for leisure activities organized by capitalist enterprises. The new railway companies provided cheap excursion tickets and Lancashire cotton workers could go to Blackpool for the day. In 1841 Thomas Cook organized his first tour, an excursion by rail from Leicester to Loughborough for a temperance meeting. Mass travel to spectator sports, especially football and horse-racing, where people could be charged for entry, was now possible. The importance of this can hardly be exaggerated, for whole new industries were emerging to exploit and develop the leisure market, which was to become a huge source of consumer demand, employment, and profit.

Capitalist production had transformed people's work and leisure lives. The investment of capital in the expectation of profit drove the Industrial Revolution and rapid technical progress increased productivity by leaps and bounds. But machines could not work on their own and it was wage labour that was central to the making of profit. The wage bill was the employer's main cost and became the focus of the conflict between the owners of capital and, as Karl Marx put it, those who owned only their 'labour power', the capacity to make money through physical work. Workers were concentrated in factories and mills, where they had to work in a continuous and disciplined manner under the supervisor's watchful eye, but also now had an opportunity to organize themselves collectively in unions. Non-work activities were expelled from work time into leisure time and daily life was now sharply divided between work and leisure. Wage labour also meant, however, that workers had money to spend on their leisure life. The commercialization of leisure created new industries that fed back into the expansion of capitalist production.

Financial capitalism

On Thursday, 23 February 1995, Nick Leeson, the manager of Baring Securities in Singapore, watched the Nikkei, the Japanese stock market index, drop 330 points. In that one day, Barings lost £143 million through the deals that he had made, though he was the only one who knew what was happening. These losses came on top of the earlier ones of some £470 million that Leeson had kept hidden from his bosses. He knew the game was up and bolted, with his wife, to a hideaway on the north coast of Borneo. Meanwhile, Barings managers, puzzling over the large sums of money that had gone missing in Singapore, tried desperately to find him. By the next morning it was clear that Baring Brothers, the oldest merchant bank in London, had sustained such huge losses that it was effectively bankrupt. Leeson tried to find his way back to England but was arrested in Frankfurt, extradited by Singapore for breaches of its financial regulations, and jailed for six and a half years.

Leeson had been trading in 'derivatives'. These are sophisticated financial instruments that *derive* their value from the value of something else, such as shares, bonds, currencies, or indeed commodities, such as oil or coffee. *Futures*, for example, are contracts to buy shares, bonds, currencies, or commodities at their *current* price at some point in the future. If you think that the price of a share is going to rise, you can buy a three months' future in it. After the three months have expired, you receive shares at the original price and make a profit by selling them at the higher price now prevailing. You can also buy *options*, which do not commit you to the future deal but allow you to decide later whether you want to go ahead or not.

The buying of futures can perform a very important function, since it enables the reduction of uncertainty and therefore risk. If the price of corn is high but the harvest is some way off, a farmer can lock into the existing price by making a deal with a merchant to sell the corn at this price in three months' time. Futures can also, however, be bought for purely speculative reasons to make money out of movements in prices. Financial futures of the kind that Leeson was trading in were more or less informed gambles on future price movements. This was what Susan Strange has called 'casino capitalism'.

Money could also be made from 'arbitrage', which exploits the small price differences that occur for technical reasons between markets. If you are able to spot these differences, calculate rapidly what they are worth, and move large sums of money very quickly, you can make big profits this way. Leeson found that he could exploit small differences, lasting less than a minute, between futures prices on the Osaka and Singapore stock exchanges. Operations of this kind could be carried out with little risk, since an immediate and calculable profit was taken from an existing, if short-lived, price difference.

Why then did things go so wrong for Leeson? He started down a slippery slope when he created a special error account, no. 88888, supposedly to handle innocent dealing and accountancy mistakes. This was the place where he hid his losses and he also found a way of concealing the accumulated end-of-the-month deficits by getting the Singapore 'back office' to make temporary but illegal transfers of money between various accounts. This and other manipulations bamboozled the auditors, who should have uncovered what was going on.

The existence of 88888 allowed Leeson to gamble with Barings' money. He could build his reputation by taking risks and trading aggressively on the futures markets, since any losses could be hidden. These *could* be covered by later trades and at one time he came close to breaking even, but if he had then closed 88888 down this would have ended the operation that made him the star dealer of Barings. Eventually his losses built up again and accumulated to the point at which they could no longer be concealed just by switching money around.

At this point he plunged into selling options, which, unlike futures, could immediately raise money to cover the monthly shortfalls in 88888. Leeson was gambling heavily on future price movements and the Tokyo stock market went the wrong way. As his losses increased, he raised the stakes by selling more and riskier options, supposedly on behalf of a mythical client called Philippe. When the Nikkei fell after the Kobe earthquake, his losses became so great that he tried single-handedly to force the market up by buying large numbers of futures. The downward pressures were far too strong and the market fell. By now, the losses and liabilities that he had built up were greater than the total capital of Barings.

Why did Barings allow all this to happen? They were a merchant bank which in 1984 had ventured into stockbroking by creating Baring Securities. This was a successful move and by 1989 dealings in mainly Japanese stocks and shares were accounting for half Barings' profits. Baring Securities then moved into the increasingly fashionable activity of derivatives trading. In 1993 Barings merged its capital with that of Barings Securities and in doing so fatally removed the 'fire-wall' protecting the bank from possible losses by its securities department. This was a particularly dangerous thing to do, since senior Barings managers had a poor grasp of the new game that they had entered, while no proper management structure had been put in place and financial controls were very weak. Fraud was an ever-present danger in this financially very complex world and Barings broke a golden rule by allowing Leeson to be both a trader and the manager of the Singapore 'back office', which checked the trades and balanced the books.

Leeson was apparently a very successful dealer who was making large profits for Barings and they backed him to the hilt. Ironically, when Barings crashed his bosses had just decided to reward his 1994 activities with a £450,000 bonus. As Leeson's operations drained increasing amounts of money from London and sent Barings hunting for loans around the world to cover them, Leeson's bosses actually thought they were financing profitable deals made by their star trader. It was not only the complexities of the financial markets and the extraordinarily weak financial controls within Barings that enabled Leeson to get away with things for so long, but also the corporate hunger for ever greater profits.

What then is capitalism?

We have examined three very different examples of capitalism. The various business activities involved are about as different as they could be, but all involve the investment of money in order to make a profit, the essential feature of capitalism. It is not the nature of the activity itself that matters but the possibility of making profit out of it. Indeed, it is typical of a capitalist society that virtually all economic activities that go on within it are driven by the opportunity to make profit out of capital invested in them.

Capital is money that is invested in order to make more money. By extension the term capital is often used to refer to money that is *available* for investment or, indeed, any asset that can be readily turned into money for it. Thus, a person's house is often described as their capital, because they can turn it into capital either by selling it or by borrowing on the strength of it. Many small businesses are indeed set up in this way. It is, however, only possible to turn property into capital if its ownership is clearly established, its value can be measured, its title can be transferred, and a market exists for it. A characteristic feature of the development of capitalist societies is the emergence of institutions that enable the conversion of assets of all kinds into capital. Hernando de Soto has argued persuasively that it is the absence of these institutions, above all functioning systems of property law, that frustrates the emergence of local capitalisms in the Third World. He claims that an enormous amount of value that is locked up in property cannot therefore be realized and put by entrepreneurs to productive use.

Capitalists existed before capitalism proper. Since the earliest times merchants have made money by investing in goods that they sold at a profit. As we saw with the East India Company, a merchant capitalism of this kind could be highly organized and very profitable, but it was an activity that involved only a small part of the economy. Most people's livelihoods did not come from economic activities financed by the investment of capital. In capitalism proper the whole economy becomes dependent on the investment of capital and this occurs when it is not just trade that is financed in this way but production as well.

Capitalist production is based on wage labour. A clear line of division and conflict emerges between the owners of capital, who own what Karl Marx called 'the means of production', and those who sell their labour in exchange for wages. The means of production are the workplace, the machinery, and the raw materials, which in pre-capitalist societies were owned not by the owners of capital but by the craftsmen who made the goods. A wage (or salary) is the price paid by the employer for labour sold by the worker. Just as a capitalist will invest money in any activity that brings a profit, a worker can find employment in any activity that pays a wage.

In a capitalist society, both capital and labour have an abstract and disembedded quality, since both are separated from specific economic activities and are therefore able in principle to move into any activity that suitably rewards them. In real life this mobility is constrained by the existing skills and experience of both the owners of capital and workers, and by the relationships and attachments that they have formed. The potential mobility of capital and labour is, nonetheless, one of the features of capitalist societies that gives them their characteristic dynamism.

Wage labour is both free and unfree. Unlike slaves, who are forced to work by their owners, wage labourers can decide whether they work and for whom. Unlike the serfs in feudal society, who were tied to their lord's land, they can move freely and seek work wherever they choose. These freedoms are, on the other hand, somewhat illusory, since in a capitalist society it is difficult to survive without paid work and little choice of work or employer may be available. Wage labourers are also subject to tight control by the employer and, as we saw in the cotton mills, capitalist production meant a new kind of disciplined and continuous work. Workers had become, as Marx put it, 'wage slaves'.

The importance of wage labour is not only its role in production but also its role in consumption. Wage labourers cannot themselves produce what they need or may wish to consume, they have to buy it, thereby providing the demand that activates a whole range of new capitalist enterprises. This applies not only to their food and clothing and personal possessions but to their leisure activities as well. As we saw earlier, capitalist production rapidly led to the creation of whole new industries based on the commercialization of leisure. This double role of wage labour, which enabled the dynamic interaction of production and consumption, explains why capitalist production expanded so very rapidly once it had got going.

Markets, like merchants, are nothing new, but they are central to a capitalist society in a quite new and more abstract way. This is because production and consumption are divorced – people do not consume what they produce or produce what they consume – and are linked only through the markets where goods and services are bought and sold. Instead of being a place where you can buy some extra item that you do not produce yourself, markets become the only means by which you can obtain anything. They are no longer located just in market-places but exist wherever buyers and sellers make their exchanges and, nowadays, this commonly means in some electronic space where prices are listed and deals registered. This applies not only to goods and services but also to labour, money, and capital. The wage, that is the price, for labour is established on a labour market, where employers compete for labour and workers compete for jobs. Money itself is bought and sold on currency markets. The ownership of companies is bought and sold in stock exchanges.

As we saw with the cotton mills, markets generate intense competition between capitalist enterprises. They compete in many different ways by, for example, exploiting labour more efficiently or using technical innovation to reduce costs or market products more effectively. Competition forces companies into constant change as they seek to beat the competition or at least keep up with it. Some of course fail and go under, throwing their employees out of work. This competitiveness, which contrasts strongly with the monopolistic practices of merchant capitalism, makes capitalist production exceptionally dynamic.

Capitalist enterprises have, nonetheless, found ways of reducing competition. Those with an edge over their rivals may relish the cut and thrust of competition, but this also creates uncertainty, reduces profits, and causes bankruptcies. Companies thus form trade associations to regulate competition. The market can be rigged by agreeing not to engage in price competition or deciding that all will pay the same wage rates. Competition can also be reduced by mergers and take-overs which concentrate production in fewer hands. There is in capitalism always a tension between competition and concentration, which are equally characteristic of it.

Since prices change, any market provides an opportunity to make money through speculation. This occurs when something is bought in the expectation of selling it, without increasing its value by processing it in some way, at a higher price in the future. It can occur in relation to almost any commodity. It may be grain, it may be a currency, it may be a derivative, it may be a slave. Speculation of this kind is often regarded as an unproductive and parasitic activity that is wholly separable from the real economy where goods and services are produced. Unproductive it may often be, but it is not just a means of making money through speculation but also a way of avoiding risk. Since the relationship between supply and demand is always changing, markets are unstable. The building up and storage of stocks is a means of insuring against some adverse price movement that could destroy profit and wipe out a business. Trading in futures, of the kind that Leeson speculated in, is another way of reducing uncertainty and originated long ago as a sophisticated way of protecting producers and traders against unpredictable future movements in prices.

The huge growth in the trading of currency during the 1980s and 1990s followed the shift from fixed to floating exchange rates in the 1970s, which created much greater uncertainty about future currency values. One way of reducing this uncertainty was to 'hedge' one's bets by buying currency futures. So, though the vast bulk of trading in currency futures is undoubtedly speculative, the expansion of this market and the financial innovations associated with it were grounded in real economic needs.

The same argument applies to the speculative trading of company shares. The existence of markets for capital is central to capitalism. They are essential to its functioning since they bring together those seeking to finance economic activities and those with money to invest. Since the stock market prices of companies change, as their economic situation and profitability changes, there are inevitably opportunities for speculating on future price movements. Speculation is not something separate from capitalism but an inevitable outgrowth of its essential machinery.

So, the answer to our question is that capitalism involves the investment of money to make more money. While merchants have long done this, it is when production is financed in this way that a transformative capitalism comes into being. Capitalist production depends on the exploitation of wage labour, which also fuels the consumption of the goods and services produced by capitalist enterprises. Production and consumption are linked by the markets that come to mediate all economic activities. Markets enable competition between enterprises but also generate tendencies towards concentration in order to reduce uncertainty. Market fluctuations also provide the basis of a speculative form of capitalism, which may not be productive but is, nonetheless, based on mechanisms that are central to the operation of a capitalist economy.

Consider
1. What is capitalism?
2. Based on the materials in this book and relevant additional sources, characterise some of the major stages in the historical development of capitalism.
3. What is neoliberalism?
4. How does neoliberalism shape contemporary dynamics of globalisation? Again, you may need additional sources to fully answer this question.

5.4 The network society

Finally, I add yet another perspective to my discussion of modernity and the problem of social cohesion. As mentioned above, sociologists have for a long time tended to imagine societies as clearly bounded *nation states*. While nations and nationalism are clearly still significant in the contemporary world, this perspective may not be fully up-to-date any more. In recent years, sociologists have begun to look at forms of social organisation, social solidarity, social bonds and communities that exist beyond – or even regardless of – the boundaries of nation states. It is in this sense that adopting a global perspective is central to contemporary sociology.

The idea of the network society provides one particularly important perspective on the growing importance of social ties beyond national borders. One of its key proponents is the Spanish sociologist Manuel Castells (e.g. Castells 2000). Castells' arguments depart from the monumental social transformations of the postmodern period that we have already explored:

> Toward the end of the second millennium of the Christian era several events of historical significance transformed the social landscape of human life. A technological revolution, centered around information technologies, began to reshape, at accelerated pace, the material basis of society. Economies throughout the world have become globally interdependent, introducing a new form of relationship between economy, state, and society, in a system of variable geometry. (Castells 2000: 1)

Castells then goes on to consider a broad range of social, cultural and political changes that characterise contemporary life. His main concern, however, lies with the consequences of the 'technological revolution' and the emergence of new forms of fast mass communication and information technology, in particular the Internet. He argues that *networks*, in particular electronic information networks, are the new constitutive elements of social life, surpassing previous, more closely localised forms of social organisation. These information networks radically alter the meaning of time and space, allowing the instant transmission of information and the formation of social ties across vast distances. Through networks, social interaction is disembedded from real physical space, instead taking the form of virtual *flows* of information, ideas and meanings.

The international system of financial markets is one key instance of such networks, being built around the immediate transmission of data across the globe and tying economic processes all around the world to each other more closely than ever. It is, among other factors, due to this global network of financial markets that an economic crisis in the USA in 2008 quickly turned global or that the bankruptcy of the Greek state would have repercussions across all of Europe and beyond.

Another central example are the already much-mentioned virtual social networks. Facebook, Myspace and so forth allow you to build a network of contacts, acquaintances and friendships with people all around the world, and the degree of closeness you experience with your online friends has become largely independent of their physical location in the world. At the same time, the way you present yourself online and engage with others may often be significantly different from your offline persona. It is for these reasons that virtual social networks have profoundly altered the nature of human social interaction in the span of just a few years.

In the following, you will read from the work of another key theorist of the network society, the Dutch sociologist Jan van Dijk. While van Dijk's account of the network society differs somewhat from the approach formulated by Manuel Castells, both scholars do agree that social relationships in the contemporary world are being fundamentally re-shaped. In the reading below, van Dijk describes these changes in some detail.

Reading

Van Dijk, J. (2006), *The Network Society: Social Aspects of New Media*, 2nd edn, London: SAGE, pp. 1–3, 19–20, 32–6, 191–4

A new infrastructure for society

New roads are being built at tremendous speed and yet we hardly notice. After all, the countryside is not being cleared by bulldozers and covered with rails, canals or asphalt. These roads are for information and communication. Apparently they are part of an abstract, barely visible reality. We might see them as yet another cable running into our homes. We do not realize that they are making us dependent on yet another technology in our life. We are not only tied to roads, electricity cables, water pipes, gas lines, sewers, postboxes, telephone wires and cable television, but also to computer networks such as the Internet.

Contemporary literature abounds with expressions such as 'we live in a connected world', 'a connected age', a 'human web' and a 'web society'. At first sight this seems rather peculiar because simultaneously there is much talk about individualization, social fragmentation, independence and freedom. On second thoughts this coincidence is not that strange because both tendencies might be two sides of the same coin. At least, that is argued in this book. 'The world may never have been freer, but it has also never been so interdependent and interconnected' (Mulgan, 1997: 1).

At the individual level the use of networks has come to dominate our lives. Counting the time spent on broadcast networks, telephony and the Internet we can add between five and seven hours of leisure time a day on average in a developed society. Not to mention the hours spent with them at work and at school. Observing social networking by individuals we could add several hours spent in all kinds of meetings. Individualization and smaller households packed with technology to make us more independent from others, have not made us less social human beings.

Almost every organization in the developed world has become completely dependent on networks of telephony and computers. When they break down, the organization simply stops working. Long before they became so dependent on these media networks organizations had already split in separate organizations, departments and teams that still worked together in an extensive division of labour. These days organizations do not finish products or services all by themselves. This is done in cooperation and competition inside and between economic networks.

At the level of society and on a global scale we can see that media networks, social networks and economic networks reach into the farthest corners and edges of the world. Our world has become truly globally connected. With the swift spread of satellite TV, mobile telephony and the Internet, developing countries such as China and India rapidly transform from pre-industrial societies into industrial mass societies and partly even post-industrial network societies. The meaning of these terms will be fully explained below.

With little exaggeration, we may call the 21st century the age of networks. Networks are becoming the nervous system of our society, and we can expect this infrastructure to have more influence on our entire social and personal lives than did the construction of roads for the transportation of goods and people in the past. In this sense 'information highway' is an appropriate term. The design of such basic infrastructures is crucial for the opportunities and risks to follow. We did not foresee what the consequences would be of our choice in the early 20th century of predominantly small-scale private transportation instead of large-scale public transport. But now we are only too well aware of the consequences. Traffic congestion, environmental degradation and global warming are all too evident.

The potential consequences of choosing a certain kind of communication infrastructure and embedding this infrastructure in our social and personal lives may be less visible, but it will be just as severe.

Continuing this line of argument, at stake here is not only the ecology of nature – that is, transportation of information and communication will partly replace transportation of goods and people – but also 'social ecology'. Therefore, when the new media arrived in the 1980s, some people were talking about the 'pollution' of our social environment by the new media penetrating our private lives. According to them, the new media were reducing, diminishing and even destroying the quality of face-to-face communications and were making relationships at work more formal (Kubicek, 1988). They would result in privacy reduction and total control from above. In the 1990s these *dystopian* views were replaced by *utopian* views of the new media substantially improving the quality of life and of communication. A 'new economy' and a new era of prosperity, freedom and online democracy was looming ahead.

In the first Dutch edition of this book (van Dijk, 1991), I championed a wide public debate about such presumed outcomes of the new media. This call was partly heeded. Especially between 1994 and 1998, a huge boost was given to discussion of the opportunities of the Internet and the perspective of the so-called electronic highway, a term introduced in the United States in 1993 as 'information superhighway'. The discussion in those years was largely theoretical. Utopian and dystopian views were listed and opposed in an abstract and rather speculative manner.

In the first decade of the 21st century we are able to develop a more balanced or *syntopian* view (Katz and Rice, 2002) of new media development after more than 25 years of experience. This time we are able to draw conclusions based on facts and empirical investigations. This is the main objective of this book.

This book demonstrates how the most fundamental values of our society are at issue when it comes to the development of new information and communication technologies, in which networks are already setting the tone.

Social equality is at stake, since certain categories of people participate more than others in the information society. Some profit from its advantages, while others are deprived. Technology allows for a better distribution of knowledge. Its complexity and costs, however, may serve to intensify existing social inequalities, or even create large groups of 'misfits' – people who do not fit in with the information society.

The fact that the new media enable well-informed citizens, employees and consumers to have more direct communication with, and participation in, institutions of decision-making should, in principle, strengthen *democracy*. On the other hand, because the technology is susceptible to control from above, democracy could be threatened. Some would argue that *freedom*, for example the freedom of choice for consumers, will increase because of the interactivity offered by this technology. Others paint a more pessimistic picture, and predict that freedom will be endangered by a decrease in privacy for the individual as a registered citizen, a 'transparent' employee and a consumer screened for every personal characteristic, and by the growing opportunities for central control.

For certain groups of people (disabled, sick and elderly people) as well as for society as a whole, *safety* can be improved by all kinds of registration and alarm systems. At the same time, safety seems to decrease because we have become dependent on yet another type of technology. And a very vulnerable technology at that.

The *quantity and quality of social relationships* might improve if communication technology enables us to get in touch easily with almost everybody, even over long distances. On the other hand, they might decrease because they invite particular people to withdraw into computer communication and to interact only with safe, self-chosen social environments. In this way new media communication may become a complete substitute for face-to-face communication, causing the quality of communication to be diminished in certain respects.

The *richness of the human mind* may increase owing to the diversity of impressions we gather through these new media. On the other hand, it may also be reduced because these impressions are offered out of context in schematic, (pre-)programmed and fragmented frames. And because it is available in huge amounts, information can never be fully processed by the recipient.

[. . .]

The network society and other classifications

Several concepts are available to indicate the type of society that evolves under the influence of the use of information and communication technology. The most popular concept is the information society. In this book that concept is used in combination with the concept network society to typify contemporary developed and modern societies marked by a high level of information exchange and use of information and communication technologies (ICTs). In the concept of an information society, the changing *substance* of activities and processes in these societies is emphasized. In the concept of a network society, attention shifts to the changing organizational *forms* and (infra)structures of these societies.

I start with my own complete definitions of these types of society and continue with a number of qualifications of these definitions and their relationships with other classifications such as capitalist society and (post-)modern society.

In an information society the information intensity of all activities becomes so high that this leads to:

- an organization of society based on science, rationality and reflexivity;
- an economy with all values and sectors, even the agrarian and industrial sectors, increasingly characterized by information production;

- a labour market with a majority of functions largely or completely based on tasks of information processing requiring knowledge and higher education (hence, the alternative term *knowledge society*);
- a culture dominated by media and information products with their signs, symbols and meanings.

It is the intensity of information processing in all these spheres that allows us to describe it as a new type of society. The common denominator of the changes produced by the increasing information intensity of all activities is the semi-autonomous character of information processing. Most activities in contemporary society are dedicated to *means*, in this case means of processing and producing information. These activities tend to keep a distance from their ultimate aims and to gather their own momentum and reason to exist. Manuel Castells (1996) even claims that information has become an independent source of productivity and power.

The network society concept emphasizes the form and organization of information processing and exchange. An infrastructure of social and media networks takes care of this. So the network society can be defined as a social formation with an infrastructure of social and media networks enabling its prime mode of organization at all levels (individual, group/organizational and societal). Increasingly, these networks link all units or parts of this formation (individuals, groups and organizations). In western societies, the individual linked by networks is becoming the basic unit of the network society. In eastern societies, this might still be the group (family, community, work team) linked by networks.

[...]

From mass society to network society

Now we are ready to understand the main characteristics of the network society as compared to that of the mass society. This comparison is made in Table 2.2. It will serve as a summary of the argument in this section and an introduction to the following chapters where the network society is described in detail.

The mass society was defined earlier in this chapter as a social formation with an infrastructure of groups, organizations and communities ('masses') that shapes its prime mode of organization at all levels. The main components of this formation are all kinds of relatively large collectivities. Historically, the mass society characterizes the first phase of the era of the global web as it is called by the McNeills (2003). This society evolved during the industrial revolution when large concentrations of people came together in industrial towns and trading centres. Typical of these concentrations was that the traditional communities already existing in neighbourhoods and villages were largely maintained when they were combined on a larger scale in cities and nations.

Table 2.2 A typology of the mass society and the network society.

Characteristics	Mass Society	Network Society
Main components	Collectivities (Groups, Organizations, Communities)	Individuals (linked by networks)
Nature of components	Homogeneous	Heterogeneous
Scale	Extended	Extended and Reduced
Scope	Local	'Glocal' (global and local)
Connectivity and Connectedness	High within components	High between components
Density	High	Lower
Centralization	High (few centres)	Lower (polycentric)
Inclusiveness	High	Lower
Type of community	Physical and unitary	Virtual and diverse
Type of organization	Bureaucracy Vertically integrated	Infocracy Horizontally differentiated
Type of household	Large with extended family	Small with diversity of family relations
Main type of communication	Face-to-face	Increasingly mediated
Kind of media	Broadcast mass media	Narrowcast interactive media
Number of media	Low	High

The basic components of mass society are large households and extended families in the rather tight communities of a village or a city neighbourhood. In large companies, other mass associations appear, such as closely cooperating shifts and departments. The basic components or units of the mass society are homogeneous. This does not mean that internal conflict or opposition is absent, but that all units concerned largely reveal the same characteristics and social structures. For example, the large households consist of standard nuclear families with a mother, father and many children. Local communities also are relatively homogeneous or unitary and they are marked by physical proximity.

The mass society is marked by scale extension. Corporations, governments and other organizations grow larger and larger and they become bureaucracies. They spread across nations and the world at large to create a global web of 19th-century empires and multinationals. However, the scope of the mass society remains local: the organization of its basic components is tied to particular places and communication is still overwhelmingly local. The mass society is an assembly and connection of relatively homogeneous separate local places.

These basic components or units of the mass society are marked by the physical co-presence of their members. This means high connectivity inside and relatively low connectivity outside. The mass society is very much clustered with strong ties of high density (in local communities and extended family structures) and it contains relatively few weak ties connecting these clusters at long distances in diffuse network structures.

The internal relations in the units of the mass society are centralized. Bureaucratic and vertically integrated modes of organization prevail. are relatively few very influential centres: the national, regional and local state, the army, a number of large corporations, churches or other cultural institutions and a limited number of mass media. The complement of centralization is that the inclusiveness of relations is high as well. The number of connected members is high and few of them are isolated or excluded. The mass society is marked more by solidarity than the network society.

In the mass society, every unit (community, household) has access to only one or perhaps a few of each type of mass media, such as one local newspaper, followed by one national newspaper and one or a few radio and television channels. So, the number of media is relatively low as compared to the current standards in network societies. Essentially, they are all broadcast media. However, generally speaking, face-to-face communication is much more important than mediated communication in the mass society.

[. . .]

In the course of the 20th century, the structures of the mass society were gradually replaced by the structures of the network society. This happened first of all in developed or modern societies. The reasons for this replacement will be discussed in the following chapters, as they derive from problems of organization and communication in the economic, political and cultural systems and the general social infrastructure of these societies. The characteristics of the network society are described below in order to compare them with the mass society.

As has been argued above, in the contemporary process of individualization, the basic unit of the network society has become the individual who is linked by networks. Traditional local collectivities such as communities, extended families and large bureaucracies are fragmenting. This is caused by simultaneous scale extension (nationalization and internationalization) and scale reduction (smaller living and working environments). Other kinds of communities arise, consisting of people who on the one hand continue to live and work in their own families, neighbourhoods and organizations, but on the other hand frequently move around in large-scale social networks that are much more diffuse than the traditional ones. Daily living and working environments are getting smaller and more heterogeneous, while the range of the division of labour, interpersonal communications and mass media extends. So, the scale of the network society is both extended and reduced as compared to the mass society. The scope of the network society also is both global and local, sometimes indicated as 'glocal'. The organization of its components (individuals, groups, organizations) is no longer tied to particular times and places. Aided by information and communication technology, these coordinates of existence can be transcended to create virtual times and places and to simultaneously act, perceive and think in global and local terms.

The social units of the network society are fragmented and dispersed. This means that the density of contacts and ties *within* these units is relatively low as compared to traditional families, neighbourhoods, communities and organizations in the mass society. Instead, the elements of these units, the individuals, select their own contacts and ties *beyond* these units. Using all kinds of telecommunication they develop an extremely high level of connectivity between themselves as individuals and accordingly between the units of the network society of which they are a part.

Networks are relatively flat and horizontal, so-called heterarchical social structures. However, this does not mean that they do not have centres. Think about the spider in the web. Networks usually do not have a single centre. They are polycentric, as some nodes are (much) more important than others. For this reason, the network society is less centralized in the sense of having single centres in the economy, politics, government, culture and community life. They are replaced by a multitude of centres cooperating and competing with each other.

The network society is less inclusive than the mass society. You may be a member of some part of the mass society by birth or ascription. In the individualized network society you have to fight for a particular place. You have to show your value for every network. Otherwise you will be isolated in, or even excluded from, the network. In the network society, you have to stand firm as an individual. You are not that easily taken along in solidarity by proximate people.

In the network society, face-to-face communication remains the most important kind of communication in many ways. However, gradually it is also partly replaced and supplemented by mediated communication. A multitude of interpersonal and mass communication media are used for this purpose. Broadcast mass media reaching everyone are accompanied by, and partly replaced by, narrowcast interactive media reaching selected audiences. They lead to all kinds of new communication forms and groupings between interpersonal and mass communications, such as chat and instant messaging groups, virtual teams at work and virtual communities of interest. Virtual communities add to the thinned out physical communities of the network society with their small and diversely composed households. [. . .]

Living in a digital culture

Views differ as to which technical part of the new media has the greatest cultural impact. Many think it is the fact that they are digital. At least, this word is very popular in all kinds of prefixes: digital revolution, digital city and even digital being (Negroponte, 1995). Used in this way, the word suggests more than it says. Chapter 1 explained that digitalization is only one of the technical characteristics of the new media. What effects could it have on culture? To answer this question we will have to dig deeper than is usual in popular accounts of digitalization.

Digitalization means that every item can be translated into separate bytes consisting of strings of ones and zeros (called bits). This applies to images, sounds, texts and data. They can be produced and consumed in separate pieces and combined in every manner imaginable. From now on, every item can be presented on screens and accompanied by sound. All items can be stored on digital data carriers and retrieved from them in virtually unlimited amounts and at virtually unlimited speed. In the preceding sentences, digital technology and cultural impact have already been linked. Thus, at this point in the discussion, the reader can gather that digitalization increases the *chances* of:

- a standardization and differentiation of culture;
- a fragmentation of culture;
- a collage of culture;
- an acceleration of culture;
- a visualization of culture;
- a larger quantity of culture.

Pre-programming and creativity

In popular literature on the new media, the suggestion is made that these media will create unlimited choice from our sizeable cultural heritages and a new creative potential among the population, as people are enabled to create their own works of art and other products with multimedia. In *The Road Ahead* (1995), Bill Gates claimed ICT will offer new ways for people to express themselves. Apparently, ICT offers 'unprecedented artistic and scientific opportunities to a new generation of geniuses' (p. 154). Indeed, these opportunities do exist for people with the means and the skills to use them. However, the chances that we are dealing with a 'new and original type of work', in the terms of Dutch copyright law, are decreasing. More and more often we will be processing, reworking or adapting things other people have created. This is just the next phase in the evolution of art. In the course of (modern) history, the work of art has been taken away from the artist step by step and put into the hands of consumers. After the era of large-scale technical reproducibility of art (Benjamin, 1968), we are now entering an era enabling people to create their 'own' works of art consisting of all the bits and pieces of the cultural heritage. Multimedia encourage users to make all sorts of video collages and images, to sample and compose pieces of music from a CD, to decide the ending of a film by picking one from several scripts, and to create their own abstract Mondrian-style painting from red, yellow and blue squares. Of course, professional and popular art have always been a matter of reworking and adapting the cultural heritage. But now we are taking one essential step further. Qualitatively more means are inserted between source and result. There is more than pencil, pen and ink on paper and paint on canvas. The means of production offered by digital media are (pre-)programmed themselves and they partly work automatically. They only have to be adapted by the user to gain some craft. The material worked upon is not empty, but it is filled with existing cultural content. In this way, creativity is put in an entirely different perspective.

The same can be said of the presumed infinite options in digital media. In fact, the whole thing is about options from a menu, in other words entirely pre-programmed. Usually, the user is able to make general choices only. Allowing users to choose from details would require too much preprogramming work.

Anyway, these options do lead to both a differentiation and a standardization of culture. The amount of content from which one can choose is increasing. At the same time, however, the elements of this content increasingly resemble one another. Everything is arranged in similar (menu) structures. Sources of information that used to be separate are combined in multimedia. Under certain circumstances, this may lead to diluting sources of information and eroding contents (see below).

Fragmentation and collage

Digitalization causes a technical division of analogue sources into bits and bytes. This enables an unrestricted division of the content of these sources. Digitalization and processing of analogue sources by multimedia equipment have already had a fragmenting effect on our culture. Michael Heim (1987) pointed out this trend some years ago by analysing changes in text caused by word processing. Text is provided with a pointed structure. The argument is structured in advance and divided into separate subjects, items and paragraphs. Items can easily be added or deleted later on – which may result in some loss of the course of the argument. Another example is the structure of the Internet. The content of web sites is spread over several pages and images which can all be accessed in one click. In this way, the traditional linear processing of content is replaced by the making of links, jumps and associations.

Finally, we come to the content of pieces of music and films processed by using interactive programs. Interactive music CDs are composed of separate, accumulated layers and fragments that may be easily isolated, manipulated, sampled and (re)combined. This *modularization* quickly causes the unity of a creative work to be lost. For the idea is to give listeners the opportunity to create their own collages. Many traditional artists, designers and producers find this anathema. They think the unique construction and coherence they have made is the essence of their creation. They dissociate themselves from the results obtained by the consumer, or accept them only because it pays to do so.

Acceleration

Digitalization allows a considerable increase in the production, dispersion and consumption of information and the signals of communication. In hardware, 'fast' has become the key word: fast computers, fast modems, fast lines, fast programs. The hunger for speed is never appeased. This gives all the more reason to believe that the popular assumption of the irrelevance of time in the new media is wrong. On the contrary, the importance of time is radicalizing (see Chapter 7). Saving time is immediately followed by new needs to be filled and created.

The need for speed is determined by motives in the economy (maximization of profits on the surplus value of working time in capitalism), the organization (efficiency) and consumption (immediate fulfilment of needs). Driven by a swift increase in technical capacities, these motives call into existence a *culture of speed*, (Miller and Schwarz, 1998; Virilio, 1988). This means our culture changes substantially as well. The following examples may be useful. First, expressions of culture date quickly. Trends follow each other at high speed. In the modern world, various trends exist side by side, competing for popularity. Second, information is sent in increasing amounts, ever more frequently and at ever higher speed just to attract attention. This phenomenon is called information and communication overload (see below). The result is shallowness in the perception of cultural expressions, a fact producers are anticipating and reinforcing. Furthermore, communication and language have increased to such a speed that we cannot sit down to think about a message, such as writing a letter or starting a conversation. Instead, we immediately pick up the phone and give ad hoc answers by telephone, or by email. Language also changes under the influence of the new media. This will be discussed in the next chapter. It acquires an abrupt style (like staccato) and contains increasing amounts of jargon with innumerable abbreviations. The final example is the rising importance of images in our culture, a type of data that is presented and consumed much more quickly than the others (speech, text and numbers).

Consider
1. What, from a sociological point of view, is a network?
2. What, according to Jan van Dijk, are the key characteristics of the network society?
3. How does the network society differ from the preceding 'mass society'? Describe each difference in detail and provide relevant examples.
4. How do you yourself form part of the social relationships of the network society, as described by Jan van Dijk?
5. Do we really live in a network society? Critically discuss the assumptions made by either Jan van Dijk or Manuel Castells. Answering this question will require you to do further background reading of your own.
6. Is the whole world integrated equally into the network society? Explain your reasoning through relevant examples. In order to answer this question, you will need to consider other sections of this book and do further background research of your own.

5.5 Rationalisation

The global rise of capitalism is closely linked to broader social, cultural and economic dynamics of modern life which sociologists have described as 'rationalisation'. To make sense of this, let's consider some examples of how the term 'rational' is used in contemporary everyday life. First, it is not uncommon to read in the news that this or that business company is undergoing 'rationalisation'. What this means is that the company is looking to make its operations more efficient, often by reorganising its administrative structure, and often by sacking staff deemed surplus to requirements. Second, in colloquial English, we use the expression 'be rational' to ask someone to reconsider plans that seem to run counter to the person's best interests. Imagine that your friend, who has few financial means, inherits a sum of money that would allow her to pay for her tuition fees and living expenses for a full year. Instead, she decides to use the funds to pay for an expensive three-months holiday over the summer. Hearing about this, you ask your friend to 'be rational', consider her long-term future, and place her studies first.

Both examples are good approximations to the sociological meaning of rationalisation. To clarify this, we need to return to the work of Max Weber (initially discussed in Chapter 3). As evident, for instance, in his work on the Protestant work ethic and the rise of capitalism, Weber understood modernity as the inexorable progress of a certain form of rationality, that is to say *a certain form of understanding the world and acting upon this understanding*. Weber distinguished between forms of rationality based primarily, on the one hand, upon *values*, *feelings* or *habit* and, on the other hand, upon the systematic calculation of the most expedient means to achieve a specific goal. The latter he called *instrumental rationality*, and he described its spread as a driving force of modern life. If my company is facing bankruptcy, and, in response, I decide to lay off half my employees as a means to reducing costs, this would be an example of an instrumentally rational means-ends calculation. On the contrary, I might hang on to my employees due to a deeply felt attachment to them, or because I firmly believe that dismissing them would be an injustice, or just because the daily routines of the company have become so routinised for me that I cannot imagine any changes.

Weber originally constructed his arguments more than a century ago, and they are built upon research that reaches even further back into history. However, other sociologists have extended the study of rationalisation throughout the twentieth and into the twenty-first century. Rationalisation is a major sociological issue because of its often ambivalent consequences. On the one hand, the reorganisation of social life has had many consequences that could be considered positive – consider rationally organised industrial production enabling the mass production of cheap goods previously unaffordable for most, or the emergence of large-scale educational bureaucracies coordinating the provision of public education. On the other hand, however, many contemporary sociologists share Max Weber's (1905/2009) view that rationalisation amounts to a growing 'disenchantment of the world'. Rationalisation erodes the traditions that make human life colourful and distinctive, and it leads to alienation by forcing individuals into an 'iron cage' (Weber 1905/2009) of standardised, efficient routines that belie their individuality.

The work of American sociologist George Ritzer (2010) is widely seen as a particularly powerful analysis of rationalisation in contemporary life. Writing about the 'McDonaldization of society', Ritzer evokes the image of the fast-food restaurant to describe rationalisation at work today:

Reading

George Ritzer (2010), 'An introduction to McDonaldization' in *McDonaldization: The Reader*, London: Sage, pp. 3–4 and 15–22

1

An Introduction to McDonaldization

George Ritzer

Ray Kroc (1902–1984), the genius behind the franchising of McDonald's restaurants, was a man with big ideas and grand ambitions. But even Kroc could not have anticipated the astounding impact of his creation. McDonald's is the basis of one of the most influential developments in contemporary society. Its reverberations extend far beyond its point of origin in the United States and in the fast-food business. It has influenced a wide range of undertakings, indeed the way of life, of a significant portion of the world. And having rebounded from some well-publicized economic difficulties, that impact is likely to expand at an accelerating rate in the early 21st century.

However, this is not a book about McDonald's, or even about the fast-food business, although both will be discussed frequently throughout these pages. I devote all this attention to McDonald's (as well as to the industry of which it is a part and that it played such a key role in spawning) because it serves here as the major example of, and the paradigm for, a wide-ranging process I call *McDonaldization* – that is,

> the process by which the principles of the fast-food restaurant are coming to dominate more and more sectors of American society as well as of the rest of the world.

McDonaldization has shown every sign of being an inexorable process, sweeping through seemingly impervious institutions (e.g., religion) and regions (European nations such as France) of the world.

The success of McDonald's itself is apparent: In 2006, its revenues were $21.6 billion, with operating income of $4.4 billion. McDonald's, which first began operations in 1955, had 31,667 restaurants throughout the world at the beginning of 2007. Martin Plimmer, a British commentator, archly notes:

> There are McDonald's everywhere. There's one near you, and there's one being built right now even nearer to you. Soon, if McDonald's goes on expanding at its present rate, there might even be one in your house. You could find Ronald McDonald's boots under your bed. And maybe his red wig, too. [. . .]

The Dimensions of McDonaldization

Why has the McDonald's model proven so irresistible? Eating fast food at McDonald's has certainly become a "sign" that, among other things, one is in tune with the contemporary lifestyle. There is also a kind of magic or enchantment associated with such food and its settings. The focus here, however, is on the four alluring dimensions that lie at the heart of the success of this model and, more generally, of McDonaldization. In short, McDonald's has succeeded because it offers consumers, workers, and managers efficiency, calculability, predictability, and control. . . .

Efficiency

One important element of the success of McDonald's is *efficiency*, or the optimum method for getting from one point to another. For consumers, McDonald's (its drive-through is a good example) offers the best available way to get from being hungry to being full. The fast-food model offers, or at least appears to offer, an efficient method for satisfying many other needs, as well. Woody Allen's orgasmatron offered an efficient method for getting people from quiescence to sexual gratification. Other institutions fashioned on the McDonald's model offer similar efficiency in exercising, losing weight, lubricating cars, getting new glasses or contacts, or completing income tax forms. Like their customers, workers in McDonaldized systems function efficiently by following the steps in a pre-designed process.

Calculability

Calculability emphasizes the quantitative aspects of products sold (portion size, cost) and services offered (the time it takes to get the product). In McDonaldized systems, quantity has become equivalent to quality; a lot of something, or the quick delivery of it, means it must be good. As two observers of contemporary American culture put it, "As a culture, we tend to believe deeply that in general 'bigger is better.'" People can quantify things and feel that they are getting a lot of food for what appears to be a nominal sum of money (best exemplified by McDonald's current "Dollar Menu," which played a key role in recent years in leading McDonald's out of its doldrums and to steadily increasing sales). In a recent Denny's ad, a man says, "I'm going to eat too much, but I'm never going to pay too much." This calculation does not take into account an important point, however: The high profit margin of fast-food chains indicates that the owners, not the consumers, get the best deal.

People also calculate how much time it will take to drive to McDonald's, be served the food, eat it, and return home; they then compare that interval to the time required to prepare food at home. They often conclude, rightly or wrongly, that a trip to the fast-food restaurant will take less time than eating at home. This sort of calculation particularly supports home delivery franchises such as Domino's, as well as other chains that emphasize saving time. A notable example of time savings in another sort of chain is LensCrafters, which promises people "Glasses fast, glasses in one hour." H&M is known for its "fast fashion."

Some McDonaldized institutions combine the emphases on time and money. Domino's promises pizza delivery in half an hour, or the pizza is free. Pizza Hut will serve a personal pan pizza in 5 minutes, or it, too, will be free.

Workers in McDonaldized systems also emphasize the quantitative rather than the qualitative aspects of their work. Since the quality of the work is allowed to vary little, workers focus on things such as how quickly tasks can be accomplished. In a situation analogous to that of the customer, workers are expected to do a lot of work, very quickly, for low pay.

Predictability

McDonald's also offers *predictability*, the assurance that products and services will be the same over time and in all locales. The Egg McMuffin in New York will be, for all intents and purposes, identical to those in Chicago and Los Angeles. Also, those eaten next week or next year will be identical to those eaten today. Customers take great comfort in knowing that McDonald's offers no surprises. People know that the next Egg McMuffin they eat will not be awful, although it will not be exceptionally delicious, either. The success of the McDonald's model suggests that many people have come to prefer a world in which there are few surprises. "This is strange," notes a British observer, "considering [McDonald's is] the product of a culture which honours individualism above all."

The workers in McDonaldized systems also behave in predictable ways. They follow corporate rules as well as the dictates of their managers. In many cases, what they do, and even what they say, is highly predictable.

Control

The fourth element in the success of McDonald's, *control*, is exerted over the people who enter the world of McDonald's. Lines, limited menus, few options, and uncomfortable seats all lead diners to do what management wishes them to do – eat quickly and leave. Furthermore, the drive-through (in some cases, walk-through) window invites diners to leave before they eat. In the Domino's model, customers never enter in the first place.

The people who work in McDonaldized organizations are also controlled to a high degree, usually more blatantly and directly than customers. They are trained to do a limited number of things in precisely the way they are told to do them. This control is reinforced by the technologies used and the way the organization is set up to bolster this control. Managers and inspectors make sure that workers toe the line.

A Critique of McDonaldization: The Irrationality of Rationality

McDonaldization offers powerful advantages. In fact, efficiency, predictability, calculability, and control through nonhuman technology (that is, technology that controls people rather than being controlled by them) can be thought of as not only the basic components of a rational system but also as powerful advantages of such a system. However, rational systems inevitably spawn irrationalities.

The downside of McDonaldization will be dealt with most systematically under the heading of the irrationality of rationality; in fact, paradoxically, the irrationality of rationality can be thought of as the fifth dimension of McDonaldization.

Criticism, in fact, can be applied to all facets of the McDonaldizing world. As just one example, at the opening of Euro Disney, a French politician said that it will "bombard France with uprooted creations that are to culture what fast food is to gastronomy." Although McDonaldization offers many advantages (explained later in this chapter), the book's focus is on the great costs and enormous risks of McDonaldization. McDonald's and other purveyors of the fast-food model spend billions of dollars each year detailing the benefits of their system. Critics of the system, however, have few outlets for their ideas. For example, no one sponsors commercials between Saturday-morning cartoons warning children of the dangers associated with fast-food restaurants.

Nonetheless, a legitimate question may be raised about this critique of McDonaldization: Is it animated by a romanticization of the past, an impossible desire to return to a world that no longer exists? Some critics do base their critiques on nostalgia for a time when life was slower and offered more surprises, when at least some people (those who were better off economically) were freer, and when one was more likely to deal with a human being than a robot or a computer. Although they have a point, these critics have undoubtedly exaggerated the positive aspects of a world without McDonald's, and they have certainly tended to forget the liabilities associated with earlier eras. As an example of the latter, take the following anecdote about a visit to a pizzeria in Havana, Cuba, which in some respects is decades behind the United States:

> The pizza's not much to rave about – they scrimp on tomato sauce, and the dough is mushy.
>
> It was about 7:30 P.M., and as usual the place was standing-room-only, with people two deep jostling for a stool to come open and a waiting line spilling out onto the sidewalk.
>
> The menu is similarly Spartan. . . . To drink, there is tap water. That's it – no toppings, no soda, no beer, no coffee, no salt, no pepper. And no special orders.
>
> A very few people are eating. Most are waiting. . . . Fingers are drumming, flies are buzzing, the clock is ticking. The waiter wears a watch around his belt loop, but he hardly needs it; time is evidently not his chief concern. After a while, tempers begin to fray.
>
> But right now, it's 8:45 P.M. at the pizzeria, I've been waiting an hour and a quarter for two small pies.

Few would prefer such a restaurant to the fast, friendly, diverse offerings of, say, Pizza Hut. More important, however, critics who revere the past do not seem to realize that we are not returning to such a world. In fact, fast-food restaurants have begun to appear even in Havana (and many more are likely after the death of Fidel Castro). The increase in the number of people crowding the planet, the acceleration of technological change, the increasing pace of life – all this and more make it impossible to go back to the world, if it ever existed, of home-cooked meals, traditional restaurant dinners, high-quality foods, meals loaded with surprises, and restaurants run by chefs free to express their creativity.

It is more valid to critique McDonaldization from the perspective of a conceivable future. Unfettered by the constraints of McDonaldized systems, but using the technological advances made possible by them, people could have the potential to be far more thoughtful, skillful, creative, and well-rounded than they are now. In short, if the world was less McDonaldized, people would be better able to live up to their human potential.

We must look at McDonaldization as both "enabling" and "constraining." McDonaldized systems enable us to do many things we were not able to do in the past; however, these systems also keep us from doing things we otherwise would do. McDonaldization is a "double-edged" phenomenon. We must not lose sight of that fact, even though this book will focus on the constraints associated with McDonaldization – its "dark side."

Illustrating the Dimensions of McDonaldization: The Case of IKEA

An interesting example of McDonaldization, especially since it has its roots in Sweden rather than the United States, is IKEA. Its popularity stems from the fact that it offers at very low prices trendy furniture based on well-known Swedish designs. It has a large and devoted clientele throughout the world. What is interesting about IKEA from the point of view of this book is how well it fits the dimensions of McDonaldization. The similarities go beyond that, however. For example, just as with the opening of a new McDonald's, there is great anticipation over the opening of the first IKEA in a particular location. Just the rumor that one was to open in Dayton, Ohio, led to the following statement: "We here in Dayton are peeing our collective pants waiting for the IKEA announcement." IKEA is also a global phenomenon – it is now in 34 countries (including China and Japan) and sells in those countries both its signature products as well as those more adapted to local tastes and interests.

In terms of *efficiency*, IKEA offers one-stop furniture shopping with an extraordinary range of furniture. In general, there is no waiting for one's purchases, since a huge warehouse is attached to each store (one often enters through the warehouse), with large numbers of virtually everything in stock.

Much of the efficiency at IKEA stems from the fact that customers are expected to do a lot of the work:

- Unlike McDonald's, there are relatively few IKEAs in any given area; thus, customers most often spend many hours driving great distances to get to a store. This is known as the "IKEA road trip."

- On entry, customers are expected to take a map to guide themselves through the huge and purposely maze-like store (IKEA hopes, like Las Vegas casinos, that customers will get "lost" in the maze and wander for hours, spending money as they go). There are no employees to guide anyone, but there are arrows painted on the floor that customers can follow on their own.
- Also upon entry, customers are expected to grab a pencil and an order form and to write down the shelf and bin numbers for the larger items they wish to purchase; a yellow shopping bag is to be picked up on entry for smaller items. There are few employees and little in the way of help available as customers wander through the stores. Customers can switch from a shopping bag to a shopping cart after leaving the showroom and entering the marketplace, where they can pick up other smaller items.
- If customers eat in the cafeteria, they are expected to clean their tables after eating. There is even this helpful sign: "Why should I clean my own table? At IKEA, cleaning your own table at the end of your meal is one of the reasons you paid less at the start."
- Most of the furniture sold is unassembled in flat packages, and customers are expected to load most of the items (except the largest) into their cars themselves. After they get home, they must break down (and dispose) of the packaging and then put their furniture together; the only tool supposedly required is an Allen wrench.
- If the furniture does not fit into your car, you can rent a truck on site to transport it home or have it delivered, although the cost tends to be high, especially relative to the price paid for the furniture.
- To get a catalog, customers often sign up online.

Calculability is at the heart of IKEA, especially the idea that what is offered is at a very low price. Like a McDonald's "Dollar Menu," one can get a lot of furniture – a roomful, even a houseful – at bargain prices. As with value meals, customers feel they are getting value for their money. (There is even a large cafeteria offering low-priced food, including the chain's signature Swedish meatballs and 99-cent breakfasts.) However, as is always the case in McDonaldized settings, low price generally means that the quality is inferior, and it is often the case that IKEA products fall apart in relatively short order. IKEA also emphasizes the huge size of its stores, which often approach 300,000 square feet or about four to five football fields. This mammoth size leads the consumer to believe that there will be a lot of furniture offered (and there is) and that, given the store's reputation, most of it will be highly affordable.

Of course, there is great *predictability* about any given IKEA – large parking lots, a supervised children's play area (where IKEA provides personnel, but only because supervised children give parents more time and peace of mind to shop and spend), the masses of inexpensive, Swedish-design furniture, exit through the warehouse and the checkout counters, boxes to take home with furniture requiring assembly, and so on.

An IKEA is a highly *controlled* environment, mainly in the sense that the maze-like structure of the store virtually forces the consumer to traverse the entire place and to see virtually everything it has to offer. If one tries to take a path other than that set by IKEA, one is likely to become lost and disoriented. There seems to be no way out that does not lead to the checkout counter, where you pay for your purchases.

There are a variety of *irrationalities* associated with the rationality of IKEA, most notably the poor quality of most of its products. Although the furniture is purportedly easy to assemble, many are more likely to think of it as "impossible-to-assemble." Then there are the often long hours required to get to an IKEA, to wander through it, to drive back home, and then to assemble the purchases.

Consider
1. What are the main dimensions of McDonaldization which Ritzer identifies? Give examples for each.
2. Visit a fast-food outlet in your area and observe. What examples of efficiency, calculability, predictability and control can you notice? Is there anything that contradicts Ritzer's observations?
3. Beyond the world of fast-food restaurants, give other examples of rationalisation in contemporary social life.
4. Critically examine Ritzer's McDonaldization thesis in the light of the three paradigms of globalisation discussed above. To what extent are Ritzer's arguments compatible with assumptions about hybridisation or a 'clash of civilisations'?

5.6 Risk and reflexive modernisation

The preceding discussion of rationalisation might seem to suggest that, for better or worse, modern life is becoming ever more organised and predictable. Through social processes such as those identified by George Ritzer, control over almost every aspect of our everyday life seems to have become achievable. When we go for lunch, we know with great certainty how long it will take to order a meal at McDonald's, sit down to eat it, and make our way back to work. When we take a plane from London to Mexico City, we know exactly how long the flight will last and which route the plane will take. A host of well-rehearsed routines ensures our onboard safety, and we are insured and legally protected in case something untoward does happen.

This, however, is a rather incomplete portrayal of modernity's consequences for our lives. As much as modernity has made social life rationally controlled and predictable, it also has brought about man-made risks of an unprecedented scope. On Friday, 11 March 2011, a particularly massive earthquake took place off the eastern coast of

Japan, provoking a huge tsunami that wrecked wide swathes of coastal land. This natural disaster spilled over into a man-made disaster when the coastal Fukushima Daiichi nuclear power plant suffered a string of nuclear meltdowns. Radioactive materials began to be released into the atmosphere, and the radiation leaks do not seem to have been contained at the time these words are being written. On 10 August 2011, journalist Amy Goodman wrote in the *Guardian* newspaper:

> In recent weeks, radiation levels have spiked at the Fukushima nuclear power reactors in Japan, with recorded levels of 10,000 millisieverts per hour (mSv/hr) at one spot. This is the number reported by the reactor's discredited owner, Tokyo Electric Power Co, although that number is simply as high as the Geiger counters go. In other words, the radiation levels are literally off the charts. Exposure to 10,000 millisieverts for even a brief time would be fatal, with death occurring within weeks.

There are thus strong indications that the destroyed power plant will be a source of serious health risks for an unpredictable and maybe very long amount of time.

Even though the dangers posed by nuclear radiation have been long known, power plants using nuclear reactors have been popular and widely used throughout the world for nearly 60 years. On the one hand, they constitute a predictable, reliable source of energy for our everyday needs, thus fitting the pattern of modern rationalisation. On the other hand, however, the catastrophic collapse of safety measures in nuclear reactors is a distinct possibility, with consequences that can hardly be predicted, controlled, or contained. In this sense, modern efforts at rationalising social life may have deeply irrational, unintended consequences.

The risks inherent in modern life have famously been captured by German sociologist Ulrich Beck (1986/2000). Beck argues that, as modernity has unfolded, the problem of the risks *generated by technological and economic development* has risen to ever greater prominence. Modernisation has become *reflexive*, in that it is not any more simply concerned with controlling the external, natural world and improving the human condition. Rather, societies are forced to constantly look back upon the potentially catastrophic consequences of their development and seek to mitigate them.

A central feature of these man-made risks – nuclear meltdowns, nuclear war, environmental pollution, global warming, etc. – is that they have the *potential to destroy human civilisation*. For example, global warming, caused by an increased concentration of so-called greenhouse gases in the atmosphere due to industrial production, deforestation, etc., has been widely predicted to cause floods, droughts and unprecedented heat waves in this century already. However, in spite of their scope, these risks tend to be *invisible* to direct observation in everyday life. As a result, they become subject to complex *scientific controversies* that may be hard for laypeople to follow. In the context of controversial public debates about high-profile risks, the boundaries between scientific knowledge and lay knowledge may come to be blurred, and science may come to be a source of uncertainty, rather than security. How unhealthy exactly is it to eat fast food or drink alcohol? Expert opinions on both topics abound, and, more often than not, they contradict each other. Without a degree in biochemistry or medicine, how do you know whose advice to follow? How will this advice affect your choices when it comes to eating a hamburger or drinking a glass of wine? Much depends on it, at least in terms of your personal wellbeing. Still more depends on it when it comes to controversies about the safety of nuclear power plants, as the preceding example suggests. In this sense, in late modernity, unprecedented risks abound, and science may have become a source of fundamental uncertainty.

Reading

Beck, U. (1986/2000), *Risk Society*, Cambridge: Polity Press, pp. 19–27 and 87–90

On the Logic of Wealth Distribution and Risk Distribution

In advanced modernity the social production of *wealth* is systematically accompanied by the social production of *risks*. Accordingly, the problems and conflicts relating to distribution in a society of scarcity overlap with the problems and conflicts that arise from the production, definition and distribution of techno-scientifically produced risks.

This change from the logic of wealth distribution in a society of scarcity to the logic of risk distribution in late modernity is connected historically to (at least) two conditions. First, it occurs – as is recognizable today – where and to the extent that *genuine material need* can be objectively reduced and socially isolated through the development of human and technological productivity, as well as through legal and welfare-state protections and regulations. Second, this categorical change is likewise dependent upon the fact that in the course of the exponentially growing productive forces in the modernization process, hazards and potential threats have been unleashed to an extent previously unknown.

To the extent that these conditions occur, one historical type of thinking and acting is relativized or overridden by another. The concepts of 'industrial' or 'class society', in the broadest sense of Marx or Weber, revolved around the issue of how socially produced wealth could be distributed in a socially unequal and *also* 'legitimate' way. This overlaps with the new *paradigm of risk society* which is based on the solution of a similar and yet quite different problem. How can the risks and hazards systematically produced as part of modernization be prevented, minimized, dramatized, or channeled? Where they do finally see the light of day in the shape of 'latent side effects', how can they be limited and distributed away so that they neither hamper the modernization process nor exceed the limits of that which is 'tolerable' – ecologically, medically, psychologically and socially?

We are therefore concerned no longer exclusively with making nature useful, or with releasing mankind from traditional constraints, but also and essentially with problems resulting from techno-economic development itself. Modernization is becoming *reflexive*; it is becoming its own theme. Questions of the development and employment of technologies (in the realms of nature, society and the personality) are being eclipsed by questions of the political and economic 'management' of the risks of actually or potentially utilized technologies – discovering, administering, acknowledging, avoiding or concealing such hazards with respect to specially defined horizons of relevance. The promise of security grows with the risks and destruction and must be reaffirmed over and over again to an alert and critical public through cosmetic or real interventions in the techno-economic development.

Both 'paradigms' of inequality are systematically related to definite periods of modernization. The distribution of socially produced wealth and related conflicts occupy the foreground so long as obvious material need, the 'dictatorship of scarcity', rules the thought and action of people (as today in large parts of the so-called Third World). Under these conditions of 'scarcity society', the modernization process takes place with the claim of opening the gates to hidden sources of social wealth with the keys of techno-scientific development. These promises of emancipation from undeserved poverty and dependence underlie action, thought and research in the categories of social inequality, from the class through the stratified to the individualized society.

In the welfare states of the West a double process is taking place now. On the one hand, the struggle for one's 'daily bread' has lost its urgency as a cardinal problem overshadowing everything else, compared to material subsistence in the first half of this century and to a Third World menaced by hunger. For many people problems of 'overweight' take the place of hunger. This development, however, withdraws the legitimizing basis from the modernization process, the struggle against obvious scarcity, for which one was prepared to accept a few (no longer completely) unseen side effects.

Parallel to that, the knowledge is spreading that the sources of wealth are 'polluted' by growing 'hazardous side effects'. This is not at all new, but it has remained unnoticed for a long time in the efforts to overcome poverty. This dark side is also gaining importance through the over-development of productive forces. In the modernization process, more and more *destructive* forces are also being unleashed, forces before which the human imagination stands in awe. Both sources feed a growing critique of modernization, which loudly and contentiously determines public discussions.

In systematic terms, sooner or later in the continuity of modernization the social positions and conflicts of a 'wealth-distributing' society begin to be joined by those of a 'risk-distributing' society. In West Germany we have faced the beginning of this transition since the early 1970s at the latest – that is my thesis. That means that two types of topics and conflicts overlap here. We do not *yet* live in a risk society, but we also no longer live *only* within the distribution conflicts of scarcity societies. To the extent that this transition occurs, there will be a real transformation of society which will lead us out of the previous modes of thought and action.

Can the concept of risk carry the theoretical and historical significance which is demanded of it here? Is this not a primeval phenomenon of human action? Are not risks already characteristic of the industrial society period, against which they are being differentiated here? It is also true that risks are not an invention of modernity. Anyone who set out to discover new countries and continents – like Columbus – certainly accepted 'risks'. But these were *personal* risks, not global dangers like those that arise for all of humanity from nuclear fission or the storage of radioactive waste. In that earlier period, the word 'risk' had a note of bravery and adventure, not the threat of self-destruction of all life on Earth.

Forests have also been dying for some centuries now – first through being transformed into fields, then through reckless overcutting. But the death of forests today occurs *globally*, as the *implicit* consequence of industrialization – with quite different social and political consequences. Heavily wooded countries like Norway and Sweden, which hardly have any pollutant-intensive industries of their own, are also affected. They have to settle up the pollution accounts of other highly industrialized countries with dying trees, plants and animal species.

It is reported that sailors who fell into the Thames in the early nineteenth century did not drown, but rather choked to death inhaling the foul-smelling and poisonous fumes of this London sewer. A walk through the narrow streets of a medieval city would also have been like running the gauntlet for the nose. 'Excrement piles up everywhere, in the streets, at the turnpikes, in the carriages . . . The façades of Parisian houses are decomposing from urine . . . the socially organized constipation threatens to pull all of Paris into the process of putrescent decomposition' (Corbin 1984: 41ff.). It is nevertheless striking that hazards in those days assaulted the nose or the eyes and were thus perceptible to the senses, while the risks of civilization today typically *escape perception* and are localized in the sphere of *physical and chemical formulas* (e.g. toxins in foodstuffs or the nuclear threat).

Another difference is directly connected to this. In the past, the hazards could be traced back to an *under*supply of hygienic technology. Today they have their basis in industrial *over*production. The risks and hazards of today thus differ in an essential way from the superficially similar ones in the Middle Ages through the global nature of their threat (people, animals and plants) and through their *modern* causes. They are risks *of modernization*. They are a *wholesale product* of industrialization, and are systematically intensified as it becomes global.

The concept of risk is directly bound to the concept of reflexive modernization. *Risk* may be defined as a *systematic way of dealing with hazards and insecurities induced and introduced by modernization itself*. Risks, as opposed to older dangers, are consequences which relate to the threatening force of modernization and to its globalization of doubt. They are *politically reflexive*.

Risks, in this meaning of the word, are certainly as old as that development itself. The immiseration of large parts of the population – the 'poverty risk' – kept the nineteenth century holding its breath. 'Threats to skills' and 'health risks' have long been a theme of automation processes and the related social conflicts, protections (and research). It did take some time and struggle to establish social welfare state norms and minimize or limit these kinds of risk politically. Nevertheless, the ecological and high-tech risks that have upset the public for some years now, which will be the focus of what follows, have a new quality. In the afflictions they produce they are no longer tied to their place of origin – the industrial plant. By their nature they endanger *all* forms of life on this planet. The normative bases of their calculation – the concept of accident and insurance, medical precautions, and so on – do not fit the basic dimensions of these modern threats. Atomic plants, for example, are not privately insured or insurable. Atomic accidents are accidents no more (in the limited sense of the word 'accident'). They outlast generations. The affected even include those not yet alive at the time or in the place where the accident occurred but born years later and long distances away.

This means that the calculation of risk as it has been established so far by science and legal institutions *collapses*. Dealing with these consequences of modern productive and destructive forces in the normal terms of risk is a false but nevertheless very effective way of legitimizing them. Risk scientists normally do so as if there is not the gap of a century between the local accidents of the nineteenth century and the often creeping, catastrophic potentials at the end of the twentieth century. Indeed, if you distinguish between calculable and non-calculable threats, under the surface of risk calculation new kinds of *industrialized, decision-produced incalculabilities and threats* are spreading within the globalization of high-risk industries, whether for warfare or welfare purposes. Max Weber's concept of 'rationalization' no longer grasps this late modern reality, produced by successful rationalization. *Along with the growing capacity of technical options [Zweckrationalität] grows the incalculability of their consequences.* Compared to these global consequences, the hazards of primary industrialization indeed belonged to a different age. The dangers of highly developed nuclear and chemical productive forces abolish the foundations and categories according to which we have thought and acted to this point, such as space and time, work and leisure time, factory and nation state, indeed even the borders between continents. To put it differently, in the risk society the unknown and unintended consequences come to be a dominant force in history and society.

The social architecture and political dynamics of such potentials for self-endangerment in civilization will occupy the center of these discussions. The argument can be set out in five theses:

(1) Risks such as those produced in the late modernity differ essentially from wealth. By risks I mean above all radioactivity, which completely evades human perceptive abilities, but also toxins and pollutants in the air, the water and foodstuffs, together with the accompanying short- and long-term effects on plants, animals and people. They induce systematic and often *irreversible* harm, generally remain *invisible*, are based on *causal interpretations*, and thus initially only exist in terms of the (scientific or anti-scientific) *knowledge* about them. They can

thus be changed, magnified, dramatized or minimized within knowledge, and to that extent they are particularly *open to social definition and construction*. Hence the mass media and the scientific and legal professions in charge of defining risks become key social and political positions.

(2) Some people are more affected than others by the distribution and growth of risks, that is, *social risk positions* spring up. In some of their dimensions these follow the inequalities of class and strata positions, but they bring a fundamentally different distributional logic into play. Risks of modernization sooner or later also strike those who produce or profit from them. They contain a *boomerang effect*, which breaks up the pattern of class and national society. Ecological disaster and atomic fallout ignore the borders of nations. Even the rich and powerful are not safe from them. These are hazards not only to health, but also to legitimation, property and profit. *Connected* to the recognition of modernization risks are *ecological devaluations and expropriations*, which frequently and systematically enter into contradiction to the profit and property interests which advance the process of industrialization. Simultaneously, risks produce *new international inequalities*, firstly between the Third World and the industrial states, secondly among the industrial states themselves. They undermine the order of national jurisdictions. In view of the universality and supra-nationality of the circulation of pollutants, the life of a blade of grass in the Bavarian Forest ultimately comes to depend on the making and keeping of international agreements. Risk society in this sense is a world risk society.

(3) Nevertheless, the diffusion and commercialization of risks do not break with the logic of capitalist development completely, but instead they raise the latter to a new stage. There are always losers but also winners in risk definitions. The space between them varies in relation to different issues and power differentials. Modernization risks from the winners' points of view are *big business*. They are the insatiable demands long sought by economists. Hunger can be sated, needs can be satisfied, but *civilization* risks are a *bottomless barrel of demands*, unsatisfiable, infinite, self-producible. One could say along with Luhmann that with the advent of risks, the economy becomes 'self-referential', independent of the surrounding satisfaction of human needs. But that means: with the economic exploitation of the risks it sets free, industrial society produces the hazards and the political potential of the risk society.

(4) One can *possess* wealth, but one can only be *afflicted* by risks; they are, so to speak, *ascribed* by civilization. [Bluntly, one might say: in class and stratification positions being determines consciousness, while in risk positions *consciousness determines being*.] Knowledge gains a new political significance. Accordingly the political potential of the risk society must be elaborated and analyzed in a sociological theory of the origin and diffusion of *knowledge about risks*.

(5) Socially recognized risks, as appears clearly in the discussions of forest destruction, contain a peculiar political explosive: what *was* until now *considered unpolitical becomes political* – *the elimination of the causes in the industrialization*

process itself. Suddenly the public and politics extend their rule into the private sphere of plant management – into product planning and technical equipment. What is at stake in the public dispute over the definition of risks is revealed here in an exemplary fashion: not just secondary health problems for nature and mankind, but the *social, economic and political consequences of these side effects* – collapsing markets, devaluation of capital, bureaucratic checks on plant decisions, the opening of new markets, mammoth costs, legal proceedings and loss of face. In smaller or larger increments – a smog alarm, a toxic spill, etc. – what thus emerges in risk society is the *political potential of catastrophes.* Averting and managing these can include a *reorganization of power and authority.* Risk society is a *catastrophic* society. In it the exceptional condition threatens to become the norm.

Scientific Definition and Distributions of Pollutants

The debate on pollutant and toxic elements in air, water and foodstuffs, as well as on the destruction of nature and the environment in general, is still being conducted exclusively or dominantly in the terms and formulas of *natural* science. It remains unrecognized that a social, cultural and political meaning is inherent in such scientific 'immiseration formulas'. There exists accordingly a danger that an environmental discussion conducted exclusively in chemical, biological and technological terms will inadvertently include human beings in the picture only as *organic material.* Thus the discussion runs the risk of making the same mistake for which it has long and justly reproached the prevailing optimism with respect to industrial progress; it runs the risk of atrophying into a discussion of nature *without* people, without asking about matters of social and cultural significance. Particularly the debates over the last few years, in which all arguments critical of technology and industry were once again deployed, have remained at heart *technocratic* and *naturalistic.* They exhausted themselves in the invocation and publication of the pollutant levels in the air, water and foodstuffs, in relative figures of population growth, energy consumption, food requirements, raw material shortages and so on. They did so with a passion and a singlemindedness as if there had never been people such as a certain Max Weber, who apparently wasted his time showing that without including structures of social power and distribution, bureaucracies, prevailing norms and rationalities, such a debate is either meaningless or absurd, and probably both. An understanding has crept in, according to which modernity is reduced to the frame of reference of technology and nature in the manner of perpetrator and victim. The social, cultural and political risks of modernization remain hidden by this very approach, and from this way of thinking (which is also that of the political environmental movement).

Let us illustrate this with an example. The Rat der Sachverständigen für Umweltfragen (Council of Experts on Environmental Issues) determines in a report that 'in mother's milk beta-hexachlorocyclohexane, hexachlorobenzol and DDT are often found in significant concentrations' (1985: 33). These toxic substances are contained in pesticides and herbicides that have by now been taken off the market. According to the report their origin is undetermined (33). At another point it is stated: 'The exposure of the population to lead is not dangerous on average' (35). What is concealed behind that statement? Perhaps by analogy the following distribution. Two men have two apples. One eats both of them. Thus they have eaten *on average* one each. Transferred to the distribution of foodstuffs on the global scale this statement would mean: 'on average' all the people in the world have enough to eat. The cynicism here is obvious. In one part of the Earth people are dying of hunger, while in the other the consequences of overeating have become a major item of expense. It may be, of course, that this statement about pollutants and toxins is *not* cynical, that the *average* exposure is also the *actual* exposure of *all* groups in the population. But do we know that? In order to defend this statement, is it not a prerequisite that we know what other poisons the people are forced·to inhale and ingest? It is astonishing how *as a matter of course* one inquires about 'the average'. A person who inquires about the average already excludes many socially unequal risk positions. But that is exactly what that person cannot know. Perhaps there are groups and living conditions for which the levels of lead and the like that are 'on average harmless' constitute a *mortal danger*?

The next sentence of the report reads: 'Only in the vicinity of industrial emitters are dangerous concentrations of lead sometimes found in children.' What is characteristic is not just the absence of any social differentiations in this and other reports on pollutants and toxins. It is also characteristic *how* differentiations are made – along *regional* lines with regard to emission sources and according to *age* differences – both criteria that are rooted in *biological* (or more generally, natural scientific) thinking. This cannot be blamed on the expert committees. It only reflects the general state of scientific and social thought with regard to environmental problems. These are generally viewed as matters of nature and technology, or of economics and medicine. What is astonishing about that is that the industrial pollution of the environment and the destruction of nature, with their multifarious effects on the health and social life of people, which only arise in highly developed societies, are characterized by a *loss of social thinking*. This loss becomes caricature – this absence seems to strike no one, not even sociologists themselves.

People inquire about and investigate the distribution of pollutants, toxins, contamination of water, air, and foodstuffs. The results are presented to an alarmed public on multi-colored 'environmental maps', differentiated along regional lines. To the extent that the state of the environment is to be presented in this way, this mode of presentation and consideration is obviously appropriate. As soon as *consequences for people* are to be drawn from it, however, the underlying thought *short-circuits*. Either one implies broadly that *all* people are *equally* affected in the identified pollution centers – independent of their income, education, occupation and the associated eating, living and recreational opportunities and habits (which would have to be proved). Or one ultimately excludes people and the extent of their affliction entirely and speaks only about pollutants and their distributions and effects on the region.

The pollution debate conducted in terms of natural science correspondingly moves between the false conclusion of social afflictions based on biological ones, and a view of nature which excludes the selective affliction of people as well as the social and cultural meaning connected to it. At the same time what is not taken into consideration is that *the same* pollutants can have quite *different* meanings for *different* people, according to age, gender, eating habits, type of work, information, education and so on.

What is particularly aggravating is that investigations which start from individual pollutants can *never* determine the concentration of pollutants *in people*. What may seem 'insignificant' for a single product, is perhaps extremely significant when collected in the 'consumer reservoirs' which people have become in the advanced stage of total marketing. We are in the presence here of a *category error*. A pollution analysis oriented to nature and products is incapable of answering questions about safety, at least as long as the 'safety' or 'danger' has anything to do with the people who swallow or breathe the stuff. What is known is that the taking of several medications can nullify or amplify the effect of each individual one. Now people obviously do not (yet) live by medications alone. They also breathe the pollutants in the air, drink those in the water, eat those in the vegetables, and so on. In other words, the insignificances can add up quite significantly. Do they thereby become more and more insignificant – as is usual for sums according to the rules of mathematics?

On the Knowledge Dependence of Modernization Risks

Risks like wealth are the object of distributions, and both constitute positions – risk positions and class positions respectively. In each case, however, one is concerned with a quite different good and a quite different controversy on its distribution. In the case of social wealth, one is dealing with consumer goods, incomes, educational opportunities, property, etc. as desirable items in scarcity. By contrast, risks are an *incidental* problem of modernization in *undesirable abundance*. These must be either eliminated or denied and reinterpreted. The *positive logic of acquisition* contrasts with a *negative logic of disposition*, avoidance, denial, and reinterpretation.

While such things as income and education are consumable goods that can be experienced by the individual, the existence of and distribution of risks and hazards are *mediated on principle through argument*. That which impairs health or destroys nature is not recognizable to one's own feeling or eye, and even where it is seemingly in plain view, qualified expert judgment is still required to determine it 'objectively'. Many of the newer risks (nuclear or chemical contaminations, pollutants in foodstuffs, diseases of civilization) completely escape human powers of direct perception. The focus is more and more on hazards which are neither visible nor perceptible to the victims; hazards that in some cases may not even take effect within the lifespans of those affected, but instead during those of their children; hazards in any case that require the 'sensory organs' of science – *theories, experiments, measuring instruments – in order to become visible or interpretable as hazards at all*. The paradigm of these hazards is the gene-altering effects of radioactivity, which, as the reactor accident at Three Mile Island shows, imperceptibly abandon the victims completely to the judgments, mistakes and controversies of experts, while subjecting them to terrible psychological stresses. [. . .]

Ambivalences: Individuals and the Developed Labor Market

At the core of this section lies the assessment that we are eye witnesses to a social transformation within modernity, in the course of which people will be *set free* from the social forms of industrial society – class, stratification, family, gender status of men and women – just as during the course of the Reformation people were 'released' from the secular rule of the Church into society. The argument can be outlined in seven theses.

(1) In the welfare states of the West, reflexive modernization dissolves the traditional parameters of industrial society: class culture and consciousness, gender and family roles. It dissolves these forms of the conscience collective, on which depend and to which refer the social and political organizations and institutions in industrial society. These detraditionalizations happen in a *social surge of individualization*. At the same time the *relations* of inequality remain stable. How is this possible? Against the background of a comparatively high material standard of living and advanced social security systems, the people have been removed from class commitments and have to refer to themselves in planning their individual labor market biographies.

The process of individualization has previously been claimed largely for the developing bourgeoisie. In a different form, however, it is also characteristic of the 'free wage laborer' in modern capitalism, of the dynamics of labor market processes. labor mobility education and changing occupation. The entry into the labor market dissolves such bindings and is connected over and over again with 'liberations' [*Freisetzungen*] in a double sense from traditional networks and the constraints of the labor market. Family, neighborhood, even friendship, as well as ties to a regional culture and landscape, contradict the individual mobility and the mobile individual required by the labor market. These surges of individualization do compete with the experiences of a collective fate (mass unemployment and deskilling); however, under the conditions of a welfare state, class biographies, which are somehow ascribed, become transformed into reflexive biographies which depend on the decisions of the actor.

(2) With respect to the interpretation of *social inequality*, therefore, an ambivalent situation arises. For the Marxist theoretician of classes as well

as for the investigator of stratification, it may be that not much has changed. The separations in the hierarchy of income and the fundamental conditions of wage labor have remained the same. On the other hand, ties to a social class recede mysteriously into the background for the actions of people. Status-based social milieus and lifestyles typical of a class culture lose their luster. The tendency is towards the emergence of individualized forms and conditions of existence, which compel people – for the sake of their own material survival – to make themselves the center of their own planning and conduct of life. Increasingly, everyone has to choose between different options, including as to which group or subculture one wants to be identified with. In fact, one has to choose and change one's social identity as well and take the risks in doing so. In this sense, individualization means the variation and differentiation of lifestyles and forms of life, opposing the thinking behind the traditional categories of large-group societies – which is to say, classes, estates, and social stratification.

In Marxist theories the antagonism between classes was linked once and for all to the 'essence' of industrial capitalism. This conceptualizing of historical experience into a permanent form can be expressed as the *law of the excluded middle*: *either* capitalism exits the stage of world history through the only door open to it – the intensifying class struggle – with the 'big bang of revolution', and then reappears through the back door, with transformed relationships of ownership, as socialist society; *or* the classes struggle and struggle and struggle. The individualization thesis asserts the excluded middle, that the dynamism of the labor market backed up by the welfare state has diluted or dissolved the social classes *within* capitalism. To put it in Marxist terms, we increasingly confront the phenomenon of a capitalism *without* classes, but with individualized social inequality and all the related social and political problems.

(3) This tendency to the 'classlessness' of social inequality appears as a textbook example in the distribution of mass unemployment. On the one hand, the proportion of the unemployed who have been without work for a long time is rising, as is the proportion of people who have left the labor market, or never entered it at all. On the other hand, the constancy of the number of unemployed by no means implies a constancy of registered cases and affected persons. In Germany during the years from 1974 to 1983, roughly 12.5 million people, or *every third* gainfully employed German, were unemployed at least once. Simultaneously there are growing gray zones between registered and unregistered unemployment (among housewives, youths, early retirers) as well as between employment and underemployment (flexibilized work hours and forms of employment). The broad distribution of more or less temporary unemployment thus coincides with a growing number of long-term unemployed and with new hybrids between unemployment and employment. The culture of social classes is unable to provide a context of orientation for this. Intensification *and* individualization of social inequalities interlock. As a consequence, problems of the system are lessened politically and transformed into personal failure. In the detraditionalized

modes of living, a *new immediacy for individual and society* arises, the immediacy of *crisis and sickness*, in the sense that social crises appear to be of individual origin, and are perceived as social only indirectly and to a very limited extent.

(4) The 'freeing' relative to status-like social classes is joined by a 'freeing' relative to *gender status*, as reflected primarily in the changed condition of *women*. The most recent data speak clearly: it is not social position or lack of education but *divorce* which is the trap-door through which women fall into the 'new poverty'. This is an expression of the extent to which women are being cut loose from support as spouses and housewives, a process which can no longer be checked. The spiral of individualization is thus taking hold *inside* the family: labor market, education, mobility – everything is doubled and trebled. Families become the scene of a continuous juggling of diverging multiple ambitions among occupa- tional necessities, educational constraints, parental duties and the monotony of housework. The type of the 'negotiated family' comes into being, in which indi- viduals of both genders enter into a more or less regulated exchange of emotional comfort, which is always cancellable.

(5) Even these quarrels between the sexes, which occur as matters for the indi- viduals involved, have another dimension. From a theoretical point of view, what happens between a man and a woman, both inside and outside the family, follows a general pattern. These are the consequences of reflexive modernization and the private parameters of industrial society, since the industrial social order has always divided the indivisible principles of modernity – individual freedom and equality – and has ascribed them by birth to only one gender and with- held them from the other. Industrial society *never* is and *never* was possible *only* as industrial society, but always as half industrial and half *feudal* society, whose feudal side is not a relic of tradition, but the *product* and *foundation* of industrial society. In that way, as industrial society triumphs, it has always promoted the dissolution of its family morality, its gender fates, its taboos relative to marriage, parenthood and sexuality, even the reunification of housework and wage labor.

(6) This brings out clearly the special features of present-day individualization (by comparison to apparently similar ones in the Renaissance or the early indus- trial age). The new aspect results from the consequences. The place of hereditary estates is no longer taken by social classes, nor does the stable frame of reference of gender and the family take the place of social classes. *The individual himself or herself becomes the reproduction unit of the social in the lifeworld*. What the social is and does has to be involved with individual decisions. Or put another way, both within and outside the family, the individuals become the agents of their educational and market-mediated subsistence and the related life planning and organization. Biography itself is acquiring a reflexive project.

This differentiation of individual conditions in the developed labor market society must not, however, be equated with successful emancipation. In this sense, individualism does not signify the beginning of the self-creation of the world by the resurrected individual. Instead it accompanies tendencies toward the *institutionalization* and *standardization* of ways of life. The detraditionalized individuals become dependent on the labor market, and *with that*, dependent on education, consumption, regulations and support from social laws, traffic planning, product offers, possibilities and fashions in medical, psychological and pedagogical counseling and care. All of this points to the special forms of control which are being established here.

(7) Correspondingly, individualization is understood here as a historically contradictory *process of societalization*. The collectivity and standardization of the resulting 'individual' modes of living are of course difficult to grasp. Nevertheless, it is precisely the eruption and the growing awareness of these contradictions which can lead to *new socio-cultural commonalities*. It may be that social movements and citizens' groups are formed in relation to modernization risks and risk situations. It may be that in the course of individualization expectations are aroused in the form of a desire for a 'life of one's own' (in material, temporal and spatial terms, and in structuring social relationships) – expectations which however face social and political resistance. In this way *new social movements* come into existence again and again. On the one hand, these react to the increasing risks and the growing risk consciousness and risk conflicts; on the other hand, they experiment with social relationships, personal life and one's own body in the numerous variants of the alternative and youth subcultures. Not least of all, therefore, communities are produced from the forms and experiences of the protest that is ignited by administrative and industrial interference in private 'personal life', and develop their aggressive stance in opposition to these encroachments. In this sense, on the one hand the new social movements (ecology, peace, feminism) are expressions of the new risk situations in the risk society. On the other, they result from the search for social and personal identities and commitments in detraditionalized culture.

Consider
1. What does Ulrich Beck understand by 'risk'? How does his use of the term differ from its colloquial meaning?
2. 'The concept of risk is directly bound to the concept of reflexive modernization. Risk may be defined as a systematic way of dealing with hazards and insecurities induced and introduced by modernization itself. Risks, as opposed to older dangers, are consequences which relate to the threatening force of modernization and to its globalization of doubt.' Discuss.
3. To what extent do you live in a 'risk society'? Based on Ulrich Beck's definition, draw up list of risks to which you are exposed in your everyday life.
4. To what extent, and how, are contemporary risks global in nature? Answer this question in reference to one of the following cases:

   (a) Nuclear energy
   (b) Genetically manufactured crops
   (c) Global warming.

   In order to be able to answer the question, you will need to conduct additional background research.

5.7 Consumer culture

The concepts of risk and rationalisation together draw attention to general developmental tendencies in the modern world. In the remainder of this chapter, we will consider more concrete expressions of global modernity. We will begin with the issue of consumer culture.

Many of the examples used in this book, such as fast food or smart phones, belong to the realm of consumer culture. We might provisionally define consumer culture as *a way of life based upon the identification with particular goods and services, grounded in a socio-economic system that encourages the desire for such identification.* Consider the following example: In 2006, Apple launched a series of TV advertisements to promote the sales of Macintosh computers. Notably, these advertisements did not simply highlight the superior functionality of a Macintosh. Instead, they emphasised that owning one is a trait of 'cool' people: Under the slogan 'I'm a PC. – I'm a Mac', they displayed two people, one a supposedly typical owner of Windows PCs and one an Apple customer. The former came across as a stressed, overweight, somewhat unhealthy workaholic, while the latter appeared casual, relaxed and creative.

This marketing campaign alludes to the fact that the ownership of high-tech goods such as computers is today not purely a matter of getting work done efficiently. Instead, the computer and its brand name may stand for personal qualities we want ourselves and others to believe we own. Apple has firmly established an association between the Macintosh brand and the traits 'cool' and 'creative', and this association plays a significant role in many people's choice to buy these relatively expensive computers. Moreover, this is not an isolated example. Rather, the consumption of branded goods and services, from clothing to electronics, is a major part of many people's ways of life throughout the world, shaping the ways they think and feel about themselves.

This way of life has been deliberately encouraged by major corporations in the latter part of the twentieth century. Instead of concentrating on the efficient production of goods and services, recent decades were characterised by an increasing attention to marketing, brands and matters of image in the competition for customers. As sociologists Scott Lash and Celia Lury (2007) argue, the purchase and ownership of branded things does not only allow us to identify with the traits for which they stand. Rather, it also serves as a marker of difference, setting us apart from others. The Apple advertising campaign shows this very clearly. Not only does it enable Macintosh users to feel cool about themselves, it also gives them the entitlement to look down upon decidedly uncool and technically handicapped PC owners.

With the rise of global capitalism, consumer culture has also become globalised. The spread of fast-food chains such as McDonald's is a clear marker of this development, as is the popularity which many other products and brands enjoy. Apple's 'I'm a Mac' campaign was broadcast globally from the USA to Japan. Western luxury goods enjoy an unprecedented popularity among the newly affluent Chinese middle class, and China has recently begun to turn into the world's largest consumer of branded luxury goods (Goodman 2008). At the same time, the inability to partake in consumer culture may also serve as a marker of deprivation and social exclusion. A conspicuous feature of the London riots of August 2008 were reports about looters' particular attention to shops selling brand clothes, electronics, jewellery, etc. Perhaps this might be understood as an indication of the frustration felt by many of those who, cut off from regular employment and access to education, are unable to join in the consumerism that dominates London life today.

Reading

Williams, Raymond (2006), 'Advertising: The Magic System', in Williams, R. *Culture and Materialism: Selected Essays*, London: Verso, pp. 170–2, 177–86

Advertising: the Magic System

1. History

It is customary to begin even the shortest account of the history of advertising by recalling the three thousand year old papyrus from Thebes, offering a reward for a runaway slave, and to go on to such recollections as the crier in the streets of Athens, the paintings of gladiators, with sentences urging attendance at their combats, in ruined Pompeii, and the fly-bills on the pillars of the Forum in Rome. This pleasant little ritual can be quickly performed, and as quickly forgotten: it is, of course, altogether too modest. If by advertising we mean what was meant by Shakespeare and the translators of the Authorized Version – the processes of taking or giving notice of something – it is as old as human society, and some pleasant recollections from the Stone Age could be quite easily devised.

The real business of the historian of advertising is more difficult: to trace the development from processes of specific attention and information to an institutionalized system of commercial information and persuasion; to relate this to changes in society and in the economy: and to trace changes in method in the context of changing organizations and intentions.

The spreading of information, by the crier or by handwritten and printed broadsheets, is known from all periods of English society. The first signs of anything more organized come in the seventeenth century, with the development of newsbooks, mercuries and newspapers. Already certain places, such as St Paul's in London, were recognized as centres for the posting of specific bills, and the extension of such posting to the new printed publications was a natural development. The material of such advertisements ranged from offers and wants in personal service, notices of the publication of books, and details of runaway servants, apprentices, horses and dogs, to announcements of new commodities available at particular shops, enthusiastic announcements of remedies and specifics, and notices of the public showing of monsters, prodigies and freaks. While the majority were the simple, basically factual and specific notices we now call 'classified', there were also direct recommendations, as here, from 1658:

> That Excellent, and by all Physicians, approved China drink, called by the Chineans Tcha, by other nations *Tay* alias *Tee*, is sold at the Sultaness Head Cophee-House in Sweeting's Rents, by the Royal Exchange, London.

Mention of the physicians begins that process of extension from the conventional recommendations of books as 'excellent' or 'admirable' and the conventional adjectives which soon become part of the noun, in a given context (as in my native village, every dance is a Grand Dance). The most extravagant early extensions were in the field of medicines, and it was noted in 1652, of the writers of copy in news-books:

> There is never a mountebank who, either by professing of chymistry or any other art drains money from the people of the nation but these arch-cheats have a share in the booty – because the fellow cannot lye sufficiently himself he gets one of these to do't for him.

Looking up, in the 1950s, from the British Dental Association's complaints of misleading television advertising of toothpastes, we can recognize the advertisement, in 1660, of a 'most Excellent and Approved DENTIFRICE', which not only makes the teeth 'white as Ivory', but

> being constantly used, the Parties using it are never troubled with the Tooth-ache. It fastens the Teeth, sweetens the Breath, and preserves the Gums and Mouth from Cankers and Imposthumes.

Moreover

> the right are onely to be had at Thomas Rookes, Stationer, at the Holy Lamb at the east end of St Paul's Church, near the School, in sealed papers at 12d the paper.

In the year of the Plague, London was full of

> SOVEREIGN Cordials against the Corruption of the Air.

These did not exactly succeed, but a long and profitable trade, and certain means of promoting it, were now firmly established.

With the major growth of newspapers, from the 1690s, the volume of advertisements notably increased. The great majority of them were still of the specific 'classified' kind, and were grouped in regular sections of the paper or magazine. Ordinary household goods were rarely advertised; people knew where to get these. But, apart from the wants and the runaways, new things, from the latest book or play to new kinds of luxury or 'cosmatick' made their way through these columns. By and large, it was still only in the pseudo-medical and toilet advertisements that persuasion methods were evident. The announcements were conventionally printed, and there was hardly any illustration. Devices of emphasis – the hand, the asterisk, the NB – can be found, and sailing announcements had small woodcuts of a ship, runaway notices similar cuts of a man looking back over his shoulder. But, in the early eighteenth century, these conventional figures became too numerous, and most newspapers banned them. The manufacturer of a 'Spring Truss' who illustrated his device, had few early imitators.

A more general tendency was noted by Johnson in 1758:

> Advertisements are now so numerous that they are very negligently perused, and it is therefore become necessary to gain attention by magnificence of promises and by eloquence sometimes sublime and sometimes pathetick. Promise, large promise, is the soul of an advertisement. I remember a wash-ball that had a quality truly wonderful – it gave *an exquisite edge to the razor*! The trade of advertising is now so near to perfection that it is not easy to propose any improvement.

This is one of the earliest of 'gone about as far as they can go' conclusions on advertisers, but Johnson, after all, was sane. Within the situation he knew, of newspapers directed to a small public largely centred on the coffee-houses, the natural range was from private notices (of service wanted and offered, of things lost, found, offered and needed) through shopkeepers' information (of actual goods in their establishments) to puffs for occasional and marginal products. In this last kind, and within the techniques open to them, the puffmen had indeed used, intensively, all the traditional forms of persuasion, and of cheating and lying. The mountebank and the huckster had got into print, and, while the majority of advertisements remained straightforward, the influence of this partic-ular group was on its way to giving 'advertising' a more specialized meàning. [. . .]

Yet still in the 1850s advertising was mainly of a classified kind, in specified parts of the publication. It was still widely felt, in many kinds of trade, that (as a local newspaper summarized the argument in 1859)

> it is not *respectable*. Advertising is resorted to for the purposes of introducing inferior articles into the market.

Rejecting this argument, the newspaper (*The Eastbourne Gazette and Fashionable Intelligencer*) continued:

> Competition is the soul of business, and what fairer or more legitimate means of competition can be adopted than the availing oneself of a channel

to recommend goods to public notice which is open to all? Advertising is an open, fair, legitimate and respectable means of competition; bearing upon its face the impress of free-trade, and of as much advantage to the consumer as the producer.

The interesting thing is not so much the nature of this argument, but that, in 1859, it still had to be put in quite this way. Of course the article concluded by drawing attention to the paper's own advertising rates, but even then, to get the feel of the whole situation, we have to look at the actual advertisements flanking the article. Not only are they all from local tradesmen, but their tone is still eighteenth-century, as for example:

> To all who pay cash and can appreciate
> Good and Fine Teas
> Charles Lea
> Begs most respectfully to solicit a trial of his present stock which has been selected with the greatest care, and paid for before being cleared from the Bonded warehouses in London . . .

In all papers, this was still the usual tone, but, as in the eighteenth century, one class of product attracted different methods. Probably the first nationally advertised product was Warren's Shoe Blacking, closely followed by Rowland's Macassar Oil (which produced the counter-offensive of the antimacassar), Spencer's Chinese Liquid Hair Dye, and Morison's Universal Pill. In this familiar field, as in the eighteenth century, the new advertising was effectively shaped, while for selling cheap books the practice of including puffs in announcements was widely extended. Warren's Shoe Blacking had a drawing of a cat spitting at its own reflection, and hack verses were widely used:

> The goose that on our Ock's green shore
> Thrives to the size of Albatross
> Is twice the goose it was before
> When washed with Neighbour Goodman's sauce.

Commercial purple was another writing style, especially for pills:

> The spring and fall of the leaf has been always remarked as the periods when disease, if it be lurking in the system, is sure to show itself. (Parr's Life Pills, 1843).

The manner runs back to that of the eighteenth-century hucksters and mountebanks, but what is new is its scale. The crowned heads of Europe were being signed up for testimonials (the Tsar of all the Russias took and recommended Revalenta Arabica, while the Balm of Syriacum, a 'sovereign remedy for both bodily and mental decay', was advertised as used in Queen Victoria's household). Holloway, of course a 'Professor', spent £5,000 a year, in the 1840s, spreading his Universal Ointment, and in 1855 exceeded £30,000.

Moreover, with the newspaper public still limited, the puffmen were going on the streets. Fly-posting, on every available space, was now a large and organized trade, though made hazardous by rival gangs (paste for your own, blacking for the others). It was necessary in 1837 to pass a London act prohibiting posting without the owner's consent (it proved extremely difficult to enforce). In 1862 came the United Kingdom Bill-posters Association, with an organized system of special hoardings, which had become steadily more necessary as the flood of paste swelled. Handbills ('throwaways') were distributed in the streets of Victorian London with extraordinary intensity of coverage; in some areas a walk down one street would collect as many as two hundred different leaflets. Advertising vans and vehicles of all sorts, such as the seven-foot lath-and-plaster Hat in the Strand, on which Carlyle commented, crowded the streets until 1853, when they were forbidden. Hundreds of casual labourers were sent out with placards and sandwich boards, and again in 1853 had to be officially removed from pavement to gutter. Thus the streets of Victorian London bore increasingly upon their face 'the impress of free trade', yet still, with such methods largely reserved to the sellers of pills, adornments and sensational literature, the basic relation between advertising and production had only partly changed. Carlyle said of the hatter, whose 'whole industry is turned to *persuade* us that he has made' better hats, that 'the quack has become God'. But as yet, on the whole, it was only the quack.

The period between the 1850s and the end of the century saw a further expansion in advertising, but still mainly along the lines already established. After the 1855 abolition of Stamp Duty, the circulation of newspapers rapidly increased, and many new ones were successfully founded. But the attitude of the Press to advertising, throughout the second half of the century, remained cautious. In particular, editors were extremely resistant to any break-up in the column layout of their pages, and hence to any increase in size of display type. Advertisers tried in many ways to get round this, but with little success.

[. . .]

3. Transformation

The strange fact is, looking back, that the great bulk of products of the early stages of the factory system had been sold without extensive advertising, which had grown up mainly in relation to fringe products and novelties. Such advertising as there was, of basic articles, was mainly by shopkeepers, drawing attention to the quality and competitive pricing of the goods they stocked. In this comparatively simple phase of competition, large-scale advertising and the brand-naming of goods were necessary only at the margin, or in genuinely new things. The real signs of change began to appear in the 1880s and 1890s, though they can only be correctly interpreted when seen in the light of the fully developed 'new' advertising of the period between the wars.

The formation of modern advertising has to be traced, essentially, to certain characteristics of the new 'monopoly' (corporate) capitalism, first clearly evident in this same period of the end and turn of the nineteenth century. The Great Depression which in general dominated the period from 1875 to the middle 1890s (though broken by occasional recoveries and local strengths) marked the turning point between two modes of industrial organization and two basically different approaches to distribution. After the Depression, and its big falls in prices, there was a more general and growing fear of productive capacity, a marked tendency to reorganize industrial ownership into larger units and combines, and a growing desire, by different methods, to organize and where possible control the market. Among the means of achieving the latter purposes, advertising on a new scale, and applied to an increasing range of products, took an important place.

Modern advertising, that is to say, belongs to the system of market-control which, at its full development, includes the growth of tariffs and privileged areas, cartel-quotas, trade campaigns, price-fixing by manufacturers, and that form of economic imperialism which assured certain markets overseas by political control of their territories. There was a concerted expansion of export advertising, and at home the biggest advertising campaign yet seen accompanied the merger of several tobacco firms into the Imperial Tobacco Company, to resist American competition. In 1901, a 'fabulous sum' was offered for the entire eight pages of *The Star*, by a British tobacco advertiser, and when this was refused four pages were taken, a 'world's record', to print 'the most costly, colossal and convincing advertisement ever used in an evening newspaper the wide world o'er'. Since the American firms retaliated, with larger advertisements of their own, the campaign was both heavy and prolonged. This can be taken as the first major example of a new advertising situation.

That this period of fundamental change in the economy is the key to the emergence of full-scale modern advertising is shown also by radical changes within the organization of advertising itself. From the eighteenth century, certain shops had been recognized as collecting agencies for advertisements, on behalf of newspapers. In the nineteenth century, this system (which still holds today for some classified advertisements) was extended to the buying of space by individual agents, who then sold it to advertisers. With the growth in the volume of advertising, this kind of space-selling, and then a more developed system of space-brokerage, led to a growth of importance in the agencies, which still, however, were virtually agents of the Press, or at most intermediaries. Gradually, and with increasing emphasis from the 1880s, the agencies began to change their functions, offering advice and service to manufacturers, though still having space to sell for the newspapers. By the turn of the century, the modern system had emerged: newspapers had their own advertising managers, who advanced quite rapidly in status from junior employees to important executives, while the agencies stopped selling space, and went over to serving and advising manufacturers, and booking space after a campaign had been agreed. In 1900 the Advertisers Protection Society, later the Incorporated Society of British Advertisers, was formed: partly to defend advertising against such attacks as those of SCAPA, partly to bring pressure on newspapers to publish their sales figures, so that campaigns might be properly planned. Northcliffe, after initial hesitations about advertising (he had wanted to run *Answers* without it), came to realize its possibilities as a new basis for financing newspapers. He published his sales figures, challenged his rivals to do the same, and in effect created the modern structure of the Press as an industry, in close relation to the new advertising. In 1917 the Association of British Advertising Agents was founded, and in 1931, with the founding of the Audit Bureau of Circulations, publishing audited net sales, the basic structure was complete.

It is in this same period that we hear first, with any emphasis, of advertising as a profession, a public service, and a necessary part of the economy. A further aspect of the reorganization was a more conscious and more serious attention to the 'psychology of advertising'. As it neared the centre of the economy, it began staking its claims to be not only a profession, but an art and a science.

The half-century between 1880 and 1930, then, saw the full development of an organized system of commercial information and persuasion, as part of the modern distributive system in conditions of large-scale capitalism. Although extended to new kinds of product, advertising drew, in its methods, on its own history and experience. There is an obvious continuity between the methods used to sell pills and washballs in the eighteenth century ('promise, large promise, a quality truly wonderful') and the methods used in the twentieth century to sell anything from a drink to a political party. In this sense, it is true to say that all commerce has followed the quack. But if we look at advertising before, say, 1914, its comparative crudeness is immediately evident. The 'most costly, colossal and convincing advertisement' of 1901 shows two badly-drawn men in tails, clinking port-glasses between announcements that the cigarettes are five a penny, and the slogan ('The Englishman's Toast – Don't be gulled by Yankee bluff, support John Bull with every puff') is in minute type by comparison with 'Most Costly' and 'Advertisement'. Play on fear of illness was of course normal, as it had been throughout quack advertising, and there were simple promises of attractiveness and reputation if particular products were used. But true 'psychological' advertising is very little in evidence before the First War, and where it is its techniques, both in appeal and in draughtsmanship and layout, are crude. Appropriately enough, perhaps, it was in the war itself, when now not a market but a nation had to be controlled and organized, yet in democratic conditions and without some of the older compulsions, that new kinds of persuasion were developed and applied. Where the badly-drawn men with their port and gaspers belong to an old world, such a poster as 'Daddy, what did YOU do in the Great War' belongs to the new. The drawing is careful and detailed: the curtains, the armchair, the grim numb face of the father, the little girl on his knee pointing to her open picture-book, the boy at his feet intent on his toy-soldiers. Alongside the traditional appeals to patriotism lay this kind of entry into basic personal relationships and anxieties. Another poster managed to suggest that a man who would let down his country would also let down his sweetheart or his wife.

The pressures, of course, were immense: the needs of the war, the needs of the economic system. We shall not understand advertising if we keep the argument at the level of appeals to taste and decency, which advertisers should respect. The need to control nominally free men, like the need to control nominally free customers, lay very deep in the new kind of society. Kitchener, demanding an Army, was as startled by the new methods as many a traditional manufacturer by the whole idea of advertising, which he associated with dubious products. In both cases, the needs of the system dictated the methods, and traditional standards and reticences were steadily abandoned when ruin seemed the only alternative.

Slowly, after the war, advertising turned from the simple proclamation and reiteration, with simple associations, of the earlier respectable trade, and prepared to develop, for all kinds of product, the old methods of the quack and the new methods of psychological warfare. The turn was not even yet complete, but the tendencies, from the twenties, were evident. Another method of organizing the market, through consumer credit, had to be popularized, and in the process changed from the 'never-never', which was not at all respectable, to the primly respectable 'hire-purchase' and the positively respectable 'consumer credit'. By 1933, a husband had lost his wife because he had failed to take this 'easy way' of providing a home for her. Meanwhile Body Odour, Iron Starvation, Night Starvation, Listlessness and similar disabilities menaced not only personal health, but jobs, marriages and social success.

These developments, of course, produced a renewed wave of criticism of advertising, and, in particular, ridicule of its confident absurdities. In part this was met by a now standard formula: 'one still hears criticism of advertising, but it is not realized how much has been done, within the profession, to improve it' (for example, a code of ethics, in 1924, pledging the industry, *inter alia* 'to tell the advertising story simply and without exaggeration and to avoid even a tendency to mislead'. If advertisers write such pledges, who then writes the advertisements?). The 'super-sensitive faddists' were rediscovered, and the 'enemies of free enterprise'. Proposals by Huxley, Russell, Leavis, Thompson and others, that children should be trained to study advertisements critically, were described, in a book called *The Ethics of Advertising*, as amounting to 'cynical manipulation of the infant mind'.

But the most significant reply to the mood of critical scepticism was in the advertisements themselves: the development of a knowing, sophisticated, humorous advertising, which acknowledged the scepticism and made claims either casual and offhand or so ludicrously exaggerated as to include the critical response (for example, the Guinness advertisements, written by Dorothy Sayers, later a critic of advertising). Thus it became possible to 'know all the arguments' against advertising, and yet accept or write pieces of charming or amusing copy.

One sustained special attack, on an obviously vulnerable point, was in the field of patent medicines. A vast amount of misleading and dangerous advertising of this kind had been repeatedly exposed, and eventually, by Acts of 1939 and 1941, and by a Code of Standards in 1950, the advertisement of cures for certain specified diseases, and a range of misleading devices, was banned. This was a considerable step forward, in a limited field, and the Advertising Association was among its sponsors. If we remember the history of advertising, and how the sellers of ordinary products learned from the quack methods that are still used in less obviously dangerous fields, the change is significant. It is like nothing so much as the newly-crowned Henry the Fifth dismissing Falstaff with contempt. Advertising had come to power, at the centre of the economy, and it had to get rid of the disreputable friends of its youth: it now both wanted and needed to be respectable.

4. Advertising in Power

Of the coming to power there was now no question. Estimates of expenditure in the inter-war years vary considerably, but the lowest figure, for direct advertising in a single year, is £85,000,000 and the highest £200,000,000. Newspapers derived half their income from advertising, and almost every industry and service, outside the old professions, advertised extensively. With this kind of weight behind it, advertising was and knew itself to be a solid sector of the establishment.

Some figures from 1935 are interesting, showing advertising expenditure as a proportion of sales:

Proprietary medicines	29.4%
Toilet goods	21.3%
Soaps, polishes etc	14.1%
Tobacco	9.3%
Petrol and oil	8.2%
Cereals, jams, biscuits	5.9%
Sweets	3.2%
Beer	1.8%
Boots and Shoes	1.0%
Flour	0.5%

The industry's connections with its origins are evident: the three leading categories are those which pioneered advertising of the modern kind. But more significant, perhaps, is that such ordinary things as boots, shoes and flour should be in the table at all. This, indeed, is the new economy, deriving not so much from the factory system and the growth of communications, as from an advanced system of capitalist production, distribution and market control.

Alongside the development of new kinds of appeal came new media. Apart from such frills as sky-writing, there was commercial radio, not yet established in Britain (though the pressure was there) but begun elsewhere in the 1920s and beamed to Britain from the 1930s. Commercial television, in the 1950s, got through fairly easily. Among new methods, in this growth, are the product jingle, begun in commercial radio and now reaching classic status, and the open alliance between advertisers and apparently independent journalists and broadcasters. To build a reputation as an honest reporter, and then use it either openly to recommend a product or to write or speak about it alongside an advertisement for it, as in the evening-paper 'special supplements', became commonplace. And what was wrong? After all, the crowned heads of Europe, and many of our own Ladies, had been selling pills and soaps for years. The extension to political advertising, either direct or by pressure-groups, also belongs, in its extensive phase, to this period of establishment; in the 1950s it has been running at a very high rate indeed.

The only check, in fact, to this rapidly expanding industry was during the last war, though this was only partial and temporary, and the years since the war, and especially the 1950s, have brought a further spectacular extension. It is ironic to look back at a book published in wartime, by one of the best writers on advertising, Denys Thompson, and read this:

> A second reason for these extensive extracts is that advertising as we know it may be dispensed with, after the war. We are getting on very well with a greatly diminished volume of commercial advertising in wartime, and it is difficult to envisage a return to the 1919-1939 conditions in which publicity proliferated.

Mr Thompson, like Dr Johnson two centuries earlier, is a sane man, but it is never safe to conclude that puffing has reached its maximum distension. The history, rightly read, points to a further major growth, and to more new methods. The highly organized field of market study, motivation research, and retained sociologists and psychologists, is extremely formidable, and no doubt has many surprises in store for us. Talent of quite new kinds is hired with increasing ease. And there is one significant development which must be noted in conclusion: the extension of organized publicity.

'Public Relations'

Advertising was developed to sell goods, in a particular kind of economy. Publicity has been developed to sell persons, in a particular kind of culture. The methods are often basically similar: the arranged incident, the 'mention', the advice on branding, packaging and a good 'selling line'. I remember being told by a man I knew at university (he had previously explained how useful, to his profession as an advertiser, had been his training in the practical criticism of advertisements) that advertisements you booked and paid for were really old stuff; the real thing was what got through as ordinary news. This seems to happen now with goods: 'product centenaries', for example. But with persons it is even more extensive. It began in entertainment, particularly with film actors, and it is still in this field that it does most of its work. It is very difficult to pin down, because the border-line between the item or photograph picked up in the ordinary course of journal-ism and broadcasting, and the similar item or photograph that has been arranged and paid for, either directly or through special hospitality by a publicity agent, is obviously difficult to draw. Enough stories get through, and are even boasted about, to indicate that the paid practice is extensive, though payment, except to the agent, is usually in hospitality (if that word can be used) or in kind. Certainly, readers of newspapers should be aware that the 'personality' items, presented as ordinary news stories or gossip, will often have been paid for, in one way or another, in a system that makes straightforward advertising, by comparison, look respectable. Nor is this confined to what is called 'show business'; it has certainly entered literature, and it has probably entered politics.

The extension is natural, in a society where selling, by any effective means, has become a primary ethic. The spectacular growth of advertising, and then its extension to apparently independent reporting, has behind it not a mere pressure-group, as in the days of the quacks, but the whole impetus of a society. It can then be agreed that we have come a long way from the papyrus of the run-away slave and the shouts of the town-crier: that what we have to look at is an organized and extending system, at the centre of our national life.

5. The System

In the last hundred years, then, advertising has developed from the simple announcements of shopkeepers and the persuasive arts of a few marginal dealers into a major part of capitalist business organization. This is important enough, but the place of advertising in society goes far beyond this commercial context. It is increasingly the source of finance for a whole range of general communica-tion, to the extent that in 1960 our majority television service and almost all our newspapers and periodicals could not exist without it. Further, in the last forty years and now at an increasing rate, it has passed the frontier of the selling of goods and services and has become involved with the teaching of social and personal values; it is also rapidly entering the world of politics. Advertising is also, in a sense, the official art of modern capitalist society: it is what 'we' put up in 'our' streets and use to fill up to half of 'our' newspapers and magazines: and it commands the services of perhaps the largest organized body of writers and artists, with their attendant managers and advisers, in the whole society. Since this is the actual social status of advertising, we shall only understand it with any adequacy if we can develop a kind of total analysis in which the economic, social and cultural facts are visibly related. We may then also find, taking advertising as a major form of modern social communication, that we can understand our society itself in new ways.

It is often said that our society is too materialist, and that advertising reflects this. We are in the phase of a relatively rapid distribution of what are called 'consumer goods', and advertising, with its emphasis on 'bringing the good things of life', is taken as central for this reason. But it seems to me that in this respect our society is quite evidently not materialist enough, and that this, paradoxically, is the result of a failure in social meanings, values and ideals.

It is impossible to look at modern advertising without realising that the material object being sold is never enough: this indeed is the crucial cultural quality of its modern forms. If we were sensibly materialist, in that part of our living in which we use things, we should find most advertising to be of an insane irrelevance. Beer would be enough for us, without the additional promise that in drinking it we show ourselves to be manly, young in heart, or neighbourly. A washing-machine would be a useful machine to wash clothes, rather than an indication that we are forward-looking or an object of envy to our neighbours. But if these associations sell beer and washing-machines, as some of the evidence suggests, it is clear that we have a cultural pattern in which the objects are not enough but must be validated, if only in fantasy, by association with social and personal meanings which in a different cultural pattern might be more directly available. The short description of the pattern we have is *magic*: a highly organized and professional system of magical inducements and satisfactions, functionally very similar to magical systems in simpler societies, but rather strangely coexistent with a highly developed scientific technology.

This contradiction is of the greatest importance in any analysis of modern capitalist society. The coming of large-scale industrial production necessarily raised critical problems of social organization, which in many fields we are still only struggling to solve. In the production of goods for personal use, the critical problem posed by the factory of advanced machines was that of the organization of the market. The modern factory requires not only smooth and steady distributive channels (without which it would suffocate under its own product) but also definite indications of demand without which the expensive processes of capitalization and equipment would be too great a risk. The historical choice posed by the development of industrial production is between different forms of organization and planning in the society to which it is central. In our own century, the choice has been and remains between some form of socialism and a new form of capitalism. In Britain, since the 1890s and with rapidly continuing emphasis, we have had the new capitalism, based on a series of devices for organizing and ensuring the market. Modern advertising, taking on its distinctive features in just this economic phase, is one of the most important of these devices, and it is perfectly true to say that modern capitalism could not function without it.

Yet the essence of capitalism is that the basic means of production are not socially but privately owned, and that decisions about production are therefore in the hands of a group occupying a minority position in the society and in no direct way responsible to it. Obviously, since the capitalist wishes to be successful, he is influenced in his decisions about production by what other members of the society need. But he is influenced also by considerations of industrial convenience and likely profit, and his decisions tend to be a balance of these varying factors. The challenge of socialism, still very powerful elsewhere but in Britain deeply confused by political immaturities and errors, is essentially that decisions about production should be in the hands of the society as a whole, in the sense that control of the means of production is made part of the general system of decision which the society as a whole creates. The conflict between capitalism and socialism is now commonly seen in terms of a competition in productive efficiency, and we need not doubt that much of our future history, on a world scale, will be determined by the results of this competition. Yet the conflict is really much deeper than this, and is also a conflict between different approaches to and forms of socialism. The fundamental choice that emerges, in the problems set to us by modern industrial production, is between man as consumer and man as user. The system of organized magic which is modern advertising is primarily important as a functional obscuring of this choice.

Consider
1. What is consumer culture? Give a sociological definition in your own words and illustrate it with relevant examples.
2. What, according to Raymond Williams, is the role which advertising plays in consumer culture?
3. 'The popularity of "consumer", as a way of describing the ordinary member of modern capitalist society in a main part of his economic capacity, is very significant. [. . .] This metaphor drawn from the stomach or the furnace is only partially relevant even to our use of things. Yet we say "consumer", rather than "user", because in the form of society we now have, and in the forms of thinking which it almost imperceptibly fosters, it is as consumers that the majority of people are seen. We are the market, which the system of industrial production has organized. We are the channels along which the product flows and disappears. In every aspect of social communication, and in every version of what we are as a community, the pressure of a system of industrial production is towards these impersonal forms' (Williams 2006: 187). Discuss.
4. Compare how Raymond Williams's characterisation of consumer culture might apply to any TWO of the following:
   (a) Pop music
   (b) Smart phones
   (c) Holiday travel
   (d) University degrees.

5.8 Communication, media and everyday life

We now turn to another running thread in our discussion so far: the issue of communication. An unavoidable aspect of social life is our *communication* with others. By talking, listening, and watching others, we learn about society and engage with its beliefs, values and norms. The process of *socialisation* through which children go to become adults can be understood as a process of communication with parents, teachers and others who are tasked with seeing us through the first years in our lives. Even when we are by ourselves, we engage in communication. In *internal conversations* which play out in our minds all the time, we consider our wishes and feelings in the light of norms and moral values we have learned, we envisage how others may react to our behaviour, and we may even engage in imagined conversations with them!

Ultimately, thus, the forms of communication that are prevalent in society form an important part of the problems of community life, social cohesion and anomie in modernity that have troubled sociology since its beginning. The reason for this lies in important historical transformations in the social dynamics of communication. Prior to the technological breakthroughs that began in the early nineteenth century, human social interaction and communication were predominantly *localised* and *unmediated*, and most individuals acquired their understanding of the world through the people immediately surrounding them. This even holds for societies spread across vast geographical distance, such as the Roman or Chinese empires. While trade, politics and migration did facilitate a measure of awareness of the world at large, the lives of the vast majority of people remained firmly embedded in their local communities.

As we have seen, globalisation and modernisation have fundamentally altered this pattern, *compressing time and space* and enabling, by the beginning of the twenty-first century, instant communication between practically any two places in the world. The emergence and rapid proliferation of technologies such as the telegraph, the telephone, the radio, the television, mobile phones and the internet lie at the heart of this fundamental transformation of communication. Today, *mediated communication* dominates the life experience of a very large part of humanity.

In this context, *mass media* play a particularly important role. The term mass media is frequently used to refer to *organisations that make use of modern communication technologies to address a large number of individuals simultaneously across large distances*. Newspaper and magazine printing, radio, television, cinema and the internet are all examples of such technologies. The significance of mass media lies in their impact on our life experience and major social institutions. By transporting a constant stream of images and stories into our homes, technologies such as television and the internet now shape *what* we know about the world and *how* we know about it. Family life has been dramatically altered by the advent of television, and watching TV together or by ourselves is an important aspect of our routines in our homes. Cinema tells us stories that can be deeply emotional or thought-provoking. Likewise, public life has become increasingly reliant on the use of mass media. Companies rely on advertising, as in the case of Apple's 'I'm a Mac' campaign. The viability of governments and success in election campaigns depends on the effective use of mass media to convince voters of the impor-tance of policies and political positions. Mass media organisations themselves have become an important part of social life. Media industries play a significant role in the economy and politics of many countries: giant media corporations employ thousands and have the ability to shape the outcome of elections.

Yet, the age of mass media, as exemplified by television, may already have passed. Television began to spread around the world from the 1950s onwards, based on the production of cheap electronics. In the age of the network society, TV more and more forms a backdrop for new, cutting-edge developments. This concerns, in particular, the advent of new, personalised forms of mass media use. Digital television makes it possible to tailor TV programming to our preferences and ignore what we do not wish to watch. The internet today allows us to easily develop and display our own content. Social networking sites connect millions, but their presentation and functions can to some extent be adjusted to our preferences. At its core, a smart phone is as much a tele-phone as was a twentieth-century rotary dial, but it also allows us to choose from thou-sands of additional applications. The social impact of these new, personalised media is captured vividly in the following reading.

Reading

Baym, N. (2010), *Personal Connections in the Digital Age*, Cambridge: Polity Press, pp. 1–12

1

New forms of personal connection

There have never been more ways to communicate with one another than there are right now. Once limited to face to face conversation, over the last several millennia we have steadily developed new technologies for interaction. The digital age is distinguished by rapid transformations in the kinds of technological mediation through which we encounter one another. Face to face conversation, landline telephone calls, and postal mail have been joined by email, mobile phone calls, text messaging, instant messaging, chat, web boards, social networks, photo sharing, video sharing, multiplayer gaming, and more. People have always responded to new media with confusion. In this time of rapid innovation and diffusion, it's natural to be concerned about their effects on our relationships.

When first faced with a new barrage of interpersonal communication media, people tend to react in one of two ways, both of which have long cultural histories. On the one hand, people express concern that our communication has become increasingly shallow. For many, the increased amount of mediated interaction seems to threaten the sanctity of our personal relationships. For others, new media offer the promise of more opportunity for connection with more people, a route to new opportunities and to stronger relationships and more diverse connections. Both perspectives reflect a sense that digital media are changing the nature of our social connections. Over time, as people get used to new communication media, we come to see them in more nuanced ways. Eventually they become so taken for granted they are all but invisible. These moments in which they are new and the norms for their use are in flux offer fresh opportunities to think about our technologies, our connections, and the relationships amongst them.

The purpose of this book is to provide a means of thinking critically about the roles of digital media, in particular the internet and the mobile phone, in personal relationships. Rather than providing exuberant accounts or cautionary tales, this book provides a theoretical and data-grounded primer on how to make sense of these important changes in relational life. I began paying attention to these issues in 1990, launched my first research project into interpersonal communication over the internet in 1991, and began teaching courses in communication and new technology in Communication departments in 1994. The material in this book draws on my research projects, observations, and the large and growing body of scholarship on how digital media affect our interpersonal lives to offer frameworks for evaluating and understanding these changes.

New media, new boundaries

Digital media raise a variety of issues as we try to understand them, their place in our lives, and their consequences for our personhood and relationships with others. When they are new, technologies affect how we see the world, our communities, our relationships, and our selves. They lead to social and cultural reorganization and reflection. In her landmark study of nineteenth-century popular scientific magazines, Carolyn Marvin (1988) showed how a new technology such as electricity, the telegraph, or the telephone creates a point in history where the familiar becomes unfamiliar, and therefore open to change. This leads to anxiety. While people in ancient times fretted about writing and Victorians fretted about electricity, today we are in "a state of anxiety not only about the PC, but in relation to technology more generally" (D. Thomas, 2004: 219).

The fundamental purpose of communication technologies from their ancient inception has been to allow people to exchange messages without being physically co-present. Until the invention of the telegraph in the 1800s, this ability to transcend space brought with it inevitable time delays. Messages could take years to reach their audience. The telegraph changed that by allowing real-time communication across long distances for the first time. People may have reeled in the face of writing and publishing, but it was little compared to how we reeled and continued to reel in the face of this newfound power to collapse time and space. After millennia as creatures who engage in social interaction face to face, the ability to communicate across distance at very high speeds disrupts social understandings that are burned deep into our collective conscience. Digital media continue these disruptions and pose new ones. They raise important questions for scholars and lay people alike. How can we be present yet also absent? What is a self if it's not in a body? How can we have so much control yet lose so much freedom? What does personal communication mean when it's transmitted through a mass medium? What's a mass medium if it's used for personal communication? What do private and public mean anymore? What does it even mean to *be* real?

Kenneth Gergen (2002) describes us as struggling with the "challenge of absent presence," worrying that too often we inhabit a "floating world" in which we engage primarily with non-present partners despite the presence of flesh-and-blood people in our physical location. We may be physically present in one space, yet mentally and emotionally engaged elsewhere. Consider, for instance, the dinner partner who is immersed in his mobile phone conversation. Since he is physically present, yet simultaneously absent, the very nature of self becomes problematic. Where is "he?" The borders between human and machine, the collapse of which was celebrated in Haraway's (1990) "Cyborg manifesto," and between self and body, are thrown into flux. In a time when some people feel that their "real self" is expressed best online (McKenna, Green, & Gleason, 2002), long-distance romances are built and maintained through electronic contact, and spaces for our media are built right into the clothing we wear, how do we know where, exactly, true selves reside? Furthermore, what if the selves enacted through digital media don't line up with those we present face to face, or if they contradict one another? If someone is nurturing face to face, aggressive in one online forum, and needy in another online forum, which is real? Is there such a thing as a true self anymore? Was there ever?

The separation of presence from communication offers us more control over our social worlds yet simultaneously subjects us to new forms of control, surveillance, and constraint. Naomi Baron (2008) argues that new media offer us "volume control" to regulate our social environment and manage our encounters. We can create new opportunities to converse. We can avoid interactions, talking into a mobile phone (or pretending to) to avoid a co-present acquaintance or letting calls go to voice mail. We can manipulate our interactions, doing things like forwarding nasty emails or putting people on speakerphone. We can use nonverbally limited media such as text messages or emails to shelter us from anxiety-inducing encounters such as flirting or ending relationships. But, just as we can use these media to manage others more strategically, others can also more easily manage us. Our autonomy is increasingly constrained by the expectation that we can be reached for communication anytime, anywhere, and we will owe an appropriate and timely response. We are trapped by the same state of "perpetual contact" (Katz & Aakhus, 2002) that empowers us.

One of the most exciting elements of new media is that they allow us to communicate personally within what used to be prohibitively large groups.

This blurs the boundary between mass and interpersonal communication in ways that disrupt both. When people gather in an online space to talk about a television show, they are a mass communication audience, but the communication they have with one another is both interpersonal, directed to individuals within the group, and mass, available for anyone to read. If, as increasingly happens, the conversations and materials these fans produce for one another are incorporated into the television show, the boundaries between the production and reception of mass media are blurred as well. Furthermore, what is personal may become mass, as when a young woman creates a videolog for her friends, which becomes widely viewed on YouTube. The ability for individuals to communicate and produce mediated content on a mass scale has led to opportunities for fame that were not available outside of the established culture industries before, but confusion about the availability and scale of messages has also led to unplanned broadcast of what was meant to be private.

This is just one way in which the boundaries between public and private are implicated in and changed by digital media. Internet users, especially youth, have been decried for revealing private information through online activities. Mobile phone users have been assailed for carrying on private conversations in public spaces (and shooting nasty looks at those who don't pretend not to notice). Puro (2002: 23) describes mobile phone users as "doubly privatizing" public space since they "sequester themselves non-verbally and then fill the air with private matters." Homes, especially in affluent societies, exhibit a "privatized media rich bedroom culture" (Livingstone, 2005) in which people use media to create privacy and solitude. All of this happens in a cultural moment when individualism is increasingly defined through consumerist practices of purchasing mass mediated and branded products (Gergen, 1991; Livingstone, 2005; Walker, 2008).

At the heart of this boundary flux is deep confusion about what is virtual – that which seems real but is ultimately a mere simulation – and what is real. Even people who hang out and build relationships online contrast it to what they do "IRL" (In Real Life), lending credence to the perception that the mediated is unreal. Digital media thus call into question the very authenticity of our identities, relationships, and practices (e.g. Sturken & Thomas, 2004). Some critics have noted that these disruptions are part and parcel of a movement from modern to postmodern times in which time and space are compressed, speed is accelerated, people are ever more mobile, communication is person-to-person rather than place-to-place, identities are multiple, and communication media are ubiquitous (e.g. Fornås, Klein, Ladendorf, Sundén, & Sveningsson, 2002; Haythornthwaite & Wellman, 2002; Ling, 2004). Others have emphasized how, within these cultural changes, digital media are made mundane, boring, and routine as they are increasingly embedded in everyday lives and social norms coalesce around their use (e.g. Haythornthwaite & Wellman, 2002; Humphreys, 2005; Ling, 2004). The first perspective forms a necessary backdrop for contextualizing and making sense of the second, but the emphasis in this book is on the mundane and the everyday, on how people incorporate digital media into their routine practices of relating and with what consequences.

Plan of the book

In the remainder of this chapter I identify a set of key concepts that can be used to differentiate digital media and which influence how people use them and with what effects. I then offer a very brief overview of the media discussed in this book and a discussion of who does and who doesn't make use of them. Chapter 2 is an orientation to the major perspectives used to understand the interrelationships between communication technology and society and an exploration of the major themes in popular rhetorics about digital media and personal connection. Chapter 3 examines what happens to messages, both verbal and nonverbal, in mediated contexts. Chapter 4 addresses the group contexts in which online interaction often happens, including communities and social networks. The remaining two chapters explore dyadic relationships. Chapter 5 shows how people present themselves to others and first get to know each other online. Chapter 6 looks at how people use new media to build and maintain their relationships. Finally, the conclusion returns to the question of sorting myths from reality, arguing against the notion of a "cyberspace" that can be understood apart from the mundane realities of everyday life and for the notion that what happens online may be newer, but is no less real.

Seven key concepts

If we want to build a rich understanding of how media influence personal connections, we need to stop talking about media in overly simplistic terms. We can't talk about consequences if we can't articulate capabilities. What is it about these media that changes interaction and, potentially, relationships? We need conceptual tools to differentiate media from one another and from face to face (or, as Fortunati, 2005, more aptly termed it, "body to body") communication. We also need concepts to help us recognize the diversity amongst what may seem to be just one technology. The mobile phone, for instance, is used for voice, texting, and also picture and video exchange. The internet includes interaction platforms as diverse as YouTube, product reviews on shopping sites, email and Instant Messaging (IM), which differ from one another in many ways. Seven concepts that can be used to productively compare different media to one another as well as to face to face communication are interactivity, temporal structure, social cues, storage, replicability, reach, and mobility.

The many modes of communication on the internet and mobile phone vary in the degrees and kinds of *interactivity* they offer. Consider, for instance, the difference between using your phone to select a new ringtone and using that phone to argue with a romantic partner, or using a web site to buy new shoes rather than to discuss current events. Fornås and his co-authors (2002: 23) distinguish several meanings of interactivity. Social interactivity, "the ability of a medium to enable social interaction between groups or individuals," is what we are most interested in here. Other kinds include technical interactivity, "a medium's capability of letting human users manipulate the machine via its interface," and textual interactivity, "the creative and interpretive interaction between users (readers, viewers, listeners) and texts." "Unlike television," writes Laura Gurak (2001: 44), "online communication technologies allow you to talk back. You can talk back to the big company or you can talk back to individual citizens." Rafaeli and Sudweeks (1997) posit that we should see interactivity as a continuum enacted by people using technology, rather than a technological condition. As we will see in chapters to come, the fact that the internet enables interactivity gives rise to new possibilities – for instance, we can meet new people and remain close to those who have moved away – as well as old concerns that people may be flirting with danger.

The *temporal structure* of a communication medium is also important. Synchronous communication, such as is found in face to face conversations, phone calls, and instant messages, occurs in real time. Asynchronous communication media, such as email and voicemail, have time delays between messages. In practice, the distinction cannot always be tied to specific media. Poor connections may lead to time delays in a seemingly synchronous online medium such as Instant Messaging. Text messaging via the telephone is often asynchronous, but needn't be. Ostensibly asynchronous email may be sent and received so rapidly that it functions as a synchronous mode of communication.

The beauty of synchronous media is that they allow for the very rapid transmission of messages, even across distance. As we will see, synchronicity can enhance the sense of placelessness that digital media can encourage and make people feel more together when they are apart (Baron, 1998; Carnevale & Probst, 1997; McKenna & Bargh, 1998). Synchronicity can make messages feel more immediate and personal (O'Sullivan, Hunt, & Lippert, 2004) and encourage playfulness in interaction (Danet, 2001). The price of synchronicity, however, is that interactants must be able to align their schedules in order to be simultaneously engaged. Realtime media are also poorly suited to hosting interaction in large groups, as the rapid-fire succession of messages that comes from having many people involved is nearly impossible to sort through and comprehend, let alone answer. There is a reason that dinner parties are generally kept to a small collection of people and at large functions guests are usually seated at tables that seat fewer than a dozen. Accordingly, most online chat rooms and other real-time forums have limits on how many can participate at one time.

With asynchronous media, the costs and benefits are reversed. Asynchronous communication allows very large groups to sustain interaction, as seen in the social network sites and online groups like fan forums, support groups, and hobbyist communities addressed in Chapter 4. Asynchronicity also gives people time to manage their self-presentations more strategically. However, word may filter more slowly through such groups and amongst individuals. We can place fewer demands on others' time by leaving asynchronous messages for people to reply to when they like, but we may end up waiting longer than we'd hoped, or receive no reply at all. One of the biggest changes wrought by digital media is that even asynchronous communication can happen faster than before. Time lags are created by the time it takes a person to check for new messages and respond, not by the time messages spend in transit. In comparison to postal mail, the internet can shave weeks off interactions.

Most of the questions surrounding the personal connections people form and maintain through digital media derive from the sparse *social cues* that are available to provide further information regarding context, the meanings of messages, and the identities of the people interacting. As Chapter 3 will address in more detail, rich media provide a full range of cues, while leaner media provide fewer. Body-to-body, people have a full range of communicative resources available to them. They share a physical context, which they can refer to nonverbally as well as verbally (for instance, by pointing to a chair). They are subject to the same environmental influences and distractions. They can see one another's body movements, including the facial expressions through which so much meaning is conveyed. They can use each other's eye gaze to gauge attention. They can see one another's appearance. They can also hear the sound of one another's voice. All of these cues – contextual, visual, and auditory – are important to interpreting messages and creating a social context within which messages are meaningful.

To varying degrees, digital media provide fewer social cues. In mobile and online interactions, we may have few if any cues to our partner's location. This is no doubt why so many mobile phone calls begin with the question "where are you?" and also helps to explain some people's desire to share GPS positioning via mobile applications. The lack of shared physical context does not mean that interactants have no shared contexts. People communicating in personal relationships share relational contexts, knowledge, and some history. People in online groups often develop rich in-group social environments that those who've participated for any length of time will recognize.

Though, as we will address in more depth in chapter 6, much of our mediated interaction is with people we know face to face, some media convey very little information about the identities of those with whom we are communicating. In some circumstances, this renders people anonymous, leading to both opportunity and terror. In lean media, people have more ability to expand, manipulate, multiply, and distort the identities they present to others. The paucity of personal and social identity cues can also make people feel safer, and thus create an environment in which they are more honest. Chapter 5 examines these identity issues.

Media also differ in the extent to which their messages endure. *Storage*, and, relatedly, *replicability*, are highly consequential. Unless one makes an audio or video recording of telephone and face to face conversations (practices with laws governing acceptable practice), they are gone as soon as they are said. Human memory for conversation is notoriously poor. To varying degrees, digital media may be stored on devices, web sites, and company backups where they may be replicated, retrieved at later dates, and edited prior to sending (Carnevale & Probst, 1997; Cherny, 1999; Culnan & Markus, 1987; Walther, 1996). Synchronous forms like IM and Skype require logging programs that most users are not likely to have. Those that are asynchronous can be easily saved, replicated and redistributed to others. They can also be archived for search. Despite this, online messages may feel ephemeral, and indeed web sites may be there one day and different or gone the next.

Media also vary in the size of an audience they can attain or support, or *reach*. Gurak (2001: 30) describes reach as "the partner of speed," noting that "digitized discourse travels quickly, but it also travels widely . . . One single keystroke can send a message to thousands of people." Face to face communication is inherently limited to those who can fit in the same space. Even when amplified (a form of mediation in itself), physical space and human sensory constraints limit how many can see or hear a message as it's delivered. The telephone allows for group calls, but the upper limit on how many a group can admit or maintain is small. In contrast, many forms of digital communication can be seen by any internet user (as in the case of websites) or can be sent and, thanks to storage and replicability, resent to enormous audiences. Messages can reach audiences both local and global. This is a powerful subversion of the elitism of mass media, within which a very small number of broadcasters could engage in one-to-many communication, usually within regional or geographic boundaries. The gatekeeping function of mass media is challenged as individuals use digital media to spread messages much farther and more widely than was ever historically possible (Gurak, 2001). Future chapters will address how enhanced reach allows people to form new communities of interest and new relationships.

Finally, media vary in their *mobility*, or extent to which they are portable – enabling people to send and receive messages regardless of location – or stationary – requiring that people be in specific locations in order to interact. The mobile phone represents the paradigm case of mobility, making person-to-person communication possible regardless of location. The clunky personal computer tied to a desk requires that the user be seated in that spot. Landline phones require that people be in the building where that number rings. In addition to offering spatial mobility, some digital media allow us to move between times and interpersonal contexts (Ishii, 2006). Mobile media offer the promise that we need never be out of touch with our loved ones, no matter how long the traffic jam in which we find ourselves. When stuck with our families, we may import our friends through our mobile devices. As we'll see in Chapter 6, mobile media give rise to microcoordination (Ling, 2004) in which people check in with one another to provide brief updates or quickly arrange meetings and errands. However, more than other personal media, mobile phones threaten autonomy, as we may become accountable to others at all times. Schegloff (2002), one of the first to study telephone-mediated interaction, suggests mobile media don't create perpetual contact so much as offer the perpetual possibility of making contact, a distinction some exploit by strategically limiting their availability (Licoppe & Heurtin, 2002).

These seven concepts help us begin to understand the similarities and differences between face to face communication and mediated interaction, as well as the variation amongst different kinds of digital interactions. Face to face communication, like all the forms of digital media we will be discussing, is interactive. People can respond to one another in message exchanges. Face to face communication is synchronous. It is also loaded with social cues that make one another's identities and many elements of social and physical context apparent (although, as we will return to in Chapter 5, this does not guarantee honesty). Face to face conversations cannot be stored, nor can they be replicated. Even when recorded and, for example, broadcast, the recording loses many elements of the context that make face to face communication what it is. As discussed above, face to face communication has low reach, limiting how many can be involved and how far messages can spread. Face to face communication may be mobile, but only so long as the interactants are moving through space together. This combination of qualities grants face to face a sort of specialness. The full range of cues, the irreplicability, and the need to be there in shared place and time with the other all contribute to the sense that face to face communication is authentic, putting the "communion" in communication.

In contrast, some forms of mediated interaction are asynchronous, enabling more message planning and wider reach, but a potentially lower sense of connection. Media such as Skype or other video chat technologies offer many social cues – voice, facial expression, a window into the physical surroundings – but lack critical intimacy cues including touch and smell. Most digital media have fewer social cues than that, limiting interaction to sounds or even just words. By virtue of their conversion into electronic signals, all digital media can be stored, though particular interactions may not be. Even when conversations and messages are not stored, however, they may leave traces such as records of which phone numbers called which other ones, which IP addresses visited which websites, or how many tweets a person has twittered. Digital messages are easily replicated if they are asynchronous, but less so if they are synchronous. The reach of digital media can vary tremendously depending on the medium. A phone call generally remains a one-to-one encounter as does much instant messaging and chat, but emails, mailing lists, discussion groups, and websites are among the digital modes that can have extraordinary reach. Digital media are becoming increasingly mobile as the internet and mobile phone converge into single devices, meaning that these technologies make communication possible in places where it wasn't before, but also that they can intrude into face to face conversations where they never could before. As a result, people can have very different experiences with different media, yet none may seem to offer the potential for intimacy and connection that being face to face does. These distinctions all bring with them important potential social shifts, which the remainder of this book will address.

Consider
1. 'There have never been more ways to communicate with one another than there are right now.' Discuss.
2. According to Nancy Baym, what is the significance of digital media in contemporary social life?
3. Describe in your own words the seven key concepts Baym uses to distinguish different media forms. Illustrate each of these concepts with examples.
4. Gather information on the history of the World Wide Web. How old is it? When did its use become widespread throughout the world? Are there any major differences in access to it in different parts of the world? What economic, social, political, and cultural consequences of the rise of the Web can you identify?

5.9 Cities

A thorough discussion of globalisation and life in the modern world requires that we further examine the role of *cities*. Earlier on, we suggested that cities play a crucial role in modern life and have been of significant interest to sociologists for a long time. This interest forms part of wider sociological concerns with the *social organisation of space*. From the point of view of the sociological imagination, space and the way in which it is organised can be understood as the outcome of historically and geographically specific social relations (cf. Bhambra 2007: 9–12). For example, social space plays an important role in Erving Goffman's (1959) analysis of the ways in which ordinary people in the USA of the mid twentieth century managed the impressions which others formed of them. Goffman (1959: 146ff.) distinguishes between the 'front regions' and the 'back regions' of our everyday lives. While we will pay heightened attention to social norms of proper conduct in the front regions of public space, we may often feel able to 'let go' when we return to the back regions of private space. Attending a lecture, you know that you are being observed by the lecturer and dozens of other students, some of them strangers, and you therefore are likely to control your behaviour according to the norms pertaining to public academic settings. In contrast, when you return to your home, you are either alone or only in the company of close friends and family, and you will feel relaxed and able to do things that you would not wish strangers to watch.

The recognition of the socially constructed nature of urban space has shaped respective sociological enquiry from the outset. The sociological exploration of urban life, for example, played a major role in the Chicago School of Sociology, one of the earliest sociology programmes in the USA. Robert E. Park, a key figure in the Chicago School, argued:

> The city [. . .] is something more than a congeries of individual men and of social conveniences – streets, buildings, electric lights, tramways, and telephones, etc.; something more, also, than a mere constellation of institutions and administrative devices – courts, hospitals, schools, police, and civil functionaries of various sorts. The city is, rather, a state of mind, a body of customs and traditions, and of the organized attitudes and sentiments that inhere in these customs and are transmitted with this tradition. The city is not, in other words, merely a physical mechanism and an artificial construction. It is involved in the vital processes of the people who compose it; it is a product of nature, and particularly of human nature. (Park 1925/1967: 1)

Describing the city as a 'state of mind' and 'a body of customs and traditions', Park could hardly be more explicit in pointing to the ways in which historically and geographically particular forms of social life shape the nature of urban space.

Urbanisation, that is to say the increasing accumulation of populations in large settlements, has been a feature of human life for a very long time. It was initially set in motion approximately 12,000 years by the Agricultural Revolution, that is, the discovery of technologies of farming and animal domestication that allowed relatively large groups of people to become sedentary and abandon nomadic ways of life. Since this period, cities have remained focal points of government, administration, trade, education and artistic life around the world. At the height of the Roman Empire in the first century CE, its capital, Rome, encompassed more than a million inhabitants. In the mid thirteenth century, Hangzhou, the capital of the Chinese Song Dynasty, was the largest city in the world, with around two million residents.

However, in spite of these enormous concentrations of human populations, social life in these times still revolved to a very large extent around agriculture and rural life, be it in Europe or in China. The Industrial Revolution of the eighteenth century changed this, leading to an unprecedented growth of cities at first in Europe and then all around the world. This was due to a new demand for industrial labourers – factory workers, miners, etc. – in the industrialising cities, as well as the willingness of people to leave the countryside in search of a better standard of living.

The twentieth century and the beginning of the twenty-first century have witnessed an accelerated rhythm of urbanisation and the emergence of *megacities* encompassing 8 million residents or more. In some societies, accelerated urbanisation has entailed significant social problems. In Mexico, a country of 112 million people, 21 million live in the Mexico City metropolitan area, 4 million reside in the western metropolis of Guadalajara, another 4 million are concentrated in Monterrey in the north, and so forth. As a consequence, Mexican agriculture has faced problems of stagnation and under-production, due to the abandonment of the countryside, and the country's megacities are confronting mounting challenges when it comes to the maintenance of urban infrastructure and living conditions.

At the same time, globalisation has brought about a network of *world cities* concentrating economic and financial resources and power and dominating global economic exchanges. The work of Dutch sociologist Saskia Sassen has been foundational to the sociological analysis of the role of world cities in globalisation. In at least superficial affinity to Manuel Castells's (2000) theses about the network society (see Chapter 6), Sassen (1991: 3) argues that the large-scale international debt crisis of the early 1980s and other socio-economic developments at the international level throughout the 1960s and the 1970s ended the dominance of large US transnational corporations. 'Yet the international economy did not simply break into fragments. The geography and composition of the global economy changed so as to produce a complex duality: a spatially dispersed, yet globally integrated organization of economic activity' (Sassen 1991: 3). On this base, thus Sassen, world cities have come to occupy an important strategic role in processes of socio-economic globalisation. The following is an extract from her book *The Global City: New York, London, Tokyo* (1991) which explores this development in some detail.

Reading

Sassen, S. (1991), *The Global City: New York, London, Tokyo*, Princeton: Princeton University Press, pp. 3–10.

One

Overview

For centuries, the world economy has shaped the life of cities. This book is about that relationship today. Beginning in the 1960s, the organization of economic activity entered a period of pronounced transformation. The changes were expressed in the altered structure of the world economy, and also assumed forms specific to particular places. Certain of these changes are by now familiar: the dismantling of once-powerful industrial centers in the United States, the United Kingdom, and more recently in Japan; the accelerated industrialization of several Third World countries; the rapid internationalization of the financial industry into a worldwide network of transactions. Each of these changes altered the relation of cities to the international economy.

In the decades after World War II, there was an international regime based on United States dominance in the world economy and the rules for global trade contained in the 1945 Bretton Woods agreement. By the early 1970s, the conditions supporting that regime were disintegrating. The breakdown created a void into which stepped, perhaps in a last burst of national dominance, the large U.S. transnational industrial firms and banks. In this period of transition, the management of the international economic order was to an inordinate extent run from the headquarters of these firms. By the early 1980s, however, the large U.S.

transnational banks faced the massive Third World debt crisis, and U.S. industrial firms experienced sharp market share losses from foreign competition. Yet the international economy did not simply break into fragments. The geography and composition of the global economy changed so as to produce a complex duality: a spatially dispersed, yet globally integrated organization of economic activity.

The point of departure for the present study is that the combination of spatial dispersal and global integration has created a new strategic role for major cities. Beyond their long history as centers for international trade and banking, these cities now function in four new ways: first, as highly concentrated command points in the organization of the world economy; second, as key locations for finance and for specialized service firms, which have replaced manufacturing as the leading economic sectors; third, as sites of production, including the production of innovations, in these leading industries; and fourth, as markets for the products and innovations produced. These changes in the functioning of cities have had a massive impact upon both international economic activity and urban form: Cities concentrate control over vast resources, while finance and specialized service industries have restructured the urban social and economic order. Thus a new type of city has appeared. It is the global city. Leading examples now are New York, London, and Tokyo. These three cities are the focus of this book.

As I shall show, these three cities have undergone massive and *parallel* changes in their economic base, spatial organization, and social structure. But this parallel development is a puzzle. How could cities with as diverse a history, culture, politics, and economy as New York, London, and Tokyo experience similar transformations concentrated in so brief a period of time? Not examined at length in my study, but important to its theoretical framework, is how transformations in cities ranging from Paris to Frankfurt to Hong Kong and São Paulo have responded to the same dynamic. To understand the puzzle of parallel change in diverse cities requires not simply a point-by-point comparison of New York, London, and Tokyo, but a situating of these cities in a set of global processes. In order to understand why major cities with different histories and cultures have undergone parallel economic and social changes, we need to examine transformations in the world economy. Yet the term *global city* may be reductive and misleading if it suggests that cities are mere outcomes of a global economic machine. They are specific places whose spaces, internal dynamics, and social structure matter; indeed, we may be able to understand the global order only by analyzing why key structures of the world economy are *necessarily* situated in cities.

How does the position of these cities in the world economy today differ from that which they have historically held as centers of banking and trade? When Max Weber analyzed the medieval cities woven together in the Hanseatic League, he conceived their trade as the exchange of surplus production; it was his view that a medieval city could withdraw from external trade and continue to support itself, albeit on a reduced scale. The modern molecule of global cities is nothing like the trade among self-sufficient places in the Hanseatic League, as Weber understood it. The first thesis advanced in this book is that the territorial dispersal of current economic activity creates a need for expanded central control and management. In other words, while in principle the territorial decentralization of economic activity in recent years could have been accompanied by a corresponding decentralization in ownership and hence in the appropriation of profits, there has been little movement in that direction. Though large firms have increased their subcontracting to smaller firms, and many national firms in the newly industrializing countries have grown rapidly, this form of growth is ultimately part of a chain. Even industrial homeworkers in remote rural areas are now part of that chain. The transnational corporations continue to control much of the end product and to reap the profits associated with selling in the world market. The internationalization and expansion of the financial industry has brought growth to a large number of smaller financial markets, a growth which has fed the expansion of the global industry. But top-level control and management of the industry has become concentrated in a few leading financial centers, notably New York, London, and Tokyo. These account for a disproportionate share of all financial transactions and one that has grown rapidly since the early 1980s. The fundamental dynamic posited here is that the more globalized the economy becomes, the higher the agglomeration of central functions in a relatively few sites, that is, the global cities.

The extremely high densities evident in the business districts of these cities are one spatial expression of this logic. The widely accepted notion that density and agglomeration will become obsolete because global telecommunications advances allow for maximum population and resource dispersal is poorly conceived. It is, I argue, precisely because of the territorial dispersal facilitated by telecommunication that agglomeration of certain centralizing activities has sharply increased. This is not a mere continuation of old patterns of agglomeration; there is a new logic for concentration. In Weberian terms, there is a new system of "coordination," one which focuses on the development of specific geographic control sites in the international economic order.

A second major theme of this book concerns the impact of this type of economic growth on the economic order within these cities. It is necessary to go beyond the Weberian notion of coordination and Bell's (1973) notion of the postindustrial society to understand this new urban order. Bell, like Weber, assumes that the further society evolves from nineteenth-century industrial capitalism, the more the apex of the social order is involved in pure managerial process, with the content of what is to be managed becoming of secondary importance. Global cities are, however, not only nodal points for the coordination of processes (Friedmann 1986); they are also particular sites of production. They are sites for (1) the production of specialized services needed by complex organizations for running a spatially dispersed network of factories, offices, and service outlets; and (2) the production of financial innovations and the making of markets, both central to the internationalization and expansion of the financial industry. To understand the structure of a global city, we have to understand it as a place where certain kinds of work can get done, which is to say that we have to get beyond the dichotomy between manufacturing and services. The "things" a global city makes are services and financial goods.

It is true that high-level business services, from accounting to economic consulting, are not usually analyzed as a production process. Such services are usually seen as a type of output derived from high-level technical knowledge. I shall challenge this view. Moreover, using new scholarship on producer services, I shall examine the extent to which a key trait of global cities is that they are the most *advanced* production sites for creating these services.

A second way this analysis goes beyond the existing literature on cities concerns the financial industry. I shall explore how the character of a global city is shaped by the emerging organization of the financial industry. The accelerated production of innovations and the new importance of a large number of relatively small financial institutions led to a renewed or expanded role for the marketplace in the financial industry in the decade of the 1980s. The marketplace has assumed new strategic and routine economic functions, in comparison to the prior phase, when the large transnational banks dominated the national and international financial market. Insofar as financial "products" can be used internationally, the market has reappeared in a new form in the global economy. New York, London, and Tokyo play roles as production sites for financial innovations and centralized marketplaces for these "products."

A key dynamic running through these various activities and organizing my analysis of the place of global cities in the world economy is their capability for producing global control. By focusing on the production of services and financial innovations, I am seeking to displace the focus of attention from the familiar issues of the power of large corporations over governments and economies, or supracorporate concentration of power through interlocking directorates or organizations, such as the IMF. I want to focus on an aspect that has received less attention, which could be referred to as the *practice* of global control: the work of producing and reproducing the organization and management of a global production system and a global marketplace for finance. My focus is not on power, but on production: the production of those inputs that constitute the capability for global control and the infrastructure of jobs involved in this production.

The power of large corporations is insufficient to explain the capability for global control. Obviously, governments also face an increasingly complex environment in which highly sophisticated machineries of centralized management and control are necessary. Moreover, the high level of specialization and the growing demand for these specialized inputs have created the conditions for a freestanding industry. Now small firms can buy components of global capability, such as management consulting or international legal advice. And so can firms and governments anywhere in the world. While the large corporation is undoubtedly a key agent inducing the development of this capability and is a prime beneficiary, it is not the sole user.

Equally misleading would be an exclusive focus on transnational banks. Up to the end of the 1982 Third World debt crisis, the large transnational banks dominated the financial markets in terms of both volume and the nature of firm transactions. After 1982, this dominance was increasingly challenged by other financial institutions and the innovations they produced. This led to a transformation in the leading components of the financial industry, a proliferation of financial institutions, and the rapid internationalization of financial markets rather than just a few banks. The incorporation of a multiplicity of markets all over the world into a global system fed the growth of the industry after the 1982 debt crisis, while also creating new forms of concentration in a few leading financial centers. Hence, in the case of the financial industry, a focus on the large transnational banks would exclude precisely those sectors of the industry where much of the new growth and production of innovations has occurred; it would leave out an examination of the wide range of activities, firms, and markets that constitute the financial industry in the 1980s.

Thus, there are a number of reasons to focus a study on marketplaces and production sites rather than on the large corporations and banks. Most scholarship on the internationalization of the economy has already focused on the large corporations and transnational banks. To continue to focus on the corporations and banks would mean to limit attention to their formal power, rather than examining the wide array of economic activities, many outside the corporation, needed to produce and reproduce that power. And, in the case of finance, a focus on the large transnational banks would leave out precisely that institutional sector of the industry where the key components of the new growth have been invented and put into circulation. Finally, exclusive focus on corporations and banks leaves out a number of issues about the social, economic, and spatial impact of these activities on the cities that contain them, a major concern in this book and one I return to below.

A third major theme explored in this book concerns the consequences of these developments for the national urban system in each of these countries and for the relationship of the global city to its nation-state. While a few major cities are the sites of production for the new global control capability, a large number of other major cities have lost their role as leading export centers for industrial manufacturing, as a result of the decentralization of this form of production. Cities such as Detroit, Liverpool, Manchester, and now increasingly Nagoya and Osaka have been affected by the decentralization of their key industries at the domestic and international levels. According to the first hypothesis presented above, this same process has contributed to the growth of service industries that produce the specialized inputs to run global production processes and global markets for inputs and outputs. These industries – international legal and accounting services, management consulting, financial services – are heavily concentrated in cities such as New York, London, and Tokyo. We need to know how this growth alters the relations between the global cities and what were once the leading industrial centers in their nations. Does globalization bring about a triangulation so that New York, for example, now plays a role in the fortunes of Detroit that it did not play when that city was home to one of the leading industries, auto manufacturing? Or, in the case of Japan, we need to ask, for example, if there is a connection between the increasing shift of production out of Toyota City (Nagoya) to offshore locations (Thailand, South Korea, and the United States) and the development for the first time of a new headquarters for Toyota in Tokyo.

Similarly, there is a question about the relation between such major cities as Chicago, Osaka, and Manchester, once leading industrial centers in the world, and global markets generally. Both Chicago and Osaka were and continue to be important financial centers on the basis of their manufacturing industries. We would want to know if they have lost ground, relatively, in these functions as a result of their decline in the global industrial market, or instead have undergone parallel transformation toward strengthening of service functions. Chicago, for example, was at the heart of a massive agroindustrial complex, a vast regional economy. How has the decline of that regional economic system affected Chicago?

In all these questions, it is a matter of understanding what growth embedded in the international system of producer services and finance has entailed for different levels in the national urban hierarchy. The broader trends – decentralization of plants, offices, and service outlets, along with the expansion of central functions as a consequence of the need to manage such decentralized organization of firms – may well have created conditions contributing to the growth of regional subcenters, minor versions of what New York, London, and Tokyo do on a global and national scale. The extent to which the developments posited for New York, London, and Tokyo are also replicated, perhaps in less accentuated form, in smaller cities, at lower levels of the urban hierarchy, is an open, but important, question.

The new international forms of economic activity raise a problem about the relationship between nation-states and global cities. The relation between city and nation is a theme that keeps returning throughout this book; it is the political dimension of the economic changes I explore. I posit the possibility of a systemic discontinuity between what used to be thought of as national growth and the forms of growth evident in global cities in the 1980s. These cities constitute a system rather than merely competing with each other. What contributes to growth in the network of global cities may well not contribute to growth in nations. For instance, is there a systemic relation between, on the one hand, the growth in global cities and, on the other hand, the deficits of national governments and the decline of major industrial centers in each of these countries?

The fourth and final theme in the book concerns the impact of these new forms of and conditions for growth on the social order of the global city. There is a vast body of literature on the impact of a dynamic, high-growth manufacturing sector in the highly developed countries, which shows that it raised wages, reduced inequality, and contributed to the formation of a middle class. Much less is known about the sociology of a service economy. Daniel Bell's (1973) *The Coming of Post-Industrial Society* posits that such an economy will result in growth in the number of highly educated workers and a more rational relation of workers to issues of social equity. One could argue that any city representing a post-industrial economy would surely be like the leading sectors of New York, London, and increasingly Tokyo.

I will examine to what extent the new structure of economic activity has brought about changes in the organization of work, reflected in a shift in the job supply and polarization in the income distribution and occupational distribution of workers. Major growth industries show a greater incidence of jobs at the high- and low-paying ends of the scale than do the older industries now in decline. Almost half the jobs in the producer services are lower-income jobs, and half are in the two highest earnings classes. In contrast, a large share of manufacturing workers were in the middle-earnings jobs during the postwar period of high growth in these industries in the United States and United Kingdom.

Two other developments in global cities have also contributed to economic polarization. One is the vast supply of low-wage jobs required by high-income gentrification in both its residential and commercial settings. The increase in the numbers of expensive restaurants, luxury housing, luxury hotels, gourmet shops, boutiques, French hand laundries, and special cleaners that ornament the new urban landscape illustrates this trend. Furthermore, there is a continuing need for low-wage industrial services, even in such sectors as finance and specialized services. A second development that has reached significant proportions is what I call the downgrading of the manufacturing sector, a process in which the share of unionized shops declines and wages deteriorate while sweatshops and industrial homework proliferate. This process includes the downgrading of jobs within existing industries and the job supply patterns of some of the new industries, notably electronics assembly. It is worth noting that the growth of a downgraded manufacturing sector has been strongest in cities such as New York and London.

The expansion of low-wage jobs as a function of *growth* trends implies a reorganization of the capital-labor relation. To see this, it is important to distinguish the characteristics of jobs from their sectoral location, since highly dynamic, technologically advanced growth sectors may well contain low-wage dead-end jobs. Furthermore, the distinction between sectoral characteristics and sectoral growth patterns is crucial: Backward sectors, such as downgraded manufacturing or low-wage service occupations, can be part of major growth trends in a highly developed economy. It is often assumed that backward sectors express decline trends. Similarly, there is a tendency to assume that advanced sectors, such as finance, have mostly good, white-collar jobs. In fact, they contain a good number of low-paying jobs, from cleaner to stock clerk.

Consider

1. 'The city is, rather, a state of mind, a body of customs and traditions, and of the organized attitudes and sentiments that inhere in these customs and are transmitted with this tradition' (Park 1925/1967: 1). Discuss.

2. Sassen (p. 3) refers to the international economic system established after World War II through the Bretton Woods agreement, as well as to the subsequent collapse of this system. Based on appropriate background research, outline the Bretton Woods system and the reasons for its crisis from the 1970s onwards.

3. According to Saskia Sassen, what is the significance of world cities in the global economy today? Outline the four respective key points in her argument in your own words.

4. What are the transformations, from the 1980s onwards, that have brought about the rise of world cities such as London, New York, or Tokyo?

5. Beyond the economic issues discussed by Sassen, in which other ways do world cities concentrate cultural, political and social life today? Use examples from other academic sources, news media, and your personal experience to support your argument.

5.10 Work and economic life

Looking at economic life, we address another topic that has been frequently mentioned but so far not explored in detail. The term 'economy' is generally used to refer to *the ways in which the production, consumption and distribution of goods and services are organised in society*. Economic patterns and changes in modern life have been central sociological concerns since Émile Durkheim's (1984) research on the division of labour and Karl Marx's and Max Weber's (1905/2009) enquiry into the origins and consequences of capitalism. However, sociologists generally do not examine economic issues in isolation. Durkheim looked at the division of labour to analyse problems of social cohesion and anomie in modern societies. Karl Marx and Friedrich Engels were concerned about the social consequences of capitalism for the exploited and impoverished industrial proletariat. Max Weber focused on the cultural, or, more specifically, religious, roots of capitalism. In other words, economic sociology highlights the fact that patterns of economic life may have a profound impact on many other spheres of social life.

Looking at economic life in the long run, we can point to several major historical breaks. The first of these, as we saw above, was the Agricultural Revolution, which, more than 12,000 years ago, allowed humans to form stable settlements and give up a predominantly nomadic life. The second was the already much discussed Industrial Revolution, which has transformed the face of the world from the eighteenth century onwards. Finally, many scholars argue that we are now witnessing a 'digital revolution', whose impact is manifest in contemporary globalisation and the emergence of a 'network society'.

Through this digital revolution, economic life and the nature of work have changed around the world during the past 40 years. As already mentioned elsewhere, previously highly industrialised countries have experienced *de-industrialisation* and moved on to *information-based forms of economic activity*. While the coal miner and the assembly line worker represented the industrial age in countries like England, Germany, or the USA, stock brokers, software engineers, journalists, marketing specialists, etc., are at the forefront of the digital revolution. In relation to the emergence of contemporary consumer culture, industrial production has moreover shifted from the *Fordist* system of standardised mass production to *post-Fordist* patterns emphasising flexibility and highly specialised, customisable goods. Encouraged by new possibilities for cheap long-distance trade and the transport of goods, and by neoliberal government policies encouraging free trade and direct foreign investment, industrial manufacturing has shifted to new world regions. The sweatshop of 1911 stood in Manchester or Detroit, but the sweatshop of 2011 can be found in Jakarta or Mexico City.

Simultaneously, the lifetime contract not untypical of industrial labour under Fordism has been replaced by casual, flexible labour and mass unemployment. *Primary labour markets* providing stable employment with substantial benefits are often only able to absorb a limited part of the workforce, leaving many to *unemployment* or unstable, low-paid work in the *secondary labour market*. The call centre agent and the fast-food worker are emblematic representatives of this new face of work in the twenty-first century.

US sociologist Richard Sennett vividly describes the personal consequences of this destabilisation of work in the following reading:

Reading

Sennett, R. (1997), 'The New Capitalism', *Social Research* 64 (2), pp. 161–8 and 172–5

The New Capitalism
By Richard Sennett

The word *new* is a suspect word, the favored adjective of advertisers. Yet in the last twenty years profound changes in material life have occurred, changes that a score of years ago it was hard to foresee. Then, the great corporate bureaucracies and government hierarchies of the developed world seemed securely entrenched, the products of centuries of economic development and nation-building. Commentators spoke of "late capitalism" or "mature capitalism" as though earlier forces of growth had now entered an end-game phase.

Now a new chapter has opened: the economy is global and makes use of new technology; mammoth government and corporate bureaucracies are becoming both more flexible and less secure institutions. The social guarantees of the welfare states of an earlier era are breaking down, capitalism itself has become economically flexible, highly mobile, its corporate structures ever less determinate in form and in time. These structural changes are linked to a sudden and massive outpouring of productivity, new goods like computers, new services like the global financial industries. The cornucopia is for the moment full.

As a result, though, the ways we work have altered: short-term jobs replace stable careers, skills rapidly evolve; the middle class experiences anxieties and uncertainties that were, in an earlier era, more confined to the working classes.

Place has a different meaning now as well, in large part thanks to these economic changes. An earlier generation believed nations, and within nations, cities, could govern their own fortunes; now, the emerging economic network is less susceptible to the controls of geography. One measure of the changing relation between economy and place is immigration – a force perplexing cities like New York and Vienna, since the appearance of immigrants is not accidental, but tied to subtle structural changes in the economy of these cities. Yet the appearance of these strangers does not encompass the magnitude of the transformation of place we are now experiencing. A divide has opened between polity – in the sense of self-rule – and the global economy.

The culture of this new capitalist order of work and place is the focus of my own reflections – that is, what difference the new political economy makes in our ethical values, our sense of one another as social creatures, and our understanding of ourselves. As a point of departure, I'd like to put forward to you two simple propositions that seem to be emerging from this new order.

The first is that the new capitalism is impoverishing the value of work. Becoming more flexible and short-term, work is ceasing to serve as a point of reference for defining durable personal purposes and a sense of self-worth; sociologically, work serves ever less as a forum for stable, sociable relations.

The second proposition is that the value of place has thereby increased. The sense of place is based on the need to belong not to "society" in the abstract, but belong somewhere in particular. As the shifting institutions of the economy diminish the experience of belonging somewhere special at work, people's commitments increase to geographic places like nations, cities, and localities. The question is, commitments of what sort? Nationalism or ethnic localism – often expressed as hatred of immigrants or other outsiders – can indeed serve as defensive refuges against a hostile economic order, but at a steep human price. The man who hates the outside is weakened, rather than strengthened, by his hatred.

These two propositions might suggest an unrelievedly bleak view of the culture of the emerging political economy. But this is not my view. Work is a problematic frame for the self, since it tends to equate worldly success and personal worth. And the renewed value on place aroused by troubled fortunes might in fact present an opportunity – the opportunity to construct a public realm in which people think about themselves and act socially other than as economic animals, their value as citizens not dependant upon their riches.

At least, this was Hannah Arendt's hope a generation ago, when she made, in *The Human Condition* (1958), her famous distinction between labor and politics. She hoped particularly that in urban life, with its large scale and impersonality, people could conduct a civic existence that did not merely reflect, or depend upon, their personal fortunes. Today, the uncertainties of the new economy argue more than ever for a selfhood, as well as civic behavior, unchained from the conditions of labor. Yet the places in which this might occur can neither be cities of the classical kind that Arendt admired, nor can they be defensive, inward-turning localities. We need a new kind of public realm to cope with the new economy.

Growth

To make sense of the culture of the emerging political economy, we need to understand its key word, *growth*. Growth occurs, most simply, in four ways.

The simplest way is sheer increase in number, such as more ants in a colony, more television sets on the market. Growth of this sort appears in economic thinking among writers like Jean Baptiste Say, whose *loi des débouchés* postulated that "increased supply creates its own demand." That's a form of growth that appears in the modern economy, for instance, in the computer industry, the ever-increasing supply of hardware and software arousing and pushing product demand.

An increase in number can lead to alteration of structure, which is how Adam Smith conceived of growth in *The Wealth of Nations*; larger markets trigger, he said, the division of labor in work. Increase of size that begets complexity of structure has been the way government bureaucracy as well as industry have grown in the past. The technology of the new capitalism exemplifies this kind of growth in the ever more complex structure of information services linking the world.

A third kind of growth occurs through metamorphosis; a body changes its shape or structure without necessarily increasing in number. A moth turning into a butterfly grows in this way, so do characters in a novel. Much of the internal growth of modern corporations has occurred in this form. Though the press focuses on job loss and downsizing in the modern economy, radical metamorphoses in corporate structure can often occur even when the number of employees remains relatively constant; metamorphosis characterizes the restructuring of banking and other financial service industries, for instance.

Finally, a system can grow by becoming more democratic. This kind of growth is antifoundational, as John Dewey argued: the elements in a system are free to interact and influence one another so that boundaries become febrile, forms become mixed; the system contracts or expands in parts without overall coordination. Communications networks like the early Internet are obvious examples of how growth can occur democratically. Such a growth process differs from a market mechanism, in which an exchange ideally clears all transactions and so regulates all actors in the system. Resistances, irregularities, and cognitive dissonances take on a positive value in democratic forms of growth. This is why subjective life develops through something like the practice of inner democracy – interpretative and emotional complexity emerges without a master plan, a hegemonic rule, an undisputed explanation.

My own view is that this form of growth is more than a matter of pure process; the very freedom and flexibility of the process gives rise to the need for signposts, defined forms, tentative rituals, and provisional decisions that matter in future conduct, all of which help people orient themselves. And my argument is that the flexible economy is destroying exactly these formal elements that orient people in the process of truly democratic growth. Put another way, what we need to cope with the emerging political economy is to promote more truly democratic forms of flexible growth. The question is, Where? At the workplace, in the community? Are they equally possible, or equally desirable, sites for democracy?

Smith's Paradox

A cultural paradox of growth has dogged the development of modern capitalism throughout it long history: as material growth occurs, the qualitative experience of work often becomes impoverished.

The age of High Capitalism – which for convenience's sake can be said to span the two centuries following the publication of Adam Smith's *The Wealth of Nations* in 1776 – was an era that lusted for sheer quantitative growth, of the first sort I've described, but had trouble dealing with the human consequences of the second sort, in which the increase of wealth occurred through more complex economic structures.

Adam Smith argued that the division of labor, a structural complexity, was promoted by the expansion of free markets with ever greater numbers of goods, services, and laborers in circulation; a growing society seemed to him like a honeycomb, each new cell the place for ever more specialized tasks. A nail-maker doing everything himself could make a few hundred nails a day; Smith calculated if nail-making was broken down into all its component parts, and each worker did only one of them, a nail-maker could process more than forty-eight thousand nails a day. However, work experience would become more routine in the process. Breaking the tasks involved in making nails down into its component parts would condemn individual nail-makers to a numbingly boring day, hour after hour spent doing one small job.

I'll call this coupling of material growth and qualitative impoverishment Smith's Paradox – he recognized its existence but didn't name it as such. Smith's Paradox came down into our time as what we call "Fordist production," the kind of assembly-line work organized in Ford's Highland Park plant in Michigan during the First World War.

Proponents of the new order claim that Smith's Paradox is now coming to an end; modern technology promises to banish routine work to the innards of new machines, leaving ever more workers free to do flexible, nonroutine tasks. But in fact, the qualitative impoverishment has instead taken new forms.

The new technology frequently "de-skills" workers, who now tend, as the electronic janitors of robotic machines, complex tasks the workers once performed themselves. The conditions of job tenure often compound deskilling, for workers will learn to do a particular job well, only to find that work task at an end. An executive for AT&T recently summed up the aim of reorganizing work this way: "In AT&T we have to promote the whole concept of the work force being contingent, though most of the contingent workers are inside our walls. 'Jobs' are being replaced by 'projects' and 'fields of work.'" The reality now facing young workers with at least two years of college is that they will change jobs, on average, at least eleven times in the course of their working lives.

More brutally, the division of labor now separates those who get to work, and those who don't: large numbers of people are set free of routine tasks only to find themselves useless or underused economically, especially in the context of the global labor supply. Geography no longer simply separates the skilled First World from the unskilled Third World; computer code is written efficiently, for instance, in Bombay for a third to a seventh its cost in IBM home offices.

Let me say a few words more about this particular phenomenon. Statistics on job creation do not quite get at the fear of uselessness; the number of jobs, even good skilled jobs, does not dictate who will have access to them, how long the jobs can be held, or, indeed, how long the jobs will exist. Ten years ago, for instance, the U.S. economy had a deficit of computer systems analysts, today it has a surplus of such highly trained workers. And many do not, contrary to ideology, retrain well; their skills are too specific. The specter of uselessness, shadowing the lives of educated middle-class people, has now compounded the older experiential problem of routine among less-favored workers: as well as too many qualified engineers, programmers, systems analysts, there is a growing glut of lawyers, M.B.A.s, securities salesmen, and academics. The young suffer the pangs of uselessness in a particularly cruel way, since an ever-expanding educational system trains them ever more elaborately for jobs that do not exist.

The undertow connotation of uselessness, deskilling, and task labor is a dispensable self. Instead of the institutionally induced boredom of the assembly line, this experiential deficit appears more to lie within the worker, who hasn't made him or herself of lasting value to others, and so can simply disappear from view. The economic language in use today – "skills-based economy," "informational competence," "task-flexible labor," and the like – shifts the focus from impersonal conditions like the possession of capital to more personal matters of competence. Economic flexibility is legitimated by appeals to personal autonomy. While the shift in language seems psychologically empowering, in fact it can increase the burdens on the working self.

In turn, the sense of failing personally to be of much value in this economy has great sociological implications. What Michael Young feared in his prophetic essay *The Rise of Meritocracy* (1959) has come to pass: as the economy needs ever fewer, highly educated people to run it, the "moral distance" between mass and elite widens. The masses, now comprising people in suits and ties as well as those in overalls, appear peripheral to the elite productive core; the emerging economy profits by shrinking its labor base. The economy's emphasis on personal agency helps explain why welfare dependency and parasitism are such sensitive issues for people whose fortunes are now troubled in the world.

Enthusiasts for the new economy are, as they say in California, "in denial" on the subject of disposable labor. In a popular classic about modern corporations, *Re-engineering the Corporation* (1993), the authors Michael Hammer and James Champy defend "re-engineering" against the charge that it is a mere cover for firing people by asserting "downsizing and restructuring only mean doing less with less. Re-engineering, by contrast means doing *more* with less." The "less" in the last sentence reverberates with the denials of an older Social Darwinism: those who are not fit will somehow disappear.

Some tough-minded economists argue that current forms of unemployment, under-employment, deskilling, and parasitism are incurable in the emerging order, since the economy indeed profits from doing "more with less." What I wish to emphasize is that the modern economy, no more than the classical capitalist economy, offers a solution to Smith's Paradox, to the problem of impoverished work experience. The sheer increase of jobs, the reorganization of the division of labor, are not forms of growth that increase the quality of laboring experience. Instead, this qualitative impoverishment makes increasing numbers of people feel that they personally have no footing in the process of economic growth. And that lack of footing poses a profound political challenge: can we, through political means, provide people with a sense that they are worthwhile and necessary and consequent human beings?

A Coherent Self

The Victorians founded their sense of self-worth on life organized as one long project: the German values of *formation*, the English virtues of purpose, were for keeps. Careers in business, military, or imperial bureaucracies made the lifelong project possible, grading work into a clear sequence of steps. Such expectations devalue the present for the sake of the future – the present, which is in constant upheaval and which may tempt an individual into byways or evanescent pleasures. Weber thus described future-orientation as a mentality of delayed gratification. Yet this Victorian experience of cohering time has another side, which they subsumed under the ethical category of taking responsibility for one's life. Will enters into that act of taking responsibility for one's life, though in a way quite opposite from the innovatory character of the will to change from within.

In *Thus Spake Zarathustra* Nietzsche wrote, "powerless against what has been done, he is an angry spectator of all that is past. The will cannot will backwards."

But Nietzsche's contemporaries did bend the will backwards in time. The Victorians bent consciousness backwards to compose out of the dislocations, accidental changes of direction, or unused capacities of a life a record for which one had to take personal responsibility, even though these events might be beyond the actual control of the person who experienced them. Freud's early case histories, like his study of the "Wolf-Man," revolve around costs of organizing time in this cohering fashion – particularly the act of taking responsibility, with its consequent feelings of guilt, for past events beyond one's control. The poet Senancour combined the subjective time of future and past in declaring that "I live to become, but I carry the unshakable burden of what I have been." Freud remarks that such feelings of responsibility are modern sentiments, in contrast to earlier ages when people felt their life histories in the hands of the gods, God, or blind fortune.

Today, these late Victorian values of personal responsibility are as strong as a century ago but their institutional context has changed. The iron cage has been dismantled, so that individuals struggle for security and coherence in a seemingly empty arena. The destruction of institutional supports at work, as in the welfare state, leaves individuals only their sense of responsibility; the Victorian ethos now often charts a negative trajectory of defeated will, of having failed to make one's life cohere through one's work.

Twenty-five years ago (for the book *The Hidden Injuries of Class* [1973]), I interviewed workers in Boston who knew work was beyond their control, like Nietzsche's "angry spectators," yet took responsibility for what happened to them. In that generation, a catastrophe in the economy that caused a worker, say, to lose his home, roused this double consciousness of being an angry spectator and a responsible agent. Today, exactly the processes that expand the economy put workers in this double bind.

Take what happens when career paths are replaced by intermittent jobs. Many temporary workers have a dual consciousness of their work, knowing such work suits obligation-resistant companies, yet nonetheless believing that if only they had themselves managed their lives differently, they would have made a career out of their skills, and so be permanently employed. The new economic map that devalues lifelong career projects has shifted the optimal age curves of work to younger, raw employees (it used to be late twenties to middle fifties; now it's early twenties to early forties), even though adults are living longer and more vigorously. Studies of dismissed middle-aged workers find them both obsessed and puzzled by the liabilities of age. Rather than believing themselves faded and over the hill, they feel they know what to do, that they are more organized and purposeful than younger workers. Yet they blame themselves for not having made the right moves in the past, for not having prepared. Their work histories are like Senancour's burden, heavy memories.

This legacy of personal responsibility deflects anger away from economic institutions. The rhetoric of modern management indeed attempts to disguise power in the new economy by making the worker believe he or she is a self-directing agent; as the authors of *Re-engineering the Corporation* declare, in the emerging institutions "managers stop acting like supervisors and behave more like coaches." It is not false consciousness that makes such statements credible to those who are likely to suffer from them; rather, a twisted sense of moral agency.

In his *On the Dignity of Man* (1965), the Renaissance philosopher Pico della Mirandola declared, "man is an animal of diverse, multiform, and destructible nature"; in this pliant condition, "it is given to him to have that which he chooses and to be that which he wills." Man is his own maker; the chief of his works is his self-worth. In modernity, people take responsibility for their lives because the whole of it feels their making. But when the ethical culture of modernity, with its codes of personal responsibility and life purpose, is carried into a society without institutional shelters, there appears not pride of self, but a dialectics of failure in the midst of growth. Growth in the new economy depends on gutting corporate size, ending bureaucratic guarantees, profiting from the flux and extensions of economic networks. People come to know such dislocations as their own lack of direction. The ethics of responsibility becomes, ironically, and terribly, a subjective yardstick to measure one's failure to cohere.

This is why I'd like to see new discussions about social democracy enlarged beyond the frame of reference of worker self-management or collective participation. We have to think through social democracy in terms of this legacy of subjectivity, one in which time is deeply personal, in which self-management of durable time becomes an ethics of responsibility. This subjectivity now coexists with capitalist practices of metamorphosis and rupture, as a terrible duet – or, if you like, dialectics – of continuity and change.

As I've listening to this duet, I've wondered if its strength might be weakened by easing the subjective voice; that is, by lightening the burden of self-responsibility and time that people bear in modernity. And that reflection brings me back to the question of place.

Consider

1. Summarise Sennetts's argument in your own words.
2. What does Sennett understand by the 'spectre of uselessness', and how is it related to contemporary changes in the world of work?
3. 'The skills economy still leaves behind the majority; more finely, the education system turns out large numbers of unemployable educated young people, at least unemployable in the domains for which they have trained. [. . .] The economic machine may be able to run profitably and efficiently by drawing on an ever-smaller elite' (Sennett 2006: 86). Discuss.
4. Do you agree with Sennett's analysis of the world of work? Give examples that support or contradict Sennett's arguments.

5.11 Individualisation

Alongside the mobilisation of social life, sociological perspectives on *individualisation* may offer important insights into contemporary processes of modernisation and globalisation. Debates about individualisation have played an important role in Western sociology since at least the mid 1980s. They can, perhaps, be best understood in relation to long-standing preoccupations among sociologists with questions of social cohesion under conditions of modernity. Generally speaking, the term *social cohesion* refers to the question of what holds modern societies together in the context of the rapid and large-scale social changes that have been characteristic of modernisation. Many of the works of the early sociologists discussed in Chapter 3 deal with social cohesion. For example, writing about the division of labour in society, Émile Durkheim (1984) sought to address problems brought about by what he saw as a lack of mutual solidarity and community life in highly differentiated, complex European societies. Karl Marx's arguments about capitalism and class struggle (e.g. see Kamenka 1983: 125ff.) engage with the conflicts and alienation brought about by the rise of capitalism. Georg Simmel's (1971) study on life in the modern metropolis speaks of the sense of isolation and distance from others we may easily experience in the fast-paced, anonymous, sprawling cities that concentrate an ever-growing share of humanity. And so forth.

Studies by European sociologists Ulrich Beck and Anthony Giddens have had a particularly strong influence on debates about individualisation over the past two decades. For Ulrich Beck, processes of individualisation may play a significant role in contemporary or *reflexive* modernisation. According to Beck (2000), apart from generating risks on an unprecedented scale, reflexive modernisation also works to undermine the traditional social bonds that underpinned earlier stages of modern life. Where the everyday lives of industrial labourers in the early twentieth century were shaped to a large extent by the solidarities and common world views of the working class, today's call-centre operators or fast-food workers largely experience the demands of their working lives on their own, in an environment often characterised by high staff turnover, anonymity, and few chances to build close ties with co-workers. Where marriage and family ties once lasted decades or entire lifetimes, being single, living alone or in a temporary relationship, and getting divorced are, thus Beck (2000), increasingly common in societies that demand high levels of flexibility and mobility from individuals and offer little support for lasting friendships and intimate ties.

According to Beck (2000: 128), individualisation is characterised by three core dynamics. First, there is the *disembedding* of individuals from pre-established, largely fixed social bonds of, for instance, class, labour, institutionalised religion, or family and kinship. Second, there is a *loss of traditional security*. Ways of life, norms and values that may previously have been taken for granted are now open to doubt and questioning, as societies' institutions lose their capacity to act as dominant moral authorities. Third, individuals are reintegrated into *a new type of social commitment*, where they are directly confronted with the demands that governments, employers, schools and universities, and other large-scale social institutions may seek to impose on them. We might therefore imagine individualisation as a process of social atomisa-tion, which gives individuals both the freedom and the burden to fashion their own sense of self, identity and biography, and to work out their place in society by them-selves. The idea of *reflexivity* refers to precisely this capacity and need on the part of each of us to negotiate our life plans and our place in society on our own.

Drawing on the theme of reflexive modernisation, Anthony Giddens has examined issues such as self-identity (Giddens 1991) and the nature of intimate attachment in the contemporary world (Giddens 1992). In his widely cited study *The Transformation of Intimacy* (1992), Giddens points to the increasing possibility for individuals to redefine intimate relationships beyond traditional norms and bonds of social status. He writes of the rise of *pure relationships* into which people enter for their own sake and for the satisfaction intimate partners may derive from being together (Giddens 1992: 58). Pure relationships are hence at once grounded in ideals of *romantic love*, life-long and unique, and in *confluent love* (Giddens 1992: 61), that is to say love which needs to be constantly worked on and re-kindled and which may fade if left to wither:

> There is a structural contradiction in the pure relationship, centring upon commit-ment, which many of Hite's respondents acknowledge. To generate commitment and develop a shared history, an individual must give of herself to the other. That is, she must provide, in word and deed, some kind of guarantees to the other that the relationship can be sustained for an indefinite period. Yet a present-day relationship is not, as marriage once was, a 'natural condition' whose durability can be taken for granted short of certain extreme circumstances. It is a feature of the pure relation-ship that it can be terminated, more or less at will, by either partner at any particular point. For a relationship to stand a chance of lasting, commitment is necessary; yet anyone who commits herself without reservations risks great hurt in the future, should the relationship become dissolved. (Giddens 1992: 137)

Here, Giddens discusses the tensions and instability inherent in pure relationships. Begun out of love and the conviction that I have found a truly special other, I hope and expect that a relationship will last forever. At the same time, the cultural and economic pressure to remain married that may have characterised the lives of earlier generations is now gone. Moreover, alongside my relationship, I am faced with the task of personal and professional success in a social environment calling for my constant availability, mobility and flexibility. Thus (at Giddens 1992: 140), my investment in my relation-ship may fade and my partner and I may simply grow apart.

In spite of numerous criticisms, such as the failure to account for persistent boundaries and inequalities of gender, sex, class and generations (cf. Smart 2007) the work of Giddens and Beck has remained popular. It has been followed by numerous other commentar-ies on individualisation and the atomisation of social ties (e.g. Bauman 2001; Hochschild 2003; Elliott and Lemert 2006; Illouz 2007). Moreover, there have been significant recent attempts to apply theories of individualisation beyond their original European remit (e.g. Yan 2009; Hansen and Svarverud 2010). The following reading provides you with an introduction to some more recent arguments about individualisation and globalisation.

Reading

Elliott, A. and Lemert, C. (2006), *The New Individualism*, Abingdon: Routledge, pp. 79–83 and 91–6

Living in a privatized world

Coping with globalization

He was always punctual, and approached psychotherapy like it was simply one of the many business transactions he conducted daily. A good looking man, a 48-year-old hi-tech computer whizz, Larry had accumulated buckets of money during the dot.com revolution and was now a millionaire several times over. He was, on his own reckoning, 'self-made', and remarked that he really only felt secure when he was 'in control' of a situation – which, for him, meant defining how things should be. Psychotherapy was no exception.

The idea that other people could engender different emotional states or frames of mind in him was foreign. It simply never arose for his consideration. People, much like things, were there for his pleasure, his manipulation. Not that he approached the world in a cynical way, he stressed. It was just the way the world worked. Period.

'People see me as something of a control freak I know, and they may be right', he said. 'But that desire for control goes all the way down, and it is, ultimately, a result of the way my mother related to me. She always said it was important to fit in, to belong. But that was just a cover, a way of getting me to do what she wanted, to dance to her tune. And so, this is where projection comes in. I've taken what happened from my childhood, what was done to me, and I'm now putting it on others, making them dance to my tune.'

Larry's reference to 'projection' gives some indication of the way he approached psychotherapy, the latest in his various attempts to purchase care of the self. Before beginning therapy he'd got hold of all the books his psychoanalyst – a prominent and respected professional – had written. He read them intensely, as if studying for exams. He'd also immersed himself in the self-help literature. It was as if he believed the only way he could reflect on the psychological meanings of his life was to affect a kind of 'therapy-speak', as if copying a discourse promoted by experts.

The language of therapy is, in fact, a form of talk that by and large ignores the socially and historically fragile, but fundamental, division between public and private life, and perhaps nowhere is this more so than in the therapeutic injunction to free associate. The notion of 'free association' appealed to Larry's finely tuned commercial instincts: Freud's precept that the patient should be released to a kind of unconscious dreaming had become, in Larry's hands, a new way into thinking about the behavioural imperatives of the global marketplace for flexibility, fluidity and continual self-reinvention. If he could successfully organize his daily working life and manage to negotiate all sorts of significant changes within the company that he owned, then surely self-change wasn't going to be that diffi-cult. Flexibility creates dynamism in the marketplace, and so may actually induce big emotional changes in personal life also. But how to be flexible? Really flex-ible. Emotionally flexible.

Larry's desire for flexibility was somewhat constrained by his inflexible attitude that all things had to be done quickly. Speed was a supreme value in his life – the accelerating pace of technology, after all, had made him a rich man. But not so therapy, which – as Larry discovered – works with an altogether different under-standing of time. Therapy, after all, isn't exactly famous for getting fast results. A colleague had told him to read a well-known book on self-therapy, a kind of guide to becoming one's own therapist.

> Possibly you're feeling restless. Or you may feel overwhelmed by the demands of wife, husband, children, or job. You may feel unappreciated by those people closest to you. Perhaps you feel angry that life is passing you by and you haven't accomplished all those great things you had hoped to do. Something feels missing from your life. You were attracted by the title of this book and wish that you really were in charge. What to do?

Though sceptical of the Californian cult of therapy, this book – *Self-Therapy* by Janette Rainwater – struck a chord with Larry. Something certainly was missing from his life, and he was quite prepared to try self-therapy. This was all to the good he thought, since it cut out the awkwardness of having to discuss embarrassing personal problems with another person. Larry would be his own therapist. And he could work at his own pace: fast.

And so he did. Larry's dedication to 'taking charge of one's life', as the therapy-speak has it, was single-minded. He followed, almost to the letter, all of Rainwater's recommendations. He kept a journal. He sought to break with habit, with his rou-tine ways of doing things. He thought long and hard about traumatic phases of his childhood (what Rainwater calls 'autobiographical thinking' – as if there might be another kind?), especially the loss of his mother's affections during his earliest years. He thought about the future. Imagining what Rainwater terms a 'dialogue with time', he tried to envisage what his life might be like without work, without that familiar structure which he used to screen out questions about what he actually wanted to do, what he felt like doing. And he tried to think about death Rainwater-style: not as time running out but as an active engagement with the present and his own desires.

Still, all the time he was getting anxious and more depressed. His addiction to feverish work was threatening his own health and he could not seem to hold things together at work in the manner he once could. He went to see his doctor, who recommended yet another therapy, psychoanalysis, which is how his story has come to be told here.

Coming to psychoanalysis had been perhaps even more difficult for Larry than it might have been, partly because he concluded that this meant his self-therapy was a failure. Rather than viewing his experiment with self-therapy opening emotional questions which led to psychoanalysis, Larry preferred to carve up his world into neat starts and endings, successes and failures, the good and the bad.

Larry liked being analytical in analysis. He would routinely stand back from his described feeling states – as if still the self-therapist – and pronounce on his psychological condition. He spoke of resistances in himself, of projection and transference, and of repression. He had almost convinced himself that he did in fact understand what was going on in his emotional life when he did not. This posed obvious problems. Such was his desire to be always in control, to assume total knowledge, that it was anything but simple for Larry to tolerate uncertainty or ambivalence. From pop-psychology handbooks to his psychoanalyst's latest technical papers, Larry used whatever he read to protect against a fear of not-knowing.

Before Larry could pursue this fear and attempt to come to terms with its emotional significance, he needed to acknowledge his inability to feel at a loss about what he wanted and needed. This came slowly, through long and often painful therapeutic work. More often than not, any step forward would in turn generate a few backwards. His unconscious anger poured out. A workaholic, Larry knew one guaranteed way out of the emotional messiness the analysis was reflecting. Work. Feverish work.

Yet even work wasn't what is used to be for Larry. It was increasingly unable to protect him from the seemingly chaotic feelings of which he was more and more aware. In fact, it was work – or, rather, a failure to work – that brought Larry into psychoanalysis in the first place. There were two especially telling incidents. The first arose when Larry was seeking to clinch a business deal, ironically enough when using a mobile phone. The anxiety was extreme. Suddenly, it was as if there was too much confusion; Larry had to get one of his associates to take over the negotiations. The second incident occurred several months later, again when Larry was with business associates. Executives from a company based in London were in Los Angeles, seeking to finalize an agreement with Larry's company. After the first round of meetings, Larry invited the associates to dinner at an exclusive restaurant. While Larry was waiting to be seated at the restaurant, anxiety flooded in again. Intolerable anxiety. Larry felt 'temporarily deranged'. He was confused and couldn't think; he fled the restaurant.
[. . .]

Living with globalism

For those who fear globalization and its impacts, Larry's story might seem an instructive warning: a man who has 'made it', primarily through traversing the global, and one whose personal sense of satisfaction gained from capitalist society (material affluence, power, symbolic prestige) enters into sharp contradiction with the ideologies of that world (security, freedom and happiness). Larry is, on his own reckoning, self-made, autonomous, his own boss, blissfully self-determining. And yet, paradoxically, all of Larry's reflections on his life in therapy attest to a sense of displacement, decentring and division. The authorship of his own biography, he implies, is continually written over by outside forces; but also, and more interestingly, such dislocating forces penetrate to the core of his identity. Caught within the denied difference between the rhetoric and reality of global postmodernist culture, Larry is at once self-identical and decentred, manically narcissistic and defensively depressed.

Larry's reflections on the determining power of 'outside forces' provide a salutary example of the risks issuing from globalization, especially of its perceived threats and terrors. Interestingly, Larry has his own perspective on the global. During therapy, he expressed deep reservations about the intricate links between corporate power and the new global economy – reservations which reflect anxieties about the myriad ways his own life has been transformed as a consequence of globalization. The trouble with globalization, he reasoned, is that it is ultimately menacing, soul-destroying and all-controlling. The relentless commercial pressure to compete, continually to cut costs and to find more flexible and cheaper methods of service delivery cuts directly across any sense of loyalty and commitment to his staff as well as the building of a larger organizational identity. He felt saddened that money, materialism and managerialism so obviously held the upper hand over loyalty, commitment and community. From this angle, the economic and cultural consequences of globalization can only be thought of in terms of deadlock, the former displacing and disfiguring the latter. The media, he reckons, mythologizes the virtues of global forces like digital communications, especially its capacity to broaden the mind, to allow one to learn from, and experiment with, other forms of life, other cultures. But for Larry this isn't what happens at all. The something happening in our brave new world, unleashed by the unknown and unseen forces of globalization, is that which takes control of your life, both professionally and personally, rendering one defensive and depressed.

For all the wealth the new global capitalism has brought him, Larry is clearly prone to speaking a language of victimhood. The hard-nosed entrepreneur in him welcomes the greater competitiveness and intense individualism which globalization has spawned. And yet his own experience, as one whose lifestyle of globalism leaves him feeling far removed from his own emotional world as well as emotional contact with others, leads him time and again to blame external forces. And nothing, it seems, is quite such a menacing external force as globalism. Although Larry only used the term 'globalization' on rare occasions, many of the issues he was preoccupied with in therapy go to the very core of this phenomenon. In particular, corporate downsizing and constant technological change had made him permanently uneasy, self-doubting, anxiously preoccupied with matters of professional standing and social hierarchy. Torn between liberal rhetoric of the economic benefits of globalization and the realities of corporate re-engineering and general short-termism, it was as if Larry couldn't decide whether – as boss of the company – he's a winner or loser. Again, however, what comes through most clearly in therapy is his sense of a lack of emotional freedom. For Larry has come to blame the counterfeit flexibility promoted by globalizing economic forces for this sense of emotional deficit pervading his life.

As Larry speaks of it, this brave new world of corporate re-engineering and technological networking is primarily about economic globalization. Yet there is a sense also in which the global economy spills over into the cultural sphere, and at the same time transforms and reconfigures it. For example, Larry often referred to his business as a 'control machine'. When this was explored in therapy it became clear that he imagined this 'machine' as controlling not only the activities, thoughts and dispositions of both employees and senior management but also that this omnipotent force extended to the commercial operations of the organization itself – thereby filling in a range of societal connections with other communication networks, corporations and, ultimately, the global marketplace. Tellingly, it had never occurred to Larry that these fantasies about corporate surveillance or social control might be worth exploring further for himself, both for what they might suggest about his ties with other people and for the changed relations between institutional and personal life. Larry's analyst suggested that it might be fruitful to think about this some more, and in time it emerged that there was a link in Larry's mind between the corporate, technical and organized world of global systems on the one hand, and the draining or emptying out of passion, spontaneity and interpersonal engagement in personal life on the other. The more Larry immersed himself in the world of business and the dynamics of the global economy, the less sure he felt of his inner self and of his emotional connection with others. This was the theme – organized globalization contrasted with dislocations of the intimacies of personal life – that dominated many analytic sessions.

What, exactly, is the personal dislocation of which Larry speaks? What is being explored here is the fear (and, no doubt, the wish) of relinquishing personal agency. In a globalizing world, in which past ways of doing things are continually revised and overturned, personal reflexivity becomes paramount. There are of course various ways in which individuals can avoid or displace these pressures of globalism, and strategies of passivity, resigned acceptance and denial are all ways of limiting the difficult emotional task of relating inner and outer, self and world, identity and difference. And yet such strategies, notwithstanding their own emotional brittleness, run directly into conflict with the deadly worlds of globalization. Such is the heavy emphasis on individualism today that people are compelled, and daily, to be proactive or self-legislating in all aspects of life. Only those practised in the arts of escape, from day-dreaming to artistic and literary expression, manage to hold to a sense of what is tantalizing in the very thought of subjective escape. For what we need to escape from – others, work, the system – says a great deal about both ourselves and our contemporary cultural malaise.

Here is where sociology enters in an interesting way, as there has been no shortage of intellectual assessments of the conditions of political domination structuring the desire for social escape. Inspired by various kinds of literary and sociological works – from Weber's envisioned 'iron cage of bureaucracy' to Orwell's *1984* – many have portrayed the development of the modern age in terms of escalating and unstoppable levels of social control, with an accompanying radical deterioration of individual initiative and sense of personal freedom. Thus the sociological melodrama of 'Big Brother society', in which the world of organized capitalism and bureaucratic rationality produces ever-intensifying levels of private fear, foreboding and fragmentation.

Many contemporary accounts of globalization do, in fact, present an explanation of the ills of society in terms of the determining power of structures in people's lives; it is then but a short step to fill in the missing pieces of the jigsaw by uncovering how individuals, identities, desires, dispositions, environments and cultures are reshaped, usually in a brutally linear fashion, by the omnipotent forces of globalism. The central conceptual and political limitation of conceptualizing globalization purely as an external force, however, is that it prevents us from seeing with sufficient clarity the myriad ways in which individuals engage, respond, escape, reproduce or transform the whole gamut of globalizing forces that they necessarily encounter in their everyday lives. What is ironic is that such top-heavy accounts of globalism – even if they were proved an accurate account of current social realities – cannot provide an adequate means of grasping how individuals respond to both the expansive and the debilitating impacts of such worldwide transformations. People who retreat inwards, like Larry, are merely cast as the dupes of a particular Western set of ideological values or consumption patterns; what is passed over in silence is the multiplicity of emotions that shape the distinctive and idiosyncratic ways in which individuals navigate the multiple cruising speeds of globalization.

The opposite of social control, one might say, is choice. Precisely how we come to think about the scope of available choices in our lives, at any particular moment, has consequences for how we imagine the ways the world impacts upon us. In the language of some analysts of worldwide social transformations, globalization is viewed as both a condition and a consequence of people exercising choice in their daily lives. A triumph, one might think, of neo-liberal ideology? A reinstatement of the modernist dream of the free individual at precisely the historical moment when global conglomerates reign supreme? Or, perhaps, simply a consumerist discourse raised to the second power? Not necessarily, as choice in this context cannot be explained exhaustively in terms of the marketplace and the new capitalism. Those who think it feasible to speak of a more nuanced idea of how personal choice intersects with globalization have in mind, perhaps above all, the crisis (or, better, ever-erupting crises) of the late modern age, and in particular focus on the complex ways in which ordinary people reframe global troubles in terms of individual responsibilities, emotional conundrums and ethical dilemmas. Here is how Anthony Giddens, renowned sociologist and a leading figure in British Third Way politics, describes how choice is shaped by, and reshapes, globalizing processes:

> The more tradition loses its hold, and the more daily life is reconstituted in terms of the dialectical interplay of the local and the global, the more individuals are forced to negotiate lifestyle choices among a diversity of options. Of course, there are standardising influences too – most notably, in the form of commodification, since capitalistic production and distribution forms core components of modernity's institutions. Yet because of the 'openness' of social life today, the pluralisation of contexts of action and the diversity of 'authorities', lifestyle choice is increasingly important in the constitution of self-identity and daily activity.

Not so much a phenomenon 'out there', globalization is rather internal to the way we go about making choices and performing activities in daily life. Globalization is not merely constraint, a kind of brake, on personal autonomy, though undoubtedly it sometimes feels like this. For Giddens, the global – which penetrates to the core of lifestyle options – is inextricably bound up with the local, the way we live now.

Consider
1. How do Elliott and Lemert characterise the relationship between individualisation and globalisation? How does Larry's story illustrate this relationship?
2. How would you define individualisation? Use the reading and the preceding introduction to support your arguments.
3. How relevant is the idea of individualisation to the society you live in? Why?
4. Now return to sections 5.10 and 5.11. How may new forms of mobility and transformations in the world of work contribute to explaining the individualisation of modern societies?

5.12 Conclusion

This chapter has explored contemporary patterns of social change from a relatively wide range of perspectives. Each of these perspectives represents a particular lens or standpoint from which you could begin to think about the nature of contemporary social life and the shape of things to come. Given the particularity of these standpoints, it is also important to emphasise that each of them can only give you a somewhat partial and incomplete image of the social world. Social change tends to proceed in a *non-linear* manner. This means that processes of global change might best be understood as general tendencies that manifest themselves in very specific ways in different places and that may entail a variety of consequences.

The inexorable global spread of capitalism serves well to illustrate this point. It is uncontroversial to argue that capitalist forms of social, economic and cultural life are pervasive around the world today. There is, however, less agreement upon the nature and consequences of capitalism's global dominance. In line with the theories of globalisation outlined in section 5.2, some would argue that capitalism's spread has gone hand in hand with a trend towards the homogenisation or, often, Americanisation, of social life. Other scholars emphasise that capitalism has been moulded to suit a variety of locally specific beliefs and practices. In spite of these differences, even many supporters of the homogenisation thesis acknowledge a notable degree of variability in globalisation's manifestations and consequences.

Sociologist Ronald Robertson (1997) consequently writes of the *glocalisation*, rather than the globalisation, of social life, merging the terms globalisation and localisation. With this term, Robertson refers to the simultaneity and co-existence of globalising and localising trends in the development of contemporary societies. On the one hand, there are far-reaching dynamics of social change at work that encompass all of us, regardless of our place in the world. On the other hand, these dynamics may be incorporated into or offset and remoulded by cultural, economic, political, etc., forces that pertain to specific societies and social groups.

It is in this sense that, writing about the global spread of McDonald's fast food restaurants as an emblem of a broad trend towards the capitalist rationalisation of social life, George Ritzer (2010) acknowledges that eating at McDonald's may mean many different things and take notably different shapes in different societies. A simple illustration of this point involves searching for international McDonald's TV advertisements on websites such as YouTube or Google Video. A direct comparison of different national websites of McDonald's will also do. In any case, you will find that the culinary sensibilities to which the restaurant chain speaks in different countries are quite notably dissimilar! For examples, beef burgers feature quite prominently on the website of McDonald's UK, but are nowhere to be found at McDonald's India, where chicken plays a much bigger role.

The sociological concepts discussed in this chapter will therefore be most useful and inspiring if you draw on them with caution, avoiding blanket generalisations and considering what, if anything at all, they might mean in particular times and places. Draw on them to sensitise yourself to the social processes you would like to explore, without expecting universal truths!

The debate: Globalisation and social inequality

From here, we will move on to look at the ways in which social inequalities and divisions shape our lives. A good starting point for this discussion is to consider how globalisation and some of the most recent and cutting-edge social, cultural, economic and technological developments have created new, sharp, painful forms of inequality. One of these forms of inequality is the *digital divide*. The idea that we now live in a network society (see above) does not mean that the emergent networks of social, cultural and economic exchange

are evenly structured and generally accessible without substantial complications. Recent research, for instance, has emphasised the existence of a substantial *digital divide*, that is, the gap in access to computers and the internet that
exists between individuals, groups and countries today. Jan van Dijk argued as
recently as 2005 that:

> the digital divide is far from closed. In most parts of the world, it is still
> widening. The gap between developed and developing countries is extremely
> wide, and it is growing. Even in the most developed high-tech societ-
> ies, where the division in physical access has stopped broadening, about one
> quarter, or even one third, of the population has no access to computers and
> the Internet. (van Dijk 2005: 2)

Globalisation in this sense brought with it new forms of social inequalities – a
subject matter to be explored in more detail in the next chapter. The exposure of
people and societies to the forces of the network society – global financial markets,
new technologies of communication and travel, academic and intellectual
exchange, and so forth – is differentiated by the basic economic and technological
means to take part in networks in the first place. When individuals or societies lack
access to and knowledge about computers, internet-based communication, etc.,
they are barred from many crucial developments and opportunities.

To give one example, at the time these words are written, an important debate
is taking place about the ways in which access to cutting-edge research is skewed
in favour of highly networked, highly affluent researchers and universities,
typically located in highly networked and highly affluent societies. As part of
their professional development, considerable pressure is put on academics to
publish their research in leading journals in their field. These leading journals are
very often published by commercial publishing houses, which charge considerable access fees. These fees are indeed so considerable that universities and
researchers in many or most parts of the world cannot afford to pay them (see
thecostofknowledge.com for more information on this). The very latest work in
virtually all academic fields is easily accessible to anyone with a computer and an
internet connection – and a credit card that allows her or him to overcome pay-
walls that may charge £30, £50 or more for even single journal articles. Lacking
access to new discoveries and ideas, these universities and researchers are in
many ways 'left behind', and their work is considerably slowed at the very least.
In turn, elite institutions and academics are able to maintain and reproduce their
privileged status by virtue of their exclusive access to new research. Currently,
campaigns are in progress to raise awareness of this problem and entice researchers to publish in free open-access journals. As of mid 2012, the results of these
campaigns remain unclear.

Discuss

1. What is the extent of the digital divide *between* societies worldwide? What is the extent of the digital divide *within* societies worldwide? Look for information on both questions and give relevant examples.
2. What are the origins of the digital divide? What are its consequences?
3. In the light of the digital divide, to what extent and in which ways do we really live in a global network society?

Works cited

Bauman, Z. (2001), *The Individualized Society*, Cambridge: Polity Press.

Beck, U. (1986/2000), *Risk Society: Towards a New Modernity*, London: Sage.

Bhambra, G. K. (2007), 'Sociology and Postcolonialism: Another 'Missing' Revolution?', *Sociology* 41(5): 871–84.

Castells, M. (2000), *The Rise of the Network Society*, Oxford: Blackwell Publishers.

Durkheim, É. (1984), *The Division of Labour in Society*, Basingstoke: Macmillan.

Elliott, A. and C. Lemert (2006), *The New Individualism: The Emotional Costs of Globalization*, London: Routledge.

Giddens, A. (1991), *Modernity and Self-Identity: Self and Society in the Late Modern Age*, Cambridge: Polity Press.

Giddens, A. (1992), *The Transformation of Intimacy: Love, Sexuality and Eroticism in Modern Societies*, Cambridge: Polity.

Goodman, D. S. G., ed. (2008), *The New Rich in China: Future Rulers, Present Lives*, Abingdon: Routledge.

Hansen, M. H. and R. Svarverud, eds (2010), *iChina: The Rise of the Individual in Modern Chinese Society*, Copenhagen: Nordic Institute of Asian Studies.

Hochschild, A. R. (2003), *The Commercialization of Intimate Life: Notes from Home and Work*, Berkeley: University of California Press.

Illouz, E. (2007), *Cold Intimacies: The Making of Emotional Capitalism*, Cambridge: Polity Press.

Kamenka, E., ed. (1983), *The Portable Karl Marx*, New York: Penguin Books.

Lash, S. and C. Lury (2007), *Global Culture Industry: The Mediation of Things*, Cambridge: Polity Press.

Park, R. E. (1925/1967), 'The City: Suggestions for the Investigation of Human Behavior in the Urban Environment' in *The City*, edited by R. E. Park, E. W. Burgess and R. D. McKenzie, Chicago: The University of Chicago Press (pp. 1–46).

Ritzer, G. (2010), *The McDonaldization of Society 6*, Thousand Oaks: Pine Forge Press.

Robertson, R. (1997), 'Glocalization: Time-Space and Homogeneity-Heterogeneity', in *Global Modernities*, edited by M. Featherstone, S. Lash and R. Robertson, London: Sage: 25–44.

Sassen, S. (1991), *The Global City: New York, London, Tokyo*, Princeton: Princeton University Press.

Sennett, R. (2006), *The Culture of the New Capitalism*, New Haven: Yale University Press.

Smart, C. (2007), *Personal Life : New Directions in Sociological Thinking*, Cambridge: Polity Press.

van Dijk, J. A. G. M. (2005), *The Deepening Divide: Inequality in the Information Society*, Thousand Oaks: Sage.

van Dijk, J. (2006), *The Network Society: Social Aspects of New Media*, 2nd edn, London: SAGE.

Waters, M. (1995), *Globalization*, London: Routledge.

Weber, M. (1905/2009), *The Protestant Ethic and the Spirit of Capitalism, with Other Writings on the Rise of the West*, New York: Oxford University Press.

Williams, R. (2006), *Culture and Materialism*, London: Verso.

Yan, Y. (2009), *The Individualization of Chinese Society*, Oxford: Berg.

6 Social inequalities and globalisation

6.1 Introduction

In this chapter, we will focus on social divisions and inequalities. The systematic analysis of the ways in which simple differences between social groups may turn into sharp divisions, inequalities and, often, conflict and exploitation has always been a major concern for sociologists. Sociological research has served to disqualify many myths and stereotypes about the causes of inequalities. It highlights how inequalities are *socially constructed*: rather than resulting from natural, somehow biologically or psychologically inherent traits of social groups, inequalities are shaped by social processes that are often so persistent that they become an invisible, taken-for-granted part of common sense. Such inequalities often operate in terms of processes of *social stratification*, that is, social systems by which people and social groups are ranked in a hierarchical order. Moreover, they are closely associated with the organisation of *social power* and the *ability of individuals and social groups to achieve goals against the resistance of others*.

In many Latin American countries, notable inequalities between different social and ethnic groups are widespread. These inequalities have deep historical roots. The countries of contemporary Latin America emerged from the conquest and occupation of a large part of the Americas by Spanish invaders from the early sixteenth century onwards. Spanish elites quickly rose to power and began to control social, economic and political life. Colonial society was composed of many groups, including Spaniards and other Europeans, indigenous populations, and Africans who had first arrived through the transatlantic slave trade. From this mix, a complex *caste system* emerged, in order to allow the Spanish elites to maintain power. A caste system can be defined as a *form of social stratification within which an individual's position is inherited or otherwise ascribed*. In colonial Spanish society, this led to sharp distinctions between European-born elites and *criollos* (that is, descendants of Europeans born in America) on the one hand and members of lower-ranked castes on the other. A vast, complex, and often inconsistent list of terms emerged to classify the latter. The term *mestizo*, for instance, was used to designate the descendants of a Spanish father and an indigenous mother. Further down in the hierarchy, we find *castizos*, descended from a Spanish father and a *mestizo* mother. Of a yet lower status, the child of a Spanish father and a *castizo* mother would be an *espomolo*. The child of a Spaniard and a black African would be a *mulato*, and the mulato's child with a Spaniard would a *morisco*, who, in turn, would have an *albino* child with a Spanish father. And so forth. While the term *mestizo* is still frequently used, the other labels and the hierarchy they denote have long since been abandoned. Nonetheless, an attentiveness to issues of ethnicity and skin colour does persist in many parts of Latin America.

This example illustrates basic sociological points about social inequalities. First, it highlights the association of inequalities with the organisation of social power. The caste system of the Spanish viceroyalties was a direct outcome of colonial conquest by military force and the control of the occupied territories by foreign elites, who sought legitimacy by placing themselves at the top of the caste hierarchy. This, moreover, points us to the social constructedness of inequalities. The caste system rendered people unequal by virtue of their birth and their traits supposedly biologically inherited from parents of a better or lesser origin. However, the fact that the castes suddenly emerged after the conquest of the Americas and then faded away as the Latin American nations gained their independence in the nineteenth century shows that, rather than being biologically grounded or 'natural', the caste system was the outcome of the convergence of very specific social factors under very particular historical circumstances. For the caste system to become a meaningful part of everyday life, people in the colonies had to be convinced of it and believe that, in a social and biological sense, the castes and resulting hierarchies did really exist. Social inequalities can become powerful elements of social life when people are convinced that others are not only different, but also in some sense inferior, and when power in society is distributed in ways that encourage disdain for others to spill over into outright oppression or exploitation.

On the following pages, we will consider some basic forms of social inequality that are prominent in contemporary sociological research. Where relevant, we will tie these inequalities to the broader themes of modernisation and globalisation that have informed much of our argument so far.

6.2 Race, ethnicity and racism

'Race', 'ethnicity' and 'racism' are all terms you are familiar with. Precisely for this reason, it is somewhat difficult to approach them from a sociological perspective. This is because they have acquired common-sense meanings which vary considerably in their usage. For US Americans, it is very common to speak of different 'races' to designate people of different national, cultural and physical characteristics. The German equivalent of 'race' – *Rasse* – fell out of favour after it was used by the National Socialist dictatorship (1933–45) to justify genocide, the Holocaust and the propagation of war on a massive scale. The use of the term is now fairly firmly associated with fascism and extreme right-wing politics. In this sense, you might wish to take the following definitions as starting points in your exploration of a particularly intricate subject matter.

Let us begin with 'race'. The notion that there are human races emerged alongside the development of modern biology from the eighteenth century onwards and is thus very much a modern creation. Certain scholars, for instance, attempted to apply newly developed principles of biological classification to distinguish different kinds of human beings. For instance, around the middle of the nineteenth century, Joseph Arthur Comte de Gobineau, a French writer, published *An Essay on the Inequality of Human Races*, in which he sought to explain the survival and failure of civilisations across human history. De Gobineau argued:

> The fall of civilizations is the most striking, and, at the same time, the most obscure, of all the phenomena of history. [. . .] But what is this seed, this principle of death? [. . .] We moderns are the first to have recognized that every assemblage of men, together with the kind of culture it produces, is doomed to perish. (de Gobineau 1853–55/1915: pp. 1–3)

With 'the assemblage of men', de Gobineau referred to miscegenation, or intermarriage among members of different human races. In his view, this would dilute superior traits inherent in different races and doom civilisation to decline and extinction. Further on in the text (pp. 205ff.), de Gobineau moreover elaborates a hierarchy of human races and points to the superiority of an Aryan 'master race'. His work served as a major inspiration for the German National Socialists. It is a prime example of *scientific racism*, that is, the use of pseudo-scientific arguments to justify inequalities among social groups.

In biological terms, the application of the category of race to human beings is erroneous and does not fit the taxonomy used to classify living organisms. From a sociological point of view, we might therefore define race as *groups of people who share supposed biological traits that are held to be socially significant* . The belief in the biologically derived psychological and cultural inequality of human races was so powerful in 1930s' Germany that it led to the murder of approximately six million European Jews. Therefore, 'race' is closely linked to *'racialisation', that is, the establishment of social hierarchies based on supposed biological inequalities*. *Racism*, then, could be defined as *belief that such hierarchies of race are factually accurate*.

Given the strong taint that permeates the idea of race, many sociologists instead prefer to write about *ethnicity*, a term which refers to the common cultural and historical heritage of social groups. While there is no such thing as a German race, it does make sense to think of Germans as an ethnic group. Likewise, one could characterise the inhabitants of Turkey as members of various ethnic groups, according to significant historical and cultural differences. Moreover, an examination of the sizeable communities of Turkish migrants in Germany would lead to significant questions about ethnicity and cultural heritage. These communities are examples of *diasporas* who have moved abroad from their homeland. While such diasporas may retain deep roots in the society they left, their beliefs, values and norms may also be modulated by life in their new home. This example shows that the concept of ethnicity leads to the consideration of questions that can hardly be captured through the idea of 'race'.

Earlier on, we argued that race thinking and scientific racism emerged with the onset of high modernity. To conclude our discussion of this subject matter, we will explore this link in greater depth. For this, we turn to Zygmunt Bauman's analysis of the origins of the Holocaust. Bauman (1989) forcefully argues that the Holocaust cannot be understood as a singular historical event. Rather, its occurrence is tightly bound up with central cultural, social and political tendencies in modernity.

Reading

Bauman, Z. (1989), *Modernity and the Holocaust*, Cambridge: Polity Press, pp. 12–18 and 56–60

The meaning of the civilizing process

The etiological myth deeply entrenched in the self-consciousness of our Western society is the morally elevating story of humanity emerging from pre-social barbarity. This myth lent stimulus and popularity to, and in turn was given a learned and sophisticated support by, quite a few influential sociological theories and historical narratives; the link most recently illustrated by the burst of prominence and overnight success of the Elias's presentation of the 'civilizing process'. Contrary opinions of contemporary social theorists (see, for instance, the thorough analyses of multifarious civilizing processes: historical and comparative by Michael Mann, synthetic and theoretical by Anthony Giddens), which emphasize the growth of military violence and untrammelled use of coercion as the most crucial attributes of the emergence and entrenchment of great civilizations, have a long way to go before they succeed in displacing the etiological myth from public consciousness, or even from the diffuse folklore of the profession. By and large, lay opinion resents all challenge to the myth. Its resistance is backed, moreover, by a broad coalition of respectable learned opinions which contains such powerful authorities as the 'Whig view' of history as the victorious struggle between reason and superstition; Weber's vision of rationalization as a movement toward achieving more for less effort; psychoanalytical promise to debunk, prise off and tame the animal in man; Marx's grand prophecy of life and history coming under full control of the human species once it is freed from the presently debilitating parochialities; Elias's portrayal of recent history as that of eliminating violence from daily life; and, above all, the chorus of experts who assure us that human problems are matters of wrong policies, and that right policies mean elimination of problems. Behind the alliance stands fast the modern 'gardening' state, viewing the society it rules as an object of designing, cultivating and weed-poisoning.

In view of this myth, long ago ossified into the common sense of our era, the Holocaust can only be understood as the failure of civilization (i.e. of human purposive, reason-guided activity) to contain the morbid natural predilections of whatever has been left of nature in man. Obviously, the Hobbesian world has not been fully chained, the Hobbesian problem has not been fully resolved. In other words, we do not have as yet enough civilization. The unfinished civilizing process is yet to be brought to its conclusion. If the lesson of mass murder does teach us anything it is that the prevention of similar hiccups of barbarism evidently requires still more civilizing efforts. There is nothing in this lesson to cast doubt on the future effectivenes of such efforts and their ultimate results. We certainly move in the right direction; perhaps we do not move fast enough.

As its full picture emerges from historical research, so does an alternative, and possible more credible, interpretation of the Holocaust as an event which disclosed the weakness and fragility of human nature (of the abhorrence of murder, disinclination to violence, fear of guilty conscience and of responsibility for immoral behaviour) when confronted with the matter-of-fact efficiency of the most cherished among the products of civilization; its technology, its rational criteria of choice, its tendency to subordinate thought and action to the pragmatics of economy and effectiveness. The Hobbesian world of the Holocaust did not surface from its too-shallow grave, resurrected by the tumult of irrational emotions. It arrived (in a formidable shape Hobbes would certainly disown) in a factory-produced vehicle, wielding weapons only the most advanced science could supply, and following an itinerary designed by scientifically managed organization. Modern civilization was not the Holocaust's *sufficient* condition; it was, however, most certainly its *necessary* condition. Without it, the Holocaust would be unthinkable. It was the rational world of modern civilization that made the Holocaust thinkable. 'The Nazi mass murder of the European Jewry was not only the technological achievement of an industrial society, but also the organizational achievement of a bureaucratic society.' Just consider what was needed to make the Holocaust unique among the many mass murders which marked the historical advance of the human species.

> The civil service infused the other hierarchies with its sure-footed planning and bureaucratic thoroughness. From the army the machinery of destruction acquired its military precision, discipline, and callousness. Industry's influence was felt in the great emphasis upon accounting, penny-saving, and salvage, as well as in factory-like efficiency of the killing centres. Finally, the party contributed to the entire apparatus an 'idealism', a sense of 'mission', and a notion of history-making . . .
>
> It was indeed the organized society in one of special roles. Though engaged in mass murder on a gigantic scale, this vast bureaucratic apparatus showed concern for correct bureaucratic procedure, for the niceties of precise definition, for the minutiae of bureaucratic regulation, and the compliance with the law. [Kuper 1981, 121]

The department in the SS headquarters in charge of the destruction of European Jews was officially designated as the Section of Administration and Economy. This was only partly a lie; only in part can it be explained by reference to the notorious 'speech rules', designed to mislead both chance observers and the less resolute among the perpetrators. To a degree much too high for comfort, the designation faithfully reflected the organizational meaning of activity. Except for the moral repulsiveness of its goal (or, to be precise, the gigantic scale of the moral odium), the activity did not differ in any formal sense (the only sense that can be expressed in the language of bureaucracy) from all other organized activities designed, monitored and supervised by 'ordinary' administrative and economic sections. Like all other activities amenable to bureaucratic rationalization, it fits well the sober description of modern administration offered by Max Weber:

> Precision, speed, unambiguity, knowledge of the files, continuity, discretion, unity, strict subordination, reduction of friction and of material and personal costs – these are raised to the optimum point in the strictly bureaucratic administration . . . Bureaucratization offers above all the optimum possibility for carrying through the principle of specializing administrative functions according to purely objective considerations . . . The 'objective' discharge of business primarily means a discharge of business according to *calculable rules* and 'without regard for persons.'

There is nothing in this description that warrants questioning the bureaucratic definition of the Holocaust as either a simply travesty of truth or a manifestation of a particularly monstrous form of cynicism.

And yet the Holocaust is so crucial to our understanding of the modern bureaucratic mode of rationalization not only, and not primarily, because it reminds us (as if we need such a reminder) just how formal and ethically blind is the bureaucratic pursuit of efficiency. Its significance is not fully expressed either once we realize to what extent mass murder on an unprecedented scale depended on the availability of well-developed and firmly entrenched skills and habits of meticulous and precise division of labour, of maintaining a smooth flow of command and information, or of impersonal, well-synchronized co-ordination of autonomous yet complementary actions: on those skills and habits, in short, which best grow and thrive in the atmosphere of the office. The light shed by the Holocaust on our knowledge of bureaucratic rationality is at its most dazzling once we realize the extent to which *the very idea of the* Endlösung *was an outcome of the bureaucratic culture.*

We owe to Karl Schleuner the concept of the twisted road to physical extermination of European Jewry: a road which was neither conceived in a single vision of a mad monster, nor was a considered choice made at the start of the 'problem-solving process' by the ideologically motivated leaders. It did, rather, emerge inch by inch, pointing at each stage to a different destination, shifting in response to ever-new crises, and pressed forward with a 'we will cross that bridge once we come to it' philosophy. Schleuner's concept summarizes best the findings of the 'functionalist' school in the historiography of the Holocaust (which in recent years rapidly gains strength at the expense of the 'intentionalists', who in turn find it increasingly difficult to defend the once dominant single-cause explanation of the Holocaust – that is, a vision that ascribes to the genocide a motivational logic and a consistency it never possessed).

According to the functionalists' findings, 'Hitler set the objective of Nazism: "to get rid of the Jews, and above all to make the territory of the Reich *judenfrei*, i.e., clear of Jews" – but without specifying how this was to be achieved.' Once the objective had been set, everything went on exactly as Weber, with his usual clarity, spelled out: 'The "political master" finds himself in the position of the "dilettante" who stands opposite the "expert", facing the trained official who stands within the management of administration.' The objective had to be implemented; how this was to be done depended on the circumstances, always judged by the 'experts' from the point of view of feasibility and the costs of alternative opportunities of action. And so the emigration of German Jews was chosen first as the practical solution to Hitler's objective; it would resulted in a *judenfrei* Germany, were other countries more hospitable to Jewish refugees. When Austria was annexed, Eichmann earned his first accolade for expediting and streamlining the mass emigration of Austrian Jewry. But then the territory under Nazi rule began to swell. At first the Nazi bureaucracy saw the conquest and appropriation of quasi-colonial territories as the dreamt-of opportunity to fulfil the *Führer's* command in full: *Generalgouvernment* seemed to provide the sought-after dumping ground for the Jewry still inhabiting lands of Germany proper, destined for racial purity. A separate reserve for the future 'Jewish principality' was designated around Nisko, in what was, before the conquest, central Poland. To this, however, German bureaucracy saddled with the management of the former Polish territories objected: it had already enough trouble with policing its own local Jewry. And so Eichmann spent a full year working on the Madagascar project: with France defeated, her far-away colony could be transformed into the Jewish principality that failed to materialize in Europe. The Madagascar project, however, proved to be similarly ill-fated, given the enormous distance, the volume of necessary ship-space, and the British navy presence on the high seas. In the meantime the size of the conquered territory, and so the number of Jews under German jurisdiction continued to grow. A Nazi-dominated Europe (rather than simply the 'reunited *Reich*') seemed a more and more tangible prospect. Gradually yet relentlessly, the thousand-year *Reich* took up, ever more distinctly, the shape of a German-ruled Europe. Under the circumstances, the goal of a *judenfrei* Germany could not but follow the process. Almost imperceptibly, step by step, it expanded into the objective of *judenfrei* Europe. Ambitions on such a scale could not be satisfied by a Madagascar, however accessible (though according to Eberhard Jäckel there is some evidence that still in July 1941, when Hitler expected the USSR to be defeated in a matter of weeks, the vast expanses of Russia beyond the Archangel-Astrakhan line were seen as the ultimate dumping ground for all Jews inhabiting Europe unified under German rule). With the downfall of Russia reluctant to materialize, and the alternative solutions unable to keep pace with the fast-growing problem, Himmler ordered on 1 October 1941 the final stop to all further Jewish emigration. The task of 'getting rid of the Jews' had been found another, more effective means of implementation: physical extermination was chosen as the most feasible and effective means to the original, and newly expanded, end. The rest was the matter of co-operation between various departments of state bureaucracy; of careful planning, designing proper technology and technical equipment, budgeting, calculating and mobilizing necessary resources: indeed, the matter of dull bureaucratic routine.

The most shattering of lessons deriving from the analysis of the 'twisted road to Auschwitz' is that – in the last resort – *the choice of physical extermination as the right means to the task of* Entfernung *was a product of routine bureaucratic procedures*: means-ends calculus, budget balancing, universal rule application. To make the point sharper still – the choice was an effect of the earnest effort to find rational solutions to successive 'problems', as they arose in the changing circumstances. It was also affected by the widely described bureaucratic tendency to goal-displacement – an affliction as normal in all bureaucracies as their routines. The very presence of functionaries charged with their specific tasks led to further initiatives and a continuous expansion of original purposes. Once again, expertise demonstrated its self-propelling capacity, its proclivity to expand and enrich the target which supplied its *raison d'être*.

> The mere existence of a corpus of Jewish experts created a certain bureaucratic momentum behind Nazi Jewish policy. Even when deportations and mass murder were already under way, decrees appeared in 1942 prohibiting German Jews from having pets, getting their hair cut by Aryan barbers, or receiving the Reich sport badge! It did not require orders from above, merely the existence of the job itself, to ensure that the Jewish experts kept up the flow of discriminating measures.

At no point of its long and tortuous execution did the Holocaust come in conflict with the principles of rationality. The 'Final Solution' did not clash at any stage with the rational pursuit of efficient, optimal goal-implementation. On the contrary, *it arose out of a genuinely rational concern, and it was generated by bureaucracy true to its form and purpose*. We know of many massacres, pogroms, mass murders, indeed instances not far removed from genocide, that have been perpetrated without modern bureaucracy, the skills and technologies it commands, the scientific principles of its internal management. The Holocaust, however, was clearly unthinkable without such bureaucracy. The Holocaust was not an irrational outflow of the not-yet-fully-eradicated residues of pre-modern barbarity. It was a legitimate resident in the house of modernity; indeed, one who would not be at home in any other house.

This is not to suggest that the incidence of the Holocaust was *determined* by modern bureaucracy or the culture of instrumental rationality it epitomizes; much less still, that modern bureaucracy *must* result in Holocaust-style phenomena. I do suggest, however, that the rules of instrumental rationality are singularly incapable of preventing such phenomena; that there is nothing in those rules which disqualifies the Holocaust-style methods of 'social-engineering' as improper or, indeed, the actions they served as irrational. I suggest, further, that the bureaucratic culture which prompts us to view society as an object of administration, as a collection of so many 'problems' to be solved, as 'nature' to be 'controlled', 'mastered' and 'improved' or 'remade', as a legitimate target for 'social engineering', and in general a garden to be designed and kept in the planned shape by force (the gardening posture divides vegetation into 'cultured plants' to be taken care of, and weeds to be exterminated), was the very atmosphere in which the idea of the Holocaust could be conceived, slowly yet consistently developed, and brought to its conclusion. And I also suggest that it was the spirit of instrumental rationality, and its modern, bureaucratic form of institutionalization, which had made the Holocaust-style solutions not only possible, but eminently 'reasonable' – and increased the probability of their choice. This increase in probability is more than fortuitously related to the ability of modern bureaucracy to co-ordinate the action of great number of moral individuals in the pursuit of any, also immoral, ends.

[. . .]

The modernity of racism

An important thing happened to the Jews on the road to modernity. They had embarked on that road while set securely aside, segregated and enclosed behind stony or imaginary walls of the *Judengasse*. Their estrangement was a fact of life, like air or mortality. It did not call for mobilization of popular feelings, sophisticated arguments or alertness of self-appointed vigilantes; diffuse and often uncodified, yet on the whole well-co-ordinated habits, sufficed to reproduce the mutual repellence which guarded the permanence of separation. All this changed with the advent of modernity, with its dismantling of legislated differences, its slogans of legal equality and the strangest of its novelties; citizenship. As Jacob Katz put it,

> When Jews lived in the ghetto, and immediately after they left it, accusation against them came from citizens who enjoyed the legal status denied the Jews. These accusations were designed only to justify and reconfirm the status quo and provide a rationale for keeping Jews in an inferior legal and social position. Now, however, the accusations were levelled by citizens as citizens who were equal before the law, and the purpose of these indictments was to show that Jews were unworthy of the legal and social position conferred upon them.

As it were, it was not just moral or social worth that was at stake. The problem was infinitely more intricate. No less was involved than the designing of previously unpractised mechanisms, and acquiring of hitherto unthought-of skills – both necessary to produce *artificially* what was in the past given *naturally*. In pre-modern times, Jews were a caste among castes, a rank among ranks, an estate among estates. Their distinctiveness was not an issue, and habitual, virtually unreflective, practices of segregation effectively prevented it from becoming one. With the rise of modernity, separation of the Jews did become an issue. Like everything else in modern society, it had now to be manufactured, built up, rationally argued, technologically designed, administered, monitored and managed. Those in charge of pre-modern societies could assume the leisurely and confident attitude of gamekeepers: left to its own resources, society would reproduce itself year by year, generation after generation, with scarcely a noticeable change. Not so its modern successor. Here, nothing could be taken for granted any more. Nothing should grow unless planted, and whatever would have grown on its own must have been the wrong thing, and hence a dangerous thing, jeopardizing or confounding the overall plan. The gamekeeper-like complacency would be a luxury one could ill afford. What was needed instead was the posture, and skills, of a gardener; one armed with a detailed design of the lawn, of the borders and of the furrow dividing the lawn from the borders; with a vision of harmonious colours and of the difference between pleasing harmony and revolting cacophony; with determination to treat as weeds every self-invited plant which interferes with his plan and his vision of order and harmony; and with machines and poisons adequate to the task of exterminating the weeds and altogether preserve the divisions as required and defined by the overall design.

Separation of the Jews had lost its naturalness, suggested in the past by the territorial segregation and reinforced by profuse and obtrusive warning signs. It seemed instead hopelessly artificial and brittle. What used to be an axiom, a tacitly accepted assumption, became now a truth one had to demonstrate and prove; and 'essence of things' hidden behind phenomena that apparently contradicted it. New *naturalness* now had to be laboriously *constructed* and grounded in an authority different from that of the evidence of sensual impressions. As Patrick Girard put it,

> The Jewish assimilation into surrounding society and the disappearance of social and religious distinctions had led to a situation in which Jews and Christians could not be differentiated. Having become a citizen like any other and mixing with Christians through marriage, the Jew was no longer recognizable. This fact had significant weight for anti-Semitic theorists. Edouard Drumont, the author of the pamphlet *Jewish France*, wrote: 'A Mr Cohen, who goes to synagogue, who keeps kosher is a respectable person. I don't hold anything against him. I do have it in for the Jew who is not obvious'.
>
> One finds similar ideas in Germany, where Jews in ritual curls and caftans were less scorned . . . than their coreligionists, the German patriots of Jewish persuasion who imitated their Christian countryman . . . [M]odern anti-Semitism was born not from the great difference between groups but rather from the threat of absence of differences, the homogenization of Western society and the abolition of the ancient social and legal barriers between Jews and Christians.

Modernity brought the levelling of differences – at least of their outward appearances, of the very stuff of which symbolic distances between segregated groups are made. With such differences missing, it was not enough to muse philosophically over the wisdom of reality as it was – something Christian doctrine had done before when it wished to make sense out of the factual Jewish separation. Differences had to be created now, or retained against the awesome eroding power of social and legal equality and cross-cultural exchange.

The inherited religious explanation of the boundary – the rejection of Christ by the Jews – was singularly unfit for the new task. Such an explanation inevitably entailed the possibility of exit from the segregated field. As long as the boundary remained clearly drawn and well marked, that explanation served a good purpose. It provided the needed element of flexibility which tied the fate of men to their assumed freedom to earn salvation or commit a sin, to accept or to reject the Divine grace; and it achieved it all without in the slightest detracting from the solidity of the boundary itself. The same element of flexibility, however, would prove disastrous once the practices of segregation had become too half-hearted and lackadaisical to sustain the 'naturalness' of the boundary – making it instead a hostage to human self-determination. The modern world-view, after all, proclaimed the unlimited potential of education and self-perfection. Everything was possible, with due effort and good will. Man was at birth a *tabula rasa*, an empty cabinet, later to be covered and filled, in the course of the civilizing process, with contents supplied by the levelling-up pressure of shared cultural ideas. Paradoxically, referring the differences between the Jews and their Christian hosts solely to the distinction of creed and connected rituals, appeared well geared to the modern vision of human nature. Alongside the renunciation of other prejudices, the abandonment of Judaist superstitions, and the conversion to a superior faith, seemed to be proper and sufficient vehicles of self-improvement; a drive only to be expected, and on a massive scale, on the road to the final victory of reason over ignorance.

What truly threatened the solidity of old boundaries was not, of course, the ideological formula of modernity (though it did not strengthen it either), but the refusal of the secularized modern state to legislate differentiated social practices. This was all right as long as the Jews (Drumont's 'Mr Cohen') themselves refused to follow the state in its drive towards uniformity, and stuck to their own discriminating practices. Real confusion was caused by those ever-more-numerous Jews, who did take up the offer and accomplish the conversion, either in its bequeathed, religious form, or in its modern form of cultural assimilation. In France, Germany, in the German-dominated part of Austro-Hungary, the likelihood that all Jews would sooner or later be 'socialized', or would 'self-socialize', into non-Jews, and hence would become culturally indistinguishable and socially invisible, was quite real. In the absence of old customary and legally supported practices of segregation, such absence of visible marks of difference could only be tantamount to wiping out the boundary itself.

Under conditions of modernity, segregation required a modern method of boundary-building. A method able to withstand and neutralize the levelling impact of allegedly infinite powers of educatory and civilizing forces; a method capable of designating a 'no-go' area for pedagogy and self-improvement, of drawing an unencroachable limit to the potential of cultivation (a method applied eagerly, though with mixed success, to all groups intended to be kept permanently in a subordinate position – like the working classes or women). If it was to be salvaged from the assault of modern equality, *the distinctiveness of the Jews had to be re-articulated and laid on new foundations, stronger than human powers of culture and self-determination.* In Hannah Arendt's terse phrase, Judaism has to be replaced with Jewishness: 'Jews had been able to escape from Judaism into conversion; from Jewishness there was no escape.'

Unlike Judaism, Jewishness had to be, emphatically, stronger than human will and human creative potential. It had to be located at the level of natural law (the kind of law that ought to be discovered, and then taken account of and exploited for human benefit, but which cannot be wished away, tampered with, or neglected – at least, not without terrible consequences). It is of such a law that Drumont's anecdote was meant to remind his readers: '"Do you want to see how blood speaks?" a French duke once asked his friends. He had married a Rothschild from Frankfurt in spite of his mother's tears. He called his little son, pulled a golden louis from his pocket and showed it to him. The child's eyes lit up. "You see," continued the duke, "the semitic instinct reveals itself straight away".' Some time later Charles Maurras would insist that 'what one is determines one's attitude from the beginning. The illusion of choice, of reason, can only lead to personal *déracinement* and political disaster.' To neglect such a law may only be done at one's own, and common, peril – or so we learn from Maurice Barrès: 'Caught up in mere words a child is cut off from all reality: Kantian doctrine uproots him from the soil of his ancestors. A surplus of diplomas creates what we may call, after Bismarck, a "proletariat of graduates". This is our indictment of the universities; what happens to their product, the "intellectual", is that he becomes an enemy of society.' The product of conversion – be it religious or cultural – is not the change, but *loss* of quality. On the other side of conversion lurks a void, not another identity. The convert loses his identity without acquiring anything instead. Man *is* before he *acts*; nothing he does may change what he is. This is, roughly, the philosophical essence of racism.

Consider
1. What was the Holocaust? Answer this question in reference to the reading and relevant background research of your own.
2. Summarise Bauman's argument in the reading in your own words.
3. How does the Holocaust genocidal racism, according to Bauman, exemplify modern forms of rationality?
4. What is the relevance of the Holocaust to a sociological understanding of racism?

6.3 Social class and socio-economic stratification

The concept of social class in very basic terms refers to *patterns of socio-economic stratification among social groups in a particular society*. With this discussion of class, we return to another long-standing concern of sociology. Around the middle of the nineteenth century, Karl Marx and Friedrich Engels developed a powerful body of theory on the differentiation and inequality of social classes to explain large-scale poverty and the exploitation of industrial workers. Marx and Engels highlighted economic factors to account for class inequality, specifically pointing to unequally distributed ownership of the means of production as a root cause. They argued that class struggle based on economic inequalities is a driving force of social change across human history, culminating in the terminal confrontation between proletariat and industrial bourgeoisie under conditions of capitalism:

> The history of all hitherto existing society is the history of class struggles. Freeman and slave, patrician and plebian, lord and serf, guild-master and journeyman, in a word, oppressor and oppressed, stood in constant opposition to one another, carried on an uninterrupted, now hidden, now open fight, a fight that each time ended, either in a revolutionary reconstitution of society at large, or in the common ruin of the contending classes. [. . .] The modern bourgeois society that has sprouted from the ruins of feudal society has not done away with class antagonisms. It has but established new classes, new conditions of oppression, new forms of struggle in place of the old ones. Our epoch, the epoch of the bourgeoisie, possesses, however, this distinct feature: it has simplified class antagonisms. Society as a whole is more and more splitting up into two great hostile camps, into two great classes directly facing each other – bourgeoisie and proletariat. (Marx and Engels 1848/1983: pp. 203f.)

Marx and Engels' work has been foundational to sociological studies of class and socio-economic stratification and remains so to date. However, it also has notable limitations. As the statement that the 'history of all hitherto existing society is the history of class struggles' would suggest, their arguments are driven by *economic determinism*, that is to say an emphasis on the causal power of economic structures to the exclusion of other factors.

Later theorists have developed alternative models of socio-economic stratification, or have modified the Marxist approach. Max Weber proposed a tripartite model, in which economically determined social class interacts with considerations of social status in terms of honour, prestige and religion and with political affiliations to determine individuals' relative position in society. French sociologist Pierre Bourdieu (2003) in turn drew attention to the role of cultural factors in the context of class inequalities. Bourdieu points to the importance of notions of taste and refinement that set members of different social classes apart. An appreciation of opera, the ability to select the right glass for a certain wine, and ownership of sophisticated furniture all may declare one's membership among social elites. In contrast, working-class taste, while potentially distinctive, remains on the horizon of superior elite taste and is thus by its very nature regarded as inferior.

Based on these and many other approaches, sociologists have developed sophisticated models of societies' class structures. These models are often built around the distinction between three broad groups: a small upper class, comprising aristocrats, capitalists, corporate executives, celebrities, etc.; a middle class, consisting of often highly educated and well-earning professionals, mid-level managers, bureaucrats, teachers, and so forth; and a working class of frequently poorly trained and poorly remunerated manual labourers in industry, agriculture and service work.

Recent debates in Western Europe have been particularly concerned with the possible demise of social class and the individualisation of socio-economic inequality. For example, some sociologists argue that transformations of capitalism and developments such as the rise of flexible, unstable labour have eliminated the sense of community and the consciousness of a common socio-economic position that previously bound working class people together (Beck 2000). Call-centre workers, fast-food employees and supermarket workers may face considerable hardship and exploitation, but they often experience these as purely personal problems and not as a predicament they share with many others (Sennett 1998; Sennett 2006). Proponents of class theories argue that, while their nature may have changed, broad social divisions along class lines remain a powerful force in society with, for instance, upper classes remaining tightly bounded and continuing to share common world views, experiences and interests.

In the context of globalisation and the extension of networks of industrial production, commerce, trade, culture, and politics across national boundaries, another important problem has come to the fore. This concerns the relevance of the concept of class, originally developed to examine European societies, at the global level and in societies whose historical development has differed fundamentally from European patterns.

The following reading is taken from *Distinction*, a seminal and widely cited work by Pierre Bourdieu (2003). *Distinction* illustrates the complexities of arguments about class, highlighting the ways in which the seemingly innocuous choices we make in everyday life work to establish our position in society.

Reading

Bourdieu, P. (2003), *Distinction: A Social Critique of the Judgement of Taste*. New York: Routledge, pp. 1–7

There is an economy of cultural goods, but it has a specific logic. Sociology endeavours to establish the conditions in which the consumers of cultural goods, and their taste for them, are produced, and at the same time to describe the different ways of appropriating such of these objects as are regarded at a particular moment as works of art, and the social conditions of the constitution of the mode of appropriation that is considered legitimate. But one cannot fully understand cultural practices unless 'culture', in the restricted, normative sense of ordinary

usage, is brought back into 'culture' in the anthropological sense, and the elaborated taste for the most refined objects is reconnected with the elementary taste
for the flavours of food.

Whereas the ideology of charisma regards taste in legitimate culture as a gift
of nature, scientific observation shows that cultural needs are the product of
upbringing and education: surveys establish that all cultural practices (museum
visits, concert-going, reading etc.), and preferences in literature, painting or music,
are closely linked to educational level (measured by qualifications or length of
schooling) and secondarily to social origin. The relative weight of home background and of formal education (the effectiveness and duration of which are
closely dependent on social origin) varies according to the extent to which the
different cultural practices are recognized and taught by the educational system,
and the influence of social origin is strongest – other things being equal – in
'extra-curricular' and avant-garde culture. To the socially recognized hierarchy of
the arts, and within each of them, of genres, schools or periods, corresponds a
social hierarchy of the consumers. This predisposes tastes to function as markers
of 'class'. The manner in which culture has been acquired lives on in the manner
of using it: the importance attached to manners can be understood once it is
seen that it is these imponderables of practice which distinguish the different –
and ranked – modes of culture acquisition, early or late, domestic or scholastic,
and the classes of individuals which they characterize (such as 'pedants' and
mondains). Culture also has its titles of nobility – awarded by the educational
system – and its pedigrees, measured by seniority in admission to the nobility.

The definition of cultural nobility is the stake in a struggle which has gone on
unceasingly, from the seventeenth century to the present day, between groups
differing in their ideas of culture and of the legitimate relation to culture and to
works of art, and therefore differing in the conditions of acquisition of which
these dispositions are the product. Even in the classroom, the dominant definition of the legitimate way of appropriating culture and works of art favours those
who have had early access to legitimate culture, in a cultured household, outside of scholastic disciplines, since even within the educational system it devalues
scholarly knowledge and interpretation as 'scholastic' or even 'pedantic' in favour
of direct experience and simple delight.

The logic of what is sometimes called, in typically 'pedantic' language, the 'reading' of a work of art, offers an objective basis for this opposition. Consumption is,
in this case, a stage in a process of communication, that is, an act of deciphering,
decoding, which presupposes practical or explicit mastery of a cipher or code.
In a sense, one can say that the capacity to see (*voir*) is a function of the knowledge (*savoir*), or concepts, that is, the words, that are available to name visible
things, and which are, as it were, programmes for perception. A work of art has
meaning and interest only for someone who possesses the cultural competence,
that is, the code, into which it is encoded. The conscious or unconscious implementation of explicit or implicit schemes of perception and appreciation which
constitutes pictorial or musical culture is the hidden condition for recognizing

the styles characteristic of a period, a school or an author, and, more generally, for the familiarity with the internal logic of works that aesthetic enjoyment presupposes. A beholder who lacks the specific code feels lost in a chaos of sounds and rhythms, colours and lines, without rhyme or reason. Not having learnt to adopt the adequate disposition, he stops short at what Erwin Panofsky calls the 'sensible properties', perceiving a skin as downy or lace-work as delicate, or at the emotional resonances aroused by these properties, referring to 'austere' colours or a 'joyful' melody. He cannot move from the 'primary stratum of the meaning we can grasp on the basis of our ordinary experience' to the 'stratum of secondary meanings', i.e., the 'level of the meaning of what is signified', unless he possesses the concepts which go beyond the sensible properties and which identify the specifically stylistic properties of the work. Thus the encounter with a work of art is not 'love at first sight' as is generally supposed, and the act of empathy, *Einfühlung*, which is the art-lover's pleasure, presupposes an act of cognition, a decoding operation, which implies the implementation of a cognitive acquirement, a cultural code.

This typically intellectualist theory of artistic perception directly contradicts the experience of the art-lovers closest to the legitimate definition; acquisition of legitimate culture by insensible familiarization within the family circle tends to favour an enchanted experience of culture which implies forgetting the acquisition. The 'eye' is a product of history reproduced by education. This is true of the mode of artistic perception now accepted as legitimate, that is, the aesthetic disposition, the capacity to consider in and for themselves, as form rather than function, not only the works designated for such apprehension, i.e., legitimate works of art, but everything in the world, including cultural objects which are not yet consecrated – such as, at one time, primitive arts, or, nowadays, popular photography or kitsch – and natural objects. The 'pure' gaze is a historical invention linked to the emergence of an autonomous field of artistic production, that is, a field capable of imposing its own norms on both the production and the consumption of its products. An art which, like all Post-Impressionist painting, is the product of an artistic intention which asserts the primacy of the mode of representation over the object of representation demands categorically an attention to form which previous art only demanded conditionally.

The pure intention of the artist is that of a producer who aims to be autonomous, that is, entirely the master of his product, who tends to reject not only the 'programmes' imposed a priori by scholars and scribes, but also – following the old hierarchy of doing and saying – the interpretations superimposed a posteriori on his work. The production of an 'open work', intrinsically and deliberately polysemic, can thus be understood as the final stage in the conquest of artistic autonomy by poets and, following in their footsteps, by painters, who had long been reliant on writers and their work of 'showing' and 'illustrating'. To assert the autonomy of production is to give primacy to that of which the artist is master, i.e., form, manner, style, rather than the 'subject', the external referent, which involves subordination to functions – even if only the most elementary one, that of representing, signifying, saying something. It also means a refusal to recognize any necessity other than that inscribed in the specific tradition of the artistic discipline in question: the shift from an art which imitates nature to an art which imitates art, deriving from its own history the exclusive source of its experiments and even of its breaks with tradition. An art which ever increasingly contains reference to its own history demands to be perceived historically; it asks to be referred not to an external referent, the represented or designated 'reality', but to the universe of past and present works of art. Like artistic production, in that it is generated in a field, aesthetic perception is necessarily historical, inasmuch as it is differential, relational, attentive to the deviations (*écarts*) which make styles. Like the so-called naive painter who, operating outside the field and its specific traditions, remains external to the history of the art, the 'naive' spectator cannot attain a specific grasp of works of art which only have meaning – or value – in relation to the specific history of an artistic tradition. The aesthetic disposition demanded by the products of a highly autonomous field of production is inseparable from a specific cultural competence. This historical culture functions as a principle of pertinence which enables one to identify, among the elements offered to the gaze, all the distinctive features and only these, by referring them, consciously or unconsciously, to the universe of possible alternatives. This mastery is, for the most part, acquired simply by contact with works of art – that is, through an implicit learning analogous to that which makes it possible to recognize familiar faces without explicit rules or criteria – and it generally remains at a practical level; it is what makes it possible to identify styles, i.e., modes of expression characteristic of a period, a civilization or a school, without having to distinguish clearly, or state explicitly, the features which constitute their originality. Everything seems to suggest that even among professional valuers, the criteria which define the stylistic properties of the 'typical works' on which all their judgements are based usually remain implicit.

The pure gaze implies a break with the ordinary attitude towards the world, which, given the conditions in which it is performed, is also a social separation. Ortega y Gasset can be believed when he attributes to modern art a systematic refusal of all that is 'human', i.e., generic, common – as opposed to distinctive, or distinguished – namely, the passions, emotions and feelings which 'ordinary' people invest in their 'ordinary' lives. It is as if the 'popular aesthetic' (the quotation marks are there to indicate that this is an aesthetic 'in itself' not 'for itself') were based on the affirmation of the continuity between art and life, which implies the subordination of form to function. This is seen clearly in the case of the novel and especially the theatre, where the working-class audience refuses any sort of formal experimentation and all the effects which, by introducing a distance from the accepted conventions (as regards scenery, plot etc.), tend to distance the spectator, preventing him from getting involved and fully identifying with the characters (I am thinking of Brechtian 'alienation' or the disruption of plot in the *nouveau roman*). In contrast to the detachment and disinterestedness which aesthetic theory regards as the only way of recognizing the work of art for what it is, i.e., autonomous, *selbständig*, the 'popular aesthetic' ignores or refuses the refusal of 'facile' involvement and 'vulgar' enjoyment, a refusal which is the basis of the taste for formal experiment. And popular judgements of paintings or photographs spring from an 'aesthetic' (in fact it is an ethos) which is the exact opposite of the Kantian aesthetic. Whereas, in order to grasp the specificity of the aesthetic judgement, Kant strove to distinguish that which pleases from that which gratifies and, more generally, to distinguish disinterestedness, the sole guarantor of the specifically aesthetic quality of contemplation, from the interest of reason which defines the Good, working-class people expect every image to explicitly perform a function, if only that of a sign, and their judgements make reference, often explicitly, to the norms of morality or agreeableness. Whether rejecting or praising, their appreciation always has an ethical basis.

Popular taste applies the schemes of the ethos, which pertain in the ordinary circumstances of life, to legitimate works of art, and so performs a systematic reduction of the things of art to the things of life. The very seriousness (or naivety) which this taste invests in fictions and representations demonstrates a contrario that pure taste performs a suspension of 'naive' involvement which is one dimension of a 'quasi-ludic' relationship with the necessities of the world. Intellectuals could be said to believe in the representation – literature, theatre, painting – more than in the things represented, whereas the people chiefly expect representations and the conventions which govern them to allow them to believe 'naively' in the things represented. The pure aesthetic is rooted in an ethic, or rather, an ethos of elective distance from the necessities of the natural and social world, which may take the form of moral agnosticism (visible when ethical transgression becomes an artistic *parti pris*) or of an aestheticism which presents the aesthetic disposition as a universally valid principle and takes the bourgeois denial of the social world to its limit. The detachment of the pure gaze cannot be dissociated from a general disposition towards the world which is the paradoxical product of conditioning by negative economic necessities – a life of ease – that tends to induce an active distance from necessity.

Although art obviously offers the greatest scope to the aesthetic disposition, there is no area of practice in which the aim of purifying, refining and sublimating primary needs and impulses cannot assert itself, no area in which the stylization of life, that is, the primacy of forms over function, of manner over matter, does not produce the same effects. And nothing is more distinctive, more distinguished, than the capacity to confer aesthetic status on objects that are banal or even 'common' (because the 'common' people make them their own, especially for aesthetic purposes), or the ability to apply the principles of a 'pure' aesthetic to the most everyday choices of everyday life, e.g., in cooking, clothing or decoration, completely reversing the popular disposition which annexes aesthetics to ethics.

In fact, through the economic and social conditions which they presuppose, the different ways of relating to realities and fictions, of believing in fictions and the realities they simulate, with more or less distance and detachment, are very closely linked to the different possible positions in social space and, consequently, bound up with the systems of dispositions (habitus) characteristic of the different classes and class fractions. Taste classifies, and it classifies the classifier. Social subjects, classified by their classifications, distinguish themselves by the distinctions they make, between the beautiful and the ugly, the distinguished and the vulgar, in which their position in the objective classifications is expressed or betrayed. And statistical analysis does indeed show that oppositions similar in structure to those found in cultural practices also appear in eating habits. The antithesis between quantity and quality, substance and form, corresponds to the opposition – linked to different distances from necessity – between the taste of necessity, which favours the most 'filling' and most economical foods, and the taste of liberty – or luxury – which shifts the emphasis to the manner (of presenting, serving, eating etc.) and tends to use stylized forms to deny function.

The science of taste and of cultural consumption begins with a transgression that is in no way aesthetic: it has to abolish the sacred frontier which makes legitimate culture a separate universe, in order to discover the intelligible relations which unite apparently incommensurable 'choices', such as preferences in music and food, painting and sport, literature and hairstyle. This barbarous reintegration of aesthetic consumption into the world of ordinary consumption abolishes the opposition, which has been the basis of high aesthetics since Kant, between the 'taste of sense' and the 'taste of reflection', and between facile pleasure, pleasure reduced to a pleasure of the senses, and pure pleasure, pleasure purified of pleasure, which is predisposed to become a symbol of moral excellence and a measure of the capacity for sublimation which defines the truly human man. The culture which results from this magical division is sacred. Cultural consecration does indeed confer on the objects, persons and situations it touches, a sort of ontological promotion akin to a transubstantiation. Proof enough of this is found in the two following quotations, which might almost have been written for the delight of the sociologist:

'What struck me most is this: nothing could be obscene on the stage of our premier theatre, and the ballerinas of the Opera, even as naked dancers, sylphs, sprites or Bacchae, retain an inviolable purity.'

'There are obscene postures: the stimulated intercourse which offends the eye. Clearly, it is impossible to approve, although the interpolation of such gestures in dance routines does give them a symbolic and aesthetic quality which is absent from the intimate scenes the cinema daily flaunts before its spectators' eyes . . . As for the nude scene, what can one say, except that it is brief and theatrically not very effective? I will not say it is chaste or innocent, for nothing commercial can be so described. Let us say it is not shocking, and that the chief objection is that it serves as a box-office gimmick. . . . In *Hair*, the nakedness fails to be symbolic.'

The denial of lower, coarse, vulgar, venal, servile – in a word, natural – enjoyment, which constitutes the sacred sphere of culture, implies an affirmation of the superiority of those who can be satisfied with the sublimated, refined, disinterested, gratuitous, distinguished pleasures forever closed to the profane. That is why art and cultural consumption are predisposed, consciously and deliberately or not, to fulfil a social function of legitimating social differences.

Consider

1. Summarise Bourdieu's arguments in your own words.
2. What might Bourdieu mean when he writes of an 'economy of cultural goods'? Can you think of any examples?
3. 'Taste classifies, and it classifies the classifier.' Discuss.
4. What, if anything, does your taste reveal about your class position? Formulate your answer using sociological concepts and ideas. Give examples to support your argument.
5. Bourdieu's *Distinction* primarily considers the role of culture and consumption in socio-economic stratification. Which other factors contribute to patterns of stratification and class divisions in society? Look at the above reading, as well as other relevant sources, to answer this question.
6. In recent years, China has become one of the biggest importers of luxury goods worldwide. What does this reveal about the changes in the stratification of Chinese society? How could you use Bourdieu's arguments about taste and consumption to look at (some) Chinese people's new predilection for luxury? These questions require you to do some background research. There is both substantial media coverage (do look online) and academic research on the subject matter.

6.4 Sex and gender

Let us begin with an extract from a recent study on sexual harassment in Japan:

Among stereotyped images of Asian women, Japanese women predominate, portrayed as Madame Butterfly: obedient, modest, chaste and doll-like. As with all myths, however, such images have never reflected the reality of Japanese women, and contemporary Japanese women conform less and less to the stereotype. One of the most rapid changes in recent years is the increase in sexual activity of young women. [. . .] Women have become more accepting of sex among unmarried persons and more tolerant of divorce over the last thirty years. Women have also become more active in other areas. Their workforce participation has been growing since the 1960s, with women comprising 41 per cent of those employed in 2007. [. . .] Yet transnational statistics show that Japanese women hold only 10 per cent of managerial positions in their country's economy, a surprisingly small percentage compared to 58 per cent in the Philippines and 43 per cent in the United States [. . .]. Female representation is also low in the political arena at both the national and local levels. [. . .] In such conditions, sexual harassment in the office is a critical problem because it is reinforced by the power imbalance between the sexes and enabled by the popular attitude towards sexuality. In fact, the very rapidity with which awareness of the concept of sexual harassment has spread in Japan reflects the impact of this problem on the society. (Kazue 2008: 52)

Sociologist Muta Kazue here builds a complex image of the contemporary situation of Japanese women. Her argument, first of all, is about the ways in which societies make distinctions in terms of sex and gender. In a very basic sense, *sex* refers to biologically based distinctions between male and female, on the base of bodily make-up and observable bodily features. Differences in chromosomes and hormone levels would be an example of the former, while visible sexual characteristics are instances of the latter. In sociological usage, sex is distinct from *sexuality*, which concerns experiences and practices that are tied in with erotic desire.

Gender, in contrast, indicates the social organisation of perceived differences between male and female. This concerns *gender identity*, that is to say our subjective perceptions and experiences of how we are male or female. Gender is also a matter of our everyday *performance* or enacting of how we are male or female: through processes of socialisation, we come to understand the norms, values and beliefs that are attached to being a man or a woman, and we act towards them, sometimes endorsing them and sometimes challenging or creatively transcending them (Butler 1999; West and Zimmerman 2000). Importantly, however, gender is not only a matter of *difference*; it is likewise an arena in which powerful social *hierarchies* are constructed and played out. Raewyn Connell thus argues that societies are structured by a *gender order*, 'a historically constructed pattern of power relations between men and women and definitions of femininity and masculinity' (Connell 1987). Workplaces, families, government, the law – these are just some examples of the arenas in which a gender order is put into practice. Given the ways in which power relations in many of these arenas favour men, and gender orders around the world often sustain women's subordination, many sociologists have come to write about *patriarchy*. *Patriarchy* literally means 'rule of fathers'. In sociological terms, it refers to patterns of social organisation that lead to men's systematic domination and exploitation of women. Patriarchy entails gender-based stratifications of society in which material resources, political power and forms of cultural expression are generally controlled by men.

Muta Kazue's discussion of sexual harassment in Japan illustrates such sociological conceptualisations of gender quite well. Her arguments about the under-representation of women in the workforce, boardrooms and centres of political control of Japanese society suggest its *patriarchal organisation*. *Power relations* in the Japanese gender order seem to systematically encourage male domination, and it brings with it a *gendered division of labour* that limits women's participation in paid labour, politics and the public sphere. This impression is furthered by Kazue's suggestion that the everyday *performance* of gender relations may include substantial levels of sexual harassment.

However, Kazue also points to notable changes in gender identities and performances, concerning issues such as sex or paid employment. Her point that sexual harassment has been recognised as a critical problem is a further indicator of change. Such change in gender orders is often the outcome of transformative *gender politics*. Through social movements, government intervention, changes in the law, intellectual movements, and sustained public debates, changes in the gendered hierarchies of society can be actively brought about. The success of feminist activists and scholars in enhancing women's rights over the past century or so is one notable example here. Another important contemporary example of gender politics is the increasing acceptance of same-sex relationships. For instance, various countries around the world – among others, the UK, the Netherlands, Germany, France, Canada, parts of the USA and Mexico – have recently passed laws that allow for same-sex unions and marriages. In some cases, the USA being particularly notable, such change has come about in the context of significant political struggle – so much so that some commentators have written of 'culture wars'! The following reading unpacks some of the respective issues.

Reading

Monro, Surya (2005), *Gender Politics*, London: Pluto Press, pp. 10–22

Gender Theory

We live in a world that is deeply structured by sex and gender. The categorisation of people as 'male' or 'female' permeates our society on every level, including our language, relationships, social institutions, and academic debates. On a social level, biological determinism, or the belief that we act in certain ways because of our physical make-up, is rife. This is the case despite the changes that have occurred over the past century in the way that gender and sexuality are constructed, and high levels of cross-cultural gender and sexual variance. The development of constructionist, or 'nurture', approaches, and, more recently, post-structuralist (and postmodernist) theories, has disrupted biologically determinist approaches to gender and sexuality, but at the same time, evidence to support the existence of some biological basis for gender differences continues to emerge (see for example Swaab 1995).

This chapter provides a critical overview of some of the key issues and bodies of theory concerning gender, in order to provide a basis for theorising gender and sexual diversity, and begins an exploration of different ways of conceptualising gender pluralism. The chapter is divided into four separate, but related, sections: the first is titled 'Trans and Gender/Sexual Orientation Complexity'; the second, titled, 'Intersectionality', focuses on the intersections between social characteristics such as 'race', class, and sexuality. This part of the chapter provides a foundation for the later focus on gender, and includes an illustrative case study of gender and sexual diversity in India. The third section is titled 'Overview of Existing Theories' and the fourth, 'Gender Pluralist Theory'. It is important to point out that some authors conceptualise gender as being determined by processes concerning sexual orientation, others see sexuality as resulting from gender, whilst still others see gender and sexuality as being interwoven, so that our gender identities are shaped by our sexual orientation and vice versa (see Richardson 2000d). Whilst holding ultimately to the latter viewpoint, I focus this discussion on gender, because the process of gender ascription in infancy seems to precede the ascription of sexual identities, serving in practice as a foundation for later categorisation. I would also like to note that although I provide an indication of the importance of intersectionality, dealing in any depth with cross-cultural variations in gender and sexual categorisation is outside of the scope of this book. Interested readers can refer to Feinberg (1996), Herdt (1994), Bullough and Bullough (1993), Ramet (1997) and Prieur (1998). Similarly, analysis of disability and gender/sexual fluidity and multiplicity is an important area, which I do not deal with here (see for example Blackburn 2002). I also do not address some of the other relevant issues, such as challenges to gender norms amongst non-trans people, which are widely discussed in the feminist and masculinities literature.

Trans and Gender/Sexual Orientation Complexity

This section explores the ways in which gender and sexual diversity challenges rigid gender and sexual orientation binaries in the West. Most Western people are brought up to think that being 'male' or 'female' is a crucial aspect of identity – and that 'female' and 'male' are the only options available. Transgender and intersex challenge this normalisation of gender binaries. Sexual orientation categories are also disrupted when people have non male/female genders, or experience gender fluidity, because the notions of 'lesbian', 'gay', 'heterosexual/straight', and 'bisexual' are based on male and female categorisation.

Gender Diversity

Gender diversity provides a challenge to the gender binary system in a number of ways – via intersex, third or other genders, gender fluidity, positions outside of gender, gender fuck and gender queer. Whilst the majority of trans people and cross-dressers exist within a gender binary system, identifying as either male or female, there are a range of other people who are gender diverse. Gender diversity which challenges the gender binary system includes:

1. Intersex, which disrupts the binary system on two levels: on a physical level, as the various conditions subsumed under the umbrella term of intersex involve physiological characteristics (for example chromosomal, hormonal and gonadal) which are other than (or a mixture of) those conventionally associated with males and females; and in terms of identity, as research

contributions showed that in some cases intersex people wish to have an identity that is other, or in addition to, male or female (projects (a) and (d)).

2. People who are born as male or female but seek to identify as androgynous, third, fourth, or other sexes or genders, or as non-gendered. Some of my research contributors (projects (a) and (d)) identified as other than male or female. For example, Simon Dessloch, a female-to-male (FTM) trans person, said that he felt himself to be in between, or neither, or both, or third sex. Similarly, Christie Elan Cane, who started life as female, said in 1998:

> I don't feel male or female, and I say that I'm basically third gender because I can't identify as male or female . . . I mean I'm still trying to unravel how I wanted to be. I wondered whether maybe I could be part of both, which is not how I feel any longer but I sort of went through several stages along, trying to express and figure out how I felt, but now I feel I'm neither. I can't relate to male and female.

3. 'Third space' as opposed to 'third sex or gender' (see Bornstein 1994, Nataf 1996, Garber 1992). 'Third space' allows for the articulation of various gendered identities, without these identities being solidified into clear categories.

4. Gender fluidity amongst trans people during the period that they are changing sex (and in some cases, later). For example contributor Zach Nataf described the way that, during the early stages of his transition from female to male, he felt more like a man on some days and more transgendered on others, and that this depended to an extent on who he was with (see also Bornstein 1994).

5. Fluidity amongst other gender diverse people, including drag kings and queens, cross-dressers and transvestites. Butch dyke Hamish described gender fluidity as a state in itself, whilst gender transient Phaedra Kelly said:

> It's about a discipline of duality with an open mind, without changing sex with hormones, with pills, with injections or surgery, living one's dualism as much as possible. If I am Phaedra, I allow elements of Bruce through, and there is no self-hating or loathing going on. If I am Bruce I allow elements of Phaedra – it's horses for courses, but like the transvestite, and to some degree the trans person living full-time, I live with a separate identity. I have accepted my separate identity as well.

6. Transsexuality as a space beyond gender binarisms. Cameron (1996) sees transsexuality as an in-between place outside of gender duality, while Stone argues that 'a trans person currently occupies a position which is nowhere, which is outside of the binaried oppositions of gendered discourse' (1991: 295). Some contributors mirrored this, for example Christie Elan Cane discussed moving beyond the gender system and being non-gendered.

7. 'Gender fuck', which refers to conflicting sex/gender signals. In some cases these are consciously taken on as part of identity (see Halberstam 2002). Kate N'Ha Ysabet explained that:

> if I have a penis and big tits that's gender fuck, if I wore makeup and butch clothing that's gender fuck. And what's quite interesting is that androgyny is acceptable because there's a reason for that, but gender fuck isn't, because people go 'oh, OK' but with gender fuck it's this thing of 'shit, I'm getting two sets of signals' and it feels like you're having a drum and bass mix on one side and classical music on the other and you're going 'Oh my God which am I going to listen to?'

8. 'Gender queer': this is any type of trans identity that is not always male or female. It is where people feel they are a mixture of male and female.
9. Non-gendered people – people who refuse to be defined in a gendered way.
10. Intentional eunuchs (see for example <http://bmeworld.com/smooth/>), who may or may not have sexual reasons for their castration.
11. Multiple genders (sometimes called 'gender pluralism'). This is where an individual has a number of differently gendered personalities, and is non-pathological.
12. Gender variant people's reproduction. This includes FTM trans people who have had babies after starting their gender transition (stopping hormone treatment in order to conceive and deliver, but continuing to identify as male) (More 1998), male-to-female (MTF) trans people who store sperm in order to be able to parent after transition, and trans people who parent in alternative ways, for example in a lesbian relationship after one partner has had gender reassignment surgery.
13. Unintentional gender variance following surgical removal of gonads or genitals due to illness (see for example <http://prostrate-help.org/caeunuc.htm> which documents a survivor of prostate cancer identifying as a eunuch). Of course, many people who have had this type of surgery will continue to identify as male or female.

The gender pluralism and multiplicity, which are evident amongst some trans and intersex people, disrupt culturally entrenched notions of gender binarism. They provoke discussions of a society in which there are more than two types of gender, and in which for some people, gender is fluid or multiple. Gender pluralism has important implications for systems of sexual orientation, as well as for theory concerning gender and sexuality.

Sexual Orientation

The sexual orientation categories that are used in the West – lesbian and gay, heterosexual, and bisexual, are based on the gender binary system. In other words, being heterosexual means being attracted to people of the opposite sex, whereas being lesbian or gay entails same-sex attraction, and bisexuality involves attraction to both males and females. Our system of sexual orientation categorisation is problematised by gender diversity (see Rothblatt 1995) physically, in terms of sexual expression, and socially, in terms of identity. Gay, lesbian, and heterosexual sexualities rely on the notion that people are only attracted to people of one sex (this can also be termed 'monosexual'), that there are only two sexes and genders, and that people can be identified as clearly falling within one of them. The term 'bisexuality', whilst allowing for polysexual attraction (desire for people of more than one sex) also implies two sexes and genders. As I have shown above, gender diversity sometimes involves gender fluidity and non-male/female genders. Whilst the majority of people can relate to notions of same-sex or opposite-sex attraction, the categories of LGB (lesbian, gay, and bisexual) and heterosexual are insufficient in describing, for example, attraction between an androgyne and someone who identifies as gender transient. Sexual orientation categories based on the gender binary system are disrupted by gender diversity. The genitals of some gender diverse people are physiologically 'other' than those usually associated with women and men, although, of course, these people may identify as male or female. For example at the 1998 Transgender Film Festival Del LaGrace Volcano (an initially female bodied person who took testosterone) displayed photographs of his and other people's phalloclits, which resemble small penises enwreathed in labial lips. Sex between people with non-standard genitals is unlikely to fit heterosexual, gay, or lesbian sexual norms. As FTM trans person James Green told me: 'First of all I never had sex as a woman, and I will never have sex as a man. You know, I will always in that sense be other. And I cannot pretend that I'm not a transgender male.'

The destabilisation of sexual orientation categorisation that gender diversity can provoke may elicit a number of different types of (often overlapping) response. I will list these briefly here, before exploring them in more depth:

- alternative types of sexual orientation are developed, for example 'polysexual';
- individuals and groups continue to use existing definitions, whilst acknowledging their limitations;
- there is overlap of categories when people move around different gender subject positions;
- the signals associated with gender diverse and LGB images conflict, causing tensions between different groups;
- gender diversity and the tensions it provokes are channelled into sexual expression, for instance, contributor Zach Nataf said 'Once you've realised how unfixed gender is already, then sex, then sexuality, you know, gets thrown up [for questioning], you know it's just open.'

Alternative types of sexual orientation include those documented by Queen (1997): 'omnisexual', (attracted to multiple genders), and 'pansexual', a term coined by Firestone (1970) to mean diverse, unbounded desire. Other alternatives include for instance 'trannie lover'. These terms are not widely used, even in the sexual fringes where people are conversant with sexual orientation fluidity. Individuals and groups continue on the whole to use existing definitions, even when they do not fit very well. For example, Annie Cox, a MTF trans person, defined herself as a 'woman who loved woman' although she has a penis, whilst Rosario (1996) describes a study of the partners of gay FTM trans people who were happy with their partners having vaginas, despite identifying as gay. These issues also apply to the category of bisexual:

John: Some bisexuals are aware of the way in which gender diversity problematises the category of bisexual . . . I am careful to say I am attracted to more than one gender. We need strategically to use 'bisexual' as it's known – I am uncomfortable with pansexual and omnisexual. Bisexual is sufficient to freak people out, if we go further, it is even more alienating than with bisexuality.

Interviewer: *You don't see 'bisexual' as binaried?*

John: No – I am uncomfortable about the 'bi' aspect and the 'sexuality' aspect. I want an equivalent to 'lesbian' or 'gay' [in which lifestyle and political aspects are acknowledged].

Interviewer: *What are the implications of this for third or intersex people?*

John: There's an option of being monosexual – you could only be attracted to one type . . . I think sexual identity comes from gender identity, and if you identity as male or female you can slot into gay and lesbian categories. It's much easier.

Overlap of categories occurs when people move through a number of different spaces or identities. For example contributor Kate More said 'the only space I don't occupy, I think, is bisexual. And yet, in every way taking gay, lesbian, straight, whatever into consideration. Taking all three roles, that would make me bisexual I suppose.' This kind of statement is confusing for people who use mainstream sexual orientation categories, which tend to assume a single sexual identity being taken over a period of months or years – people do not generally think of someone being 'gay' for a couple of hours, then 'heterosexual' for the next couple of hours. People who are fluid about their desires might identify as bisexual. However, it is also possible to be bisexual and in a monogamous relationship for years, perhaps 'freezing' someone to an extent in an identity as 'heterosexual' or 'gay' or 'lesbian' – but also illustrating the way in which desire and sexuality mean more than physical sexual expression.

Gender and sexual orientation fluidity or multiplicity may cause conflicts within the cultures associated with sexual minorities. This is because signals that challenge gender stereotypes have historically been used by gay men and lesbians as a way of identifying themselves – butch and camp are important aspects of lesbian and gay culture. For example More (1996) described how MTF trans person and camp gay signifiers conflict, disrupting the delicately cross-gendered discourses of the lesbian and gay communities. She discussed the way in which transgender implodes the established divide between gender and sexuality, in which femininity and masculinity, can, for example, be associated with hetero-sexuality, and cross-gender identities associated with the lesbian and gay cultures.

Another, very different way of dealing with gender and sexual orientation fluid-ity and contradiction is found in various fringe sexual scenes. Some of the people involved in trans, fetish, or sex work worlds eroticise gender and sexual orien-tation dissonance and multiplicity (see Nataf 1996). This takes place amongst some gender diverse people, for example:

> If you open something up on the other person about their own gender posi-tion where they've not actually had that kind of question about themselves before, that gives them access to more material for desire and different ways of being sexual . . . they can then take that into a situation with a non-transgender person and open that up for everyone, so that it becomes, in fact it can become a gift. (Zach Nataf)

The fetish scenes provide a space where erotic transgression can take place within semi-public, rather than private, settings. Cross-dressing is an established part of the fetish and sadomasochistic scenes, as is 'gender play' (where different gender identities are enacted in a sexual context). Some of the contributors to research project (a) discussed gender play – for example I met a lesbian who dragged (cross-dressed) as a man and had sex with women as a man, and another les-bian who had several male sub-personalities that she used for sexual purposes. Gender play is also part of some transvestite identities – for example contributor Yvonne Sinclair described auto-erotic activity: 'to see an erect penis poking out from very pretty knickers, a frilly petticoat, and there it is, this woman who's got a prick and bollocks'. Gender diversity is also evident on the sex work scene, where certain types of transgender sex workers (usually 'she males' or preoperative MTF trans people) attract the interest of (usually male) clients – again, this is segregated away from mainstream society (see Evans 1993). Transgender categories are sexu-alised in unequal ways, reflecting unequal social relations. For instance, sex work primarily revolves around the eroticisation of the she male as gender ambiguous, enabling heterosexual male expression of what is possibly, in some cases same-sex attraction, without disruption of the gender binaried, patriarchal system.

Overall, the complexity that is apparent when gender and sexual orientation categories become fluid and multiple is managed in a number of ways, including continuing with the current, inadequate system, creating alternatives, and eroti-cising dissonance within certain subcultures that are segregated away from the mainstream.

Intersectionality

This section aims to contextualise gender and sexuality, indicating the way in which they are related to other structuring forces. Historically, many of the characteristics that are now routinely seen by social scientists as being social constructs, such as 'race', class, and gender, were once thought to have a biological basis. Praxis (theory and politics) that has moved on from this position has tended to focus on one or two social structuring mechanisms, such as class, sexuality and gender, or 'race', sometimes obscuring or reinforcing other systems of domination. Authors such as McClintock (1995) have explored the ways in which different social characteristics interact. McClintock argues that race, gender and class are related realms of experience, but that they cannot simply be yoked together. They come into existence in, and through, relationship to each other, 'if in contradictory and conflictual ways' (1995: 5). These complex relationships were demonstrated in research project (b), where some contributors discussed 'race', class and gender as 'adding onto' each other, whilst others saw them as combining in specific ways. For example, a black lesbian community member noted that a middle-class black gay man is likely to have very different experiences to those of a working-class black gay man.

Some authors have attempted to produce integrated models of social inequalities. For instance, Weber (2001) provides an analysis of the ways in which social characteristics structure US society. She outlines the way in which 'every social situation is affected by society wide historical patterns of race, class, gender, and sexuality that are not necessarily apparent to the participants and that are experienced differently depending on the race, class, gender and sexuality of the people involved' (Weber 2001: 19). According to Weber these social characteristics are structured in a hierarchical way, forming systems of oppression, in which certain groups have historically gained power and control over assets and other people, so that some groups become dependent on other groups and are exploited by them. This dynamic is masked by ideologies, so that inequalities are seen as being the result of a group's traits rather than social inequities. Structural inequality continues because members of privileged groups benefit from arrangements, and this is supported by a lack of wider awareness of the experiences of subordinated groups. The dynamics are not uniform – some people's experiences are different from the general pattern – and they are malleable to an extent.

Analysis of power and social inequality can utilise a number of theoretical bases, for example group-based approaches (including Marxism and radical feminism), in which certain groups (middle- and upper-class people, men) are seen to have power and to exploit others in a systematic way, and post-structuralism, in which power is seen as fluid and located in multiple places. I will draw primarily on post-structuralist approaches. For the post-structuralist author Foucault, power operates productively through the heterogeneous micro-relations that form social life (Sawicki 1991) – in other words, everything we do is part of wider power relations, challenging or reinforcing social norms. The mechanism of hegemonic (dominant) power is 'the construction of the subject by a discourse that weaves knowledge and power into a coercive structure that "forces the individual back on himself [sic] and ties him to his own identity in a constraining way"' (Alcoff 1995: 415). This means that people internalise dominant ideologies and end up thinking that their own position in society is justified, and that society is fair and equal. So, if they are in a subordinate position, it must be 'their own fault', or if in a privileged position, they think they are 'naturally' better or more deserving. For post-structuralists, power is constantly disputed via competing discourses (sets of ideas), so that subjectivity (a person's experience of themselves) is a site of conflict (Weedon 1994). The various discourses associated with race, class, gender, sexuality, age, ability and other characteristics interact in different ways for different people – and these people resist them in varied ways, for instance someone might challenge sexism but perpetrate racism.

The interrelationship of different discourses may be particularly complex for people with fluid genders or sexualities, as they are likely to experience marked changes in social context, meaning that they are affected by very different, sometimes conflicting, sets of discourses at different times. For instance, a MTF trans person may have learnt 'masculine' skills (such as car mechanics) whilst living as a man, but when she goes through GRS (Gender Reassignment Surgery) she may feel under pressure to abandon these due to social pressure to conform to feminine norms – but may also be influenced by feminist critiques of gender stereotyping.

Case Study: Gender and Sexual Diversity in India

What does intersectionality mean in practice? In this case study, which uses material from research project (c), I provide a snapshot of gender and sexuality categorisation in India, highlighting the ways that gender, sexuality, caste/class and processes of globalisation interact. Gender variance in India has ancient, even prehistoric, roots. According to one text, 'The Hijra communities in India have a recorded history of more than 4000 years' (PUCL-K 2003: 17). Hijras, who are born as intersex or as male (some undergo castration), trace their origins to the myths in the ancient Hindu scriptures of the Ramayana and Mahabharata. Hijras belonged to the 'Eunuch' culture that was common across the Middle East and India, where Eunuchs worked as guards, advisers, and entertainers (PUCL-K 2003). Other forms of gender pluralism in ancient India were also socially accepted. Gender variant women took roles as mercenaries, advisers, and religious people, and same-sex sexual expression is also documented, often taking place alongside opposite-sex relationships (Penrose 2001); 'traditionally, sexuality has always been more fluid, less rigidly categorised [than in the West]. Western naming, for many Indians, does not correspond to the amorphous nature of sexual experience' (Seabrook 1997). With the advent of British colonialism, the established social position of gender variant people was under-mined, for example the British removed the land rights of the Hijra communities. Indigenous sexualities were also suppressed by the British, and to some extent by Islam (Seabrook 1997).

Current exploratory research in India (project (c)) shows that there are different systems of gender and sexuality classification operating simultaneously, set against the backdrop of ancient systems of gender variance, dominant patriarchal norms, and post-colonialism. These systems are being integrated to some extent by the growing LGBT communities, which bridge indigenous and Western systems of categorization, and are reportedly inclusive of Hijras and Kothis (effeminate gay trans people). Gender or sexually variant Indians who are born female have fewer options than those born as male. They can identify as lesbian or transsexual, but these possibilities are often only available to the middle and upper classes. In theory, people born as male, on the other hand, can identify as gay, transgender, cross-dresser, Kothi or Hijra. In practice, these choices are heavily structured by caste/class and location. As Seabrook (1997) says, 'there are men who call themselves gay in India, but they are overwhelmingly middle class, English speaking, and privileged'.

According to Seabrook (1997), the undefined same-sex expression that was present prior to British rule still takes place to an extent in the slums and vil-lages, whilst amongst the less affluent urban dwellers, a heavily gendered system of male classification has emerged. Men who have sex with men are divided into two categories – the 'karte hain' (those who do) and the 'karvate hain' (those who are done to). Same-sex sexual expression is not linked with gay identification. For instance, one Kothi contributor told me that 'some hetero-sexual men like anal sex. If I do sex with a straight man, fucking him, he gets some pleasure from anal sex. Homosexuality is about attraction, it's not physi-cal.' Heterosexual identification is usual amongst the giriyas, or active partners. Kothis seem to identify more with transgender than gay identities – although some of the Kothis I met identified as gay. Kothis are further subdivided into feminine and masculine Kothis, reflecting the gender binaried nature of Indian society.

The Kothi and Hijra systems seem to exist side by side, overlapping to some degree. The extent to which Hijras do, or do not, identify as third sex is debatable:

> Hijras are akwas [not castrated] and nirvana [castrated] – some Hijras are akwas, so biologically they are men. They are mostly homosexual though they may be married with kids, but this is due to convenience, they are not bisexual. These are the Kothis, who cross over into the Hijra communities. Less than 1 per cent are intersex and 5 per cent have been castrated . . . they would not speak about this to most people because it is not in their interest. (Sexual health organisation worker)

This contributor pointed out that Hijras occupy a position in society that is simultaneously revered and stigmatised, and that they cultivate the mystique associated with this. They are seen as having the power to curse or bless people, due to their spiritual heritage, and they are also seen as having a huge potential for embarrassment because they threaten to expose themselves physically if they are not paid. The Hijras utilise these sources of power, retaining a somewhat secure position in society. This means that they can beg, and are less harassed by the police than other gender and sexual minorities. In addition, there are some designated political seats for Hijras, and Hijra involvement in party politics is well documented in the newspapers. Hijras are using their third-sex status to advantage, marketing themselves as 'incorruptible Eunuchs' (Chakraborty 2002). As one contributor said, 'they are seen as not being part of the mainstream, which then allows them to have a place in the mainstream'. However, most Hijras belong to the poorer castes and classes, and economic marginalisation structures their experiences very heavily. As Gupta says, 'Hijras might have an accepted place in Indian society, but it is a place pretty much at the bottom of the heap – making them not only a sexual but also a highly deprived social minority' (2002: 21).

Overall, therefore, it appeared that three main types of gender and sexual classification are current in India – unclassified sexual activity, the Hijra and Kothi systems (where transgender and same-sex expression are merged but are heavily structured by the gender binary system), and Western systems. These three forms of categorisation illustrate intersectionality because their operation is a product of caste, class, and colonialism-related inequalities, as well as the gender and sexuality inequalities that permeate Indian society. The Hijras, by occupying a social position in opposition to the binary system, have carved out a social space in which mainstream norms are rejected or revised, perhaps challenging, but not escaping, other structuring factors.

The sex/gender classification system in India provides an illustration of intersectionality. Intersectionality, or the way in which different social structuring factors interact, forms a crucial backdrop for discussions concerning gender and sexuality, as people's gender and sexual identities, as well as their positions in society, are formed in relation to factors such as class, ethnicity, and nationality.

Consider

1. How is gender social?
2. How do gender *differences* and *inequalities* shape social life in the contemporary world? Answer this question using sociological concepts and examples of your own.
3. How may families be sites of gender inequalities? Illustrate your answer with relevant contemporary examples.
4. How may workplaces be sites of gender inequalities? Illustrate your answer with relevant contemporary examples.

5. 'We live in a world that is deeply structured by sex and gender. The categorisation of people as "male" and "female" permeates our society on every level, including our language, relationships, social institutions, and academic debates. On a social level, biological determinism, or the belief that we act in certain ways because of our physical make-up, is rife' (Monro 2005, p.10). Discuss.
6. Summarise Monro's characterisation of gender diversity, sexual orientation and intersectionality in your own words. Give relevant examples of your own.
7. Investigate contemporary changes in the social recognition of same-sex relationships around the world. How can these changes be explained?

6.5 Reconsidering social inequalities: a research project

At this point, it is a good idea to take a step back from the exploration of social inequalities and ask what it has achieved so far. To begin with, it may have drawn your attention to the ways in which race, class, gender and sexuality define people's position in society and create differences and inequalities. Moreover, we have suggested a very basic toolkit of sociological concepts you can use to think about these inequalities.

It is also important to point out, however, that the distinctions we have set up between different forms of social inequality are somewhat artificial. Race, class, gender and sexuality are important in defining how we are and where we are located in society. Nonetheless, no individual can be reduced to their race, class, gender or sexuality, and the ways in which people's biographies intersect with broader currents of history cannot be explained through such a reduction. Sociologists train their gaze on specific forms of difference and inequality in order to be able to study them in sufficient detail. In doing so, they are forced to abstract from the complexity of everyday life and single out those themes and issues they can explore in manageable ways.

With such abstractions comes the temptation to engage in generalisations. For instance, looking at gender inequalities, it is easy to focus solely on the workings of patriarchy in societies around the world. However, such an approach disregards the – actually rather obvious – fact that women's and men's positions in society are also stratified by hierarchies of race, class, etc. Therefore, conclusions drawn about, say, white middle-class women in London may only be of limited relevance to illegal Mexican immigrants in the USA, Afro-Brazilians, or the descendents of immigrants from the Indian subcontinent now living in the UK. What this means is that our positions in society are always defined through the *intersection* of multiple social processes that create difference and inequality: race and class and gender and sexuality and age and health and disabilities . . . and so on. Figure 6.1 illustrates this idea.

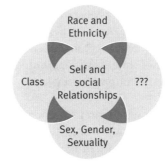

Figure 6.1   The intersection of social inequalities

This project allows you to explore the intersection of social inequalities in detail. Let's begin with a reading by US sociologist Patricia Hill Collins. Her works, particularly her 1990 book *Black Feminist Thought*, have gained widespread acclaim for the attention they devote to problems of *intersectionality*.

Reading

Hill Collins, Patricia (2000), *Black Feminist Thought* (2nd edn), New York: Routledge: pp. 1–3 and 13–19

The Politics of Black Feminist Thought

In 1831 Maria W. Stewart asked, "How long shall the fair daughters of Africa be compelled to bury their minds and talents beneath a load of iron pots and kettles?" Orphaned at age five, bound out to a clergyman's family as a domestic servant, Stewart struggled to gather isolated fragments of an education when and where she could. As the first American woman to lecture in public on political issues and to leave copies of her texts, this early U.S. Black woman intellectual foreshadowed a variety of themes taken up by her Black feminist successors (Richardson 1987).

Maria Stewart challenged African-American women to reject the negative images of Black womanhood so prominent in her times, pointing out that race, gender, and class oppression were the fundamental causes of Black women's poverty. In an 1833 speech she proclaimed, "Like King Solomon, who put neither nail nor hammer to the temple, yet received the praise; so also have the white Americans gained themselves a name . . . while in reality we have been their principal foundation and support." Stewart objected to the injustice of this situation: "We have pursued the shadow, they have obtained the substance; we have performed the labor, they have received the profits; we have planted the vines, they have eaten the fruits of them" (Richardson 1987, 59).

Maria Stewart was not content to point out the source of Black women's oppression. She urged Black women to forge self-definitions of self-reliance and independence. "It is useless for us any longer to sit with our hands folded, reproaching the whites; for that will never elevate us," she exhorted. "Possess the spirit of independence. . . . Possess the spirit of men, bold and enterprising, fearless and undaunted" (p. 53). To Stewart, the power of self-definition was essential, for Black women's survival was at stake. "Sue for your rights and privileges. Know the reason you cannot attain them. Weary them with your importunities. You can but die if you make the attempt; and we shall certainly die if you do not" (p. 38).

Stewart also challenged Black women to use their special roles as mothers to forge powerful mechanisms of political action. "O, ye mothers, what a responsibility rests on you!" Stewart preached. "You have souls committed to your charge. . . . It is you that must create in the minds of your little girls and boys a thirst for knowledge, the love of virtue, . . . and the cultivation of a pure heart." Stewart recognized the magnitude of the task at hand. "Do not say you cannot make any thing of your children; but say . . . we will try" (p. 35).

Maria Stewart was one of the first U.S. Black feminists to champion the utility of Black women's relationships with one another in providing a community for Black women's activism and self-determination. "Shall it any longer be said of the daughters of Africa, they have no ambition, they have no force?" she questioned. "By no means. Let every female heart become united, and let us raise a fund ourselves; and at the end of one year and a half, we might be able to lay the corner stone for the building of a High School, that the higher branches of knowledge might be enjoyed by us" (p. 37). Stewart saw the potential for Black women's activism as educators. She advised, "Turn your attention to knowledge and improvement; for knowledge is power" (p. 41).

Though she said little in her speeches about the sexual politics of her time, her advice to African-American women suggests that she was painfully aware of the sexual abuse visited upon Black women. She continued to "plead the cause of virtue and the pure principles of morality" (p. 31) for Black women. And to those Whites who thought that Black women were inherently inferior, Stewart offered a biting response: "Our souls are fired with the same love of liberty and independence with which your souls are fired. . . . [T]oo much of your blood flows in our veins, too much of your color in our skins, for us not to possess your spirits" (p. 40).

Despite Maria Stewart's intellectual prowess, the ideas of this extraordinary woman come to us only in scattered fragments that not only suggest her brilliance but speak tellingly of the fate of countless Black women intellectuals. Many Maria Stewarts exist, African-American women whose minds and talents have been suppressed by the pots and kettles symbolic of Black women's subordination (Guy-Sheftall 1986). Far too many African-American women intellectuals have labored in isolation and obscurity and, like Zora Neale Hurston, lie buried in unmarked graves.

Some have been more fortunate, for they have become known to us, largely through the efforts of contemporary Black women scholars (Hine et al. 1993; Guy-Sheftall 1995b). Like Alice Walker, these scholars sense that "a people do not throw their geniuses away" and that "if they are thrown away, it is our duty as artists, scholars, and witnesses for the future to collect them again for the sake of our children, . . . if necessary, bone by bone" (Walker 1983, 92).

This painstaking process of collecting the ideas and actions of "thrown away" Black women like Maria Stewart has revealed one important discovery. Black women intellectuals have laid a vital analytical foundation for a distinctive standpoint on self, community, and society and, in doing so, created a multifaceted, African-American women's intellectual tradition. While clear discontinuities in this tradition exist – times when Black women's voices were strong, and others when assuming a more muted tone was essential – one striking dimension of the ideas of Maria W. Stewart and her successors is the thematic consistency of their work.

If such a rich intellectual tradition exists, why has it remained virtually invisible until now? In 1905 Fannie Barrier Williams lamented, "The colored girl . . . is not known and hence not believed in; she belongs to a race that is best designated by the term 'problem,' and she lives beneath the shadow of that problem which envelops and obscures her" (Williams 1987, 150). Why are African-American women and our ideas not known and not believed in?

The shadow obscuring this complex Black women's intellectual tradition is neither accidental nor benign. Suppressing the knowledge produced by any oppressed group makes it easier for dominant groups to rule because the seeming absence of dissent suggests that subordinate groups willingly collaborate in their own victimization (Scott 1985). Maintaining the invisibility of Black women and our ideas not only in the United States, but in Africa, the Caribbean, South America, Europe, and other places where Black women now live, has been critical in maintaining social inequalities. Black women engaged in reclaiming and constructing Black women's knowledges often point to the politics of suppression that affect their projects. For example, several authors in Heidi Mirza's (1997) edited volume on Black British feminism identify their invisibility and silencing in the contemporary United Kingdom. Similarly, South African businesswoman Danisa Baloyi describes her astonishment at the invisibility of African women in U.S. scholarship: "As a student doing research in the United States, I was amazed by the [small] amount of information on Black South African women, and shocked that only a minuscule amount was actually written by Black women themselves" (Baloyi 1995, 41).

Despite this suppression, U.S. Black women have managed to do intellectual work, and to have our ideas matter. Sojourner Truth, Anna Julia Cooper, Ida B. Wells-Barnett, Mary McLeod Bethune, Toni Morrison, Barbara Smith, and countless others have consistently struggled to make themselves heard. African women writers such as Ama Ata Aidoo, Buchi Emecheta, and Ellen Kuzwayo have used their voices to raise important issues that affect Black African women

(James 1990). Like the work of Maria W. Stewart and that of Black women transnationally, African-American women's intellectual work has aimed to foster Black women's activism.

[. . .]

Developing Black Feminist Thought

Starting from the assumption that African-American women have created independent, oppositional yet subjugated knowledges concerning our own subordination, contemporary U.S. Black women intellectuals are engaged in the struggle to reconceptualize all dimensions of the dialectic of oppression and activism as it applies to African-American women. Central to this enterprise is reclaiming Black feminist intellectual traditions (see, e.g., Harley and Terborg-Penn 1978; Hull et al. 1982; James and Busia 1993; and Guy-Sheftall 1995a, 1995b).

For many U.S. Black women intellectuals, this task of reclaiming Black women's subjugated knowledge takes on special meaning. Knowing that the minds and talents of our grandmothers, mothers, and sisters have been suppressed stimulates many contributions to the growing field of Black women's studies (Hull et al. 1982). Alice Walker describes how this sense of purpose affects her work: "In my own work I write not only what I want to read – understanding fully and indelibly that if I don't do it no one else is so vitally interested, or capable of doing it to my satisfaction – I write all the things *I should have been able to read*" (Walker 1983, 13).

Reclaiming Black women's ideas involves discovering, reinterpreting, and, in many cases, analyzing for the first time the works of individual U.S. Black women thinkers who were so extraordinary that they did manage to have their ideas preserved. In some cases this process involves locating unrecognized and unheralded works, scattered and long out of print. Marilyn Richardson's (1987) painstaking editing of the writings and speeches of Maria Stewart, and Mary Helen Washington's (1975, 1980, 1987) collections of Black women's writings typify this process. Similarly, Alice Walker's (1979a) efforts to have Zora Neale Hurston's unmarked grave recognized parallel her intellectual quest to honor Hurston's important contributions to Black feminist literary traditions.

Reclaiming Black women's ideas also involves discovering, reinterpreting, and analyzing the ideas of subgroups within the larger collectivity of U.S. Black women who have been silenced. For example, burgeoning scholarship by and about Black lesbians reveals a diverse and complex history. Gloria Hull's (1984) careful compilation of the journals of Black feminist intellectual Alice Dunbar-Nelson illustrates the difficulties of being closeted yet still making major contributions to African-American social and political thought. Audre Lorde's (1982) autobiography, *Zami*, provides a book-length treatment of Black lesbian communities in New York. Similarly, Kennedy and Davis's (1994) history of the formation of lesbian communities in 1940s and 1950s Buffalo, New York, strives to understand how racial segregation influenced constructions of lesbian identities.

Reinterpreting existing works through new theoretical frameworks is another dimension of developing Black feminist thought. In Black feminist literary criticism, this process is exemplified by Barbara Christian's (1985) landmark volume on Black women writers, Mary Helen Washington's (1987) reassessment of anger and voice in *Maud Martha*, a much-neglected work by novelist and poet Gwendolyn Brooks, and Hazel Carby's (1987) use of the lens of race, class, and gender to reinterpret the works of nineteenth-century Black women novelists. Within Black feminist historiography the tremendous strides that have been made in U.S. Black women's history are evident in Evelyn Brooks Higginbotham's (1989) analysis of the emerging concepts and paradigms in Black women's history, her study of women in the Black Baptist Church (1993), Stephanie Shaw's (1996) study of Black professional women workers during the Jim Crow era, and the landmark volume *Black Women in the United States: An Historical Encyclopedia* (Hine et al. 1993).

Developing Black feminist thought also involves searching for its expression in alternative institutional locations and among women who are not commonly perceived as intellectuals. As defined in this volume, Black women intellectuals are neither all academics nor found primarily in the Black middle class. Instead, all U.S. Black women who somehow contribute to Black feminist thought as critical social theory are deemed to be "intellectuals." They may be highly educated. Many are not. For example, nineteenth-century Black feminist activist Sojourner Truth is not typically seen as an intellectual. Because she could neither read nor write, much of what we know about her has been recorded by other people. One of her most famous speeches, that delivered at the 1851 women's rights convention in Akron, Ohio, comes to us in a report written by a feminist abolitionist some time after the event itself (Painter 1993). We do not know what Truth actually said, only what the recorder claims that she said. Despite this limitation, in that speech Truth reportedly provides an incisive analysis of the definition of the term *woman* forwarded in the mid-1800s:

> That man over there says women need to be helped into carriages, and lifted over ditches, and to have the best place everywhere. Nobody ever helps me into carriages, or over mud puddles, or gives me any best place! And ain't I a woman? Look at me! Look at my arm! I have ploughed, and planted, and gathered into barns, and no man could head me! And ain't I a woman? I could work as much and eat as much as a man – when I could get it – and bear the lash as well! And ain't I a woman? I have borne thirteen children, and seen them most all sold off to slavery, and when I cried out with my mother's grief, none but Jesus heard me! And ain't I a woman? (Loewenberg and Bogin 1976, 235)

By using the contradictions between her life as an African-American woman and the qualities ascribed to women, Sojourner Truth exposes the concept of woman as being culturally constructed. Her life as a second-class citizen has been filled with hard physical labor, with no assistance from men. Her question, "and ain't I a woman?" points to the contradictions inherent in blanket use of the term *woman*. For those who question Truth's femininity, she invokes her status as a mother of thirteen children, all sold off into slavery, and asks again, "and ain't I a woman?" Rather than accepting the existing assumptions about what a woman is and then trying to prove that she fit the standards, Truth challenged the very standards themselves. Her actions demonstrate the process of deconstruction – namely, exposing a concept as ideological or culturally constructed rather than as natural or a simple reflection of reality (Collins 1998a, 137–45). By deconstructing the concept *woman*, Truth proved herself to be a formidable intellectual. And yet Truth was a former slave who never learned to read or write.

Examining the contributions of women like Sojourner Truth suggests that the concept of *intellectual* must itself be deconstructed. Not all Black women intellectuals are educated. Not all Black women intellectuals work in academia. Furthermore, not all highly educated Black women, especially those who are employed in U.S. colleges and universities, are *automatically* intellectuals. U.S. Black women intellectuals are not a female segment of William E. B. DuBois's notion of the "talented tenth." One is neither born an intellectual nor does one become one by earning a degree. Rather, doing intellectual work of the sort envisioned within Black feminism requires a process of self-conscious struggle on behalf of Black women, regardless of the actual social location where that work occurs.

These are not idle concerns within new power relations that have greatly altered the fabric of U.S. and Black civil society. Race, class, and gender still constitute intersecting oppressions, but the ways in which they are now organized to produce social injustice differ from prior eras. Just as theories, epistemologies, and facts produced by any group of individuals represent the standpoints and interests of their creators, the very definition of who is legitimated to do intellectual work is not only politically contested, but is changing (Mannheim 1936; Gramsci 1971). Reclaiming Black feminist intellectual traditions involves much more than developing Black feminist analyses using standard epistemological criteria. It also involves challenging the very terms of intellectual discourse itself.

Assuming new angles of vision on which U.S. Black women are, in fact, intellectuals, and on their seeming dedication to contributing to Black feminist thought raises new questions about the production of this oppositional knowledge. Historically, much of the Black women's intellectual tradition occurred in institutional locations other than the academy. For example, the music of working-class Black women blues singers of the 1920 and 1930s is often seen as one important site outside academia for this intellectual tradition (Davis 1998). Whereas Ann duCille (1993) quite rightly warns us about viewing Black women's blues through rose-colored glasses, the fact remains that far more Black women listened to Bessie Smith and Ma Rainey than were able to read Nella Larsen or Jessie Fauset. Despite impressive educational achievements that have allowed many U.S. Black women to procure jobs in higher education and the media, this may continue to be the case. For example, Imani Perry (1995) suggests that the music of Black women hip-hop artists serves as a new site of Black women's intellectual production. Again, despite the fact that hip-hop contains diverse and contradictory components (Rose 1994) and that popularity alone is insufficient to confer the title "intellectual," many more Black women listen to Queen Latifah and Salt 'N' Pepa than read literature by Alice Walker and Toni Morrison.

Because clarifying Black women's experiences and ideas lies at the core of Black feminist thought, interpreting them requires collaborative leadership among those who participate in the diverse forms that Black women's communities now take. This requires acknowledging not only how African-American women outside of academia have long functioned as intellectuals by representing the interests of Black women as a group, but how this continues to be the case. For example, rap singer Sister Souljah's music as well as her autobiography *No Disrespect* (1994) certainly can be seen as contributing to Black feminist thought as critical social theory. Despite her uncritical acceptance of a masculinist Black nationalist ideology, Souljah is deeply concerned with issues of Black women's oppression, and offers an important perspective on contemporary urban culture. Yet while young Black women listened to Souljah's music and thought about her ideas, Souljah's work has been dismissed within feminist classrooms in academia as being "nonfeminist." Without tapping these nontraditional sources, much of the Black women's intellectual tradition would remain "not known and hence not believed in" (Williams 1987, 150).

At the same time, many Black women academics struggle to find ways to do intellectual work that challenges injustice. They know that being an academic and an intellectual are not necessarily the same thing. Since the 1960s, U.S. Black women have entered faculty positions in higher education in small but unprecedented numbers. These women confront a peculiar dilemma. On the one hand, acquiring the prestige enjoyed by their colleagues often required unquestioned acceptance of academic norms. On the other hand, many of these same norms remain wedded to notions of Black and female inferiority. Finding ways to temper critical responses to academia without unduly jeopardizing their careers constitutes a new challenge for Black women who aim to be intellectuals within academia, especially intellectuals engaged in developing Black feminist thought (Collins 1998a, 95–123).

Surviving these challenges requires new ways of doing Black feminist intellectual work. Developing Black feminist thought as critical social theory involves including the ideas of Black women not previously considered intellectuals – many of whom may be working-class women with jobs outside academia – as well as those ideas emanating from more formal, legitimated scholarship. The ideas we share with one another as mothers in extended families, as othermothers in Black communities, as members of Black churches, and as teachers to the Black community's children have formed one pivotal area where African-American women have hammered out a multifaceted Black women's standpoint. Musicians, vocalists, poets, writers, and other artists constitute another group from which Black women intellectuals have emerged. Building on African-influenced oral traditions, musicians in particular have enjoyed close association with the larger community of African-American women constituting their audience. Through their words and actions, grassroots political activists also contribute to Black women's intellectual traditions. Producing intellectual work is generally not attributed to Black women artists and political activists. Especially in elite institutions of higher education, such women are typically viewed as objects of study, a classification that creates a false dichotomy between scholarship and activism, between thinking and doing. In contrast, examining the ideas and actions of these excluded groups in a way that views them as subjects reveals a world in which behavior is a statement of philosophy and in which a vibrant, both/and, scholar/activist tradition remains intact.

Objectives of the Volume

African-American women's social location as a collectivity has fostered distinctive albeit heterogeneous Black feminist intellectual traditions that, for convenience in this volume, I call *Black feminist thought*. Investigations of four basic components of Black feminist thought – its thematic content, its interpretive frameworks, its epistemological approaches, and its significance for empowerment – constitute the core of this volume. All four components have been shaped by U.S. Black women's placement in a political context that is undergoing considerable change. Thus, Black feminist thought's core themes, interpretive frameworks, epistemological stances, and insights concerning empowerment will reflect and aim to shape specific political contexts confronting African-American women as a group.

In this volume, I aim to describe, analyze, explain the significance of, and contribute to the development of Black feminist thought as critical social theory. In addressing this general goal, I have several specific objectives. First, I summarize selected core themes in Black feminist thought by surveying their historical and contemporary expression. Drawing primarily on the works of African-American women scholars and on the thought produced by a wide range of Black women intellectuals, I explore several core themes that preoccupy Black women thinkers. The vast majority of thinkers discussed in the text are, to the best of my knowledge, U.S. Black women. I cite a range of Black women thinkers not because I think U.S. Black women have a monopoly on the ideas presented but because I aim to demonstrate the range and depth of thinkers who exist in U.S. Black civil society. Placing the ideas of ordinary African-American women as well as those of better-known Black women intellectuals at the center of analysis produces a new angle of vision on Black women's concerns. At the same time, Black feminist thought cannot be developed in isolation from the thought and actions of other groups. Thus, I also include the ideas of diverse thinkers who make important contributions to developing Black feminist thought. Black women must be in charge of Black feminist thought, but being in charge does not mean that others are excluded.

Using and furthering an interpretive framework or paradigm that has come to be known as race, class, and gender studies constitute a second objective of *Black Feminist Thought*. Rejecting additive models of oppression, race, class, and gender studies have progressed considerably since the 1980s. During that decade, African-American women scholar-activists, among others, called for a new approach to analyzing Black women's experiences. Claiming that such experiences were shaped not just by race, but by gender, social class, and sexuality, works such as *Women, Race and Class* by Angela Davis (1981), "A Black Feminist Statement" drafted by the Combahee River Collective (1982), and Audre Lorde's (1984) classic volume *Sister Outsider* stand as groundbreaking works that explored interconnections among systems of oppression. Subsequent work aimed to describe different dimensions of this interconnected relationship with terms such as *intersectionality* (Crenshaw 1991) and *matrix of domination*. In this volume, I use and distinguish between both terms in examining how oppression affects Black women. Intersectionality refers to particular forms of intersecting oppressions, for example, intersections of race and gender, or of sexuality and nation. Intersectional paradigms remind us that oppression cannot be reduced to one fundamental type, and that oppressions work together in producing injustice. In contrast, the matrix of domination refers to how these intersecting oppressions are actually organized. Regardless of the particular intersections involved, structural, disciplinary, hegemonic, and interpersonal domains of power reappear across quite different forms of oppression.

My third objective is to develop an epistemological framework that can be used both to assess existing Black feminist thought and to clarify some of the underlying assumptions that impede its development. This issue of epistemology raises some difficult questions. I see the need to define the boundaries that delineate Black feminist thought from other arenas of intellectual inquiry. What criteria, if any, can be applied to ideas to determine whether they are in fact Black and feminist? What essential features does Black feminist thought share with other critical social theories, particularly Western feminist theory, Afrocentric theory, Marxist analyses, and postmodernism? Do African-American women implicitly rely on alternative standards for determining whether ideas are true? Traditional epistemological assumptions concerning how we arrive at "truth" simply are not sufficient to the task of furthering Black feminist thought. In the same way that concepts such as woman and intellectual must be challenged, the process by which we arrive at truth merits comparable scrutiny. While I provide a book-length treatment of these theoretical concerns in *Fighting Words: Black Women and the Search for Justice*, here I focus on the distinguishing features of a Black feminist epistemology.

I aim to use this same epistemological framework throughout the volume. Alice Walker describes this process as one whereby "to write the books one wants to read is both to point the direction of vision and, at the same time, to follow it" (1983, 8). This was a very difficult process for me, one requiring that I not only develop standards and guidelines for assessing U.S. Black feminist thought but that I then apply those same standards and guidelines to my own work while I was creating it. For example, in Chapters 2 and 10 I argue that Black women intellectuals best contribute to a Black women's group standpoint by using their experiences as situated knowers. To adhere to this epistemological tenet required that, when appropriate, I reject the pronouns "they" and "their" when describing U.S. Black women and our ideas and replace these terms with the terms "we," "us," and "our." Using the distancing terms "they" and "their" when describing my own group and our experiences might enhance both my credentials as a scholar and the credibility of my arguments in some academic settings. But by taking this epistemological stance that reflects my disciplinary training as a sociologist, I invoke standards of certifying truth about which I remain ambivalent.

Consider

1. How and why, according to Collins, is Black Feminist thought being suppressed? Summarise her arguments in your own words.
2. How does Collins explain the need for Black Feminist scholarship and activism? Summarise her arguments in your own words.
3. Define intersectionality and the matrix of domination in your own words. Give relevant examples to illustrate your definitions.

Debate: Highlighting inequalities

Now let us take the debate further. Our look at inequalities so far has been anything but comprehensive. There are many other ways in which human beings are different and unequal, exploited and divided in society, and some of these ways are receiving increasing public attention. Consider any one of the following issues:

1. Age and generations
2. Health and illness
3. Disabilities
4. Any other form of social inequality that can be reasonably defined as such.

Now explain in your own words why you believe that the issue you have chosen is socially and sociologically significant. To do so, you need to look into it quite systematically. You might choose an international perspective, or you might consider any one particular place in the world. Look for academic publications, official reports, media coverage and other public documents. What are the patterns of inequality that have been reported regarding your chosen issue? What sociological concepts, if any, have been used to describe them? How are they being addressed? How are they related to other forms of social inequality? Write a report on your findings.

6.6 Global inequalities and global poverty

So far, we have explored the ways in which societies are internally stratified. Race, class, gender, sexuality, age, disabilities and other characteristics differentiate individuals and social groups. Moreover, they establish hierarchies in terms of power, recognition by others, and access to the resources we need to live and live well. However, as we have already seen in previous chapters, it is not sufficient to look only at social inequalities within individual societies. Over the past centuries, a global social system has slowly taken shape, within which societies are closely tied together through the spread of fashions, values and beliefs, commerce, the production and consumption of goods, transnational friendships and marriages, warfare and imperial conquest, and so forth. Some scholars, such as Manuel Castells (2000) argue that we now live in one global network society. However, the very same forces that have tied societies together have also driven them apart, creating a tight web of inequity, exploitation and disparate life chances. Alongside debates about social inequalities within societies, it is necessary to look at the ways in which *global social inequalities* cut across borders in the contemporary world. The remainder of this chapter will consider questions surrounding these global inequalities.

The *Human Development Index* (HDI) is one key indicator of global inequalities. Compiled by the United Nations Development Programme for its annual Human Development Reports, it uses indicators of health, education and living standards to measure and compare the overall quality of life in countries across the world. Countries are assigned values between '1' (highest human development) and '0' and ranked in four groups, from 'very high human development' to 'low human development'. The HDI is meant to serve as a tool for the systematic improvement of the quality of life across the planet. However, it also points to global hierarchies and inequalities in terms of the life chances of people in different societies. In the 2011 HDI, Norway (with a human development value of 0.943), Australia (0.929), The Netherlands (0.910), the USA (0.910), and New Zealand (0.908) were firmly established at the top, while the Democratic Republic of the Congo (0.286), Niger (0.295), Burundi (0.316), Mozambique (0.322), and Chad (0.328) languish at the bottom (http://hdr.undp.org/en/media/HDR_2011_EN_Table1.pdf). A glance at previous reports reveals that this has not changed dramatically over the years, with largely the same countries forming the top and the bottom of the global pecking order. The Human Development Index reveals a radically unequal world and a world in which inequality seems lasting and firmly entrenched.

The image of global inequality conjured by the HDI needs to be amended with more specific statements about the distribution of global inequalities. Societies are not uniform, and certain social groups suffer more than others from major forms of inequality and exploitation. Let us consider the case of *global poverty*. The World Bank defines poverty as follows:

> Poverty is 'pronounced deprivation in well-being.' The conventional view links well-being primarily to command over commodities, so the poor are those who do not have enough income or consumption to put them above some adequate

minimum threshold. This view sees poverty largely in monetary terms. Poverty may also be tied to a specific type of consumption; for example, people could be house poor or food poor or health poor. These dimensions of poverty often can be measured directly, for instance, by measuring malnutrition or literacy. The broadest approach to well-being (and poverty) focuses on the capability of the individual to function in society. Poor people often lack key capabilities; they may have inadequate income or education, or be in poor health, or feel powerless, or lack political freedoms. (http://siteresources.worldbank.org/INTPA/Resources/429966-1259774805724/Poverty_Inequality_Handbook_Ch01.pdf)

According to the World Bank, in 2008, 22.4 per cent of the world population, or 1,289 million people, lived in extreme poverty, having to get by with only about $1.25 per day. World Bank data likewise reveal that global poverty is concentrated in certain regions of the world, most notably Africa and the Indian subcontinent. In turn, across the world certain people, such as women, children and the elderly, are much more likely to experience severe poverty than others. Entrenched inequalities of gender, age, race, and so forth, work to ensure that poverty is much more likely for certain parts of the world population than for others. The following reading raises critical questions about the nature of global poverty, and ties it to considerations of social justice. While Thomas Pogge, its author, is not a sociologist, he writes in the spirit of the sociological imagination, and his work has done much to inspire sociological debates in recent years.

Reading

Pogge, Thomas (2010), *Politics as Usual*, Cambridge: Polity Press, pp. 10–13, 20–24 and 57–62

What Is Global Justice?

1.0 Introduction

A literature search on "global justice" finds this to be a newly prominent expression. There were more books and essays on global justice in the first few years of the new millennium than in the preceding one, at least as far as computers can tell. Of course, some of the broad topics currently debated under the heading of "global justice" have been discussed for centuries, back to the beginnings of civilization. But they were discussed under different labels, such as "international justice," "international ethics," and "the law of nations." This chapter explores the significance of this shift in terminology. Having been involved in this shift for more than three decades, I realize that there is likely to be a personal element in my account of it, which is due to the specific motives and ideas that have animated my thinking and writing. This is not an objective scholarly report from a distance, which, in any case, would be hard to write at this early time.

For centuries, moral reflection on international relations was focused on matters of war and peace. These issues are still important and much discussed. Since World War II, however, other themes have become more prominent due to increasing global interdependence and an erosion of sovereignty. The United Nations and the *Universal Declaration of Human Rights* reflect efforts to establish globally uniform minimum standards for the treatment of citizens within their own countries. The Bretton Woods institutions and later the World Trade Organization powerfully shape the economic prospects of countries and their citizens. Global and regional organizations, most notably the UN Security Council and the European Union, have acquired political functions and powers that were traditionally thought to belong to national governments.

These developments are in part a response to the horrors of World War II. But they are also fueled by technological innovations that limit the control governments can exert within their jurisdictions. Thus, industrialization has massive effects that no country can avoid – effects on culture and expectations, on biodiversity, climate, oceans, and atmosphere. New communication technologies make it much harder to control the information available to a national population. And many of the goods demanded by more affluent consumers everywhere require ingredients imported from foreign lands. The traditional concerns with the just internal organization of societies and the moral rules governing warfare leave out some highly consequential features of the modern world.

1.1 The extent of global poverty

After some delay, academic moral reflection has responded to these developments. Beginning in the early 1970s, philosophers and others have asked probing questions about how the emergence of a post-Westphalian world modifies and enlarges the moral responsibilities of governments, corporations, and individuals. These debates were driven also by the realization that world poverty has overtaken war as the greatest source of avoidable human misery. Many more people – some 360 million – have died from hunger and remediable diseases in peacetime in the 20 years since the end of the Cold War than perished from wars, civil wars, and government repression over the entire twentieth century. And poverty continues unabated, as the official statistics amply confirm: 1,020 million human beings are chronically undernourished, 884 million lack access to safe water, and 2,500 million lack access to basic sanitation; 2,000 million lack access to essential drugs; 924 million lack adequate shelter and 1,600 million lack electricity; 774 million adults are illiterate; and 218 million children are child laborers.

Roughly one third of all human deaths, 18 million annually, are due to poverty-related causes, easily preventable through better nutrition, safe drinking water, cheap rehydration packs, vaccines, antibiotics, and other medicines. People of color, females, and the very young are heavily overrepresented among the global poor, and hence also among those suffering the staggering effects of severe poverty. Children under the age of 5 account for over half, or 9.2 million, of the annual death toll from poverty-related causes. The overrepresentation of females is clearly documented.

Such severe deficits in the fulfillment of social and economic human rights also bring further deficits in civil and political human rights in their wake. Very poor people – often physically and mentally stunted as a result of malnutrition in infancy, illiterate due to lack of schooling, and much preoccupied with their family's survival – can cause little harm or benefit to the politicians and officials who rule them. Such rulers have far greater incentives to attend to the interests of agents more capable of reciprocation: the interests of affluent compatriots and foreigners, of domestic and multinational corporations, and of foreign governments.

1.2 The moral significance of global poverty

Three facts make the great ongoing catastrophe of human poverty deeply problematic, morally.

First, it occurs in the context of unprecedented global affluence that is easily sufficient to eradicate all life-threatening poverty. Suppose we think of the very poor narrowly as those who suffer the deprivations detailed above – lack of access to safe food and water, clothing, shelter, basic medical care, and basic education. This narrow and absolute definition of severe poverty corresponds roughly to the World Bank's "$2.50 per day" poverty line, according to which a household is poor just in case the local cost of its entire consumption, per person per day, has less purchasing power than $2.50 had in the United States in 2005. Although 48 percent of the world's population, 3,085 million human beings, were reportedly living below this poverty line in 2005 – on average, 45 percent below it – their collective shortfall from this line amounts to only 2 percent of global household income. A 2 percent shift in the distribution of global household income could wholly eradicate the severe poverty that currently blights the lives of nearly half the human population.

While the income ratio between the top and bottom decile of the human population is a staggering 273:1, their wealth ratio is ten times greater still. In 2000 the bottom half of the world's adults together owned 1.1 percent of global wealth, with the bottom 10 percent having only 0.03 percent, while the top 10 percent had 85.1 percent and the top 1 percent had 39.9 percent. Severe poverty today is avoidable at a cost that is tiny in relation to the incomes and fortunes of the affluent – vastly smaller, for instance, than the Allies' sacrifice in blood and treasure for victory in World War II.

Second, the unprecedented global inequalities just described are still increasing relentlessly. For the 1988–98 period, Branko Milanovic finds that, assessed in terms of purchasing power parities (PPPs), the Gini measure of inequality among persons worldwide increased from 62.2 to 64.1, and the Theil from 72.7 to 78.9. He adds that real incomes among the poorest 5 percent of world population (identified by PPP comparison) *declined* 20 percent during 1988–93 and another 23 percent during 1993–8, even while real global per capita income rose 5.2 percent and 4.8 percent respectively. I confirm and update his findings with other, more intuitive data below. There is a clear pattern: global inequality is increasing as the global poor are not participating proportionately in global economic growth.

Third, conditions of life anywhere on earth are today deeply affected by international interactions of many kinds and thus by the elaborate regime of treaties and conventions that profoundly and increasingly shape such interactions. Those who participate in this regime, especially in its design or imposition, are morally implicated in any contribution it makes to ever-increasing global economic inequality and to the consequent persistence of severe poverty.

[...]

1.6 The global institutional order contributes to severe poverty

The global institutional order is causally related to the incidence of morally significant harms in two main ways. First, its rules may affect individuals indirectly, by co-shaping the national institutional order under which they live. The four international privileges accorded even to highly illegitimate rulers provide an obvious example. By enabling despotic rulers and juntas to entrench themselves in power and by giving potential such oppressors strong incentives to try to take power by force, these privileges facilitate and foster oppressive and corrupt government in many less developed countries where the resource sector is a large part of the national economy and where ordinary citizens have few means to resist their oppression.

Secondly, the rules of the global institutional order may affect people more directly. Consider, for example, the current WTO treaty system, which permits the affluent countries to protect their markets against cheap imports (agricultural products, textiles and apparel, steel, and much else) through tariffs, anti-dumping duties, quotas, export credits, and huge subsidies to domestic producers. Such protectionist measures reduce the export opportunities from poor countries by constraining their exports into the affluent countries and also, in the case of subsidies, by allowing less efficient rich-country producers to undersell more efficient poor-country producers in world markets. In the absence of these constraints, poor countries would realize welfare gains in excess of $100 billion annually (comparable to current official development assistance or ODA) and reductions of several hundred million in the number of poor. The magnitude of this amount suggests that the *WTO Treaty's* high tolerance for rich-country protectionism greatly aggravates severe poverty in the less developed countries. If the WTO treaty system did not allow the protectionist measures in question, there would be much less poverty in the world today.

Another important example of the direct impact of the global institutional order is the globalization of intellectual property rights through the TRIPS (Trade-Related Aspects of Intellectual Property Rights) component of the *WTO*

Treaty. Under TRIPS, WTO members are required to adjust their domestic laws so as to grant 20-year monopoly patents on a wide range of innovations, which, most importantly, include advanced seeds and medicines. In this way, TRIPS has dramatically curtailed the access poor people have to cheap generic versions of advanced medicines. The absence of generic competition multiplies the prices of advanced medicines – often 10- to 15-fold – and thereby effectively excludes the poor. In addition, this globalized monopoly patent regime strongly discourages pharmaceutical innovators from doing any research and development focused on the diseases concentrated among the global poor – diseases that kill millions each year. It is obvious that pharmaceutical research could be incentivized differently: governments could reward any newly developed medicine in proportion to its impact on the global disease burden on condition that this medicine is sold at the (competitively determined) lowest feasible cost of production and distribution. Under this alternative regime, both deadly defects of the TRIPS regimes would be avoided: the price of advanced medicines would be vastly lower, which would greatly expand access to such medicines by the world's poor, and there would be many new medicines developed for the neglected diseases that continue to ravage the world's poorest populations.

Much more could and should be said about these three examples: about the four privileges that fuel and perpetuate oppression and civil war in many poor countries, about the rules that shelter the protectionism practiced by the affluent countries, and about the rules that exclude the global poor from the benefits of pharmaceutical innovation. But the point here is not to demonstrate injustice, but merely to illustrate what institutional moral analysis applied to the global institutional order would look like. In the next chapter, I will take a closer look at the ways in which the global institutional order contributes to severe poverty.

1.7 Global poverty is foreseeable and avoidable

Insofar as the current design of the global institutional order does turn out to entail substantial excesses of violence and severe poverty with consequent excesses of mortality and morbidity (relative to some alternative design), we might go on to ask who bears responsibility for the existing design and whether these responsible parties could have foreseen and could reasonably have avoided these excesses.

The governments of the more powerful developed countries, especially the so-called G-7, have played the dominant role in designing the post-Cold War global institutional order. In shaping this order, those governments have given much weight to the interests of their domestic business and finance elites and rather little weight to the interests of the poor and vulnerable populations of the less developed countries. The resulting global institutional order is arguably unjust insofar as the incidence of violence and severe poverty occurring under it is much greater than would have been the case under an alternative order whose design would have given greater weight to the interests of the poor and vulnerable. As the G-7 countries are reasonably democratic, their citizens share responsibility for the global order their governments have built as well as for the comparative impact of this order upon human lives. At least this is the kind of moral diagnosis that moves center-stage as normative debates about international relations shift from the *international ethics* to the *global justice* paradigm by extending institutional moral analysis beyond the state.

Two objections are often advanced against this moral diagnosis by defenders of the adequacy of the international-ethics paradigm. Objection One asserts that the global institutional framework cannot be unjust because its participants have consented to it – *volenti non fit iniuria*. Objection Two asserts that it cannot be wrong for the affluent countries' governments to design and impose the present global order because their primary responsibility is to their own people, not to foreigners. Let me conclude by briefly responding to these two objections in turn.

Objection One holds that the global institutional order is immune from moral criticism insofar as it has been freely consented to also by the poorer and less powerful states. The objector would allow that, in some cases, the consent given – to the WTO treaty system, for example – was perhaps problematic. He would be willing to entertain the possibility that some weak states were negotiating under considerable duress and also lacked the expertise to work out whether the asymmetrical market access rules they were being offered were better or worse for them than remaining outside the WTO. Our objector might even be willing to consider that perhaps the bargaining power of states entering the negotiations was inappropriately affected by historical crimes, such as colonialism. Still, the objector would insist, insofar as states have freely and competently consented to common rules, these rules are morally unobjectionable.

A proponent of the new global-justice paradigm would reject this reasoning as question-begging. The objection *assumes* what needs to be shown: namely that the only morally relevant question about a global institutional order is whether it does wrong to any of its member states. This is precisely the point challenged by the global-justice paradigm, with the claim that it is relevant for the moral assessment of a global institutional order how it treats individual human beings. As I argue in the next chapter (section 2.4.2), insofar as the present design of the global institutional order foreseeably produces a large excess of avoidable mortality and morbidity, it cannot be justified through even the unanimous consent of the world's governments.

Objection Two holds that it is the very point and purpose of governments to represent and promote the interests of their people. It is therefore entirely appropriate and permissible for affluent countries' governments to do their utmost to shape the global institutional order in the best interest of their citizens.

There is evidently some truth in this objection. Surely a government is not required to give equal weight to the interests of all human beings worldwide. Rather, it is permitted to be partial by showing special concern for the interests of its own people, present, and future. But there are obvious ethical limits to a government's partiality; for example, insofar as it is impermissible for a country's citizens to kill innocent foreigners in order to advance their economic interests, it is likewise impermissible for these citizens' government to do so on their behalf.

The limits on permissible government partiality with regard to the shaping of the global institutional order are less familiar but no less compelling. Quite generally, partiality is legitimate only in the context of a "level playing field," broadly conceived as including fair rules impartially administered. This idea is familiar and widely accepted in many contexts: it is permissible for persons to concentrate on promoting their own interests, or those of their group, sports team, or relatives, provided they do so in the context of a fair competition. Because such a fair setting is a moral precondition for permissible partiality, such partiality cannot extend to the subversion of the level playing field. To the contrary, those who are *partial* in favor of their own group must, as a condition of the permissibility of such partiality, also be *im*partially concerned for preserving the fairness of the larger social setting.

In a domestic setting, for example, it is entirely permissible for you to concentrate your time and money on securing a good education for your own children, at the expense of other children whose education you could also promote. Yet it would be morally wrong for you to seek to promote your children's prospects by using your political influence to oppose equal access to education for children whose gender, color, religion, or class differs from that of your own children. In short: partiality of concern is alright within a minimally fair setting, but not alright when it seeks to undermine the minimal fairness of this setting itself. The minimal fairness of the terms of the competition must not itself become an object of this competition. And the justice limit to a government's partiality in favor of its own citizens forbids, then, partial conduct that undermines the minimal fairness of the global institutional order. An appeal to permissible partiality cannot justify the imposition, by the most powerful governments on the rest of the world, of an unjust global institutional order under which a majority of humankind is foreseeably and avoidably deprived of anything resembling a fair start in life.

The First UN Millennium Development Goal: A Cause for Celebration?

3.0 Introduction

In the *UN Millennium Declaration* of the year 2000, the 191 member states of the UN committed themselves to the goal "to halve, by the year 2015, the proportion of the world's people whose income is less than one dollar a day and the proportion of people who suffer from hunger." This is the first and most prominent of what have come to be known as the eight UN Millennium Development Goals (MDGs).

The commitment to this goal, in such a prominent text, has been widely celebrated. The governments of the world have finally united behind the goal of eradicating hunger and extreme poverty, defined as the inability to afford "a minimum, nutritionally adequate diet plus essential non-food requirements." And they have not merely endorsed this goal in a vague and general way, but have committed themselves to a concrete path with a precise intermediate target. Given the abject poverty in which so many human beings subsist today, this highly official and highly visible commitment is surely reason for celebration. – Isn't it?

I am not so sure. In any case, I want to offer some skeptical reflections that we might ponder before judging the goal our governments have set in our names.

3.1 Reflection one – on halving world poverty

The goal of halving extreme poverty and hunger by 2015 is not new. It was very prominently affirmed, for instance, four years earlier, at the World Food Summit in Rome, where the 186 participating governments declared: "We pledge our political will and our common and national commitment to achieving food security for all and to an ongoing effort to eradicate hunger in all countries, with an immediate view to reducing the number of undernourished people to half their present level no later than 2015." An "immediate" view that budgets 19 years to solve merely half a problem is not especially ambitious, to be sure, but at least the pledge seemed definite and firm.

Is the first MDG then merely a reaffirmation of a commitment made earlier? Well, not exactly. Looking closely at the two texts, we find a subtle but important shift. While the earlier *Rome Declaration* spoke of halving by 2015 the *number* of undernourished, the later *Millennium Declaration* speaks of halving by 2015 the *proportion* of people suffering from hunger and extreme poverty.

Substituting "proportion" for "number" makes a considerable difference. The relevant proportion is a fraction consisting of the number of poor people in the numerator and "the world's people" in the denominator. With world population expected to increase by 2015 to about 120 percent of what it was in 2000, a reduction in the number of poor to 60 percent of what it was in 2000 suffices to cut the proportion in half. The *Rome Declaration* promised a 50 percent reduction in the number of poor by 2015. The *Millennium Declaration* promised only a 40 percent reduction in this number.

In highlighting this revision, I attach no importance to whether governments focus on the number of poor people or their proportion. My concern is with the dilution of the 2015 goal and with the effort to obscure this dilution. The dilution can be expressed in either idiom: the number of poor is to be reduced by 50 percent according to the *Rome Declaration* and by only 40 percent according to the *Millennium Declaration*. Or: the proportion of poor is to be reduced by 58.33 percent according to the *Rome Declaration* and by only 50 percent according to the *Millennium Declaration*. Either formulation makes apparent that the goalposts were moved.

The significance of the dilution can be gauged in terms of the World Bank's current poverty statistics. These figures show 1,656 million extremely poor people in 1996, and the *Rome Declaration* thus promised that this number will be no more than 828 million in 2015. The same figures show that there were

1,665 million extremely poor people in 2000 – 27.2 percent of world population then. And the *Millennium Declaration* thus promised that this number will be no more than 993 million in 2015 – 13.6 percent of the expected world population in 2015. The subtle shift in language quietly adds 165 million to the number of those whose extreme poverty in 2015 will be deemed morally acceptable – an extra 165 million human beings for whom "a minimum, nutritionally adequate diet plus essential nonfood requirements" will be out of reach. This dilution was successfully obscured from the public, and kept out of the media, by opaquely switching from "number" to "proportion" while retaining the language of "halving poverty by 2015."

Since its celebrated adoption by the UN General Assembly, the poverty promise has undergone further revision, in two respects. The current UN statement and tracking of MDG-1 express the poor not as a "proportion of the world's people," but as a "proportion of people in the developing world." This change is significant because the population of the developing world grows faster than that of the world at large. Because such faster population growth accelerates the rise in the denominator of the proportion, a smaller reduction in the numerator suffices to halve the proportion.

The other change is that the current UN statement of MDG-1 backdates the baseline to 1990, thus envisioning that the halving should take place "between 1990 and 2015" rather than between 2000 and 2015. This change is significant because, lengthening the period in which population growth occurs, it further inflates the denominator and thereby diminishes even more the needed reduction in the number of poor. The population of the developing countries in 2015 is expected to be 146 percent of what it was in 1990. Therefore a reduction of the number of poor to 73 percent of what it was in 1990 suffices to cut that proportion in half.

It is worth nothing that the creative accounting is not confined to MDG-1. The most recent MDG report states quite generally that "the baseline for the assessment is 1990, but data for 2000 are also presented, whenever possible, to provide a more detailed picture of progress since the Declaration was signed." The year "1990" occurs 62 times in the *Report 2008* and not even once in the *UN Millennium Declaration*. As the UN is now phrasing MDG-4 and MDG-5, they require us to "reduce by two thirds, between 1990 and 2015, the under-five mortality rate" and to "reduce by three quarters, between 1990 and 2015, the maternal mortality ratio." What the UN General Assembly had actually agreed to promise is rather different: "By the same date [2015], to have reduced maternal mortality by three quarters, and under-five child mortality by two thirds, of their *current* rates."

One remarkable consequence of the UN's backdating of the MDG baselines is that China's massive poverty reduction in the 1990s – the number of Chinese living in extreme poverty reportedly declined by 264 million during that decade – can now be counted as progress toward achieving the MDGs. The revision of MDG-1 thus led UN Secretary-General Kofi Annan tragicomically to report to the General Assembly that for the world's most populous region – East Asia and the Pacific – the 2015 poverty target was met already in 1999, a full year before this goal had even been adopted.

How does the dual revision of MDG-1 affect the allowable number of extremely poor people in 2015? According to the current World Bank statistics, there were 1,813.4 million extremely poor people in 1990 (43.8 percent of the 1990 population of the developing countries). The new target for 2015 is therefore to reduce the number of extremely poor persons to 1,324 million (21.9 percent of the 2015 population of the developing countries). By revising MDG-1, the UN has thus raised the number of those whose extreme poverty in 2015 will be deemed morally acceptable by 331 million (from 993 to 1,324 million). Relative to the *Rome Declaration*, the target was raised by 496 million and the promised reduction in the number of extremely poor people correspondingly lowered by nearly three-fifths: from 828 to 332 million. How are Kofi Annan and the rest of us going to explain to those 496 million people that we changed our minds and that consequently they shall not have a minimum, nutritionally adequate diet plus essential non-food requirements?

Let me sum up my first reflection. MDG-1 is taken to supersede a commitment the world's governments had made years earlier, notably in the 1996 *Rome Declaration*. There they promised to reduce, by 2015, the *number* of extremely poor people to half its *present* (1996) level. The current statement of MDG-1 retains the language of halving world poverty by 2015 but also deforms this goal through three highly deliberate dilutions. First, it aims to halve the *proportion* of extremely poor people, not their number, thus taking advantage of population growth. Second, it redefines this proportion, replacing "the world's people" by "the population of the developing world," thereby taking advantage of faster growth in the latter population (and also detracting from the global moral responsibility of the affluent countries). Third, it extends the plan period backward in time, having it start in 1990 rather than at the time the commitment was made, thereby increasing population growth in the denominator and taking advantage of a reported massive poverty reduction in China.

Drawing on the currently official World Bank figures, Table 3.1 summarizes what the dilutions mean in human terms. Compared to the 1996 World Food

Table 3.1 A promise diluted.

	Baseline year	Baseline number of poor (millions)	Promised reduction by 2015	Target for 2015 (millions)	Required annual rate of reduction	Target for 2005 (millions)
World Food Summit	1996	1,656	50.0%	828	3.58%	1,193
MDG-1 as adopted	2000	1,665	40.4%	993	3.39%	1,401
MDG-1 as revised	1990	1,813	27.0%	1,324	1.25%	1,501

Summit commitment, MDG-1 as now stated by the UN *raises* the number of extremely poor people deemed morally acceptable in 2015 by 496 million (from 828 to 1,324 million) and thereby *shrinks* by more than half (from 837 to 341 million) the reduction in this number which governments pledge to achieve during the 2000–15 period. Had we stuck to the promise of Rome, our task for 2000–15 would have been to reduce the extremely poor by 837 million or 50.3 percent. MDG-1 as revised envisages a reduction by only one-fifth or only 341 million: from 1,665 million in the year 2000 to 1,324 million in 2015.

With the World Bank's 2005 figure already down to 1,376.7 million, there is little doubt that the UN will be able to announce in 2015 that the goal of halving world poverty has been achieved. But this success will depend decisively on having replaced the promise of the *Rome Declaration* – to halve between 1996 and 2015 the number of people in extreme poverty – with the promise of MDG-1 as subsequently diluted: to halve between 1990 and 2015 the proportion of people in the developing world who live in extreme poverty.

The story of the sly revisions of the grand commitment of Rome and, more generally, of how the world's governments are managing the "halving of world poverty by 2015" illustrates one main reason for the persistence of massive poverty: the poor have no friends among the global elite. Hundreds of officials in many governments and international agencies were involved in shifting the goalposts to the detriment of the poor. Thousands of economists, statisticians, and other academics understood what was happening. So did thousands of people in the media, who had been reporting on the Rome Summit and the MDGs – with some of them expressly denying that the revisions were worth reporting. Most of these privileged harbor no ill will toward poor people. They merely have other priorities. And they don't care how their pursuit of these other priorities is affecting the global poor.

Consider

1. Summarise the reading in your own words.
2. The Human Development index and the data from the World Bank presented above point to the extent of global poverty. However, they do not explain it. Based on the reading and other relevant sources, summarise sociological explanations for global poverty.
3. How might considerations about social justice be relevant to debates about global poverty? Ground your arguments in the reading as well as any other relevant sources and examples.
4. What are the Millennium Development Goals? How does Thomas Pogge criticise their perspective on global poverty? Ground your answer in the reading as well as relevant background research about the Millennium Development Goals.
5. The counterpart of extreme poverty is extreme wealth. What can you find out about the world's super rich? Specifically, consider the size of their assets, the history of their wealth, and social, cultural, and economic factors that have facilitated their economic success.

6.7 Civil society and social justice

The nature and extent of global poverty raises important questions about social solidarity and social justice. An important perspective on these issues was recently put forward by the American sociologist Jeffrey Alexander in his book *The Civil Sphere* (2006):

> This book is about justice and about the democratic institutions and beliefs that can sustain justice in our massively complex and highly stratified world. Justice depends on solidarity, on the feeling of being connected to others, on being part of something larger than ourselves, a whole that imposes obligations and allows us to share convictions, feelings, and cognitions, gives us a chance for meaningful participation, and respects our individual personalities even while giving us the feeling that we are all in the same boat. (Alexander 2006: 13)

First of all, note that Alexander introduces *normative* considerations into the discussion. Where some theorists of the social system, such as Talcott Parsons (see Chapter 4), overtly limit themselves to an analysis of the ways in which society functions in fact, Alexander also draws on questions about how we *should* live. The first sentence ties the workings of the institutions of modern societies – economy and labour market, educational system, families, state and government, and so forth – to issues of justice. In this sense, social solidarity is not only a matter of the integration of values, beliefs and norms, it is also closely connected to the individual experience of enjoying 'meaningful participation' in society.

Alexander approaches the link between social solidarity and social justice through the concept of the *civil sphere* or *civil society*. The idea of the civil sphere generally refers to the non-state, non-commercial groups and organisations that engage individuals in everyday social life, allow them to form social bonds, and offer support for a variety of concerns and problems. Schools, religious institutions, charities, trade unions and political parties are some examples of civil sphere organisations.

Alexander himself draws particular attention to the role which the women's movement and the civil rights movement have played in reshaping US society and achieving greater social justice along lines of gender and race. He acknowledges, however, that the workings of the civil sphere may also lead to greater fragmentation, exclusion and inequality. For example, he points to the long-standing problem of Antisemitism in American life. Nonetheless, Alexander argues that the civil sphere at best may enable social criticism and the active participation of citizens across the manifold social boundaries of modern societies.

One of the issues Alexander considers to sustain this idea is the problematic of multiculturalism. In the context of the growing diversification of (post)modern societies, the increasing interconnectedness of different regions of the world, and the massive processes of migration which this interconnectedness has enabled, the problem of living together with major cultural and ethnic differences has become highly significant in the USA and many other countries. In the worst case, as the example of Antisemitism and the social exclusion of American Jews show, multiculturalism may lead to the radical exclusion of those perceived as 'outsiders'. However, critical and open debates in civil societies make it possible to redefine cultural diversity and achieve inclusiveness by concentrating on the shared freedoms and obligations all citizens enjoy equally, regardless of their differences.

Jeffrey Alexander's work is important for our argument in this book in two ways. On the one hand, it introduces you to long-standing sociological concerns with social justice and social inequalities. On the other hand, it raises questions that are central to humans beings' ability to engage with each other peacefully and fairly in the context of an ever faster, ever more connected, and ever more diverse (post)modern world.

Reading

Alexander, J. (2006), *The Civil Sphere*, New York: Oxford University Press, pp. 3–9

Introduction

We live in a cynical age. Some people think might makes right, and sometimes they are the leaders of powerful countries. Sophisticated intellectuals sometimes think there is no right, and relativism becomes the order of the day. The gap between philosophy and empirical social science threatens to becomes a chasm. Once mired in analytic and technical concerns, philosophy has sprouted new branches. Today, it has become again a great moral science, filled not only with normative stipulations but with empirical assumptions about the world. Sociology has begun to grow out of its pseudo-scientific ivory tower theories and methods, and a newly cultural sociology allows us to speak centrally to the issues of public and everyday life.

In this book, the normative and empirical sciences meet, and they do so on the terrain of civil society. The premise of *Civil Sphere* is that societies are not governed by power alone and are not fueled only by the pursuit of self-interest. Feelings for others matter, and they are structured by the boundaries of solidarity. How solidarity is structured, how far it extends, what it's composed of – these are critical issues for every social order, and especially for orders that aim at the good life. Solidarity is possible because people are oriented not only to the here and now but to the ideal, to the transcendent, to what they hope will be the everlasting.

Our new moral philosophies underscore the vital significance for justice of broader and more inclusive social ties, but that they do not, in fact, tell us much about solidarity itself. When we examine the masterworks of classical and modern sociological theory, we find the same thing. Solidarity is pointed to, but it is nowhere systematically interpreted or explained.

Where can we look for a better theory? In 1980, a momentous and effervescent social movement arose in Poland. It was called Solidarity. After a year and a half of extraordinary success, it was repressed, but it marked the first chapter of a democratic narrative that has continued to this day. The theorists and leaders of Solidarity said they were fighting for a civil society, and those who followed them in time often followed their civil society banner as well.

Civil society is an idea that has been heard from before. In the wake of Solidarity and its successor democratic revolutions, there has been a great revival of civil society talk, but too much of it echoes earlier times. We need a new concept of civil society as a civil *sphere*, a world of values and institutions that generates the capacity for social criticism and democratic integration at the same time. Such a sphere relies on solidarity, on feelings for others whom we do not know but whom we respect out of principle, not experience, because of our putative commitment to a common secular faith.

The idea that there can be a secular faith has been anathema to modern sociology, which has falsely equated being modern with being beyond belief. I challenge this old-fashioned perspective of modernity. In its place, I introduce the idea of democracy as a way of life. Democracy is not a game governed by technical rules. It is a world of great and idealizing expectations, but also overwhelming feelings of disgust and condemnation. It is a competitive scene of partisan conflict, but also cosmopolitan disinterest and love. Democratic life shifts back and forth between a transcendental language of sacred values of the good and profane symbols of evil, but these shifts are mediated by institutions that push for agreement in difference, such as voting, the rule of law, and the ethics of office.

Civil society is not a panacea. Modernity is strewn with the detritus of civil societies, shipwrecks, such as the Third Republic in France and the Weimar Republic in Germany, whose carcasses came near to suffocating the twentieth century. The discourse of civil society can be as repressive as liberating, legitimating not only inclusion but exclusion.

The structure of civil society may rest upon a cultural structure, but it is hardly merely discursive in its shape and form. It is filled with institutions, organizations of communication and regulation. To see what these institutions are up to, we need to recognize first the world of public opinion, which is the sea inside of which the civil sphere swims. Public opinion is the middle ground between the generalities of high-flown discourse and the ongoing, concrete events of everyday life. It is filled with collective representations of ideal civility, but it is also defined by strong expressions of negativity. For every "yes" and "I agree" there is, in every poll, the responses of "no" and "strongly disagree." There are often, in fact, "feeling thermometers" to register, in numeric terms, just how strongly are the passions of civil life. It is no wonder that public opinion has a real, if nonbinding, force.

The communicative institutions of civil society are composed in part of mass media. Newspapers and television news are factual media; they record, but they also select and reconstruct in civil terms what "actually goes on" in a society's life. Fictional media – such as novels, movies, and television comedies and dramas – do much the same thing, but at a temporal remove from immediacy and under the guise of high and popular art. Mass media institutions respond to opinion, but they also structure and change it. Public opinion polls seem merely to measure opinion, to make it scientifically factual, but actually they construct it in a palpable way. Civil associations, such as Mothers against Drunk Driving or Moveon.Org, are also vital communicative institutions in civil life. It is traditional to equate such civil associations with voluntary associations, but I am skeptical about taking this path. Voluntariness characterizes the Girl Scouts, hospital volunteers, and the PTA. Each of these is a good thing, but they do not project communicative judgments in the wider civil sphere.

The representations that pour forth from the communicative institutions of civil society have influence but not power in the more instrumental sense. This is why, even in the quashed and confined civil spheres of authoritarian societies, communicative institutions can often project representations that have some communicative force. To the degree that a society is democratic, however, the broad solidarity that constitutes "the people" must have teeth in it. There must, in other words, also be institutions of a more regulative kind, which means they need access to the violence monopolized by the state. Voting and party competition create civil power. They allow representatives of civil society not only to insert themselves into state bureaucracy but to formally control it. To represent civil power, however, is not necessarily to serve it. It is because power potentially corrupts that we speak of the duties and ethics of "office." Office can be thought of as a regulative institution. A product of centuries of religious and political conflict, office functions as an invisible kind of control that warns and periodically publicizes and pollutes actions of the powerful when they slide toward self-interest alone.

Voting, party conflict, and office are essential in the construction of social solidarity, and they go beyond merely persuasive force because they have access to the law. It is of more than passing interest that law has rarely been a compelling subject for either empirical or theoretical sociology, still less for social theory more broadly defined. When law has been discussed, moreover, it has usually been treated merely as the means to gain some economic interest or political end, not as a means for establishing civil solidarity. Drawing on certain trends in jurisprudential philosophy, I propose to rethink law as a form of symbolic representation. Law highlights, stereotypes, and pollutes actions that are considered threatening to civil society. The regulatory power of such legal representations is extraordinary. They constitute simultaneously symbolic constructions and normative judgments, and, in the name of the civil community, they can draw upon coercion and even control the bureaucratic state. Even while such control is exercised for the civic good, it often legalizes exclusion and domination at the same time. Law applies the sacred principles of civil discourse case by case, in real historical time; in order to do so, it must identify and punish the profane.

Civil society can thus be thought of as an independent sphere. It has "its own" ethics and institutions. But the civil sphere is not separated and ideal; it must exist in the real world. It must be located in time and space. As civil society settles down into everyday social systems, its contradictions become apparent. Real civil societies are created by social actors at a particular time and in a particular place. These founders and their qualities are lionized. It might perhaps be thought one of the abiding misfortunes of civil society that this founding, the actors who did it and the place where it occurred, tend almost always to be seen through a sentimental and nostalgic gaze. The qualities of the founders and the place of their creation are sacralized; they are taken, somehow, as the very essence of civility. The founders' ethnicity, race, gender, class, and sex are essentialized, and so is the city, region, or nation in which these qualities were first displayed. By an alchemy that is less mysterious than it is mystifying, these arbitrary qualities become transformed into necessary qualifications. Those who follow are judged as worthy or unworthy in relation.

All this contradicts the utopian aspirations of civil society, but there is more. The civil sphere is bounded by what might be called "noncivil" spheres, by such worlds as state, economy, religion, family, and community. These spheres are fundamental to the quality of life and to the vitality of a plural order, and their independence must be nurtured and protected. At the same time, their concerns and interests often seem to threaten the civil sphere. The goods they produce and the powers they sustain are sectoral not societal, particularistic not universalistic. The hierarchies in these non-civil spheres often interfere with the construction of the wider solidarity that is the sine qua non of civil life.

Real civil societies are contradictory and fragmented. These dynamics create the conditions for suppressing the very existence of the civil sphere. They also create the possibility for its civil repair. The ideals of civil society are never completely negated. They hold before us alternative possibilities, and from these general principles there emerge counterproposals for reform. It is the idea of civil solidarity that allows divisions to be reconstructed. That solidarity can be broadened is the project of civil repair.

But civil repair does not happen just like that. Ideals don't just realize themselves. In considering the dynamics of civil societies, social movements must be given pride of place. They are accordions that inflate and deflate civil contradictions, instruments that supply the melodies, in major and minor keys, for expressing its divisions and for repairing or suppressing them. To see how this accordion is played, social movements must be rethought. They are not motivated simply by cognitive perceptions of rational interest, and their success hardly depends on mobilizing resources in the material sense. Social movements are rooted in subjectivity and dependent on symbolic communication. Anchored in the idealized discourses and communicative institutions of the civil sphere, social movements have one foot in some particular injustice and the other in promises about the general good. This reflects the duality of social position in complex social systems and fragmented civil spheres. The civil rights and feminist movements were not only about the particular interests of racial and gender groups. They were about the reconstruction of social solidarity, about its expansion and repair. To be successful, they had to convince people outside their groups; they could do so only by interweaving their particular struggles with universal civil themes.

Those who are excluded from civil societies do not gain entrance through the struggles of social movements alone, but through more indirect and incremental processes of incorporation. In the recent life and times of social theory, "assimilation" has become almost a dirty word. In fact, however, it represents, in terms of the promises of civil society, a tremendous achievement. Members of out-groups are, in principle, allowed to become members of the society on condition that they keep their stigmatized qualities hidden behind the wall of private life. Allowing persons to be separated from their qualities, assimilation gives members of stigmatized groups an out. If they learn to wear the primordial camouflage of the core group, they can become members. This is a cruel paradox, but over the last centuries it has often been accepted as the price for entry into civil life. In the course of the twentieth century, other options have emerged. Hyphenation suggests a more horizontal, if still asymmetrical, relationship between the qualities of core and out-group. With multiculturalism, there emerges the possibility that out-group qualities can be purified – that they can, in fact, become objects not only of tolerance but of respect and even desire. As the multicultural mode of incorporation becomes more than merely a theoretical possibility, the language of incorporation changes from integration to diversity. But the siren song of difference can attract only if it represents a variation on the chords of civil society.

If the initial story I tell is relatively uplifting, it is the dark side of civil society that dominates the latter part of the book. For two thousand years, the "Jewish question" bedeviled the history of Western civil societies. Because of the early civil ambition of Christianity and its later political, social, and legal domination, Western antagonism to Jews has never been only religious. Jews have been constructed as anticivil, as the ultimate threat to broad solidarity and the good life. When Jews were emancipated after the early modern democratic revolutions, their millennia-long demonization became ever more closely intertwined with the contradictions of civil society. Despite what seemed the rapid progress of assimilation, for European Jews these contradictions became, eventually, an iron cage, and then an inescapable chamber of death. This mass murder was not because Europeans suffered from ineradicable anti-Semitism, but because in the most powerful and aggressive European society, Germany, the civil sphere collapsed, and it became impossible to keep state violence at bay. In America, Jews did not suffer the same fate, but this was not because their qualities were acceptable. Indeed, until almost halfway through the twentieth century, the status of Jewish Americans was precarious, and in the 1920s and '30s they were increasingly excluded from civil and noncivil life. World War II changed everything. In the aftermath of the Holocaust, the relationship of Jews to the American civil sphere shifted dramatically. For the first time in history, Jewish qualities became respectable, and sometimes even attractive, to masses of non-Jewish people.

Civil society is a project. It cannot be fully achieved, even in the fullest flush of success. Nor, despite tragedy and defeat, can it ever be completely suppressed. The contradictions of civil society, divisions of race, religion, gender, and class, can seem like arbitrary and destructive intrusions into its ideal of social solidarity. In fact, however, they are civil solidarity's other side. We would not be so indignant about these contradictions if we were not so fiercely committed to the ideal of a broadly solidaristic humanity, to brotherhood and sisterhood. These contradictions, in other words, are the price of civil society. The idea of civil society is transcendental. Its discourse and institutions always reach beyond the here and the now, ready to provide an antidote to every divisive institution, every unfair distribution, every abusive and dominating hierarchy. Let us grab hold of this old new concept and theorize and study it before it is too late.

Consider

1. What is the civil sphere? Draw on the reading to formulate a definition of the concept in your own words.
2. Alexander links the civil sphere to the notion of a 'secular faith'. Explain his respective argument in your own words.
3. How are mass media foundational to the workings of contemporary civil spheres? Use Alexander's arguments as well as your own examples to support your answer.
4. 'Civil society is a project. It cannot be fully achieved, even in the fullest flush of success' (Alexander 2006: 9). Discuss in reference to problems of global inequality and global poverty.

6.8 Colonialism, imperialism and postcolonialism

Problems of social inequality and social justice in the early twenty-first century cannot be fully understood without looking at the lasting impact of *colonialism*. In a broad sense, colonialism refers to the subjugation of a territory and the people therein by an outside state or people and the imposition of new and at least partially extraneous forms of social, economic and cultural life. In a narrower sense, colonialism refers to the conquest and domination of increasingly large parts of the world by Western powers between roughly the fifteenth and the twentieth century.

Colonialism is closely associated with *imperialism*. In general, imperialism can be taken to refer to the systematic cultural, social and economic domination of an extensive assortment of territories and peoples by a single state and government. The Roman Empire, the Chinese Empire, the Ottoman Empire and the Aztec Empire are frequently cited examples in diverse historical and geographical contexts. More specifically, imperialism is often linked to processes of global domination in the latter stages of capitalist development, as a means for sustaining the economic growth of the major capitalist powers.

Imperialism may proceed through the direct colonisation of foreign territories. In 1492, European colonies covered only a small part of the world, mostly in the relative vicinity of the colonial powers. Less than two centuries later, Spain had occupied large swathes of the Americas, and other powers – particularly France, the United Kingdom, the Netherlands and Portugal – had established far-reaching footholds. By the end of the nineteenth century, Spain had lost most of its colonies, while the British Empire spanned the globe; indeed, a few colonial powers and their empires now covered most of the world.

These powers were driven to establish colonies abroad by a wide range of motivations. Colonisation was often justified with religious and cultural reasons. The obligation to convert heathen people to Christianity and thus save their souls was frequently cited, as was, to use words from a poem by British writer Rudyard Kipling (1865–1936), 'the white man's burden', that is to say the noble duty of the colonial powers to civilise, in today's language, 'underdeveloped' peoples and gradually lift them up to parity with the West.

At the same time, the growth of modern capitalism in roughly the same historical period made Western powers look abroad in the search for wealth and resources that might grant them an advantage over their competitors. For instance, as Eduardo Galeano argues, the economic development of European powers in the early stages of capitalism depended to a large extent on gold extracted by the Spanish from their American colonies:

> Between 1503 and 1660, 185,000 kilograms of gold and 16,000,000 of silver arrived at the Spanish port of Sanlukar de Barrameda. Silver shipped to Spain in little more than a century and a half exceeded three times the total European reserves – and it must be remembered that these official figures are not complete. The metals taken from the new colonial dominions not only stimulated Europe's economic development; one may say that they made it possible. Even the effect of the Persian treasure seized and poured into the Hellenic world by Alexander the Great cannot be compared with Latin America's formidable contribution to the progress of other regions. (Galeano 1971/1997: 23)

Likewise, the establishment of a large-scale plantation system, producing a variety of valuable agricultural goods, contributed greatly to the wealth of the colonial powers. The plantation system was driven by the transatlantic slave trade. At often great profit for the traders, businessmen and plantation owners involved, men and women were forced from their homes in Africa and deported across the Atlantic ocean to work on plantations in the Americas. Even after the independence of former European colonies, slavery continued for many decades in the plantation-based economies of countries such as Brazil or the southern states of the USA.

Slavery was abolished in large parts of the British Empire in 1833, in the USA in 1865 and in Brazil in 1888. The colonial world system collapsed in the wake of the Second World War, with large-scale overseas colonies largely becoming economically and politically untenable. Today, relatively few territories remain European colonies.

Nonetheless, the cultural, social, political and economic legacy of colonialism is still acutely felt around the world. On the one hand, the social, economic and cultural structures created by centuries of imperial domination remain in place in many societies. On the other hand, while direct colonial domination has become relatively rare, efforts at imperial domination are still common. David Harvey (2003), for instance, argues that contemporary US foreign and domestic policies can be understood as a 'new imperialism', geared towards shoring up capitalist interests through geopolitical domination and control over resources such as oil.

This legacy is the subject matter of an area of academic enquiry often termed 'postcolonial studies'. Postcolonial studies is interdisciplinary in nature, and scholars from a wide range of fields, such as literature, theatre, film, cultural studies, history and anthropology, have contributed to it. Its core concerns overlap in many ways with those of the sociological imagination – a fact that is increasingly being recognised by sociologists today (cf. Bhambra 2007).

Postcolonial studies is often associated with the aforementioned postmodern turn in the humanities and social sciences (see Chapter 4). Scholars associated with the field often seek to critically interrogate the cultural narratives and social patterns associated with colonialism and its legacy and unpack the norms, values and beliefs implicit in them. Nonetheless, as Larsen (2005) suggests, the territory of postcolonial analysis remains notably difficult to define and controversial, as it is associated with a vast range of social situations that have emerged in the wake of the Western colonial empires – from South African apartheid, to the emergence of nation states in the Caribbean, and Indian cinema.

One way to gain an initial understanding of postcolonial analysis is to engage with studies that were foundational to the emergence of the field. Edward Said's (1978/2003) *Orientalism* is a good starting point for this. While Said (1935–2003) was primarily a literary scholar, his work has developed a lasting influence on sociology. Said describes 'orientalism' as an ideological framework which is based on stereotypical understandings rather than factual knowledge of 'Eastern' societies. This ideological framework elides differences between Eastern societies, homogenising them into blurred cultural images of a culturally and politically weak and inferior 'Orient', and thus serves as a legitimatory tool for Western domination of the 'East'.

Reading

Said, E.W. (1978/2003), *Orientalism*, London: Penguin, pp. 1–9

Introduction

I

On a visit to Beirut during the terrible civil war of 1975–1976 a French journalist wrote regretfully of the gutted downtown area that "it had once seemed to belong to . . . the Orient of Chateaubriand and Nerval." He was right about the place, of course, especially so far as a European was concerned. The Orient was almost a European invention, and had been since antiquity a place of romance, exotic beings, haunting memories and landscapes, remarkable experiences. Now it was disappearing; in a sense it had happened, its time was over. Perhaps it seemed irrelevant that Orientals themselves had something at stake in the process, that even in the time of Chateaubriand and Nerval Orientals had lived there, and that now it was they who were suffering; the main thing for the European visitor was a European representation of the Orient and its contemporary fate, both of which had a privileged communal significance for the journalist and his French readers.

Americans will not feel quite the same about the Orient, which for them is much more likely to be associated very differently with the Far East (China and Japan, mainly). Unlike the Americans, the French and the British – less so the Germans, Russians, Spanish, Portuguese, Italians, and Swiss – have had a long tradition of what I shall be calling *Orientalism*, a way of coming to terms with the Orient that is based on the Orient's special place in European Western experience. The Orient is not only adjacent to Europe; it is also the place of Europe's greatest and richest and oldest colonies, the source of its civilizations and languages, its cultural contestant, and one of its deepest and most recurring images of the Other. In addition, the Orient has helped to define Europe (or the West) as its contrasting image, idea, personality, experience. Yet none of this Orient is merely imaginative. The Orient is an integral part of European *material* civilization and culture. Orientalism expresses and represents that part culturally and even ideologically as a mode of discourse with supporting institutions, vocabulary, scholarship, imagery, doctrines, even colonial bureaucracies and colonial styles. In contrast, the American understanding of the Orient will seem considerably less dense, although our recent Japanese, Korean, and Indochinese adventures ought now to be creating a more sober, more realistic "Oriental" awareness. Moreover, the vastly expanded American political and economic role in the Near East (the Middle East) makes great claims on our understanding of that Orient.

It will be clear to the reader (and will become clearer still throughout the many pages that follow) that by Orientalism I mean several things, all of them, in my opinion, interdependent. The most readily accepted designation for Orientalism is an academic one, and indeed the label still serves in a number of academic institutions. Anyone who teaches, writes about, or researches the Orient – and this applies whether the person is an anthropologist, sociologist, historian, or philologist – either in its specific or its general aspects, is an Orientalist, and what he or she does is Orientalism. Compared with *Oriental studies* or *area studies*, it is true that the term *Orientalism* is less preferred by specialists today, both because it is too vague and general and because it connotes the high-handed executive attitude of nineteenth-century and early-twentieth-century European colonialism. Nevertheless books are written and congresses held with "the Orient" as their main focus, with the Orientalist in his new or old guise as their main authority. The point is that even if it does not survive as it once did, Orientalism lives on academically through its doctrines and theses about the Orient and the Oriental.

Related to this academic tradition, whose fortunes, transmigrations, special-izations, and transmissions are in part the subject of this study, is a more gen-eral meaning for Orientalism. Orientalism is a style of thought based upon an ontological and epistemological distinction made between "the Orient" and (most of the time) "the Occident." Thus a very large mass of writers, among whom are poets, novelists, philosophers, political theorists, economists, and imperial administrators, have accepted the basic distinction between East and West as the starting point for elaborate theories, epics, novels, social descriptions, and political accounts concerning the Orient, its people, customs, "mind," destiny, and so on. *This* Orientalism can accommodate Aeschylus, say, and Victor Hugo, Dante and Karl Marx. A little later in this introduction I shall deal with the methodological problems one encounters in so broadly construed a "field" as this.

The interchange between the academic and the more or less imaginative meanings of Orientalism is a constant one, and since the late eighteenth century there has been a considerable, quite disciplined – perhaps even regulated – traffic between the two. Here I come to the third meaning of Orientalism, which is something more historically and materially defined than either of the other two. Taking the late eighteenth century as a very roughly defined starting point Orientalism can be discussed and analyzed as the corporate institution for dealing with the Orient – dealing with it by making statements about it, authorizing views of it, describing it, by teaching it, settling it, ruling over it: in short, Orientalism as a Western style for dominating, restructuring, and having authority over the Orient. I have found it useful here to employ Michel Foucault's notion of a discourse, as described by him in *The Archaeology of Knowledge* and in *Discipline and Punish*, to identify Orientalism. My contention is that without examining Orientalism as a discourse one cannot possibly understand the enormously systematic discipline by which European culture was able to manage – and even produce – the Orient politically, sociologically, militarily, ideologically, scientifically, and imaginatively during the post-Enlightenment period. Moreover, so authoritative a position did Orientalism have that I believe no one writing, thinking, or acting on the Orient could do so without taking account of the limitations on thought and action imposed by Orientalism. In brief, because of Orientalism the Orient was not (and is not) a free subject of thought or action. This is not to say that Orientalism unilaterally determines what can be said about the Orient, but that it is the whole network of interests inevitably brought to bear on (and therefore always involved in) any occasion when that peculiar entity "the Orient" is in question. How this happens is what this book tries to demonstrate. It also tries to show that European culture gained in strength and identity by setting itself off against the Orient as a sort of surrogate and even underground self.

Historically and culturally there is a quantitative as well as a qualitative difference between the Franco-British involvement in the Orient and – until the period of American ascendancy after World War II – the involvement of every other European and Atlantic power. To speak of Orientalism therefore is to speak mainly, although not exclusively, of a British and French cultural enterprise, a project whose dimensions take in such disparate realms as the imagination itself, the whole of India and the Levant, the Biblical texts and the Biblical lands, the spice trade, colonial armies and a long tradition of colonial administrators, a formidable scholarly corpus, innumerable Oriental "experts" and "hands," an Oriental professorate, a complex array of "Oriental" ideas (Oriental despotism, Oriental splendor, cruelty, sensuality), many Eastern sects, philosophies, and wisdoms domesticated for local European use – the list can be extended more or less indefinitely. My point is that Orientalism derives from a particular closeness experienced between Britain and France and the Orient, which until the early nineteenth century had really meant only India and the Bible lands. From the beginning of the nineteenth century until the end of World War II France and Britain dominated the Orient and Orientalism; since World War II America has dominated the Orient, and approaches it as France and Britain once did. Out of that closeness, whose dynamic is enormously productive even if it always demonstrates the comparatively greater strength of the Occident (British, French, or American), comes the large body of texts I call Orientalist.

It should be said at once that even with the generous number of books and authors that I examine, there is a much larger number that I simply have had to leave out. My argument, however, depends neither upon an exhaustive catalogue of texts dealing with the Orient nor upon a clearly delimited set of texts, authors, and ideas that together make up the Orientalist canon. I have depended instead upon a different methodological alternative – whose backbone in a sense is the set of historical generalizations I have so far been making in this Introduction – and it is these I want now to discuss in more analytical detail.

II

I have begun with the assumption that the Orient is not an inert fact of nature. It is not merely there, just as the Occident itself is not just *there* either. We must take seriously Vico's great observation that men make their own history, that what they can know is what they have made, and extend it to geography: as both geographical and cultural entities – to say nothing of historical entities – such locales, regions, geographical sectors as "Orient" and "Occident" are man-made. Therefore as much as the West itself, the Orient is an idea that has a history and a tradition of thought, imagery, and vocabulary that have given it reality and presence in and for the West. The two geographical entities thus support and to an extent reflect each other.

Having said that, one must go on to state a number of reasonable qualifications. In the first place, it would be wrong to conclude that the Orient was *essentially* an idea, or a creation with no corresponding reality. When Disraeli said in his novel *Tancred* that the East was a career, he meant that to be interested in the East was something bright young Westerners would find to be an all-consuming passion; he should not be interpreted as saying that the East was *only* a career for Westerners. There were – and are – cultures and nations whose location is in the East, and their lives, histories, and customs have a brute reality obviously greater than anything that could be said about them in the West. About that fact this study of Orientalism has very little to contribute, except to acknowledge it tacitly. But the phenomenon of Orientalism as I study it here deals principally, not with a correspondence between Orientalism and Orient, but with the internal consistency of Orientalism and its ideas about the Orient (the East as career) despite or beyond any correspondence, or lack thereof, with a "real" Orient. My point is that Disraeli's statement about the East refers mainly to that created consistency, that regular constellation of ideas as the pre-eminent thing about the Orient, and not to its mere being, as Wallace Stevens's phrase has it.

A second qualification is that ideas, cultures, and histories cannot seriously be understood or studied without their force, or more precisely their configurations of power, also being studied. To believe that the Orient was created – or, as I call it, "Orientalized" – and to believe that such things happen simply as a necessity of the imagination, is to be disingenuous. The relationship between Occident and Orient is a relationship of power, of domination, of varying degrees of a complex hegemony, and is quite accurately indicated in the title of K. M. Panikkar's classic *Asia and Western Dominance*. The Orient was Orientalized not only because it was discovered to be "Oriental" in all those ways considered commonplace by an average nineteenth-century European, but also because it *could be* – that is, submitted to being – *made* Oriental. There is very little consent to be found, for example, in the fact that Flaubert's encounter with an Egyptian courtesan produced a widely influential model of the Oriental woman; she never spoke of herself, she never represented her emotions, presence, or history. *He* spoke for and represented her. He was foreign, comparatively wealthy, male, and these were historical facts of domination that allowed him not only to possess Kuchuk Hanem physically but to speak for her and tell his readers in what way she was "typically Oriental." My argument is that Flaubert's situation of strength in relation to Kuchuk Hanem was not an isolated instance. It fairly stands for the pattern of relative strength between East and West, and the discourse about the Orient that it enabled.

This brings us to a third qualification. One ought never to assume that the structure of Orientalism is nothing more than a structure of lies or of myths which, were the truth about them to be told, would simply blow away. I myself believe that Orientalism is more particularly valuable as a sign of European-Atlantic power over the Orient than it is as a veridic discourse about the Orient (which is what, in its academic or scholarly form, it claims to be). Nevertheless, what we must respect and try to grasp is the sheer knitted-together strength of Orientalist discourse, its very close ties to the enabling socio-economic and political institutions, and its redoubtable durability. After all, any system of ideas that can remain unchanged as teachable wisdom (in academies, books, congresses, universities, foreign-service institutes) from the period of Ernest Renan in the late

1840s until the present in the United States must be something more formidable than a mere collection of lies. Orientalism, therefore, is not an airy European fantasy about the Orient, but a created body of theory and practice in which, for many generations, there has been a considerable material investment. Continued investment made Orientalism, as a system of knowledge about the Orient, an accepted grid for filtering through the Orient into Western consciousness, just as that same investment multiplied – indeed, made truly productive – the statements proliferating out from Orientalism into the general culture.

Gramsci has made the useful analytic distinction between civil and political society in which the former is made up of voluntary (or at least rational and non-coercive) affiliations like schools, families, and unions, the latter of state institutions (the army, the police, the central bureaucracy) whose role in the polity is direct domination. Culture, of course, is to be found operating within civil society, where the influence of ideas, of institutions, and of other persons works not through domination but by what Gramsci calls consent. In any society not totalitarian, then, certain cultural forms predominate over others, just as certain ideas are more influential than others; the form of this cultural leadership is what Gramsci has identified as *hegemony*, an indispensable concept for any understanding of cultural life in the industrial West. It is hegemony, or rather the result of cultural hegemony at work, that gives Orientalism the durability and the strength I have been speaking about so far. Orientalism is never far from what Denys Hay has called the idea of Europe, a collective notion identifying "us" Europeans as against all "those" non-Europeans, and indeed it can be argued that the major component in European culture is precisely what made that culture hegemonic both in and outside Europe: the idea of European identity as a superior one in comparison with all the non-European peoples and cultures. There is in addition the hegemony of European ideas about the Orient, themselves reiterating European superiority over Oriental backwardness, usually overriding the possibility that a more independent, or more skeptical, thinker might have had different views on the matter.

In a quite constant way, Orientalism depends for its strategy on this flexible *positional* superiority, which puts the Westerner in a whole series of possible relationships with the Orient without ever losing him the relative upper hand. And why should it have been otherwise, especially during the period of extraordinary European ascendancy from the late Renaissance to the present? The scientist, the scholar, the missionary, the trader, or the soldier was in, or thought about, the Orient because he *could be there*, or could think about it, with very little resistance on the Orient's part. Under the general heading of knowledge of the Orient, and within the umbrella of Western hegemony over the Orient during the period from the end of the eighteenth century, there emerged a complex Orient suitable for study in the academy, for display in the museum, for reconstruction in the colonial office, for theoretical illustration in anthropological, biological, linguistic, racial, and historical theses about mankind and the universe, for instances of economic and sociological theories of development, revolution, cultural personality, national or religious character. Additionally, the imaginative examination of things Oriental was based more or less exclusively upon a sovereign Western consciousness out of whose unchallenged centrality an Oriental world emerged, first according to general ideas about who or what was an Oriental, then according to a detailed logic governed not simply by empirical reality but by a battery of desires, repressions, investments, and projections. If we can point to great Orientalist works of genuine scholarship like Silvestre de Sacy's *Chrestomathie arabe* or Edward William Lane's *Account of the Manners and Customs of the Modern Egyptians*, we need also to note that Renan's and Gobineau's racial ideas came out of the same impulse, as did a great many Victorian pornographic novels (see the analysis by Steven Marcus of "The Lustful Turk").

And yet, one must repeatedly ask oneself whether what matters in Orientalism is the general group of ideas overriding the mass of material – about which who could deny that they were shot through with doctrines of European superiority, various kinds of racism, imperialism, and the like, dogmatic views of "the Oriental" as a kind of ideal and unchanging abstraction? – or the much more varied work produced by almost uncountable individual writers, whom one would take up as individual instances of authors dealing with the Orient. In a sense the two alternatives, general and particular, are really two perspectives on the same material: in both instances one would have to deal with pioneers in the field like William Jones, with great artists like Nerval or Flaubert. And why would it not be possible to employ both perspectives together, or one after the other? Isn't there an obvious danger of distortion (of precisely the kind that academic Orientalism has always been prone to) if either too general or too specific a level of description is maintained systematically?

My two fears are distortion and inaccuracy, or rather the kind of inaccuracy produced by too dogmatic a generality and too positivistic a localized focus. In trying to deal with these problems I have tried to deal with three main aspects of my own contemporary reality that seem to me to point the way out of the methodological or perspectival difficulties I have been discussing, difficulties that might force one, in the first instance, into writing a coarse polemic on so unacceptably general a level of description as not to be worth the effort, or in the second instance, into writing so detailed and atomistic a series of analyses as to lose all track of the general lines of force informing the field, giving it its special cogency. How then to recognize individuality and to reconcile it with its intelligent, and by no means passive or merely dictatorial, general and hegemonic context?

Consider

1. How does Edward Said define orientalism?
2. How does orientalism, in Said's account, shape the cultural and political relationships between 'East' and 'West'?

3. How, if at all, is Said's work on orientalism relevant to debates about contemporary forms of social inequality?
4. 'I have begun with the assumption that the Orient is not an inert fact of nature. It is not merely there, just as the Occident itself is not just *there* either' (italics in original). Discuss.
5. Why, if at all, should sociologists consider issues of colonialism and postcolonialism?
6. Examine the role of orientalism in contemporary Western popular culture. In particular, consider one of the following:
   (a) Hollywood movies
   (b) News coverage on 'Eastern' societies
   (c) 'Eastern' restaurants in the 'West'.

6.9 Global warming, risk and global inequalities

Issues such as colonialism or global poverty have been discussed for a relatively long time. However, contemporary processes of globalisation also involve the emergence of new forms of inequality. A key feature of globalisation is the rise of a new category of risks – risks whose reach is global, which may not be immediately visible even when we are directly exposed to them, and which therefore are subject to complex and contentious public debates (see Chapter 5). It is for this reason that sociologists such as Ulrich Beck describe the contemporary world as a 'world risk society':

> Risk society, fully thought through, means world risk society. For its axial principle, its challenges, are dangers produced by civilization which cannot be socially delimited in either space or time. In this way the basic conditions and principles of the first, industrial modernity – class antagonism, national statehood, as well as the images of linear, technical-economic rationality and control – are circumvented and annulled. (Beck 1996: 1)

Rational technological achievements that were previously identified with progress now mean unforeseeable risks. From meltdowns in nuclear reactors to a perilous reduction of biodiversity by bioengineered crops, human achievements meant to solve pressing problems have brought about new crises and disasters. Because of the resulting dynamic of risk and uncertainty, Beck argues that issues such as class struggle or conflicts between nation states matter much less than in previous stages of modernity. Radioactive clouds have no regard for national borders, and they will wreck the health of rich and poor alike.

Nonetheless, in many ways, these new risks have also exacerbated old social divisions of race, class, gender, etc., and have created inequalities on a new and unprecedented scale. The consequences of *global warming* resulting from human industrial production and mass consumption are a case in point. John Urry, a pioneer in the sociological analysis of global warming, describes its extent and likely results as follows:

> Global temperatures have risen over the past century by at least 0.74°C and this appears to be the consequence of higher levels of greenhouse gases within the Earth's atmosphere (IPCC, 2007). Greenhouse gases trap the sun's rays. As a result of this 'greenhouse' effect the Earth warms. Such greenhouse gas levels and world temperatures will significantly increase over the next few decades. Climate change, which may well be rapid and abrupt, constitutes a major transformation of human life and patterns of economic and social organization. Even the Pentagon has announced that climate change will result in a global catastrophe, costing millions of lives in wars and natural disasters. They say that its threat to global stability is far greater than that of terrorism. (Urry 2010: 193)

However, the unprecedented scale of the catastrophe does not mean that all human beings will be exposed to it to the same degree. Politicians, journalists and representatives of industry and business in many societies deny the reality of global warming. At the same time, a plethora of studies demonstrates that its effects are palpable even now and that they are the most palpable for some of the world's poorest and most underprivileged societies and social groups. Urry (2010) argues that poorer societies in the Global South will experience a drop in living standards and environmental conditions sooner and more sharply than those in the Global North. Recent research likewise suggests that some of the world's most deprived countries, for example in sub-Saharan Africa, may experience civil wars and substantial military conflicts as a result of droughts and stagnating economic growth due to global warming (Devitt and Tol 2012). A recent report by the United Nations Environment Programme concludes:

> The landlocked countries in the study region (Burkina Faso, Chad, Mali and Niger) produce the majority of the region's cereals and export to neighbouring countries. Increasing uncertainty about rainfall and the recurrence of droughts and flooding threaten food production in the region. For example, Niger was assessed in 2005 as having 2.4 million people highly vulnerable to food insecurity, including nearly 900,000 facing extreme food insecurity and 1.2 million requiring food aid. (United Nations Environment Programme 2011: 73)

In turn, long-established forms of social inequality work to ensure that certain social groups are more likely to suffer the full brunt of climate change than others. Urry (2011: 6), for instance, points out that 'women are much more likely to be the victims of such changing climates'; patriarchal social divisions in many ways lie at the root of this fact. Likewise, long-established patterns of poverty in the Sahel region of Africa mean that many of its inhabitants are ill equipped to survive the strife and additional deprivation brought about by the destabilisation of climate (United Nations Environment Programme 2011).

Reading

Urry, J. (2011), *Climate Change and Society*. Cambridge, Polity Press, pp. 5–7 and 114–21

Changing climates

Global temperatures have risen over the past century by at least $0.74°C$. This increase appears to be the result of higher levels of greenhouse gases (GHGs) in the earth's atmosphere. Such GHGs trap the sun's rays. As a result of this 'greenhouse' effect, the earth warms. The scientific evidence for such climate change is now thought to be less uncertain than when the first IPCC Report appeared in 1990. By the 2007 Report, the IPCC states that the warming of the world's climate through these increased GHGs is now 'unequivocal'. With 'business as usual' and no significant reductions in high carbon systems, the stock of GHGs could treble by the end of the century. By 2100, there is a 20 per cent risk of more than a $5°C$ increase in temperatures. If this happens, the world's physical and human geography would be transformed. Even a worldwide temperature increase of $3°C$ overall is beyond known human experience and would totally change temperature patterns, rainfall, crops, animals and human life worldwide.

The IPCC Report further shows that the concentration levels of carbon dioxide now exceed by far the natural range that scientists had identified over the past 650,000 years. Such science thus concludes that this high and rising level of carbon dioxide must result from 'non-natural' human-produced causes.

Through the IPCC, the organized actions of thousands of scientists across the globe have thus transformed public debate. In 2006 Al Gore had the surprising PowerPoint hit *An Inconvenient Truth*, and he subsequently received, with the IPCC, a Nobel Prize. The Pentagon announced that climate change will result in a global catastrophe costing millions of lives in wars and natural disasters. The threat to global stability is said to far eclipse that of terrorism, a view also expressed by Sir David King, when he was the UK Government Chief Scientist. From around 2001 onwards, there is a dramatically increased linking together in the media of the twin issues of climate change and terrorism.

This organized 'power of science' led to the worldwide mobilizing of actions and events focused upon this perceived world crisis of climate change, a crisis that is global, urgent and soluble. And this is so even though there is still huge uncertainty as to the scale, impact and speed of future climate changes. As discussed in Chapter 2, the General Circulation Models used to predict rates of GHG and temperature increases contain many 'unknowns'.

Climate change should not be understood as a single 'cause' or a single set of 'effects'. There are many elements of changing climates: increase in Arctic temperatures, reduced size of icebergs, melting of icecaps and glaciers, reduced permafrost, changes in rainfall, reduced bio-diversity, new wind patterns, more droughts and heat waves, and more frequent tropical cyclones and other extreme weather events. Moreover, recent research examining ice cores shows that, in previous glacial and inter-glacial periods, abrupt and rapid changes occurred in the earth's temperature. Earth, it is now suggested, does not engage in gradual change. Rapid changes have been the norm, not the exception.

The World Health Organization calculated as early as 2000 that over 150,000 deaths are caused each year by climate change. These changes are global but more concentrated in the 'global south', their effects are cross-generational, and women are much more likely to be the victims of such changing climates. Bangladesh in the low-lying Ganges is so far the worst-affected society, and yet produces tiny levels of carbon emissions. These emerging global relationships have been termed 'climatic genocide', with millions migrating away from the global climate change risks mainly encountered in the poor 'south'. While the planet will endure, many forms of human habitation may not if these predictions, albeit based on scientific uncertainty, are even partially correct. These climate, food, water and energy changes generate socially very uneven effects stemming from water stress, rising sea levels, loss of bio-diversity, floods, droughts, heatwaves, new diseases and enforced migration. The United Nations Development Programme (UNDP) documents how the effects of climate change that are even now apparent almost certainly heighten class, gender, ethnic and age inequalities in the contemporary world; they are increasing global 'environmental injustice' and hence likely to provoke opposition and resistance of many different forms.
[. . .]

Policy technics

Szerszynski uses the notion of 'climate technics' to examine various policies and practices that are possible in relationship to potentially changing climates, such as behaviour-change, biofuels, the nuclear option, geo-engineering and so on. Each of these is presented in bodies of academic and policy writing as the way to 'fix' the problem of climate change. Szerszynski is rightly critical of the notion that there is a single measurable problem here and especially that there is a single climate technic that will somehow fix that problem – let alone for ever! I propose to generalize this notion, suggesting we should distinguish various 'policy technics' and consider how these deal differently with what is problematic about changing climates. There are various policy technics.

First, there is the technic of constructing a *market* in emissions. This involves capping the level of emissions deemed to be appropriate, and then constructing a market or trade in emissions permits. These permits can be bought and sold – that is, traded on increasingly extensive markets. This market-based system is a neo-liberal way of dealing with the problem of reducing emissions. Such a system is favoured by politicians since this technic does not involve extra taxes, and the lack of a clear price makes them subject to backroom deals that can be carried out with various interest groups behind the scenes. The best example of this system is the European Union Emissions Trading System but this has so far effected only tiny reductions in emissions. This is partly because regulators are heavily pressured to reduce the price of permits to emit.

Second, there is climate change action *within each society*. Some commentators suggest that 'democracies' will develop at least lower emissions, given their level of development. This may be because they are better able to respond to civil society concerns and more likely to implement effective and shared programmes to limit climate change. However, this relationship seems only partly correct judging by the data. Indeed, there are various different measures of emissions that can be used here: total emissions, emissions per capita and percentage change in emissions since say 2000. Of the leading forty carbon-emitting countries in the world, the three biggest are China, the US and Russia; largest emissions per capita are found in Australia, United Arab Emirates and Singapore; and the largest increases in recent emissions since 2000 are in China, Iran and Kazakhstan. Also, we can note that major emitters within the top ten of total emissions include the 'democracies' of India, Japan, Germany, Canada and the UK. It would seem that some such 'democracies' enable the carbon interests examined in the previous chapter access to various forms of media and interest group power so that they prevent policy formation effective at limiting present and future emissions (as in north America and Australia).

It is striking that none of the Nordic democracies are in this list of the forty worst emitters, even though they are rich and have access to plentiful supplies of North Sea oil and gas (as well as some renewables). Thus a related claim might be that since 'democracy' is such a weak and minimal political form – what Walby terms 'shallow', in comparison to the ten key characteristics of 'deep democracy' – it is lower levels of inequality that may be a better context in which effective policy-making can come to limit GHG emissions.

Certainly this would be consistent with Sweden being generally reckoned, according to Giddens, to be the 'leader of the pack' in reducing emissions. Sweden has been pursuing reductions in its oil-dependence since the 1970s and plans to be oil-free by 2020. Sweden operates a carbon tax, with income tax being correspondingly reduced when the carbon tax was introduced in 1991 (Finland was the first to introduce a carbon tax in 1990). At the national level there are many environmental objectives that have to be met in Sweden. Since 1997 it has pursued a Vision Zero policy on its roads and this has reduced child fatalities, in particular through improved design and reduced vehicle speed levels.

But this is the exception. Overall, it is difficult even to measure what Halpern calls 'the hidden wealth of nations', the forms of wealth that are not well captured by relative levels or growth of a society's GDP. GDP measures the sum of market transactions within a country. Such transactions do not represent or capture either what is good for the environment or what may generate a good society with high levels of wellbeing. Indeed, increases of GDP may often go along with worsening the scale of emissions and hence reduced levels of happiness and wellbeing. There have been various efforts to develop better indicators that would build-in contributions to global climate change but getting national states to adopt these and relevant policies, such as the 'Happy Planet Index', is almost impossible (see chapter 9 below).

Third, and relatedly, there is the technic of reorganizing social life towards a thoroughgoing *localism*. This would involve international and national policies that encourage and support, through financial and other incentives, the following: distributed energy rather than centralized generation based on coal or nuclear; small-scale energy including wind, water turbines, hydro-electricity, biomass, solar and geothermal; local initiatives to source water, food, products and services; disincentives to work, study and socialize away from one's locality; incentives to find friends locally; reduced availability of long-distance transportation, especially based on oil; and the redirection of medical, retail and leisure services to being provided locally, but with much accessing of digitized information (see chapter 9 below).

Fourth, there is the technic of developing and implementing *global agreements*, especially those that are debated and ratified at global summits such as Kyoto or Copenhagen. What is most important about these, as discussed in the previous chapter, is that they provide a setting in which the world's media focus in on some array of societies and their leaders and subject them to a kind of global scrutiny and the threat of global shaming and scandal. Normally agreements are arrived at 'back-stage' out of sight but at sudden moments there can be visibility and exposure, especially because at least some of these events involve NGOs, both formally in meetings and informally through their creating a global carnival which puts those leaders on display and subjects them to some media scrutiny. Such global agreements generally pertain to maintaining current economic levels while somehow reducing the carbon emissions that such a stable level – or even rising level – of GDP presupposes. So far there are no major economies which have seriously reduced their dependence upon coal and oil: coal to produce electricity to heat homes and to power factories, and oil to move people and objects. Without global agreements not to use coal and oil, there is no possibility of slowing down the planet's likely heating, especially because 'clean coal' on a global scale, achieved through carbon capture and storage, is decades away.

Fifth, there is the policy technic of *geo-engineering* the future. This involves huge global interventions within the earth's wider metabolic processes. This would probably come about under the sway of what was viewed as a massive climate change 'crisis' so that most countries would feel that they had to sign up and which would involve a short-circuited reworking of the future. This would make existing wars of, say, terror seem puny by comparison. Under these schemes the weather as a whole would be made an object of technological control, echoing the Cold War military origins of climate change science. These geo-engineered, almost literally global, futures include: huge reflective roofs and reflective crops, space-based reflectors between the earth and sun, fertilizing the oceans to increase CO_2 absorption, massive worldwide reforestation, and stratospheric aerosols. Most of these vast schemes deal with the utter exuberance or generosity of the sun, of solar power. The sun is *the* source of power upon which the earth and life both depend but which has to be kept in its place through the use of huge amounts of countervailing energy. Such geo-engineering futures would presuppose binding global agreements and vast levels of investments which, in the post-2008 world of financial collapse and the post-2010 boost to climate scepticism through so-called 'Climategate', seem exceptionally unlikely.

Finally, there is the technic of *system change*. Here most of the twentieth-century high carbon systems come to be replaced by a cluster of low carbon systems, in housing, buildings, transport and leisure. This possibility of system change is discussed in the rest of this chapter and the next. Considerable attention is devoted to this since this seems to be the only policy technic on the table that might do the business, but it is a possible future that is fraught with risks. I begin with how such a technic presupposes a major shift in the character of twentieth-century capitalism.

Resource capitalism

I noted that almost all forms of nineteenth- and twentieth-century capitalism operated without regard for the long-term viability of their resource-base. Nature or the physical world was regarded as separate from the economy and available for its maximum transformation. This physical world was bent to the will of those developing new commodities and instruments and the forms of an increasingly mobile social life that came to characterize the twentieth century, although many criticisms of this exploitation of nature were seen from the nineteenth century onwards.

But there was little effective challenge to the view that the physical world constituted a set of resources that were available for maximum exploitation. Nature got transformed into various physical commodities and new sources of energy, especially steam and then electricity; forms of transportation, particularly the railways that flattened nature; manufactured commodities made out of iron and steel; services, involving 'fictitious capital'; and many cities, both for living in and, increasingly, staged for consumption. There was a metabolic relation between capital and nature that was laid down in Europe and then north America during the late eighteenth and nineteenth centuries. And this divide was even reflected in the very notion of a physical measurable climate to be controlled, a climate separate from its cultural reading and interpretation, a distinction rejected within previous societies.

Then in the twentieth century a cluster of powerful high carbon, path-dependent systems were set in place, locked-in through various economic and social institutions. And as the century unfolded, those lock-ins meant that the world came to be left with a high and unsustainable carbon legacy. There was what has been termed a series of 'treadmills' established, which are almost impossible to get off, let alone reverse. As a consequence, resources are used up too fast. Various critiques had developed of that process, beginning with 1960s environmentalism. And in this new century capitalism will have to be reversed so as to control those powers set in motion during the unprecedentedly high carbon twentieth century, and which various doomsday analysts consider are destined to wipe out much of the modern world (see chapter 3 above). It was the genie that got let out of the bottle and cannot be put back in.

The Great Crash of 2008 was an exceptional event because it showed that tread-mills can stop, or at least be slowed down. It also showed the need for wholly different ways of organizing economic, physical and social processes, especially highlighting extreme events, tipping points and path reversals. The year 2008 could be the forerunner of further events in which the world's resources show the capac-ity to bite back, undermining the notion of a neo-liberal world operating as though history had ended, since it seemed that there were no constraints upon economic and financial development. That same year enables the staging, as Beck puts it, of a different kind of capitalism. The Great Crash may just have allowed some of the seeds of resource capitalism to develop, by engendering perceptions, policies and practices of an alternative. It showed that there had to be an alternative.

The events of 2008 made abundantly clear that markets on occasions destroy the very conditions of the market economy; they do not *necessarily* generate the solution to economic crises. They can generate massive diseconomies and moves away from equilibria. In particular there are no obvious equilibria in financial markets since markets generate bubbles that are unsustainable in the *long* run. The private sector cannot be relied upon to solve bursting bubbles or to generate optimal levels of financialization. Markets, moreover, generate social inequalities that worsen the conditions of the poor and involve resentment-inducing con-sumption by the 'greed is good', predominantly male, rich.

The suggestion here is that there is a resource capitalism emerging, that there are some seeds of a new mode of capitalism, beyond neoliberal or disorganized capitalism. This new capitalism can be seen as rather like an archipelago, of tiny islands popping up around the world in often very unlikely and improbable locations. Nowhere is this in place but few societies do not have some such islands appearing above the surface, but there are relatively few connections yet being made between them. These islands are examined in the next chapter; they comprise many different elements, of states, civil society organizations and markets.

Resource capitalism is roughly equivalent to what others term 'ecological modernization' or 'natural capitalism'. The thesis of 'natural capitalism' involves a critique of previous capitalisms because of how capitalism fails to assign value to the largest stock of capital it employs, namely natural resources and living sys-tems, as well as the social systems that are the basis of human capital. What, the theory asks, would the economy be like if it effectively valued all forms of capital? What if the economy were organized not around the abstractions of economics and accountancy but around nature itself?

Thus, in the shift to what I call resource capitalism, nature would not be regarded as separate from the economy and hence would not be available for transfor-mation through short-term profit maximization. As in periods of war, resources would be presumed to be central to each economy-and-society. It is noteworthy that the American car industry almost overnight turned into a producer of tanks and light vehicles at the start of the US' involvement in the Second World War.

All production and consumption requires resources such as energy, materials and land. And production and consumption generate waste and emissions. Resource capitalism entails the clear recognition that there is limited capability to supply resources and to absorb pollution. How then do different economic activities influence the use of natural resources and the generation of pollution? How can these both be minimized? Resources need to be assessed not in terms of their individual components but in terms of their overall uses throughout the life-cycle of products. Which products and consumption categories have the smallest impacts across their life-cycle, and how can these be further minimized? Which materials have the lowest impacts across their life-cycle and how can their effects be further reduced? Overall, economies shift the measurement of success from that of GDP to minimizing the impact on energy, materials and land.

With resource capitalism, local, national and international states need to harbour such resources into the long term. There is the need for an 'ensuring state'. Regulations are necessary for all markets, the only issue being the form of regulation and the avoidance of perverse effects, although this is no easy task. Thus states are in the long term necessary for all successful economies; hence appropriate and fair tax revenues are especially essential and require closing tax havens.

It is already clear that societies and their 'states' differ greatly in their capacity for societal resilience in the face of catastrophic change. International organizations need to ensure that 'resources' and not 'finance' are at the heart of any programme of aid and restructuring.

Moreover, within resource capitalism, future generations are as significant as those of the present. Thus there should be no discounting the future – at least not the future of the next few decades. Within such resources, energy should be regarded as pre-eminent and short-term maximization should never be the central criterion for assessing policy. Finance is based upon utility and not upon speculation, especially against futures. Regulations are central to states that take a long-term view of resources, energy and emissions. Criteria of policy cannot then simply be that of economic wealth but must involve further notions of economic and social wellbeing.

Moreover, it is clear that, since there are financial market failures, so there can be other market failures and it may be that there will be failures of 'resources' and the generation of global crises. Crises are significant since they make *global* actions by states or state-like organizations seem necessary in order to deal with them on an appropriate scale. Moreover, solutions to crises are as much societal as economic, as much involving the real economy as the money economy, as much long-term investment as short-term profit maximization. Given that there are tipping points in financial markets, so there can be tipping points elsewhere, as in the earth's climate or the price of oil. Moreover, as the 2008 Crash reduces the size of the American economy, so it may reduce the dominance of the US over the rest of the world and hence the power of its carbon interests and of neo-liberalism.

Perceptions, practices and policies must develop fast and furiously along the lines of a resource capitalism in order that this century does not turn out to be a dark and dangerous one. In the next chapter I examine the possibilities of developing low carbon innovation within multiple systems, as one element of this putative resource capitalism. What this analysis shows is both the huge urgency and the enormous difficulties of resource capitalism getting sufficient traction, especially to link together the various islands of the archipelago.

The argument of this chapter has been that the only way of developing a capitalist 'solution' to climate change and energy security is through a resource capitalism and a widespread shifting in multiple systems to a low carbon economy-and-society. This is the sole plan on offer. In the absence of that being realized, then by the middle of this century some quite different 'societies' will be likely to develop, as outlined in chapter 9. I examine there some of the conditions and events that might emerge which would bring about different future scenarios, all of which involve very significant 'costs', with reduced income, consumption and population. Chapter 10 shows how the legacy of the twentieth century has hugely constrained the types of society that are possible by the middle of this current century. It is only a resource capitalism that would avoid some of the projected catastrophic futures discussed above in chapter 3. Neo-liberalism has to be left back in the twentieth century, as 'so twentieth-century'!

Consider
1. In which ways, if at all, does global warming illustrate the notion that we now live in a 'world risk society'?
2. How is exposure to the effects of global warming differentiated by major forms of social inequality? Base your answer on the reading as well as additional background research.
3. According to John Urry, what are the major 'policy techniques' currently used to address global warming? How effective are these? In addition to using the reading, also base your answer on further background research.
4. What does Urry understand by 'resource capitalism'? How would it address global warming and its social consequences?

6.10 Mobilities

New *mobilities* of people, goods, information, and ways of life are another central instance of social inequalities under conditions of globalisation. Internet-based social networking and portable communication devices are examples we have already explored extensively throughout the book. In a recent study, Baym, Zhang and

Lin (2004) compared the relative amounts of online, telephone, and face-to-face communication among US college students. They concluded (Loomba 2005: 315f.) that these students had integrated the internet into a variety of aspects of their everyday life and that their use of the internet seemed to merge with, rather than to diminish, other forms of social interaction. While the study's authors carefully avoid undue generalisations of their findings beyond the world of US college life, they do conclude that their findings might be indicative of a broader cultural trend (ibid.). In this sense, their research points to the new significance of online-based, mobile forms of communication today. However, as we have seen before (see Chapter 5), the *digital divide* cuts off a large part of the world population from these new forms of communication and social interaction, with often serious consequences.

The world of air travel is another particularly indicative example, as it points to both the significance of being mobile and the profound inequalities that structure people's access to mobility today. David Lyon identifies the security regimes that govern air travel and airports – passport controls, the gathering of biometric data on travellers, no-fly lists kept and exchanged by government agencies, etc. – as instances of a trend towards 'global surveillance' that has emerged in association with the rise of new forms of mobility:

> In the twenty-first century, surveillance is a global phenomenon. The capture, tracing, and processing of personal data occur today not only within local organizational settings but across national borders. Digital technologies permit the routine, real-time transfer of such data, relating to citizenship, employment, travel, and consumption, using far-flung networks that indirectly connect numerous agencies with the everyday lives of ordinary people. [. . .] It is important to remember that the growth of global surveillance is not a conspiracy. The primary reason why surveillance is globalizing is that mobility is a fundamental feature of the flexible capitalism that now dominates the world of exchange, production, and consumption. The personal information economy is an important aspect of this globalizing world, but mobile labor is as well, which means that employment records also migrate. Travelers of all kinds are emblematic of these multiple mobilities, and their data are embedded in passports, visas, and other identifying documents, are read by machines and officials, and are passed from place to place the world over. One's identity as a citizen is checked by these means and others, such as national or category-specific ID cards, which also bring the 'border' to other locations than the 'edges' of territory, thus further virtualizing it. (Lyon 2007: 30, 32)

Thus, as much as air travel has become cheaper and more accessible to many people around the world, barriers are being erected to channel and in some cases suppress mobility by means of air travel. Lyon (2007) goes on to argue that airports serve as 'data filters' tasked with classifying travellers as potential consumers of the goods and services on offer or as security threats. Benjamin Muller (2010) writes about the rise of a 'biometric border' that serves to selectively grant and deny the rights of citizenship

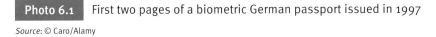

Photo 6.1 First two pages of a biometric German passport issued in 1997

Source: © Caro/Alamy

and the possibility to remain mobile. In this way, airports come to serve as sites that establish the 'risk factor' presented by travellers and assess their right to travel, according to nationality, habits, purchasing patterns, ethnicity, and so forth.

The nature of contemporary mobilities and restrictions to being mobile has attracted considerable attention among sociologists. The work of John Urry (2000; 2007) has been particularly significant in this regard. Urry (2000) argues that the rise of varied new forms of mobility is fundamentally changing the nature of social life, requiring sociologists to develop a new vocabulary that departs from the assumption of largely stationary societies enclosed within the boundaries of national states. Like Manuel Castells (2000), Urry deploys the language of trans-local, trans-national networks and flows in examining these new mobilities, and he argues that the study of these networks and flows might become the new focal point for sociological enquiry in the twenty-first century (Urry 2000: 17). Urry (2007) later distinguishes between twelve key forms of mobility in the contemporary world (see Figure 6.2).

The following is an extract from a recent book, *Mobile Lives* (Elliott and Urry 2010), which explores the impact of new forms of mobility on people's everyday lives. In particular, the extract deals with the phenomenon of 'mobile intimate relationships'.

Asylum, refugee and homeless migration	Business and professional travel	Discovery travel of students and other young people
Medical travel to spas, hospitals, etc.	Military mobility and their civilian spinoffs	Post-employment travel and retirement lifestyles
'Trailing travel' of partners, children, domestic servants, etc.	Travel and migration across the key nodes within diasporas (e.g. overseas Chinese)	Travel of service workers, especially between global cities and including the global slave trade
Tourist travel	Visiting friends and relatives, where friendship networks may also be 'on the move'	Work-related travel, such as commuting

Figure 6.2   Twelve main mobility forms

Source: based on Urry (2007: 10f.)

Reading

Elliott, A. and Urry, J. (2010), *Mobile Lives*, London: Routledge, pp. 87–91

Intimate relationships: from territorially fixed to individualized mobility

What distinguishes Robert and Gemma's contemporary 'distance relationship' from more traditional intimacies in the past? What, exactly, has changed to facilitate intimacy at-a-distance as a growing pattern? There have been three broad areas of rapid change, we suggest, which have transformed traditional relationship structures and forms of intimacy away from territorially fixed designations to more individualized and mobile patterns of relating. These areas concern globalization, transformations of intimacy and the reinvention of personal life. In what follows, we sketch some key features of this social change.

The first broad area involving massive changes to the very fabric of routine personal, social and economic life concerns globalization. Globalization, at least at the level of changes to human relationships, refers to a transformation in the dimensions of time and space between people and places, and among organizations, institutions, nations and cultures. This transformation has been interrogated with reference to the expanding scale, escalating speed, growing magnitude and deepening impact of transnational flows of people, objects, information, messages and images upon patterns of social interaction. One significant consequence of these global transformations is the 'death of distance'. While consisting of multiple processes, globalization generates increasing interconnectedness between peoples in different cultures, countries and regions and, importantly, 'unhooks' and 'dis-embeds' people from the constraints, but also the supports, of traditional structures of social interaction. In the fields of sexuality, gender and intimacy, this reorganization, reconstruction and compression of the distances between peoples and places has had dramatic implications – one result being the surge of distance relationships and commuting lifestyles, which in turn has served to intensify the dissolution of traditional structures of intimacy and family life.

The many controversies that surround globalization partly concern the extent to which an increasingly 'interconnected world' generates common global patterns. Some see the relationship between globalization and social order in terms of growing uniformity, or homogeneity. Others caution against such a view of social integration and argue that globalism does not generate a common set of experiences, values or worldviews. Yet there are emerging lines of consensus in the globalization debate, especially regarding the institutional processes facilitating compressions of time and space that underpin contemporary patterns of travel and communication across large distances. As we have seen, these institutional processes include:

- the digital infrastructure of global communications linked to new information technologies;
- communications 'on the move', with mobile telephony now more common throughout the world than conventional landlines;
- the emergence of new global business models for the provision of discount travel and cheap airfares, which has led to an explosion in international journeys, now nearing one billion arrivals annually;
- the movement of peoples throughout the global economy for work and employment, family and friendship, linked to the growth of populations and major shifts in demography;
- the emergence of global networks, comprising broad cross-border interconnections and transnational processes relating to the multiple forms of mobile social practice we outlined in Chapter 1;
- the unfolding of a new type and form of 'life politics', involving personal autonomy and self-actualization.

There are clearly many ways of conceiving and categorizing these institutional processes in terms of the global age. There are even more ways in which people seek to adapt, adjust, cope with or react against such global transformations.

The second major contemporary social development is the *transformation of intimacy*. This has been traced to many roots and identified with various events – especially the sexual revolution of the late 1960s and early 1970s, as well as feminism and the women's movements – but its central focus has been the supposed 'crisis' of the nuclear family and of marriage. Among changes, sociologists argue that few are more profound than those transforming the texture of family life. Throughout contemporary, network-driven societies in the rich north, we are moving to a situation in which nearly half of first marriages end in divorce, and divorce and separation rates are higher for second and subsequent marriages.

Among conservatives, this decline is often cast as a sign of society's moral decay. The lament attributes it to several sources, from sexual permissiveness to feminism, from new parenting arrangements to the spread of gay rights. This new era, many conservatives argue, is one that spells the end of family ties that bind. Conservative critics have consequently sought to defend traditional familial values, from speaking up 'in defence of the bourgeois family' to sounding alarms about 'generations at risk'.

The 'war over the family' that has broken out in recent decades is important for assessing changes to intimacy, relationships and sexualities. Certainly, a dramatic rise in both stepfamilies and one-parent families, as well as the sharp rise in births outside marriage, indicates that key changes are underway to the staging of everyday life in the contemporary era. And yet, although profound changes are undeniably occurring inside and outside the traditional family network, proclamations about the 'end of the family' are plainly out of step. Conservative critics do not readily acknowledge the fact that people very often remarry. The implications of this are far-reaching, and some sociologists are now suggesting that, rather than family breakdown, family life is undergoing a constructive renewal. The emergence of what has been called a 'post-familial family' is said to be taking shape, comprising a diversity of social forms and cutting across the apparent solid structures of the traditional family. From non-marital cohabitation to gay and lesbian couples, from multi-adult households to open marriages, family life is becoming increasingly diversified, reconstituted and pluralized. Jeffrey Weeks captures this point:

> Within the broad limits of the term 'family' itself there are many internal differences arising from different class, religious, racial, ethnic and political beliefs and practices . . . It is wise today to refer not to the family, as if it were a fixed form, but to families, signifying diversity.

Such transformations of family life are helping to create patterns of living best captured by the term mobile intimacy. Intimacy in conditions of intensive mobilities becomes flexible, transformable and negotiable. Mobile intimacy is fluid in both emotional and interpersonal terms. In *Liquid love*, Bauman underscores the 'looseness' and 'episodicity' of intimate relations in contemporary societies. He speaks, for example, of the rise of 'top-pocket relationships', those you can use when you need to and dispose of just as easily, as well as of the highly compartmentalized worlds of semi-detached couples (SDCs), those romantics who maintain separate pads and separate lives (a high-carbon liquid love, we might note!). Mobile intimacy involves relationships across distance and through space and is spreading to many social relations. These range from couples 'living apart together' (LATs) to 'business deals in brothels', from 'commuter marriages' to 'distance relationships', from 'love online' to 'weekend couples' and so on.

The third area in which the decline of tradition impacts upon the mobile complexity of intimate relationships is *reinventing personal life*. In contrast to industrial, solid or disciplinary forms of modernity, in which tradition or established habit inscribed self-identity within neighbourhoods based upon relatively slow forms of movement, the networked, liquid and mobile terrain of some lives today confronts people with a complex array of choices that are less clear-cut. On all standard measures, many people in parts of the world are more mobile *and* more changeable in their vocabularies of self and world. 'The great ideological certainties are giving way', writes Gilles Lipovetsky, 'before subjective singularities that may not be very original, creative, or reflective but that are more numerous and more flexible than before.' This reinvention of personal life concerns various transformations of values, lifestyles and practices. The life of choice, the do-it-yourself life, involves a radical break with neighbourhood cultures, as well as ways of doing things, and is today reflected in a growing, widespread acceptance of 'relationship experimentation' in birth control, abortion, divorce, pre-marital sex, non-married partners and open marriages (not of course that all these are remotely available in all societies!).

These changes have significantly increased the possibilities for some experimentation in some societies in terms of personal life, sexuality and intimacy. Giddens has argued that such post-traditional lifestyle concerns open out 'the mobile nature of self-identity'. By this, Giddens means to underscore the dramatic rise of choice within a plurality of possible options at the level of lifestyles and life plans. The explosion of discourses around choice is part of a new cultural tendency, and indeed compulsion, to develop life plans and relationship stories in ever more inventive ways, resulting in a heightened dramatization of what Foucault dubbed 'care of the self' in everything from psychotherapy and self-help literature to confessional television programmes and cosmetic surgery. Such lifestyle experimentation has particular application to the area of consumption in contemporary societies, as the multiplicity of choices presented within the ever-growing sectors of lifestyle consumption facilitates the adoption and enactment of novel social practices. This is somewhat akin perhaps to the idea of relationships as life choices made in a 'supermarket'. Aaron Ben-Ze'ev argues that we are witnessing the rise in 'flexible relationships'. Being able to 'love online' means that it becomes more possible to 'whet your appetite outside while eating at home'. It becomes easier, he says, to combine long-term commitment and short-term affairs through intermittent 'cyber-love'.

The degree to which today's plurality of choices confronting people in terms of personal and professional life is either experimental or disempowering is much debated. The intensification of the 'mobile nature of self-identity' is not simply about a multiplicity of choices, however important that might be in a post-traditional social order. It is also, and crucially, about the opening of potential lifestyles in situations of work, leisure, friendship or family to novel options across distances, in different neighbourhoods at different times. Whether to go as a young person for 'overseas experience' in a country the other side of the world? Whether to explore a job offer in a different country? Whether to undertake further education or training that would mean extra time away from partner or family? Whether to pursue an erotic connection with some distant other met in passing? Whether to retire to somewhere quite new and well away from established patterns of work, life and family?

These are all aspects of the mobile intensification and reinvention of personal lives relatively de-synchronized from others and especially from those living within one's local neighbourhood.

Consider

1. Examine Figure 6.2 above. To what extent does it reflect diverse experiences of mobility by people around the world? Are there any other forms of mobility that you would like to add? Support your arguments with relevant examples, from academic sources, newspaper articles, or other media items.
2. In which ways, if at all, are the twelve forms of mobility identified by Urry sites of social inequality? Provide examples to support your argument.
3. What is a biometric passport (see Photo 6.1)? Describe debates among proponents and critics of biometric passports about civil liberties and the freedom to travel. Which side of the argument do you support, and why?
4. What are the key features of mobile intimate relationships that Anthony Elliott and John Urry describe in the reading? How, if at all, do institutional transformations of globalisation, such as migration and visa regimes, support the rise of mobile intimate relationships? The second question will require you to do some background research. The issue of mobile and transnational intimate relationships is widely discussed in the academic literature and in mass media, and you should be able to find a range of examples.

6.11 Conclusion

In this chapter, we have sketched some major dimensions of social inequality in the contemporary world, pointed you to other dimensions not considered here, and drawn your attention to the complex intersections of various forms of inequality in everyday life. This discussion is of twofold importance. First, the study of patterns of inequality has been central to sociological enquiry since the beginnings of the discipline. In order to become a sociologist, you need to understand sociological perspectives on the world as it is divided by hierarchies of race, class, gender, sexuality, and so forth. Second, your engagement with these issues is of immediate importance to your engagement with the world around you. Recent research consistently portrays the world as a deeply divided place (e.g. United Nations Development Programme 2011), and it also suggests that these divisions are likely to widen in the future (e.g. Crouch 2011). It is therefore essential that you come to understand these inequalities and the ways in which they shape your own life and your engagement with others around you.

In this chapter, we have, more than anything, sought to point you to the importance of these issues. The preceding pages do not by any means give you a complete overview of sociological perspectives on inequality, and it is important that you engage with other sources to develop a more comprehensive perspective. To conclude this book, we will now move in another direction and consider in more detail the general importance of sociology today.

Works cited

Alexander, J. (2006), *The Civil Sphere*, New York: Oxford University Press.

Baer, H. and R. Long (2004), 'Transnational Cinema and the Mexican State in Alfonso Cuarón's "Y tu mamá también",' *South Central Review* 21(3): 150–68.

Baym, N., Y. Zhang. and M. Lin (2004), 'Social Interactions Across Media: Interpersonal Communication on the Internet, Telephone and Face-to-Face', *New Media and Society* 6(3): 299–318.

Beck, U. (1996), 'World Risk society as Cosmopolitan Society? Ecological Questions in a Framework of Manufactured Uncertainties', *Theory, Culture and Society* 13(4): 1–32.

Beck, U. (2000), *Risk Society: Towards a New Modernity*, London: Sage.

Bhambra, G. K. (2007), 'Sociology and Postcolonialism: Another "Missing" Revolution?', *Sociology* 41(5): 871–84.

Bourdieu, P. (2003), *Distinction: A Social Critique of the Judgement of Taste*, New York: Routledge.

Butler, J. (1999), *Gender Trouble: Feminism and the Subservion of Identity*, New York: Routledge.

Castells, M. (2000), *The Rise of the Network Society*, Oxford: Blackwell Publishers.

Connell, R. (1987), *Gender and Power*, Cambridge: Polity Press.

Crouch, C. (2011), *The Strange Non-Death of Neoliberalism*, Cambridge: Polity Press.

de Gobineau, J. A. C. (1853–55/1915), *The Inequality of Human Races*, New York: G. B. Putnam's Sons.

Devitt, C. and R. S. T. Tol (2012), 'Civil war, climate change, and development: A scenario study for sub-Saharan Africa', *Journal of Peace Research* 49(1): 129–45.

Elliott, A. and J. Urry (2010), *Mobile Lives*, London: Routledge.

Galeano, E. (1971/1997), *Open Views of Latin America: Five Centuries of the Pillage of a Continent*, New York: Monthly Review Press.

Harvey, D. (2003), *The New Imperialism*, Oxford: Oxford University Press.

Jin, D. Y. (2007), 'Transformation of the World Television System under Neoliberal Globalization, 1983 to 2003', *Television and New Media* 8(3): 179–96.

Kazue, M. (2008), 'The Making of *Sekuhara*: Sexual Harassment in Japanese Culture', in *East Asian Sexualities: Modernity, Gender and New Sexual Cultures*, edited by S. Jackson, J. Liu and J. Woo, London: Zed Books: 52–68.

Larsen, N. (2005), 'Imperialism, Colonialism, Postcolonialism', in *A Companion to Postcolonial Studies*, edited by H. Schwarz and S. Ray, Oxford: Blackwell: 23–52.

Lee, R. L. M. (2011), 'Modernity, Solidity and Agency: Liquidity Reconsidered', *Sociology* 45(4): 650–64.

Loomba, A. (2005), *Colonialism/Postcolonialism: The New Critical Idiom*, Abingdon: Routledge.

Lyon, David (2007), *Surveillance Studies: An Overview*, Cambridge: Polity Press.

Muller, B. (2010), *Security, Risk and the Biometric State: Governing Borders and Bodies*, Abingdon: Routledge.

Said, E. W. (1978/2003), *Orientalism*, London: Penguin Books.

Sennett, R. (1998), *The Corrosion of Character: The Personal Consequences of Work in the New Capitalism*, New York: W. W. Norton.

Sennett, R. (2006), *The Culture of the New Capitalism*, New Haven: Yale University Press.

United Nations Development Programme (2011), *Human Development Report 2011*, New York: Palgrave Macmillan/UNDP.

United Nations Environment Programme (2011), *Livelihood Security: Climate Change, Migration and Conflict in the Sahel*, Geneva: United Nations Environment Programme.

Urry, J. (2000), *Sociology Beyond Societies: Mobilities for the Twenty-first Century*, London: Routledge.

Urry, J. (2007), *Mobilities*, Cambridge: Polity Press.

Urry, J. (2010), 'Consuming the Planet to Excess', *Theory, Culture and Society* 27(2–3): 191–212.

Urry, J. (2011), *Climate Change and Society*, Cambridge: Polity Press.

West, C. and D. Zimmerman (2000), 'Doing Gender' in *The Gendered Society Reader*, edited by M. Kimmel, Oxford: Oxford University Press: 131–49.

7 Why sociology? Some concluding remarks

7.1 Does sociology matter?

The previous chapters introduced you to a range of sociological themes and concepts. The approach adopted for this final chapter is somewhat different. The primary objective here is to convince you of the importance of sociological reasoning. We will therefore not present new sociological perspectives but, rather, seek to explain why those considered in the earlier parts of this book are important, both for you personally and for public life at large.

Sociology's importance is perhaps not as obvious as that of other disciplines. For example, if you study medicine, you do so with the objective of furthering the health of human beings, either through medical practice as a nurse or doctor or through relevant research. A set of obvious practical objectives – improving health and contributing healthcare – is directly attached to abstract medical knowledge. This is not so in the case of contemporary sociology. We live in a time in which common sense dictates that the most important and worthwhile academic disciplines are those that provide immediate practical and economic benefits to students, business and society. Sociology does not fall into this group of instrumentally useful disciplines, and it is therefore necessary to explain what role it might play in your life and the world at large. Does sociology matter? If so, how does it matter?

Studying for a sociology degree requires you to familiarise yourself with sociological theories, the methods of sociological research, particular subject fields within the discipline, the conventions of academic reading and writing, and so forth. Among all these tasks, it is easy to lose sight of one basic fact: above all, becoming a sociologist is about looking at the world from a fresh, creative angle, discovering its previously hidden facets, and approaching social problems with a critical frame of mind. Sociology is thus not really about absorbing and reproducing factual knowledge to be tested in essays and exams. What matters most in your studies of sociology is your ability to show that you can actively use the sociological imagination and sociological knowledge to think for yourself and question the generally taken-for-granted assumptions of common sense. In the best of cases, this can be a lot of fun, and on other occasions, it may seem like a daunting challenge.

So, why study sociology? Was it a long-standing interest in social life that made you choose this degree? An earlier encounter with sociology during your school years? The fact that admission to sociology degrees is, in comparison with other courses, often easy to gain? Or maybe you were not sure at all which degree to pick (this is quite normal and common) and ended up with sociology more or less by accident? Actually, whatever your initial motivations were, there are some very good reasons for you to stick with your choice.

In a recent review of the role of education in modern societies, philosopher Martha Nussbaum (2010) distinguishes between what she terms 'education for growth' and 'education for democracy'. At its core, education for growth is geared towards training students in the basic skills necessary to perform the tasks required in complex and highly diversified economies. This approach dominates public views and media debates about higher education in many Western countries, and it finds its expression in the rhetoric of 'employability' which universities often use to attract students to their degrees. We argue that sociology suits this purpose very well, as it equips you with a broad range of knowledge and skills suitable to many professions. A degree in sociology provides you with the flexibility and adaptability that are paramount to success in contemporary labour markets.

However, Martha Nussbaum (2010) is rightly critical of a purely instrumental understanding of education driven by narrowly economic concerns. She argues that education, in enabling citizens to adopt an active, conscious role in society, is essential for the survival and success of democratic institutions. In this context, she mentions, for example:

> The ability to think well about political issues affecting the nation, to examine, reflect, argue, and debate, deferring to neither tradition nor authority [. . .] The ability to imagine well a variety of complex issues affecting the story of human life as it unfolds: to think about childhood, adolescence, family relationships, illness, death, and much more in a way informed by an understanding of a wide range of human stories, not just by aggregate data [. . .] The ability to think about the good of the nation as a whole, not just that of one's own local group [. . .] The ability to see one's own nation, in turn, as part of a complicated world order in which issues of many kinds require intelligent transnational deliberation for their resolution. (Nussbaum 2010: 25f.)

In sum, what is at stake is your ability to transcend the immediate concerns and necessities of your everyday life, understand the broader social, political and economic forces that shape the world you live in, and make well-informed, positive choices for your own future and that of others.

7.2 Three arguments in favour of sociology

Sociology allows you to develop such an active perspective on everyday life. It does so in three ways.

First, sociology enables you to see the general in the particular. This is the promise of the sociological imagination. Sociology allows you to see clearly how the manifold events in your lives are shaped by specific social forces. As C. Wright Mills (1959/1967) famously argued, sociology connects individual biography to history, and personal troubles to social processes that affect thousands or even millions at once. Consider the example of unemployment. Looking through the lens of the sociological imagination, we can demonstrate that people's failure to find paid employment very often is not the result of a lack of willingness or skills – rather, it results from much broader and often very long-term socio-economic processes, such as the replacement of human workers with machines or the decline of industrial manufacturing in some countries. Importantly, sociology is not only a statement of ambition – it consists of powerful methods, tools and theories that you can draw on to make better sense of your own life in a social context.

Second, sociology allows you to see the global in the local, and vice versa. As much as sociology connects individual lives to broader social processes, it also enables you to see how these social processes more and more transcend local, regional and national boundaries and work on a global scale. The decline of industrial manufacturing that has led to heightened unemployment in some countries is a good example. Technological developments in transport and communications during the twentieth century made it easier and easier to ship goods and spread out industrial production processes over vast distances. At the same time, certain countries – China, Indonesia and Mexico being good examples among many others – began to offer highly attractive conditions that led many companies to move their manufacturing operations there. While Detroit in the USA established its claim to fame in the early twentieth century through car manufacturing, American car companies like General Motors today often prefer to have their cars produced in Mexico. Britain was the initiator and motor of the Industrial Revolution, but today has very little industry at all. As a result, the manufacturing jobs that sustained the urban working classes for much of the nineteenth and twentieth century have largely disappeared, leading to high unemployment and a host of related social problems in traditional industrial cities like Detroit or Birmingham. Using sociological methods and theories, you can make better sense of these complex transnational social processes and move beyond simplistic notions of unemployment as purely individual failure.

Third, sociology lets you see the political in the social. The discoveries which sociology allows you to make about the social world are never politically and morally neutral. They always allow significant insights into the cultural values, mores and laws on which communities are built. The 'highly attractive conditions', for instance, that have led many US companies to relocate their manufacturing operations to Mexico since the 1970s and 1980s often consisted of extremely low salaries, extremely long working hours, and highly unsafe and hazardous working environments. Some have been highly critical of such exploitative working conditions, while others have suggested that the creation of industrial labour in Mexico also led to important opportunities, for example enabling many Mexican working class women to work outside their homes and become less dependent on their husbands (Fernández-Kelly 1983). Yet others have criticised the destitution of the working classes in the USA through the disappearance of manufacturing jobs abroad.

So what do you think, and where do you stand? You cannot answer these questions meaningfully without an understanding of the complex social, economic and political processes that drive the outlined issues. Answering difficult questions such as these is important in two ways. First, to return to Martha Nussbaum's (1995: 25) arguments, it allows you to participate actively and competently in debates about the 'political issues affecting the nation', instead of being thrown here and there by the often misleading rhetoric about important issues that pervades the public sphere. Second, the ability to understand problems grounded in complex social, economic and political connections is key to most of the jobs that are in demand in today's highly-skilled 'knowledge economy'. By engaging with the methods and tools of sociology and coming to terms with the socio-logical imagination, you can develop talents central to your progress after your degree.

7.3 Returning to the sociological imagination

The preceding arguments have important implications for sociological enquiry. In the most basic terms, you study sociology by acquainting yourself with the theories, meth-ods and salient lines of enquiry that are associated with the discipline. The knowledge of sociology you thus acquire is sufficient for you to formulate technically sound descriptions of the social world. Using sociological techniques, such as a questionnaire survey or in-depth interviews and focus groups, you can, in principle, study any social phenomenon and describe it quite accurately. This ability, however, does not yet make you a sociologist.

Market research, for example, uses a wide variety of sociological tools and techniques. Market researchers might, say, conduct a precise survey of Londoners' preferences as to electronic gadgets and conclude that 27.5 per cent prefer Apple products while 31.4 per cent enjoy all things Samsung and 41.1 per cent like everything made by Nokia. Through focus groups and interviews, researchers might also have arrived at an explanation of what makes certain products appear as eminently desirable must-haves. While such information is certainly useful to electronics companies, it has very little to do with sociology proper.

Sociology is driven by the sociological imagination: a view of the world that highlights the ways in which all our lives are shaped by, and shape, much larger social structures. C. Wright Mills explained this idea by stating: 'No social study that does not come back to the problems of biography, of history and of their intersection within a society has completed its intellectual journey' (Mills 1959/1967: 6). In connecting individual life stories to broader social-structural patterns and processes, Mills did not just offer a description of the social world and its workings. Rather, he outlined a perspective that allows sociologists to *problematise* the ways in which society works and to both analyse and critique salient social problems and inequalities. This is evident, for instance, in Mills's classic study *The Power Elite* (2000). In the first instance, *The Power Elite* offers a detailed analysis of the domination of US society by a closely circumscribed network of economic, political and military institutions:

> Within American society, major national power now resides in the economic, the political, and the military domains. Other institutions seem off to the side

of modern history, and, on occasion, duly subordinated to these. No family is as directly powerful in national affairs as any major corporation; no church is as directly powerful in the external biographies of young men in America today as the military establishment; no college is as powerful in the shaping of momentous events as the National Security Council. Religious, educational, and family institutions are not autonomous centers of national power; on the contrary, these decentralized areas are increasingly shaped by the big three, in which developments of decisive and immediate consequence now occur. (Mills 2000: 6)

However, Mills did not just seek to offer a matter-of-fact description of the organisation of social power in the USA. Rather, by drawing attention to the workings of the 'power elite', he sought to question its easy ability to dominate the lives of ordinary Americans and shape social life at will. This aspect of his work is visible in statements such as the following:

The economy—once a great scatter of small productive units in autonomous balance—has become dominated by two or three hundred giant corporations, administratively and politically interrelated, which together hold the keys to economic decisions. The political order, once a decentralized set of several dozen states with a weak spinal cord, has become a centralized, executive establishment which has taken up into itself many powers previously scattered, and now enters into each and every cranny of the social structure. The military order, once a slim establishment in a context of distrust fed by state militia, has become the largest and most expensive feature of government, and, although well versed in smiling public relations, now has all the grim and clumsy efficiency of a sprawling bureaucratic domain. (Mills 2000: 7)

In this sense, the sociological imagination has an important *ethical dimension*. Sociological enquiry seeks to offer truthful, in some sense factual, and systematic accounts of social patterns and processes. These accounts, however, are often underpinned and motivated by normative appraisals of how society works in actual fact and how it should work. Mills's work, for example, is driven by concern about the hold which a narrow, opaque elite has gained over American life. Similarly, the work of sociology's founders in many ways expresses concern about the nature of modern life. The writings of Karl Marx and Friedrich Engels (e.g. Marx and Engels 1848/1983) are clear in their preoccupation with the domination and exploitation of the working class by the industrial bourgeoisie. While Max Weber was careful to differentiate value judgements from the empirical analysis of social life (Weber 1949), many of his writings do manifest concern about the ways in which modern forms of rationality, for instance in the form of bureaucratic institutions, have re-shaped social life (Weber 1948/1991). Émile Durkheim's writings on anomie (e.g. Durkheim 1893/1984; Durkheim 1897/1970) are grounded in pressing questions about the sources of social cohesion and the fundaments on which individuals can lead meaningful lives in modern society. And so forth. Sociology does not just amount to the advocacy of certain values by which we should live. Nonetheless, values and the ethical world views in which they are grounded are central sources of the questions sociologists ask. These questions, in turn, can reveal much about the world we live in today and possibilities for improving the human condition.

All these points are illustrated by the following epilogue. In it, Ken Plummer, a British sociologist, sets out his 'critical humanist' approach to sociology. Plummer's critical humanism combines a specific approach to systematic sociological analysis with an explicit ethical world view. Critical humanism is just one of many approaches to the sociological imagination. Nonetheless, by exploring it and critically assessing its merits, you might begin to discover what your own perspective on the social world is and what kind of sociologist you want to be.

Works cited

Durkheim, É. (1893/1984), *The Division of Labour in Society*, Basingstoke: Macmillan.

Durkheim, É. (1897/1970), *Suicide: A Study in Sociology*, London: Routledge & Kegan Paul.

Fernández-Kelly, M. P. (1983), *For We Are Sold, I and My People: Women and Industry in Mexico's Frontier*, Albany: State University of New York Press.

Marx, K. and F. Engels (1848/1983), *Manifesto of the Communist Party*, in *The Portable Karl Marx*, edited by E. Kamenka, New York: Penguin Books.

Mills, C. W. (1959/1967), *The Sociological Imagination*, London: Oxford University Press.

Mills, C. W. (2000), *The Power Elite*, New York: Oxford University Press.

Nussbaum, Martha (2010), *Not for Profit: Why Democracy Needs the Humanities*, Princeton: Princeton University Press.

Weber, M. (1948/1991), 'Bureaucracy' in *Max Weber: Essays in Sociology*, edited by H. Gerth and C. W. Mills, Abingdon: Routledge: 196–244.

Weber, M. (1949), *The Methodology of the Social Sciences*, New York: The Free Press.

Epilogue: A Manifesto for a Critical Humanism in Sociology: on Questioning the Human Social World

Ken Plummer

(Emeritus Professor of Sociology, University of Essex, UK)

We can know only that we know nothing. And that is the highest degree of human wisdom. (Leo Tolstoy, *War and Peace*)

These then are my last words to you. Be not afraid of life. Believe that life is worth living and your belief will help create the fact. (William James, *The Will to Believe*, 1896)

1 Prologue: A very human animal in an all-too-human world

We are discussing no small matter, but how we ought to live. (Socrates)

Where Do We Come From? Who Are We? Where Are We Going? (Title of Oil Painting by Paul Gauguin 1897)

Man's inhumanity to man

Makes countless thousands mourn!

(Robert Burns 'Man was made to mourn', 1786)

We all dwell in an all-too-human social world. This world is created by human beings, organised and disorganised by human beings, and ultimately transformed by human beings. Born into a world we never ever made, the past becomes our prison from the moment we are born, even as we struggle to change it for our self and the next generation. For some two centuries, sociology has championed a systematic, sceptical and critical analysis of this humanly produced social world. It is not the only world, but it is the one sociologists study and it is the one that usually matters most to human beings. The proper study of this human world is the study of this human being.

The broad social facts of this human being – our humanity – are very well known. Currently, there are some seven billion of us and we are fast growing (there may have been 100 billion since the dawn of humanity – we come and go). In the twenty-first century we have become increasingly hi-tech, media-based and global. We rightly worry that we have degraded our environment catastrophically over our short history here on planet Earth. We have lived through many major vast civilisations – from Sinic (or Chinese) to Islamic (or Arabian) to African and Western. The Western world often acts as if it is a dominant world even though it is very small when compared with the rest of the world (only one in eight humans live in North America and Europe!). The past ghosts of our history always haunt us. Today, we are now organised into some 200 countries, with seven or eight major religions (and thousands of smaller ones), and some 6,000 languages. Difference and schismatic tension always pervades us, though it creates a vast global chain of inter-connections. Half of us live in cities, often brutalised; 85 per cent of us own nothing. Most of us live under an economic system of global capitalism that provides prosperity for a few while damaging many more. Indeed many groups – women, the poor, ethnic and sexual minorities of all kinds – often get violently excluded, leading wasted lives.

This human being is also, then, a troubled human being. Here we have the complexities of our lives: our ceaseless consciousness, subjectivities and desires; our struggles with our bodies and our multiple emotions; our existential predicaments; our confrontations with, and denials of, death; the inevitabilities of failure and disappointment; our ongoing ambivalence and ambiguities – all of which the literature of, say, a William Shakespeare, a Virginia Wolf, a Marcel Proust, or a James Joyce have tried to explore. Often too we are damaged by social exclusion, stigmatisation, violence and dehumanisation of all kinds. All these are also the brutal social facts of our humanity. Sociologists are charged with examining the minutiae of the everyday life of the everyday person across the ever-emergent human world.

A key challenge for this human animal must centre on the ways we hand over our human social worlds to the next generation; how we reproduce and transmit these worlds through our cultures. And we humans have done a very mixed job of this. Living on this planet over the past few millennia, we have many significant achievements to pass on. In music and the arts our creativity has soared; in science and technology our inventions have been ingenious; in health and welfare we live longer and longer and have fostered amazing skill alongside care and compassion; and in our political systems the idea of democracy has evolved where even with its tensions, there is the pursuit of justice, equality and freedom. It may not be a very good system but it is probably the best we can devise, so far. There are many good things we have done.

And yet, and despite this, throughout the history of humanity, most people have also had to live subsistence lives – poverty, poor conditions and lack of freedom are widespread amongst today's seven billion, no less than the smaller numbers of the past. We have persistently managed to create truly vast inequalities of wealth, power, privilege and prestige such that only a few can glory in the world while the vast majority live in a sorry state. The weight of the world bears upon them. Billions of human lives have become damaged and wasted over the millennia. Indeed, the history of humankind can be depicted as a long history of brutality, cannibalism, colonialism, child slaughter, cruelty, eliminationism and exterminations; of environmental destruction and exploitation; of genocides, holocausts, human conquests of indigenous peoples, inquisitions, mass slaughter and massacres; of poverty, religious crusading, revenge atrocities, slavery, torture, terrorisms, tyranny, violence, war. Oh the horrors and the banalities of universal and ubiquitous everyday cruelty and nastiness! In the twentieth century alone, some 180 million human beings were slaughtered by other human beings. And the twenty-first century is not really looking any better. Meanwhile, our value systems overall have been invaded by a commercial, market-based commodification of the human: everything now is judged in terms of a brutal monetary worth, and other values such as kindness and care are often pushed aside. Humanity, in truth, has not proved to be a very kind humanity, and its history has proved to be routinely stuffed full of the most horrendous cruelty and violence. We have not really left the world a better place for each successive generation.

The challenge for sociology is to grasp this complex, ever-changing humanly produced, lived and everyday social world; to sense that we both miraculously and terrifyingly make and remake this world ourselves; and that the challenge is for us all to work to make it a little better, if we can, in our short lifetimes. And at the heart of this challenge lies what we might call *the sociology–humanist paradox*. For whilst sociology makes us look to the general and the social, humanism makes us look to the unique human person. We always need to remind ourselves that human beings make this social world that then constrains and dominates us. We need both sociology and humanism lest we miss the link: to be both social and individual. And that is the tension that marks a humanist sociology.

2 On the human search for meaning

Man is a being in search of meaning. (Plato)

What is the highest good in all matters of action? To the name, there is almost complete agreement; for uneducated and educated alike call it happiness, and make happiness identical with the good life and successful living. They disagree, however, about the meaning of happiness. (Aristotle, *Nicomachean Ethics*, 1:4)

What makes a life significant? (William James)

So what is this 'human' of which I speak? 'The Human' is what defines us as an emergent species different from other animals or forms of life. It raises the questions about what is distinctive about us human beings when compared with others forms of life. There are biological differences – but even though apes, our nearest relatives, are only 1.5 per cent genetically different from us, there are many biological features that can be seen to make us different: we are *Homo erectus* and *Homo sapiens*. We are the animals with very large and complex brains, prehensile hands, an upright gait. Yet we are so much more than these biological features.

For we are, after all and quite profoundly, the thinking, reflexive, conscious, purposeful, sometimes rational and, maybe even moral animal. Our lives are centred on experiences, practical activities and story telling. We are relational, interactive and inter-subjective. We feel emotions and create selves and identities. We are capable of thinking beyond and outside of ourselves. We are practical beings engaged with the problems, sufferings and joys of our lives and those in the wider worlds around us. We are the little animal who creates 'dreams of a better world'. We are also the animals with distinctive human capabilities or capacities for things like creativity and music, love and hope. And ultimately we hold a belief in something akin to 'human dignity' – which is an inviolable, inherent characteristic of the human animal suggesting a kind of intrinsic worth and value. Some of these features we may indeed share with some other animal life; many of these ideas are themselves open to critique; but most of these features attributed to being human are not to be found commonly amongst other life forms, and, if they are, certainly not so complexly.

One project to help understand human animals is to examine our endless 'search for meaning' – and usually through elaborate systems. Humans are the meaning-making animals: they, almost, *have* to make sense of their own lives and of the worlds and universes around them. Throughout history, our elaborate meaning-making activity has weaved countless stories; we have come to dream our dreams, fight our fights and assemble our cultures. These 'searches for meaning' can be found in myths and legends, in philosophy and science, in metaphysics and religions, in psychology and theories of archetypes. Viktor Frankl's *Man's Search for Meaning* (1946) is a study of concentration camp survival that suggests famously that humans spend every moment of their life searching for meaning – even, maybe especially, at the extreme edges of suffering and death. We look for meaning in understanding others, in aesthetics, in imagination, in science, in Gods and the spiritual, and in material worlds and goods. Some of this pursuit of meaning is rational; some of it is emotional; some of it arises from a repressed unconscious; some of it is aesthetic and some artistic; some of it comes from tradition – handed down by generations; much of it is practical – the little 'wisdoms' developed over a lifetime.

Sociology is one of these searches for meaning.

3 On sociology

Everytime we undertake to explain something human, taken at a given moment of history – be it a religious belief, a moral precept, a legal principle, an aesthetic style, or an economic system – it is necessary to go back to its most primitive and simple form, to try to account for the characterization by which it was marked at that time and then to show how it developed and became complicated little by little, and how it became that which it is at the moment in question. (Émile Durkheim, *The Elementary Forms of the Religious Life*)

Men make their own history, but they do not make it as they please; they do not make it under self-selected circumstances, but under circumstances existing already, given and transmitted from the past. The tradition of all dead generations weighs like a nightmare on the brains of the living. (Karl Marx, *The Eighteenth Brumaire of Louis Bonaparte*)

The sociological imagination enables us to grasp history and biography and the relations between the two within society. That is its task and its promise. (C. Wright Mills, *The Sociological Imagination*)

I'd say that the twin role which we, sociologists, are called in to perform in . . . dialogue are those of defamiliarising the familiar and famialrising (taming, domesticating) the unfamiliar. (Zygmunt Bauman, *Collateral Damage: Social Inequalities in a Global Age*, 2011: 171)

One way humans try to make sense of the world is through Sociology – the discipline which tries to engage our imaginations and rationalities in the arts and sciences of critically mapping and grasping what is going on in the human social world. It is part of the search for meaning, of ways of making sense of the world. As the human world becomes larger and more complex, so the systematic study of it becomes more and more important. Over the past two hundred years it has largely moved down the scientific pathway in its study; and it has, in truth, not been a hugely successful story. Rarely, and sadly, these days, do people call upon sociologists and sociology to explain the world!

There are many versions of sociology; but at its best, Sociology can be seen as a humanistic discipline posing questions about what is taken for granted as obvious or 'natural' in our human worlds. It establishes an emancipatory project, providing us with a challenging form of thinking: a critical consciousness that can ultimately even become a way of life. At its heart, it sees that the air we breathe is social: we need other people to be human. This idea of 'the social' captures both how we relate to others (doing things together and taking others into account) and how we find ourselves constrained by a layer of reality *sui generis*, which exists independently of us. The social is both a relationship and a social fact. But this social world is full of tensions, change, contradiction and inequalities: it simply does not work well for many, many people. The challenge for sociology is to question how this social order functions and changes; and how people can make better worlds for subsequent generations. In effect, sociology can only work in societies that cherish human freedom: societies where there is an absence of coercion and the presence of autonomy. It cannot usually be found in authoritarian societies.

Sociology ultimately critically investigates and questions many things about this human social world. Sociology studies *human social actions* and how human beings come to create meanings in the world. Sociology studies *human social structures*, looking at the patterns and predictabilities of social life. Sociology investigates *human cultures*, the multilayered complex mosaics and ragbags of meanings we bring to our lives – the recipes to help us resolve everyday problems. Human beings weave webs of cultures – life designs, tool kits for life and ways of living. And in their wake we find symbols, language, communication. Sociology questions our *human material life*, which hurls us into brute realities: environments, economies and bodies, reminding us that we are both animals and cultural creatures. Intrinsically dual, we are – as Ernest Becker said in *The Denial of Death*, 'the little gods who shit'. Sociology also studies *human social differences*, telling us that all of our human social worlds are 'incorrigibly plural' as we dwell in social tensions and contradiction. Everything in social life, including sociological and humanist thinking, brings tensions, conflicts and contradictions. Sociology also studies *the inequalities between human beings that result from this*. These stratifications are organised around wealth, power and status (class), gender, ethnicity, age, health, sexualities and nationhood, and our opportunities for human social life can be severely restricted by them. Sociology researches *human social communication*: it highlights the complexities and significance of our languages, our media of communication and the role of dialogues and story telling. We are the dialogic story-telling animal. Human beings are narrators and live in a constant round of telling tales of lives and societies to each other. And all knowledge – whatever else it may be – is within this social dialogue: it is always local, contested, relational knowledge. Monologue is a problem. Sociology is also compelled to study the social as it *flows thorough human social space and social time*: all of social life as changing, as a flux, a constant flow of emergence and entropy, and it changes as it moves across situations from the most local to most global. And sociology ultimately investigates *human social conflict and social power* – our capacities and legitimacies in controlling social life.

In accounting for our human social world, sociology necessarily uses language, constructs imagery and metaphors and develops stories about it. Human society has been variously seen as a social bond creating solidarity; as a structure like a machine or an organism; as a system – even a cybernetic system; as a conflict, a war, a struggle; as a theatrical drama; as an exchange; as a conversation; as a ritual; as a language; as a form of life. Much has been written. The humanist sociologist can see it as all these things. There is no one way. In its tasks it also seeks to break down strict academic discipline boundaries by drawing in anthropology and history, psychology and biology, literature and art, philosophy and the rest.

Ultimately sociology hurls us towards some of the really big questions of life – and many of the smaller ones. Are human societies making progress and getting better – or are we heading for Armageddon? (And what does 'better' mean?) Is inequality growing when compared with earlier societies – and is it inevitable? Do all societies have crime – and do we need scapegoats and outsiders in all societies? How does our social life corrupt the environment we live in? What are the social factors that organise AIDS and can we use this understanding to alleviate the problems it is causing across the world? Why do religions generate hatred and war – as well as benevolence and kindness? And in all cases, what could we – should we – do about it? How *should* we humans work to prevent world problems, and how indeed might we make the world a better place? Is justice possible in society?

Sociology, then, is a challenging, wide-ranging and almost impossible discipline. But it is a very necessary one.

4 The challenge of humanism

First humanist rule: Proclaim the natural dignity and inherent equality of all human beings in all places and in all circumstances. (Rodrigue Tremblay, *The Code for Global Ethics: Toward a Humanist Civilization*, 2009: 17)

If there is anything distinctive about pragmatism, it is that it substitutes the notion of a better human future for the notions of 'reality', 'reason' and 'nature'. (Richard Rorty, *Philosophy and Social Hope*, 1999)

The hallmark of humanist thought is that it places the human being at the heart of its analysis: it puts our species to the forefront of our critical thinking. Human actions, creativities, moralities, ways of being, talking, feeling, suffering, joys, passions, and so forth, have to lie at the core of its concerns. People are what matter. They are not all that matter; and it may be at times that we also have to remind ourselves of our huge insignificance in the grander scheme of things. We are, indeed, only a little animal and a little species with a short time on this planet. But as a distinctive little animal, we surely ought to try to make sense of ourselves. And this is the challenge of the human – and humanism.

The challenge of diverse form of humanisms in world history may be as long as the history of humanity itself. Indeed, Alfred McLung Lee – an early, much ignored champion of a humanistic sociology – sees it everywhere:

> *Humanism has figured in a wide range of religious, political and academic movements. As such it has been identified with atheism, capitalism, classicism, communism, democracy, egalitarianism, populism, nationalism, positivism, pragmatism, relativism, science, scientism, socialism, statism, symbolic interactionism, and supernaturalism, including versions of ancient paganisms, Hinduism, Buddhism, Judaism, Roman Catholicism, Protestantism and Mohammedanism. It has also been rationalized as being opposed to each of these. It has served as an ingredient in movement against each. And these terms do not at all suggest all of humanism's ideological and social associations.* (Alfred McLung Lee, *Sociology for whom?*, 1978: 44–5)

Humanism can be initially clarified by linking it to four major ideas: The Human, the Humane, the Humanitarian and, finally, the Humanities.

The Human suggests a focus on the person, personhood, and putting this human being – this embodied, emotional, huffing and puffing little symbolic animal creature – at the centre of our thinking. By contrast, there are problems with the unhuman, the inhumane, the dehumanising, the post human and other ways of negating our personhood. *The Humane* directs us to a way of responding to other people – with a certain kindliness, sympathy and benevolence towards others. We seek to avoid inflicting pain on others and aim to be kind. *The Humanitarian* suggests people who act with regard to the best interests of humankind at large, having concern for, or helping to improve the welfare and happiness of, people. And *The Humanities* flags the broad human search for wisdoms and understanding about our humanities and the universes we live in. It engages in the literatures of cultures, their arts and sciences: from philosophy and poetry to statistics, from life stories to interviews, from art to maps, from film to drama, from documentary to journalism.

Linked to all this is a concern with the oppositions to the human: to the inhuman where we ignore people; to the inhumane where we are cruel; to the non-humanitarian where we are ungenerous and act only through self interest. In the broadest sense humanism is hence interested in the workings of its opposite form: in dehumanisation – the multiple and major social processes which degrade and rob humans of their humanities.

5 Righting the troubles with humanisms

The modern individual – objectified, analysed, fixed – is a historical achievement. There is no universal person on whom power has performed its operations and knowledge, its enquiries. Rather, the individual is the effect and object of a certain crossing of power and knowledge. He (sic) is the product of the complex strategic development in the field of power and the multiple development in the human sciences. (Foucault in Dreyfus and Rabinow, Michel Foucault: Beyond Structuralism and Power, 1982: 159–60)

So says that most influential of modern thinkers, Michel Foucault! There are many who think this wretched little human animal, us, is a very poor starting point for thinking about the human social world; and humanism has long been under attack from many different sides. Yet, there are some gross misconceptions that have often ben identified with humanists and these must be cleared up from the outset: they do a lot of harm. We have to recognise that humanisms come in many forms, and many critiques are falsely aimed.

First, humanists are often identified with Renaissance and Enlightenment thinking, but detailed study (like that found in the work of Jonathan Israel's *Radical Enlightenment* (2002) and *Democratic Enlightenment* (2011)) shows that the Enlightenment itself was a great crisis over the nature of what a human being was. Its great thinkers were in persistent disagreement over the nature of humanity and never agreed upon it being any one thing. But more than this, there have been humanists throughout history and across all cultures and religions and so it is simply wrong to identify it solely with the Enlightenment. How can the critics have missed this?

Linked to this, humanists are often mistakenly assumed to believe that there is one true universal essence of humanity (an 'unencumbered self', a 'universal man'). In so far as there are boundaries with other species this is true; but in general, humanism fosters a view of the human being as historically changing, as possibilities and potentials rather than a solitary being who strides through history as essentially the same. The nature of the human being, and humanity, is a perpetual movement.

Third, humanists are often mistakenly and dangerously seen as necessarily being atheists. Sadly, many groups like the British Humanist Association, and some academic writers too, actually foster this limited view. They make the words humanist and atheist synonymous. And this is neither fair nor correct: there have been many humanists who are spiritual. Humanists really have to recognise the world 'variety of religious experience' and, with this, the significance of, and struggles with, religious meaning in human lives across cultures and history. Humanists do get very critical, however, when such religions become institutionalised, controlling and authoritarian – presuming a level of absolutism and monologic terrorism that is unbecoming to our humanities.

And finally, humanists are often seen as cheery, simple-minded folk who like everyone to 'feel good', believe in the goodness of people, and fight the good fight for progress in the name of humanity. Well, there are some humanists like this; but much humanist writing takes a very different track. Many humanists often struggle to hold their heads up in the face of the clear and stark knowledge of the truly dreadful nature of humanity throughout its history: its bloody wars, genocides, holocaust, rapes, violence, slavery, discriminations, prejudices, inequalities and hatreds of all kind. Of 'humanity's inhumanity to humanity'. Indeed it is precisely this suffering and tragic being that drives many of them to ask the very question of how we can live with this. What kind of human is it who does so many terrifyingly terrible things? The testimonies of concentration camp survivors – Primo Levi, Bruno Bettelheim and the rest – speak to this (see Tzvetan Todorov's *Facing the Extreme: Moral Life in the Concentration Camps* 1999).

Some humanisms, then, have a very narrow version of the human. Critical Humanism identifies these narrow problems and challenges any simple unitary vision of the human.

6 On critical humanism

Modern humanism is caught in a paradoxical relation between the universalistic character of its own aspirations and the always particularistic, culture-bound terms in which these universalizing claims are made. (Pauline Johnson, *Feminism as Radical Humanism*, 1994, Allen and Unwin)

Humanistic sociology is not a difficult idea to define. For the humanistic sociologist, sociology is the study of how to make a better world. The key commitment is that people matter. (William Du Bois and R. Dean Wright, 'What is Humanistic Sociology?' *The American Sociologist*, Winter 2002, Vol. 33, No. 4: 5–36)

I . . . stress the importance of a radical humanism, alive to difference, contingency and the necessary human bond (Jeffrey Weeks, *Invented Moralities*, 1995, Columbia UP, p. 81)

Critical humanism draws upon the long-standing traditions of studying humanity while looking to change for a better world. Thus, it obviously has a focus on human subjectivity, experience and creativity: it starts with people living their daily lives. It investigates their talk, their feelings, their actions, their bodies as they move around in social worlds and experience the constraints of history and a material world of inequalities and exclusions.

But it goes way beyond this standard concern of human and becomes critical. Human beings cannot be understood if they are taken out of the contexts of time and space of which they are always a part. Thus the 'human being' is not a free-floating universal individual: rather 'it' is always stuffed full of the culture and the historical moments of which it is a part, and this history and culture is always in process and changing. Human beings 'nest' themselves in webs of contexts, relationships .To talk otherwise is to engage in the 'myth of the universal man' which critical humanism does not want to suggest.

But this also means the critical humanist acknowledges the inevitable political and ethical role of all inquiry. As they develop a naturalistic 'intimate familiarity' with the lived experiences they study, they also recognise their own (self-reflexive) part in such study. There must be a reflexive self-awareness, part of which will entail their sense of an ultimate moral and political role in moving towards a social structure in which there is less exploitation, oppression and injustice and more creativity, diversity and equality along with more human flourishing. Embracing both a *situated ethics of care* (recognition, tolerance, respects for persons, love) and a *situated ethics of justice* (redistribution, equality), they recognise that research can never be wholly neutral or value free, since the core of the inquiry is value driven: for a better world for all. Indeed, impartiality may even be suspect; a rigorous sense of the ethical and political sphere is a necessity. Just why would one even bother to do research were it not for a wider concern or value?

Ultimately, critical humanism develops accounts of human life that examine the ways these concrete human experiences are linked to social material worlds of bodies, economics and environments (and not just their inner, psychic or biological structuring). It has a very strong, pragmatic pedigree, espousing an epistemology of radical, pragmatic empiricism which takes seriously the idea that knowing is always limited and partial and should be grounded in experience. It makes no claims for grand abstractions or universalism – assuming an inherent ambivalence and ambiguity in human life with no 'final solutions', whilst simultaneously sensing both their subject's ethical and political concerns and their own in conducting such inquiries. It looks for practicalities that help make the world a better place for all.

7 The human condition: obdurate features of the human world

Plurality is the condition of human action since we are all the same, that is, human in such a way that nobody is ever the same as anyone else who ever lived, lives or will live. (Hannah Arendt, *The Human Condition*, 1958)

Within critical humanism, it is probably best to see the so-called 'Human Condition' as a flow of troubling conundrums, ambiguities and puzzles: as a precarious plurality of changing existential predicaments. Human beings dwell in a cascade of continuous and ceaseless creativities, communications, contingencies, changes, complexities, contradictions, and conflicts. That is our lot. And with this, human life requires necessarily living with ambivalence. The path to a good life and a good world is riddled with perpetual problems and dangers. It is usually neither fair nor easy. Get used to it, as they say!

Thus, we live with *creativity*. Like it or not, we humans act in the world we find ourselves in: we are creative beings (even though much is ruled by habit and the law of inertia). We act upon our environment and develop our capacities and capabilities to varying degrees (see below). We make and use tools and we cook fancy meals; we create art and music and write great thoughts; we invent sports and create cyberspace. We are a very odd little animal! We also live with *complexities*: in the vastness of space and time, we live in a plural universe – an infinite world of 'blooming buzzing confusion'. We live with *contingencies*. Human beings are surrounded throughout their lives by chance, fateful moments, contingencies. Hurled out in the universe, we live life through a cluster of precarious possibilities. We confront a constant stream of moments along with a sense that chance happenstances are the stuff of everyday lives. Contingency is one of the main constituents of the human condition. And of course we live with *changes*. Always and everywhere human social life is changing and emergent. Every day is a new day. We cannot step in the same river twice.

Above all we live with *communication*. Humanity depends on language and other symbolic forms. We are the symbol-manipulating, meaning-making animal. But symbols are always ambiguous and contested and lead to layers of confusion and misunderstanding. Communication never entails a solitary or monologic language. Humans are never alone and are dialogic, inter-subjective (i.e. with others and not simply subjective), having selves that are capable of reflexivity, reflectivity. Humans can and do communicate with themselves and others, critically because (as George Herbert Mead has it) they have selves. Human beings are able to take the roles of others, imaginatively and sympathetically, and chart their own actions in relation to these others. They live in worlds reflected in and through others and their languages. And more, they are able through language to hold conversations with others. Of course, other animals can do this too – but not in the same complex fashions which lead to cultures and histories. We are 'homo narrans', the story-telling animal. We will see more of this below.

And finally, flowing from this we live with *contradictions and conflicts* pushed by opposites, antinomies, dialectics all the time. We can find it in the tensions between love and hate, in the tensions of reason and feeling, in the debate over materialism or idealism, body or mind, virtue or vice, absolute or relativist truth, classical and romantic, agency and structure, individual or social, East and West, masculine or feminine – even between good and evil. It is found in the yin and yang (dark and light) of Chinese philosophy; and is present in many ancient Greek stories such as Dionysian and

Apollonian myths. Some cultures make dualisms and split central and a dialectic, con-flicting force for change; some live with them more easily. Living with contradiction is not easy and a key source of perpetual conflict.

These core features of our human realities we live everyday: they need constant inquiry from humanist sociologists.

8 On human potentials, capabilities and rights

What is each person able to do and to be? (Martha Nussbaum, *Creating Capabilities,* 2011: 18)

A musician must make music, an artist must paint, a poet must write if he is to be ultimately at peace with himself. What one can be, one must be. (Abraham Maslow, *On Dominance, Self-Esteem and Actualization,* 1954)

A person has to be what a person has to be. Drawing from a long line of Aristotelian reasoning which argues for the realisation of 'natural ends', human beings can be iden-tified as having distinctive, unique potentials or capabilities for life that are shaped and facilitated by the social; we may even call these their human rights. Such capabilities may vary a little from culture to culture; they are not fixed but complex and grow and change with lives. But they do hint strongly at lives that can be enabled to flourish and other lives that may be damaged or even wasted. For each individual human, we start with the unlived life and start to see how it is our social relations that help shape and enable us to flourish, or not.

What might these human capabilities, potentials, rights be? There have been many attempts to create long lists of these potentials. The humanistic psychologist Abraham Maslow probably provided the most succinct listing, and placed our needs on a hierarchy of physiological needs, security needs, social needs, esteem needs, and ultimately of actualising needs: 'Self-actualizing people have a deep feeling of identification, sympathy, and affection for human beings in general. They feel kinship and connection, as if all people were members of a single family.' Others have produced lists of multiple needs: Christian Smith's *What is a Person?* suggests some thirty capacities. But perhaps the most valuable – even if ever changing, rather long and still incomplete – listing is that by the feminist philosopher Martha Nussbaum, and so I reproduce it (in summary form) here. Human capabilities entail:

1. Life. Being able to live to the end of a human life of normal length; not dying prematurely or before one's life is so reduced as to be not worth living.
2. Bodily Health. Being able to have good health, including reproductive health; being adequately nourished; being able to have adequate shelter.
3. Bodily Integrity. Being able to move freely from place to place; having one's bodily boundaries treated as sovereign i.e. being able to be secure against

assault, including sexual assault, marital rape, and domestic violence; having opportunities for sexual satisfaction and for choice in matters of reproduction.

4. Senses, imagination, and thought. Being able to use the senses; being able to imagine, to think, and to reason – and to do these things in a "truly human" way, a way informed and cultivated by an adequate education, including, but by no means limited to, literacy and basic mathematical and scientific training; being able to use imagination and thought in connection with experiencing and producing expressive works and events of one's own choice (religious, literary, musical etc.); being able to use one's mind in ways protected by guarantees of freedom of expression with respect to both political and artistic speech and freedom of religious exercise; being able to have pleasurable experiences and to avoid non-necessary pain.

5. Emotions. Being able to have attachments to things and persons outside ourselves; being able to love those who love and care for us; being able to grieve at their absence; in general being able to love, to grieve, to experience longing, gratitude, and justified anger; not having one's emotional development blighted by overwhelming fear or anxiety, or by traumatic events of abuse or neglect. (Supporting this capability means supporting forms of human association that can be shown to be crucial in their development.)

6. Practical reason. Being able to form a conception of the good and to engage in critical reflection about the planning of one's own life. (This entails protection for the liberty of conscience.)

7. Affiliation. (a) Being able to live for and in relation to others, to recognize and show concern for other human beings, to engage in various forms of social interaction; being able to imagine the situation of another and to have compassion for the situation; having the capability for both justice and friendship. (Protecting this capability means, once again, protecting institutions that constitute such forms of affiliation, and also protecting the freedoms of assembly and political speech.) (b) Having the social bases of self-respect and non-humiliation; being able to be treated as a dignified being whose worth is equal to that of others. (This entails provisions of nondiscrimination, on the basis of race, sex, sexual orientation, religion, caste, ethnicity, or national origin.)

8. Other species. Being able to live with concern for and in relation to animals, plants, and the world of nature

9. Play. Being able to laugh, to play, to enjoy recreational activities.

10. Control over one's environment. (a) Political: being able to participate effectively in political choices that govern one's life; having the rights of political participation, free speech, and freedom of association (b) Material: being able to hold property (both land and movable goods); having the right to seek employment on an equal basis with others; having the freedom from unwarranted search and seizure. In work, being able to work as a human being, exercising practical reason and entering into meaningful relationships of mutual recognition with other workers.

(Source: adapted from *Sex and Social Justice*, 1999: 41–2; *Women and Human Development*, 2000: 78–80; *Creating Capabilities*, 2011: Ch. 2)

Of course the list is inadequate but it is a good start for thinking. The challenge for the humanist sociologist is to inspect each of these capabilities and then to empirically investigate those social conditions that enable lives to develop and flourish in these areas. Closely linked is also the task of analysing the ways in which each of these human potentials also suggests a range of human rights that need respecting.

9 The challenge of plural worlds, ethnocentrism and cosmopolitanism

For different men take joy in different actions. (Homer, *The Odyssey*)

Now the blindness in human beings . . . is the blindness with which we are all inflicted in regard to the feelings of creatures and people different from ourselves. We are practical beings, each of us with limited functions and duties to perform. Each is bound to feel intensely the importance of his (sic) own duties and the significance of the situations that these call forth. But this feeling is in each of us a vital secret, for sympathy with which we vainly look to others. The others are too much absorbed in their own vital secrets to take an interest in ours. Hence the stupidity and injustice of our opinions, so far as they deal with the significance of their lives. Hence the falsity of our judgments, so far as they presume to deal in an absolute way on the value of other person's conditions or ideals . . . What is the result of all these considerations . . .? It is negative in one sense, but positive in another. It absolutely forbids us to be forward in pronouncing on the meaninglessness of forms of existence other than our own; and it commands us to tolerate, respect, and indulge those whom we see harmlessly happy and interested in their own ways, however unintelligible they may be to us. Hands off: neither the whole truth nor the whole of good is revealed to any single observer, although each observer gains a partial superiority of insight from the peculiar position in which he (sic) stands. (William James, *On a Certain Blindness in Human Beings*, 1899/1913)

At the heart of human social life is plurality and difference. We live, as the great philosopher and psychologist William James never tired of reminding us, in a plural universe. Living with this difference is one of the greatest challenges of human life. There exists a real humanistic universalism of differences. Human beings and their differences should be treated as a key subject for the human studies. There are perpetual conflicts about these differences, the source of much human suffering, and they are not likely to go away. But they can be reduced.

Pluralism is foiled by the problem of ethnocentrism 'in which one's own group is the center of everything, and all others are scaled and rated with reference to it'. W.G. Sumner's famous term has quietly become one of the most influential of modern times, and grasps an idea so vital in appreciating one of humanity's key predicaments. We live in our own worlds; it is often very hard to grasp the worlds of others – and that they are not the same as ours. We are plagued by parochialism, provincialism and post-colonialism. And usually we do not even see this, let alone try to move beyond them.

We can find this problem everywhere and sociological humanism suggests two key strategies as central in overcoming it. Interpersonally, we need dialogue; across societies, we need cosmopolitanism. Dialogue demands understanding of the other and seeks to break down monologue. It can bring empathy and sympathy and a care and reciprocity for the other, however different they may seem. Cosmopolitanism becomes a social form or structure which stresses the recognition of these differences of others as being crucial to what counts as being human.

Cosmopolitanism suggests a social psychology of empathy, dialogue and an ability to live with differences through an ever-expanding 'circle of others' spreading across the globe. It also suggests a form of society, social structure or social solidarity where a reciprocal inter- and intra-cultural awareness of differences can become enshrined in human rights, laws, institutions and everyday practices. Cosmopolitanism suggests a politics of human differences, connecting local political struggles with global ones. It bridges world stages with local stages – through ideas like international law, global human rights, universal values and grounded ethics.

Dialogue and cosmopolitanism are crucial for humanity. As they foster an attitude of 'openness' and 'tolerance' towards difference, they will often be accompanied by a sense of irony, paradox, contradiction and contingency as a fuller appreciation of the different kinds of humanity is developed.

10 On becoming human: the process of humanisation

What most horrifies me in life is our brutal ignorance of one another. (James, cited in R. D. Richardson, *The Heart of William James*, 2006: 3)

Our humanity may, or may not, be born with us. We are certainly born with certain 'open-ended' capacities or capabilities to become human. And it is this becoming human which interests sociologists: how does it happen? How do we take a new-born baby and turn it into a fully functioning, even flourishing, human being? Or fail to do so?

The core challenge is for the infant child to become aware of others – to empathise, even sympathise with them. They grow into what Adam Smith (in his *Theory of Moral Sentiments*) saw as the 'circle of others'. We move outwards from our parents to an ever-expanding social world. And this requires a complex process containing many elements including:

1. *Communication*, in which ideas are sent from one person to another.
2. *Language*, which becomes a critical tool for this communication.

3. *Recognition* (and *identification*), where we come to acknowledge and identify who we are and how we are different from each other.

4. *Respect,* where we honour such differences of 'others'.

5. *Role taking* and *reflexivity,* where we come to see the world from the viewpoint of specific others and are able to see ourselves through the eyes of these others, and eventually the wider community too.

6. *Dialogue,* where communication is always seen as entailing at least two and never a simple monologue.

7. *Empathy,* where we come to appreciate the others' points of view.

8. *Sympathy,* where we are concerned to feel the others' points of view.

9. *Compassion,* where our empathy and sympathy leads us to want to do something for the others.

10. *Generosity, Care and Kindness,* which are key forms of human actions which help the others.

Humanistic sociology needs to understand this complex process of communication, dialogue and empathy, placing it at the heart of human social relationships and indeed social life. So much failed social life can be seen as a breakdown of this process. Often through a skewing of power relations, so much communication becomes impossible or at least one sided. People are spoken to: there is no reflexivity, no dialogue, no empathy. This is broken-down human life. (The works of many sociologists, theologians and philosophers, like Hanna Arendt, Martin Buber, Mikhail Bakhtin, Seyla Benhabib, Arthur Frank, Paulo Freire, Jurgen Habermas, George Herbert Mead, Paul Ricoeur and many others can all help us to build a deeper understanding of how we become human.)

11 A sociology of the people: being practical and pursuing the wise society

How different things would be . . . if the social sciences at the time of their systematic formation in the nineteenth century had taken the arts in the same degree they took the physical science as models. (Robert Nisbet, *Sociology as an Art Form,* 1976: 16)

There is no best way to tell a story about society. Many genres, many methods, many formats – they can all do the trick. Instead of ideal ways to do it, the world gives us possibilities among which we choose. Every way of telling the story of a society does some of the job superbly but other parts not so well. (Howard S. Becker, *Telling About Society,* 2007: 285)

The only way to prepare for social life is to engage in social life. (John Dewey, *Democracy and Education,* 1930/2010)

A humanistic sociology should be *about* all the people, *by* all the people and *for* all the people. It has to be *about all the people* because even if the focus is on just one individual, this individual has to be seen as part of a historical sweep of humanity and also part of the seven billion alive today. Their uniqueness can be studied and celebrated in a world of differences. It has to be *by all the people* in the sense that *all* the people *can* speak – any methods are suitable that allow us to get close to human experiences: those that negate this may be fine for other reasons but they are not humanistic. And finally it has to be ultimately *for all the people*: to make their worlds a better place for them and subsequent generations, a task that has to include living with their differences.

Rather sadly, the history of sociology these past two hundred years has sometimes negated these visions. It has often become either a jargon-ridden abstracted science or a rather mundane grabbing of small-scale facts assembled into incomprehensible tables. It has often drifted away from a deep and passionate concern with life as it is lived in human worlds to a rather moribund discipline that is not taken very seriously by the wider world. In many circles it has become a bad word and, in bookshops, shelves devoted to it have dwindled. In part this has been because of its obsession with theory and methodology. In sociology courses, students are often made to spend huge amounts of time on theory and methods. They are encouraged to get away from human life and take refuge in abstraction and research skills. But theory and methods are really only very pedestrian means to more important goals. We should never forget this. Theory and Methodology are only a means, and not ends in themselves.

The challenge for sociology is to grapple seriously with the impossible task of gaining wisdoms about the ways of the human social world; to put them into public debate; and to use them for emancipatory purposes. Sociology has a multitude – almost infinite – pool of human resources that it can draw upon in doing this. From great works of art throughout history (the works of say a Breughel or a Hogarth), from literature (say a Chaucer, a Shakespeare, a Tolstoy, a Dickens), to the vast archives of modern photography (a Dorothea Lange, a Sebastiao Salgado), and to the twentieth-century global art form of film (a *Tokyo Story*, an *It's a Wonderful Life*). All of this, sadly and routinely, is excluded from courses in sociology in favour of interview methods, multivariable analysis and sample design.

But the humanistic sociologist has before them a wondrous archive of human social life: of archival documents (historical, personal, all kinds) and artefacts ('stuff': personal possessions, archaeological 'finds', consumer objects); of art (painting, sculptures) and autobiographies and life stories; of diaries, documentary films and documents of all kinds (e.g. blogs, websites, club magazines); of fiction (novels, television drama (e.g. soaps) and films); of letters, maps and texts of all kinds. Above all, it has everyday people going about their everyday lives across the world waiting to be engaged in telling about their lives.

Again, the importance of this account is the way it runs against the grain of more totalising, abstract and general accounts of social life.

12 We are the story-telling animals

Stories animate human life: that is their work . . . Narrative makes the earth habitable for human beings. (Arthur W. Frank, *Letting Stories Breathe*, 2010)

All sorrows can be borne if you put them in a story or tell a story about them. (Karen Blixen, cited in Hannah Arendt, *The Human Condition*, 1958)

[There is] . . . a powerful argument for the efficacy of storytelling in advancing the ongoing and constantly transforming pursuit of social justice . . . (Schaffer and Smith, *Human Rights and Narrated Lives*, 2004: 233)

At the heart of the humanistic sociological enterprise is story telling. We are the only animals living on planet Earth to have the capability for *telling, appreciating and living* stories, as Aristotle indicates in his *Poetics*. Other animals can surely communicate: but they do not seem capable of telling and writing stories to transmit across cultures and generations. We are, then, the *story-narrating animals* ceaselessly creating stories and dwelling in *story-telling societies*. As we humans *tell* our stories, *listen* to the stories of others, and *story our lives*, our tales come to haunt, shape and transform our social worlds. We really need our stories in order to live. They are key companions through our lives: we invent, travel and die with them. They have consequences, so we should be careful with the tales we tell.

Sociology wants to take us beyond the narrow confines of our own limited worlds, and stories help us do this. At the heart of our story telling lies our human empathy with different, imaginative lives – and their different values. Stories enable concrete empathy with the worldwide common problems of humanity and, in doing this, they play a crucial moral and political role in human social life. Our everyday life drips with stories of how people live and love, work and play, hate and die.

The moral call of stories helps us hear 'different voices' and provides us with a widening expansion of our circles of empathy and the moral universes we can live in. Stories can inspire a 'moral imagination'. Through being attentive to the 'narratives of virtuous people', we can construct our sense of a good life: stories of others can help us see the possibilities of leading better lives – and sometimes worse ones.

The political call of stories inspires a political imagination. Listening to the stories of the lives of others whose world may be different from ours is a prerequisite for democratic functioning, for the working of societies seeking a respect and recognition for human differences. As we hear tales of sorrow and suffering, of outsiders and the excluded, of strangers and the marginal, of the colonised and the wretched of the earth, of the stigmatised, the outsider, and 'the other', so stories deepen our sympathies, our imaginations, our critiques of a damaged world. It is why stories are so often used by social movements, by reformers and campaigners, by educators and by humanitarian activists to provide exemplars and case studies to help us all see the need for and possibilities of social change. Stories help fashion political identities, political campaigns, imagined communities, discourses of the 'others', the literature of human rights: and, in all this, political change for a better world becomes more feasible.

13 The politics and ethics of humanism: living a better life and making a better world

We have only one story. All novels, all poetry, are built on the never ending contest in ourselves of good and evil. (John Steinbeck, *East of Eden*, 1952)

William James asks his uncle: What is a life for? And is told: Three things in human life are important. The first is to be kind. The second is to be kind. And the third is to be kind. (Cited in Robert Coles, *Handing one Another Along*, 2010: 241)

A humanistic sociology can never claim that sociology should or ever could be completely value-free. Indeed, believing in the significance of the human is itself a value position. And as human beings we live inevitably in value-drenched worlds; our search for meaning is a value world. And so, also inevitably, sociology always touches these values. It is a normative discipline and values shape the baseline assumptions of our research, our everyday practices of doing sociological theory and research (research ethics), and ultimately in the – hopefully emancipatory – ways our research is put to use. A Critical Humanistic Sociology has to study these values and put them to work.

Sociology needs to address values as part of its core agenda: how people live with values, how values are socially and historically developed in societies and people's lives, how values change, and how sociologists themselves bring values into play at every stage of their work (how they set their problems, conduct their research, and ultimately use their 'findings'). And, of course, what role stories and narratives play in all this. For stories are nothing but the conveyors of values.

In Western thought there are two grand abstract schemas of values and ethics that are often called the *Justice* stance and the *Virtue* stance. The former looks to an ethics and politics of redistribution, recognition and rights alongside issues of freedom, equality and democracy; the latter looks to human flourishing and various traits like generosity, wisdom, kindness, altruism and care alongside the rights for a 'good life'. With multiple internal conflicts, they are often also put into tension with each other. Yet we need both. Sometimes they seek grand and abstract universal principles; other times they are more gritty and espouse a down-to-earth practical reasoning and action. Yet in theories, actions and practices there is no reason why they should be held apart. They could all work together. Although the small worlds of intellectual elites have devoted huge energy to a refined finding of the one correct path through all these philosophies, there will probably never be the one way: we can suffice with examining and understanding the ways in which people struggle to put such values to everyday work in their lives. Humanists develop a grounded sense of practical everyday politics and ethics. But humanism also has to go beyond these Western views – there are also Confucian values (e.g. piety, ritual and humaneness), Buddhist values (e.g. suffering and the eight-fold path to right-living), Muslim values (e.g. firm faith, charity, good citizenship) and in a global humanism the challenge is to bring these together in the search for some kind of more global ethics and politics. There are many commonalities, for instance, across world religions and world philosophies and a challenge for the humanist is to inspect these, compare them and search for '*common grounds*'. A Global ethics may be based on the search for a Universal common ground. Many grounds have been suggested and we need to inspect them: dignity, tolerance, empathy, love. Curiously, when most ethical statements are closely examined one common theme does seem to emerge and has been called the golden rule. It is: *One should treat others as one would like to be treated oneself.* A provisional 'Ten Commandments for a Global Humanism' can be found in Rodrigue Tremblay's *The Code of Global Ethics*, 2009.

The institutional form for all these values to be discussed and cherished has to be some kind of civic culture, of which sociology will be part. Here public rational debates – aware of humanity's contingencies, confusions and contradictions, and seeking to be kind – can take place over a multitude of differences and values. It is here where ultimately some kind of universalistic solidarities about the nature of personhood and our futures is to be found.

Some possible values for a Global Humanism

Critical humanists take values very seriously and part of their work lies in the building and understanding of normative frameworks that work for a better world for all. These values are reflexive. We study and research these values, investigating the social structures that create them. At the same time we are aware of how they play back into our lives and help shape both what and how we research. They also help us scrutinise the wider political and ethical implications of our work, building an understanding of them into our daily practices as sociologists. Most centrally they can be used as starting point for seeking 'common grounds' across different conflicts groups across the world.

Quite what these values are is open to debate: they may change and they can be reshaped by arguments. I do not want to present a dogma. But at present, I suggest six major domains of value work for critical humanism. These are:

1. *The principles of global empathy and dialogue*: understanding how people make sense of others in their different social worlds. The human world cannot live with monologue but needs dialogue. Some key areas of action and discussion include the nature of the 'other', of hidden and silenced voices, of multiculturalism, of the importance of recognition, the sociology of tolerance, the norm of reciprocity, the rise of the empathic civilisation, and the role of dialogic ethics and the development of cosmopolitanism. It wants to foster the ability to live with our differences and help shape the empathic, cosmopolitan society.
2. *The principles of global care and kindness*: understanding the ways in which people look after each other – even love each other – in the world. The human world cannot live with perpetual cruelty, violence, war and hatred. Some key areas for action and discussion here include the ethics of care, the rise of the compassionate temperament and the humanitarian society, the importance of love and kindness

in human lives, and even the way we look after our environment. It wants to foster kindness for others over self interest to help shape a *Caring Society*.

3. *The principles of global justice*: understanding fairness and how equalities and inequalities shape human life. The human world cannot live with its raging poverty, brutality, competition and stark inequalities. Some key areas of action and discussion will focus on how human freedoms are restricted by intersecting social divisions across class, gender, ethnicity, health, age, sexualities and nationhood; how we can bring about a society with more social justice, redistribution, equalities and freedom – for all, not just the elite few. It wants to foster economic redistribution and interpersonal equality and respect to help shape a *Just Society*.

4. *The principles of global rights and human dignity*: understanding the rise and role of human rights debates and their significance in what it means to be a human being with human dignity. The human world cannot live by simply banishing huge swathes of people as worth nothing and condemning them to wasted lives. Some key areas for discussion here include the problem of human dignity and what it means, of modernity and universality of rights, the variety and differentiations of human rights (e.g. civil, religious, intimate), international agencies for rights and social movements for rights. It wants to foster human rights and dignity helping to shape a truly *Human Society*.

5. *The principles of global flourishing lives for all*: understanding human capabilities and the social conditions under which they can flourish. The human world cannot condemn so many people to lives that are 'wretched', 'damaged' and lacking in any kind of 'quality'. Some key areas for action and discussion centre on what is meant by human well-being, 'happiness'; what is meant by the good life and the wasted life; what are human capabilities and potentials; and what might be a 'virtuous' life. What are the good traits of humanity, which need to be cherished and valued, and what social conditions will bring this about? It wants to take seriously what it would mean to have a good life for all and help shape a *Flourishing Society*.

6. *The principles of global amelioration and social hope*: understanding the ways in which people have made better worlds in the past and how they can in the present and the future. The human world cannot live in despair, pessimism, gloom and a sense of uselessness. It must not succumb to negativism and pessimism. It needs a sense of hope and working for a better world. Some key areas for action and discussion centre on the tools of amelioration and change; the maps of utopias – past, present, real and imagined; and the problem of balancing optimism with pessimism into a realistic appraisal of future worlds. The principle of hope leads us to consider the idea of real utopias and the strategies to achieve them. It wants to help shape a *Progressive Society*.

7. *The principle of global pragmatism*: understanding that the world does not work through grand abstract theories, philosophies and plans but through small-scale, local, practical, contingent, contradictory, and endlessly pluralistic practical actions. The human world cannot live with grand designs, grand rulers and despots, or authoritarian systems of any kind which trample on the human. They simply do not work for the majority for the people who live ordinary everyday practical lives doing ordinary everyday practical actions. Some key areas for action and discussion are the

significance of local grounded politics and research; the value of ethnography and documentary methods which bring us into closer contact with other realities and worlds; a move from abstractions to details. It wants to create a practical Grounded World – grounded in people's everyday lives.

In sum:

1. Understand others
2. Be kind
3. Seek justice
4. Foster human rights and dignity
5. Encourage lives to flourish
6. Be positive and work for better worlds for all
7. Stay grounded and be practical

14 Dark hope and dreaming ahead in perpetually troubled times: key directions for a future humanistic agenda

I'm a pessimist because of intelligence, but an optimist because of will. (Antonio Gramsci, *Letter from Prison,* 19 December 1929)

What we can do is . . . make life a little less terrible and a little less unjust in every genera-tion. A good deal can be achieved in this way. (Karl Popper, 1949)

'Dreaming ahead' (Ernst Bloch)

Human beings always live in troubled times: in the past, in the present and in the future. One of the lessons of life is that troubles are indeed our lot. The world is in perpetual crisis, though more so at some times than others. Experiments in creating better worlds often fail and frequently presage disasters; grand plans are rarely achiev-able; good deeds have unintended consequences; often we confront fatal remedies and pyrrhic victories; the world is aleatory. And meanwhile human beings suffer in their billions. A glancing eye on history and recent times cannot encourage much optimism.

Take the very current moment. It is stuffed full of its own problems, though all may simply be versions of universal and long-lasting issues. As I write (in June 2012) we confront:

Conflicts, war and armed crisis – usually sectarian and often religious across countries such as Afghanistan, Burma, Colombia, Korea, Nigeria, Pakistan, Somalia, Sudan, Syria, and the so-called 'Arab Spring'. The search is on to understand – and maybe alleviate – perpetual violence and conflict, and to promote the peace process.

Economic crises linked to the breakdown of neo-liberalism and capitalism – evidenced all around the world but currently notable in the eurozone and Greece, Spain and Italy. The search is on to provide a sociological account of a new or transformed human economic system which will not cause so such human damage.

Criminality, violence, and lawlessness across the world – robbery in Cape Town; drug wars in Mexico; homicide in Rio and San Pedro Sula; kidnapping in Grozny, Chechnya; violence in Baghdad; lawlessness in Mogadishu, Somalia. The search is on to understand crime not as a simple problem of individuals in themselves but to see how sociologically crime is so very bound up with the very conditions of the way a society is run – and to seek changes within the society.

Abject poverty and extreme inequalities across the world – evidenced in slum cities, feral societies, and the manifest differences in lives between the mass outcast poor and the elite 'super-rich'. The search is on to find means to lift the poor out of their poverty and examine just how much wealth a life really needs. There is an obscenity on the planet when we live and ignore so much abject poverty of the many alongside the luxuriant and wasteful lives of the multi-billionaire few.

De-secularisation and global violence over religion – The global Jihad; Buddhist revolts in Asia – Sri Lanka, Mongolia, Tibet; Hindu nationalism; Pakistan conflicts; Pentecostalism in African countries; the clash of fundamentalisms. The search is on to understand the dynamics of both inter and intra religious conflicts and violence – and their possible expanding futures in the world.

Gender and sexual violence across the world – widespread domestic abuse, female genital mutilation, forced marriage, sex trafficking, female infanticide, rapes of all kinds (including war rape, work and sexual harassment, dowry abuse and sexual murder). And over 80 countries still outlaw homosexuality – some with the death penalty. Transgender issues remain an anomaly in many countries. The search is on to understand and change gender and sexual inequalities across the world amongst many countries and groups who actively promote this kind of hatred and discrimination.

The world crisis of the environment and population – climate change, expanding waste, water shortage, energy crisis, endangered species and population expansion with ageing populations are all putting planet Earth and the people who live on it in jeopardy. The search is on to understand this 'new catastrophism' and see what it is doing to human lives around the world.

Democratic failure and political crisis – dictatorships in North Korea, Sudan, Zimbabwe, Myanmar; genocide in Myanmar, Syria, Sudan, Uganda, Ethiopia; restrictions of freedom in China, especially in the media, a lack of equality, widespread corruption, a lack of free and fair elections. The search is on to see how authoritarianism is still prominent, inequalities pervade and how democracies – after all this time – still fail and fail badly.

And so the list goes on and on. . . .

Contemporary humanists and sociologists are charged with documenting all this bad news. It is hard to miss the wider tales of genocide, the long history of violence, wars, of gross global and local inequalities, of economic breakdown, of endless political corruption, social exclusion and environmental catastrophe. It is indeed part of the wider social imaginary that we live in 'crisis', 'bad times', or, as Immanuel Wallerstein once put it in the title of a book, *'The End of the World as We Know it'* (2001). Our newspapers, television and pundits tell us this every day. Indeed, sociologists should perhaps spend more time critiquing this widespread view instead of simply mirroring it in the language of yet another damn crisis.

So here comes a problem: with all this, sociology can easily become the moaning, grumbling discipline. Excessively critical, we only look on the dark side of life. Much sociology becomes almost obsessively *miserablist* (espousing the philosophy of pessimism), *misanthropic* (cynically believing the worst of human nature and motivation) and *melancholic* (a mental state characterised by deep depression, sadness and gloom). Some sociologists are modern-day doomsayers and apocalypse forecasters.

But dark as it indeed is, this is not the full story.

We also need a human sociology to take seriously the idea of hope and the future. Part of our work should routinely be the emancipatory project of imagining better human social worlds *for all*; and to engage in discussions about the values and practices which need to be developed to nudge us towards this potentially better world. As Ernst Bloch outlines in his magisterial volumes on *The Principle of Hope* (1938–47), we need *a sociology of hope* which might help provide some 'outlines of a better world'. What might this project look like?

We can start by seeing the significance of cultivating *a sociology of the human person* and an understanding of what it means to be human in the world. This is not meant to be a narrow understanding of the Western individual, but a wide comparative understanding of how human beings live in past and present worlds across the globe. It remembers there are over seven billion today and that this is no small project. It has to draw from psychology, genetics, anthropology and history in this challenge. We ask how have humanities changed across time and space? What may be their potential for the future? What might be meant by post-humanism and what is the challenge it brings?

Second, we need to attend to the global sufferings of humanity across the world and appraise what Jeffrey Alexander has recently called 'cultural trauma'. We need to understand our worldwide human problems. *A sociology of suffering* would document the multiple forms of personal and cultural suffering (in life, of course, but also in films, writing, art, poems), to probe their depths and become sensitive to their pains, and to think critically about how best to theorise them, conceptualise them and explain why and how people across the world often ignore, deny, facilitate or even celebrate human suffering. A critical sociology of suffering is already being developed by a few – in the work of Jeffrey Alexander, Michael Burawoy, Iain Wilkinson, Arthur Kleinman, Pierre Bourdieu, for example – and we need to promote its wider understanding in the world. We ask what are the social conditions and social processes that bring lives to suffering and despair?

Third, and by contrast, we need *a sociology of good lives*. Here we listen to (and document and analyse) the stories of all people who struggle to live helpful lives, to be good people in a difficult world – even as they fail (and perhaps most apparently in the lives of the caring professions and the like). How do they try to work to make the world a better place in their various life activities, and how do they succeed or fail? A sociology of good lives might ask how people and their groups come to look after other people and in very ordinary ways 'do good'; and the problems this brings. We ask what are the social conditions and social processes that enable people to live caring lives?

Closely linked to this would be the development of *a sociology of human capacities and flourishing*. Using something like Nussbaum's capabilities listed above we could examine how some never have opportunities to achieve fulfilled lives, whilst others do. We could examine the process through which some lives become wasted, some damaged, and others flourish. Part of this will also mean sociologist study pleasure and joy: a sociology of joy: the passion of music, the joy of dance, the skill in sport, the love of food, the pleasures of sex – and more. We ask what are the social conditions and social processes that enable people to live flourishing lives? We investigate human capabilities and examine the social conditions which lead to each capability to flourish.

But these opportunities for human capabilities are not simply individual things but are organised through the wider society and the state. Here we need to develop *a sociology of the humanitarian society and the humanitarian state*. We investigate the structures of international governance, welfare states and social protection that may facilitate capabilities; the workings of institutions that encourage the development of human rights and equality frameworks; the facilitation of care and kindness and the roles of global activism, volunteers and philanthropy; we continue to inspect the deep interconnected structures of inequalities and social exclusion that are known to have such damaging effects on social opportunity and the quality of lives; and we look to institutions that facilitate global empathy, cosmopolitanism and ethics in ensuring we recognise differences and foster peace processes across our human world.

An important part of all this must be to develop a persistent awareness of humanity's global interconnectedness (*a sociology of global humanity*) and how this is grounded in an awareness of everyday life – more and more of the seven billion people. It is a move away from the simple replication of the concerns of a small intellectual (largely university-based and Western) elite – we need to go beyond these limited worlds and look at the ordinary lives of ordinary people doing ordinary things all over the globe. (The You Tube film *A Life in a Day* is an early exemplar of this – showing how thousands across the world are keen to contribute in the documentation of different lives.) Avoiding the tyranny of elite knowledge, we ask how is social life lived by ordinary people across the globe? We ask how we can learn to avoid the ethnocentrism of our worlds, and look out to others.

And finally, we also need *a sociology of better worlds*. A key challenge for a sociological humanism is the imagination of just what better human worlds may look like. Utopias may never arrive, but visions of them are important. A sociology without visions of both imagined and real utopias becomes a directionless sociology. Sociology already has in its hands vast resources which can be studied (without huge funding) on possible better worlds. Most obviously there is the vast terrain of science fiction and its imagined worlds, its utopias and dystopias, its good lives and bad lives. Second, there is the literature of social movements of all kinds – all of which produce statements of dreams, goals, ideologies and missions. Third, there is the vast field of world religions in all their diversities and multitudes – and all of which have some ethical or political version of a City of God (or else they would not be a religion?). We could even include in this the plans and proposals also of many therapeutic groups who often border on the religious. Some of these of course are truly dangerous: but there are lessons to be learnt. Fourth, there is the great literature, drama, art, music and philosophy across the world – so much of which ultimately addresses a better world for humanity. Fifth are also international documents – of human rights, of reconciliation, of peace: so much stuff that outlines the negotiations and plans that little human beings have had in the past and the present for a better world. We could at least know about all these, have a sense of where they have failed, and more practically how they might work.

Finally, we have many experiments in social life throughout history – of what have been called attempts at 'real utopias'. We must learn from how some social experiments – like both German Nazism and Soviet Communism – have failed and wreaked havoc; and other smaller-scale conflicts have been resolved (a little?): in South Africa, in Ireland, maybe in Rwanda. There are also a hundred little daily experiments in making a better world: from the democratising push of Wikipedia to the multiple kindnesses found in the health and welfare services, through to the daily concerns of Médicins Sans Frontières and Amnesty International.

The days of the big dreams of the utopias are over. We have seen too much damage come from this. We need instead a down-to-earth pragmatism of empathy, justice, kindness and care. We have to think small in a big way. We can end on one more of William James's comments:

> *I am done with great things and big plans, great institutions and big success. I am for those tiny, invisible loving human forces that work from individual to individual, creeping through the crannies of the world like so many rootlets, or like the capillary oozing of water, which, if given time, will rend the hardest monuments of pride.* (William James, *Letters*; and also cited in James's biography by Robert D. Richardson, 2006/7: 384)

Further reading

Introductions to sociological humanisms include: Audrey Borenstein's *Redeeming the Sin: Social Science and Literature* (1979), Columbia UP; Peter Berger's classic *Invitation to Sociology* (1966), Penguin. The classic sociological introductions to humanism and sociology can be found in the works of Alfred McClung Lee especially *Toward a Humanist Sociology* (1973), New Jersey: Prentice Hall; *Sociology for Whom?* (1978), New York: Oxford University Press; *Sociology for People: Toward a Caring Profession*

(1988), Syracuse UP. For an introduction to the wider field of social science human-ism, see Robert Coles, *Handing One Another Along: Literature and Social Reflection* (2010), New York: Random House. On methodology, the classic is the appendix in C. Wright Mills, *The Sociological Imagination* (1895/1982), London: Macmillan Press. T.S. Bruyn, *The Human Perspective in Sociology* (1966), London: Sage; Ken Plummer, *Documents of Life – 2: An Invitation to a Critical Humanism* (2001), London: Sage. See also: Ken Plummer, *Sociology: The Basics* (2010), Abingdon: Routledge.

The work of William James is crucial of understanding modern humanism. For an overview and collection of writings, see *The Heart of William James*, edited by Robert Richardson (2010) Harvard. Short introductions to varieties of humanism include: Peter Cave, *Humanism: A Beginner's Guide* (2009), Oxford: Oneworld; Tony Davies, *Humanism* (1997), Abingdon: Routledge; Richard Norman, *On Humanism* (2004), Abingdon: Routledge. A useful anthology collecting the ideas of many past humanist thinkers is Margaret Knight's *Humanist Anthology* (1961), London: Rationalist Press. On the recent history of the nature of humanity, see Joanna Bourke, *What it means to be human: Reflections from 1791 to the present* (2011) Virago. On humanity's inhu-manity to humanity, see Jonathan Glover, *Humanity: A Moral History of the Twentieth Century* (1999), Jonathan Cape, Adam Jones, *Genocide: A Comprehensive Introduction* (2010 2nd edn), Routledge; on the ontology of the human world, look at: Dennis Ford, *The Seach for Meaning: A Short History* (2007), University of California Press. The classic of modern humanism is Hannah Arendt, *The Human Condition* (1958), Chicago. The work of Martha Nussbaum is also prominent; see especially *Cultivating Humanity* (1997) Harvard; *Creating Capabilities: The Human Development Approach* (2011), Harvard. Adam Smith's *The Theory of Moral Sentiments* (1759) is the foun-dation for much modern thinking about the person. Advanced contemporary dis-cussions of the human person can be found in Andrew Sayers, *Why Things Matter to People* (2011), Cambridge and Christian Smith, *What is a Person: Rethinking Humanity, Social Life, and the Moral Good from the Person Up* (2010), Chicago.

On global values and ethics see: Ernest Bloch, *The Principle of Hope* (three volumes: 1938–70 (1986), Blackwell; Michael J Sandel, *Justice: What's the Right Thing To Do?* (2009), Penguin; Amartya Sen, *The Idea of Justice* (2009), Allen Lane; Ronald C. Arnett, *Communication Ethics Literacy: Dialogue and Difference* (2008), Sage; Seyla Benhabib, *Dignity in Adversity: Human Rights in Troubled Times* (2012), Polity; Michael Slote, *The Ethics of Care and Sympathy* (2007), Routledge; Steven Lukes, *Liberals and Cannibals: The Implications of Diversity* (2003), Verso; Eric Olin Wright, *Envisioning Real Utopias* (2010), Verso; Kay Schaffer and Sidonie Smith, *Human Rights and Narrated Lives: The Ethics of Recognition*, (2004), Palgrave; Rodrigue Tremblay, *The Code for Global Ethics: Toward a Humanist Civilization* (2009), Victoria, BC: Trafford; Richard J. Bernstein, *The Pragmatic Turn* (2010), Polity.

Finally, some books that help orientate future humanistic research would be: Iain Wilkinson, *Suffering: A Sociological Introduction* (2005), Cambridge: Polity; Jeremy Rifkin, *The Empathic Civlization* (2009), Cambridge: Polity; Rebecca Solnit, *A Paradise Built in Hell* (2009), Harmondsworth: Penguin; Tzvetan Todorov, *Facing the Extreme: Moral Life in the Concentration Camps* (1999), London: Weidenfeld and Nicolson; Stanley Cohen, *States of Denial* (2000) Cambridge: Polity. Jeffrey C. Alexander, *Trauma: A Social Theory* (2012), Cambridge: Polity; Zygmunt Bauman, *Collateral Damage: Social Inequalities in a Global Age* (2011), Cambridge: Polity; John D. Brewer, *Peace Processes: A Sociological Approach* (2010), Cambridge: Polity.

Study questions for the manifesto

1. Values and sociology

As you have been reading this book and the readings, you will have frequently encountered what sociologists call 'the value debate'. Can sociology be value- and politics-free? Should it be? Some claim it can be. Others, whilst still stressing the importance of objectivity in research, believe it is always relevant to probe the value links in their work. Here are some opening tasks for you:

1. Gather up evidence from this book for or against values being central in sociology.
2. What kinds of values have you found in various readings in the book? Name readings and authors and then indicate the values they seem to espouse. Alternatively, find readings in the book which you think are completely value-free.
3. Suggest ways in which values find their way into sociology through:
   (a) basic underlying assumptions,
   (b) the practical research process, and
   (c) the ways in which sociology is ultimately presented and used.

2. Plummer and values

Plummer is very up front about the value stance of sociology. He takes a particular view – that of a Critical Humanist. Consider:

1. What kinds of values and politics do you find in Plummer's analysis? Make a list of them.
2. What kinds of values are these? Are they ethical guidelines on living 'good' lives or political values on social change – or both?
3. Do you agree with them? Hold these values up to scrutiny.
4. Consider what alternative kinds of value stance could be taken within sociology.

3. Critical humanism

The core of this Manifesto is an outline of the theory of Critical Humanism. As you read it, ask:

1. What are the key features of Critical Humanism?
2. How does Critical Humanism differ from Humanism: in what ways is it critical?

3. In what ways might Critical Humanism be an attempt to deal with some of the presumed critiques often made of humanism as a limited Western and Enlightenment theory?

4. Human capabilities

One key idea of the Manifesto draws from Martha Nussbaum's ideas of human capabilities.

1. What are the key human capabilities suggested by Nussbaum?
2. Could you add more to this list?
3. Do you think such capabilities are universal across history and cultures?
4. What kinds of social things might help facilitate the flourishing of these capabilities?

5. On methods

1. Although Plummer does not specifically address 'methodology' in his manifesto, a close reading will give you all kinds of ideas as to how sociology might be done. Can you suggest what these are?

6. On humanisation

Plummer provides a framework for thinking how we become human beings. Consider:

1. What might be key features of becoming human?
2. What key concepts might be developed to help us understand this process of becoming social human beings?
3. Where in the main text do you find such ideas being discussed and developed? Find specific readings that help you with this.

7. On research

1. At the end of the Manifesto, Plummer gives us the good news and the bad news. What is this?
2. Detail some of the kinds of research that he would like to see conducted in sociology in the future.
3. How might this research be done?

Index